AF572241

Azerbaijani - English Dictionary

Patrick A. O'Sullivan

Mario Severino

Valeriy Volozov

dp Dunwoody Press
Kensington, Maryland, U.S.A.

Azerbaijani - English Dictionary

All inquiries should be directed to:
Dunwoody Press, P.O. Box 400, Kensington, MD, 20895 U.S.A.

ISBN: 1-881265-18-8
Library of Congress Catalog Number: 94-69717
Printed and bound in the United States of America

To Pamela Johnson Moguet, 1956-1994, who began this book but left us before it could be finished.

"Praising what is lost makes the remembrance dearer."
William Shakespeare

Table of Contents

Preface

Azerbaijani is a Turkic language and thus part of the Altaic family of languages. It is spoken by the majority of the more than 7 million people in the Republic of Azerbaijan and by slightly fewer (6,086,000 according to a 1986 census) in two provinces of northwestern Iran, also known as Azerbaijan. Azerbaijani is to some degree mutually intelligible with modern Turkish and Turkmen. Three generations of Soviet domination has left a legacy of bureaucratic scars as well as linguistic influences on the present Republic of Azerbaijan not evident in its sister region in Iran. The Russian influence, which preceded the Soviet takeover by more than a century, as well as the Arabic influence brought with the Islamic religion in the 8th century, have all left their marks on the language of the Republic of Azerbaijan. Borrowings from these languages and others are included in this dictionary although the Russian language influence is so pervasive that it has been necessary to limit entries from that source to very common terms.

This dictionary is intended particularly for those wishing to read the literature of the Republic of Azerbaijan. It is suitable for English speaking students and users of the language who have a beginning or intermediate knowledge of Azerbaijani. Its approximately 25,000 entries include most of the words likely to be encountered in everyday speech, newspapers, non-technical journals, and general usage. The more advanced translator will be able to use A. A. Orudzhev's comprehensive four-volume monolingual Azerbaijani Dictionary, published by the Azerbaijani Academy of Sciences of the USSR (see Bibliography).

The editors particularly wish to express their great indebtedness to the authors, editors and compilers of the following works, without which the construction of this dictionary would not have been possible:

The Azerbaijani-Russian Dictionary of Kh. A. Azizbekov and staff (Baku: 1965); the four-volume monoglot Explanatory Dictionary of the Azerbaijani Language edited by A. A. Drudzhev (Baku: 1964-1987); the four volume Azerbaijani-Russian Dictionary of Professor M. T. Tagiev and his collegium (Baku: 1986). A number of other works have been consulted in the compilation of the dictionary. These, and the works just acknowledged, are listed in the Bibliography in conventional form.

The editors are grateful to the following individuals who have helped in vastly different ways in the completion of this work:

To the author of a valuable unpublished study, A Beginning Student's Guide to the Study of Azerbaijani (Washington, DC: 1990). (A compilation of reviews of textbooks, reference grammars, dictionaries and other works in Western languages which are essential to or useful in the study of the Azerbaijani language and other Turkic languages of the former USSR.)

To Naida Mamedova and Lala Seidova for their timely assistance in identifying and verifying Azerbaijani basic vocabulary in current usage.

To Stephen A. Bladey and W. Gregory Mullins for their help in solving computer problems and their valuable advice concerning formatting and printing.

And especially to John D. Murphy for the use of descriptions of the Azerbaijani language from his Azerbaijani Newspaper Reader, (Dunwoody Press, 1993). The editors are also very grateful to Mr. Murphy for his able and patient counsel on Turkic languages -- one of the great loves of his life. He has added significantly to the professional quality of the dictionary and to the editors' enjoyment in doing it.

Guide to the Construction and Use of the Dictionary

1. **Headwords**: Headwords are listed in bold type in the order of the Azerbaijani alphabet. Separate meanings of an Azerbaijani word are marked off by Arabic numerals followed by a half-parenthesis, thus:

> **боj** :*n* 1) growth, increase 2). . .

Shades of meaning which are not strictly synonymous are separated by a semi-colon : synonyms are separated by a comma. The oblique stroke is also used to indicate synonyms, and also to avoid repetition, thus:

> **абырсыз** : *adj* shameless, insolent, brazen
> **созалмаг** : *v-intr* 1) turn/grow pale 2) fade, wither, wilt. . .

2. **Colloquial and dialect variants**: Headwords in this category are cross-referenced to the normative form of the word:

> **боғмача** : see боғма 2), 3)

3. **Homonyms**: Homonyms are not listed as separate entries, but as additional meanings.

4. **Articles and infinitive markers**: In the English text the articles *a, the* are omitted before nouns unless essential to the meaning, and *to* as the marker of the infinitive is omitted before verbs

5. **Extended definitions**: In the case of terms whose basic meaning may not have wide currency, a more extensive gloss is given in italic type, thus :

> **биjар** : *n hist* corvée *labor performed by a serf or temporarily obligated peasant for the benefit of a landowner, or nobleman, in return for the use of a sector of land which can be passed on to his heir.*

6. **Scientific terms**: To avoid ambiguity in zoological and botanical terms, the international Latin name is given in italic type, together with one or more common English names, thus:

битоту : *n bot* stavesacre *Delphinium staphysagria* , a type of European larkspur from which an ointment used to kill lice is prepared

7. **Cross-references**: If a headword is cross-referenced to a specific meaning, or several meanings of another headword, the pertinent meanings are indicated in parentheses.

боғмача : see боғма (2,3)

8. **Nouns and adjectives**: Since Azerbaijani nouns may sometimes function as adjectives, and since adjectives may sometimes function as nouns, these additional functions have been listed separately when it was felt that this would be useful. The basic function is listed first. However, as a general rule, words listed only as adjectives may also be used as nouns and adverbs.

икиүзлү : *a* 1) hypocritical, two-faced, insincere, duplicitous 2) double-faced *of material* 3) dihedral *n* 4) hypocrite, double-dealer; sanctimonious person

професcор : *n* 1) professor *a* 2) professorial

9. **Verbal Nouns**: A verbal noun is entered as a headword and cross-referenced to the verb from which it is derived, thus:

јәләтмә : *vn* fr. **јәләтмәк**

10. **Verbs**: The passive, causative, and other forms of the verb have been listed separately as infinitives. A causative verb is cross-referenced to the verb from which it is derived, thus:

һопмаг : *pass* be absorbed

чаггылдатмаг : *caus of* чаггылдамаг

икиләнмәк : *v-int* 1) divide in two, be divided in two *bot* 2) bifurcate

11. **Adverbs**: As noted above, almost any adjective may modify a verb. When used adverbially, this meaning is listed under the adjective-headword, thus:

јаваш : *a* 1) quiet, gentle, slow, unhurried *adv* 2) quietly, gently, slowly

A repeated adjective may also serve as an adverb. In this case it has been entered as a separate headword, thus:

јаваш-јаваш : *adv* gradually, little by little, by easy stages, slowly

12. **Culture-specific terms**: Azerbaijani words which are specific to the culture, and which have no English equivalent (i.e. personal names, foods, articles of native costume, musical and literary terms etc) have been transliterated in the Turkic Latin alphabet scheduled for eventual general use, and accompanied by a brief definition, thus:

зурна : *n mus* zurna wind instrument

бозбаш: n bozbaş meat and pea soup

13. **Cardinal numbers**: Cardinal numbers are listed as headwords, thus:

беш : *num* five

Additionally, as a matter of user-convenience a list of the cardinal numbers from one to a thousand has been included in the grammatical section of the General Introduction.

14. **Russian loanwords:** a great number of Russian words of every kind, but largely of the international type, appear throughout contemporary journalistic texts. It has not been deemed practical to include them all, not only because of the limited scope of the dictionary, but also because their permanency as an element of the language cannot be predicted. The reader is advised to have recourse to a standard Russian-English dictionary (see bibliography). The Azerbaijani-Cyrillic alphabet, however, lacks eight of the thirty-two standard Russian-Cyrillic characters and the spelling of Russian loanwords has consequently been altered to accomodate the disparity, and also to reflect Azerbaijani pronunciation.

a) The following eight Russian-Cyrillic graphemes are not included in the Azerbaijani-Cyrillic alphabet: **ё, й, ц, щ, ъ, ь, э, ю, я.**

b) The "hard-sign" /**ъ**/, and the "soft-sign" /**ь**/ have been omitted entirely from Russian loanwords.

c) The remaining Russian-Cyrillic graphemes have been replaced as follows:

	Russian	Azerbaijani
ё/јо	**костёл**	**костјол**
й/и	**йюль**	**ијул**
щ,ш	**плащ**	**плаш**
э/е	**энциклопедия**	**енсиклопедија**
ц/с	**реакция**	**реаксија**
ю/ју	**костюм**	**костјум**
я/ја	**конфедерация**	**конфедерасија**

d) Russian-Cyrillic /**г**/ , so-called "hard-G" (a voiced uvular stop) is replaced by Azerbaijani-Cyrillic /**к**/˙ e.g.

Russian	Azerbaijani
геология	**кеолокија**.
биология	**биолокија**.

The Writing System

Azerbaijani is currently written in a variant of the Cyrillic alphabet. The letters are listed below, accompanied where possible by a very approximate English, French or Turkish equivalent.

А	а	is like the a in car
Б	б	is like the b in boy
В	в	is like the v in vest
Г	г	is a voiced uvular stop which in final position often becomes a fricative
Ғ	ғ	is a voiced uvular fricative
Д	д	is like the d in do
Е	е	is like the e in ten
Ә	ә	is like the a in hat
Ж	ж	is like the z in azure
З	з	is like the z in zoo
И	и	is like the ee in seen
Ы	ы	is like the i in girl
Ј	ј	is like the y in you
К	к	is like the c in cool, but in final position it often becomes a fricative
Ҝ	ҝ	is like the g in go
Л	л	is like the l in like
М	м	is like the m in moon
Н	н	is like the n in not
О	о	is like the o in so (without the diphthongal quality)
Ө	ө	is like the French eu in peu
П	п	is like the p in park
Р	р	is an r-sound dissimilar from English r
С	с	is like the s in so
Т	т	is like the t in ten
У	у	is like the ou in you (without the diphthongal quality)
Ү	ү	is like the French u in tu
Ф	ф	is like the f in fall
Х	х	is like the Scotch ch in loch
Һ	һ	is like the h in hat
Ч	ч	is like the ch in church
Ҹ	ҹ	is like the j in judge
Ш	ш	is like the sh in show

An official resolution has been made to replace the the Cyrillic with the Latin alphabet in the near future. The Latin letters with their Cyrillic equivalents are listed below.

A	a	(А	а)	M	m	(М	м)
B	b	(Б	б)	N	n	(Н	н)
C	c	(Ҹ	ҹ)	O	o	(О	о)
C	c	(Ч	ч)	O	o	(Ө	ө)
D	d	(Д	д)	P	p	(П	п)
E	e	(Е	е)	Q	q	(Г	г)
A	a	(Ә	ә)	R	r	(Р	р)
F	f	(Ф	ф)	S	s	(С	с)
G	g	(Ҝ	ҝ)	S	s	(Ш	ш)
G	g	(Г	г)	T	t	(Т	т)
H	h	(Һ	һ)	U	u	(У	у)
I	i	(Ы	ы)	U	u	(Ү	ү)
I	i	(И	и)	V	v	(В	в)
J	j	(Ж	ж)	X	x	(Х	х)
K	k	(К	к)	Y	y	(Ј	ј)
L	l	(Л	л)	Z	z	(З	з)

The Substantive

In considering the following nominal and verbal paradigms the following facts must be kept in mind.

1. The quality of the vowel or vowels of a suffix is determined by the final vowel of the stem or root. There are two series of harmonic vowels: the fourfold series consisting of **ы**, **и**, **у** and **ү**, and the twofold series consisting of **-а** and **-ә**. Each suffix vowel is associated exclusively with one or the other series. For example, the locative suffix is either **-да** or **-дә.** depending on the quality of the immediately preceding root or stem vowel. An awareness of this will obviate the necessity of repeating the same paradigm two or four times.

2. Final **г** often becomes **ғ** before a low vowel: **алмаг - алмаға.** Final **к** often becomes **j** before a high vowel: **көрмәк - көрмәjи.** This occurs chiefly in nominal and verbal inflection.

Azerbaijani has six cases:

Nominative	----
Genitive	**-(н)ын-**
Dative	**-а**
Definite Accusative	**-(н)ы**
Locative	**-да**
Ablative	**-дан**

Note: **(н)** occurs if the preceding form ends in a vowel.

The plural suffix **-лар/-ләр** belongs to the twofold series. It comes immediately before the case ending.

	Sing.		Pl.	
Nom.	**китаб**	book	**китаблар**	books
Gen.	**китабын**	of a book	**китабларын**	of books
Dat.	**китаба**	to a book	**китаблара**	to books
Acc.	**китабы**	the book	**китаблары**	the books
Loc.	**китабда**	in a book	**китабларда**	in books
Abl.	**китабдан**	from a book	**китаблардан**	from books

Note: The English equivalents above are possible, but not the only possible equivalents.

The possessive suffixes are:

Person	Sing.	Pl.
1st	-(ы)м	-(ы)мыз
2nd	-(ы)н	-(ы)ныз
3rd	-(с)ы	-лары

The parenthetical (ы) occurs if the preceding letter is a consonant; (с) occurs if the preceding letter is a vowel.

Person	Sing.		Pl.	
1st	**китабым**	my book	**китабымыз**	our book
2nd	**китабын**	your book	**китабыныз**	your book
3rd	**китабы**	his/her book	**китабланы**	their book

Person		Sing.		Pl.
1st	**атам**	my father	**атамыз**	our father
2nd	**атан**	your father	**атаныз**	your father
3rd	**атасы**	his/her father	**аталары**	their father

Note: The plural suffix precedes the possessive suffix.

китабларымыз	our books
аталарыныз	your fathers

The possessive suffix may be followed by case endings:

атамын	of my father
атама	to my father

Note that **-н-** is interposed between the third person possessive suffix **-сы-** and a case ending.

атасынын	of his father
атасына	to his father

A possessive construction is composed of the possessor, with or without the genitive suffix, followed by the item possessed which bears the possessive suffix. The forms without the genitive suffix are more closely knit than those with it, and may be viewed as compound nouns. Also, the notion of "possessor" is used in a broad sense and need not imply physical possession.

Examples of constructions with the genitive suffix on the first member:

университетин тәләбәләри	the students of the university
атамын ады	my father's name

Examples of constructions in which the genitive suffix is lacking:

бир гәзет мәгаләси	a newspaper article
мәдәнијјәт мәркәзи	a cultural center

The Personal Pronouns

The personal pronouns, except for a very few irregularities, are declined like nouns.

SINGULAR

	First		Second		Third	
Nom.	**мəн**	I	**сəн**	you	**о**	he,she,it
Gen.	**мəним**	my	**сəнин**	your,etc	**онун**	his,her,etc.
Dat.	**мəнə**	to me	**сəнə**		**она**	
Acc.	**мəни**	me	**сəни**		**ону**	
Loc.	**мəндə**	in me	**сəндə**		**онда**	
Abl.	**мəндəн**	from me	**сəндəн**		**ондан**	

PLURAL

	First		Second		Third	
Nom.	**биз**	we	**сиз**	you	**онлар**	they
Gen.	**бизим**	our,etc.	**сизин**	your,etc.	**онларын**	their,etc.
Dat.	**бизə**		**сизə**		**онлара**	
Acc.	**бизи**		**сизи**		**онлары**	
Loc.	**биздə**		**сиздə**		**онларда**	
Abl.	**биздəн**		**сиздəн**		**онлардан**	

Demonstrative Pronouns And Adjectives

о, онлар also occur as far demonstratives - *that, those.* When used adjectivally **о** is invariable, and may mean *that* or *those,* depending on the number of the following noun.

Examples:

О бина мəктəбдир.	That building is a school.
о вахтдан бəри	since that time
О, мараглы кираб охуjур.	He is reading an interesting book.
Онлар достдулар.	They are friends.

As a pronoun, **бу** means *this*. When used adjectivally it is invariable and may mean either *this* or *these*, depending on the number of the following noun.

Examples:

бу гәзет	this newspaper
бу инһисарлар	these monopolies
Бу кимдир ?	Who is this ?
Бу, вәзијјәти даһа да ағыр-	This can further aggravate
лашдыра билир.	the situation.

ӨЗ

өз, *self*, replaces Turkish kendi. It may take possessive and case suffixes.

Examples:

О өзү алмандыр.	He himself is German.
Бу өз ишиндир.	This is your own business.
Мәммәд өз ишини јахшы билир.	Mahmed knows his job well.

Postpositions

Azerbaijani has a number of postpositions which govern specific cases. The one most likely to confuse students of Turkish is **кими** (= Turkish gibi). Following the nominative case it means *like* or *as*;; following the dative it may be rendered *until* or *up to*.

Examples:

саралмаз бир јара кими	like an incurable wound
индијә кими көрүнмәмиш бир вәһишлик	a brutal act not seen until now

Почт саат нечәјә кими ишләјир?	Until what time is the post office open (lit. functioning.)

The Verb

Following are paradigms of the nine tenses of Azerbaijani. The word "tense" is used in a very loose sense, because aspect and mood are also very much involved.

THE -ды PAST TENSE

The Definite Past Tense, also known as the Definite Completive Tense, is used to express a single action which took place in the past. It is formed by suffixing **-ды, -ди, -ду** or **-дү** to the stem (the choice being determined by the principle of vowel harmony). To this are added the following personal endings:

	Sing.	Pl.
1st person	**-м**	**-г** (**-к** after a front vowel)
2nd person	**-н**	**-ныз/-низ/-нуз/-нүз**
3rd person	-	**лар/-ләр**

Example from **јазмаг**, to write

	Sing.		Pl.	
lst.	**јаздым**	I wrote, etc.	**јаздыг**	we wrote, etc.
2nd.	**јаздын**			**јаздыныз**
3rd.	**јазды**			**јаздылар**

The negative is formed by inserting **-ма-/-мә-** between the verb stem and the tense ending.

lst. sing, **јазмадым,** I didn't write, etc.

Examples:

Мән китабы охудум.	I read the book.
Јемәјә бир шеј тапмадым.	I did not find anything to eat.

Болгарыстандан кәлмиш	We met with delegates who
нүмајәндәләрлә көрүшдүк.	had come from Bulgaria.

Compare the equivalent Turkish forms:

yazdim, yazdin, etc. ; yazmadim, etc.

THE **-мыш** PAST TENSE

The Narrative Past Tense, also known as the Indefinite Completive Tense, is used to express an action that took place at an unspecified time in the past, and that may have present implications. It is formed by suffixing **-мыш** (or variants) to the verbal stem. To these are added the following predicative endings.

	Sing.	Pl.
1st	**-ам/-әм**	**-ыг/-ик/-уг/-үк**
2nd	**-сан/-сән**	**-сыныз/синиз/сунуз/сүнүз**
3rd	(**дыр** and variants)**-лар/-ләр**	

Example from **јазмаг**, to write

	Sing.	Pl.
1st	**јазмышам**	**јазмышыг**
2nd	**јазмышсан**	**јазмышсыныз**
3rd	**јазмыш(дыр)**	**јазмышлар**

The negative is formed by inserting **-ма/-мә** between the verb stem and the tense ending.

lst. sing. **јазмамышам,** I didn't write, etc.

Examples:

Мән бураја бир мүхбир кими кәлмишәм.	I have come here as a a journalist.
Бу өлкә һаггында чох ешит- мишдик.	We have heard a lot about this country.
Чәми ики китаб алмышам.	I bought a total of two books.

Compare the equivalent Turkish forms.
yazmişim; yazmamişim.

THE **-ыр** PRESENT TENSE

The Present Progressive Tense, also known as the Definite Incompletive, expresses an event going on or a state existing at the present time. The tense sign is a high-vowel followed by **-р**: **-ыр/-ир/-ур/-үр**. If the verb stem ends in a vowel, **-ј-** is inserted between the verb stem and the suffix. To this are added the predicative personal endings (see the previous section).

Example from **јазмаг**, to write

	Sing.		Pl.	
1st	**јазырам**	I am writing	**јазырыг**	we are writing
2nd	**јазырсан**			**јазырсыныз**
3rd	**јазыр**			**јазырлар**

The negative is formed by inserting **-м-** between the verb stem and the tense ending.

1st sing. **јазмырам**, I am not writing.

Examples:

Мән инанырым ки....	I believe that...
Һарада јашајырсыныз ?	Where do you live ?
Онлар нәјә бахырлар ?	What are they looking at?

Compare the equivalent Turkish forms :

yaziyorum; yazmiyorum.

THE **-ачаг** FUTURE TENSE

The Future Tense, as its name implies, expresses and event that will take place in the future. The tense sign is the disyllabic suffix **-ачаг/-әчәк.** The final consonant **-г** becomes **-ғ** before **-ам** or **-ыг**; final **-к** becomes **-ј-** before **-әм** or **-ик**. To this are added the predicative endings.

Example from **јазмаг**, to write

	Sing.		Pl.	
1st	**јазачағам**	I will write	**јазачағыг**	we will write
2nd	**јазачагсан**		**јазачагсыныз**	
3rd	**јазачаг(дыр)**		**јазачаглар**	

The negative is formed by inserting **-мај-/-мәј-** between the verb stem and the tense ending.

lst sing. **јазмајачам,** I will not write.

Examples:

Мән буну һеч вахт унутмајачагам.	I will never forget this.
Бизораја кедәчәјикми ?	Shall we go there ?
Мүһазирани ким охујачаг ?	Who will deliver (lit. read) the lecture ?

Compare the equivalent Turkish forms

yazacağim; yazmayacağim

THE AORIST/INDEFINITE FUTURE TENSE

The Indefinite Future, also known as the Indefinite Incompletive and Aorist, expresses habitual action or, more frequently, indefinite future action. The tense sign is **-ар-/-әр-**. If the verb stem ends in a vowel, **-ј-** is inserted between the verb stem and the tense sign. To this are added the predicative personal endings.

	Sing.		Pl.	
1st	**јазарам**	I write/will write	**јазарыг**	we write/will write
2nd	**јазарсан**			**јазарсыныз**
3rd	**јазар**			**јазарлар**

The negative is formed by inserting **-м-** before the tense sign,and changing the final **-р** of the tense sign to **-з-** in the second and third persons.

	Sing.		Pl.	
1st	**јазмарам**	I won't write	**јазмарыг**	we won't write
2nd	**јазмазсан**		**јазмазсыныз**	
3rd	**азмаз**		**јазмазлар**	

Examples:

Бу чох вахт апармаз.	This won't take much time.
Бир аздан јенә зәнк чаларам.	I will telephone again in a little while.

Мән буна чаваб верә билмәрәм. — I am unable to give an answer to that.

Compare the equivalent Turkish forms :

gelirim (I will come); gelmez (he won't come)

THE IMPERATIVE

When used in the second person the Imperative expresses a command. In the first and third persons it is often the equivalent of an English phrase introduced by "let me/us/him/her/them." On other occasions it is dependent on a previous verb and is rendered "that, in order that + verb."

Example from **јазмаг**, to write.

	Sing.	
1st	**јазым**	let me write, that I write
2nd	**јаз**	write!
3rd	**јазсын**	let him/her write
	Pl.	
1st	**јазаг**	let us write, that we write
2nd	**јазын**	write!
3rd	**јазсынлар**	let them write

The negative is formed by inserting **-ма(ј)/-мә(ј)** between the verb stem and the tense ending.

јазмасын	let him not write
јазмаіын	don't you (pl.) write

The Turkish equivalents of the above are :yazmasin and yazmayınız.

Examples:

Давам един !	Continue !
Горхмаіын! Биз бурадаіыг.	Do not fear ! We are here.
Кәл мүһазирәни динләјәкю	Come (sing.), let's listen to the lecture.

Дәрс јүғү 12 **саата енлиридсин.**	Let the teaching load be reduced to 12 hours.
Мән арзу едирәм ки, мүһарибә тезликлә сона јетсин.	I wish that the war would quickly come to an end.

THE OPTATIVE

The Optative is characterized by the mood sign **-(j)a/-(j)ә** followed by the personal endings. It normally follows another verb.

Example from **јазмаг**, to write

	Sing.		Pl.	
1st	**јазам**	that I write	**јазаг**	that we write
2nd	**јазасан**		**јазасыныз**	
3rd	**јаза**		**јазалар**	

The negative is formed by inserting **-мај-/мәј-** between the verb stem and the optative ending.

јазмајам, etc.

Compare the equivalent Turkish forms:

yazayım, yazasın,etc.

THE CONDITIONAL

The Conditional Mood is used to express a condition or a hypothesis. In English a conditional clause is ordinarily introduced by the conjunctions "if" or "unless." The mood sign is the low-vowel suffix **-са-/-сә-** to which are added the personal endings.

Example from **јазмаг**, to write

	Sing.		Pl.	
1st	**јазсам**	if I write	**јазсаг**	if we write
2nd	**јазсан**		**јазсаныз**	
3rd	**јазса**		**јазсалар**	

Note: The 1st plural after the mood sign **-сә-** ends in -**сәк.,** e.g., **көрсәк**, if we see.

The negative is formed by inserting **-ма-/-мә-** between the verb stem and the mood ending.

1st. **јазмасам,** if I don't write.

Examples:

Зәһмәт олмаса, јерләримизи бизә көстәрин.	Please (lit. if it is not trouble), show us our places.
Биз онлара узунмүддәтли јардым көстәрсәк...	If we grant (lit. show) show them long-term aid...
Чәтин олса да...	Although it it difficult...
Сијасәтчи олмасам да...	Although I am not a politician...

Compare the equivalent Turkish forms:

yazsam, yazmasam.

THE NECESSITATIVE

The Necessitative, as its name implies, expresses the notion that an action should, ought, or must take place. The characteristic sign is the disyllabic suffix **-малы/-мәли** which is followed by the predicative personal endings.

Example from **јазмаг**, to write

	Sing.		Pl.	
1st	**јазмалыјам**	I must write	**јазмалыјыг**	we must write
2nd	**јазмалысан**		**јазмалысыныз**	
3rd	**јазмалыдыр**		**јазмадылар**	

The negative is formed by inserting **-ма-/-мә-** between the verb stem and the personal ending.

1st **јазмамалыјам** I must not write

Examples :

Мән кетмәлијәм	I must be going.
Унутмамалыјыг ки...	We must not forget that....
Сиз билмәлисиниз ки....	You should know that...

Compare the Turkish equivalents:

1st yazmalıyım, I must write; yazmamalıyım, I must not write.

THE -a/-ə билмәк CONSTRUCTION

билмәк as a primary verb means "to know." Following another verb ending in **-a/-ə** it functions as an auxiliary expressing potentiality .

Examples:

Башлаjа биләрикми ?	Can we begin ?
Бу гыш ачлыг ола билер.	There may be famine this winter.
Халга чох шеј верә билмәдик.	We were not able to give the people many things.

DERIVED FORMS OF THE VERB

Of the several derived forms of the Verb the ones to be illustrated here are the Causative and the Passive. A verb be made causative by suffixing **-дыр** (or variants) or, less frequently, **-т** to the stem of the verb.

Examples:

билмәк	to know
билдирмәк	to make known
өлмәк	to die
өлдүрмәк	to kill
Һава дәјишир	The weather is changing
вәзиjјәти дәјишдирмәк үчүн	in order to change the situation

A verb may be made passive by suffixing **-ыл-** or, less frequently, **-ын** to the stem of the verb or to a preceding causative suffix.

Example:

өлдүрмәк	to kill
өлдүрүлмәк	to be killed
Нүвә силаһлары чыхарылмышды.	Atomic weapons have been taken out.
Дирломатик мүнасибәтләр јарадылыр.	Diplomatic relations are being established.

AUXILIARIES

In addition to their function as tense/mood markers **-ды-, -мыш-** and **-са-** are used as a part of the auxiliary to form compound tenses. The Past Auxiliary **-лы-** is illustrated here. For a detailed account see Underhill, pages 181-188.

Гардашым Москваја кетмишди.	My brother went/ had gone to Moscow.
Мәним анам јүзләрчә дастан билирди.	My mother used to know hundreds of legends.
чүнки Бакыда 220 мин ермәни јашајарды	because 220 Armenians used to live in Baku

THE INFINITIVE

The Infinitive, as in Turkish, is characterized by the suffix **-маг/-мәк.** It may be fully declined. The locative of the Infinitive followed by **-дыр** forms a present continuous tense.

Examples:

галмаг	to remain
галмамаг	not to remain
Јағыш јамаға башлады.	It began to rain.
Китаб охумағы, мусиги дин- ләмәји вә идмаднысевирәм.	I like to read books, to listen to music and sports.

THE SHORT INFINITIVE

The Short Infinitive, also known as the Noun of Action, ends in **-ма/-мә.** It often occurs in the dative and accusative cases.

Examples:

мәктублардан сечмәләр	selections from letters
Азәрбајчанывн истиглалиј̌ј̌әт газанмасы	Azerbaijan's gaining independence
космик шүаланма шәраитиндә көрмә вә ешитмә	seeing and hearing under conditions of cosmic radiation

PARTICIPLES

The Subject Participle **-ан/-ән** may be used as a noun, a simple adjective and, most importantly, a relative participle modifying a noun and governing previous elements in the clause. Although it is usually called a present participle, in practice it expresses an action concurrent with that of the main verb of the clause.

Examples:

бизә мә'лум олан фактлары көрә	according to the facts known to us
һеч бир күнаһы олмајан аламлар	men having no guilt
Мәним бурад охујан бир достум вар	I have a friend who studies here.

мүгәддәс торпағымызы горуіан икид оғуллар	the brave sons who are protecting our sacred land

The Subject Participle **-мыш** (and variants) differs from the participle in **-ан/-ән** in that it refers to an action occurring before that of the main verb.

Examples:

е'лан олунмамышыш мүһарибә	an undeclared war, a war that had not been declared
өлкәниздә баш вермиш тарики дәјишикликләр	historic changed that had taken place (lit. given head) in our country.

The Objective Participle in **-дыг-** may be used as a noun, a simple adjective, and a relative particple modifying a noun and governing preceding elements of the clause.

Examples:

алдығым китаб	the book which I bought
кәллијимиз гатар	the train on which we came
ешитдијимә көрә	according to what I have heard

VERBAL ADVERBS

In a succession of verbal forms in a sentence usually only the final verb is suffixed for tense and person. One such non-final form is **-ыб** (corresponding to Turkish **-ip**), but unlike Turkish **-ip**, it frequently occurs in final position, equivalent in meaning to the **-мыш** past.

Examples:

Һәп икиси Һәр күн чајын гырағына кәлиб орада көрү-шүрмүшләр.	Every day both of them would come to the bank of the river and would meet there.
Ораја даһа 4 баталјон көндәрилиб.	Four additional battalions were sent there.
Јелтсин гејд едиб ки...	Yeltsin noted that....

Another non-final form of the verb takes the suffix **-араг/-әрәк.** In translation it may often be equated with English forms in -ing.

Examples:

буна бахмаjараг	regardless of this, lit. not looking at this
Түркиjә ордусунун jүксәк мәһсәбли забитинә истинад едәрәк...	relying on a high-ranking officer of the Turkish army...

Invariable **-кән** differs from other verbal adverbial suffixes in that it is usually suffixed to the indefinite future tense sign **-ар/-әр**. In translation it is the equivalent of English *while or when.*

Examples:

һәлә орта мәктәбдә охуjаркән	while still studying in secondary school..
Парка кедиркән достума раст кәлдим.	While going to the park I met my friend.

NON-VERBAL PREDICATES

The predicative endings (see the **-мыш** past tense) can be used with non-verbal as well as many verbal tenses and moods.

Examples:

Мән әминәм ки...	I am sure that..
Сән нечәсән ?	How are you (sing.)?
Сиз нечәсиниз ?	How are you (pl.)?
Биз jахшыjыг.	We are well.

1	**бир**	30	**отуз**
2	**ики**	31	**отуз бир**
3	**үч**	40	**гырх**
4	**дөрд**	41	**гырз бир**
5	**беш**	50	**әлли**
6	**адты**	51	**әлли бир**
7	**једди**	60	**алтмыш**
8	**сәккиз**	61	**алтмыш бир**
9	**доггуз**	70	**јетмиш**
10	**он**	71	**јетмиш бир**
11	**он бир**	80	**сәксән**
12	**он ики**	81	**сәксән бир**
13	**он үч**	90	**дохсан**
14	**он дөрд**	91	**дохсан бир**
15	**он беш**	100	**јүз**
16	**он алты**	101	**јүз бир**
17	**он једди**	200	**ики јүз**
18	**он сәккиз**	300	**үч јүз**
19	**он доггуз**	400	**дөрд јүз**
20	**ијирми**	500	**беш јүз**
21	**ијирми бир**	1000	**мин**

1995 **мин доггуз дохсан беш**

ABBREVIATIONS

a	adjective
adv	adverb
agric	agriculture
anat	anatomy
astron	astronomy
biol	biology
bot	botany
caus	causative verb
chem	chemistry
cmp	compound
coll	collective noun
colloq	colloquial
conj	conjunction
deic	deictic
derog	derogatory
dim	diminutive
econ	economics
elev	elevated language
exp	expression
fig	figurative
fin	financial
geog	geography
geol	geology
gram	grammatical
hist	historical
hort	hortative
intj	interjection
intr	intransitive (verb)
intro-wd	introductory word
iron	ironic
leg	legal term
ling	linguistics
lit:	literally means
math	mathematics
med	medical
mil	military
min	mineralogy
mus	music
myth	mythology
n	noun
n-cmp	compound noun
neg	negative
num	numeral, number
o.s.	oneself
obs	obsolete
onom	onomatopoeia
ord	ordinal
part	particle
pass	passive
phys	physics
poet	poetry
polit	political terminology
pred	predicative
prf	prefix
pro	pronoun
ptc	participle
qw	question word
r	rare
Ru	Russian loan word
rel	relative
relig	religion
s.o	someone
sp	sports
s.t.	something
tech	technology
text	textile
typ	typography/printing
v	verb
v-adv	verbal adverb
v-cmp	compound verb
v-intr	intransitive verb
v-pass	passive verb
vet	veterinary medicine
v n	verbal noun (gerund)
vulg	vulgar
zool	zoology

Bibliography

Alderson, A. D. and I. Fahir, eds. The Concise Oxford Turkish Dictionary. Oxford: Clarendon Press, 1959.

Austin, Paul M. "Russian Loanwords In the Proposed Reform of Soviet Turkic Alphabets" General Linguistics, Vol. 13, No 1. University Park, PA, and London: Pennsylvania State University Press, 1973.

Avery, C. Robert, et al. Contemporary Turkish-English Dictionary. Istanbul: Redhouse Press, 1983.

Azizbekov, Kh. A., et al. Азәрбаjанча-Русча Лүғәт (Azerbaijani-Russian Dictionary). Baku: Azerbaijan State Publishing House, 1985.

Bailey, Liberty H. Hortus Third: A Concise Dictionary of Plants. New York: Macmillan, 1976.

Budagova, Z. I., Sh. M. Saadiev, and A. K. Alexperov Самоучитель Азербайджанского Языка („Self-Instruction Manual in the Azerbaijani Language"). Baku: Elm Publishing House, 1977.

Callaham, Ludmilla Russian-English Chemical and Polytechnical Dictionary, 3rd ed. New York: Wiley, 1975.

Dal', Vladimir I. Толковый Словарь Живого Велико-русского Языка („Dictionary of the Great-Russian Living Language"), 4 volumes. Moscow:Russkij Yazyk, 1981.

Deny, Jean, et al. Philologiae Turcicae Fundamenta. Wiesbaden: Franz Steiner, 1959.

Ercilasun, Ahmet B., et al. Karşilaştirmali Türk Lehçeleri Sözlügü ("A Comparative Dictionary of Turkish Dialects"). Ankara: Kültür Bakanlığı, 1991.

Fernald, Merrit L. Gray's Manual Of Botany, vol. 2. Portland, Oregon: Dioscorides Press, 1987.

Haim, Suleyman The Shorter Persian-English Dictionary. Teheran: Librairie-Imprimerie Béroukhim, 1961.

Householder, F. W. and M. Lotfi "Azerbaijan- English Vocabulary" in Basic Course in Azerbaijani (Uralic and Altaic Series 45). Bloomington: Indiana University, and the Hague: Mouton, 1965.

Katzner, Kenneth English-Russian, Russian-English Dictionary. New York: John Wiley & Sons, 1984.

Khalilov, Y. G. and M. I. Yavlalov Deutsch-Azerbaidschanisch-Russisches Wörterbuch Für Gesellschäftliche Disziplinen. Baku: Maarif, 1965.

Lewis, G. L. Turkish Grammar. Oxford: Clarendon Press, 1985.

Miller, B. V. Персидско-Русский Словарь ("Persian-Russian Dictionary"). Moscow: State Publishing House for Foreign and National Language Dictionaries,1960.

Murphy, John D. Azerbaijani Newspaper Reader. Kensington, MD: Dunwoody Press 1993.

Orudzhev, A. A., ed., et al. Азербаjчан Дилинин Изали Лүғати ("Explanatory Dictionary of the Azerbaijani Language"), 4 volumes. Baku: Azerbajani State Publishing House (vol. 1) 1964, (vol. 2) 1965, (vol. 3) 1983, (vol. 4) 1987.

Orudzhev, A. G., S. D. Melikov, and A. A. Efendiev, eds. Русско-Азербайданский Словарь („ Russian-Azerbaijani Dictionary"), 2 volumes, 2nd ed., rewritten and expanded. Baku: Azerbaijanian Academy of Sciences Publishing House, 1956.

Ozhegov, S. I. Словарь Русского Языка ("Dictionary of the Russian Language"). Moscow: Soviet Encyclopedia Publishers, 1972.

Redhouse, Sir James New Redhouse Turkish-English Dictionary. Istanbul: Redhouse Press, 1983.

Rubinchik, Yu. A., ed., et al. Персидско-Русский Словарь ("Persian-Russian Dictionary") 2 volumes. Moscow: Soviet Encyclopedia Publishers, 1970.

Sari, M. Turkish-English-Arabic Lexicon. Istanbul: Gonca Yayinevi, n.d.

Simson, C. G. "Recent Changes in the Orthography of the Soviet Azerbaydzhani Language," Central Asian Review, vol. 7, pp 139-144. London, 1959.

Smirnitskij, A. I. Russian-English Dictionary. Moscow: Russky Yazyk Publishers, 1991.

Tagiev, M. T., Chief Editor, et al. Азербаjчанча-Русча Лүғәт ("Azerbaijani-Russian Dictionary"), 4 volumes. Baku: "Elm" Publishing House, 1986.

Underhill, R. Turkish Grammar, 3rd Edition. Cambridge, MA: Massachusetts Institute of Technology, 1980.

Ushakov, D. N., ed., et al. Толковый Словарь Русского Языка ("Explanatory Dictionary of the Russian Language"), 4 volumes. Moscow: Soviet Encyclopedia Publishers, 1935.

The Dictionary

a

а : first letter of the Azerbaijani alphabet

аб : *n* water *Persian, obsolete, occurs mainly in classical literature*

аба : *n* cassock *clerical garment worn by Moslem clerics*

абад : *a* populated; equipped with modern amenities

абадан : *a* populated; well maintained; equipped with modern amenities or conveniences

абаданлащдырылмаг : *v* 1) be well maintained *of an area* 2) become equipped with modern amenities

абаданлащдырмаг : *v* 1) maintain an area well 2) equip with modern amenities

абаданлашмаг : *v* become well maintained

абаданлыг : *n* 1) equipping with services and utilities 2) region or district with good amenities, modern conveniences

абадланмаг : *v* 1) come to be well maintained 2) come to be provided with modern amenities /conveniences

абадлащдырмаг : *v* bring *some place* to a well maintained condition

абадлашма : *v* equipping with services and utilities

абадлашмаг : *v* be equipped with modern amenities, be built/completed, be populated/settled, prosper, flourish

абадлыг : *n* state of being equipped with services and utilities

абадча : *a* comfortable, well-organized, well-equipped

абажур : *n Ru* lamp-shade

абасбәји : *n* variety of pear

аббасиләр : *n* Abbasids *Moslem dynasty 750-1258 AD*

аббасы : *n* 20 kopeck silver coin

аббасылыг : *n* s.t. worth 20 kopecks

абгора : *n* sour juice of unripe grapes used as a seasoning for food

абдал : *n* fool, simpleton, dolt

абдаллашма : *vn* **абдаллашмаг**

абдаллашмаг : *v* 1) grow stupid/foolish 2) grow careless/ negligent/slovenly

абдаллыг : *n* 1) stupidity, ignorance, idiocy 2) negligence, slovenliness

абдалчасына : *adv* 1) foolishly, idiotically 2) negligence, slovenliness

абдан : *n* reservoir, storage pond/pool

абдәст : *n* see **ajarјолу**

абзас : *n Ru* 1) indented line *indicating a paragraph* 2) paragraph *text between two indented lines*

абид : *n relig* 1) pilgrim, ascetic 2) *a* devout, pious, religious 3) Abid *masculine first name*

абиданә : *n* see **абидчәсинә**

абидә : *n* monument , memorial

абидләшмәк : *v* become devout, pious, religious

абидлик : *n* piety, devotion, religiousness

абидчәсинә : *adv* piously, religiously, ascetically

аби-зәмзәм : *n* water from the sacred well, "Zemzem", not far from the Mohammedan shrine, the Kaaba in Medina

аби-нејсан : *n* April rains

аби-һәјат : *n myth* 1) nectar, elixir of life 2) legendary fountain of youth

абы : *a* blue, pale blue, sky blue

абыр : *n* 1) decency, dignity 2) shame 3) sense of honor

абырлама : *v* 1) from **абырламаг** 2) *n* reproach, reproof, rebuke, blame

абырламаг : *v* reproach *with*, shame, put to shame, make ashamed *of s.t.*

абырландырмаг : *v* make s.o. feel ashamed, bring s. o. to a decent, self-respecting state of mind

абырланмаг : *n* take on/assume a seemly, respectable appearance, change externally for the better, become respectable/neat/tidy *being ashamed of one's earlier actions*

абырлы : *a* 1) diffident, bashful, shy; decent, proper, moral 2) modest, sound, reputable

абырлылыг : *n* diffidence, modesty, decency, propriety, decorum

абырсыз : *a* shameless, insolent, brazen

абырсыз-абырсыз : *adv* shamelesssly, brazenly, insolently, cheekily

абырсызлыг : *n* 1) shamelessness, impudence, effrontery 2) vulgarity, indecency 3) dishonor, disgrace, disgraceful conduct

абырсызча, абырсызчасына : *adv* insolently, shamelessly, bold-facedly, cynically

абыр-һәја : *n* modesty, decency, decorum

абытәһәр, абыјачалан : *a* slightly blue

абкәрдән : *n* ladle, dipper, scoop

абкүшт : *n* 1) see **бозбаш** 2) a pea soup made with meat

абнабат : *n* hard candy, fruit drops

абнос : *n bot* Yew *Taxus El*

аборт : *n* abortion

абриз : *n* see **ajarjoлу**

абстраксија : *n* abstraction

абунә : *n* subscription

абунәчи : *n* subscriber

абхаз : *n* Abkhazian

абхазија : *n* Abkhazia

аб-һава : *n* weather ; climate

абшерон : *n* 1) Apsheron peninsula *a* 2) Apsheron

аваданлыг : *n* 1) equipment, stock, inventory 2) household equipment

аваз : *n* voice

авазымаг : *v* grow pale

авазлашмаг : *v* call to one another, exchange shouts

авазлы : *a* loud-voiced, full-throated, stentorian

авам : *n* 1) ignoramus, unlettered person *a* 2) ignorant ; simple 3) illiterate

авам-авам : *adv* ignorantly, simple-mindedly

авамлыг : *n* ignorance

авамфриб : *n* demagogue

авамчасына : see **авам-авам**

аванд : *a* 1) successful, fortunate *n* 2) front side, right side of s.t.

аванс : *n* smaller part of salary paid in the middle of the month *in the Soviet Union*

авар : *n* 1) oar 2) an Avar

авара : *n* 1) idler, slacker, loafer 2) tramp 3) two-year-old buffalo calf

авара-авара : *adv* idly

авараланмаг : *v* become a loafer/idler; idle, loaf

аваралашмаг : *v* become/turn into an idler/loafer

аваралыг : *n* idleness, loafing, inactivity

авара-сәркәрдан : *n* tramp, unemployed person, homeless person

аварачылыг : *n* idleness, unemployment

аварија : *n* 1) accident *a* 2) accident[al], emergency

аварлаја-аварлаја : *n* rowing *action*

аварлама : *n* rowing *occupation, sport*

аварламаг : *v* row, scull

аварлы : *a* oared, equipped with oars

аварчәкән : *n* oarsman, rower

аварчы : *n* see **аварчәкән**

аварчылыг : *n* occupation/pursuit/profession of rowing

авиасија : *n* 1) aviation *a* 2) aviation

авизо : *n fin* aviso, letter of advice

авкит : *n min* augite *a dark-colored variety of aluminous pyroxene, occuring in igneous rock*

аврал : *n nav* 1) work involving all hands; a clean sweep fore and aft 2) emergency work, rush job

авропа : *n* 1) Europe *a* 2) European *pertaining to Europe*

авропалащдырмаг : *v* Europeanize s.o.

авропалашмаг : *v* be/become Europeanized

авропалы : *n* European

авропачылыг : *n* Europeanism, Westernism

австралија : *n* 1) Australia *a* 2) Australian

австралијалы : *n* Australian

австрија : *n* 1) Austria *a* 2) Austrian

австријалы : *n* Austrian

автобус : *n* 1) bus *a* 2) bus

автовағзал : *n Ru* bus station

автограф : *n* autograph

автозавод : *n* automobile/automotive plant/factory

автокран : *n* truck crane

автократија : *n* autocracy

автомат : *n* automatic machine ; *mil* machine gun, machine carbine , U.S. Tommy gun

автоматик : *a* 1) automatic *adv* 2) automatically

автомашин : *n* automobile, car, automotive vehicle

автомеханик : *n* auto mechanic, automotive mechanic

автомобил : *n* 1) automobile, car, automotive vehicle *a* 2) automobile, car

автореферат : *n* 1) abstract or concise description of a book or article prepared by the author 2) author‘s abstract *of dissertation etc*, abstract of thesis *prepared by degree candidates*

авторитет : *n* authority

агибәт : *n* future

агибәтли : *a* future

агил : *n* 1) sage, wise man *a* 2) wise, sage

агиланә : *adv* wisely, sagely

агробиологиja : *n* agricultural biology; agrobiology *pseudo-science invented by an official protègè of Stalin, Trofim Lisenko, in the late 40's*

агрокимиja : *n* agricultural chemistry

агрометеоролокиja : *n* agricultural meteorology

агроном : *n* agronomist

агрономик : *a* agronomic

агрономлуг : *n* 1) agronomy .2) the agronomic profession

агротехника : *n* agricultural technology, agrotechnics, agricultural engineering

агротехники : agrotechnological

аг : *a* 1) white *n* 2) coarse white calico 3) white of the eye; white of an egg 4) impudent, beyond-the-beyond

аг турп : *n* turnip

ага : *n* 1) master, owner 2) lord *title of nobility* ; 3) title applied to the Sayyids *the supposed descendants of Mohammed through his elder son Hussein* 4) father *solemn address to one's father*

агаз : *n* foreword, preface

агазадә : *n* Master's son and heir

агаjана : *adv* nobly, aristocratically

агаланмаг : *v* pose as a lord/ master, assume a noble title

агалыг : *n* 1) supremacy, rule, sway, dominion 2) noble house, palace, estate, manor

агаппаг : *a* snow-white

агара-агара : *n* showing up white

агаранты : *n* see **агарты** 1)

агардан : *n* 1) whitewasher 2) scribe, copyist

агардылмаг : *v* be whitewashed

агардычы : *n* 1) whitewasher, painter *a* 2) whitewashed, painted white

агарма : *vn* from **агармаг**

агармаг : *v* turn/grow white, show up white, become white/grey [haired]

агартдырмаг : *caus.* of **агартмаг**

агарты : *n* 1) milk products 2) an almost imperceptable whiteness, white spot

агартма : *n* 1) whitewashing 2) recopying

агартмаг : *v* 1) whiten, whitewash; 2) recopy 3) clean till s.t. is white/till s.t. is spotlessly clean

агатәбиәт : *a* well-behaved,well brought up

агачалан : *a* see **агымсов**

агач : *n* 1) tree 2) stick, cudgel, staff, cane 3) see **агач-угач** *a* 4) arboreal

агач-агач : *n* game played with sticks

агачаjаг : *n* stilts

агачаохшар : *a* tree-like, arborescent

агачасына : *adv* nobly, aristocratically, lordly

агачгыран : *n* wood-cutter, lumberjack

агачгурбагасы : *n* *zool* tree frog *Rana pipiens*

агачгурду : *n* *zool* Capricorn beetle *fam. Cerambycidae*

агачдәлән : *n* woodpecker *Picida L*

агачламаг : *v* beat, thrash, hit with a stick

агачлы : *a* having trees, wooded

агачлыг : *n* 1) wooded place *a* 2) well-wooded

агачсаггызы : *n* soft resin

агач-угач : *n* timber, lumber, construction lumber, scrap construction timber

агаччилалаjан : *n* wood-polisher *person*

агбагыр : *n* 1) coward *a* 2) cowardly, timorous, faint-hearted

агбалыг : *n* *zool* 1) sturgeon *Acipenseridae* 2) Also a.

агбаш : *a* 1) white-haired, grey-haired *n* *fog* 2) Mullah

агбәдән : *a* white-bodied

агбәниз : *a* pale, white-faced

агбәхт : *n* lucky fellow, Fortune's child, fair-haired boy

агбәхтли : *a* lucky, fortunate

агбирчәк : *n* 1) grey-haired old woman, elderly woman with grey hair, *fig* 2) elderly housewife, respectable woman

агбыг : *a* grey-moustached

агганад : *a* white-winged

аггарын : *a* *zool* white-bellied

агвардиja : *n* *hist* White Guard *Forces opposing the Bolshevik Army during the Russian revolution and Civil War*

агвардиjачы : *n* White Guardsman see **агвардиja**

агызыл : *n* platinum

агговаг : *n* Poplar tree *Populus L*

аггуjруг : *a* white-tailed

агдамар : *a* *bot* white-veined

ағдаш : *n* 1) white stone 2) Agdash *city in Central Azerbaijan*

ағдиш : *a* white-toothed

ағзыачыг : *n* 1) gawker 2) scatterbrain, thoughtless person

ағзыбәрк : *a* close-mouthed, capable of keeping a secret

ағзыбәрклик : *n* capability to keep a secret, close-mouthedness

ағзыбир : *n* cell *in prison*

ағзыбош : *n* 1) chatterbox, gasbag, windbag; gossip, leaker, one unable to keep a secret; *a* 2) garrulous, gabby 3) characterless, weak-willed

ағзыбошлуг : *n* 1) talkativeness, inability to keep a secret 2) weakness of will, lack of character

ағзыбүтөв : *a* see **ағзыбәрк**

ағзыбүтүн : *a* see **ағзыбәрк**

ағзыгара : *a* 1) black-muzzled' *n* 2) wolf 3) wolf-hound, sheep-dog

ағзыдуалы : *a* pious, religious

ағзыәјри : *a* crooked-mouthed, wry-mouthed

ағзыјава : *n* foul-mouthed person, garbage-mouth

ағзыјасты : *a* speaking slowly/quietly/drawlingly

ағзыјекә : *a* wide-mouthed

ағзыјелли : *a* arrogant, smug, self-satisfied, haughty

ағзыјыртыг : *n* see **ағзыбош**

ағзыкәсәрли : *a* speaking authoritatively/weightily /impressively

ағзыкәсәрлилик : *n* 1) authoritativeness, impressiveness 2) one whose opinion is respected

ағзыкөпүклү : *a* foaming at the mouth

ағзыкен : *a* wide-mouthed *of a vessel/ jar*

ағзыкөјчәк : *n* chatterbox, talkative/garrulous person

ағзыкөјчәклик : *n* garrulity, gabbiness, talkativeness

ағзыодлу : *a* 1) speaking heatedly, agitatedly 2) heated, agitated 3) heatedly, agitatedly

ағзыпәртөв : *n* foul-mouthed person, one prone to profanity, garbage-mouth

ағзыпозуг : *a* see **ағзыпәртөв**

ағзыпүстә : *n* woman with a small mouth, woman with a pretty, well-shaped mouth *like a pistachio*

ағзысөјүшлү : *n* one who frequently uses obscenities

ағзыһарфа : *a* 1) vulgar, unrestrained in words and expressions *n* 2) foul-mouthed person, garbage-mouth

ағзыһарфалыг : *n* foul language, ribaldry, profanity

ағзыһәрзә : *a* see **ағзыһарфа**

ағзычырыг : *a* see **ашзыбош**

ағы : *n* 1) elegy; ritual lamentation, keening, mournful, plaintive singing; 2) poison

ағыз : *n* 1) mouth; pharynx 2) opening, aperture, lid of a dish/pot 3) cutting edge, sharp side of a blade 4) muzzle of a firearm 5) door, entrance

ағыз ачмаг : *v* ask, request

ағыздан гачырмаг : *v* blurt out

ағзына сөз атмаг : *v* prompt; instigate

ағзыны арамаг : *v* assay

ағызбаағыз : *n* overfilled, filled to the brim

ағызбары : *adv* orally, by heart

ағыз-бурунлу : *a* neatly dressed, respectable ; of imposing appearance

ағыздан : *adv* orally, by heart

ағызјуммадан : *adv* incessantly, nonstop endlessly, without shutting up for a moment *talking*

ағызјуммаз : *a* unceasing, incessant *of talking*, garrulous, talkative

ағызлашдырмаг : *v* compel s.o. to exchange angry words

ағызлашма : *n* quarrel, squabble

ағызлашмаг : *v* 1) quarrel, exchange angry words 2) seek counsel from, ask advice of have a short talk with s.o.

ағызлы : *n* eloquent, silver-tongued

ағызлыг : *n* 1) see **гыф** 2) plug, cork 3) see **ағызоту**

ағызоту : *n* priming powder, primer, fuse

ағызсыз : *a* see **дилсиз-ағызсыз**

ағызучу : *adv* 1) groundlessly, unsoundly *speak* 2) by the way, off the cuff

ағыл : *n* reason, intellect, judgement

ағыл чатмаг : *v* comprehend, understand, get the idea

ағыла кәтирмәк : *v* remember

ағлы кәсмәк : *v* perceive, become aware *of*

ағылама : *n* poisoning

ағыламаг : *v* poison

ағыланмаг : *v* be poisoned

ағылјана : *adv* at random, by guess,

ағылкәсән : *a* probable, likely, reasonable, sensible

ағылкәсмәз : *a* improbable, unlikely, inadmissable

ағылкәсмәјән : *a* see **ағылкәсмәз**

ағыллaндырмаг : *v* make to see reason, make s.o. see the error of his ways

ағылланмаг : *v* grow wiser, come to see reaason,

ағыллы : *a* clever, intelligent, sensible, reasonable

ағыллы-ағыллы : *adv* cleverly, reasonably, wisely, intelligently

ағыллы-башлы : *a* 1) rather decent/proper 2) quite suitable , quite high quality, quite worthwhile *adv* 3) as it should be 4) decently, properly, gravely

ағыллы-камаллы : *a* reasonable, intelligent; quite decent, honest, respectable

ағыллылыг : sense, wisdom, reasonableness

ағыллыча : *adv* wisely, sensibly, intelligently

ағылсыз : *a* stupid, imprudent, senseless

ағылсызлыг : *n* senselessness, stupidity, folly

ағылсызчасына : *adv* crazily, rashly

ағылумулмаз : *n* person of diminished responsibility, dunce

ағымсов : *a* whitish

ағымтыл : *a* see **ағымсов**

ағымтраг : *a* see **ашымсов**

ағыр : *a* difficult, hard, slow; painful, grievous

ағыр-ағыр : *adv* 1) slowly, awkwardly 2) solemnly

ағырешидән : *a* slightly deaf, hard of hearing, hearing-impaired

ағырлатмаг : *v* burden, make heavier, aggravate, make harder

ағырлашдырычы : *a* aggravating *i.e. circumstances*

ағырлашдырмаг : *v* see **ағырлатмаг**

ағырлашмаг : *v* grow/become heavy/heavier, become complicated, grow worse

ағырлыг : *n* 1) weight 2) heaviness 3) burden 4) load, cargo

ағыр-санбаллы : *a* weighty, ponderous, strong *argument*

ағыр-сәнкин : *a* solemn, serious, earnest, grave

ағыр-сәнкинләшмәк : *v* settle down, become staid/ respectable

ағыр-сәнкинлик : *n* steadness, sedateness, respectability

ағыртәрпәнән : *a* awkward, clumsy; difficult to lift

ағыртәрпәнишли : *a* see **ағыртәпәнән**

ағыртәһәр : *a* 1) somewhat heavy, heavyish *fig* 2) rather hard *adv* 3) with some difficulty

ағырхасиjjәт : *n* difficult person, one who is hard to get along with

ағырхасиjjәтли : *n* see **ағырхасиjjәт**

ағычы : *n* professional mourner *woman paid to perform ritual lamentations at a funeral*

ағјағыз : *a* see **ағбәниз**

ағјал : *a* white-maned, white-crested

ағјаллы : *a* see **ағјал**

ағјол : *n astron* the Milky Way, the Galaxy

ағкирпик : *a* white-lashed

ағкөјнәк : *a* white-shirted, wearing a white shirt

ағкилә : *n* large-fruited white grape variety

ағкөвдәли : *a bot* white-stemmed, white-trunked

ағкөз : *n zool* variety of carp *Cyprinus carpio*

ағкүн : *n* a happy, carefree life

ағлабатан : *a* 1) probable; possible; acceptable, admissible 2) reasonable, sensible

ағлабатмаз : *a* hardly probable, unacceptable, inadmissible

ағлабатмазлыг : *n* improbability; unacceptability

ағлаған : *n* 1) cry-baby, complainer *a* 2) tearful, whining

ағладычы : *a* lamentable, deplorable; sorrowful, evoking tears

ағлаја-ағлаја : *n* weeping, crying, shedding tears

ағлајыб-сытгамаг : *v* beg, plead with tears in one's eyes

ағлајыш : *n* weeping, crying

ағлакәлмәз : *a* 1) improbable, inconceivable *adv* 2) improbably, inconceivably

ағлакирмәз : *a* see **ағлакәлмәз**

ағлама : *vn* fr.. **ағламаг**

ағламаг : *v* cry, sob, weep

ағламсынмаг : *v* shed a few tears, be unable to keep from weeping

ағлар : *a* 1) lamentable, deplorable 2) whining *n* 3) Whites *Forces opposed to Reds*

ағлар-күләр : *a* tragicomical, producing laughter and tears at the same time

ағласығмаз : *a* improbable, incredible inconceivable, unthinkable

ағласығмазлыг : *n* inconceivability, improbability

ағлатмаг : *v* cause to weep, evoke tears

ағлашдырмаг : *v* cause common/joint weeping

ағлашма : *n* 1) general weeping 2) general weeping for a deceased person

ағлашмаг : *v* weep in common

ағлыг : *n* whiteness

ағмаја : *a* white; plump *of a baby*

ағмала : *n* first coat of plaster

ағнаг : *n* 1) place where animals rest on hot days 2) site in the mountains where soil has slipped down 3) pot-hole

ағнаја-ағнаја : *adv* falling over, rolling over; turning from one side to the other

ағнамаг : *v* turn from one side to the other

ағнатмаг : *v* lower; move a mass; drive away

ағнашма : *adv* lying, rolling on the floor/the ground

ағнашмаг : *v* roll on the floor together

ағот : *n bot* feather grass *Stipa L*

ағры : *n* pain, rheumatic pain, ache; ailment, illness

ағры-ачы : *n* pain, rheumatic pain

ағры-ачысыз : *adv* painlessly

ағрыдычы : *a* evoking/causing pain

ағрыкәсән : *a* relieving pain, palliative

ағрымаг : *v* be ill/ailing, have pain, be painful, hurt

ағрысыз : *a* painless

ағрытмаг : *v* cause pain/illness

ағсаггал : *a* 1) white-bearded *n* 2) elder, tribal leader, venerable/ estimable person

ағсаггаллыг : *n* state of being an elder

ағсач : *a* white-haired, grey-haired

ағсачлы : *a* white-haired, grey-haired

ағсифәт *a* 1) white-faced 2) white-faced person

ағсөјүд : *n bot* white willow *Salix Alba L.*

ағтәһәр : *a* whitish

ағтикан : *n bot* Buckthorn *Rhamnus L.*

ағуш : *n* 1) embraces 2) womb; 3) lap, bosom *of nature*

ағүзлү : *a* white-faced ; having a clear conscience

ағчил : *a* speckled with white spots

ағчичәкли : *a* white-flowered, having white blossoms

ағча : *a dim* 1) white *n* 2) woman's ornament made of silver coins 3) coin

ағчагајын : *n bot* birch-tree *Betulaceae*

ағчаганад : *n zool* mosquito, gnat

ағчаговаг : *n bot* Aspen

ағчамаја : *a* see **ағмаја**

ағчијәр : *n* 1) coward *a* 2) cowardly, faint-hearted

ағчијәрлик : *n* cowardice, faint-heartedness

ағшам : *n bot* fir tree, silver fir *Abies*

ад : *n* name; title, fame; rank, degree

ад алмаг : *v* become famous

ад гојмаг : *v* name, give a name

ад чәкмәк : *v* mention

ады батмаг : *v* lose reputation

ады чәкилмәк : *v* be proposed as a candidate

ада : *n* island

адаб : *n* decency, politeness, good manners

адаг : *n* first steps of a child

адаг-адаг : *adv* slowly, with childlike, uncertain steps

ададовшаны : *n* rabbit

адалы : *n* islander

адам : *n* man, person, human being

адамајовушмаз : *n* see **адамдангачан**

адамалдадан : *n* cheat, fraud, swindler

адамаохшамаз : *n* 1) freak, monster *a* 2) unprepossessing, uncomely

адамаохшар : *a* anthropomorphous, anthropoid, human-like

адамбашы : *adv* per capita

адамбоју : *a* of human size

адамдангачан : *n* misanthrope, unsocial person; hermit, anchorite

адамјана : *adv* humanly, in a human way, rationally

адамјејән : *n* cannibal

адамкөкү : *n bot* mandrake *Mandragora officinalis L.*

адамкүлдүрән : *a* 1) funny, laughable *n* 2) joker

адамлыг : *n* 1) humanity 2) *in conjunction with numerical terms* per x persons

адамојнадан : *n* mocker, scoffer

адамөтүрән : *n* guide *one who knows an area*

адамсевмәз : *n* see **адамдангачан**

адамсыз : *a* 1) unpopulated, deserted 2) having no family, defenseless 3) homeless

адамсызлыг : *n* 1) solitude 2) defenselessness 3) absence of human beings

адамтаныјан : *n* physiognomist *one skilful in the practice of discerning character by features of the face or forms of the body*

адамчасына : *adv* humanly, in a human way; mercifully

адамчыг : *n derog* 1) little fellow, little man 2) poor fellow

адамчығаз : *n* see **адамчыг**

адамчыл : *a* 1) bloodthrsty, rapacious *n* 2) *animal* beast of prey; *bird* raptor, *human* plunderer, spoiler

адахлама : *n* engagement, betrothal

адахламаг : *n* become/get engaged/betrothed

адахландырмаг : *v* see **адахламаг**

адахланмаг : *v* be engaged

адахлы : *n* 1) fiance 2) fiancee, bride *a* 3) engaged, betrothed

адахлыбазлыг : *n* traditional secret meeting of the engaged couple *usually with the knowledge and consent of the mother*

адачајы : *n bot* sage *Salvia L*

адачыг : *n* islet, small island

адаш : *n* namesake, person bearing the same name

адашлыг : *n* state or condition of having the same name

адбаад : *adv* by name

адгојма : *n* naming, giving a name *i.e to a child*; name day

адда-будда : *adv* with interruptions, brokenly, here and there

аддамаг : *v* step over, get over go over; trespass

аддатмаг : *v* carry *somewhere else* transport, convey, take across

аддым : *n* step

аддым-аддым : *adv* step by step, slowly

аддымбааддым : *adv* step by step; on the track *of s.t. / s.o.*

аддымбасды : *n kind of children's game*

аддымбашы : *adv* often; here and there

аддымлајан : a stepping, treading *used to describe a type of power-shovel, or excavator*

аддымлама : *n* military pace, parade step

аддымламаг : *v* tread, stroll, march, stride

аддымлатмаг : *caus.* of **адымламаг**

аддымлы : *n* one walking with large strides

аддымлыг : *n* pace *after numerals refers to the distance in paces*

аддымөлчән : *n* pedometer

адә е! *interj* hey, you!

адәм : *n* Adam in the Bible, the first man, the progenitor of the human race

адәмдәнгалма : *a colloq* ancient, dating from the time of Adam, preserved from Adam‘s time

адәт : *n* custom, habit; tradition, ritual

адәт олмаг : *v* have o.'s period

адәтдәнкәнар : *a* unusual, out of the ordinary, non-traditional; unaccustomed, unwonted

адәтдәнхарич : *a* see **адәтдәнкәнар**

адәтән : *adv* usually, normally, as always

адәткәрдә : *a* prone *to* used *to*, inclined *to*

адәтсиз : *a* unused *to*, unaccustomed, unwonted

адәтчә : *adv* usually, as usual, according to habit/ custom/tradition/ritual

ади : *a* 1) usual, ordinary 2) simple, commonplace

адил : *a* 1) fair, just 2) Adil *masculine first name*

адиланә : *adv* fairly, justly

адилик : *n* simplicity, ordinariness; commonplaceness, conventionality

ады : *adv* quite, absolutely; at all

адыбатмыш : *a* forgotten, consigned to oblivion

адыбилинмәз : *a* unknown

адыкеј : *n* 1) an Adighe/Adygei *a* 2) Adighe *pertaining to the Adighei, a small Circassian nation in the North Caucasus*

адыкејчә : *adv* in the Adighe/ Adygei language

адына : *n colloq* Friday

адјал : *n* blanket *distorted form of the Russian word* 'одеяло'

адландырмаг : *v* name, give a name *to* ; call

адланмаг : *v* be named/called/titled

адлы : *a* famous, well-known; by the name of; nominal *in various meanings*

адлыг : *a gram* nominative

адлы-санлы : *a* honored, respected, having a good reputation

адмирал : *n* admiral

адмираллыг : *n* 1) position or rank of an admiral 2) Admiralty

ад-сан : *n* glory, fame; reputation

адсыз : *a* nameless, anonymous

адсыз-сансыз : *a* obscure, unknown *person*

аеродром : *n Ru* airfield

аз : *a* little, few

аз гала : *adv* almost

азад : *a* 1) free 2) Azad *common masculine first name*

азад еләмәк : *v* free, let go

азадә : *a* see **азад**

азадәлик : *n* see **азадлыг** :

азадлыг : *n* freedom, liberty

азадлыгсевән : *a* freedom-loving

азадфикирли : *a* 1) free-thinking *n* 2) free-thinker

азадфикирлилик : *n* free thought

азадхаһ : *a* freedom-loving

азадча : *adv* freely, easily, at will

азадчасына : *adv* see **азадча**

аз-аз : *adv* little by little; occasionally

азајланмаг : *v* complain; lament; nag; grumble

азалан : *a* 1) reducing, diminishing *n* 2) minuend

азалдылмаг : *v* be lessened/cut short/ reduced/subtracted

азалма : *vn* fr.. **азалмаг**

азалмаг : *v* lessen, be reduced/diminished

азалтдырмаг : *v* cause s.o. to lesson/cut short/reduce

азалтма : *n* lessening, cutting short, reduction

азалтмаг : *v* cause lessening/cutting short/reduction

азан : *a* 1) wandering, roaming *n* 2) person who has lost his way 3) Moslem call to prayer

азанчы : *n* muezzin

азар : *n* illness, disease, pain; epidemic; trouble, worry

азар-безар : *n* every kind of ailment

азаркәздирән : *n* disease carrier

азарладан : *a* disease-causing

азарладычы : *a* see **азарладан**

азарлама : *a* falling ill, contracting a disease

азарламаг : *v* get sick, fall ill

азарлатмаг : *v* cause illness/disease

азарлы : *a* sore, painful

азарлы-азарлы : *a* very sore, very painful

азарлылыг : *n* sickliness

азарсыз : *a* 1) free of disease, not sick 2) inoffensive, incapable of offending

азартөрәдән : *a* infectious, contagious

азархана : see **хәстәхана**

азачыг : *adv* a little bit, slightly

азбиликли : *a colloq* ill-informed, not very well informed, not quite with it

азбудаглы : *a* sparsely branched

азвахтлы : *a* see **азмүддәтли**

азгазанчлы : *a* unprofitable, not lucrative; having a low income

азгидалы : *a* unnutritious

азғын : *a* 1) wandering, roaming 2) frenzied, unrestrained, wild 3) out-of-control

азғынлашмаг : *v* 1) become frenzied, be in a frenzy 2) be unrestrained, be out of control, be wild/frenzied/delirious

азғынлыг : *n* 1) lack of restraint; state of delirium; ungovernability 2) dissolution, dissipation, licentiousness, profligacy

азданышан : *a* taciturn, silent, uncommunicative

аздан-чохдан : *adv* 1) any *amount n* 2) more or less, some quantity

аздырылмаг : *v* be led astray, be put off one‘s route

аздырмаг : *v* confuse, mix up; divert; lead astray

аздыртмаг : *caus.* of **азмүддәтли**

азәрбајчан : *n* 1) Azerbaijan *a* 2) Azerbaijan, Azerbaijani

азәрбајчанлы : *n* Azerbaijanian, Azerbaijani *person*

азәрбајчанча : *adv* in Azerbaijani *language*

азәри : *n* see **азәрбајчанлы**

Азәринформ : *n* Azerbaijan News Agency

азәричә : *adv* see **азәрбајчанча**

азишләнән : *a* rare, rarely used, seldom used, not in common use

азы : *adv* at least, minimally

азыдиши : *n* molar

азыхмаг : *v* 1) worsen, grow worse *med* 2) grow complicated, have complications set in *of an illness*

азјашлы : *a* under age, juvenile, minor

азкәлирли : *a* unprofitable, unremunerative

азкөрүнән : *a* 1) barely visible/noticeable 2) rarely encountered

азлыг : *n* 1) minority 2) small in number/quanity 3) shortage

азма : *v* fr.. **азмаг**

азмаг : *v* 1) lose one's way; err, be mistaken 2) become corrupted, spoiled ; grow impudent

азман : *n* 1) six year old he-goat 2) huge, tremendous

азмә'луматлы : *a* of little knowledge, ill-informed

азмәнфәәтли : *a* not very profitable

азмүддәтли : *a* short-term, of short duration

азот : *n* nitrogen

азотлашдырма : *n* nitrogenization

азотлу : *a* nitrous

азсавадлы : *a* semi-literate, functionally illiterate, half-educated

азсајлы : *a* being few in numbers; minority

азтанынан : little-known

азтапылан : *a* 1) rare, uncommon 2) in short supply

азтәһәр : *adv* not quite enough, barely sufficient

азтәһсилли : *a* poorly educated

азтәчрүбәли : *a* inexperienced, having little experienced

азторпаглы : *a* having insufficient *arable* land

азторпаглылыг : *n* shortage of arable land

азтутумлу : *a* not capacious, not roomy, of insufficient capacity *vessel, container*

азугә : *n* food supply, food reserve

азушаглы : *a* having few children

аз-чох : *adv* 1) more or less 2) a little, some, some quantity, any *amount*

азча : *adv* just a little bit, a trifle, a wee bit

азча-азча : *adv* just a very little bit, in small doses, little by little, a bit at a time

азчана : *adv* a little bit

азшахәли : *a* see **азбудаглы**

аид : *postp.* 1) relating to, pertinent/pertaining to 2) concerning, about, in connection with 3) as regards,belonging *to*

аидијјәт : *n* state/condition of belonging to/being related to, being applicable, pertaining to s.t.

аилә : *n* family

аиләви : *a* familial, family

аиләдар : *n* family man *one devoted to his family*

аиләли : *a* domestic; having a family

аиләпәрәст : *n* see **аиләдар**

аиләсиз : *a* single, without a family

аиләчилик : *n* nepotism

ај : *n* 1) month 2) moon

аја : *intj* used to express surprise; Really! Well! Oh no! Huh!

ајаг : *n* leg, foot

ајаг еләмәк : *v* take s.o. as a partner

ајаг олмаг : *v* take part

ајаг сахламаг : *v* slow down

ајагдан чәкмәк : *v* be hostile to each other

ајаға дүшмәк : *v* lower, go down *of prices*

ајаға чәкмәк : *v* cock *a gun*

ајағыны дирәмәк : *v* be stubborn, obstinate

ајаг-ајаға : *adv* step by step, in step together

ајагалты : *n* doormat; rug

ајаг-баш : *adv* topsy-turvy, head-over-heels

ајаггабы : *n* footwear, foot gear

ајаггабыбичән : *n* leather-cutter *one who cuts out leather parts for shoe-making*

ајаггабылы : *a* wearing shoes, shod

ајаггабыстан : *n* footwear/shoe merchant/seller, footwear shopping center

ајаггабысыз : *a* see **ајагјалын**

ајагданчәкән : *n* mean, ill-intentioned, underhanded person

ајагјалын : *a* 1) barefoot/barefooted 2) barefoot

ајагјолу : *n* restroom, bathroom

ајагкирәси : *n* see **ајагһагты**

ајагламаг : *v* trample down, tramp on s.t.

ајагланмаг : *v* be trampled on

ајаглатдырмаг : *caus.* of **ајагламаг**

ајаглатмаг : *caus.* of **ајагламаг**

ајаглашмаг : *v* be in step, achieve equality *with s.o.*

ajaглы : *a* 1) having feet, legs *adv* 2) quickly

ajaгсejри : *n* stroll, walk, promenade

ajaгсыз : *a* legless, having no feet/legs

ajaгучу : *adv* in passing by, while passing by

ajaгүстү : *adv* see **ajaгучу**

ajaгhaгты : *n* fee charged for a visit/session

ajaгчы : *n* 1) errand boy 2) pedlar

ajaғыачыг : *a* suffering from diarrhea

ajaғыбағлы : *n* see **гәбиз**

ajaғыjүнкүл : *a* 1) energetic, enterprising, successful *n* 2) an energetic, enterprising, "go-ahead" individual, a "go-getter"; a successful, enterprising, enterpreneurial person

ajaғыпәрдәлиләр : *a zool* web-footed

ajaғысүрүшкән : *n* whore, prostitute

ағычарыглы : *n* maker of bast sandals/shoes

ajaз : *a* 1) clear, cloudless *of a winter sky* *n* 2) clear, cold weather 3) *both masculine and feminine first name*

ajaзымаг : *v* 1) become clearer and colder *in winter* 2) freshen, refresh *o.s.*

ajaзытмаг : *v* refresh *s.o.*

ajaма : *n* nickname

ajбaaj : *adv* monthly, on a monthly basis

ajбашы : *n* 1) menstruation, monthly period

ajғыр : *n* stud-horse *lit. and fig.*

ajғырлашмаг : *v* 1) become a stud-horse *lit. and fig*

ajдын : *a* 1) clear, limpid 2) distinct 3) understandable, intelligible, indisputable 4) *very popular masculine first name*

ajдын-ашкар : *a* 1) clear, obviously, indisputably *adv* 2) clearly, obviously, indisputably

ajдынлатмаг : *v* clarify, make clear, explain

ajдынлашдырылмаг : *v* 1) be explained, cleared, clarified 2) be revealed; developed

ajдынлашдырылмаз : *a* inexplicable

ajдынлашдырычы : *a* explanatory, interpretive *of notes to a document*

ajдынлашдырма : *n* 1) explanation, clarification 2) development

ajдынлашдырмаг : *v* explain, clarify, make understandable

ajдынлашма : *v* from **ajдынлашмаг**

ajдынлашмаг : *v* beome clear/obvious; become apparent; be developed

ajдынлыг : *n* 1) clarity, distinctness *fig* 2) moonlight

ajдынча : *a* 1) completely clear *adv* 2) clearly, convincingly

ajә : *n* verse of the Koran

ajәндә : *n* future

ajин : *n* cult, ritual, ceremony

ajы : *n* 1) bear 2) *fig.* rude person

ajыбаласы : *n* unburnt brick made of clay mixed with straw

ajыбоған : *n orig. adjective* unripe pear; inripe, inedible fruit *usually pear*

ajыг : *a* 1) alert, keen 2) sober; awake 3) conscious

ajыглыг : *n* 1) vigilance, watchfulness 2) sobriety ; state of alert wakefulness 3) reality

ajыг-саjыг : *adv* 1) with clear mind and full consciousness; watchfully, vigilantly, keenly *a* 2) watchful, vigilant 3) sober

ajыдөшәjи : *n bot* fern *Filicineae L*

ajылыг : *n* 1) area having a large bear population 2) *fig* awkwardness, crudity; ignorance

ajылмаг : *v* 1) wake up, awaken 2) sober up; take a "morning-after drink", take a hair of the dog that bit you 3) come to one's senses, collect one's wits 4) improve (of a sick person)

ajылтмаг : *v* 1) awaken *s. o.* 2) sober *s. o.* up

ajын-ojун : *n* trifles; belongings, one's things; utensils

ajыojнадан : *n* bear-trainer

ajыпәнчәси : *n bot* Acanthus

ajырычы : *n* sorter, separator

ajырма : *v* fr. **ajырмаг**

ajырмаг : *v* 1) separate, divide, set apart, isolate 2) disconnect, disjoin 3) move apart

ajыхана : *n* premises where bears are kept

ajычасына : *adv* boorishly, awkwardly, bearishly

ajлы : *a* lunar

ajлыг : *n* 1) monthly pay/salary/wages *a* 2) monthly

ajлыгчы : *n* temporary employee, freelancer

ajлыгчылыг : *n* short-term employment

ajлы-улдузлу : *a* clear, starry *of night*

ajна : *n* 1) mirror 2) window *in some Azerbaijani dialects*

ajнабәнд : *a* furnished/hung with mirrors *n* 2) mirrored gallery

ajналамаг : *v* 1) install glass, glaze 2) polish

ajналы : *a* 1) mirror, smooth-surfaced 2) glass

ajнасалан : *n* glazier, glass-cutter

ajнасыз : *a* 1) without glass, unglazed 2) without mirror, mirrorless

ajначы : *n* 1) glazier, glass-cutter 2) dealer in mirrors; master mirror-maker

ajпара : *n* half moon; crescent moon ; sickle moon

ajран : *n* ayran *salty drink made of sour milk*

ajранашы : *n* soup made of ayran and rice

ajранлыг : *n* that which is required for preparing ayran

ajры : *a* 1) other, different 2) separate, special *adv* 3) separately, specially

ajры дүшмәк : *v* part, get separated

ajры салмаг : *v tr* part, set apart

ajры-ajры : *adv* separately

ajрыготу : *n bot* couch grass, quitch grass, quick grass *Agropyron Lepens L*

ajрылыг : *n* 1) separation, living apart 2) difference, distinction; divergence 3) isolation

ajрылыгда : *adv* separately

ajрылма : *n* 1) parting 2) breaking up, dismemberment; differentiation

ajрылмаг : *v intr* 1) part 2) become dismembered, break up 3) get separated, get divorced

ajрылмаз : *a* 1) inseparable 2) ever present *chem* 2) undecomposable *adv* 4) continually, constantly, permanently

ajрым : *n* Ayrum *group of Azerbaijanis who used to live in the north of Armenia*

ajры-сечкилик : *n* bias, prejudice, partiality

ajрыч : *n* intersection, crossroads

ajрыча : *adv* separately

ajсыз : *a* moonless

ajсорлар : *n* Aissor *ethnic group in the Caucasus speaking modern Aramaic*

ajүзлү : *a* 1) round-faced, moon-faced 2) beautiful

aj-haj : *intj* expression of contempt

академија : *n* academy

академик : *n* academician

академик : *a* academical

акасија : *n* acacia *the locust tree*

акварел : *n* 1) watercolor *a* 2) watercolor

аквариум : *n* aquarium

аккорд : *n* chord

акропол : *n* Acropolis

аксент : *n* accent

аксептасија : *n fin* acceptance *agreement to pay a bill of exchange, draft, order, or the like according to its terms*

аксиз : *n obs* excise, excise tax *tax on consumer goods*

аксиома : *n* axiom

акт : *n* deed, document, bill

актив : *n polit* activist ranks, most active members

актиниум : *n chem* Actinium

актјор : *n* 1) actor *a* 2) actor's

актјорлуг : *n* acting

актуал : *a* topical

актуаллыг : *n* topicality

акустика : *n* acoustics

акаh : *a* versed in, conversant with, well-informed about

акент : *n* 1) agent *a* 2) agent, agent's

акентлик : *n* 1) agency; secret/intelligence service, clandestine agent network 2) work/profession of an agent

акентура : *n Ru* secret service, intelligence network

ал : *a* 1) red, scarlet 2) purest

ала : *a* 1) multicolored; with varying coats *animals* 2) spotted, speckled *n* 3) vitiligo/leucoderma, *a skin disease characterized by white spots*

ала-бабат : *adv* 1) tolerably, so-so, not bad, passably *a* 2) passable, tolerable; slapdash

алабајдаг : *n* person with a bad reputation

алабалыг : *n zool* sig *species of freshwater salmon*

алабахта : *n zool* wood-pigeon *Columba palumbus*

алабаш : *a* 1) having a head of varied color 2) nickname for a dog 3) illegal bus *Baku slang*

ала-бәзәк : *a* 1) multi-colored, piebald 2) having coats of various colors *animals*

ала-бәзәклик : *n* diversity of colors

ала-бишмиш : *a* 1) half raw, partly cooked *n* 2) incompletely cooked/ partly cooked food

ала-була : see **ала-вәзәк**

алаг : *n* 1) weed 2) weeding

алаганад : *n zool* a finch, siskin *genus Spinus*

алагапы : *n* 1) arch, triumphal arch, gates 2) see **дарваза**

ала-гара : *a* 1) see **чызмагара** 2) angry

ала-гаранлыг : *n* 1) semidarkness, twilight 2) early morning, dawn, first light

алагарға : *n* jay; any of various corvine birds

алагарын : *a* 1) still hungry, not quite full/satisfied *adv* 2) half hungrily, unsatiatedly

алагвуран : *n* see **алагуран**

алагкеш : *n* weeder *person*

алаглама : *v* weeding, removal of weeds

алагламаг : *v* weed

алаглы : *a* overgrown with weeds

ала-голаj : *adv* see **ала-бабат**

ала-гора : *n* unripe grapes

алагчалан : *n* weeder *person*

алагчы : *n* see **алагчалан**

аладаг : *n* bare/treeless/bald mountain

ала-дәjмиш : *a* unripe, unripened

ададодаг : *a* having a white blaze, or marking on the mouth *of a horse*

алаj : *n* regiment

алаj-алаj : *adv* regiment after regiment

ала-jарым : *a* 1) partial, incomplete, insufficient *adv* 2) partially, incompletely, insufficiently 3) see **ала-jарымчыг**

ала-jарымчыг : *a* unfinished, incomplete, not qiute ready, half done

ала-jетишмиш : *a* see **ала-дәjмиш**

ала-кал : *a* see **ала-дәмиш**

ала-көлкә : *n* partial shadow

алакөз : *a* grey-eyed

алаланма : *v* fr. **алаланмаг**

алаланмаг : *v* show/appear particolored/many-colored

алалы : *a* 1) spotted, stained 2) having white spots on the skin 3) overgrown with weeds

алалыг : *n* place/ area covered with weeds

алана : *n* alana *dried fruit filled/stuffed with crushed nuts, spices and sugar*

алапача : *n* piebald/skewbald animal *one with white marks on the haunches*

ала-пөртү : *a* half-raw

ала-сүтүл : *a* 1) half-ripe{ned], unripe 2) undercooked

ала-тала : *a* 1) random, randomly placed *adv* 2) randomly, every-which-way

ала-торан : *n* daybreak, first light

алаф : *n* fodder

алафлама : feeding cattle with fodder

алафламаг : *v tr* feed *cattle*

алафсатан : *n* fodder-merchant, cattle-feed dealer

алафсызлыг : *n* lack of fodder/forage grass

ала-чалпов : *n* 1) last month of winter 2) snow mixed with rain

ала-чиj : *a* raw, undercooked

алачыг : *n* kibitka *nomad's tent* felt tent, yurt

алача : *a* dappled *of a horse*

алачаг : *n* amount due; credit

алачаганад : *v* see **алагамаг**

алачаглы : *n* money-lender, creditor

алачадимдик : *n zool* crossbill *Genus Loxia* ; a finchlike bird having points on its mandibles that cross each other when the beak is closed

алачаланмаг : *v* show/appear particolored, take on/assume a varied coloration

алачалы : *a* motley, variegated, multicolored; spotty

алачалыг : *n* diversity of colors

алачәһрә : *n zool* tomtit, blue titmouse *family Paridae*

алаша : *n* see **jабы**

албалы : *n* 1) sour cherry *a* 2) sour cherry

албан : *n* 1) an Albanian, native of Albania 2) name of an ancient people who lived in the territory of Azerbaijan prior to the tenth century A. D. 2) see **арнауд**

албанија : *n* Albania *both the modern country in the Balkan peninsula and the ancient country in the territory of Azerbaijan*

албанча : *adv* in Albanian *language*

албом : *n* album

албухара : *n* the albukhara plum *an elongated sweet-sour plum*

алвер : *n* trade, commerce

алверчи : *n* 1) dealer, trader 2) profiteer, speculator

алверчилик : *n* 1) dealing, trading 2). profiteering, speculation

ал-гырмызы : *a* scarlet, bright red

алгыш : *n* applause, welcome

алгышламаг : *v* applaud; welcome

алгышланмаг : *v intr* win applause; be welcome

алгы-сатты : *n* buying and selling

алдадылмаг : *v intr* 1) be deceived 2.) be seduced

алдадычы : *a* false, deceptive; tempting 2) seductive, alluring

алдадычылыг : *n* deceptiveness, seductiveness

алданма : *n* deception, trickery, fraud

алданмаг : *v intr* be cheated/deceived; be misled/led astray

алдатмаг : *v* 1) cheat, deceive, mislead, defraud, lead astray 2) lure, allure, seduce

алдырмаг : *caus of* **алмаг**

алдыртмаг : *caus of* **алдмаг**

алә е! *intej* hey, you!

ал-әлван : *a* colorful, highly colored; bright, vivid

аләм : *n* 1) world, universe 2) kingdom

аләм-ашкар : *a* well-known, universally known; evident, obvious

аләмкир : *a* 1) world, worldwide, world embracing *n* 2) expansionist, aggressor

аләмшүмул : *a* famous, well-known

аләт : *n* 1) tool, instrument 2) appliance, device

аләтгајыран : *n* toolmaker

али : *a* 1) supreme, highest, superior *n* 2) Ali *masculine first name*

алим : *n* scientist; scholar

алиманә : *adv* see **алимчәсина**

алимент : *n* alimony

алимәгам : *a* 1) high-ranking *n* 2) high-ranking official, VIP

алимәнсәб : *n* court official/dignitary

алимлик : *n* learning, erudition, good education

алимчәсинә : *adv* scentifically, as befits a scientist

аличаһ : *a* notable, distinguished, holding high office

аличәнаб : *a* generous, magnanimous

аличәнаблыг : *n* generosity, magnanimity

аличәнаблыгла : *adv* generously, magnanimously

аличәнабчасына : see **адичәнаблыгла**

алы : see **кавалы**

алыб-сатма : *n* fr. **алыб-сатмаг**, reselling, resale, speculation

алыб-сатмаг : *v* resell, redistribute

алыг : *n* saddle-blanket, horse-blanket, horse-cloth

алым : *n* duty, toll, fee

алын : *n* forehead

алынлыг : *n* 1) forehead covering/cover *traditional woman's headgear* 2) browband *part of a horse's bridle*

алынмаг : *v* 1) be purchased, bought 2) be taken, taken away; be received/gotten/procured 3) be borrowed 4) be conquered

алынмаз : *a* 1) unconquerable 2) inalienable 3) inaccessible

алынсыз : *a* having a low *lit 'no'* forehead, stupid, ignorant

алысын : *n* second-mowing grass, second growth grass

алычы : *n* buyer, customer

алычылыг : *a* buying, purchasing, customer

алыш-вериш : *n* trade, commerce

алыш-веришчи : *n* speculator, profiteer

алышган : *a* 1) combustible, inflammable 2) *cigarette* lighter

алышганлыг : *n* 1) inflammability, combustibility..2) capacity of quick and facile adaptability

алышдым-јандым : *n* alyshdym-jandym, a type of silk fabric

алышдырычы : *a* ignition, igniting, firing

алышдырмаг : *v* 1) ignite, kindle, set on fire 2) train, accustom *to*

алышыг : *n* 1) dry twigs and brush used to start a fire, kindling *wood* 2) tinder

алышмаг : *v intr* 1) catch fire, burst into flames 2) get accustomed to, get used to

алјанаг : *a* red/rosy-cheeked

алјанаглы : *a* see **алјанаг**

алјанс : *n* alliance, union *usually for wicked purposes*

алкогол : *n* alcohol

алкоголизм : *n* alcoholism

алкоголлу : *a* alcoholic

алкоголсуз : *a* non-alcoholic

алкоголчу : *n* alcoholic, dipsomaniac, alcohol-addicted/dependent person

алланмаг : *v intr* 1) redden, flush 2) see **алданмаг**

аллаф : *n* grain dealer; shopkeeper; inn-keeper

аллафлыг : *n* grain dealership; profession of shopkeeper/innkeeper

аллаh : *n* 1) God *a* 2) God['s]

аллаhпәрәст : *a* religious, devout, pious

аллаhсыз : *n* 1) atheist, unbeliever *a fig* 2) without conscience; heartless

аллаhсызлыг : *n* 1) atheism 2) lawlessness; cruelty; immorality

аллаhсызчасына : *adv* in a Godless, immoral way

аллашдырмаг : *v intr* flush, redden

аллашма : *v* fr. **аллашмаг**

аллашмаг : *v* redden, show/display red *color*

аллыг : *n* 1) redness 2) scarlet coloration 3) see **әнлик**

аллы-әлванлы : *a* 1) multicolored; beautiful 2) decorated with flowered patterns

аллы-күллү : *a* 1) beautiful 2) decorated with flowers

алма : *n* 1) apple *a* 2) apple-like, apple *v* 3) from **алмаг**

алмаг : *v* 1) buy, purchase 2) take; receive; borrow 3) take away 4) subjugate, conquer, occupy 5) exact from, charge money

алмаз : *n* diamond

алмаjанаг : *a* red-cheeked; having good complexion

алмалыг : *n* 1) apple orchard 2) *anat* pelvic socket

алман : *n* 1) a German *a* 2) German

алманија : *n* Germany

алманах : *n* anthology, literary miscellany

алмандин : *n* almandine *precious stone*

алманча : *adv* in German

алмачыг : *n* 1) small apple 2) cheek bone

алныачыг : *a* 1) honest, faithful, irreproachable *n* 2) person with a clear conscience

алныјекә : *a* 1) having a prominent forehead, broad browed *n* (zool) 2) species of fish of the mullet family

ало : *intj* Hello! *telephone greeting*

алов : *n* flame

аловландырмаг : *v* 1) set on fire 2) excite, arouse strongly, evoke anger

аловландырычы : *n* 1) igniter *a* 2) igniter, ignition

аловланма : *v intr* flame, blaze; be ablaze

аловланмаг : *v intr* 1) flame., blaze, be ablaze, flame up, flare up, blaze up, take fire *fig* 2) become strongly excited

аловлатмаг : *v* see **аловландырмаг**

аловлу : *a* flaming, flame

аловсуз : *a* flameless

алп : *n* 1) the Alps *a* 2) Alpine

алт : *n* bottom, bottom part *of s.t.*

алтдан : *adv* from below, underneath, below

алты : *num* six

алтыаварлы : *a* six-oared

алтыаjаг, алтыаjаглы : *a zool* hexapod, six-legged

алтыаjлыг : *a* 1) six month, of six months *n* 2) six month old child

алты-алты : *adv* by sixes, by units of six

алтыачылан : *a* six-shot *firearm*

алтыбармаг : *n* 1) person born with six fingers or six toes *a* 2) six-fingered or six-toed

алтыбашлы : *a* six-headed

алтыбучаг : *n* hexagon

алтыбучаглы : *a* hexagonal

алтыганад, алтыганадлы : *a* six-winged

алтыдүjмә, алтыдүjмәли : *a* six-inch

алтыиллик : *a* 1) six-year *n* 2) six year period

алтыjанлы : *a* see **алтытәрәфли**

алтыjашар : six-year-old *used of animals*

алтыкүнлүк : *a* 1) six-day *n* 2) six day period

алтыләчәкли : *n bot* six-petaled

алтылыг : *n* six, a"sixer" *term for something consisting of six units, or six persons*

алтымәртәбә : *a* six-storied

алтымәртәбәли : *a* six-storied

алтымисралы : *a* hexameter

алтынчы : *num* sixth

алтырәгәмли : *a math* six-digit

алтысаатлыг : *a* six-hourl[y]

алтысинифли : *a* sixth-grade, classified into six categories

алтысүтунлу : *a* six-column[ed]

алтытарлалы : *a agr* six-field

алтытарлалыг : *n agr* six-field area

алтытәрәфли, алтыүзлү : *n* 1) hexagon *a* 2) hexagonal

алтыча : *num* just six, six in all

алтычәркәли : *a* six-row

алтычилдли : *a* six-volume

алтычилдлик : *n* six-volume set, six-volume edition

алткөјнәк : *n* undershirt

алткәмәри : *n* brassiere

алтлыг : *n* 1) tray, pan, drip pan, saucer *vessel placed under a flower-pot* 2) stand, base

алтмыш : *num* sixty

алтмыш-алтмыш : *adv* by sixties, in groups of sixty

алтмышынчы : *num* sixtieth

алтмышјашлы : *a* sixty-year old

алтмышча : *num* just sixty, sixty in all

алт-үст : *adv* upside-down, topsy-turvy

алудә : *a* addicted to, having a mania for, mad about, having a hobby of/a passion for

алудәлик : *n* addiction, mania, hobby, infatuation, passion (for)

алунит : *n min* alunite, alumstone

алүминиум : *n* aluminium

алча : *n* cherry plum

алчаг : *a* 1) low, short, 2) base, foul, vile *adv* 3) low *n* 4) scoundrel

алчагајарлы : *a* poor quality, base alloy, low efficiency

алчагбој, алчагбојлу : *a* short *of a person*

алчагдабан : *a* low-heeled

алчагкөвдәли : *a bot* short-trunked, short-stemmed

алчагландырмаг : *v tr* lower

алчагланмаг : *v intr* lower

алчаглатмаг, алчаглашдырмаг : *v* see **алчагдандырмаг**

алчаглашмаг : *v* 1) see **алчагланмаг** 2) become lower in quality

алчаглыг : *n* 1) meanness, baseness 2) infamy, vileness 3) low place

алчагтәһәр : *a* 1) somewhat low, lowish *adv* 2) somewhat low

алчагча : *a dim* 1) low *adv* 2) a wee bit low

алчагчасына : *adv* meanly, wickedly, basely

алчалан : *a* 1) descending 2) humiliating, degrading *oneself*

алчалдылмаг : *v intr* 1) be lowered 2) be humiliated

алчалдычы : *a* humiliating

алчалыг : *n* plum orchard

алчалма : *v* fr. **алчатмаг**

алчалмаг : *v* 1) lower, let down 2) humble, humiliate, abase

алчалтдырмаг : *v caus of* **алчалмаг**

алчалтмаг : *v* 1) bring down, lower 2) humiliate, put down

алчачыг : *a* rather short *of a person n dim* 2) short person, a "shorty"

алчы : *n* standing position of a knucklebone *used in a game*

амадә : *a* 1) ready *adv* 2) on the alert, at the ready

амадәлик : *n* readiness, preparedness

амал : *n* ideas, notion, concept

амалгама : *n chem* amalgam

амалгамалашдырма : *v chem* amalgamating, amalgamization

амалгамалашма : *n chem* amalgamization

аман : *n* 1) mercy 2) term, period *of time*, opportunity *intj* 3) Oh!, Ah!

аман-заман : *a* 1) only, sole *adv* 2) only

аманы : *a* 1) temporary; not durable 2) temporarily, for the time being

амансыз : *a* 1) cruel, merciless, brutal *adv* 2) cruelly, mercilessly, brutally

амансызлыг : *n* mercilessness, cruelty, brutality

амансызча, амансызчасына : *adv* cruelly, mercilessly, brutally

амбырағыз : *n* wide-mouthed person

америка : *n* 1) America *a* 2) American

америкалы : *n* an American

американ : *n* 1) see **америкалы** *a* 2) American

амил : *n* factor

амир : *n* ruler, sovereign

амиранә : *a* 1) authoritative *adv* 2) authoritatively

амма : *conj* but, however

аммиак : *n chem* ammonia, ammonium hydrate

аммиаклы : *a chem* ammoniac

аммониум : *n chem* ammonium

ампер : *n phys* ampere

аму-дәрја : *n* Amu-Dar'ya *river in Central Asia*

амчых : *n vulgar* vagina

ан : *n* 1) instant, moment 2) time

ана : *n* 1) mother, mom, mama *a* 2) maternal

ана-бала : *n* mother and child

ана-бачы : *n* 1) mother and sister 2) friends *of two women*

анабир, анаданбир : *a* uterine *referring to children having the same mother but different fathers*

анадандоғма : *a* inborn, genetic, hereditary

анаданкәлмә : *a* 1) inborn, innate, hereditary *fig* 2) naked

анализ : *n* analysis

аналитик : *n* 1) analytics *a* 2) analytical

аналы-балалы : *n* mother and her children *collectively*

аналыг : *n* 1) motherhood, maternity 2) stepmother

ананас : *n* 1) pineapple 2) pineapple

анархия : *n Ru* anarchy

анасыз : *n* motherless child

анатомија : *n* anatomy

анатомик : *a* anatomical

анач : *n* 1) brood *animal* 2) stock *main stem of a plant*

аначыг, аначығаз : *n* mommy

аначлашмаг : *intr* 1) become big/large/mature 2) be grown up; become experienced, sophisticated

анаша : *n* hashish

анашачәкән : *n* hashish smoker

анашачы : *n* hashish dealer; hashish addicted

анбаан : *adv* any minute

анбар : *n* warehouse, depot; cellar; barn

анбардар : *n* warehouseman, storehouseman

анбарламаг : *v* store in a barn

анбарчы : *n* see **анбардар**

ангара : *n* 1) Ankara *capital of Turkey* 2) the Angara *river in Siberia*

ангыра-ангыра : *n* roaring

ангырмаг : *v* bray *of a donkey* , heehaw

ангырты : *n* 1) roar, roaring 2) wild scream caused by intense pain

ангыртмаг : *v* make/cause to roar

ангутбоғаз : *a* long-necked

анд : *n* oath, vow, solemn promise

анд ичмәк : *v* swear, take oath

анд-аман : *in combn* **анд-аман етмәк** try in every way to assure

андыр : *n* 1) clothing left by a dead person, dead person's clothes *a* 2) damned, ill-starred, ill-fated

андырмаг : *v* hint at, drive at, imply 2) resemble s.o.

андлашмаг : *v* take a mutual vow, swear to one another

ани : *a* 1) momentary, instantaneous, instant *adv* 2) momentarily, instantly, in a wink

анилик : *n* instantaneity, instantaneousness

анылмаг : *v intr* be mentioned/referred to

анкет : *n* 1) questionnaire *a* 2) questionnaire

анкил : *n zool* eel

анкина : *n med* quinsy, sore throat

анлаг : *n* understanding, conscience, perception

анлаглыг : *a* sensible, intelligent, quick on the uptake, quick-minded, clever, quick-witted, sharp, bright

анлагсыз : *a* dumb, dull, stupid

анлагсызлыг : *n* dumbness, stupidity, dull-wittedness

анладылмаз : *a* 1) inexplicable *adv* 2) inexplicably

анлаја-анлаја : *n* understanding, getting, grasping

анлајан : *a* 1) comprehending, understanding, bright, sensible *n* 2) bright, understanding, intelligent person

анлајыш : *n* 1) understanding, perception 2) comprehension, reason

анлама : *v* from **анламаг**

анламаг : *v* understand, perceive, grasp

анламаз : *a* 1) stupid, slow, slow-witted *n* 2) ignoramus

анламазлыг : *n* ignorance, dumbness, stupidity

анлатдырмаг : *caus* of **анлатмаг**

анлатмаг : *v* explain, elucidate, make clear

анлашылмаг : *v* 1) be/become clear, understandable 2) be explained/laid out/made clear

анлашылмаз : *a* ununderstandable, unclear, little understood; unattainable

анлашылмазлыг : *n* vagueness, lack of clarity; misunderstanding

анлыг : *n* 1) moment *a* 2) momentary *adv* 3) momentarily

анмаг : *v* remember, bring/recall to mind

аноним : *n* 1) anonymous author/work *a* 2) anonymous

анормал : *a* abnormal

анры : *adv* over there, in that direction

анры-бəри : *adv* 1) here and there, hither and thither 2) see **хырда-мырда, хырда-пара**

ансамбл : *n* ensemble, group, crew

антарктида : *n* the Antarctic

антарктик : *a* Antarctic

антена : *n* antenna

антик : *a* antique, ancient

антипод : *n* 1) antipode, an exact opposite *geog* 2) the Antipodes, a place or region on the opposite side of the earth

антоложи : *a* anthological

антолокија : *n* anthology

антрасит : *n* hard coal, anthracite

анчаг : *conj* 1) but, however 2) only, just

анчаг-анчаг : *adv* with great difficulty

апағ : *a* very white, quite white, completely white

апаjдын : *a* very clear, quite clear, completely clear

апарат : *n* apparatus, device, machine, mechanism

апарылма : *n* 1) withdrawal, carrying off 2) conducting

апарылмаг : *pass* 1) be carried away 2) be conducted *business*

апарычы : *a* 1) leading *n* 2) leader, conductor, chief

апар-кəтир : *n* red tape *bureaucratic : lit. 'take and 'bring'*

апарма : *v fr.* **апарма**

апармаг : *v* 1) take, carry away 2) win, gain

апартмаг : *caus of* **апармаг**

апачыг, ап-ашкар : *a* absolutely/quite clear, open

апокеj : *n astron.* 1) apogee 2) topmost point; climax, culmination

апостроф : *n* apostrophe

апрел : *n* April

аптек : *n* pharmacy, drugstore

аптекчи : *n* pharmacist

ар : *n* 1) shame 2) pride, self esteem

ара : *n* 1) interval, space..2) distance, range 3) middle 4) break, respite

ара вермəк : *v* give an interval, give a rest

ара вурмаг : *v* create hostilities

ара гарышмаг : *v* be in a state of mess, disorder

ара гат : *n* gasket

ара дүзəлтмəк : *v* improve relations

араjа дүшмəк : *v* 1) interfere 2) be a middle-man

араjа сөз салмаг : *v* gossip

арасыны кəсмəк : *v* block

араба : *n* wagon, cart; carriage

арабачы : *n* wagon-driver, carter

арабачылыг : *n* profession of wagon-driver/carter

ара-бəрə : *n* border, frontier; limit

ара-бəрəсиз : *a* 1) incessant, constant, uninterrupted *adv* 2) incessantly, constantly, uninterruptedly

арабир : *adv* 1) sometimes, from time to time 2) here and there 3) rarely

аравуран : *n* trouble-maker, provacateur; rebel, mutineer

араг : *n* 1) vodka 2) liquor

арагарыщдыран : *n* trouble-maker, provocateur, meddler

арагарыщдырычы : *a* trouble-making, meddling, provocative

арагарыщдырма : *v* provocation, trouble-making

араг-вараг : *adv* rummaging *used with the verb 'еләмәк'*

араг-вараг еләмәк : search carefully, search, turning everything upside down

арагчəкəн : *n* vodka distiller

арагчын : *n* skullcap of Central Asian type

арадабир : *adv* see **арабир**

арадүзəлдəн : *n* go-between; *the one* filling the gap

араз : *n* Arax *name of a river*

араjычы : *n* seeker, searcher, researcher

араjыш : *n* notice; verification; letter of information

аракəсмə : *n* partition, separation, alienation

аралама : *v fr.* **араламаг**

араламаг : *v* 1) move apart, separate 2) take apart 3) open slightly, half open

араланмаг : *v intr* 1) be moved apart, be separated 2) go away, disperse 3) be disjointed, taken to pieces 4) move off, move away from 5) break up *of clouds*

аралашдырылмаг : *v* be parted/separated/set apart

аралашдырмаг : *v* part, separate, set apart

аралашмаг : *v intr* 1) part, break up, go separate ways 2) stop quarreling/ fighting

аралы : *adv* 1) at intervals 2) at some distance 3) partly open, half open

аралыг : *n* 1) interval, gap, clearance 2) distance 3) middle

аралыгчы : *n* mediator, go-between

аралыгчылыг : *n* mediation

арам : *a* 1) calm, quiet *adv* 2) calmly, quietly *a* 3) incessant, constant, uninterrupted

арамаг : *v* see **арамаг**

арам-арам : *adv* quietly, calmly; slowly

арамла : *adv* unhurriedly

арамсыз : *a* 1) incessant, constant 2) restless, uneasy 3) unrestrained *adv* 4) incessantly, constantly 5) uneasily

арамсызлыг : *n* 1) concern, uneasiness 2) tirelessness, indefatigibility 3) wildness, lack of restraint

арамча : *adv* quietly

аран : *n geol* 1) lowland, low place, low place *a* 2 low-lying

аранлы : *n* see **аранчы**

аранлыг : *n* low-lying place/site/area

аранмаг : *v* see **ахтарылмаг**

аранчы : *n* lowlander

арасыкәсилмәз : *a* incessant, ceaseless

арасында : *adv* between

ара-сыра : *adv* see **арабир**

арат : *n* watering of ploughed land *before sowing*

аратдыра-аратдыра : *adv* rummaging around; searching, researching

аратламаг : *v* water ploughed land *before sowing*

арачы : *n* mediator, middle-man, go-between

арачылыг : *n* mediation

аращдырычы : *n* researcher; investigator

аращдырма : *v fr.* **аращдылмаг**

аращдырмаг : *v geol* 1) research, investigate; analyze 2) dig; rummage, dig into

арва : *n* weight of package/packing/crate

арвад : *n* 1) wife, spouse *f* 2) woman; wench

арвадағыз, арвадағызлы : *a* anxious to please women; henpecked, under the thumb of a wife

арвадаохшар : *n* see **арвадсифәт**

арвадбаз : *n* womanizer, seducer

арвадбазлыг : *n* womanizing, philandering, skirt-chasing

арвадланмаг : *v* pose as a mature, married woman

арвадлашмаг : *v* become effeminate; become a woman

арвадлы : *a* 1) married *n* 2) married man

арвадлыг : *n* 1) womanliness 2) woman's domestic and housekeeping skills

арвадсевән : *a* womanizing, given to womanizing

арвадсифәт : *a* effeminate

арвадсыз : *a* wifeless, having no wife/woman

арвад-ушаг : *n* family members, family *collective*

арвадхасиjjәт : *a* effiminate; meek, timid

арвадчасына : *adv* in a feminine way

арвадчыг, арвадчығаз : *n* wife *dim.* little woman

арвалы : *n* gross weight

арвана : *n* Bactrian/two-humped she-camel

арвасыз : *n* net weight

аргадаш : *n* friend *Turkish arkadaş, in occasional current use*

арғаз : *a* see **узундраз**

арғалы : *n* Caucasian mountain sheep

арғач : *n* weft *cloth*

арғачламаг : *v* 1) let go, let pass 2) quicken the pace, walk faster

арғачлыг : *n* thread suitable for/intended for the weft *cloth*

ард : *n* 1) back, back part 2) continuation

ардынча : *postp* following, behind

ардыч : *n bot* juniper *Junipera L.*

ардычыл : *n* 1) follower *a* 2) successive, consecutive *adv* 3) consistently, steadily

ардычыллыг : *n* sequence; consistency, steadiness

ардычлыг : *n* juniper thickets

арәстә : *a* ready; gathered

арзу : *n* 1) wish, desire; dream, reverie 2) Arzu *very popular first name, both masculine and femimine*

арзуламаг : *v* desire, wish; daydream *of*

арзуман : *n* 1) giant *a* 2) gigantic, huge, tremendous

ариф : *a* 1) learned, wise; enlightened 2) Arif *masculine first name; see also* ***'Рауф'***

арифанә : *adv* see **арифчәсинә**

арифләшмәк : *v* become wise/enlightened/learned; be erudite

арифлик : *n* wisdom; state of enlightenment

арифчәсинә : *adv* wisely; professionally *as befits an expert*

ары : *n* bee

арыг : *a* thin, lean, meager; exhausted

арыгапан : *n zool* blue titmouse, tit *order Passeriformes L*

арыглама : *n* emaciation, wasting away

арыгламаг : *v* become emaciated, waste away, grow thin and hollow-cheeked

арыглатмаг : *v caus* exhaust *s.o.* wear out, make thin, cause to lose flesh, bring to a state of emaciation

арыглыг : *n* leanness, thinness, emaciation

арыг-уруг : *a* emaciated, scraggy, skinny

арыгушу : *n zool* tomtit, blue titmouse, blue tit *order Passeriformes L*

арыгча : *a* slender, slim, lean, puny, frail

арыгчаг : *a* fragile, frail, small-sized, petite

арыг-чырыг : *a* see **аргыча**

арыдычы : *n* grain-sorter

арыјабахан : *n* apiarist, bee-keeper

арыјејән : *n* a species of vulture, an accipitral raptor *Accipitridae L*

арынмаг : *v* be sorted *of grain*

арысахлајан : *n* bee-keeper, apiarist

арытдырмаг : *v caus* of **арытламаг**

арытлајычы : *n* see **арыдычы**

арытлама : *v fr.* **арытламаг**

арытламаг : *v* sort out, select *of grain*

арытлатдырмаг : *v caus* from **арытламаг**

арытлатмаг : *v caus* from **арытламаг**

арытмаг : *v* see **арытламаг**

арыхана : *n* beehive

арыханачы : *n* bee-keeper, apiarist

арычы : *n* see **арыханачы**

арычылыг : *n* apiculture, bee-keeping

арктик : *a* Arctic

арктика : *n* the Arctic

аркентина : *n* 1) Argentina *a* 2) Argentine

арлы-намуслу : *a* deserving, worthy, honest; decent

армаған : *n obs* gift

армадил : *n* armadillo *family Dacipodidae*

армуд : *n* 1) pear *a* 2) pear

армудлуг : *n* pear orchard

армуду : *a* pear-shaped *tea glass*

ар-намус : *n* honor, self-respect, self-esteem

арнауд : *n* an Albanian

арнаудча : *adv* in Albanian language

арпа : *n* 1) barley *a* 2) barley

арпаламаг : *v* feed livestock with barley

арпалыг : *n* cavity, pitting in equine molars

арпачыг : *n* foresight, front sight *on the muzzle of a firearm*

арсыз : *a* thoughtless, unconcerned; shameless; careless

арсыз-арсыз : *adv* thoughtlessly, unconcernedly

арсызламаг, арсызланмаг, : *v* loose self-respect, become shameless

арсызлашмаг : *v* see **арсызламаг, арсызланмаг,**

арсызлыг : *n* unconcern; carelessness; shamelessness

арсызчасына : *adv* 1) unconcernedly 2) shamelessly

арслан : *n* see **аслан**

артдырмаг : *v* see **артырмаг**

артел : *n Ru* 1) artel *a cooperative association of workmen* *a* 2) artel

артист : *n* 1) actor *a* 2) actor's

артистлик : *n* profession of an actor

артистчәсинә : *a* in an actor's manner

артыг : *postp* 1) more, over beyond *a* 2) superfluous *n* 3) surplus, remainder 4) leavings, leftovers *a* 5) significant, important *adv* 6) more; already

артыг-артыг : *adv* enough and to spare

артыглама : *n* exceeding, excess, surplus, overfulfilment

артыглыг : *n* surplus, redundancy, excess

артыг-уртуг : *n* 1) remnants 2) left-overs

артығы : *n* 1) the greatest, the maximum, the upper limit 2) surpluses

артым : *n* 1) growth, increase, addition 2) litter, offspring *animals* 3) increase *in the weight of bread over that of the flour used*

артымлы : *a* 1) giving/yielding an increase/surplus/growth 2) propagating itself, breeding, spawning

артымсыз : *a* 1) not giving/yielding an increase/surplus/growth 2) poorly propagating itself, unsuccessfully breeding/spawning

артырылмаг : *v* be increased/supplemented/added to

артырма : *n* addition, augmentation, increment, increase

артырмаг : *v* 1) add, increase, grow, multiply 2) accumulate money 3) supplement

артычаг : adv more than necessary, enough and to spare

артма : n growth, increase, multiplication

артмаг : v grow, increase, rise

арх : ditch, trench, irrigation ditch/channel

арха : *n* 1) back *fig* 2) defense, defender, support *mil* 3) rear

архадан : *adv* behind; behind the back

архаик : *a* archaic

архајын : *a* 1) quiet, calm, unhurried *adv* 2) calmly, unhurriedly *a* 3) confident *adv* 4) confidently

архајын-архајын : *adv* utterly calmly, light-heartedly, with complete unconcern

архајынлатмаг : *v* calm, quiet, sooth; give hope *to*, reassure

архајынлащдырмаг : *v* see **архајынлатмаг**

архајынлашмаг : *v* 1) be calmed, reassured 2) be freed from labors, cares, burdens

архајынлыг : *n* calm, quiet, tranquility; confidence, certitude; self-confidence, self-assurance

архајынчылыг : *n* 1) complacency *adv* 2) calmly, securely, safely

архајынча : *adv* very quietly, calmly, unhurriedly, confidently

архаланмаг : *v* be guided by s.o; enjoy s.o.'s protection, patronage; rely on s.o. *for help*

архалы : *a* enjoying s.o.'s protection/patronage; having support

архалыг : *n* short, quilted coat

архасыз : *a* defenseless, unprotected, alone, lacking support, resources

архасызлыг : *n* defenselessness, absence of support, resources

архасына дүшмәк : *v* chase s.o.

архач : *n* fence in resting place for cattle in a field, a corral

архачламаг : *v* drive a herd *cattle etc.* into a resting place, a corral

архачланмаг : *v* be driven into a resting place/corral/stockade *of cattle*

археложи : *a* archeological

археолокија : *n* archeology

архив : *n* 1) archives. *a* 2) archival

архивчи : *n* archivist

архившүнас : *n* archivist, specialist in archival science

архившүнаслыг : *n* archival science

аршын : *n* *Ru* arshin *unit of linear measure–0,711 m*

аршын-аршын : *adv* in/by arshins

аршынламаг : *v* 1) measure in arshins 2) walk in long, arshin-long strides

аршынмалы : *n* manufactory *(archaic : a textile factory)*

аршынмалчы : *n* textile worker

аршынһесабы : *adv* in arshins

аршынчы : *n* retail textile merchant

ас : *n* ace *playing cards*

аса : *n* rod, staff, stick, walking-stick

асајиш : *n* calm, tranquility, security, peace

асан : *a* 1) easy, uncomplicated, not difficult *adv* 2) easily, simply

асанлатмаг : *v* see **асанлащдырмаг**

асанлащдырылмаг : *v* be facilitated/made easier/simplified

асанлащдырма : *n* facilitation, simplification

асанлащдырмаг : *v* facilitate, simplify

асанлашмаг : *v* be facilitated, be simplified

асанлыг : *n* easiness, simplicity

асантәһәр : *a* 1) rather simple *adv* 2) rather simply

асанча : *adv* simply

асанчасына : *adv* see **асанча**

асар : *n* 1) *literary* works 2) monuments, relics 3) tracks, traces, signs, marks, indications

асари-әтигә : *n* relics of the past/of antiquity; archeological relics/monuments/remains

асбест : *n* *min* 1) asbestos *a* 2) asbestos

асгы : *n* 1) cloakroom 2) suspender[s}

асгырдычы : *a* sneezing, sternutative, sternutatory, giving rise to a sneeze

асгырыг : *n* sneezing, sternutation

асгырмаг : *v* sneeze

асгырты : *n* see **асгырыг**

асгыртмаг : *caus of* **асгырмаг**

аси : *n* 1) rebel, revolutionary, trouble-maker *a* 2) refractory, rebellious

асија : *n* 1) Asia *a* 2) Asiatic

асијалы : *n* an Asian

асилик : *n* rebelliousness, insubordination, state of rebellion/mutiny

асиман : *n* sky, heaven; bottomlessness

асылан : *n* 1) hanged man, gallows bird *colloq a* 2) hanging

асылы : *a* 1) hanging, pendant 2) dependent *on*

асылылыг : *n* dependence

асылмаг : *v* 1) hang 2) be hanged, executed by hanging 3) impose o.s. on ; beg, implore insistently

асычы : *n* cloakroom attendant

аслан : *n* 1) lion 2) leonine

асма : *v fr.* **асмаг**

асмаг : *v tr* 1 hang, hang up, suspend, hang up 2) be hanged, executed by hanging 3) put food on the fire for cooking

асмалыг : *n* fruit stored in a bag which is hung up

аснас : *n* four-handed card game played with 20 cards, aces, kings, queens and tens *gambling game*

аспирант : *n* graduate student *candidate for a graduate degree*

аспирантлыг : *n* graduate study; course of graduate studies

аста : *a* 1) quiet 2) slow 3) careful 4) see **аста-аста**

аста-аста : *adv* 1) quietly 2) slowly 3) carefully

астакәл : *a* sluggish, clumsy, awkward

асталыг : *n* 1) slowness 2) sluggishness 3) carefulness

астана : *n* threshold

астар : *n* 1) lining 2) wrong side *i.e. clothes* 3) first coat, base coat, primer *paint*

астарламаг : *v* put in/sew in the lining, line

астарлатдырмаг, астарлатмаг : *caus of* **астарламаг**

астарлы : *a* lined, provided with a lining *garment*

астарлыг : *n* 1) lining material *a* 2) lining

астарсыз : *a* unlined

астма : *n* asthma

астроном : *n* astronomer

астрономија : *n* astronomy

астрономик : *a* astronomical

асудә : *a* 1) quiet, calm, tranquil; free; light-hearted, carefree *adv* 2) quietly, calmly, tranquilly; freely; light-heartedly, in a carefree manner

асудәләнмәк : *v intr* 1) be free *from work, responsibilies etc.* 2) be/become calm, quiet, settle down

асудәләшмәк : *v pass* see **асудәләнмәк**

асудәлик : *n* 1) leisure, rest, peace 2) calmness

асфалт : *n* 1) asphalt *a* 2) asphalt

асфалтбасан : *n* asphalt worker, worker engaged in laying asphalt pavements; asphalt roller

асфалтлама : *n* asphalting, laying asphalt pavements

асфалтламаг : *v* asphalt, lay asphalt, pave with asphalt

асфалтланмаг : *v pass* be asphalted, be paved with asphalt

асфалтлатдырмаг : *caus. of* **асфалтламаг**

асфалтлатмаг : *caus. of* **асфалтламаг**

асфалтлы : *a* asphalted

асфалтчы : *n* see **асфалтбасан**

ат : *n* 1) horse 2) knight *chess a* 3) horse, equine

ата : *n* 1) father *a* 2) father['s], paternal

аталар сөзү : *n* proverb

ата-ана : *n* relatives, relations, kinsfolk

ата-аналы : *a* having a father and mother

ата-баба : *n* forefathers, ancestors

ата-бабадан : *adv* 1) *lit* from ancestral time 2) of old, ancestrally bequeathed

ата-бала : *n* father and son/father and daughter

атабахан : *n* groom, stable-man

атабир : *a* consanguine, of the same blood, having the same father

атаданбир : *a* see **атабир**

атадангалма : *n* 1) inheritance 2) innate quality

аталыг : *n* 1) paternal feelings, obligations, debts *to children* 2) stepfather

атамалы : *n* property inherited from a father

атаман : *n* ataman *North Caucasian or Cossack chieftain*

атаманлыг : *n* the function and state of being an ataman

ата-оғул : *n* father and son

ат-араба : *n* trace *part of harness*

ат-ат : *n* game of 'playing horse/horsie'

атачыг : *n* pappa, daddy *affectionate term for father*

атачығаз : *n* see **атачыг**

атбаз : *n* horse-lover

атбазлыг : *n* love of horses, passion for horses

атты : *n* cross-beam, cross-bar, tie-beam, cross-brace

атдырмаг : *v* 1) *caus. of* **атмаг** 2) cut off, cut off, sever

атдыртмаг : *caus of* **атмаг**

атеизм : *n Ru* atheism

атәш : *n* 1) fire 2) gunfire 3) Fire! *command*

атәшбаз : *n* pyrotechnist

атәшбазлыг : *n* pyrotechnics

атәшин : *a* 1) flaming, blazing *adv* 2) flamingly, blazingly, hotly

атәшкеш : *n* 1) poker 2) scraper

атәшкәдә : *n* Zoroastrian/fire-worshippers' temple

атәшли : *a* fire, igneous

атәшпәрәст : *n* fire-worshipper, Zoroastrian

атәшпәрәстлик : *n* Zoroastrianism/ fire-worship

атәшфәшан : *n* illumination; pyrotechnics, fireworks

атәшфәшанлыг : *n* see **атәшфәшан**

атыб-тутмаг : *v* toss up and catch, catch in the hands

атыла-атыла : *adv* at a gallop

атылма : *v fr.* **атылмаг**

атылмаг : *v* 1) throw o.s., fling o.s. 2) be thrown, tossed 3) spring, jump, jump over, leap 4) rush at, make a run 5) resound, ring out *e.g. 'a shot'* 6) comb, card, scutch *cotton, wool*

атым : *n* 1) charge, cartridge, shot 2) dose

атымлыг : *n* quantity, dose *used after a numeral*

атынты : *n* waste, waste products, scrap

атычы : *n* 1) rifleman, gunner *tech.* 2) stripper, beater/scutcher, worker who prepares wool or cotton for weaving

атычылыг : *n* 1) accuracy in shooting 2) the profession of scutching cotton/wool

атыш : *n* 1) accusing, complaining *of a person's manner* 2) firing *gunnery*

атышдыртмаг : *n caus of* **атышмаг**

атышма : *n* 1) skirmish, exchange of gunfire 2) squabble, quarrel

атышмаг : *v intr.* 1) skirmish, exchange gunfire/shots 2) exchange angry words with one another, squabble, quarrel

атлаз : *n* 1) satin 2) satin, satiny

атландырма : *n* seat *manner of riding a horse*

атландырмаг : *v* 1) ride *on horseback* 2) dispatch a man on horseback

атланыш : *n* see **һоппаныш**

атланмаг : *v* mount a horse

атлантик : *a* Atlantic

атлас : *n geol.* atlas

атлы : *a* 1) riding *pertaining to riding on horseback*, cavalry *n* 2) horseback rider 3) one having a horse

атма : *vn* 1) **атмаг** *a* 2) throwing, flinging, casting; missile

атмаг : *v* 1) throw, toss, toss up, fling 2) fire, shoot..3) take *medicine* 4) beat *pulse* 5) beat, scutch 6) abandon, leave, drop

атмаралы : *a* eloquent, expressive; well-versed

атмача : *n* cue *theatrical*

атмилчәји : *n zool* gadfly, horsefly *Tabanidae L*

атминән : *n* rider, horseman

атмосфер : *n* 1) atmosphere 2) atmospheric

атом : *n* 1) atom *a* 2) atmospheric

атотаран : *n* one who grazes/pastures horses

атөјрәдән : *n* horse-trainer

атсифәт : *n* horsefaced man

атсыз : *a* horseless *referring to a poor peasant*

аттестат : *n* certificate *various uses*

аттестасија : *n* 1) attestation, certification *a* 2) attestation[al]

атүстү : *adv* hurriedly, on the run

атһаат : *n mil* continuous fire

атчибини : *n* see **атмилчәја**

атчы : *n* horse-breeder; horseman

атчылыг : *n* horse-breeding

атчыл : *n* see **атбаз**

аул : *n* village, settlement *in Daghestan and Central Asia*

афат : *a* bright, smart

афәрин : *intj* Bravo!, Well done!

афәт : *n* unexpected misfortune

афәти-чан : *n* heart-breaker, great beauty

афијәт : *n* health *equiv. to* 'God Bless You!' *said when someone sneezes*

афина : *n* Athens

афиша : *n* sign, announcement, placard

афоризм : *n* aphorism

африка : *n* 1) Africa *a* 2) African

африкалы : *n* an African

афтаб : *n* sun *Arabic, not in common use*

афтафа : *n* metal pitcher/jug with spout *used in bathroom for personal hygiene*

афтафа-ләјән : wash-stand with metal pitcher and basin

ах : *intj* Oh! Eh! What a...!

ахар : *a* 1) current; flowing 2) flow; drainage

ахар-бахар : *n* panorama, beautiful view, lovely landscape

ахар-бахарлы : *n* area pleasing/attractive/beautiful in appearance

ахачаг : *n* bed, channel *river*

ахдырмаг : *v* see **ахытмаг**

ахирәт : *n* the other world, the world beyond

ахирәтсиз : *a* 1) unbelieving, sinful *n* 2) sinner, infidel

ахирүләмр : *intro-wd* in the final analysis, after all is said and done

ахы : *conj part* well; you know

ахыдылма : *n* floating along the current/stream

ахыдылмаг : *v* be floated along the current/stream

ахым : *n* current, direction *of water*

ахын : *n* 1) current, flow 2) influx, inrush, rush

ахын-ахын : *adv* in a continuous flow, en masse

атанты : *n* alluvium, deposition *stream*

ахыр : *n* end, outcome *terminal conclusion*

ахырда : *adv* finally, after all

ахырынчы : *a* last

ахыркы : *a* see **ахырынчы**

ахырсыз : *a* endless, infinite, interminable

ахыр-ухур : *n* remainder; *colloq* left-overs, remnants

ахытдырмаг : *caus. of* **ахытмаг**

ахытмаг : *v* 1) spill, pour out, make flow 2) set afloat on a river, launch onto the current 3) inadvertantly let s.t. be carried of in the water

ахычы : *a* flowing; floating

ахычылыг : *n* flow, fluidity, liquid state

ахышма : *v fr.* **ахышмаг**

ахышмаг : *v* flow together, gather in one place; gush out, pour out

ахма : *v* fr. **ахмаг**

ахмаг : *v* 1) flow, stream *n* 2) fool, simpleton, ninny *a* 3) foolish, stupid

ахмагламаг, ахмаглашмаг : *v* grow stupid

ахмаглыг : *n* stupidity, idiocy, foolishness

ахмагчасына : *adv* stupidly, idiotically

ахмаз : *n* 1) sewage 2) pond

ахнащдырмаг : *caus of* **ахнашмаг**

ахнашмаг : *v intr* flow together, gush *out* , gather together in one place

ахсаг : *a* 1) lame, limping 2) lame person

ахсаглыг : *n* lameness, limping

ахсамаг : *v* 1) limp 2) *fig* lag behind, be unsuccessful

ахсатмаг : *caus of* 1) **ахсамаг** 2) hamper

ахта : *n* 1) eunuch 2) pitted, with stones removed (fruits)

ахталама : *v* of **ахталамаг**

ахталамаг : *v* 1) castrate, neuter 2) pit, clean of pits [fruits]

ахталанмаг : *v intr* be castrated/neutered 2) be pitted/cleaned of pits *fruits*

ахталатдырмаг : *caus of* **ахталамаг**

ахталатмаг : *caus of* **ахталамаг**

ахталыг : *a* earmarked for pit removal *fruits*

ахтарылмаг : *v* 1) turn up, be found 2) be looked for, be the object of search, be subject to search

ахтарычы : *n* 1) seeker, searcher 2) intelligence agent/officer; *mil* scout

ахтарыш : *n* 1) search, investigation 2) reconnaissaance, intelligence *a* 3) investigative 4) intelligence, reconnaissance, reconnoitering

ахтарма : *n* search, searching, quest, investigation

ахтармаг : *v* search, investigate, look for, reconnoitre, find out about

ахтартдырмаг : *caus of* **ахтармаг**

ахтартмаг : *caus of* **ахтармаг**

ахтачы : *noun* 1) pitter *one who removes the pits/stones from fruits* 2) castrater/gelder *specialist who castrates male animals*

ахунд : *n* muslim theologian/divine, Muslim clergyman

ахур : *n* feed trough, manger

ах-уф : *n* whimpering, whining, sniveling

ахшам : *n* 1) evening *a* 2) in the evening

ахшамбазары : *n* evening market/bazaar *normally much cheaper*

ахшамкы : *a* evening

ахшамламаг : *v* 1) become evening, draw on to evening 2) stay until evening 3) spend/stay the night, sleep over

ахшамлыг : *a* 1) evening, intended for evening 2) *after numerals* intended/meant/destined for the indicated number of evenings

ахшамүстү : *adv* towards evening,in the evening

аһ : *intj* Ah!, Oh!, Oh what a . . .

аһа : *intj* Aha!, Oh!, Really!, Indeed!, Well really! 2) (sigh, groan)

аһ-вај : *intj* Oy-vey! *sad sighs, moans, sobbing, cries, whimpers*

аһәнк : *n* 1) harmony, assonance 2) rhythm 3) coordination

аһәнкдар : *a* harmonious, melodious, musical, rhythmic

аһәнкдарлыг : *n* harmony, assonance, musicality

аһәнкдарча : *adv* harmoniously, assonantly, melodiously,musically

аһәнкдарчасына : see **аҺәнкдарча**

аһәнкли : *a* see **аҺәнкдар**

аһәнксиз : *a* inharmonious, unmelodious, dissonant

аһәнксизлик : *n* disharmony, cacaphony, dissonance

аһәнрүба : *n* magnet

аһәстә : *a* 1) quiet, slow, careful *adv* 2) quietly, slowly, carefully *mus* 3) piano, adagio

аһәстә-аһәстә : *adv* quietly, slowly

аһәстәлик : *n* care, caution, slowness, quietness

аһ-зар : *n* groan, *loud* cry, whimper

аһыл : *a* elderly

аһылланмаг, аһыллашмаг : *v* attain a ripe old age

аһыллыг : *n* old age, declining years

аһ-налә : *n* cry of distress, unhappiness, groaning

аһу : *n zool* gazelle

аһубахышлы : *n* 1) pretty, languorous look, appearance *of a woman a* 2) having beautiful eyes *of a woman*

аһуіеришли : *a* having a gracious, flowing walk/gait

аһукөзлү : *n* woman with beautiful eyes

аһ-уф : *intj* see **аһ-вај**

аһ-фәған : *intj* see **аһ-вај**

ачар : *n* key *to a lock*

ачаргаіыран : *n* locksmith *in particular the one specialized in key-making*

ачарлы : *a* locking, equipped with a key

ачарсыз : *a* keyless *not equipped or provided with a key*

ачарчы : *n* steward *man in charge of a household*

ачарчылыг : *n* the profession of steward *man in charge of a household or establishment*

ачдырмаг : *caus of* **ачмаг**

ачдыртмаг : *caus of* **ачмаг**

ачыг : *a* 1) open, wide-open 2) direct, candid, frank; obvious 3) bright, light; pale 4) uncovered, undisguised; barefaced

ачыг-абы : *a* pale-blue

ачыг-ајдын : *a* 1) completely clear/evident/apparent *adv* 2) completely clearly, quite apparently

ачыг-ачығына : *adv* see **ачыгча**

ачыг-ашкар : *a* 1) evident, obvious *adv* 2) evidently, obviously

ачыгбәниз : *a* fresh-faced, pleasant-faced *of a person*

ачыг-бәнөвшәји : *a* pale-lilac *lilac*

ачыг-гәһвәји : *a* pale coffee-colored, light brown

ачыг-гырмызы : *a* vermilion, crimson

ачыгдан-ачыға : *adv* see **ачыгча**

ачыг-јашыл : *a* light-green

ачыгкөзлү : *a* observant, watchful; quick on the uptake

ачыгкөзлүлүк : *n* vigilance, foresight, keenness of observation

ачыг-көј : *a* light-blue

ачыгламаг : *v* clarify, explain

ачыглыг : *n* 1) spaciousness, wide-open space[s)], open area 2) clarity, obviety 3) frankness, openness 4) blank, gap; omission

ачыгрәнкли : *a* light-colored

ачыг-сары : *a* light-yellow

ачыг-сачыг : *a* 1) familiar, free and easy, overly free *of conduct* *adv* 2) with undue familiarity, unconstrainedly *conduct, manners*

ачыг-сачыглыг : *n* undue familiarity, lack of discipline, licentiousness, dissoluteness

ачыгтәhәр : *a* rather light *of color*

ачыгүрәкли : *a* sincere, frank, open-hearted

ачыгфикирли : *a* clear-thinking, sensible

ачыгфикирлилик : *n* good sense, judiciousness, freedom of thought

ачыгча : *adv* openly, frankly, directly, straight, point-blank

ачыгчасына : *adv* see **ачыгча**

ачылыш : *n* 1) opening 2) beginning

ачылышма : *v* *fr.* **ачылышмаг**

ачылышмаг : *v* *intr* 1) accustom/habituate o.s. to, make o.s. familiar with 2) conduct o.s. in a free and easy manner, become unduly familiar 3) become sociable

ачылмаг : *v* *pass* see **ачмаг**

ачма : *v* *fr.* **ачмаг**

ачмаг : *v* *tr* 1) open 2) reveal 3) untie 4) roll, roll out *dough*

ач : *a* hungry

ачар : *n* an Adzhar, an Adzharian *ethnic group of Moslem Georgians living on the Georgian-Turkish border*

ач-ачына : *adv* on an empty stomach

ачгарына : *adv* on an empty stomach

ачгурсаг : *a* see **ачкөз**

ачдырмаг : *v* arouse hunger

ачиз : *a* helpless, weak, pitiable; inactive

ачизанә : *adv* 1) helplessly 2) humbly,submissively, in most lowly manner

ачиз-ачиз : *adv* helplessly

ачизләнмәк : *v* become helpless, lose ability/capacity

ачизләшмәк : *v* become helpless

ачизлик : *n* helplessness, incapability, weakness, debility

ачизчә, ачизчәсинә : *adv* helplessly

ачы : *a* 1) bitter *a* 2) sharp, harsh, stinging, sarcastic

ачы-ачы : *adv* 1) sarcastically, maliciously, spitefully 2) bitterly

ачыг : *n* anger

ачыгычы : *n* cress, peppergrass *Lepidium L*

ачыгла : *adv* see **ачыгча**

ачыгландырмаг : *v* make angry, anger

ачыгланмаг : *v* shout at

ачыглы : *a* 1) angry *adv* 2) angrily

ачыглы-ачыглы : *adv* angrily

ачыглылыг : *n* irascibility

ачыгча : *adv* for spite; on principle

ачыдыл : *a* 1) malicious, cutting, caustic; slanderous 2) venomous

ачыдилли : *a* see **ачыдыл**

ачыдиллилик : *n* 1) malicious speech, causticity 2) malice, spitefulness

ачыламаг : *v* speak sarcastically, offend

ачыландырмаг : *v* make bitter, embitter

ачыланмаг : *v* see **ачылашмаг**

ачылашдырмаг : *v* impart a slight bitter taste; have a bitter taste

ачылашмаг : *v* turn/become bitter

ачылыг : *n* bitterness, bitter taste

ачымаг : *v* 1) regret s.t. deplore s.t., be sorry that, sympathize with, feel for 2) ferment, rise *dough* 3) turn bitter/rancid

ачымсов : *a* somewhat bitter, bitterish

ачыначаг,ачыначаглы : *a* pitiful, pathetic, pitiable, worthy of pity; lamentable, regretable

ачындырычы : *a* evoking pity

ачындырмаг : *v* pain, distress, grieve

ачпенчәр : *n* bitter-tasting *inedible* green/green vegetable

ачытәрә : *n* see **вәзәра**

ачытәhәр : *a* rather bitter, bitterish

ачытма : *n* 1) leaven, yeast 2) ferment, fermentation

ачытмаг : *v* leaven; make sour

ачытмалы : *a* leavened; sour, acid

ачытмасыз : *a* unleavened ; fresh

ачыхәмрә : *n* see **ачытма** (1)

ачыхмаг : *v* *intr* 1) feel/grow/get hungry 2) see **ачылашмаг**

ачыча : *a* see **ачы** (1,2)

ачышдырмаг : *v* give rise to/cause an itch

ачышмаг : *v* see **кичишмәк**

ач-јалавач : *a* 1) hungry 2) indigent, poor; ragamuffin

ачкөдән : *a* see **дәләгарын**

ачкөз : *a* greedy, avid, insatiable

ачкөзлүк : *n* greed, insatiability, avidity

ачкөзчәсинә : *adv* greedily, insatiably, avidly

ач-ләләјүн : *a* hungry, starved, ravenous

ачлыг : *n* 1) hunger; starvation 2) hunger strike *colloq*

ачмаг : *v* feel hungry, get hungry

аш : *n* 1) kasha *cooked grain or groats* 2) pilaf/pilau, pilav *Oriental dish of rice, raisins, spice, and a meat or fowl sauce* 3) see **ашы**

ашағы : *a* 1) low *n* 2) bottom, bottom part

ашағыда : *adv* below, underneath

ашағыдан : *adv* from below, from the bottom

ашағы-јухары : *adv* up-down

ашбашы : *n* "ashbashi" *sauce made with chicken or other meat and served with pilaf*

ашгабад : *n* Ashkhabad *capital of Turkmenistan*

ашгар : *n* admixture; alloy

ашгарлы : *a* mixed, adulterated, impure

ашгарсыз : *a* see **чылха**

ащдырмаг : *caus of* **ашырмағ**

ащдыртмаг : *caus of* **ашырмағ**

ашиг : *a* lovelorn, in love, infatuated

ашиганә : *a* 1) love, amorous *adv* 2) amorously

ашиглик : *n* being in love, love

ашигчәсинә : *n* amorously

ашы, ашы мајасы : *n* 1) vaccine 2) tannin, tannin extract

ашыг : *n* 1) ashug *folk narrator in the Caucasus* 2) knucklebone or piece used in a traditional game *a* 2) ashug *adjectival form of 1*

ашыг-ашыг : *n* children's game with sticks

ашыглыг : *n* 1) the profession of ashug *folk narrator in the Caucasus* 2) tibio-astragalus joint *the articulation between the shin and the foot*

ашыгсајағы : *adv* in the manner of an ashug, in imitation of an ashug see '**ашыг**'

ашылама : *n* 1) innoculation, vaccination, shot 2) tanning, the process of tanning *a* 2) tanning, tannic

ашыламаг : *v* 1) innoculate, vaccinate 2) tan

ашыланмаг : *v-pass* 1) be innoculated, vaccinated 2) be tanned, undergo the tanning process

ашылатдырмаг : *caus of* **ашыламаг**

ашылы : *a* innoculated, vaccinated

ашындырмаг : *v* 1) weather, erode, wear away, deface 2) corrode, eat away

ашындыртмаг : *caus of* **ашындырмаг**

ашынма : *n* weathering, erosion, wearing away, wear and tear

ашынмаг : *pass* 1) be weathered/eroded/worn away 2) be corroded/eaten away

ашыры : 1) *of space* beyond 2) *of time* in

ашырылмаг : *pass* 1) be thrown one after another 2) be capsized, turned over

ашырым : *n* crossing, passage, pass; transition

ашырма : *n* 1) *from* **ашырмаг** 2) suspenders, braces; shoulder strap

ашырмаг : *n* 1) throw one after another 2) overturn *fig* 3) eat

ашкар : *a* 1) clear, apparent, evident *adv* 2) clearly, apparently, evidently

ашкарда : *adv* in one's waking hours

ашкарлыг : *n* clarity, obviousness, evidentness

ашкарча, ашкарчасына : *adv* clearly, obviously, evidently

ашлыг : *n* 1) intended for/earmarked for/ set aside for kasha/pilaf *of rice, vegetables, meat etc.* 2) after numerals indicates the required amount of a given ingredient for the quantity of kasha/pilaf being prepared

ашмаг : *v* cross, go across, get over, step over

ашна : *n* 1) friend 2) acquaintance 3) lover, mistress

ашнабаз : *n* womanizer

ашнабазлыг : *n* 1) relationship of godparents to parents, or of godparents 2) see '**арвадбазлыг**'

ашналашмаг : *v* make friends with, become acquainted with

ашналыг : *n* 1) acquaintance 2) friendship

ашпаз : *n* cook, culinary/cookery expert

ашпазбашы : *n* chief/senior cook, chef

ашпазлыг : *n* 1) profession of cook/chef 2) cookery

ашпазхана : *n* 1) kitchen 2) dining room, dining hall, refectory

ашсүзән : *n* colander

ашура : *n* the tenth day of the month of Muharram, the first month of the Muslim calendar, the anniversary of the death of Imam Hussein in Kerbala

ашхана : *n* dining room, dining hall; restaurant

ашханачы : *n* manager, owner of a dining establishment, restaurant

б

б : second letter of the Azerbaijani alphabet

ба : *intj* expresses feeling of delight, "admiration, surprise, fear,"Well!", "Wow!" "Really!" Is it possible?"

баб : *a* 1) suitable in age, in character; equal, even *n* 2) a pair 3) chapter *in a book*

баба : *n* 1) grandfather, grandpa *a* 2) simple, ordinary, commonplace, humble, modest

бабадангалма : *n* inherited property, ancestral property

бабал : *n* fault, sin

бабасил : *n* 1) hemorrhoids, piles *a* 2) hemorrhoidal

бабасилоту : *n* peachwort *Polygonum Persicaria L.*, a grass of the buckwheat family *Polygonaceae*

бабат : *a* 1) tolerable, fair, satisfactory, mediocre, middling, not too bad *adv* 2) tolerably, so-so, o.k

бабатлашдырмаг : *v* improve, bring to a satisfactory state, make acceptable, satisfactory

бабатлашмаг : *intr v* become satisfactory/acceptable, be improved, improve

бабатча : *adv* acceptably, satisfactorily, not too bad

бабаханы : *n* babakhan *golden coin used as women's decoration in former times*

бабачыг, бабачығаз : *n* grandpa, grampy

баби : *n* 1) Babist, a follower of the Bab *Arabic-Gate; original name Mirza Ali ibn Radhik b. 1820–d. 1850. This movement was the immediate predecessor of the modern Bahai movement.*

бабил : *n* Babylon *ancient capital of Babylon*

бабилик : *n* the teachings of the Bab *also known as the Bahai Scriptures*

бабилистан : *n* Babylonian Empire

баблашмаг : *v* 1) be of an appropriate age 2) become a pair; become even *versus odd*

баварија : *n* Bavaria

баваријалы : *n* a Bavarian

баггал : *n* grocer

баггалијјә : *n* 1) groceries *collective* ; grocery store *a* grocery

баггаллыг : *n* the grocer's profession

бағ : *n* 1) garden ; dacha *weekend or summer house outside of the city* 2) cord, string, twine; binding, band

баға : *n* turtle-frog group *collective concept specifically embracing frogs and turtles*

бағајарпағы : *n* *bot* plantain, ribwort *Plantago L sp.*

бағбан : *n* gardener

бағбанлыг : *n* profession of gardener

бағбанчылыг : *n* see **бағбанлыг**

бағбелләјән : *n* garden laborer *especially one engaged in turning over the soil*

бағдаты : *n* 1) silk head scarf/kerchief 2) plaster ceiling 3) see **таван**

бағдаш : *n* see **бардаш**

бағыр : *n* 1) liver, liver of animal *as food* *a* 2) hepatic, liver 3) breast, heart *fig. in a number of expressions*

бағыр-бејин : *n* pate made with liver, brain and sometimes fatty sheep's tail

бағырышмаг : *v* bawl/yell all together, raise a general howl

бағырмаг : *v* howl, roar, bellow

бағырсаг : *n* gut, intestine

бағырсаггурду : *n* *zool* helminth, intestinal worm

бағырсагјыған : *n* collector/gatherer of raw intestines/casings

бағырсагсыз : *a* *zool* anenterous (of animals without stomach or intestine)

бағыртдырмаг : *caus of* **бағырмаг**

бағырты : *n* loud, peremptory shout/yell

бағыртмаг : *v* evoke or cause *by one's actions* a loud shout/yell *from another person*

бағышлама : *n* 1) donation 2) forgiveness, pardon, absolution, exculpation

бағышламаг : *v* 1) give, make a present, bestow *upon* , grant, reward *with*, give without obligation 2) forgive, pardon, exculpate 3) spare, have mercy on, give amnesty to

бағышланмаг : *v intr* 1) be bestowed/granted 2) be forgiven/ pardoned/ amnestied

бағышланмаз : *a* unpardonable, unforgiveable, inexcusable

бағышлатдырмаг : *caus of* **бағышламаг**

бағлајычы : *n gram* conjunction

бағлајычысыз : *a* asyndetic, omitting conjunctions

бағлама : *v* 1) from **бағламаг** 2) bundle *articles tied up in a cloth*, bunch, batch, pack *several identical objects packed together* 3) parcel, package 4) riddles in verse form, recited by ashug, or Caucasian folk poet-musicians to one another in competitions

бағламаг : *v* 1) tie up/together, bind up, fasten 2) close/close up, lock, fasten 3) clasp, hook up 4) conclude *agreement, treaty* 5) cover, sheathe, envelop

бағланмаг : *v pass* 1) be tied up/together, bound up, fastened 2) be closed/closed up/locked/fastened

бағлы : *a* 1) tied up/together, bound up, fastened 2) closed, closed up, locked 3) connected, linked

бағлыг : *n* locality completely covered by gardens or orchards

бағлылыг : *n* dependence *upon*, attachment *to*

бағры чатламаг : *v* be racked with pain, terrified, horrified

бағсалан : *n* bodkin *kind of blunt needle used for threading cord or elastic tape*

бағча : *n* small orchard, flower garden, front garden

бағчакарлыг : *n* flower beds, small garden

бағчиjәләjи : *n bot* 1) garden strawberry *Fragaria elaterol or F. viridis L a* 2) strawberry

бағчы : *n* gardener, horticulturalist

бад : *n* 1) rim/edges of the "tendir" *clay bread oven see'* **тәндир**' 2) wind

бадаг, бадалаг : *n* backheel *wrestling*, a maneuver with the foot used to trip an opponent

бадам : *n* 1) almond *a* 2) almond

бадамы : *a* almond-shaped

бадамлы : *a* almond

бадамлыг : *n* area planted with almond trees, almond orchard

бадамчөрәjи : *n* pastry made of rich *short* dough, cut in the shape of daisies

бадамчыг : *n anat* tonsil

бадбан : *n* kite

бадбуду : *n* roasted corn kernels; corn flakes; corn-meal mush

бадә : *n* beaker, jigger, glass

бадымчан : *n* 1) eggplant *a* 2) eggplant

бадымчаны : *a* dark violet

бадjа : *n* milk-pail, milk-trough

баз : *n* 1) lover *of*, enthusiast *for*, fan, supporter *ordinarily appears as a word-formant postposition*

база : *n Ru* base, foundation

базар : *n* 1) market, bazaar 2) Sunday

базар ертәси : *n* Monday

базарбашы : *n* 1) senior supervisor of a market/bazaar 2) instigator of disorder *fig*

базары : *a* 1) mass-produced *not made to order* 2) cheap, poorly made

базарлыг : *n* purchases

базбурудлу : *a* well-put-together, stately, imposing

базы : *n* 1) terrace, embankment between rows, or sectors of a field 2) plow shaft 3) watershed

базу : *n* upper arm

баис : *n* 1) culprit, instigator, ringleader, author *of a crime* 2) reason

баjаг : *adv* recently, not long ago, the other day, lately

баjагдан : *adv* 1) long ago, ages ago 2) already, since *as in* "long since")

баjагкы : *a* recent; aforementioned

баjағы : *a* vulgar, common; commonplace, trite, trivial, banal

баjағылыг : *n* banality, commonplaceness, triteness

баjаз : *n* prayer book

баjан : *n Ru* bayan *Russian-style accordion*

баjанчалан : *n* bayan player

баjат : *a* 1) not fresh, going bad *of food* 2) stale *of bread*

баjаты : *n* 1) bayaty *generic name for a verse form in Azerbaijani folk music* 2) sad, doleful, songs and melodies with lamentations used in mourning for the dead

баjаты-күрд : *n* bayaty-kurd *a genre of mugam, Azerbaijani folk music*

баjатымаг : *v* lose freshness, grow stale *bread*

баj-баj : *intj* expresses sorrow, regret, inner pain; Alas! Woe is me! etc.

бајгуш : *n* 1) owl 2) person who always "cries the blues", predicts the worst

бајғын *a* unconscious, fainting

бајғынлыг : *n* fainting, syncope, loss of consciousness, unconscious state

бајылма : *n* faint, syncope, unconsciousness

бајылмаг : *v* faint, lose consciousness, fall in a faint

бајыр : *n* 1) exterior of premises, the outside 2) vessel, receptacle *a* 3) external, exterior, outer, outside

бајырда : *adv* in the street, outside

бајраг : *n* flag, banner

бајрагдар, бајрагчы : *n* standard bearer

бајрам : *n* 1) holiday, feast, festival *a* 2) festive, holiday

бајрамағзы, бајрамгабағы : *n* 1) eve/day before a holiday *a* 2) holiday *taking place in the period immediately preceding the holiday*

бајрамлашмаг : *v* give one another holiday greetings

бајрамлыг : *n* 1) holiday gift *a* 2) intended for the holiday

бајрамсајағы : *a* holiday

бајтар : *n* veterinarian, veterinary surgeon

бајтарлыг : *n* 1) veterinary science, veterinary medicine *a* 2) veterinary, veterinary medical

бакир : *a* 1) virginal, innocent *n* 2) virgin *male*

бакиранә : *adv* virginally, innocently

бакирә : *a* 1) virginal; innocent *n* 2) virgin

бакирәлик, бакирлик : *n* virginity

баккара : *n* bacarrat *gambling game in which winnings are decided by comparing cards held by the players with cards held by the banker*

бактерија : *n* bacteria *simplest form of vegetable microorganism*

бактериоложи : *a* bacteriological

бактериолокија : *n* bacteriology

Бакы : *n* Russian

бал : *n* 1) honey *a* 2) honey *n* ball *formal social assembly for dancing* 3) ball *meteorological evaluation*

бала : *n* 1) child, baby; little boy 2) young *animals*

бала-бала : *a and adv* see **балача-балача**

балабан : *n* balaban, small wind instrument similar to a zurna *kind of clarinet*

балабанчы : *n* balaban player *musician*

балабанчылыг : *n* balaban-playing *occupation*

балаг : *n* 1) buffalo calf less than one year old 2) hem *of skirt; rare*

балаламаг : *v* to give birth *about animals*

балалы : *a* 1) with litter, with young 2) nursing *animals*

балалыг : *n* uterus *animals*

балахана : *n* belvedere, upper story of a building; mezzanine

балача : *a* 1) small, little *n* 2) child, infant, juvenile

балача-балача : *adv* 1) little by little, a little at a time, gradually *a* 2) tiny *children, babies and so on*

балачаландырмаг : *v* see **балачалатмаг**

балачаланмаг : *v intr* grow/become smaller; become petty *fig*

балачалатмаг, балачалашдырмаг : *v* make small; reduce the significance of *fig*

балачалашдыртмаг : *caus* make grow smaller

балачалыг : *n* little bit, trifle, bagatelle

балачыг, балачығаз : *n* tiny/wee child, tiny baby

балба : *n* thick cabbage soup

балверән : *a* melliferous, nectariferous

балгабаг : *n* 1) pumpkin, gourd *a* 2) dull, obtuse, dull-witted, talentless, undistinguished

балдыз : *n* sister-in-law

балдыр : *n anat* 1) shin, shank 2) calf, calf muscles

балдырыачыг : *n* ragamuffin, ragged fellow, tramp, down-and-outer

балерина : *n* ballerina

балетбазлыг : *n* balletomania, enthusiasm for the ballet

балзам : *n* balm

балзамламаг : *v* embalm

балина : *n* 1) whale *a* 2) whale, cetaceous

балыг : *n* 1) fish *a* 2) fish

балыггулағы : *n* shell, cockle shell

балыггурудан : *n* 1) fish-smoker *person a* 2) fish-smoking

балыгдашыјан : *n* one employed in the transportation of fish *fishing industry and fish-processing plant*

балыгдузлајан : *n* fish-salter *person*

балыгәти : *n* muscle

балыгјејән : *a* fish-eating, ichthyophagous

балыгјујан : *n* fish-washer *one who washes fishes and prepares them for market*

балыгсатан : fish merchant

балыгсызлыг : *n* absence, lack of fish of fish

балыгтәмизләјән : *n* fish-cleaner *person*

балыгтутан, балыгчы : *n* fisherman

балыгудан : *n* heron *fam Ardeidae*

балыгчы : *n* 1) fisherman *a* 2) fish, fish-catching, fishing

балыгчылыг : *n* fishing, fishery, fishing industry

балынч : *n* see **балыш**

балыш : *n* pillow, cushion

балышлыг : *a* cushion, pillow, pad

балышүзү : *n* pillow case

баллы : *a* 1) melliferous, nectariferous *plants, herbs etc* 2) mellifluous, mellifluent *voice etc* 3) honeyed; spread with honey *bread etc*

баллыбаба : *n* *bot* nettle *Lamium sp.*

баллыча : *n* *bot* lungwort *Pulmonaria Officinalis L*

балнеоложи : *a* balneological *pertaining to the science of treating diseases by baths and the mineral water springs*

балнеолокија : *n* balneology *the science of treating diseases by bath and the waters of mineral springs*

балон : *n* balloon

балта : *n* 1) ax 2) chisel, gouge *used in the oil industry*

балтагајыран : *n* ax-maker; blacksmith who forges axes

балталама : *n* chopping, cutting, felling with an ax

балталамаг : *v* 1) chop, cut, fell with an ax *fig* 2) demolish, wreck, ruin, annihilate

балталанмаг : *v* be cut down, felled with an ax

балтачы : *n* woodcutter

бамбалача : *a* very small, tiny

бамбашга : *a* completely different, other

бамбылы : *n* 1) shallow, frivolous person 2) ragamuffin

бамәзә : *n* joker, clown, comedian

бамијә : *n* 1) bamiya *pastry delicacy* 2) okra, gumbo *Hibiscus esculentus*

бан : *n* 1) rooster's crow 2) basket

бандерол : *n* little package or parcel *sent by mail*

бандероллу : *a* sent as a little parcel or package

бандеролчу : *n* wrapper *person who wraps packages, parcels etc.*

бандура : *n* bandura 1) *Ukrainian stringed instrument similar to a large mandolin* 2) *slang* any big and clumsy object

бандурчалан : *n* bandura player

бани : *n* founder, initiator

банк : *n* bank

банка : *n* jar, can

банкагојан, банкадүзән, банкасалан *n* *med* person who applies cupping glasses *treatment in a traditional medicines*

банктутан : *n* banker in card games

банламаг : *v* crow *rooster*

банлашмаг : *v* call to one another *roosters*

бар : *n* fruit, harvest, yield

барабан : *n* drum

барабанчалан : *n* drummer

баракаллаһ : *intj* see **афәрин**

барама : *n* cocoon *silkworm*

барамаајыран : *n* cocoon sorter *silk industry*

барамаачан : *n* cocoon winder *silk industry*

барамабәсләјән : *n* silkworm feeder *silk industry*

барамабоған : *n* master silkworm cocoon processing craftsman

барамадашыјан : *n* carrier of silkworm cocoons *silk industry*

барамајыған : *n* collector of silkworm cocoons *silk industry*

барамасахлајан : *n* see **барамачы**

барамасечән : *n* sorter/grader of silkworm cocoons *silk industry*

барамачы : *n* silkworm breeder, sericulturist

барамачылыг : *n* silkworm breeding, sericulture

барат : *n* monetary transfer *by mail, telegraph*

бараталан : *n* *fin* drawer *person paying by a bill of exchange*

баратаеләјән : *n* *fin* drawee *person who draws a bill of exchange*

барбар : *n* 1) barbarian *a* 2) barbaric

барбаризм : *n* barbarism

барбарлыг : *n* barbarism, barbarity

барбарчасына : *adv* barbarically

бардаг : *n* clay pitcher with a narrow neck

бардан : *n* large sack

барданлыг : *n* material suitable for, or used for making sacks

бардаш : *adv* cross-legged

барелјеф : *n* 1) bas relief *a* 2) bas relief

барә : *postp* concerning, about, as regards, à propos of

бариум : *n* 1) barium *a* 2) barium

бары : *n* stone, brick or adobe enclosure/wall

бары : *conj* although, if only, at least

барынмаг : *v* derive benefit *from*, become rich, make a fortune

барыт : *n* 1) gunpowder, powder *a* 2) gunpowder, powder

барыттабы : *n* powder flask, powder horn

барышдырычы : *n* 1) conciliator, peacemaker, compromiser *a* 2) conciliatory, peacemaking, appeasing

барышдырычылыг : *n* conciliatoriness, spirit of compromise, appeasement

барышдырма : *n* reconciliation

барышдырмаг : *n* reconcile, conciliate

барышыг : *n* peace, armistice, truce; reconciliation; agreement

барышма : *n* see **барышыг**

барышмаг : *v* 1) be reconciled with, make it up with 2) come to an agreement *about*

барышмаз : *a* irreconcilable, intransigent, uncompromising

барышмазлыг : *n* irreconcilability, intransigence

барланмаг : *v* bear fruit, be productive *fruit trees*

барлы : *a* fruitful, productive

бармаг : *n* 1) finger 2) spoke *of wheel*

бармагарасы : *adv* through the fingers

бармагламаг : *v* 1) touch with a finger *med* 2) palpitate

бармаглыг : *n* screen, grating, grid; lattice

бармагсыз : *a* missing one or more fingers, fingerless

бармагчалыг : *n* pad, or palm-cover of leather or other material used by certain workers to protect their fingers against injury

бармен : *n Ru* bartender

барсыз : *a* barren, sterile, fruitless

басабас : *n* crowd, jam, hurly-burly, hubbub

басгы : *n* 1) pressure, force 2) press, paper-weight

басгын : *n* 1) attack, raid, foray, swoop, sudden attack 2) invasion, descent

басгынчы : *n* robber, brigand, raider

басгынчылыг : *n* robbery, brigandage

басдаламаг : *v* trample, step on s.t.

басдыг : *n* see **сучуг**

басдырылмаг : *v* 1) be interred 2) be buried 3) be recovered 4) be planted, dug into the ground 5) be "covered" by a sire/stud/male breeding-animal *animal husbandry*

басдырма : *v* 1) from **басдырмаг** *n* 2) basturma *meat which has been cut up and seasoned with onion and pepper to use in shashlik, and other cooked meat dishes*

басдырмаг : *v* 1) inter *bury ceremonially, according to rite* 2) dig in/into, dig into the ground, plant; bury, bury in 3) recover, cover anew 4) plant *tree* 5) couple *with;* pair *with*, mate *with* 6) cover, shelter, conceal, hide

басдыртмаг : *caus of* **басдырмаг**

басил : *n* bacillus, bacterium

басыб-кәсмәк : *v* boast *of, about;* brag *of, about*; engage in self-advertisement; become entangled in lies, become an inveterate liar

басыглыг : *n* flatness

басылыш : *n* printing, imprint

басылма : *n* 1) compression, pressing, squeezing 2) blow, defeat 3) printing, imprint

басылмаг : *pass* 1) be compressed, squeezed, contracted; be pressed upon 2) be conquered, overcome 3) have published, be published, be printed 4) be crammed into, stuffed into; be crowded into

басылмаз : *a* 1) invincible; insuperable 2) victorious, triumphant

басылмазлыг : *n* invincibility

басырыг : *n* 1) crowded state, tightness, heaped up/piled up state 2) throng, crush, crowding *a* 3) crowded, cramped, piled up, heaped up, conglomerated, pressed, squeezed

басма : *n* 1) pressure, compression, squeezing 2) typographic impression, printing, imprint *a* 3) printed, stamped

басмаг : *v* 1) press, squeeze 2) vanquish, conquer, overcome, fight down, bring down 3) cover completely/all over; get overgrown with 4) attack, make a raid 5) block up, obstruct 6) run over s.o. 7) print, imprint 8) guzzle, gobble, gobble up, devour

басманахыш : *n* design applied to textile material

басмарламаг : *v* 1) raid, swoop down upon 2) seize, seize unexpectedly/ by surprise 3) press hard *of military forces*

басмахана : *n* see **мәтбәә**

басмачы : *n* 1) basmatch *member of anti-Soviet, pan-Turanian rebel group in Central Asia* 2) robber, member of a smash-and-grab gang *typ* 2) pressman

басмачылыг : *n* the Basmachi Pan-Turanian movement in Central Asia in 1921

басһабас : *n* see **басабас**

батаг : *n* 1) sticky mud 2) bog, quagmire

батаглашмаг : *v* turn into swamp

батаглыг : *n* swamp, swampy place

батаған : *a* unsteady, unstable; hesitating, unstately

баталјон : *n* 1) battalion *a* 2) battalion

баттын : *a* 1) destroyed, annihilated, wiped out; lost 2) hollow, sunken 3) missing, vanished, passed from view *n* 4) hopeless, unrepayable debt

батдаг : *n* 1) mud 2) swamp, bog

баты : *n* see **кунбатан**

батыг : *n* 1) hollow, cavity, depression 2) dimple *a* 3) hollow, concave, sunken 4) deaf, grown deaf 5) hoarse, husky

батыглыг : *n* concavity

батырылмаг : *v* 1) be plunged, immersed, submerged 2) be soiled, dirtied, stained 3) be ruined, destroyed, wiped out 4) be driven into, be stuck into

батырылмаз : *a* nonsubmersible, non-immersible

батырма : *v* of **батырмаг**

батырмаг : *v* 1) drown, sink, submerge, dive into the water, dip 2) soil, make dirty 3) plunge, thrust into, stick into 4) destroy, wipe out 5) pollute, defile

батыртдырмаг : *caus of* **батырмаг**

батлаг : *n* see **батаг**

батма : *v* 1) from **батмаг** 2) ruin, bankruptcy, crash, failure

батмаг : *v intr* 1) dive into, plunge into, dip onesef into 2) sink, drop, 3) sink, go down, go to the bottom 4) set, go down *of heavenly bodies* 5) soil oneself, become dirty 6) be missing, perish 8) be pressed in *v* 9) overpower, overcome

батмаз : *a* non-submersible, non-immersible

батман : *n* batman *old unit of weight whose value varies between 3 and 8 kilograms*

бафта : *n* galloon, cording, braid

бафталы : *a* faced/trimmed/ edged with cording or braid

бафтатохујан, бафтачы : *n* see **шәрбаф**

бах : *part* 1) Look! Listen! Be careful! 2) Here! There! Here's. . .!

бахар : *n* 1) view, landscape *adv* 2) depending *on*, in accordance with *who, when, where*

бахдыгча : *adv* the more one looks, the more.. . .

бахдырмаг : *v* subject to scrutiny, show

бахылыш : *n* review, inspection, survey, examination

бахылмаг : *v pass* 1) be examined, scrutinized, be investigated/looked into 2) be under observation, under surveillance

бахым : *n* 1) surveillance, observation 2) care, concern, charge

бахымсыз : *a* neglected, stray, uncared for

бахымсызлыг : *n* neglect

бахычы : *n* 1) supervisor, inspector, examiner, caretaker 2) fortune teller *f.*

бахыш : *n* 1) look, glance 2) review, inspection, survey

бахышмаг : *v* exchange glances *with*

бахја : *n* needlework

бахјалама : *v fr.* **бахјаламаг**

бахјаламаг : *v* stitch, backstitch

бахјаланмаг : *pass* be stitched

бахјалатдырмаг : *caus of* **бахјаланмаг**

бахјалатмаг : *v* make s.o. stitch

бахмаг : *v* 1) look, glance, observe 2) look after, take care of, keep an eye *on* 3) put under surveillance, conduct surveillance; pay attention *to s.t.* 4) examine, try *a court case*

бахмадан : *adv* without a glance, paying no attention, regardless *of*, irrespective *of*

бахмајараг : *postp* in spite of, despite, notwithstanding

бахмалы : *a* worth looking at, paying attention

бахталамаг : *v* see **удузмаг**

баһ : *intj; expression of surprise, amazement* Oh! Wow! Really!

баһа : *a* dear, expensive, costly

баһадыр : *n* 1) epic hero, man of courage, brave spirit 2) bogatyr *term used for the archetypical hero in Russian folk epics; a* 2) heroic, courageous, bogatyr-like, 3) Bahadır *masculine first name*

баһадырлыг : *n* heroic qualities, heroism, courage

баһаландырмаг : *n* raise the price *of*

баһаланма : *n* rise in price, increase in prices

баһаланмаг : *v* rise *of prices* , go up, get more "pricey"

баһалатмаг : *v* see **баһаландырмаг**

баһалашмаг : *v* see **баһаланмаг**

баһалы : *a* 1) dear, expensive 2) valuable, precious

баһалыг : *n* dearness, expensiveness

баһар : *n* 1) spring *a* 2) spring

баһатәһәр : *a* 1) rather dear, rather expensive 2) It's rather expensive *one word sentence*

баһачы, баһачыл : *n* swindler, cheat

баһо : *intj* see **баһ**

бач : *n* tribute *hist* ; duty, assessment

бача : *n* flue, flue-pipe, chimney

бачаглы : *n* see **әшрәфи**

бачадандүшмә : *n* accidental/unexpected acquisition, windfall

бачанаг : brother-in-law, wife's sister's husband

бачардыгча : *adv* as much as possible, to the extent possible, insofar as possible

бачарыг : *n* 1) ability, skill, knack; 2) capability 3) efficacy, effectiveness 4) art

бачарыглы : *a* 1) able, skillful, versatile 2) efficient, effective 3) talented, gifted

бачарыглылыг : *n* good management skills; inclination to entrepreneurship

бачарыгсызлыг : *n* 1) inability, lack of skill 2) inactivity, inertia

бачармаг : *v* be able to/know how to cope/deal with s.t.; be able to/be in a position to do s.t.

бачатәмизләјән : *n* chimney sweep[er]

бачы : *n* sister

бачыгызы : *n* niece *sister's daughter*

бачылыг : *n* 1) stepsister 2) vowed/promised sister *refers to an Orthodox Church ceremony in which women solemnly swear to be sisters* 3) woman friend *of a woman* 4) the close relationship of sister to sister

бачыоғлу : *n* nephew *sister's son*

бачычыг, бачычығаз : *n dim* sister, sis

бач-хәрач : *n colloq hist* 1) tribute 2) bribe

бач-хәрачсыз : *a* without tribute; duty-free

баш : *n* 1) head *a* 2) head, cephalic, cerebral 3) main, chief, principal; senior 4) general; main, arterial *n* 5) beginning, commencement; upper reaches, source *of a river* 6) summit; crown *of a tree* 7) prime minister, premier, chief-, head- *first part of compounds* 8) top, summit, peak

баш ағрытмаг : *v* cause trouble, be pain in the neck

баш алыб кетмәк : *v* leave quickly, without warning, split

баш апармаг : *v* rush, dash

баш вермәк : *v* happen, take place

баш вурмаг : *v* 1) dive 2) cut one's hair

баш галдырмаг : *v* start uprising

баш гачырмаг : *v* avoid *e.g. military draft*

баш гојмаг : *v* perish, peril

баш гошмаг : *v* interfere

баш әјмәк : *v* behave, act humbly

баш ишләтмәк : *v* use one's brains

баш көтүрүб гачмаг : *v* flee

баш тапмаг : *v* understand, comprehend, be aware

баш тутмаг : *v* become true, real

баш үстә : *intrj* please! sure! I sure will!

баш чәкмәк : *v* stop by, pay brief visits

баша батмаг : *v* be perceivable, clear, understandable

баша вурмаг : *v* 1) think over 2) accomplish, complete 3) reproach

баша дүшмәк : *v* understand

баша кечирмәк : *v* put s.o. on an honorable seat around the table

баша кәлмәк : *v* be accomplished, become a reality

баша салмаг : *v* explain

баша чыхмаг : *v* 1) be finished, completed 2) become selfish, brazen, impudent

башдан еләмәк : *v* get rid of s. t. or s.o.

башдан чыхартмаг : *v* confuse, mislead s.o.

башы ачылмаг : *v* get free from work

башы бағланмаг : *v* be sequestrated

башы гарышмаг : *v* be too busy, preoccupied

башы чыхмаг : *v* have knowledge of s.t.

башына бурахмаг : *v* leave uncared, unattended

башына дөнүм : *n* my dear, darling, honey

башына чәкмәк : *v* drink in one sip

башабаш : *adv* even-steven, tit-for-tat, break-even, with neither profit or loss in an exchange

башабәла : *a* 1) restless, fidgety, difficult *n* 2) poor excuse for a man

башаг : *n* 1) ear, spike *of wheat, corn etc.* 2) individual ears spikes *of wheat, corn etc* left in the stubble after reaping

башагланмаг : *v* see **сүнбүлләнмәк**

башағрысы : *n* 1) headache 2) row, noise; fuss, bustle; procrastination

баш-ајаг : *adv* 1) head over heels, topsy-turvy, the wrong way round

башакәлмәз : *a* unrealizable, chimerical, fanciful

башалты : *n* headrest, pillow

башапаран : *a* 1) unbridled *n* 2) person without restraints, one who does not know where to draw the line in conduct

башасалан : *n* interpreter, commentator, expounder

баш-баша : *adv* together, tete a tete, two together, head to head

башбилән : *a* clever, bright; reasonable, sensible; understanding

башга : *a* 1) other; different; special, particular *postp* besides, apart from

башгалашмаг : *v intr* change, alter, become different

башгалыг : *n* another/a differing/different condition

башгасы : *n* another person; another example/sort/kind

башгырд : *n* 1) a Bashkir *a* 2) Bashkir, Bashkirian

башгырдыстан : *n* Bashkiria

башгырдча : *adv* in Bashkirian *language*

баш-гулаг : *n* look, aspect, appearance, physiognomy : **баш-гулаг апармаг** 1) to begin to speak, to get on the nerves *of* , to pester with empty chatter 2) to start shouting/crying, to start screaming shrilly/yelping

баштакы : *a* being at the head/in first place

баштан : *adv* firstly, at first, at the beginning

баштан-баша : *adv* entirely, wholly, generally, universally, fully, from beginning to end

баштансовма : *adv* 1) superficially, perfunctorially, anyhow *badly, carelessly* , in a slap-dash manner, hurriedly *a* 2) superficial, perfunctory, slap-dash, cobbled-up, carelessly-done

баштащы : *n* headstone, grave-stone/marker

башыаловлу : *adv* excitedly, agitatedly, confusedly

башыачыг : *a* 1) bare-headed, hatless *adv* 2) with head bare

башыашағы : *adv* 1) headfirst 2) in a downward direction *a* 3) quiet, modest, retiring

башыбағлы : *a* 1) depending/ being dependent *on s.o.* 2) secret, sealed *official letter* 3) provisionally contracted for; contracted for on s. o.'s down payment *goods or other property* 4) described in a search and seizure document so as to to facilitate the investigation *property*

башыбатмыш : *a* 1) hopeless, lost, wretched *pred* 2) Damn him!, May he drop dead! That wretch!

башыбәлалы : *a* 1) unlucky, unsuccessful, ill-starred 2) long-suffering

башыбәрк : *a* 1) spirited *horse* 2) strong, enduring *person*

башыбош : *a* 1) empty-headed, dim-witted, stupid 2) loose, lax *in morals, conduct*

башыдашлы : *a* 1) unlucky, ill-starred *n* unlucky individual, victim of misfortune

башыдолу : *a* intelligent, sensible 2) fond of the bottle, drunk, drunken, intoxicated

башыдумук : *a* occupied with s.t.

башыәтли : *a* rich, well-off, well-to-do

башыјекә : *a* 1) large-headed, macrocephalic 2) uncompromising, opinionated

башыјекәлик : *n* 1) large-headedness, macrocephaly 2) petty tyranny, pig-headedness, wilfulness

башыкүллү : *a* unfortunate, pitiable, humble

башыләчәкли : *n* woman *lit. head-kerchiefed*

башыөртүлү : *a* with head covered, wearing headgear *about women*

башыпапаглы : *n* 1) one who wears a head covering/hat *fig* 2) man, fellow

башыпозуг : *n* bashibazouk *one belonging to the class of mounted Turkish irregular soldiers famous for their cruelty; synonym of a strong, stupid and cruel man*

башыпозуглуг : *n* anarchy; mess, disorder

башысојуг : *a* erroneous; hasty, careless, unsystematic

башысоіуглуг : *n* error-proneness, precipateness; carelessness, negligence

башыуча : *a* with clear/clean conscience

башыучалыг : *n* honor, esteem, integrity

башкәсән : *n* cutthroat, bandit, thug

башкичәлдичи : *a* giddy, dizzy; dizzying, vertiginous, causing dizziness, vertigo

башкичәлләнмә *n* dizziness, vertigo

башкичәлләнмәси : *n* see **башкичәлләнмә**

башлама : *n* undertaking

башламаг : *v* begin, commence, undertake, start

башланғыч : *n* 1) beginning, commencement 2) introduction 3) prologue

башланыш : *n* beginning

башланмаг : *v intr* begin, be begun

башлы : *a* intelligent, sensible

башлы-башына : *adv* uncontrolledly, wilfully; haphazardly, of its own accord

башлы-башыналыг : *n* 1) freedom, licence; self-will, willfulness; excess 2) arbitrariness, anarchy

башлыг : *n* 1) bashlyk *male headcover covering the whole head down to shoulders* 2) headline of a stereotype, or electroplate; typographic illustration 3) addition, increment to s.t. *usually in an exchange*

башлыча : *a* chief, principal, fundamental, basic

башмаг : *n* bashmak, Turkish slipper having an open back

башмагсеіри : *n* walk, stroll, promenade

башмагчы : *n* 1) shoemaker, cobbler, bashmak-maker *Turkish slippers* 2) small insect

башмагчылыг : *n* profession of bashmak-maker/shoemaker

башсағлығы : *n* condolences on the occasion of a death

башсыз : *a* 1) headless 2) senseless, brainless 3) without supervision/oversight/guidance

башсыз-аіагсыз : *a* disconnected, incoherent *of speech*

башсызлыг : *n* 1) stupidity, senselessness 2) absence of a leader, leaderlessness, anarchy 3) arbitrariness

башсындыран : *a* 1) puzzling *n* 2) puzzle, conundrum

баштутмаз : *a* 1) impractical, unfeasible, unrealizable *adv* 2) not soon

башчы : *n* leader, chief, supervisor, head

башчылыг : *n* supremacy, domination; leadership, command

без : *n* coarse calico

безар : *a* 1) experiencing aversion, repugnance, disgust *n* 2) person oppressed by some negative feeling *boredom, depression*

бездирмәк : *v* pester, bother, bore, worry, plague, vex, annoy

безикдиричи : *a* importunate, persistent, boring, vexing, tedious

безикдиричилик : *n* importunity, peskiness, bothersomeness

безикдирмәк : *v* see **бездирмәк**

безикмәк : *v intr* become loathesome/repulsive, become bored, annoyed, feel revulsion

безмәк : *v* feel s. t. to be a burden, find s.t. hard

беіин : *n* brain

беіинә вурмаг : *v* to think over

беіинли : *a* 1) possed of a brain 2) intelligent, brainy, smart

беіинсиз : *a* brainless, stupid, senseless

беіинсизлик : *n* brainlessness, stupidity, senselessness

беіинчик : *n anat* cerebellum

беінәлмиләл : *n hist* 1) the International *International Marxist organization a* 2) International *pertaining to the international movement*

беінәлмиләлчи : *n* internationalist

беінәлмиләлчилик : *n* internationalism

беінәлхалг : *a* international

беінибош : *a* empty-headed, senseless, feeble-minded

беіт : *n* dystich, couplet

беітләшмә : *n* bouts rimés *fr. lit. "rhymed endings" words and syllables in rhyme, to which verses have to be fitted, in a written or oral contest*

беітләшмәк : *v* compete in the improvisation of verses or rhymed couplets

бел : *n* 1) waist 2) spinal column 3) spade, iron shovel

бел бағламаг : *v* be hopeful, rely on s.o. or s.t.

белбағы : *n* sash, girdle, belt

белетаж : *n* first floor; dress circle *theater*

белә : *pro* 1) such, so 2) similar *to*, like *adv* 3) even *not only but even*

белә-белә : *pro* such, similar *things, persons etc*

беләликлә : *introd word* 1) and so. . ., and thus. . ., this being so. . . etc.

беләчә : *adv* so, in this manner, thus

белибағлы : *n ornith* hen-harrier, or harrow *Cyrcus Cyaneus*

белибүкүк : *a* crooked, bent, hunched

белләмәк : *v* dig, dig up, dig over again *with a spade*

белләнмәк : *pass* be dug up, be dug over again *with a spade*

беллэтдирмәк : *caus of* **белләмәк**

беллэтмәк : *caus of* **белләмәк**

белорус : *n* a Belorussian

белорусија : *n* Belorussia

белорусча : *adv* in Belorussian *language*

белчика : *n* 1) Belgium *adv* 2) Belgian

белчикалы : *n* a Belgian

бензин : *n* 1) gasoline, petrol *a* 2) gasoline, gas, petrol

бензинөлчән : *n* filling station attendant, worker dispensing gasoline

бетәр : *a* 1) worse *than* 2) strong[er], violent[er] *adv* 3) strongly, violently

бетон : *n* 1) concrete *a* 2) concrete

бетонламаг : *v* concrete, treat with concrete, lay concrete

бетонлатдырмаг : *caus of* **бетонламаг**

бетонлатмаг : *caus of* **бетонламаг**

бетончу : *n* concrete worker

беһ : *n* deposit, down payment

беһбуд : *n* knife with a long, thin blade often used for criminal purposes

беһишт : *n* 1) Paradise *a* 2) paradisical

беһләшмәк : *v* conclude a transaction by putting down a deposit, a down-payment

бечә : *n* 1) cockerel 2) young swarm of bees *bot* 3) sprout, sprig, scion, graft

бечәрилмәк : *v* 1) be tilled; be cultivated 2) be raised/grown

бечәрмә : *n* cultivation, working *of land, soil* 2) breeding, propagation *plants, crops etc*

бечәрмәк : *v* 1) till; cultivate *soil etc* 2) grow, raise, cultivate; breed, propagate 3) tend, farm

беш : *num* five

бешајлыг : *a* five-monthly

бешаршынлыг : *a* five-arshin *about 13 feet*

бешатылан, бешачылан : *n* five-shot firearm *rifle, revolver*

бешбармаг : *n* brass-knuckles, knuckle-dusters

бешбашлы : *a* five-peaked *lit. five-headed; refers to mountain formation*

бешбетәр : *a* much worse, worse by far

беш-беш : *adv* by fives

бешбөлкүлү : *a poetry* pentametric, five metric foot

бешбучаг : *n* pentagon

бешбучаглы : *a* pentagonal

бешверстлик : *a* five-verst *about 6 miles*

бешгат, бешгатлы : *a* five-ply, five-layered

бешгәпиклик : *n* 5 kopek coin *no longer exists*

бешдаш : *n* children's game consisting of tossing pebbles and catching them on the fly

бешик : *n* cradle

бешиллик : *n comunist econ* 1) five-year plan *a* 2) five-year

бешинчи : *a* fifth

бешјашар : *a* five-year-old *animals*

бешкилолуг : *a* five-kilogram

бешкушәли : *a* five-terminal

бешкүл : *a* see **бешбучаглы**

бешкүнлүк : *n* 1) five-day period *a* 2) five-day

бешлик : *n* 1) five-ruble note 2) a "five" *playing cards*

бешманатлыг : *n* 1) five-ruble note *a* 2) five-ruble

бешметрлик : *a* five-meter

бешмәртәбә, бешмәртәбәли : *a* five-story

бешрәгәмли : *a math* five-digit

бешсимли : *a mus* five-string

бешсинифли : *a* fifth-grade *school*

бештарлалы : *a agr* five-field *system*

бештонлуг : *n* 1) five-tonner *truck a* 2) five-ton

бешүзлү : *n geom* 1) pentahedron *a* 2) pentahedron

бешһечалы : *a gram* five-syllable

бешчә : *adv* just five; exactly five

бешчилдли : *a* five-volume

бешчилдлик : *n* five-volume set

бәбә : *n* baby, infant, little one, small child

бәбәк : *n* pupil *of the eye*

бәбир : *n* *zool* leopard

бәғәлә : *n* *bot* see **моруг**

бәд : *a* bad, evil, nasty *Persian, largely in compounds*

бәдаје : *a* artistic; tasteful; aesthetically pleasing

бәдајепәрәст : *n* aesthete

бәдајепәрәстлик : *n* aestheticism

бәдаһәтән : *adv* at once, straight away, suddenly, unexpectedly, without warning

бәдбәхт : *a* unhappy, unfortunate, hapless unlucky, ill-starred

бәдбәхтлик : *n* misfortune, calamity, adversity

бәдбин : *n* 1) pessimist *a* 2) pessimistic

бәдбинанә : *adv* see **бәдбинчәсинә**

бәдбинләшмәк : *v intr* become a pessimist

бәдбинлик : *n* pessimism

бәдбинчәсинә : *adv* pessimistically

бәдбиһесаб : *a* 1) ungrateful, thankless 2) not recognizing a debt/obligation, not carrying out one's obligations

бәдәбәддә : *adv* if worse comes to worst, at worst

бәдәви : *n* Bedouin *nomadic Arab*

бәдәл : *n* 1) substitute, replacement; imitation, ersatz 2) ransom *a* 3) fake, false, counterfeit

бәдәмәл : *n* malefactor

бәдән : *n* *anat* 1) body 2) organism

бәдәннүма : *a* full-length *used only in compounds* : **бәдәннүма ајна/ күзкү** full-length mirror

бәдәнсиз : *a* immaterial, incorporeal

бәдәнчә : *adv* corporeally, bodily, materially, physically

бәдәсил : *a* of humble birth; ignoble, base

бәдәфкар : *n* deliberate/confirmed criminal, malefactor

бәдәхлаг : *a* loathsome, vile, amoral

бәдзат : *n* shrewd person, old fox, sly fox, one who doesn't miss a trick

бәдиә : *n* see **бәдјә**

бәдии : *a* artistic, refined, poetic, aesthetic

бәдиијјат : *n* art, aesthetics

бәдиилик : *n* 1) artistry, artistic merit; romanticism *as a trait of human personality* 2) capacity to go beyond the everyday, or what common sense would dictate 3) capacity to use apposite literary citations in a suitable situation

бәдир : *n* see **бәдр**

бәдјә : *n* 1) two-line, or four-line folk verse, usually humorous, and topical, sung in a lively manner 2) improvisation

бәдјәдејән, бәдјәчи : *n* improvisor

бәдјумн : *n* unlucky sign

бәдку : *n* perennial naysayer

бәдкулуг : *n* negation of everything

бәдкуман : *a* mistrustful, distrustful, suspicious

бәдкуманлыг, бәдкуманчылыг : *n* suspicion, mistrust, distrust

бәдләкәр : *a* see **ејбәчәр**

бәдлик : *n* 1) failure, misfortune, ill-luck 2) obstinacy, stubbornness, obduracy

бәдмәзһәб : *a* unreliable, untrustworthy; belonging to a wrong religious denomination

бәдмүшк : *n* *bot* crack willow *Salix fragilis*

бәднал : *a* balking at being shoed *horse*

бәднам : *a* 1) disgraced, defamed, discredited, dishonored, shamed 2) notorious

бәднамлыг, бәднамчылыг : *n* shame, disgrace, dishonor

бәднәзәр : *n* evil eye

бәднәфс : *n* egotist

бәднәфслик : *n* 1) egotism 2) excess

бәднијјәт : *a* disloyal, ill-intentioned

бәднијјәтлик : *n* disloyalty, perfidiousness, bad intentions

бәдр : *n* full moon

бәдраһ : *a* see **бәдрәфтар**

бәдрәнк : *a* unattractive, unsightly; unpleasing of hue

бәдрәфтар : *n* rude, quarrelsome, discourteous person

бәдрәфтарлыг : *n* quarrelsomeness, discourtesy

бәдрләнмәк : *v* become full *moon*; reach full moon

бәдсифәт : *a* 1) see **бәдрәфтар** *n* 2) see **бәдсурәт**

бәдсурәт : *n* mug, ugly face

бәдтәр : *a* see **бетәр**

бәдтинәт : *a* see **идбар**

бәдхаб : *a* sleepless

бәдхаблыг : *n* insomnia

бәдхасијјәт : *n* person having a bad character, a vicious, depraved person

бәдхасиjjәтлик : *n* bad character, depravity, lack of self-restraint, intemperance

бәдхаһ : *n* 1) malevolent, spiteful person *a* 2) malevolent, spiteful, gloating, maliciously rejoicing in others' misfortune

бәдхаһлыг : *n* malevolence, spite

бәдхәрч : *n* 1) prodigal, wastrel, spendthrift, squanderer *a* 2) extravagant, wasteful, spendthrift *attr.*

бәдхәрчлик : *n* prodigality, extravagance; squandering, dissipation

бәдһагг : *a* unpunctual, lax in meeting one's monetary obligations, insolvent

бәдһаглыг : *n* unpunctuality/unrealiabiliity in meeting monetary obligations, insolvency

бәдһал : *a* in grave condition *illness*

бәдһеjбәт : *n* 1) ugly person *a* 2) ugly, deformed, misshapen, monstrous

бәдһәрәкәт : *a* 1) obscene, indecent, improper; affected, mincing *n* 2) poser, affected person

бәдһәрәкәтлик : *n* 1) indecency, obscenity 2) affectedness, attitudinizing

бәдчинс : *a* 1) not purebred, unpedigreed 2) poor quality *attr*

бәзәк : *n* 1) attire, finery, adornment, decoration 2) embellishment

бәзәк-дүзәк : *n* embellishment, decoration, appointments

бәзәкли : *a* smart, well-dressed, decorated, adorned, well-appointed

бәзәксиз : *a* unadorned, plain, undecorated

бәзәмәк : *v* 1) dress up, array, decorate 2) *fig* exaggerate, embellish, embroider, paint a picture of

бә'зән : *adv* sometimes, from time to time, now and then

бәзәндирмәк : *v* decorate, smarten up

бәзәндиртмәк : *caus of* **бәзәмәк**

бәзәниб-дүзәнмәк : *v intr* array o.s. in, dress up

бәзәнмәк : *v intr* 1) array o.s. in, dress up 2) adorn oneself, doll o.s. up, smarten o.s. up

бәззаз : *n* retailer of dress materials/drapery

бәззазлыг : *n* trade/commercial dealing in cotton textiles, dress materials, drapery etc.

бәззат : *a* shrewd, canny, arch; able

бә'зи : *a* some

бәзиләри, бә'зи пара : *n* some people *often with disapproval*

бәзир : *n* linseed, flaxseed

бәзкәк : *n* kind of bustard, a steppe-dwelling bird, characterized by s shrill whistling caused by air passing through the wing feathers in flight *Otis tetrax sp.*

бәj : *n* 1) Bey, nobleman; *when added after a first name signifies a polite address to a man; strongly associated with the pro-Turkish policy of the People's Front of Azerbaijan* 2) fiance, bridegroom

бәjаз : *a* 1) white 2) Bayaz *feminine first name*

бәjан : *n* exposition, account, description; communication, explanation, pronouncement; revelation *title of Bab's book*

бәjанат : *n* statement, declaration, explanation

бәjаннамә : *n* declaration

бәjәндирмәк : *v* secure approval; try to have s.o. correct s.t./set s.t. straight

бәjәндиртмәк : *caus of* **бәjәнмәк**

бәjәнилмә : *n* approval

бәjәнилмәк : *v* please, be to the liking of, be approved 2) be to the taste of s.o. 3) be accepted

бәjәнмә : *n* approval

бәjәнмәк : *v* 1) pick, choose, select; find to be good/appropriate/worthy 2) approve, accept

бәjзадә : *n hist* son of a Bey, nobleman's son

бәjирмә, бәjирти : *n* bleating *goat*

бәjирмәк : *v* bleat *goat*

бәjлик : *n* 1) rank/status of a Bey, rank/status of nobility; nobility *coll* 2) holdings, estates of a nobleman *a* 2) noble, high born

бәкарәт : *n* virginity, physical chastity, innocence *of a young maiden*; chastity

бәкмәз : *n* bekmez, boiled-down juice of grapes, or mulberries *used medicinally*

бәла : *n* 1) calamity, disaster, misfortune, adversity, trouble *a* 2) *fig* bright, smart, sharp

бәлағәт : *n* eloquence

бәлағәтли : *n* eloquent

бәлалы : *a* disastrous, calamitous, ill-starred, unlucky

бәлғәм : *n med* 1) phlegm 2) uncontrollable impulse to cough

бәлғәмли : *a* mucous

бәләд : *a* 1) knowing/familiar with an area 2) familiar with/informed about/dedicated to some particular thing/area of knowledge

бәләдиjjә : *n* 1) municipality *a* 2) municipal

бәләдиjjәләшдирмә : *n* municipalization

бәләдиjjәләшдирмәк : *v* municipalize

бәләдләмәк : *v* plan, project *itinerary, work etc*

бәләдләшмәк : *v* make o.s. familiar with, get to know *an area, a work project etc*

бәләдлик : *n* knowledge, familiarity *with an area, a type of work etc*

бәләдчи : *n* guide

бәләдчилик : *n* guiding, the profession of guide

бәләк : *n* 1) swaddling clothes 2) baby wrapped in swaddling clothes

бәләкбағы : *n* swaddling bands/clothes; band/strip which is wound around an infant on top of the swaddling clothes

бәләмәк : *v* wrap in swaddling clothes

бәләнмәк : *pass* 1) be wrapped in swaddling clothes 2) see **буланмаг** (2)

бәләшмәк : *v* see **булашмаг**

бәли : *pass* yes; hello! *on the phone*

бәли-бәли : *v* assenting, being a yes-man, saying yes uncritically *lit. yes-yes*

бәлим : *n* straw remaining in a field after harvest

бәлкә : *intro wd* perhaps, maybe, it is possible that

бәлли : *a* 1) clear, evident, apparent 2) known *to*

бәлчәм : *n* phlegm

бәм : *n mus* 1) bass *lowest male voice*, low notes *a* 2) bass

бәнд : *n anat* joint, articulation 2) dam, dike 3) stanza, strophe, couplet 4) clamp, fastener; cover plate, tie-plate 5) tie,band 6) catch, clip, hasp

бәнд-бәнд : *a* 1) jointed, articulated, hinged *adv* 2) joint by joint 3) paragraph by paragraph, item by item

бәнд-бәрә : *n* passage, crossing

бәндә : *n* slave; servant

бәндәм : *n agr* 1) tie made of twisted, or braided straw, used for binding grain sheaves 2) graft, slip, cutting *bot* 3) fruit stem

бәндәр : *n* port

бәндләмә : *n* fastener, connector, coupling

бәндләмәк : *v* tie, bind, fasten, attach, connect, clamp

бәндсиз : *a* unarticulated, unsegmented, unjointed

бәнәк : *n* small red birthmarks/moles on face or body

бәнзәдилмә : *n* likening, comparison

бәнзәдилмәк : *v* bear a resemblance *to*, resemble s.o, s.t.

бәнзәjиш, бәнзәмә : *n* similarity, likeness, resemblance

бәнзәмәз : *a* unlike, dissimilar

бәнзәмәк : *v* resemble, be like

бәнзә(мә)мәзлик : *n* dissimilarity

бәнзәр : *a* like, similar, analogous, resembling s.o, s.t.

бәнзәтмә : *n* imitation; likening

бәнзәтмәк : *v* 1) liken to; imitate, make like s.t. 2) identify with, as; mistake s.o for s.o. else

бәниз : *n* 1) face; look, aspect, appearance 2) complexion, color of the face

бәнкоту : *n bot* henbane *Hyosciamus niger L*

бәнна : *n* mason, bricklayer

бәнналыг : *n* occupation of mason, bricklayer

бәнөвшә : *n* 1) *bot* violet *a* 2) violaceous *pertaining to violet*

бәнөвшәjи : *a* violet *color*

бәнөвшәлик : *n* area lush with violets

бәрабәр : *a* 1) equal, on a par, tantamount *adv* 2) equally, in equal portions, on a level *with*, equally *with*, on a level, all the same 3) together, in common, jointly, along with

бәрабәрбучаглы : *a* equiangular

бәрабәрjанлы : *a geom* iscoceles

бәрабәрләмәк : *v* see **бәрабәрләшдирмәк**

бәрабәрләшдирилмәк : *v* be levelled/made ready

бәрабәрләшдирмә : *n* levelling, equalization

бәрабәрләшдирмәк : *v* equalize, level

бәрабәрләшдиртмәк : *caus of* **бәрабәрләшдирмәк**

бәрабәрләшмә : *n* equalizing, evening, levelling

бәрабәрләшмәк : *v* come alongside, be made equal *to*, be put on a par *with*, match s.o.

бәрабәрлик : *n* equality, parity

бәрабәрсизлик : *n* inequality, disparity

бәрабәрчилик : *n* egalitarianism

бәрабәрчә : *adv* equally, in equal parts

бәраәт : *n* justification

бәрбад : *a* 1) destroyed, ruined 2) annihilated 3) disorderly 4) very bad, nasty

бәрбадлыг : *n* breakdown, disintegration, ruin, devastation

бәрбәр : *n* barber; hairdresser

бәрбәрлик : *n* profession of barber/hairdresser

бәрбәрхана : *n* barber shop, hairdresser's shop

бәрг : *n* brightness, brilliance, gloss, luster, shine

бәргәрар : *a* firm, hard, solid, strong

бәрә : *n* 1) ambush, lurking place, blind *in hunting* 2) ford, crossing, portage 3) ferry

бәрәкәт : *n* 1) plenty, abundance 2) profusion, sufficiency, fertility, productivity

бәрәкәтли : *a* plenteous, abundant, profuse, lush, fruitful, productive 2) high-yielding *grain*

бәрәкәтсиз : *a* skimpy, insufficient

бәрәкәтсизлик : *n* insufficiency, paucity, shortage, scantiness

бәрәлмәк : *v* have one's eyes popping out of their sockets

бәрәлтмәк : *v* have one's eyes wide open; goggle at

бәрзәх : *n* *geog* isthmus, neck of land

бәри : *adv* 1) hither, in this direction 2) from *directional*

бәрк : *a* 1) hard, firm 2) loud 3) strong 4) steep 5) fast, quick

бәрк-бәрк : *adv* very firmly

бәркдән : *adv* loudly, out loud, aloud

бәркидилмәк : *v intr* become stronger, be fastened, be secured

бәркимә : *n* hardening

бәркимәк : *v intr* 1) harden, become hard, set 2) get stronger, be tempered

бәркитмә : *n* strengthening

бәркитмәк : *v* 1) strengthen, fasten together, fasten tightly/firmly, attach 2) make hard 3) temper

бәркишмәк : *v intr* 1) be tempered, hardened 2) harden, set *liquid*

бәрклик : *n* 1) toughness, hardness, condition or state of toughness, and hardness *fig* 2) stinginess, miserliness, niggardliness

бәрли-бәзәкли : *a* well-dressed, elegant, smart; adorned, decorated, embellished

бәрни : *n* glazed *ceramic or glass* cupping-glass

бәрпа : *n* 1) restoration, reconstruction; rebirth, revival *a* 2) of restoration/reconstruction

бәс : *adv* enough; but, and *at the beginning of a sentence*

бәсдир : *pred* that's enough!, that'll do!

бәсирәт : *n* foresight, perspicacity, insight

бәсирәтли : *a* foresighted, perspicatious, insightful

бәсирәтсиз : *a* shortsighted, imperceptive, lacking perspicacity

бәсирәтсизлик : *n* shortsightedness, lack of insight, apperception, improvidence

бәсит : *a* simple, straightforward, not complex

бәситләшдирмәк : *v* simplify, make less complex

бәситләшмәк : *pass* be simplified, be made less complex

бәситлик : *n* primitiveness, crudity

бәсләјичи : *a* 1) nourishing, nutritious 2) fostering, cultivating *n* 3) breadwinner

бәсләјиш, бәсләмә : *n* 1) feeding; rearing, raising, bringing up 2) educating

бәсләмәк : *v* 1) feed, nourish 2) educate, bring up 3) cultivate

бәсләнмәк : *pass* 1) be fed, nourished; be brought up, reared 2) be grown, cultivated

бәсләтдирмәк : *caus of* **бәсләмәк**

бәсләтмәк : *v* see **бәсләмәк**

бәсрә : *n* Basra *city in Iraq*

бәстәбој : *a* 1) short, low *stature, height* *n* 2) short person

бәстәкар : *n* *mus* composer

бәстәкарлыг : *n* *mus* 1) composition 2) profession of composer

бәстәләјән : *n* *typol* stitcher

бәстәләмә : *n* 1) composition *in various meanings*, assembling, putting together *typog* 2) stitcher

бәстәләмәк : *v* *mus* 1) compose *typog* 2) stitch

бәт-бәниз : *n* see **бәниз**

бәтн : *n* womb

бәхт : *n* 1) luck, fortune, good fortune 2) fate

бәхтәбәхт : *adv* on the off chance, luckily, fortunately, as luck would have it

бәхтәвәр : *a* 1) happy, lucky, fortunate *n* 2) lucky

бәхтәвәрлик : *n* happiness, luck, good fortune, prosperity

бәхтигара : *a* 1) unhappy, unlucky, unfortunate *n* 2) unlucky person, failure

бәхтијар : *a* 1) happy, lucky, blessed *n* 2) lucky person

бәхтијари : *n* Bakhtiari, a powerful nomadic tribe ranging between Isfahan and Kermanshah in Iran

бәхтијарлыг : *n* luck, good fortune, felicity, success

бәхтли : *a* lucky, fortunate, successful

бәхтлик : *n* luck, good fortune

бәхтсиз : *a* unlucky, unhappy, unsuccessful, ill-starred, ill-fated

бәхш етмәк : *v* give, grant, bestow

бәхшиш : *n* gift, donation, present *given in order to influence someone*

бәһаи : *n* see **баби**

бәһанә : *n* pretext, excuse

бәһанәчи : *a* 1) overparticular, captious, niggling *n* 2) caviller, faultfinder, nitpicker

бәһанәчилик : *n* captiousness, faultfinding, nitpicking

бәһ-бәһ : *intj* Bravo!, It's marvellous wonderful, lovely !, Excellent!, Splendid!

бәһәр : *n* see **бәһрә** 2)

бәһрә : *n* 1) use, advantage, benefit 2) harvest, crop, yield *hist* 3) rent paid in money instead of services under a feudal system

бәһрәли : *a* fruitful, prolific, productive, producing high yield

бәһрәсиз : *a* sterile, barren, unfruitful, unproductive

бәһрәсизлик : *n* bad harvest, crop failure, poor crop

бәһс : *n* 1) argument, controversy, dispute, discussion 2) theme/subject of a discussion/a talk

бәһсәбәс : *adv* 1) in competition 2) adversarially, in an adversial manner

бәһсләшмәк : *v* 1) argue, dispute, engage in controversy 2) compete *with*, contend *with*

бәшәр : *n* man, mankind

бәшәри : *adv* humanly, in a human manner

бәшәријјәт : *n* humanity, mankind

биабыр : *a* disgraced, shamed, discredited

биабырчы : *a* 1) disgraceful, shameful, shameless, shocking *n* 2) hooligan, scamp

биабырчылыг : *n* shame, disgrace, scandal, outrage, disgraceful conduct

биабырчасына : *adv* shamefully, disgracefully

биар : *a* 1) unconcerned; lacking all self-respect *n* 2) shameless fellow

биарлыг : *n* unconcern, indifferrentism

бибәр : *n* capsicum; cayenne pepper; green or red pepper

биби : *n* aunt *father's side*

бибигызы : *n* female first cousin *daughter of paternal side aunt*

бибинәвәси : *n* second cousin *male or female* on father's sister's side. *Second cousins are the children of first cousins. Also used informally for any cousin beyond the first degree of kinship*

бибиоғлу : *n* first cousin *son of aunt on father's side*

бивахт : *a* 1) inopportune, untimely, unseasonable *adv* 2) inopportunely, tardily

бивеч : *a* unfit, good-for-nothing, useless

бивәфа : *a* unfaithful, inconstant *in friendship or love* 2) traitor, betrayer

бигејрәт : *a* unconcerned, careless, lacking in self-respect, lacking in social conciousness

бигејрәтләшмәк : *v* become unconcerned, careless, lacking in self-respect, lacking in social consciousness

бигејрәтлик : *n* carelessness, lack of concern, self-respect, social consciousness

бигәрәз : *a* impartial, unbiased, just

биданә : *n* species of mulberry tree

бидмишк : *n bot* see **бәдмүшк**

биәдәб : *a* unseemly, discourteous, impolite, ill-mannered; indecent

биәдәблик : *n* unseemliness, discourteousness, impoliteness, oafishness, ill-breeding

биз : *pro* 1) we *n* 2) awl

бизанс : *n* 1) Byzantium *a* 2) Byzantine

бизбурун : *a* 1) sharp-nosed *fig* 2) pointed, tapered

бизимки : *pro* our, belonging to us

бизләмәк : *v* 1) sharpen, make sharp/pointed 2) pierce/prick with an awl *fig* 3) urge on, goad, hurry, urge on s.o.

бизләнмәк : *pass* be urged on, hurried

бизнес : *n* business

бизчә : *adv* as we think, in our opinion; as we would have it ; according to our custom

бизшәкилли : *a* awl-shaped

биихтијар : *adv* 1) involuntarily, automatically 2) without permission

бијабан : *n* desert, wilderness

бијан : *n* *bot* licorice *Glycyrriza Glabra* licorice root

бијар : *n* *hist* corvée *labor performed by a serf, or temporarily obligated peasant for the benefit of a landowner, or nobleman, in return for the use of a sector of land which can be passed on to his heir*

бикар : *a* 1) unoccupied, free of the obligation to work 2) idle, unemployed

бикара : *a* unimportant, of little use; useless, of poor quality, needless

бикарлашмаг : *v* become unfit, unimportant, useless

бикарламаг, **бикарлашмаг** : *v* *intr* be released from work, become idle, unemployed

бикарлыг, **бикарчылыг** : *n* idleness

бикеф : *a* sad, melancholy, gloomy, despondent, mournful, depressed

бикеф-бикеф : *adv* sadly, gloomily, sadly, mournfully, depressedly

бикефлик, : *n* sadness, mournfulness, depression, gloom

бикефчилик : *n* see **бикефлик**,

биканә : *a* indifferent, unconcerned

биканәлик : *n* indifference, lack of concern

билаваситә : *adv* immediately, straight away, directly, at once

билаихтијар : *adv* see **биихтијар**

билатәхир : *adv* immediately, forthwith, urgently

билдир : *adv* last year

билдирилмәк : *pass* be declared/announced, be informed, be brought to the notice *of* ; be in communication *with*

билдириш : *n* announcement, notice

билдирки : *a* last year's

билдирмәк : *v* inform, notify, announce, communicate, declare, report, let know

билдирчин : *n* *zool* quail *Coturnix coturnix*

билдирчинбаз : *n* person who keeps/owns/raises quail

билет : *n* 1) ticket *a* 2) ticket

билетәбахан : *n* ticket-collector

билетјохлајан : *n* see **билетәбахан**,

билә-билә : *adv* wittingly, purposly, intentionally, knowingly, consciously

biləк : *n* wrist, carpus

биләрәкдән : *adv* see **билә-билә**

биләрзик : *n* bracelet

билик : *n* knowledge

биликли : *a* expert, learned, erudite, knowledgeable, widely-read

биликсиз : *n* 1) ignoramus *a* 2) ignorant *about* , not well-informed *about*

биликсизлик : *n* lack of knowledge, absence of knowlewdge

билинмәз : *a* unknown, unknowable

билинмәк : *v* become known; get to know, be revealed, be discovered, come to light

биличи : *a* 1) well-informed, wise *n* 2) expert 3) sorcerer, sorceress , wizard, fortune-teller

билјард : *n* 1) billiard table; billiards *a* 2) billiard

билјон : *num* billion

билки : *n* see **билик**

билмәдән : *adv* by chance, by accident, unexpectedly; God knows *how* 2) at random, by guesswork

билмәк : *v* 1) know 2) recognize, learn, find out 3) be able *to* 4) be possible

билмәмәзлик : *n* ignorance, lack of knowledge; lack of possibility

билмәррә : *adv* completely, absolutely, quite

билмәчә : *n* charade

бимар : *a* see **хәстә**

бимбиз : *a* 1) greatly sharpened/tapered 2) bristly, setaceous

бимә'на : *a* nonsensically absurd, absurd in the extreme

бимә'рифәт : *a* see **мә'рифәтсиз**

бина : *n* 1) building, premises, structure, installation 2) foundation, substructure, base

бинакузарлыг : *n* 1) disposition 2) meeasssure, action

бинамус : *a* see **намуссуз**

бинә : *n* 1) farmstead 2) primitive encampment

бинәва : *a* 1) poor, pitiful, pitiable, helpless *n* 2) poor fellow, poor thing

бинәсиб : *a* unfortunate, hapless, having no place of one's own

бинт : *n* *Ru* bandage

бинтләмәк : *v* bandage

биокимја : *n* 1) biochemistry *a* 2) biochemical

биокенез : *n* *biol* 1) biogenesis *generation of life, living things* *a* 2) biogenetic

биоложи : *a* biological

биолокија : *n* biology

бир : *num* 1) one *pro* 2) some *or other* one, a, any *expressing unity pro* 3) some *indefinite quantity*

бир аз : *adv* a little bit

бир аздан : *adv* soon, in the nearest future

бир ајаг : *adv* one time, one way

бир аләм : *adv* a lot of

бир белә : *adv* so much, that much

бир вахт : *adv* some times, at some points

бир гәдәр : *adv* certain number, certain quantity of s.t.

бир даhа : *adv* one more time

бир дә : *adv* one more time; more than that

бир зад : *pro* something, some stuff

бир јол : *adv* one time, once

бир кәс : *pro* somebody, someone

бир нәфәр : *pro* somebody, someone

бир нечә : *pro* some

бир тәhәр : *pro* somehow

бирадамлыг : *n* 1) quantity sufficient for one person *a* 2) single-seated, single-seater

бирадлы : *a* of the same name

бирајаглы : *a* one-legged

бирајлыг : *a* monthly

бирарвадлы : *n* monogamous man *one who for various reasons does not take advantage of the Islamic law permitting up to four wives*

бирарвадлылыг : *n* monogamy *condition of men who chose to have only one wife*

биратлы : *a* one-horse

бирбаш, бирбаша : *adv* 1) unceasingly, non-stop 2) directly 3) right now, right away

бирбашлы : *a* one-headed, monocephalous

бирбејтли : *n* single-verse poem *traditional poetic form consisting of two to four lines*

бирбәбир : *adv* one at a time; by the piece

бирбәндли : *a* see **бирбуғумлу**

бир-бир : *adv* one at a time; by the piece

бир-бирә : *adv* one on one *fighting, combat*

бирбуғумлу : *a* single jointed, one-jointed

бирбујнузлу : *a* one-horned, unicornous

бирбурчлу : *a* see **биртумурчуглу**

бирвәзнли : *a* monometric *poetry*

birганадлы : *a* *bot* single-lobed

биргат : *a* single; wholesome; one-layered

биргәләмә : *adv* continuously, uninterruptedly, in one go, in one breath, with a single stroke

биргәпиклик : *n* one-kopek coin *no longer exists*

биргијмәтли : *a* equivalent, of equal worth, synonymous

бирголлу : *a* one-handed, one-armed

биргулаглы : *a* one-eared

бирдамарлы : *a* *bot* single-veined

бирдәјәрли : *a* see **биргимәтли**

бирдән : *adv* 1) at once, at one go, at one fell swoop 2) suddenly, all of a sudden, unexpectedly

бирдән-бирә : *adv* suddenly, at one fell swoop, all of a sudden, unexpectedly

бирдәфәлик : *a* 1) unique, one-time 2) once and for all 3) at a sitting 4) disposable

бирдилимә : *adv* indefatigably, unceasingly, without taking a breath

бирдирәкли : *a* single-column, single shaft, single-post

бирдирсәкли : *a* single-track

бирдишичикли : *a* *bot* unisexual

бирдишли : *a* single-toothed, one-toothed

бирдынаглы : *a* *zool* solid-ungulate

бирдодаглы : *a* one-lipped

бирдорлу : *a* single-masted

биревли : *n* members of a single family

биревчикли : *a* *bot* monoecious

бирелли : *n* fellow countryman, person from the same district

бирелллилик : *n* friendly association of people from the same area

бирееркәкчикли : *a* *bot* unisexual

бирә : *n* *zool* flea

бирә-бир : *adv* see **бир-бир, бир-бирә**

бирәбитдән : *n* *orn* mountain finch, also called brambling or bramline *Frigilla montifringilla L*

бирәди : *adv* at once, at one go, wholesale, in a body; wholly, as a whole

бирәдили,бирәдилик : *adv* once and for all, conclusively, finally, irrevocably

бирәлли : *a* 1) one-handed *n dial* 2) large copper tankard, or mug

бирәсаслы : *a* *gram* 1) single-stem, having but one stem *chem* 2) single base *referring to a substance which, being added to an acid, neutralizes it*

биржа : *n* 1) *stock* exchange *a* 2) exchange *exchange-related*

биржачы : *n* stockbroker

бири : *pro* one, someone, somebody

бирикдирмә : *n* 1) concentration, accumulation; economy,savings 2) account summary 3) collated balance *sheet*

бирикдирмәк : *v* 1) accumulate, save up, amass, heap up 2) combine, collate data *in a bookkeeping department*; compose a summary/report

бирикинти : *n* 1) accumulation *geol* 2) alluvium

бирикмәк : *v* be accumulated/gathered together, be consolidated

бирикүн : *n* day after tomorrow

бириллик : *a* one-year, of one year's duration; one year old

биринчи : *a* first, primary, initial

биринчилик : *n* first-place, championship

бириси : *pro* someone, a certain, a kind of

бирисикүн : *adv* see **бирикүн**

бирјанлы : *a* 1) single-breasted 2) one-sided, unilateral

бирјарпаглы : *a bot* monophyllous, having or composed of one leaf

бирјашар : *a* 1) one-year old, yearling *n* 2) yearling, one year old animal

бирјашлы : *a* one-year

бирјерли : *a* 1) single-seated, single-seater *n* 2) fellow countryman, person from the same district

бирјерлилик : *n* friendly society of persons coming from the same district

бирјоллуг : *adv* at once, at a sitting; once and for all

бирјувалы : *a orn* of/from the same nest

биркилолуг : *a* kilogram

биркүвәнли : *a* single-humped, dromedary (of camels)

биркә : *adv* together, jointly, in common, collectively

биркәлик : *n* commonality, joint/corporative/common action, nature or structure

биркөвдәли : *a bot* single-stalked/stemmed

биркөзлү : *a* one-eyed

биркүнлүк : *a* one-day

бирләпәли : *a bot* monocotyledinous; mononuclear, uninucleate

бирләчәкли : *a bot* single-petaled

бирләшдирилмәк : *v* be united/joint

бирләшдиричи : *a* uniting, joining

бирләшдирмәк : *v* unite, join/bring together, combine, connect

бирләшмә : *n* unity, unification, combination, confluence, aggregation

бирләшмәк : *pass* be united, be unified, joined, brought together, combined, connected

бирләшмиш : *a* united

бирлик : *n* 1) oneness 2) unification 3) unity, solidarity

бирликдә : *adv* together, jointly, cooperatively

бирманатлыг : *n coll* one ruble

бирмәкикли : *a* shuttle-flight

бирмә'налы : *a* synonymous

бирмә'налылыг : *n* synonymity

бирмәртәбә, бирмәртәбәли : *a* one-story, single story

бирнәфәрлик : *a* one-man, one-person, individual

бирнәфәсә : *adv* at one go, at a stretch; at one draught *of drinking*, without a break, not stopping, without taking a breather

бирнөвлү : *a* homogeneous, uniform; similar

бирнүвәли : *a* see **бирләпәли**

бировуз : *n* something borrowed *without fee* for temporary use *another's clothing, jewelry etc.*

бирохлу : *a cryst* uniaxial, monoaxial; *biol* haplocaulescent

бирөлчүлү : *a* of the same caliber

бирөфкәли : *a med* pertaining to one lung *as in single versus double pneumonia*

бирпара : *pro plu* some

бирпәрдәли : *a* one-act

биррәгәмли : *a* synonomous

биррәнкли : *a* monochrome, monochromatic

биррәнклилик : *n* condition or state of being monochrome, of one color

бирсаплы : *a* unifilar, single cut, single thread *screw* , single-thread *textile*

бирсәсли : *a* monotonous

бирсәслилик : *n* monotony

биртајлы : *a* univalve

биртәбәгәли : *a* single-layer, single-ply, one-ply

биртәкәрли : *a* one-wheel

биртәрәфли : *a* one-sided, unilateral

биртәрәфлилик : *n* one-sidedness, unilateral nature; limited approach

биртипли : *a* monotypic

биртонлу : *a* single-tone, one-tone

биртохумлу : *a* monocotyledonous

биртумурчуглу : *a bot* single-bud *may refer to stem, branch or shoot of a plant, with rudimentary leaves and unexpanded flowers*

бируҹлу : *a* single terminal, one-peaked, with just one top

бирүзлү : *a* unilateral, one-sided

бирфазалы : *a* single-phase, monophase, uniphase

бирфамилиjалы : *n* person bearing the same surname

бирһечалы : *a ling* monosyllabic

бирһәдли : *n math* term, a single term, monomial

бирһүркүҹлү : *a* see **бирkүвәнли**

бирһүҹejрәли : *a* one-celled, unicellular

бирчархлы : *a* one-wheeled

бирчәк : *n* curl[s]

бирчәкләмәк : *v* seize s.o. by the hair *during a fight*

бирчәкләшмәк : *v* seize one another by the hair *during a fight*

бирчәкли : *a* curly-haired, curly-headed

бирчәксиз : *a* straight-haired *not having curls*

бирчичәкли : *a* single-flowered, producing a single bloom

бирҹә : *num* 1) one only, only one, just one 2) unitary, singular

бирҹә-бирҹә : *adv* one by one

бирҹәркәли : *a* single-row, in one row, unilinear, single

бирчиjәрли : *a* see **бирөфкәли**

бирҹилдли : *a* one-volume

бирҹилдлик : *n* single volume

бирҹинсли : *a* homogeneous, uniform, similar; single sex

бирҹинслилик : *n* homogeneity, uniformity, similarity; single-sexness

бирчүрлүк : *n* monotony, sameness

биршаһылыг : *n* five kopek piece

биршәкилли : *a* uniform, having the same appearance

биршәһәрли : *a* from the same city

бисавад : *a* illiterate

бисмут : *n chem* 1) bismuth *a* 2) bismuth

бисти : *n* twenty kopek piece

бит : *n* louse

битаб : *a* weak, feeble; tired

битәрәф : *a* 1) neutral, impartial 2) non-party *not belonging to the Communist Party*

биртәрәфлик : *n* 1) neutrality, impartiality 2) state/condition of not belonging to the Communist Party

битәрәфҹә, битәрәфҹәсинә : *adv* neutrally, impartially

битирилмәк : *pass* 1) be finished/completed 2) be fully grown, be grown up

битирмәк : *v* grow, grow up 2) complete, finish, conclude, consummate

битишдиричи : *a* connective, connecting

битишдирмә : *v* 1) from **битишдирмәк** 2) conjunction, combination

битишдирмәк : *v* 1) combine, join *together* 2) sew/stitch together, glue together 3) adapt *to*, adjust *to*, attach *to* fix *to*, fasten *to*

битишик : *a* 1) joined, fastened 2) united, contiguous, adjoining, adjacent 3) glued, adhering, attached, spliced *to*

битишмә : *n* 1) blending, merging 2) joining, splicing, fusion 3) uniting

битишмәк : *v* 1) unite, join, fuse, splice 2) cicatrize *wound*

битки : *n* 1) plant *a* 2) vegetable, plant

биткибити : *n zool* aphid, plant louse *Aphididae L*

биткин : *a* finished, complete, completed; ripe; mature

биткинлик : *n* completeness, finish, consummation; ripened nature, maturity

биткичилик : *n* plant growing

битли : *a* lousy, louse-ridden

битлилик : *n* lousiness, infestation by lice

битмәз, битмәз-түкәнмәз : *a* inexhaustible, unending, limitless

битмәк : *v* grow, sprout, spring up *plants* 2) take *of a graft, a cutting* 3) be completed, finished

битоту : *n bot* stavesacre *Delphinium staphysagria*, a type of European Larkspur from which an ointment used to kill lice is prepared

бихәбәр : *a* ill-informed, unaware *of*

биһал : *a* weak, debilitated from illness

биhəја : *a* 1) shameless, impudent *n* 2) shameless person 3) smart aleck, brazen/impudent person

биhəјалыг : *n* shamelessness, impudence, effrontery, impertinence

биhөрмəт : *a* see **hөрмəтсиз**

биhөрмəтлик : *n* see **hөрмəтсизлик**

биудə : *a* vain, futile, idle, unrealizable, unavailing

биhуш : *a* senseless, unconscious

биhушдары : *n* narcotic, intoxicant, drug, sleep-inducing substance

биhушлуг : *n* 1) amnesia 2) syncope/faint/fainting, semi-consciousness

бичарə : *a* 1) helpless, unfortunate, poor, pitiful, pathetic *n* 2) poor fellow, poor creature

бичдирмəк : *caus of* **бичмəк**

бичдиртмəк : *caus of* **бичмəк**

бичəнəк : *n* 1) mowing, haymaking 2) hayfield

бичили : *a* cut *out*

бичилмəк : *pass* 1) be mowed, reaped, be mowed down 2) be cut out

бичим : *n* 1) form, fashion, style, cut *of garment* 2) figure, build, proportion[s] *of a person*

бичимли : *a* well-proportioned, well-built, shapely *of a person*

бичимсиз : *a* ill-proportioned, not well-built, clumsy, awkward, ungainly, shapeless

бичимсизлəшмəк : *v* become disfigured/distorted; become poorly proportioned, not well-built

бичимсизлик : *n* condition of being poorly built/ill-proportioned, awkwardness, disproportionateness, shapelessness

бичин : *n* harvest, mowing-time, reaping-time

бичинчи : *n* 1) reaper 2) mower *person*

бичинчилик : *n* occupation/work/profession of a reaper, a mower

бичичи : *n* cutter *person*

бичмə : *n* 1) mowing, haymaking 2) cutting *out*

бичмəк : *v* 1) reap, cut, mow 2) mow, scythe *hay* 3) cut *out*

бич : *a* 1) illegitimate/out-of-wedlock/love child 2) mongrel 3) cheat, scoundrel, rascal, knave

бич-бич : *adv* 1) cunningly 2) maliciously, spitefully

бичəк : *n* 1) *bot* chick-pea *Cicer* 2) seedling, sprout

бичлик : *n* cunning, guile, trickery, cheating, swindling

бичов : *n* Georgian *slightly ironic*

бишəрəф : *a* see **шəрəфсиз**

бишəрəфлик : *n* see **шəрəфсизлик**

бишир-дүшүр : *n* cooking

бишириб-дүшүрмəк : *v* cook, *colloq* concoct, whip up, throw s.t. together

биширилмəк : *v intr* cook

биширмəк : *v* 1) cook, cook up, concoct 2) bake 3) bake *bricks etc*

биширтдирмəк : *caus of* **биширмəк**

биширтмəк : *caus of* **биширмəк**

бишкин : *a* 1) well-baked *fig* 2) experienced *fig* 3) battle-hardened, "been through the mill"

бишкинлик : *n* 1) experience *fig* 2) seasoning *in the sense of the state of having been through the mill, having graduated from the school of hard knocks, of not being wet behind the ears.*

бишмəк : *v intr* 1) cook, bake *fig* 2) become experienced/seasoned

бишмиш : *a* 1) cooked, baked 2) experienced, seasoned *n* 3) food, meal, dish, hot food, meal-ready-to-eat, victuals, *coll* grub, chow

бишүүр : *a* inactive, unenterprising, incapable, unskilful, slow(-witted), not-too sharp

бығ : *n* moustache hair, moustache *zool* 2) tentacle, feeler, antenna *of an insect* 3) curl, lock

бығалты : *adv* quietly, on the sly

бығыш : *a ironic* see **бығлы**

бығјағы : *n* bribe, graft; gift, present

бығлы : *a* mustachioed, with a big mustache; *of animals* whiskered, tentacled

бығсыз : *a* not having a mustache, clean-shaven

быж-быж : *adv onomatopoetic* swarming; see **быж-быж быжылдамаг**

быж-быж быжылдамаг : *v* swarm *bees, insects fig* people

быј : *intj expressing fright, objection, dissatisfaction* Ah!, Oh!

быппылы : *a* tiny, wee

бычаг : *n* 1) knife *a* 2) knife['s]

бычаггајыран : *n* see **бычагчы**

бычагитиләјән : *n* knife sharpener *agent*

бычагламаг : *v* knife, stab, inflict a knife wound

бычанланмаг : *pass* be knifed, stabbed, wounded with a knife

бычаглашма : *v* knifing one another, stabbing one another; knife-fight

бычаглашмаг : *v* wound one another with a knife, stab one another

бычагчы : *n* cutler *specialist in the manufacture of knives*

бычгы : *n* hack-saw

бычгыбалығы : *n zool* saw-fish *genus Pristis sp.*

бычгылама : n sawing, sawing out

бычгыламаг : *v* saw

бычгычы : n sawyer, woodcutter

бычылган : *n* disease of the skin beneath a horse's hoof

блокада : *n Ru* blockade

блузка : *n* blouse *worn by women*

БМТ : *n* the UNO

боа : *n zool* boa

боғаз : *n* 1) throat 2) neck *of a bottle/vessel geol* 3) strait, sound 4) pregnant animal

боғазалты : *n* bogazaltı *a feminine ornament consisting of a ribbon going from temple and ending up below the chin*

боғаздөјмә : *n* quarrel, altercation

боғазлама : *n* 1) grasping by the throat, throttling 2) cutting, cutting off, 3) slaughter

боғазламаг : *v* 1) grasp by the throat, throttle 2) cut, cut off 3) stab *to death*, slaughter *of an animal*

боғазлашмаг : *v* 1) grasp one another by the throat, throttle one another 2) quarrel 3) quarrel *with*, wrangle *with*, squabble *with*

боғазлыг : *n* gravidity, pregnancy *animals*

боғанаг : *n* closeness, stuffiness, humid heat

боғдурмаг : *caus of* **боғмаг**

боғдуртмаг : *caus of* **боғмаг**

боғма : *v* 1) from **боғмаг** 2) diphtheria, croup *disease of the throat* 3) all five fingers, palm with five fingers

боғмаг : *v* smother, stifle, strangle, throttle; squeeze 2) suppress 3) cause suffocation, asphyxia 4) sink, drown *in waters*

боғмача : *v* see **боғма** (2,3)

боғуг : *a* 1) muffled, indistinct, hoarse, husky wheezy *voice* 2) smothered, repressed

боғулмаг : *v intr* 1) suffocate, feel that one is suffocating, unable to breathe 2) choke 3) drown

боғунуг : *a* see **боғуг** 1)

боғучу : *a* stifling, suffocating, asphyxiating

боғучулуг : *n* suffocation, asphyxiation

боғушдурмаг, **боғушдуртмаг** : *caus of* **боғушмаг**

боғушма : *n* fight, squabble, falling out

боғушмаг : *v* fight, squabble, bicker, quarrel *with*, fall out *with*

боғча : *n* 1) knot 2) bundle

боз : *a* 1) grey 2) type of skin lesion caused by parasitic mites, scabies *in humans* mange *in dogs and other animals* 3) cock-pheasant

бозалаг : *n* variety of St. John's Wort, sp. *family Hypericacaceae*

бозармаг : *v* 1) turn/become grey 2) fade, lose color 3) be impertinent, be rude *to*

бозартма : *n* bozartma *meat dish similar to a ragout* 2) a baked pudding

бозартмаг : *v* make, cause to become grey

бозбаш : *n* bozbaş *meat and pea soup*

бозгыр : *n* dry steppe

бозговурма : *n* see **бозартма**

боз-гонур : *a* grey-brown

бозлуг : *n* 1) greyness, drabness 2) monotonous, unvegatated landscape/area

бозумсов, **бозумтул** : *a* greyish, light-grey

боj : *n* 1) growth, increase 2) height 3) length 4) dimension, size

боj вермәк : *v* be enough, sufficient

боjа : *n* dye

боjа-боj : *adv* along s.t.; one after another

боjаг : *n* see **боjа**

боjагәзән : *n n* 1) color-grinder *worker who grinds coloring agents, or materials for use in dyes* 2) pestle in which coloring agents or materials are ground 3) machine slab, or vessel in/on which coloring agents or materials are ground for use in dyes

боjагхана : *n* dye works/factory

боjагчы : *n* 1) dyer *a* 2) dye

боjагчылыг : *n* profession of dyer

боjама : *n* dyeing, applying dyes

боjамаг : *v* dye, apply dye *to*

боjана : *n* anise, anise-seed *Pimpinella anisum L*

боjанма : *v* fr. **боjанмаг**

бојанмаг : *pass* 1) be dyed/colored 2) be daubed/spattered *with dye*

бојар : *n hist* 1) boyar *member of a class of the Russian hereditary aristocracy prior to the 18th century a* 2) boyar('s)

бојарлыг : *n hist coll* the boyars, the nobility

бојарчасына : *adv* in the manner of/like a boyar, in a lordly manner

бојатдырмаг : *caus of* **бојамаг**

бојатмаг : *v* hand over to be dyed; request or insist *forcefully* that s.t. be dyed

бој-бухун : *n* figure, frame, build, carriage, bearing *of a person*

бој-бухунлу : *a* tall, strapping, well-proportioned, shapely

бојкот : *n Ru* boycott

бојланмаг : *v* 1) lean out, hang out, show oneself, look out 2) look somewhere with neck stretched out, look stretching o.s. out 3) grow up, grow taller

бојлу : *a* 1) tall, strapping 2) pregnant, gravid

бојлу-бухунлу : *a* see **бој-бухунлу**

бојмадәрән : *n bot* yarrow, millfoil *Achillea millefollium L*

бојнуәјри : *a* crook-necked, having a long, crooked neck

бојнујоғун : *a* 1) thick-necked 2) careless, unconcerned

бојнујоғунлуг : *n* carelessness, unconcernedness

бојөлчән : *n* device for measuring height/stature

бојсуз : *a* short *of stature*

бојсуз-бухунсуз : *n* dumpy/tubby person, person of short, ungainly build, squat person

бојудолу : *a* pregnant

бојун : *n* 1) neck 2) collar

бојун гачырмаг : *v* avoid, dodge

бојунча : *adv* along, throughout, lengthwise

бојнуна алмаг : *v* admit *one's guilt*

бојнуна гојмаг : *v* impose; hold s.o. responsible for s.t.

бојнуна көтүрмәк : *v* assume responsibility

бојнуну вурмаг : *v* to decapitate

бојундуруг : *v* yoke

бокс : *n* 1) crew-cut, closely cropped hair; *a* crew-cut *hair* 2) box *sports*

боксчу : *n* boxer, pugilist

боксчулуг : *n* profession of boxer/pugilist

бол : *a* 1) abundant, plentiful, lavish *adv* 2) abundantly, plentifully, lavishly

бол-бол : *adv* abundantly, very much

болгар : *n* 1) a Bulgar, a Bulgarian *a* 2) Bulgarian

болгарија : *n* Bulgaria

болгарча : *adv* in Bulgarian *language*

болланмаг : *v* see **боллашмаг**

боллашдырмаг : *v* make abundant, multiply, augment

боллашмаг : *v* abound *in*, be rich *in*, add, increase, appear in abundance

боллуг : *n* abundance, luxuriance, sufficiency, plenitude

боллуча : *a* surplus, redundant

бол-сал : *a* spacious, roomy, wide

болткәсән : *n* bolt-threader

болшевик : *n* 1) Bolshevik *a* 2) Bolshevik

болшевиксајағы *adv* in a Bolshevik manner

болшевикчәсинә : *adv* see **болшевиксајағы**

болница : *n Ru* hospital

бомба : *n* 1) bomb *a* 2) bomb

бомбадашыјан : *n* bomber, bomber-aircraft

бомбаламаг : *v* bomb

бомбардман : *n* 1) bombing *a* 2) bombing, bombardment

бомбардманчы : *n* bomber pilot

бомбачы : *n nav* 1) depth-charge mortar/launcher *av* 2) bombardier

бомбеј : *n* Bombay *Indian city*

бомбоз : *a* completely/quite grey

бомбош : *a* completely/absolutely empty

бон : *n* monetary instruments *checks, certificates etc.*

боран : *n* snow-storm, blizzard

бораны : *n* burani *meat stewed with vegetables or greens*

боранлы : *a* blizzardy, blustery, stormy *referring to snowstorms*

боркес : *n* bourgeois *a size of type, about nine points*

бору : *n* 1) pipe, conduit 2) chimney 3) tube *in various senses*

борудашыјан : *n* flatbed truck *designed to carry pipes*

борч : *n* 1) debt, loan *fig* 2) obligation, duty, responsibility

борчверән : *n* creditor, lender

борчлу : *n* 1) debtor, borrower *a* 2) obligated, indebted

борчлулуг : *n* debts, *total* indebtedness

борш : *n Ru* borshch *Ukrainian style cabbage soup with tomatoes*

босман : *n nav* 1) boatswain 2) boatswain['s]

бостан : *n* 1) vegetable garden *a* 2) water-melons, melons, and gourds. . . .

бостанлыг : *n* locality where many water-melon, melon and gourd plantations are located

бостанчы : *n* water-melon, melon, and gourd grower

бостанчылыг : *n* water-melon, melon, and gourd growing/cultivation

ботаника : *n Ru* botany

бочкагајыран, бочкачы : *n* cooper, master-barrelmaker

бочкачылыг : *n* professsion, or business of cooper/barrelmaker

бош : *a* 1) empty, idle *not functioning or in use* 2) unoccupied, free, vacant 3) uninhabited, desolate 4) not-loaded, blank 5) vain, empty, futile, unavailing 6) weak 7) insignificant, piddling 8) friable, crumbly, loose 9) foolish, nonsensical

боша чыхармаг : *v* refute

боша чыхмаг : *v* prove to be false

бошалдылмаг : *pass* 1) be free *for s.o. else's use*, be lying idle *for s.o. else's use* 2) be empty, drained, evacuated

бошалдычы : *n* 1) unloader, off-loader *agent a* 2) discharging, unloading

бошалма : *v* 1) from **бошалмаг** *phys* 2) discharging

бошалмаг : *v* 1) be emptied, discharged, unloaded, freed *for further use* 2) weaken, be enervated 3) become empty/deserted, become depopulated

бошалтдырмаг : *caus of* **бошалтмаг**

бошалтмаг : *v* 1) empty, drain 2) pour out, lay/spread out 3) free 4) unload *cargo etc* 5) unload a weapon, by firing, or extracting the cartridge, shell, or charge 5) evacuate 6) weaken, debilitate

бошама : *n* 1) divorce, annulment, dissolution of a marriage *a* 2) divorce

бошамаг : *v* divorce, grant a wife a divorce

бошанмаг : be/get divorced, get/obtain/receive a divorce from a husband

бошараг : *adv* rather weakly

бошатдырмаг : *caus of* **бошамаг**

бошатмаг : *caus of* **бошамаг**

бош-бикар : *a* unemployed, having no work whatsoever

бошбоғаз : *n* 1) talker, windbag, babbler, phrase-monger; buffoon *a* 2) talkative, loquacious, garrulous

бошбоғазлыг : *n* idle talk, twaddle, chatter; buffoonery

бош-бош, бош-бошуна : *adv* 1) senselessly, to no purpose 2) idly, in vain

бошгаб : *n* plate

бошданышан : *n* talker, windbag, phrase-monger

бошданышма : *n* phrase-mongering, mere verbiage, idle talk, twaddle

бошкәзән : *n* idler, lounger

бошламаг : *v* 1) release, let go, free, liberate 2) leave, abandon

бошлатмаг : *v* weaken

бошлуг : *n* 1) emptiness, void; *anat* cavity 2) unnecessary freedom, loosenedness 3) vacuum

боштәһәр : *a* rather weak, weakish

бөв : *anat* phalanx *one of the bones articulating with the bones of the fingers*

бөғәлә : *n bot* see **моруг**

бөјәләк : *n* gadfly

бөјрәк : *n anat* 1) kidney *a* 2) kidney, nephritic

бөјрәкүстү : *a anat* suprarenal

бөјүдүлмәк : *v pass* be reared, brought up, educated 2) be increased, enlarged

бөјүдүчү : *a* enlarged, increased, augmented

бөјүк : *a* large, big, great, huge, monumental 2) senior, elder 3) grown, grown up, adult *n* 4) chief, head

бөјүк-бөјүк : *adv* arrogantly, superciliously, insolently; pompously,

бөјүкләнмәк : *v* 1) grow, increase, grow large 2) put on airs, give o.s. airs, pose as a superior person

бөјүклүк : *n* 1) size, dimension[s] 2) vastness, immensity, enormity 3) seniority; importance, significance 4) grandeur, greatness

бөјүклү-кичикли : *adv* both great and small alike; all, from small to great

бөјүктәһәр : *a* 1) rather big, large, on the large/big side *adv* 2) rather/somewhat largely

бөјүкчә : *a* large enough, sufficiently large

бөјүмә : *n* growth, increase, expansion

бөјүмәк : *v* 1) grow, increase, grow up 2) be on the increase, broaden/widen 3) be raised, rise, rise above 4) acquire/ gain/ significance/ force/ importance/ authority

бөјүр : *n* side

бөјүрә-бөјүрә : *adv* alongside *of*, side by side, close by

бөјүрдән : *adv* at the side *of*, on the side, from the side

бөјүрмә, бөјүртү : *n* lowing, mooing *cow*; bellowing *bull*

бөјүрмәк : *v* low, moo *of cow, bull*

бөјүрткән : *n bot* blackberry *fam. Rosaceae genus Rubus*

бөјүртмәк : *v* cause to low, moo, bellow *cattle*

бөјүрүшмә : *n* lowing, mooing, bellowing by an entire herd *cattle*

бөјүрүшмәк : *v* low, moo, bellow all together *cattle*

бөјүтмә : *v* fr. **бөјүтмәк**

бөјүтмәк : *v* 1) grow, cultivate, bring up 2) increase, enlarge, extend 3) overstate, exaggerate, inflate 4) raise, elevate

бөлән : *n math* 1) divisor, denominator *tech* 2) separator 3) distributor

бөлкү : *n* 1) sharing, division, allotment, distribution 2) scale, range

бөлмә : *n* 1) division, dividing, distributing, allotment 2) section, department, sector *a* 3) separating; fractionating

бөлмәк : *v* 1) divide, share, distribute 2) cut, subdivide, parcel *out*, split up 3) allot, apportion

бөлүк : *n* 1) part 2) group, crowd *mil* 3) detachment 3) company

бөлүк-бөлүк : *adv* 1) in/by groups, detachments, companies 2) into smithereens

бөлүкләчәкли : *a bot* polypetalous *having petals free and distinct*

бөлүнән : *n math* 1) dividend *a* 2) divisible, divisible without remainder *by*

бөлүнмә : *n* 1) divisibility 2) division, distribution, *hist* schism, dissent *polit* split 3) partition[ing]

бөлүнмәз : *a* 1) indivisible, inseparable *adv* 2) inseparably

бөлүнмә : *n* indivisibility

бөлүнмәк : *pass* 1) be divisible, be divided, be split up 2) be distributed, allotted 3) be partitioned off

бөлүчү : *a* 1) separating; fractionating; distributing, distributive *n* 2) separator, separating agent, distributor

бөлүшдүрмә : *n* distribution, division, share, sharing, allotment, allocation

бөлүшдүрмәк : *v* distribute, allot, apportion, divide, share among o.s.

бөлүшдүрүлмәк : *pass* be divided, distributed among s.o.'s

бөлүшмә : *n* share, sharing, division, distribution among o.s.

бөлүшмәк : *v* share with; divide, distribute among o.s.

бөрк : *n* see **папаг**

бөһд : *n* shock *therapy applied in mental disorders*

бөһран : *n* crisis

бөһранлы : *a* crisis-related

бөһтан : *n* slander, calumny

бөһтанчы : *n* slanderer, calumniator

бөһтанчылыг : *n* salndering, calumniating, tale-bearing

бөчәк : *n* see **чүчү**

бразилија : *n* 1) Brazil *a* 2) Brazilian

бразилијалы : *n* a Brazilian

брәһмә : *n* Brahma *Hindu deity; the primordial essence; supreme being of the Universe*

брәһмән : *n* Brahman/Brahmin *member of the sacerdotal caste in India; the first of the four ancient Indian varnas*

брәһмәнизм : *n* Brahmanism/Brahminism *the religious and the social system of the Brahmans*

бриллјант : *n* 1) cut diamond; brilliant *diamond of the finest cut a* 2) brilliant *referring to cut diamonds*

британија : *n* 1) Britain *a* 2) British, Britannic

британијалы : *n* Briton

бромлу : *a chem* bromine; bromide

бронх : *n anat* bronchi

бронхиал : *a anat* bronchial

брошүр : *n* leaflet

бруселлјоз : *n med* brucellosis *any of several infectious diseases caused by a parasitic Gram-negative bacterium, genus Brucella, as Bang's disease in cattle and undulant fever in humans*

бу : *deic* this

бу күн : *adv* today

бу саат : *adv* now, right now

бугәләмун : *n* chameleon *lizard indigenous to southern lands*

буғ : *n* steam, vapor

буға : *n* 1) bull, stud-bull, bull employed as a breeder *astron* 2) Taurus *constellation*

буғда : *n* 1) wheat *a* 2) wheat, wheaten

буғдабити : *n zool* 1) Anguillulidae, small almost minute nematode worms living in the soil and in decaying organic matter 2) worms *vermes* , maggots

буғдајы : *a* see **гарабуғдајы**

буғдакәпәнәји : *n zool* owlet or cutworm moth *Noctuidae; an agricultural pest*

буғландырмаг : *v* evaporate, vaporize

буғланма : *n* evaporization, vaporization

буғланмаг : *v intr* evaporate; fume

буғум : *n* 1) articulation, joint *bot* 2) internode

буғумајаглылар : *n zool* arthropoda

буғумлу : *a zool* articulate, jointed; segmented

буғумсуз : *a* 1) inarticulate *bot* 2) sessile *leaf attachment without nodes*

буғур : *a* huge, enormous

буғхана : *n* steam-room *in a bathhouse*

буд : *n* 1) thigh; hip 2) haunch 3) ham 4) see **сағры**

будаг : *n* 1) branch, twig, bough, limb; knot *gram* 2) subordinate clause

будагланма : *n* branching, ramification

будагланмаг : *v intr* branch, ramify; fork, divide

будаглы : *a* branchy

будамаг : *v* cut off, clip, prune, trim; fell, cut down

буданмаг : *v pass* be cut off, trimmed, pruned *branches*

бударлама : *n* slapping, whipping

бударламаг : *v* slap; whip, lash

будатдырмаг, **будатмаг** : *caus of* **будамаг**

буддапәрәстлик : *n* Buddhism

будка : *n* 1) box, booth, stall *in various senses* ; *mil* sentry booth *a* attributive of all senses in 1)

будкачы : *n* policeman on duty *in a box or booth*

буз : *n* 1) ice *a* 2) icey

бузгајыран : *n* 1) ice-maker *a* 2) ice-making

бузгыран : *n* ice-breaker *ship*

бузкәсән : *n* ice-cutter *light ice-breaker*

бузлаг : *n* 1) ice-house 2) glacier

бузлама : *n* 1) freezing, iceing up *geol* glaciation

бузламаг : *v* freeze, ice up

бузлу : *a* icey, covered with ice

бузлуг : *n* ice-covered area

бузов : *n* 1) calf *a* 2) calf['s]

бузовабахан : *n* veal

бузовбурну : *n* see **гарғадузу**

бузовламаг : *v* calve

бузовчу, **бузовотаран** : *n* herdsman of a herd of young cattle

бузсатан : *n* ice-merchant

бузхана : *n* ice-house, ice-storage house; refrigerator

бузчу : *n* see **бузсатан**

буј : *n* buoy

бујнуз : *n* 1) horn 2) tentacle, palpus; *anthropoda* antenna *a* 3) horned

бујнузламаг : *v* pierce with horns, gore; butt

бујнузлашма : *n* butting one another *of horned animals*

бујнузлашмаг : *v* strike/hit one another with horns, butt *horned animals*

бујнузлу : *a* horned

бујнузсуз : *a* hornless

бујурма : *n* 1) command, behest 2) assent, approbation, welcome *used in reference to arrival of an important person*

бујурмаг : *v* 1) command, enjoin, order 2) welcome; deign, be pleased, favor, regard with favor

бујуртма : *a* custom-ordered, to order, made to order *shoes etc*

бујуруг : *n* command, behest, instruction

бујурунуз : *expr* Please; Come in; Sit down *a polite invitation to an action*

булаг : *n* 1) source, spring, wellhead *water welling up from a natural aquifer a* 2) attributive uses of terms in 1)

булама : *n* kneading, mixing *liquids* 2) milk mixed with beestings *the first milk after calving, colostrum*

буламаг : *v* 1) mix liquid 2) soil, stain, dirty 3) wag *tail* 4) shake *head* 5) pollute, defile, foul

буламач : *n* thick soup with noodles, peas and other ingredients

буландырмаг : *v* stir up, make opaque *by stirring up sediment*

буланыг : *a* turbid; dull, lackluster, cloudy

буланыглашма : *n* turbidity, cloudiness

буланыглашмаг : *v* grow turbid

буланыглыг : *n* turbidity, muddiness, cloudiness

буланмаг : *v* 1) grow/become turbid 2) soil .o.s., make o.s. dirty

буланты : *n* dregs

булашдырмаг : *v* soil, stain, make dirty

булашыг, булашыглы : *a* soiled, dirty, greasy, smeared, unwashed *of dishes*

булашмаг : *pass v* to be soiled, stained, dirty

булвар : *n* avenue, boulevard

булдог : *n* 1) bulldog *a* 2) bulldog

булка : *n small* loaf or large roll

булкабиширән : *n* baker

булкачы : *n* retail merchant selling bread, rolls and buns

булуд : *n* 1) cloud 2) sponge 3) large plate

булудланмаг : *pass* be covered with clouds/storm clouds, be overcast

булудлу : *a* cloud-covered, covered with storm clouds

булудлуг : *n* cloudiness

булудсуз : *a* cloudness

бумбуз : *a* very cold, icey, ice-cold, freezing cold

бундан бәри : *adv* since

бунсуз : *adv* aside from this, any way

бунча : *adv* so

бунчуғаз : *pro* only this, this and this alone

бура : *adv* here *in this direction, hither*

бураған : *n* 1) whirlwind, tornado 2) see **бурулған**

бурада : *adv* here *in this location*

бурадакы : *a* 1) local, of this place 2) located here

бурадача : *adv* right here, on this spot

бураз : *n* rope, cable, hawser

буралы : *a* 1) local, of this place 2) *n* local inhabitant

бурахдырмаг, бурахдыртмаг : *caus of* **бурахмаг**

бурахылыш : *n* 1) output *in various senses a* 2) output

бурахылмаг : *pass* be set free, put out; be released, let go

бурахычы : *n* publisher

бурахмаг : *v* 1) let go, pass; free, release 2) allow, permit

бурғу : *n* 1) drill, bit, auger, brace and bit 2) pipe, *small* tube, jet

бурғуламаг : *v* drill

бурдурмаг : *caus of* **бурмаг**

бурма : *n* 1) twisting, turning, involution 2) castrating, neutering *a* 3) screw-shaped, spiral 4) rotary, rotatory, rotatable 5) twisted

бурмаг : *v* 1) twist, turn, curl, crimp 2) turn around 3) *tech* screw up 4) castrate, neuter

бурнуәјри : *a* crooked-nosed

бурнујекә : *a* big-nosed

буру : *n* gripes, colic due to stomach upset/indigestion

буруг : *a* 1) twisted, curled, frizzled, crimped 2) castrated, neutered *n* 3) oil well, oil well derrick 4) tuft of combed wool

буруг-буруг : *a* spiral, helical

буруггазан : *n* borer, driller

бурулған : *n* 1) whirlpool, vortex; gulf, the deep, abyss 2) pool, slough

бурулмаг : *v intr* 1) turn, spin, gyrate; twist, become twisted 2) be castrated, emasculated, gelded, neutered 3) turn

бурум-бурум : *adv* in puffs, in clouds/wreaths *steam, clouds*

бурумланмаг : *v intr* curl *up*, wreath, swirl

бурун : *n* 1) nose 2) toe *of shoe*, toes *front part of foot geol* 3) cape, promontory *a* 4) nose, forward part *of*, bow *end*

бурунадөјмә : *n* kind of a simple card game

бурун-буруна : *adv* nose-to-nose, face-to-face, closeely

бурунламаг : *v* force out, eject, oust, shove out, chuck out, drive out

буруновмасы : *n* shaking, shock

буруноту : *n* snuff

бурунсуз : *a* noseless; spoutless *i.e. pot*

бурунтаг : *n* 1) muzzle; rope halter *used on camels, horses, donkeys* 2) clamp, tourniquet

бурунтагламаг : *v* put on a muzzle, rope halter, clamp, or tourniquet

бурхуг, бурхулма : *n* dislocation

бурхулмаг : *v* dislocate 2) unscrew, twist *off*, turn inside out

бурч : *n* 1) castle tower, bastion *astron* 2) a zodiacal sign

бурчутмаг : *v* sway while walking

бусә : *n* see **өпуш**

бута : *n* 1) almond-shaped pattern *on fabric* 2) crucible, cupel *shallow absorbent vessel used in assaying gold and silver ores*

буталы : *a* decorated with a pattern/design; in/with an almond-shaped pattern

бутерброд : *n* sandwich

бутулка : *n* 1) bottle *a* 2) bottle

буфет : *n* cafeteria, snack-shop

буфетчи : *n* cafeteria attendant

бухаг : *n* double chin

бухар : *n* steam, evaporation, fumes

бухарлы : *n* a Bukharian *native or resident of Bukhara, a city in Uzbekistan with predominantly Tajik population*

бухары : *n* fire-place

бухарландырма : *n* evaporation, concentration, steaming

бухарланма : *n* evaporation, evaporating, vaporization

бухарланмаг : *v* evaporate, fume

бухархана : *n* steam room *analogous to a sauna in Turkish or Russian bathhouse*

бухов : *n* irons *restraints for prisoners, arrestees* fetters, shackles

бухովламаг : *v* bind with metal; *fig* shackle

буховланмаг : *v* be put into chains, be shackled

буховлатдырмаг, буховлатмаг : *caus of* **буховланмаг**

буховлу : *a* in leg-irons, with iron shackles on the legs

бухур : *n* incense, frankincense

бухурдан : *n* censer, thurible *vessel for burning incense*

бухчу : *n* saw

буһу : *n* see **јапалаг**

бучаг : *n* angle

бучагөлчән : angle gage, goniometer

бучуғаз : *pro* only this, just this, exactly this

бучургад : *n* hoist, windlass, capstan *ship*

бучургадчы : *n* winch operator

будрəјə-будрəјə : *adv* stumbling

будрəк : *a* stumbling

будрəмə : *n* 1) stumbling *fig* deviation from the straight path/from the truth

будрəмəк : *v intr* stumble, make a misstep, make an error

будчə : *n* 1) budget *a* budgetary

буздум : *n anat* coccyx

бузмə : *n* 1) compression, cinstriction, wrinkling 2) gather, frill, flounce *clothing*

бүзмəк : *v* 1) tighten, draw/pull together 2) press, squeeze; wrinkle/crinkle *up*, corrugate

бүзмəли : *a* corrugated, pleated, fluted, goffered, crimped

бүзүк : *a* tightened, drawn together; wrinkled, corrugated

бүзүлмə : *n* see **бүзүшмə**

бүзүлмəк : *n* writhe, squirm

бүзүчү : *a* astringent, tart, sharp

бүзүшдүрмəк : *v* wrinkle

бүзүшдүрүчү : *a* see **бүзүчү**

бүзүшмə : *n* shrivelling *up* , shrinking

бүзүшмəк : *v* 1) shrivel, shrink 2) nestle down, curl up

бүкдəрилмəк : *v intr* coil, roll up, be rolled up

бүкдəрмə : *n* yarn, thread; twisting, spinning *thread*

бүкдəрмəк : *v* twist, rollup; spin *thread*

бүкдəртмəк : *caus of* **бүкдəрмəк**

бүкдүрмəк : *caus of* **бүкмəк**

бүкмəк : *v* 1) muffle up *in* , wrap up *in* , fold up 2) close, close up *typol* 4) fold *pages*

бүкүк : *a* 1) bent, curved, crooked; folded *n* 2) bend; flexion

бүкүлмəк : *v* 1) be folded up, be bent,/curved 2) turn, swing 3) wrap up *in*

бүкүлү : *a* 1) bent, curved, folded 2) rolled up, wrapped up

бүкүм : *a* see **бүкүк** 2)

бүкүчү : *n* page-folding machine operator *printing*

бүкүш : *a* see **бүкүк** 2)

бүлбүл : *n* 1) nightingale *a* 2) nightingale['s]

бүллур : *n* 1) cut-glass, crystal *a* 2) cut-glass, crystal

бүлөвдашы : *n* whetstone, grindstone

бүлөвлəмəк : *v* sharpen, grind, whet, sharpen on a whetstone/grindstone

бүлөвлəнмəк : *pass* 1) be sharpened on a whetstone/grindstone 2) be smoothed out, become smooth; be rubbbed off, worn away, be polished, burnished

бүлөвлəтдирмəк : *caus of* **бүлөвлəмəк**

бүлөвлəтмəк : *caus of* **бүлөвлəмəк**

бүлөвхана : *n* knife-sharpening establishment

бүлөвчү : *n* knife-grinder/sharpener

бүнөврә : *n* foundation, substructure, groundwork

бүнөврәли : *a* 1) well-founded, basic, sound, solid *adv* 2) basically; soundly

бүнөврәсиз : *a* 1) groundless, unfounded, unsound *adv* 2) unsoundly, weakly

бүркү : *n* sultry heat, stuffiness

бүркүлү : *a* close, sweltering; hot, burning, sultry

бүрмәләмәк : *v* 1) crumple; 2) wrap, muffle up

бүро : *n* bureau; office

бүрократ : *n* bureaucrat

бүрократизм, бүрократлыг : *n* bureaucratism, red tape

бүрократик : *a* bureaucratic

бүрократчасына : *adv* bureaucratically

бүрүмә : *v fr.* **бүрүмәк**

бүрүмәк : *v* 1) muffle up, wrap up 2) fit tightly, envelop, cover; surround

бүрүндүрмәк : *v* see **бүрүмәк**

бүрүнмәк : *pass* 1) be muffled up, be wrapped *up* 2) be surrounded

бүрүнч : *n* 1) brass *a* 2) brass

бүрүнчәк : *n* shawl, veil; yashmak, chador *head covering traditionally worn by Moslem women*

бүрүнчәкли : *a* wrapped in a shawl, veil; yashmak, chador

бүрүшдүрмәк : *v* knit, wrinkle the brow

бүрүшдүрүчү : *a* astringent, tart

бүрүшмәк : *v* 1) shiver, huddle o.s. up, be contorted 2) knit one's brow, be covered with wrinkles, be all wrinkled up 3) fade, wither

бүрүштә : *a* well-baked; toasted *bread*

бүрүшүк : *a* 1) wrinkled *n* 2) wrinkle

бүрч : *n* 1) tower *astron* 2) constellation

бүсат : *n* luxury, splendor; merriment, mirth, festival

бүсбүтүн : *adv* fully, in entirety, wholly

бүт : *n relig* idol

бүтөв : *a* whole, entire

бүтөвлүк : *n* wholeness, entirety; integrety

бүтпәрәст : *n* idol worshipper

бүтпәрәстлик : *n relig* idolatry

бүтүн : *pro* 1) all 2) whole

бүтүнлүк : *n* 1) safety 2) wholesome nature 3) generic nature

бүтүнлүклә : *a* wholly, entirely

бүхур : *n* incense

В

в : third letter of the Azeri alphabet

вавејла : *intj* 1) expresses grief/sorrow *n* 2) cry, moan, groan

вагтылдамаг : *v* 1) hoot *owl* 2) yelp, bark 3) talk on and on, talk nonsense, chatter boringly

ваге олмаг : *v* happen, take place

вагиә : *n* 1) event, happening, occurrence, circumstance 2) dream

вагон : *n* railroad car *passenger or freight*

вагонабахан : *n* railroad car inspector

вагонгајыран : *n* railroad car builder-assembler *worker at a factory manufacturing the RR cars*

вагонгајырма : *a* railroad car construction and assembly

вагонгошан : *n* railroad-car-coupler *person*

вагонет : *n* trolley, dolly, cart *small wheeled conveyance or trucks for conveying loads as in a factory or mine*

вагонјағлајан : *n* railroad car oiler *person*

вагонсүрән : *n* streetcar/tram driver

вагранка : *n met* cupola, cupola furnace *pig-iron smelting furnace*

ваг : *n zool* Bittern *Exobricus exilis L*

вағзал : *n* 1) railroad station *a* 2) railroad station

вадар : *a* forced, constrained

вади : *n* valley *of a dried river* wadi

ваз : *n* 1) vase 2) jump, spring, leap *animals*

ваиз : *n* preacher, interpreter of religious dogma/law/doctrine

ваизлик : *n* preaching, propagation of religious dogma

вај : *intj* expresses pain, distress, fear, surprise

вајылдамаг : *v* sigh, moan, groan

вајылты : *n* moan, groan, sighing, whimpering

вајсыланмаг : *v* express o.'s grief/regret by various appropriate exclamations

вакс : *n* shoe polish

ваксламаг : *v* polish *shoes*

вал : *n* 1) shaft, spindle *rotating metal cylinder* 2) phonograph record

валај, валајлама : *n* rocking, tossing, swaying

валајламаг, валајланмаг : *v intr* rock, sway

валеһ : *a* 1) charmed, enraptured; amazed, wonder-struck, suprised 2) *used as a masculine first name*

валеһедичи : *a* charming, delightful; striking, captivating

вали : *n* deputy; governor *in a traditional Moslem society*

валидеjн : *n* 1) parents *a* 2) parental

валјута : *n* currency; monetary system; foreign *convertible* currency; monetary unit

валлаһ : *intj* Really and truly!, Honest to God!, I swear to God! Believe it or not!

валс : *n* waltz

ванадиум : *n chem* vanadium

ванна : *n* 1) bath *a* 2) bath, bathing

вар : *a* 1) Existent, present *n* 2) Belongings, possessions, wealth *v* 3) There is / there are *with possessive suffixes;* have *e.g.* **кцтабым вар** *to have a book*

2) there is, there are *n* 3) property; fortune

вардырмаг : *v* lead there, lead as far as

вар-дөвләт : *n* riches, wealth, fortune, property

варидат : *n* income, revenue

вариjјәт : *n* see **вар-дөвләт**

вариjјәтли : *a* well-off, well-to-do

варис : *n* heir, legatee

варислик : *n* inheritance

вариссиз : *a* childless, having no descendants

варыныjеməз : *a* stingy, niggardly, miserly *n* miser, skinflint; *lit* the one who does not eat what he has

вар-јох : *n* all that there is, all property, all substance, all wealth

вар-кәл : *n* walking about, pacing back and forth

варландырмаг : *v* enrich, make wealthy

варланма : *n* enrichment

варланмаг : *v introd* grow rich, become wealthy, make a fortune

варлы : *a* 1) rich, wealthy, well-to-do *n* 2) rich/man person, wealthy man/person

варлыг : *n* 1) reality 2) being, essence 3) existence

варлылыг : *n* prosperity, wealth

填мармаг : *v* reach, attain

васвасы : *a* 1) hypochondriac 2) fastidious; squeamish 3) punctilious, overscrupulous

васвасылыг : *n* 1) hypochondria, over-anxiousness about one's health 2) fastidiousness 3) squeamishness, overscrupulousness

васитә : *n* 1) mediation, intercession 2) way, mode, means

васитәли : *a* indirect, oblique; having a mediator, a go-between

васитәсиз : *a* 1) immediate, direct, straightforward *adv* 2) immediately, directly

васитәчи : *n* mediator, intercessor

васитәчилик : *n* mediation, intercession

вассал : *n* 1) vassal *a* 2) vassal, subject

вассаллыг : *n* vassalage

вахт : *n* 1) time 2) period, term

вахташыры : *a* 1) periodic *adv* 2) periodically, from time to time

вахтында : *adv* 1) on time, in due course, in good time; at the right time, opportunely 2) punctually, exactly

вахткечирмә : *n* pastime, killing time

вахткән : *adv* in advance, in good time, beforehand

вахтлы : *a* 1) urgent, time-sensitive *adv* 2) at a fixed date, *attrib* fixed date

вахтлы-вахтында : *adv* 1) in good time, in proper time 2) punctually, exactly

вахтөлчән : *n* chronometer, timekeeper

вахтсыз : *a* 1) premature, inopportune, ill-timed *adv* 2) prematurely, inopportunely 3) at the wrong time

вахтчәкән : *a* watch *pertaining to a watch e.g. watch*

ваһә : *n* oasis

ваһид : *n math* 1) unit *a* 2) united, common, indivisible 3) only, sole

ваһидлик : *n* unity

ваһимә : *n* 1) fear, terror, panic 2) spectre, ghost, phantom, apparition

ваһимәләндирмәк : *v* terrify, horrify; frighten, scare

ваһимәләнмәк : *pass* be seized by fright, be frightened, terrified, scared

ваһимәли : *a* 1) terrible, fearful, frightful,terrifying, horrifying 2) panic; panicky

вачиб : *a* necessary, needful, vital, pressing, obligatory

вачиблик : *n* necessity; urgency, importance

вашаг : *n* *zool* lynx

ведрә : *n* bucket, pail

ведрәгајыран : *n* tinsmith

вејл : *a* 1) idle, idling, inactive, lounging *n* 2) sloven, sloppy individual; scatterbrain 3) good-for-nothing loafer, goldbricker

вејл-вејл : *adv* idly, unconcernedly

вејлләнмә : *n* loafing, goldbricking, playing truant *children*

вејлләнмәк : *v* *intr* hang round idly, hang around, loiter, loaf

вејллик : *n* idleness, loafing, about, goldbricking

векетариан : *n* 1) vegetarian *person* *a* 2) vegetarian

векетарианлыг : *n* vegetarianism

векетасија : *n* *bot* vegetation *a* 2) vegetation, vegetal

векетатив : *a* vegetative

векәсирә : *a* weak, puny, sickly *of a child*

велосипед : *n* 1) bicycle *a* 2) bicycle, cycling

велосипедчи : *n* bicyclist, cyclist

венетсија : *n* 1) Venice *a* 2) Venetian

венетсијалы : *n* Venetian, resident of Venice

вентил : *n* valve

вентилјасија : *n* 1) ventilation *a* 2) ventilator, ventilating

вентилјатор : *n* ventilator, fan, blower

вентилјаторчу : *n* ventilating system maintenance man

вердирмәк, вердиртмәк : *caus of* **вермәк**

верәчәк : *n* debt, indebtedness

верәчәкли : *n* debtor

верилиш, верилмә : *n* *radio/ TV* transmission, broadcast

верилмәк : *v* *intr* 1) give o.s. up *to* , surrender 2) be handed out, distributed 3) be presented, offered

веричи : *n* 1) supplier, giver *tech* 2) transducer, sender

верки : *n* 1) tax, assessment 2) talent, ability, gift *personal capability*

веркиверән : *n* tax-payer

веркијыған : tax-collector

веркисиз : *a* tax-free, tax-exempt, non-taxable

верkүл : *n* comma

вермә : *v* fr. **вермәк**

вермәк : *v* give, return, give back, give out, impart; hand over, pass, issue *a document*

верст : *n* verst *unit of measure = 1.067 km*

верстһесабы : *adv* in versts

вертолјот : *n* helicopter

веч : *v* getting out *used only in combinations* **вечдән чыхмаг**, go out of use

вечсиз : *a* 1) unnecessary, useless, good-for-nothing, unfit *n* 2) idler, loafer

вә : *conj* and

вәба : *n* 1) cholera *a* 2) cholera

вәгф : *n* vakuf *Arabic : bequest to a piouis foundation* ; charitable/philanthropic bequest; land lot belonging to a mosque as a result of such a bequest

вә'д : *n* promise, vow

вә'дә : *n* 1) fixed term; fixed time 2) vow, promise

вә'дәләшмәк : *v* arrange, agree *on*, come to an agreement/understanding *about time etc* ; fix a time *for meeting etc*

вә'дәли : *a* fixed date, at a fixed date, having a fixed date

вә'дәсиз : *a* with no fixed term, without time- limit, open-ended

вә'дәхилаф : *a* 1) failing to observe the date of execution *of some promised action* ; unfaithful to a promise *n* 2) person in violation of term of promised execution; person who has not kept a promise

вәз : *n* see **вәзи**

вә'з : *n* preaching, sermon; instructions, explanation *of religious dogma; Arabic*

вәзәри : *n* *bot* garden peppergrass *Lepidium Sativum L.*

вәзи : *n* *anat* gland, glandule

вәзијјәт : *n* position, situation, circumstances

вәзили : *a* glandular

вәзир : *n* 1) vizier, minister *chess* 2) queen

вәзифә : *n* 1) duty, obligation; function 2) task, job

вәзифәли : *a* official

вәзифәпәрәст : *n* careerist

вәзифәпәрәстлик : *n* careerism

вәзн : *n* 1) weight *mus* 2) rhythm, time; *poetry* metre

вәзнә : *n* 1) cartridge loop[s] on a Circassian tunic 2) loop for a pencil on a map case

вәзнли : *a* 1) weighty 2) heavy, ponderous 3) rhythmic

вәкаләт : *n* authority, power; plenary power[s]; power of attorney

вәкаләтнамә : *n* 1) letter of attorney; authorization 2) credentials, letters of credence

вәкил : *n* 1) plenipotentiary, attorney, barrister, representative 2) trial lawyer, defender; advocate

вәкиллик : *n* 1) authority, powers, plenary power[s] 2) profession of trial lawyer, attorney 3) the legal profession, the Bar

вәл : *n* threshing board *pulled by horses over grain to be threshed*

вәлвәлә : *n* alarm, commotion, turmoil, panic

вәләмбә : *n* eyelid[s]

вәләмир : *n* *bot* wild oats *Avena Fatua L.*

вәләс : *n* *bot* hornbeam *Carpinus*

вәлиәһд : *n* heir to a throne

вән : *n* see **көјрүш**

вәнкилдәмәк : *v* *intr.* whine, yelp *dog*

вәр : *n* 1) layer, stratum 2) zone, belt

вәрдәнә : *n* rolling pin *dough*

вәрдәнәләмә : *n* rolling out dough

вәрдәнәләмәк : *v* 1) roll out dough 2) roll, smooth *soil*

вәрдиш : *n* acquired habit, practice, custom

вәрдишли : *a* habitual, customary, according to practice

вәрәг : *n* sheet *of paper*

вәрәг-вәрәг : *adv* page after page

вәрәгләмәк : *v* turn over, leaf through *pages*

вәрәгләтдирмәк, вәрәгләтмәк : *caus of* **вәрәгләмәк**

вәрәгә : *n* card, leaflet, flyer

вәрәм : *n* 1) tuberculosis *a* 2) tubercular, consumptive

вәрәмләмәк : *v* contract tuberculosis

вәрәмли : *a* tubercular, consumptive

вәрәнә : *n* wide belt, or strap for transporting heavy objects

вәрәнәчи : *n* a laborer who transports heavy loads or objects by dragging them with a strap

вәрасәт : *n* inheritance

вәрәсә : *n* heir, legatee, successor

вәрәсәсиз : *a* without an heir/successor

вәрјан : *n* see **кудаз**

вәровуд : *n* 1) consideration, judgement 2) calculation

вәровурдламаг : *v* 1) judge, consider 2) calculate

вәсаит : *n* 1) means, resources 2) property

вәсатәт : *n* intercession, petitioning, entreaty

вәсатәтчи : *n* intercessor, mediator

вәсвәсә : *n* 1) doubt 2) delusion

вәси : *n* executor *of s.o. will*

вәсигә : *n* certification, verification

вәсијјәт : *n* 1) precept, behest, ordnance 2) will

вәсијјәтнамә : *n* written will

вәсмә : *n* dye/coloring for eyebrows

вәссалам : *expression indicating finality* and that's it!

вәсф : *n* praise

вәсфәкәлмәз : *a* indescribable

вәтәкә : *n* fishing zone :

вәтән : *n* native land, Fatherland, Motherland

вәтәндаш : *n* citizen

вәтәндашлыг : *n* 1) citizenship *a* 2) civic, citizen['s]

вәтәнпәрвәр : *n* patriot

вәтәнпәрвәрлик : *n* 1) patriotism *a* 2) patriotic

вәтәнпәрвәрчәсинә : *adv* patriotically

вәтәнпәрәст : *n* see **вәтәнпәрвәр**

вәтәнпәрәстлик : *n* see **вәтәнпәрвәрлик**

вәтәр : *n* *biol* 1) notochord *anat* 2) sinew, tendon

вәфа : *n* faithfulness, loyalty, devotion

вәфалы : *a* faithful, loyal, devoted, constant

вәфасыз : *a* 1) disloyal, unfaithful, inconstant 2) unreliable *in friendship/ love relationship, promises* *n* 3) traitor, betrayer

вәфасызлыг : *n* treason, disloyalty, perfidy; unfaithfulness

вәфат : *n* decease, death, departure, passed

вәһдәт : *n* unity

вәһј : *n* *relig* revelation

вәһшәт : *n* fear, terror

вәһши : *a* 1) wild, savage *n* 2) savage, primitive man

вәһшијана : *adv* see **вәһшичәсинә**

вәһшиләшмә : *n* running wild

вәһшиләшмәк : *v* grow wild, run wild; become brutalized

вәһшилик : *n* wildness, savagery, brutality

вәһшичәсинә : *adv* savagely, barbarously, rapaciously, predatorily

вәчд : *n* ecstasy, joy, delight; good mood

взвод : *n* platoon

вида : *n* farewell, leave-taking, parting

видалашма : *n* 1) see **вида** *a* 2) valedictory, farewell

видалашмаг : *v* 1) say goodbye *to* , take leave *of* , take final leave *of* , part *with*

виза : *n* visa

визјала : *n* see **фырфыра**

вилајәт : *n* 1) province, region; *hist* oblast, krai *in the Soviet Union* *a* 2) provincial, regional

винт : *n* screw; propeller

винтачан, винтбуран : *n* screwdriver

винтвары, винтәбәнзәр, винтәохшар *a* screw-shaped, spiral

винткәсән : *n* screw plate, die, tap

винтләмә : *v* *fr.* **винтләмәк**

винтләмәк : *v* screw, screw up, screw in, screw on

винтләнмәк : *pass* be screwed in, be screwed on

винтли : *a* screw, equipped with a screw, spiral, helical

виран : *a* demolished, wrecked, destroyed, devastated

виранедичи : *a* ruinous, devastating

виранә, виранәлик : *n* wreck, ruin

вирд : *n* constantly repeated saying, favorite thought/expression

виски : *n* whiskey

вич-вичә : *n* tremble, tremor, shiver

вичдан : *n* conscience *sense of moral responsibility*

вичданлы : *a* conscientious, honest

вичданлылыг : *n* conscientiousness, honesty, sense of moral responsibility, uprightness

вичдансыз : *a* unscrupulous, dishonest, shameless, lacking any sense of moral responsibility

вичдансызлыг : *n* unscrupulousness, dishonesty, shamelessness, lack of any sense of moral responsibility

вичдансызча, вичдансызчасына : *adv* unscrupulously, shamelessly, dishonestly, lacking any sense of moral responsibility

вичә : *n* see **вич-вичә**

виш : *n* string, cord, twine, thin, strong rope

вишнә : *n* *Ru* sour cherry

выз-выз : *n* *zool* scarab beetle *Lamellicornia L*

вызылдамаг : *v* hum, buzz, drone

вызылдатмаг : *v* 1) cause to buzz/hum/drone 2) fling, hurl, toss

вызылты : *n* hum, buzz, drone

выјылдамаг : *v* howl, begin to howl, raise a howl

выјылты : *n* howling

вневедомственный : *a* *Ru* extra-jurisdictional, beyond the jurisdiction *of a particular, ministry, department etc.*

военкомат : *n* *Ru* military comissariat *in the Soviet Union organization responsible for the military draft , military service record-keeping etc*

волгабоју : *adv* the Volga region

вообще : *adv* *Ru* in general, generally speaking

временный : *a* *Ru* temporary, provisional

вулкан : *n* *Ru* volcano

вулканизасија : *n* 1) vulcanization *a* 2) vulcanized

вураған : *a* 1) given to butting *cow* *n* 2) an animal given to butting *usually a cow*

вурағанлыг : *n* tendency to butt *usually about a cow*

вуран : *n* *math* 1) multiplier 2) see **вураған**

вурғу : *n* *gram* accent, stress

вурғугабағы : *a* *ling* pretonic

вурғулу : *a* *ling* accented, tonic

вурғун : *n* *med* 1) stroke, paralysis, apoplexy *a* 2) in love *with* , enamored 3) *pseudonym of a famous Azerbaijani Soviet poet*

вурғусуз : *a* unaccented, unstressed

вурдурмаг, вурдуртмаг : *caus of* **вурмаг**

вурма : *v* 1) from **вурмаг** *math* 2) multiplication

вурмаг : *v* 1) strike, hit 2) wound or kill with a weapon *math* 3) multiply 4) hit the target with a shot from a firearm *fig* 5) start up with a jerk, dart 6) sting 7) cut, clip, shear 8) make a shot, injection

вурнухма : *n* fuss, bustle

вурнухмаг : *v* throw o.s. about, bustle, fuss *about*

вур-тут : *adv* in all

вуруг : *n* *math* factor

вурулан : *n math* multiplicand

вурулмаг : *v* 1) be wounded or killed 2) be subjected to blows *math* 3) increase, multiply, be multiplied 4) fall in love, be captivated *by*

вуруш : *n* see **вурушма**

вурушган : *n* pugnacious *n* 2) pugnacious fellow, bully, troublemaker

вурушдурмаг : *v* set one person against another; quarrel *with,* fall out *with*

вурушма : *n mil* 1) battle, combat, engagement, action, skirmish 2) fight, scuffle, melee

вурушмаг : *v* fight *with* , join battle *with*

вурhавур : *n* brawl fight scuffle

вурhај : *adv* see **далбадал**

вурчатласын : *n* pandemonium, bedlam, hubbub

вүгар : *n* importance, pride, merit, gravity, sedateness

вүгарла : *adv* with an air of importance, with dignity grandly, proudly, gravely

вүгарлы : *a* important; proud; sedate

вүс'әт : *n* 1) spaciousness, extensiveness, space; width 2) scope, range, compass

вүс'әтли : *a* spacious, wide, broad

вүҹуд : *n* 1) body 2) person, individual; being, creature

Г

г : fourth letter of the Azeri alphabet

габ : *n* tableware, plates and dishes, crockery

габа : *a* 1) rude, uncouth *adv* 2) rudely

габаг : *n* 1) front, front side, fore part *n bot* 2) pumpkin, gourd *postp* 3) before

габа-габа : *adv* rudely, impolitely; indelicately, unrestrainedly

габаг-габаға, габаг-гаршы : *adv* 1) face to face, vis-a-vis 2) meeting/bumping into one another *two-people*

габагда : *adv* 1) in front, ahead 2) earlier, before, formerly, in the past

габагдакы : *a* front, forward, located in/up front

габагдан : *adv* 1) at/from the front, in front 2) before, earlier, in advance, in good time

габагкы : *a* 1) former, previous, preceding 2) front, forward, located in/up front

габагламаг : *v* 1) outstrip, take the lead over 2) let know before, give advance notice, warn

габагланмаг : *pass* 1) be given advance notice, be informed beforehand, be forewarned 2) be outstripped *by*

габаглар, габагларда : *adv* see **габагда** 2)

габаглашмаг : *v* 1) meet face to face 2) compete, contend

габагча : *adv* at first, firstly, before, earlier, formerly

габагчадан : *adv* beforehand, in good time, preliminarily

габагчыл : *a* 1) foremost, headmost, advanced *n* 2) leader, front-runner

габаға : *adv* forward, ahead

габағардан : *n* see **галајчы**

габағыалынмаз : *a* irresistible, inevitable

габалашдырмаг : *v* make rude, coarse s.o., s.t.

габалашмаг : *v* grow/become rude/coarse

габалыг : *n* 1) rudeness, crudeness, coarseness 2) uncouthness, roughness

габан : *n* 1) wild boar *a* 2) wild boar['s]

габар : *n* 1) blister 2) corn, callus, callosity

габар-габар : *a* 1) covered with blisters 2) covered with calluses

габардин : *n* 1) Kabardian *member of a Circassian ethnic group in the Northern Caucasus* 2) gabardine *a wollen cloth*

габарыг : *a* 1) convex *adv* 2) convexly

габарыгланмаг : *v* bubble, effervesce

габарыглыг : *n* 1) convexity 2) relief, hilliness, unevenness

габарланмаг : *pass* be covered with blisters/calluses

габарлатмаг : *v* make callous

габарлы : *a* 1) covered with blisters 2) knobby, knobbly 3) callous

габарлыг : *n med* 1) swelling; blister; tubercle 2) unevenness, hilliness

габарма : *vn* 1) fr. **габармаг** *geog* 2) high tide, high water

габармаг : *v intr* 1) swell, distend, inflate 2) bristle 3) be impudent/impertinent/insolent

габарты : *n* convexity

габартмаг : *v* blow up, inflate

габарчыг : *n* 1) small abscess, boil; blister 2) hummock, tussock 3) small blister, bleb; hillock

габача,габачасына : *adv* rudely, discourteously, crudely

габгалаjлаjан : *n* see **галачы**

габ-гачаг : *n* *coll* tableware, the dishes; pots and pans

габгыран : *n* *bot* see **зәнчироту**

габдүзәлдән : *n* potter

габил : *a* skilful, clever, talented, able, gifted

габиллиjjәт : *n* 1) ability, capability, intelligence,skill, know-how 2) quality, merit, virtue

габиллиjjәтли : *a* see **габил**

габиллиjjәтсиз : *a* unskilful, untalented, ungifted

габиллиjjәтсизлик : *n* lack of ability, inability, incapability, lack of talent

габилләшмәк : *v* become able, skilful, proficient

габыг : *n* 1) bark, rind, peel, rind skin, sheath, shell, wrapper 2) cover *of book*

габыг-губуг : *n* husk-like, pellicle-like scabs

габыгтурду : *n* *zool* bark beetle *family Scolytidae*

габыгланмаг : *v* be covered with, become covered with bark

габыглы : *a* covered with bark/shell/pellicle/thin skin/shell/husk etc

габыглыг : *a* *publ* intended/earmarked/set aside for covers *books, pamphlets, magazines etc.*

габыгсыз : *a* 1) having no shell/husk/skin/pellicle 2) peeled, cleaned of bark/pellicle/skin/husk etc

габыгүстү : *n* *bot* cuticle

габырға : *n* *anat* 1) rib *a* 2) rib, costal

габырғаалты : *a* *anat* subcostal, under the ribs

габырғаарасы : *a* *anat* intercostal

габырғалы : *a* strong, vigorous, robust, thickset, sturdily built *of a person*

габырғаүстү : *a* *anat* subcostal, under the ribs

габjалаjан : *n* 1) sponger *fig* 2) toady, bootlicker, sycophant, one who fawns on another

габjуjан : *n* dishwasher

габлаjычы : *n* packer

габлама : *v* packing

габламаг : *v* pack, pack s.t. into s.t. else

габланмаг : *v* *intr* pack up, do o.'s packing

габлатдырмаг, габлатмаг : *caus of* **габламаг**

габлашдырмаг : *v* put in, insert; pack/wrap/bale up, stow

габсечән : *n* grader of glassware in the glass industry

габсындыран : *n* *bot* see **зәнчироту**

гавазаг : *a* bulky, occupying too much space

гавал : *n* tambourine

гавалгаjыран : *n* expert maker of tambourines

гавалчалан, гавалчы : *n* tambourine player

гавраjыш : *n* perception

гавраjышлы : *a* perceptive

гаврама : *n* 1) perception 2) scope

гаврамаг : *v* 1) take in, perceive, cognize, acquire 2) comprehend

гавранмаг : *pass* 1) be taken in, mastered, learned 2) be comprehended

гаггылдамаг : *v* 1) laugh loudly/boisterously, burst out laughing, start roaring with laughter 2) cackle, cluck

гаггылдатмаг : *caus of* **гаггылдамаг**

гаггылдашмаг : *v* 1) laugh loudly/boisterously *by many people together* ; excite general laughter 2) set up a cackling *by many people together*

гаггылты : *n* 1) loud/boisterous laughter 2) cackling

гагго : *n* *zool* golden-eye, a large diving duck of Europe and North America *Bucephala Clangula*

гагум : *n* *zool* ermine

гаға : *n* dad, daddy; uncle *when addressing to an older man*

гағаjы : *n* *zool* seagull, tern

гағала : *v* compound-verb element; used only in compounds : **гағала чалмаг** : cackle

гағылдамаг : *v* 1) cackle 2) roar with laughter

гағылдашмаг : *v* 1) cackle *by many together* 2) roar with laughter *many together*

гағылты : *n* 1) cackling 2) roaring with laughter

гада : *n* ailment, illness; misfortune, adversity

гадан алым : *intrj of address* my dear, my darling, my little one!

гада-бала : *n* misfortune, adversity, trouble, calamity, vicissitudes of life, of fate

гадаг : *n* rivet/rivet pin; pivotal axis of scissors

гадагаjтаран : *n* *bot* see **боjмадәрән**

гадаған : *n* 1) prohibition, ban, distraint *a* 2) prohibited, forbidden

гадир : *a* powerful, big, great, mighty, almighty, all-powerful, omnipotent 2) able, capable, competent

гадын : *n* 1) woman *a* 2) woman's, female, feminine

гадынсифәт : *a* 1) effeminate *n* 2) man with an unstable, changeable character/nature

гадынхасиј̌јәт : *a* feminine, womanly

гадынчасына : *adv* in a feminine way

гадынчыг : *n* ironically friendly form of address to a woman *lit. little woman* doll

гаж : *n* see **бәнд**

газ : *n* 1) goose 2) gas 3) chiffon *cloth* *a* 3) goose['s] 4) gas, gaseous 5) chiffon

газабахан : *n* goose-herd *one who tends a flock of geese*

газајағы : *n bot* meadow rue *Thalictrum maius*

газалаг : *n* gig, little hansom

газалагчы : *n* carter, carrier, owner of a gig, a little hansom

газамат : *n* 1) prison, jail *a* 2) prison, jail

газан : *n* 1) boiler; cauldron *a* 2) boiler; cauldron

газангајыран : *n* 1) boiler-maker 2) boiler maintenance man 3) stoker, furnace-man

газандырмаг : *v* serve as the reason, or motive for s.o.'s advantaage, profit, assistance; earn

газанылмаг : *pass* be earned, acquired, gained

газанмаг : *v* earn, receive profit, benefit, gain

газантәмизләјән : *n* boiler-cleaner *person*

газанхана : *n* boiler-room, boiler house

газанча : *n* small cauldron, pot, kettle

газанчы : *n* 1) boilermaker 2) boiler installer-fitter

газанч : *n* 1) earnings 2) profit[s], gain

газанчлы : *a* profitable, lucrative, remunerative, advantageous

газанчпајы : *n* bonus

газанчсыз : *a* unprofitable, unlucrative, non-remunerative

газаохшар : *a* gaseous, gasiform

газатан : *n* gas projector

газах : *n* 1) Kazakh *city in Azerbaijan* 2) a Kazakh *a* 3) Kazakh

газахча : *adv* in Kazakh *language*

газдырмаг, газдыртмаг : *caus of* **газмаг**

газы : *n* Cadi, a Muslim Judge *specialist in religious law*

газыг : *n* 1) excavated pit 2) hollow, depression, ditch

газыг-газыг : *a* excavated

газыјычы : *n* engraver, etcher; carver

газылмаг : *pass* be dug out/excised/carved out/engraved

газыма : *n* carving; engraving

газымаг : *v* cut out, carve, carved out, engrave

газынты : *n* 1) excavations 2) scrapings

газытдырмаг, газытмаг : *caus of* **газымаг**

газланмаг : *pass* 1) be converted into a gas 2) be gassed, aerated

газлашдырма : *n* gas-pipe lines construction, production of gas

газлашдырмаг : *v* lay gas-pipe lines

газлы : *a* 1) gaseous 2) gasified *fig* 3) haughty, arrogant, self-satisfied

газма : *n* 1) digging 2) boring, drilling 3) dugout, cave 4) mine, pit, hollow *a* 5) drill, drilling, bore, boring

газмаг : *v* 1) dig, burrow, excavate, trench 2) bore, drill *n* 3) crust

газмагланмаг : *v* be covered up with a crust

газмачы : *n* 1) borer, driller 2) miner 3) sapper *US combat engineer*

газмачылыг : *n* profession of driller, miner

газөлчән : *n* gas meter, manometer, pressure gage

гаиб : *a* 1) absent 2) secret, hidden, concealed; 3) extinct

гаибанә : *adv* without seeing, by default

гаја : *n* 1) big rock, cliff 2) block

гајалы : *a* rocky

гајалыг : *n* rocky, precipitous terrain

гајаһөрүмчәји : *n* tarantula *poisonous spider*

гајғанаг : *n* fried eggs

гајғы : *n* concern, care; support

гајғыкеш : *a* concerned, careful, responsive, supportive

гајғыкешлик : *n* solicitude, anxiety, preoccupation

гајғыландырмаг : *v* worry about, look after, take care of

гајғылы : *a* 1) solicitous 2) anxious *about* , concerned, preoccupied

гајғысыз : *a* unconcerned, careless

гајғысызлыг : *n* unconcern, carelessness, negligence

гајғысызча, гајғысызчасына : *adv* unconcernedly, carelessly, negligently

гајда : *n* 1) rule, statute, procedure, regulation[s] 2) custom 3) method of production/work

гајда-ганун : *n* procedure, regulation[s]

гајдаја салмаг : *v* straighten out, put into order

гајдалы : *a* 1) right, true, correct, exact *adv* 2) according to procedure, in order, correctly

гајдасыз : *a* 1) disorderly, incorrect *adv* 2) in disorder, incorrectly

гајдасызлыг : *n* disorderliness; turmoil, lack of social order

гајә : *n* 1) goal, aim, aspiration, wish, ideal 2) limit, bound

гајыг : *n* 1) boat *a* 2) boat, boating

гајыгчы : *n* boatman; ferryman

гајыгчылыг : *n* profession of boatsman, ferryman; boating

гајыдан : *a* 1) reverting, recurring, returning 2) recurrent; return

гајыдан баш : *adv* on the way back

гајыдыш : *n* return; recurrence

гајым : *a* 1) strong, firm *adv* 2) fast, strong; hard

гајын : *n* 1) brother-in-law 2) *term applied to any in-law relationship*

гајынағачы : *n* birch tree *Betula L*

гајынана : *n* mother-in-law

гајынарвады : *n* sister-in-law

гајыната : *n* father-in-law

гајырылмаг : *v* be made, prepared, manufactured

гајырма : *n* 1) preparation, making, manufacture 2) counterfeiting *a* 3) false, imitation, counterfeit, artificial 4) home-made

гајырмаг : *v* 1) make, manufacture, fashion 2) repair, mend

гајыртдырмаг, гајыртмаг : *caus of* **гајырмаг**

гајытма : *n* 1) return, recurrence 2). reflection, rebound, recoil *a* 2) return, returning, recurring

гајытмаг : *v* 1) return, go back *phys* 2) reflect

гајытмаз : *a* 1) irrevocable, irretrievable *adv* 2) irrevocably, irretrievably

гајыш : *n* belt, strap, leather band

гајышбалдыр : *n* thin, but hardy man *lit. 'belt calf'*

гајмаг : *n* specially cooked cream

гајмагланмаг : *v* form cream, form a layer of cream *milk*

гајмагчичәји : *n* *bot* buttercup, crowfoot *Ranunculus*

гајнаг : *n* 1) weld, welding seam, welding 2) spring, source

гајнагламаг : *v* weld

гајнагчы : *n* welder

гајнајыб-гарышмаг : *v* *intr* grow together, intergrow, coalesce, run together, flow together, intermingle

гајнама : *n* 1) boiling, effervescence 2) spring, source, fountain

гајнамаг : *v* *intr* 1) boil, boil up 2) well out/spout/ spirt as a spring

гајнанмыш : *a* boiled

гајнар : *a* 1) boiling, hot *fig* 2) seething, bubbling

гајнатдырмаг : *v* make boil

гајнатмаг : *v* boil

гајнашма : *n* fuss, bustle; crowd, crush

гајнашмаг : *v* crowd, fuss, bustle swarm, teem

гајсава : *n* "kaysava" *dish from dried apricots*

гајсаг : *n* 1) film *film on a surface of a liquid* 2) crust, incrustation formed on the surface of soil after a rainfall, sprinkling, or irrigation

гајсагламаг, гајсагланмаг : *v* *intr* crust, get crusted over

гајсар : heaves, broken wind *form of emphysema in domestic animals*

гајсы=гајсу : *n* *"kaysi"* apricot see **әрик**

гајтаг : *n* see **чыхдаш**

гајтағы : *n* lezghinka *strenuous Caucasian dance*

гајтан : *n* cord

гајтанламаг : *v* lace up, tie together

гајтанланмаг : *pass* be laced up, be tied together

гајтарылмаг : *pass* 1) be returned, given back, reflected, repulsed 2) be won back, recouped

гајтарылмаз : *a* irreversible, irrevocable

гајтарычы : *n* 1) reflector, deflector *a* 2) reflecting, reverberatory, deflecting; returning, reentering

гајтарма : *n* 1) return, returning 2) reflection, reverberation, repulse, repulsion, recoil

гајтармаг : *v* 1) return, give back 2) reflect, recoil; render 3) win back

гајтартдырмаг, гајтартмаг : *caus of* **гајтармаг**

гајчы : *n* scissors, shears

гајчылама : *n* shearing, clipping

гајчыламаг : *v* cut with scissors, cut, clip

гајчыланмаг : *pass* be cut off, cut with scissors, be clipped, sheared

гајчылатдырмаг, гајчылатмаг : *caus of* **гајтармаг**

гала : *n* 1) fortress, castle 2) see **газамат** *a* 3) fortress

галабәји : *n hist* 1) governor of a town 2) commander of a fortress

галаг : *n* heap, pile, stack

гала-гала : *adv* staying, continuing to stay

галаг-галаг : *adv* in piles/heaps/stacks

галагламаг : *v* assemble, put together in a pile/heap, pile up, heap up/together

галагланмаг : *pass* be assembled/put together in a pile/ heap, be piled up, heaped up

галај : *n* 1) tin *a* 2) tin

галајлама : *n* tinning, tinplating

галајламаг : *v* tin, tinplate, blanch

галајланмаг : *pass* be tinned, tinplated, blanched

галајлатдырмаг : *v* request, have s.o. tin, tinplate, blanch

галајлатмаг : *v* request, have s.o. tin, tinplate, blanch

галајлы : *a* tinned, tinplated, blanched

галајчы : *n* tinsmith, tinner

галајчылыг : *n* profession of tinsmith, tinner

галама : *v* fr. **галамаг**

галамаг : *v* 1) stoke *furnace* 2) heap up, pile up, stack up

галан : *a* 1) the rest of *n* 2) remainder, rest, residue

галанмаг : *pass* 1) be stoked *furnace* 2) be piled/heaped,/stacked up

галатдырмаг : *caus* **галамаг**

галғы : *n* see **галыг**

галдырылмаг : *pass* be raised/lifted up/taken away

галдырым : *n* see **јохуш**

галдырычы : *n* 1) crane operator *a* 2) lift, lifting, crane, hoisting, hoist

галдырма : *v* fr. **галдырмаг**

галдырмаг : *v* 1) lift, hoist 2) raise *high* , lift

галдыртмаг : *caus of* **галдырмаг**

галиб : *n* conqueror, victor, winner

галибанә : *a* 1) victorious, conquering *adv* 2) victoriously

галибијјәт : *n* victory

галибијјәтли : *a* victorious

галыб : *n* see **гәлиб** 1)

галыг : *n* 1) remains, residue 2) shortage, arrears 3) vestige, remnant *math* 4) remainder

галын : *a* 1) thick 2) dense *woods* 3) gross, coarse *gram* 4) hard, unpalatalized *vowels, consonants* **галынгабыг** : *a* thick-skinned, thick-rinded *fruit*

галынгафа : *a* 1) dull-witted *n* 2) blockhead, nitwit

галынгаш : *a* heavy eyebrowed, thick-browed

галындодаг : *a* thick-lipped

галынламаг, галынланмаг : *v* grow thick, dense

галынлатмаг, галынлашдырмаг : *v* thicken, make thicker

галынлашмаг : *v* 1) thicken, become thicker 2) coarsen, grow coarse/rude 3) grow rich

галынлыг : *n* 1) thickness 2) density *geol* 3) width of a vein/stratum

галынсач : *a* thick-haired/tressed, bushy-haired, shaggy

галлач : *n* 1) person with a generous nature *a* 2) generous

галмаг : *v* stay; remain; be left

галмагал : *n* 1) noise, racket 2) loud quarrel, brawl, uproar, row

галмагаллы : *a* quarrelsome, rowdy

галмагалчы : *n* brawler, trouble-maker, rowdy, disorderly person

галош : *n* galosh

галстук : *n* necktie

галтаг : *n* saddletree *wooden saddle base*

галхаг : *a* convex, arched, bulging, raised

галхан : *n* shield *for deflecting blows*

галханаохшар : *a* 1) shield-shaped, *bot* 2) peltate

галханбалығы : *n zool* flatfish, flounder *Pleuronectes*

галханвары, галханшәкилли : *a* see **галханаохшар**

галхызмаг : *v* see **галырмаг**

галхышма : *n* unrest, ferment, rumblings, revolt

галхышмаг : *v* 1) revolt, rise up 2) arise, rise all together

галхмаг : *v* 1) rise, arise, stand up 2) rise up, advance

гамарламаг : *v* grasp with the hand, seize, grab

гамашдырычы : *n* blinding, dazzling

гамашдырмаг : *v* blind, dazzle, cause eye irritation *because of strong light*

гамашыг : *n* 1) bitter taste in the mouth 2) temporary blindness caused by bright light 3) general state of psychological confusion

гамашмаг : *v* 1) become sick and tired 2) be temporarily blinded by bright light *colloq* 3) be completely confused, be completely mixed up

гамгалаг : *n* chip, sliver

гамәт : *n* stature, build, carriage, bearing

гамәтли : *a* well-proportioned

гамыш : *n* 1) reed, rush, cane *a* 2) reed, rush, cane

гамышит : *n* 1) pressboard made of reeds *used in construction a* 2) attributive of 1)

гамышјыған : *n* reed cutter *person*

гамышлыг : *n* cane/reed/rush thicket, locality overgrown with reeds/canes/rushes

гамус : *n* 1) encyclopedia 2) dictionary

гамчы : *n* whip, lash, knout

гамчыламаг : *v* lash, whip, flog, scourge

гамчыланмаг : *v* undergo flogging, thrashing

гамчылатдырмаг, гамчылатмаг *caus of* **гамчыламаг**

ган : *n* 1) blood *a* 2) blood, bloody

ган ағламаг : *v* weep, sob bitterly

ган көрмәк : *v* menstruate, have one's period

ганы гајнамаг : *v* have a good attitude *toward s.o.*

ганы гаралмаг : *v* be upset; be very angry, infuriated

ганы гачмаг : *v* become pale

ганыны алмаг : *v* take a revenge, retaliate

гана-ган : *adv* eye for an eye, blood for blood *reciprocally vengefully*

ганад : *n* 1) wing 2) leaf, wing *of a door* 3) blade, vane 4) flank, side

ганадајаглы : *a zool* 1) pteropodal *having the foot expanded into lobes* ; relating to the Pteropoda *group of gastropod mollusks*

ганадаохшар : *a zool* pterygoid[al] *having the shape of a wing*

ганадвары : *a bot* see **ганадшәкилли**

ганадгујруг : *a zool* pterycaudal

ганадыјекә : *a* winged

ганадландырмаг : *v* 1) inspire, lend wings to 2) cheer up, encourage

ганадланмаг : *pass* 1) be inspired 2) be cheered up, be encouraged

ганадлы : *a* winged, having wings

ганадсыз : *a* wingless

ганадүстү : *n* elytra, wing-cases

ганадшәкилли : *a* wing-shaped, *zool* pterygoid

ганазлығы : *n* anemia

ганамаг : *v* 1) flow *of blood* 2) bleed

ганатмаг : *v* cause bleeding, wound

ганахма : *n* hemorrhage, bleeding

ганачаг : *n* 1) politeness, courtesy, civility 2) conscientiousness 3) clearness, cleverness, intelligibility, quickness of apprehension

ганачаглы : *a* 1) courteous, civil 2) clever, quick, bright 3) conscientious

ганачагсыз : *a* 1) uneducated, crude, uncivil 2) slow-witted 3) irresponsible, thoughtless *n* 4) ignoramus

ганачагсызлыг : *n* 1) slowness, dullness, slow-wittedness 2) discourtesy, incivility

ганбаһасы : *n* vendetta

ганбур : *a* see **донгар**

ганверән : *n* donor *of blood*

гангал : *n bot* milk thistle, lady's thistle *Sylibum Marianum*

ган-ган : *adv only in compound* ' **ган-ган демәк**' : *v* thirst for blood, be bloodthirsty, lust for blood

гангаралыгы, гангаралтысы : *n* trouble, nuisance, annoyance, quarrel, misunderstanding

гангарышмасы : *n* incest

гангурудан : *n bot* yarrow, millefoil *Achillea millefollia L.*

гандал, гандалаг : *n* shackles, fetters, handcuffs

гандалламаг : *v* shackle, put into irons, handcuffs

гандырмаг : *v* give to understand, explain s.t. to s.o., make s.o. understand s.t., make understand, convince

гане : *a* contenting o.s. *with* , satisfying o.s. *that* , convinced

ганичән : *a* 1) bloodthirsty *n* 2) bloodsucker, extortioner, exploiter, tyrant

ганичәнлик : *n fig* blood-sucking, bloodthirstiness

ганыг : *n* 1) satisfaction; peace, tranquillity 2) see **гисас**

ганыгаралыг : *n* see **гангаралыгы, гангаралтысы**

ганырмаг : *v* unscrew, twist

ганысојуг : *a* 1) cool, composed; indifferent, phlegmatic 2) unpleasant, disagreeable, not likeable, unattractive

ганысојуглуг : *n* coolness, composure; indifference, phlegm

ганыширин : *a* likeable, attractive person

ганкетмә, ганкетмәси : *n* bleeding, hemorrhage

ганкөрмә : *n* menstruation

ганлы : *a* 1) bloody; with blood, containing some blood, blood-stained 2) sanguinary *n* 3) blood enemy

ганлыбычаг : *n* sworn enemy, blood enemy

ганлылыг : *n* 1) blood enmity *med* 2) plethora *suberabundance of blood in the entire system or in one organ*

ганмаг : *v* understand, perceive

ганмаз : *a* 1) slow-witted, dull, stupid *a* 2) ignoramus, fool, blockhead; boor

ганмазлыг : *n* ignorance, slowness, slow-wittedness; boorishness

ганмазчасына : *adv* ignorantly; boorishly

ганов : *n* ditch, trench

гановуз : *n* kanaus *coarse silken fabric*

гансағылма, гансағылмасы : *n* 1) hemorrhage 2) bruise

гансыз : *a* 1) bloodless, anemic *fig* 2) callous, heartless, cool, apathetic

гансызлашдырмаг : *v* exsanguinate, drain of blood; exhaust, wear out *the enemy*

гансызлашмаг : *v* 1) become anemic 2) be exsanguinated/drained of blood; become exhausted, worn out

гансызлыг : *n med* 1) anemia *fig* 2) callousness, heartlessness, coolness, coldness

гансоран : *n* 1) bloodsucker *fig* 2) parasite, extortioner *a* 3) bloodthirsty

гантар : *n* see **гапан**

гантарға : *n* bridle and bit

гантарғаламаг : *v* bridle *a horse* , put a bridle on a horse

гантарғаланмаг : *pass* be bridled *a horse also fig*

гантарғалы : *a* bridled

гантәмизләјән : *a* blood-purifying

ган-тәр : *n lit.* blood and perspiration : **ган-тәрә батмаг** : sweat profusely, be steeped in perspiration

гантөкмә : *n* bloodshed

ганун : *n* law

гануназидд : *a* 1) unlawful *adv* 2) unlawfully, illegally

ганунауjғун : *a* 1) legal, lawful *adv* 2) legally, lawfully

ганунауjғунлуг : *n* legality, lawfulness

ганунверичи : *n* 1) legislator, law-giver *a* 2) legislative

ганунверичилик : *n* legislation

гануни : *a* lawful, legal

ганунилэшдирилмәк : *pass* be legalized/legitimized, be made lawful

ганунилэшдирмәк : *v* legalize, legitimize, legitimate

ганунилэшмәк : *v* become a law, become legitimate/legitimized

ганунилик : *n* lawfulness, legality

ганунлашдырмаг : *v* see **ганунилэшмәк**

гануннамә : *n* code, collection of laws

ганунпозан : *n* lawbreaker, transgressor, delinquent

ганунсуз : *a* 1) lawless, illegal, unlawful, illicit *adv* 2) lawlessly, illegally, unlawfully, illicitly

ганунсузлуг : *n* 1) illegality, lawlessness, illegal action 2) unlawfulness

ганчыг : *n* bitch

гапаг : *n* cover, lid, cap, top

гапаглы : *a* capped, lidded, having a cap/lid, closed with a cap/lid/top

гапаған : *n* 1) spiteful person *lit ' biting'* ; ill-tempered dog *a* 2) snarling, growling *of a dog*

гападылмаг : *pass* be closed/shut/locked

гапаз : *n* blow on the head with the open palm; box on the ear/head

гапазламаг : *v* give a box/slap on the head

гапазланмаг : *v* receive/get a box/slap on the head

гапазлашмаг : *v* give one another a box/slap on the head

гапалы : *a* closed/shut/locked

гапама : *n* 1) closing/shutting, corking 2) locking, fastening

гапамаг : *v* 1) close/shut/lock; cork 2) lock/fasten

гапан : *n* 1) decimal weights 2) weighing machine

гапандар : *n* see **гапанчы**

гапанмаг : *pass* 1) be closed/shut/corked 2) be locked, fastened

гапанчы : *n* weigher, weigh-master

гапатдырмаг, гапатмаг : *caus of* **гапамаг**

гапгара : quite/completely black, jet-black, ebony-black

гапдырмаг, гапдыртмаг : *caus of* **гапмаг**

гапы : *n* door

гапы-бача : *n* 1) collective name for all the exits, outlets, openings or apertures in the walls of a building, house or apartment 2) collective name for a house and yard, a farmstead, a peasant holding including outbuildings, kitchen-garden, orchard etc

гапы-гапы : *adv* along the yards/courtyards; from house to house

гапыгулу : *a* court *pertaining to a royal court*

гапылмаг : *v intr* be carried away *by* , fascinated by; give o.s. up to, be fascinated *by*

гапысыачыг : *a* hospitable

гапычы : *n* door-man, porter, hall-porter

гапычылыг : *n* the occupation of door-man, porter, hall-porter

гапыщдырмаг : *v* snatch away; take away bit by bit

гапышмаг : *v* 1) bite one another, be given to biting 2) fight *of animals* ; bicker, squabble

гаплан : *n* 1) ounce, snow leopard *a* 2) attributive of 1)

гапма : *n* biting

гапмаг : *v* 1) bite 2) seize

гапчаг : *n* bast-fiber bag, sack, mat bag

гар : *n* 1) snow *a* 2) snowy, snow

гара : *adv* 1) black, dark *n* 2) dry land, earth

гарабагара : *adv* 1) in/on the track/trail *of* 2) attentively, tenaciously, letter for letter

гарабағыр : *n* see **гарачијәр**

гарабасан : *n* clairvoyant, medium, one who communicates with spirits

гарабасма : *n* ghost, spirit, spectre

гарабатдаг : *n zool* cormorant *genus Phalacrocorax*

гарабаш : *n* 1) servant *of both sexes* ; maid 2) slave, bondswoman

гарабашаг : *n* 1) buckwheat *a* 2) buckwheat

гарабәниз : *n* see **гарашын**

гарабәхт : *a* unfortunate, ill-fated, unlucky

гарабибәр : *n bot* betel *Piper betle, an Asiatic climbing plant whose leaves are eaten with limes*

гарабығ : *a* black-moustached

гарабуғдаjы : *n* see **гараjаныз**

гараваш : *n* see **гарабаш**

гаравәлли : *n* anecdote, far fetched story, cock-and-bull story

гарагабаг : *a* 1) sullen, gloomy, morose, sombre, cheerless *n* 2) unsociable person

гарагазан : *n* blind-man's buff

гарагалпаг : *n* 1) Kara-Kalpak *nation in Central Asia* *a* 2) Kara-Kalpak

гарагалпагча : *adv* in Kara-Kalpak *language*

гараганад : *a* black-winged

гарагарын : *n* black-bellied

гарагаш : *a* black-browed

гарагышгырыг : *n* hubub, hullabaloo, uproar

гараговаг : *n bot* Black poplar *tree Populus negra*

гарагонур : *a* dark brown

гарагорху : *n* intimidation, bullying, threat, menace

гарагуjруг : *a* black-tailed

гара-гура : *n* scrawl, hen-scratching, illegible/undecipherable writing

гарагуш : *n* 1) eagle *a* 2) eagle, aquiline

гарағат : *n* 1) currant[s] *a* 2) currant

гарағач : *n bot* 1) elm *Ulmus* *a* 2) elm

гарадәнизчи : *n* sailor of the Black Sea Fleet

гарадәрили : *a* black-skinned, dark-skinned

гарадимдик : *a* black-billed *birds*

гарадинмəз : *a* taciturn, silent, not talkative, reserved, reticent

гарадиш : *a* 1) black-toothed *n* 2) ram more than three years old

гарадөш : *a* black-breasted

гараж : *n* garage

гаразырпы : *a* 1) unpolished, uncouth, clumsy, awkward *n* 2) big, strong and awkward person

гарајағыз : *a* see **гарашын**

гарајал : *a* black-maned

гарајаныз : *a* see **гарашын**

гарајара : *n* *med* anthrax

гарајаха : *a* importunate, persistent, nagging

гарајахалыг : *n* importunateness, persistency, constant nagging

гарајонча : *n* *bot* 1) lucerne, alfalfa *Medicago sativa* *a* 2) alfalfa, lucerne

гаракəһəр : *a* dark bay *horse's color*

гаракилə : *n* *bot* whortleberry, bilberry, European blueberry *Vaccinnium myrtillus* *a* 2) attributive of 1)

гаракөз, гаракөзлү : *a* dark-eyed

гаракүл : *n* 1) karakul, astrakhan *fur, fleece from karakul* *a* 2) karakul, astrakhan

гаракүн, гаракүнлү : *a* 1) unhappy, unfortunate, ill-starred, hapless, down on one's luck *n* 2) poor, unfortunate creature, poor devil

гаракүруһ : *n* *hist* the Black Hundred[s] *in pre-revolutionary Russia a party of extreme antisemitic reactionaries who used terror terror and violence against the Liberal and Radical parties*

гаракүруһчу : *n* member of the Black Hundred[s]

гаралама : *v* fr. **гараламаг**

гараламаг : *v* 1) blacken, shade; soil, dirty 2) cross out, strike out, daub 3) concentrate attention on s.t., choose, select, mark a place

гараланмаг : *pass* 1) be crossed out 2) be stained, soiled 3) be besmirched, blackmailed, marked out, singled out *by s.o.*

гаралдылмаг : *v* see **гараланмаг** 1)

гаралыг : *n* blackness

гаралма : *n* blackening

гаралмаг : *v* turn/become/grow black

гаралты : *n* dark spot, silhouette, shadow

гаралтмаг : *v* 1) make black, dark 2) cover with black, blacken, shade, darken, cloud, overshadow

гарамал : *n* cattle

гарамтыл : *a* blackish, dark

гарамуг : *n* *bot* cockle, corncockle *Agrostemma githago. Seeds are poisonous*

гарангуш : *n* *zool* swallow

гаранлыг : *n* 1) darkness, obscurity *a* 2) dark, gloomy, sombre, pitch-dark

гаранлыгламаг : *v* grow/get/become dark

гаранлыглашдырылмаг : be darkened/blacked out

гаранлыглашдырма : *n* darkening

гаранлыглашдырмаг : *v* darken, black out, obscure

гаранлыглашма : *n* darkening

гаранлыглашмаг : *v* grow/get/become dark

гарапача : *n* *zool* chamois *Rupicapra rupicapra*

гарапəнчə : *a* black-pawed

гарасаггал, гарасаггаллы : *a* black-bearded

гарасаггыз : *n* pitch, tar

гарасач, гарасачлы : *a* black-haired, dark-haired

гарасы : *n* rough sketch, draft, outline

гарател : *a* black curly haired

гаратојуг : *n* *zool* thrush *fam. Turdidae*

гараторпаг : *n* chernozem, black earth

гараторпаглы : *a* chernozem, black earth

гаратохмаг : *n* 1) spade[s] *suit of playing cards* *a* 2) attributive of 1)

гарахəшил : *n* salamata *dish similar to kasha*

гарачы : *n* 1) gypsy 2) beggar, pauper *fig* 3) babbler, shouter *a* *fig* 4) greedy, avaricious, mean *a* 5) gypsy, romany

гарачылыг : *n* 1) begging, cadging 2) clamorousness, shouting 3) avariciousness 4) begging; beggary, parasitism, sponging

гарачысајаг : *adv* 1) in Gypsy fashion 2) in Gypsy, Romany *language*

гарача : *n* *bot* ergot, spurred rye *Claviceps purpurea* ; smut *of corn*

гарачијəр : *n* liver

гараширə : *n* *a variety of black grape esteemed for its juice*

гарашын : *n* dark haired man or woman, swarthy person

гаргара : *n* 1) spool or bobbin *for thread* *med* 2) gargling *tech* 3) pulley 4) rinse, rinsing

гарға : *n zool* 1) crow *a* 2) crow['s], corvine

гарғадили : *n ling* 1) slang; also cant, "code words" or any allegorical or indirect method of concealing the real meaning from outsiders

гарғадузу : *n min* mica

гарғашалыг : *n* bustle, turmoil, commotion, confusion, disorder

гарғы : *n* 1) thin reed *a* 2) reed, rush

гарғыдалы : *n bot* 1) corn, maize *Zea mais* *a* 2) corn, maize

гарғыма : *n* damnation; imprecation, curse

гарғымаг : *v* curse, damn

гарғыш : *n* damning, cursing, calling down misfortune on s.o.'s head

гардаш : *n* 1) brother *a* 2) brotherly, fraternal

гардашарвады : *n* sister-in-law *brother's wife*

гардашгызы : *n* niece *brother's daughter*

гардашлашмаг : *v* fraternize *with*

гардашлыг : *n* 1) brotherhood, fraternity *a* 2) fraternal, brotherly 3) named/called brother, sworn *as* brother 3) stepbrother

гардашоғлу : *n* nephew *brother's son*

гардашсевән : *a* brother-loving

гардашсевәнлик : *n* brotherly love

гардашсыз : *a* brotherless, without a brother

гардашчасына : *adv* fraternally, in a brotherly way

гардашчыг, гардашчығаз : *n* little brother

гарәт : *n* 1) robbery, plunder, pillage 2) loot, ill-gotten gains, that which was amassed by robbery 3) booty

гарәтчи : *v* robber, plunderer

гарәтчилик : *n* robbery, brigandage, marauding

гары : *n* 1) old woman *a* 2) old-womanish

гарылашмаг : *v* grow old, advanced in age *a woman* , become an old woman

гарылдамаг : *v* croak, caw

гарылдашмаг : *v* croak, caw *by many together*

гарылты : *n* croaking, cawing

гарымаг : *v* remain/stay unmarried too long 2) wave the hand contemptuously at s.o. *both hands spreading the fingers*

гарын : *n* 1) stomach, belly *a* 2) abdominal

гарыналты : *n* belly-band *of a horse* ; cinch *of a saddle, girth strap*

гарынгулу : *n* 1) glutton, gourmandizer *a* 2) gluttonous

гарынгулулуг : *n* gluttony, gluttonizing

гарынәнә : *n* old woman

гарынлы : *n* 1) paunchy, big-bellied 2) see **гарынгулу**

гарынсыз : *a* paunchless, having no belly

гарынүстү : *a* belly *located on the belly*

гарыхдырычы : *a* inconsistent, confusing

гарыхдырмаг : *v* tangle, confuse, puzzle, perplex s.o.

гарыхма : *n* confusion, embarrassment, perplexity

гарыхмаг : *v* get confused, muddled

гарычыг, гарычығаз : *n* little old lady

гарыш : *n* span; inch

гарышга : *n zool* 1) ant *a* 2) ant

гарышгаjejән : *n* anteater, ant-bear *Myrmecophaga jubata*

гарыш-гарыш : *adv* span by span, inch by inch

гарышдыра-гарышдыра : *adv* mixing, blending, mixing together, stirring, agitating

гарышдырылмаг : *v* 1) meddle *with* , interfere *with* 2) interblend, commingle; be mixed, compounded 3) be moved *somewhere else* 4) be shuffled *cards*

гарышдырычы : *n* instigator, inciter

гарышдырычылыг : *n* instigation, incitement

гарышдырма : *n* mixing, stirring, agitation

гарышдырмаг : *v* 1) stir, agitate, blend, intermix, intermingle; pour out 2) shuffle *cards* 3) rumple, tousle, dishevel

гарышдыртмаг : *caus of* **гарышдырмаг**

гарышыг : *a* 1) mixed 2) tangled, confused; illegible, undecipherable; disorderly 3) heterogeneous *n* 4) mixture, blend

гарышыглы : *a* blended, with an admixture

гарышыглыг : *n* 1) confusion; illegibility 2) disorder, disturbance, agitation, commotion, hurley-burley, muddle

гарышыгсыз : *a* pure, without admixture/adulteration

гарышламаг : *v* measure with a span

гарышма : *n* 1) confusion 2) interference 3) complication *of an illness*

гарышмаг : *v* mix, interblend, mingle, get mixed up 2) interfere *in* 3) become complicated *illness* 4) bristle, stick up

гарышмамазлыг : *n* non-intervention

гарламаг : *v* 1) snow 2) cover with snow

гарлы : *a* 1) snowy 2) snow-covered

гармаг : *n* 1) hook; fish hook 2) fishing rod *v* 3) bend

гарма-гарыш, гарма-гарышыг : *a* 1) entangled, intricate, involved; disorderly, chaotic 2) incomprehensible, unintelligible

гарма-гарышыглыг : *n* 1) disorder, chaos, confusion, muddle, mess, jumble

гармагвары : *a* hooked, jagged

гармагламаг : *v* take on a hook, catch with a fish hook

гармагчыг : *n* little hook

гарамаламаг : *v* seize with the fingers, rake up wuth the hands, snatch out, intercept, grab, lay hold of, put one's paws around

гармон : *n* accordion, concertina

гармонгаjыран : *n* master accordion-maker

гармончалан, гармончу : *n* accordionist

гармончулуг : *n* profession of accordionist

гарныjекә, гарныjоғун : *a* big-bellied, paunchy

гарнытох : *a* satisfied, replete, full

гаровул : *n* guard, watch

гаровулламаг : *v* 1) guard, stand guard/watch 2) sight, range, take aim at

гаровулхана : *n* guard room, guardhouse

гаровулчу : *n* 1) watchman *a* 2) guard, watch

гаровулчулуг : *n* service/duty/work of a watchman

гарпыз : *n* water-melon

гарпыш-гарпыш : *adv* so as to cross one's path, so as to cross the line along which s.o/s.t. moves

гарпышдырмаг : *v* snatch away, snatch up

гарпышмаг : *v* grab one another

гарпма : *n* grabbing, catching, snatching, snatching out

гарпмаг : *v* snatch, seize, grab, snatch out, intercept, put one's paws around

гарпун : *v* harpoon

гарсаг : *n* 1) frill, flounce 2) tuck 3) stitch

гарсаламаг : *v* 1) burn, scorch

гарсаланмаг : *v* burn o.s., singe o.s.

гарсыма : *n* tucking, tuck *of clothing*

гарсымаг : *v* tuck, take tucks *in clothing*

гарт : *a* 1) old wolf, mature 2) tough *poultry, vegetables*

гартал : *n* 1) eagle *a* 2) eagle, aquiline

garталмаг : *v* see **гартлашмаг**

гартдамаг : *v* constantly scratch oneself

гартданмаг : *pass* be constantly scratched

гартәмизләjән : *n* snow-plow

гартымаг : *v* 1) grow to full size 2) become tough *poultry*

гартымыш : *a* 1) grown old/advanced in years 2) hardened, inveterate 3) grown tough *poultry*

гартлашмаг : *v* 1) grow old, become advanced in years 2) grow to full size, grow hardened 3) become tough *poultry*

гартлыг : *n* old age

гартмаг : *n* scab, crust

гартмагланмаг : *pass* be covered with scabs/crusts

гартмаглы : *a* covered with scabs/a crust, scab-covered, encrusted

гаршы : *a* 1) opposite *adv* 2) against, opposite

гаршы-гаршыjа : *adv* opposite, face to face, vis-a-vis

гаршыдурма : *n* resistance, opposition

гаршыламаг : *v* meet, go to meet

гаршыланмаг : *pass* be met

гаршылашдырма : *n* 1) comparison *a* 2) comparative

гаршылашдырмаг : *v* compare

гаршылашдыртмаг : *v* request/have s.o. compare

гаршылашмаг : *v* 1) be met with 2) come together for battle, measure strengths/forces

гаршылыг : *n* response *to kindness, favor etc* , remuneration, compensation

гаршылыглы : *a* 1) mutual, reciprocal 2) proceeding from opposite direction, head *as in 'head wind'* *adv* mutually, reciprocally

гаршысыалынмаз : *a* 1) irresistable 2) inevitable

гаршысында : *prep* before

гасид : *n* messenger, courier; herald

гасыг : *n* *anat* 1) groin 2) pubis 3) scrotum

гасыгүстү : *a* *anat* supraorbital, pertaining to the brow/forehead

гасырға : *n* whirlwind, tornado, hurricane

гаснаг : *n* 1) drum *component of various mechanisms in the form of a cylinder, usually hollow,* sheave *a grooved pulley, wheel* 2) crochet hook

гастрол : *n* 1) tour *theatrical etc a* 2) tour, touring

гастролчу : *n* guest artist, actor on tour

гастроном : *n* food store, grocery

гастрономик : *a* 1) gastronomic 2) pertaining to a grocery or foodstore

гат : *n* 1) layer, stratum, bed 2) storey, floor 3) fold, crimp 4) see **дəфə**

гатар : *n* 1) train 2) composition, make-up 3) file, row; caravan *any sequence of objects* ; flock, flight *birds* 3) katar an eastern melody

гатар-гатар : *adv* in files, rows, sequences; in/by flights

гатардүзəлдəн : *n* yard-master *railroad yard official whose duty it is to oversee and approve the composition of departing trains*

гатарланмаг : *v* draw up/form files/rows/ranks

гатбагат : *adv* in layers/beds/strata

гат-гарышыг : *a* 1) confused, tangled 2) displaced, moved somewhere else 3) disheveled, tousled

гат-гарышыглыг : *n* see **гарышыглыг**

гат-гат : *a* 1) folded, plicated, stratified *adv* 2) much more 3) very much more, by far more 4) in strata/layers

гат-гатлыг : *n* stratification, foliation

гатгы : *n* admixture, alloy

гатгылы : *a* alloyed; containing impurities/ admixtures

гатгысыз : *a* pure, unalloyed

гатил : *n* murderer, slayer, killer, assassin

гаты : *a* 1) thick, dense, non-liquid 2)severe, stern, strict, tough

гатыб-гатышдырмаг : *v* create confusion, muddle up

гатыг : *n* yoghurt

гатыгашы : *n* 1) soup/pottage of rice, vegetables and yoghurt *fig* 2) confusion, muddle, chaos *a fig* 3) tangled up, displaced

гатыготу : *bot* bedstraw, cleavers *Galium*

гатыгсатан : *n* seller of yoghurt

гатыгчалан : *n* yoghurt-maker *agent*

гатыланмаг : *v* see **гатылашмаг**

гатылатмаг : *v* thicken, make thick

гатылашдырычы : *n* thickener, coagulant

гатылашдырмаг : *v* see **гатылатмаг**

гатылашма : *n* thickening, coagulation

гатылашмаг : *v* thicken, grow/become thick, coagulate

гатылы : *a* with an admixture, adulterated, impure

гатылыг : *n* 1) thickness, density, viscosity 2) concentration, strength

гатылыш : *v* see **гатылма**

гатылма : *v* fr. **гатылмаг**

гатылмаг : *pass* be admixed, alloyed, be added to, be diluted

гатыр : *n* mule

гатыргујруғу : *n bot* horsetail *Equisetum*

гатырчы : *n* one who keeps mules

гатышдырылма : *v* fr. **гатышдырылмаг**

гатышдырылмаг : *pass* 1) be mixed 2) be shifted, transferred, moved elsewhere

гатышдырмаг : *v* mix, intermingle, blend

гатышыг : *n* 1) mixture 2) adulteration 3) alloy *a* 4) mixed

гатышыглыг : *n* agitation, commotion, disturbance, turmoil

гатышмаг : *pass* 1) be mixed, blended, fused 2) be mixed up *in*, implicated

гатлајычы : *n publ* folder *agent*

гатлама : *n* 1) assembling *i.e pages in a printing plant* 2) folding *printed materials a* 3) folding 4) collapsible

гатламаг : *v* 1) lay together, assemble, collate; bend 2) fold *printed materials*

гатланмаг : *pass* 1) be assembled, collated 2) be bended

гатлатдырмаг : *caus of* **гатламаг**

гатлашылмаз : *a* intolerable, unbearable *adv*

гатлашмаг : *v* 1) tolerate, bear, endure, put up *with* , accept 2) be formed into layers, stratify

гатма : *v* 1) from **гатмаг** 2) scrap of rope, bit of rope/twine

гатмаг : *v* 1) mix, blend, admix, mix in 2) join *to* , add *to*

гатма-гарышыг : *a* 1) tangled, muddled; indecipherable *n* 2) confusion, chaos

гатма-гарашыглыг : *n* confusion, muddle, mess, chaos, jumble

гатран : *n* tar, pitch

гатранламаг : *v* prime with pitch, cover, coat, smear with tar/pitch

гатранланмаг : *pass* be tarred, coated with tar/pitch

гатранлатдырмаг, гатранлатмаг : *v* request/have s.o. tar/coat with tar/smear with tar/pitch

гатранлы : *a* impregnated with tar, pitch, tarred; oil-treated

гатранхана : *n* 1) tar-pot 2) tar-works, tar factory, tar distillery

гатранчəкəн : *n* tar-extractor *agent* , tar-production specialist

гафгаз : *n* 1) the Caucasus *a* 2) Caucasian

гафгазлы : *n* a Caucasian *native/resident of the Caucasus*

гафиjə : *n* rhyme

гафиjəбаз : *n* rhymer, rhymster

гафиjəли : *a* rhymed

гах : *n* dried fruits

гахач : *n* 1) dried *dry-cured* meat *a* 2) dried *dry-cured*

гахачгаjыран : *n* smoker *agent*, meat and fish smoke-curing specialist

гахачхана : *n* smoke-house *establishment for smoke-curing meat and fish products*

гахаччы : *n* see **гахачгаjыран**

гахгаjыран, гахгурудан : *n* fruit-drier *specialist in the production of dried fruit*

гахылмаг : *pass* be stuck into, driven into, thrust/plunged into

гахынч : *n* reproach

гахмаг : *v* stick into, drive into, thrust/plunge into

гахсымаг : *v* get rotten

Гаһирə : *n* Cairo

гаһмар : *n* defender, protector, champion

гаһмарлыг, гаһмарчылыг : *n* intercession, mediation

гачаг : *n* 1) robber, brigand 2) fugitive, runaway, deserter 3) smuggler *a* 4) contraband

гачагач : *n* 1) general flight, mass escape 2) running about

гача-гача : *adv* running, while running

гачагбашы : *n* gang-leader, robber-chief

гачаг-гачаг : *n* children's game of "Robin Hood" *the generous outlaw*

гачаглыг : *n* robbery, plundering, brigandage

гачагчы : *n* smuggler

гачагчылыг : *n* the smuggler's trade

гачаған : *n* 1) runner, racer 2) fast horse

гачараг : *adv* run, running, on the double, double-quick

гачгын : *n* 1) refugee; immigrant *a* 2) fugitive

гачды-тутду : *n* run-and-catch *children's game*

гачылмаз : *a* inevitable, unavoidable

гачынмаг : *v* 1) avoid s.t./s.o. 2) abstain *from*, refrain *from* ; deviate *from*, avoid, shun s.t.

гачырдылмаг : *v* see **гачырылмаг**

гачырылмаг : *v* 1) be taken/led away, carried off, driven away, kidnapped 2) be overlooked, be lost from sight

гачырмаг, гачыртмаг : *v* 1) take/lead away, carry off 2) allow to escape, run off; allow to set free, let slip, go past

гачыш : *n* 1) run, running 2) flight, escape

гачышма : *n* 1) running about/around; *mass* flight/escape 2) track meet, competition in running

гачышмаг : *v* 1) take a run, compete in running 2) chase one another

гачма : *n* running

гачмаг : *v* 1) run, run away 2) steal away, sneak off, hide o.s. 3) evade, elude, escape, abstain/refrain *from*

гачһагач : *n* see **гачагач**

гачарлар : *n* the Kajar *Turkic tribe in Northern Iran which founded a 19th century dynasty of Iranian shahs*

гаш : *n* 1) eyebrow 2) mounted precious stone

гашалма : *n* plucking of superfluous hairs from the eyebrows of the bride before sending her in to the groom

гашанмаг : *v* urinate *animals*

гашарасы : *n* bridge of the nose

гашга : *n* 1) blaze, white spot on the forehead of an animal *a* 2) animal with a blaze, a white spot on the forehead

гашгабаг : *n* gloomy/sullen person

гашгабаглы : *a* gloomy, sullen, scowling, morose

гашгабаглылыг : *n* sullenness, moroseness, gloominess

гашгалдаг : *n zool* 1) large aquatic bird *Fulica Atra* with grey-black plumage and a bright white excrescence/tubercle on the forehead *coll* 2) bony, scrawny, skinny

гашыг : *n* spoon

гашыггаjыран : *n* spoon-maker

гашыгламаг : *v* eat/drink liquids *with a spoon*

гашыма : *n* 1) combing 2) scraping

гашымаг : *v* 1) scratch *the body* 2) scrape

гашындырмаг : *v* cause itching/the itch/scabies

гашынма : *v* 1) from **гашынмаг** 2) itching, the itch, scabies

гашынмаг : *v* 1) scratch o.s. 2) fell an itch, itch, be itching

гашынты : *n* 1) itching 2) scrapings

гашытдырмаг : *caus of* **гашымаг**

гашов : *n* curry-comb, horse-comb

гашовламаг : *v* clean with a curry-comb

гашовланмаг : *pass* be cleaned with a curry-comb

гашовлатдырмаг, гашовлатмаг : *v* request/have s.o. clean with a curry-comb, request/have s.o. curry

гашсыз : *a* having no eyebrows, eyebrowless

гашүстү : *a anat* superciliary

гвардија : *n* 1) Guards *elite military units* *a* 2) Guards

гвардијачы : *n* Guardsman *member of elite military unit*

гејбәт : *n* 1) judgement by default, judgement in absentia 2) malignant gossip, scandal, backbiting 3) squabbles, annoyances, unpleasantnesses 4) piece of scandal, whispering 5) malicious report, denunciation

гејбәтчи : *n* gossip, tale-bearer, informer, stool pigeon, slanderer, abuser, reviler

гејбәтчилик : *n* informing, denouncing, accusing

гејбәтчил : *n* scandalmonger, inveterate gossip, chronic backbiter

гејд : *n* 1) comment; proviso 2) note, marginal note 3) fact of noticing, taking care of 4) registering

гејдкеш : *a* careful, thoughtful, solicitous

гејдкешлик : *n* care, consideration, thoughtfulness, solicitude

гејдсиз : *a* careless, inconsiderate, unthoughtful

гејсизлик : *n* lack of consideration/care unthoughtfulness, unsolicitousness, indifference

гејдчи : *n* registrar

гејз : *n* anger, wrath, ire, fury, rage

гејзлә : *adv* angrily, wrathfully, furiously, irately

гејзләндирмәк : *v* anger, embitter, infuriate

гејзләнмәк : *v* become angered/incensed, fall into a rage, grow furious

гејзләтмәк : *v* see **гејзләндирмәк**

гејзли : *a* 1) angry, angered, enraged, furious, wrathful *adv* 2) irately, angrily, furiously

гејзли-гејзли : *adv* see **гејзли**

гејзлилик : *n* wrathfulness, irateness, state of rage/fury

гејр : *a* see **гејри**

гејрәт : *n* 1) courage, sense of honor, manliness 2) zeal *in the interests of production, family etc* 3) fervor, ardor

гејрәтлә : *adv* 1) zealously, fervently 2) courageously, honorably, in a manly way

гејрәтләндирмәк : *v* arouse, impart courage, hearten, inspire

гејрәтләнмәк : *v* 1) become diligent/zealous 2) be inspired, be filled with enthusiasm

гејрәтли : *a* 1) zealous, painstaking 2) standing up for one's own or s.o. else's honor/dignity

гејрәтлилик : *n* zeal, zealous relationship to business/affairs/honor

гејрәтсиз : *a* 1) not zealous, careless, indifferent, unsolicitous 2) faint-hearted, not reacting to insult or dishonor 3) cowardly

гејрәтсизлик : *n* 1) absence of zeal 2) faint-heartedness, indifference, lack of solicitude 3) dishonor, disgrace

гејрәтсизчә, гејрәтсизчәсинә : *adv* 1) faint-heartedly, unconcernedly 2) dishonestly, cowardly, disgracefully

гејри : *a* 1) other, another, different *prep* 2) as a prefix imparts a negative sense to a word as "un-, in-, non-, without-, sans-"

гејри-ади : *a* 1) unusual, uncommon, extraordinary, abnormal *adv* 2) unusually, uncommonly, extraordinarily, abnormally

гејри-гануни : *a* 1) unlawful, illegal *adv* 2) unlawfully, illegally

гејри-инсани : *a* 1) inhuman, brutal *adv* 2) inhumanly, brutally

гејри-иради : *a* see **гејри-ихтијари**

гејри-ихтијари : *a* 1) involuntary, mechanical, automatic 2) unconsciously, involuntarily, mechanically, without thinking

гејри-кафи : *a* 1) unsatisfactory *adv* 2) unsatisfactorily

гејри-мәһдуд : *a* 1) unlimited, limitless, unrestricted *adv* 2) limitlessly, unrestrictedly

гејри-мүәјјән : *a* 1) indeterminate, not fixed, indefinite *adv* 2) indeterminately, indefinitely

гејри-мүмкүн : *a* impossible

гејри-мүнтәзәм : *a* 1) uneven, irregular *adv* 2) unevenly, irregularly

гејри-мүтәшәккил : *a* 1) unorganized, disorganized *adv* 2) in an unorganized/disorganized manner

гејри-низами : *a* irregular

гејри-рәсми : *a* 1) unofficial *adv* 2) unofficially

гејри-сәмими : *a* 1) insincere *adv* 2) insincerely

гејри-тәбии : *a* 1) unnatural *adv* 2) unnaturally

гејри-үзви : *a* inorganic

гејри-һәгиги : *a* 1) inefficacious, invalid *adv* 2) invalidly

гејри-чидди : *a* 1) not serious, light, frivolous *adv* 2) not seriously, frivolously

гејри-шүури : *a* 1) mechanically, automatically

гејсәр : *n* Caesar

гәбалә, гәбаләнамә : *n* property title

гәбаһәт : *n* vileness, infamy, abomination, reprehensible act

гәбз : *n* receipt

гәбзә : *n* hilt, grip handle, shaft

гәбиз : *n* *med* constipation

гәбилә : *n* tribe, clan

гәбир : *n* 1) grave *a* 2) grave, sepulchral

гәбиргазан : *n* grave-digger

гәбиристан, гәбиристанлыг : *n* cemetery

гәбиһ : *a* infamous, foul, vile, obscene

гәбул : *n* 1) acceptance, receiving, reception *a* 2) accepting, receiving

гәбул етмәк : *v* accept

гәбуледилмәз : *a* unacceptable

гәбуледичи : *n* 1) examiner, inspector *of products in a factory* 2) receptionist 3) radio-set

гәдд : *n* stature, size, height, figure

гәддар : *a* 1) insidious, perfidious, crafty 2) fierce, cruel, pitiless, unmerciful

гәддарлыг : *n* 1) cruelty, rage, ferocity 2) despotism, tyranny

гәддарчасына : *adv* 1) cruelly, furiously 2) tyrannically, despotically

гәдд-гамәт : *n* carriage, bearing, figure, build

гәдд-гамәтли : *a* well-proportioned, well-built, shapely, stately; grandiose

гәддәмәк : *v* sharpen

гәдәк : *n* 1) blue calico *a* 2) blue calico

гәдәм : *n* step, pace

гәдәмһагты : *n* payment for a visit *to a doctor etc*

гәдәр : *n* 1) quantity *postp* 2) around, about, up to *setting a quantitive limit* 3) till, until 4) as far as

гәдәрсиз : *a* countless, innumerable, numberless

гәдәһ : *n* decanter, giblet, wine-glass

гәдим : *a* old, ancient, antique

гәдимдән : *adv* of yore, from olden days, long since; since olden times; from time immemorial

гәдими : *a* 1) old, ancient 2) antique, age-old

гәдимлик : *n* antiquity

гәдир : *n* dignity, significance, importance, worth

гәдирбилән : *a* 1) gratifying, rewarding, worthy *n* 2) shrewd *fig* conoisseur

гәдир-гијмәт : *n* see **гәдир**

гәдләмәк : *v* see **гәддәмәк**

гәза : *n* 1) sad occurrence 2) accident 3) fate, destiny

гәза-гәдәр : *n* 1) fate, destiny 2) predestination

гәзет : *n* 1) newspaper *a* 2) newspaper

гәзетсатан : *n* seller of newspapers

гәзетчи : *n* journalist

гәзетчилик : *n* 1) the newspaper business 2) journalism, the profession of journalist

гәзәб : *n* 1) wrath, fury, rage 2) bitterness, animosity

гәзәбләндирмәк : *v* 1) anger, incense, infuriate, enrage 2) embitter

гәзәбләнмәк : *v* *intr* 1) be angry *with* , become/get furious, rage, get into a rage, get mad

гәзәбли : *a* angry, irate, incensed, furious, infuriated

гәзәват : *n* Gazavat, a religious war conducted by Muslims against infidels *also 'jihad'*

гәзәл : *n* "ghazel" *Arabic* a type of lyric poetry popular in Moslem literature

гәзијјә : *n* see **гәзә** 3)

гәзил : *n* 1) goat's wool 2) string/twine made of sheep's wool

гәјјум : *n* 1) guardian, tutor 2) executor *of a will*

гәјјумлуг : *n* 1) guardianship *a* 2) guardian

гәлб : *n* 1) soul, heart 2) forged/fake document *a* 3) false, forged, fake

гәлбән : *adv* cordially, from the heart feelingly, sincerely

гәлби : *a* 1) high *adv* 2) highly

гәлбигара : *a* 1) distrustful, mistrustful. suspicious of s.t.

гәлбиләндирмәк : *v* elevate, raise, lift up higher

гәлбиләнмәк, гәлбиләшмәк *pass* be elevated, raised, lifted up higher

гәлбилик : *n* height, altitude

гәлбир : *n* sieve

гәлбирләмәк : *v* sift through a sieve

гәлбисыныг : *a* offended, hurt

гәлблик : *n* 1) forgery; falsity, falseness 2) dishonesty

гәлбсиз : *a* callous, heartless, unfeeling

гәләбә : *n* 1) victory, triumph *a* 2) victorious, triumphal/triumphant

гәләбәлик : *n* 1) populousness, overcrowding *a* 2) noisy, crowded, overcrowded

гәләви : *n chem* 1) alkali *a* 2) alkaline

гәләвиләшдирилмәк : *v* alkalize

гәләвиләшдирмәк : *v* alkalize; lixiviate, leach, leach out

гәләм : *n* 1) pen, penholder; reed pen 2) graft 3) cutting tool; chisel

гәләмдан : *n* pen case; pencil box

гәләмә : *n* 1) *bot* poplar *Populus L* *a* 2) poplar

гәләмучу : *n* pen

гәләндәр : *n* 1) "God's Fool" *simple-minded person believed to possess the divine gift of prophesy* hermit, anchorite, recluse, dervish, wandering "holy-man"

гәләндәрлик : *n* life of a dervish, God's Fool

гәләт : *n* error, mistake, inaccuracy, blunder

гәләт-гүләт : *n* a mass/tissue of errors/mistakes

гәләти-мәшһур : *n* 1) widely-recognized error *ling* 2) ingrained/deeply-rooted linguistic solecism

гәләтсиз : *a* 1) faultless, unerring *adv* 2) faultlessly, unerringly

гәлиб : *n* 1) form, mold, model, last 2) thick felt for covering a yurt, felt mat[ting] 3) construction form[s] *i.e. for cement*

гәлибгајыран : *n* molder, mold-maker

гәлибләмәк : *v* place on a last

гәлибләтдирмәк, гәлибләтмәк *caus of* **гәлибләмәк**

гәлибчи : *n* see **гәлибгајыран**

гәлиз : *a* 1) thick, oversaturated 2) pompous, bombastic, turgid *speech, writing* 3) convoluted, complicated

гәлизләндирмәк, гәлизләшдирмәк : *v* thicken, make thick, make saturated

гәлизләнмәк, гәлизләшмәк : *v intr* thicken, grow thick, coagulate, solidify

гәлизлик : *n* 1) thickness, density 2) saturation 3) bombasticism, pomposity *speech*

гәлјан : *n* hookah *an Oriental tobacco pipe having a long, flexible tube that passes through a vessel of water, thus colling the smoke, also called kalian, hubble-bubble, narghile*

гәлјаналты : *n* snack; light meal

гәлјаналтыхана : *n* snack-bar

гәлјә : *n* "galya", a dish made of vegetables and meat

гәлпә : *n* 1) splinter, sliver, fragment *a* 2) fragmentary, shrapnel

гәлсәмә : *n zool* gill[s], branchia[e]

гәлсәмәли : *a zool* gilled, branchiate

гәлсәмәсиз : *a* abranchial, without gills

гәм : *n* melancholy, sadness, grief, woe, sorrow

гәм-гүссә : *n* see **гәм**

гәмә : *n* dagger, poniard

гәмәләмәк : *v* stab, wound with a dagger

гәмәләнмәк : *pass* be stabbed/wounded with a dagger

гәмәр : *n* 1) moon 2) *Kamap a female first name*

гәмәри : *a* lunar; moon-shaped

гәмзә : *n* coquetry, affectedness

гәмзәли : *a* coquetish, arch

гәмиш : *n* 1) see **гамиш** *fig* 2) a tiresome, boring, nagging person, a bore

гәмкин : *a* 1) sad, melancholy, morose *adv* 2) sadly, morosely

гәмкин-гәмкин : *adv* see **гәмкин** 2)

гәмкинлик : *n* gloominess, moroseness, sadness, melancholy

гәмләндирмәк : *v* grieve, be sad

гәмләнмәк : *v* be sad, be melancholy, be sad, grieve *for* , mourn *over*

гәмли : *a* sad, melancholy, mournful, pained, depressed

гәмли-гәмли : *adv* see **гәмкин** 2)

гәмсиз : *a* 1) carefree, untroubled, lighthearted 2) without grief, without sadness

гәмчил : *n* knout, whip, lash

гәнаәт : *n* 1) economy, thrift, prudence 2) saving

гәнаәтбәхш : *a* 1) exhaustive, comprehensive; satisfactory *adv* 2) exhaustively, comprehensively; satisfactorily

гәнаәткар : *a* see **гәнаәтчи, гәнаәтчил**

гәнаәткарлыг : *n* see **гәнаәтчиллик**

гәнаәтләндиричи : *a* 1) satisfactory, satisfying *adv* satisfactorily

гәнаәтләндирмәк : *v* satisfy, content

гәнаәтләнмәк : *v intr* be satisfied, content o.s. *with*

гәнаәтчи, гәнаәтчил : *a* economical; thrifty

гәнаәтчиллик : *n* economy, thrift

гәнбәр : *n* 1) cobble-stone 2) gravel

гәнд : *n* 1) sugar *a* 2) sugar, sugary, sugered

гәндаб : *n* syrup; sugar water

гәндгабы, гәнддан : *n* sugar container *bowl, box etc*

гәндил : *n* chandelier

гәним : *n* hater *bitter enemy* , destroyer, tormenter, torturer

гәнимәт : *n* 1) war-booty, spoils of war 2) unexpected, propitious event

гәнимәтчи : *n* self-seeker, grabber

гәнимәтчилик : *n* self-seeking, grabbing

гәннады : *n* 1) confectioner, pastry cook *a* 2) confectioner's, pastry-cook's

гәншәр : *n* 1) opposite side *adv* 2) opposite

гәпик : *n* kopeck

гәпик-гәпик : *adv* in kopecks

гәпик-гуруш : *n* small change

гәпиклик : *a* 1) worth one kopeck *n* 2) a kopeck

гәпикчил : *n dim* kopeck

гәрар : *n* 1) decision, resolution 2) way, method of doing something

гәраркаһ : *n* 1) staff, HQ *of higher military formations* 2) halting place; camp *a* 3) staff, headquarters

гәрарлашдырмаг : *v* 1) establish, decide, determine 2) agree

гәрарлашма : *v* fr. **гәрарлашмаг**

гәрарлашмаг : *v intr* 1) be established, fixed, be determined/formed/shaped, take shape, clarify itself 2) come to an agreement

гәрарнамә : *n* 1) *written* resolution, judgement; 2) decision, resolution 2) sentence, verdict

гәрарсыз : *a* 1) evasive, shifty; restless, fidgety, uneasy 2) inconstant, fickle, changeable

гәрарсызлыг : *n* 1) fidgetiness, restlessness 2) inconstancy, fickleness, changeableness

гәрб : *n* 1) west *a* 2) western

гәрби : *a* western

гәрг : *n* immersion, submersion : **гәрг еләмәк** ***етмәк*** 1) sink *a ship* 2) dip, immerse, plunge *into water*

гәрәз : *n* 1) goal, intent, intention 2) hidden, secret intent[ion], design, object, secret thought 3) weakness *for* , predilection *for* ; malevolence, ill-will, undertone of hostility *adv* 4) in a word, in short

гәрәзлә : *adv* on purpose, purposely, with partiality, with prejudice, intentionally, deliberately

гәрәзли : *a* 1) spiteful, malicious, hostile, inimical, ill-intentioned, with malice aforethought 2) biased, ill-disposed

гәрәзсиз : *a* 1) impartial, unbiased, disinterested, unselfish *adv* 2) disinterestedly, impartially

гәрәзсизлик : *n* impartiallity, disinterestedness, unselfishness, altruism

гәрәзсизчә, гәрәзсизчәсинә : *adv* disinterestedly, no concealed motive intended, openly

гәрәнфил : *n bot* pinks *Dianthus*

гәриб : *a* 1) strange, foreign, alien, unusual, odd, queer *n* 2) foreigner, stranger, alien 3) *Karig a male first name*

гәрибә : *a* 1) remarkable, wonderful, amazing, marvelous 2) strange, queer, odd

гәрибәлик : *n* strangeness, singularity, oddity, queerness

гәриблик : *n* 1) position, situation of being a foreigner/an alien 2) solitude, loneliness 3) foreign/strange land

гәрибсәмәк, гәрибсимәк : *v* feel lonely, homesick, perplexed and alienated

гәринә : *n* 1) space of time equal to 33 years *approx. 1/3 of a century* 2) age, epoch

гәсб : *n* forcible/forced alienation, estrangement, seizure, expropriation, usurpation, appropriation

гәсбкар : *n* aggressor, invader, usurper

гәсбкарлыг : *n* 1) conquest, usurpation, invasion, aggression *a* 2) aggressive, predatory

гәсд : *n* 1) intention, design, purpose 2) attempt 3) goal, aim, determination 4) encroachment

гәсд-гәрәз : *n* malevolence, enmity

гәсдән : *adv* intentionally, on purpose

гәсдсиз : *adv* unintentionally, by accident, inadvertantly

гәсәбә : *n* village, settlement, hamlet, small town, borough

гәсидә : *n* poem of praise, elegaic verse

гәср : *n* palace, castle, tower

гәссаб : *n* butcher

гәссаблыг : *n* profession of butcher

гәссабхана : *n* butcher-shop, butcher's stall *in a market* 2) slaughterhouse, abattoir

гәт : *in compounds with verbs* : **гәт еләмәк етмәк** decide, determine, resolve, decree

гәтедичи : *a* deciding

гәти : *a* 1) categorical, decisive, final, definitive *adv* 2) categorically, finally, conclusively

гәтиjјән : *adv* categorically, absolutely, totally, not at all

гәтиjјәт : *n* resolution, resoluteness, definiteness, categoricalness

гәтиjјәтлә : *adv* resolutely, categorically, irrevocably

гәтиjјәтли : *a* decisive

гәтиjјәтсиз : *a* indecisive

гәтиjјәтсизлик : *n* indecision

гәтилик : *n* decisiveness, categoricalness

гәтл : *n* murder, homicide

гәтнамә : *n* decree, resolution

гәтрә : *n* drop

гәтрә-гәтрә : *adv* drop by drop, in drops

гәттәзә : *a* quite new

гәтфә : *n* bath towel

гәтфәләнмәк : *v* dry o.s. with a bath towel, dry o.s. off, towel o.s. down

гәфәс : *n* cage

гәфәсә : *n* shelf, shelving, set of shelves

гәфил, гәфилдән : *adv* see **гәфләтән**

гәфләт : *n* 1) ignorance, lack of information, scanty information, state of being ill-informed 2) benightedness, incomprehension 3) inattention, remissness, unconcern, carelessness, negligence *fig* 4) hibernation

гәфләтән : *adv* suddenly, all of a sudden, unexpectedly; inadvertently, by chance

гәhвә : *n* 1) coffee *a* 2) coffee

гәhвәдан : *n* coffee pot

гәhвәjи : *a* coffee-colored

гәhвәхана : *n* coffee-house, cafe

гәhгәhә : *n* *loud* laughter

гәhәт : *n* 1) shortage *a* 2) quantitatively insufficient, scant, meager

гәhәтләшмәк : *v* grow scarce, disappear, become rare, be in short supply

гәhәтлик : *n* 1) shortage, deficiency, insufficiency, inadequacy, lack 2) crop failure 3) famine

гәhрәман : *n* 1) hero, man of courage, brave spirit *a* 2) heroic

гәhрәманлыг : *n* 1) heroism, heroic deed *a* 2) heroic

гәhрәманчасына : *adv* heroically, valiantly

гәчәлә : *n* *zool* magpie *genus Pica*

гәшәнк : *a* 1) beautiful, handsome, pretty, charming, chic, delightful, smart *adv* 2) beautifully, charmingly, delightfully

гәшәнкләнмәк : *v* see **гәшәнкләшмәк** :

гәшәнкләшдирмәк : *v* color, paint, smarten up, make to look nice/well

гәшәнкләшмәк : *v* 1) grow prettier 2) spruce o.s. up, doll o.s. up 3) become beautiful, handsome, lovely

гәшәнклик : *n* 1) grace, gracefulness, elegance, 2) splendor, refinement

гәшәнкчә : *adv* beautifully, gracefully, finely, charmingly

гәшш : *n* faint, fainting fit, swoon

гиблә, гибләкаh : *n* *relig* qibla : *the direction towards Mecca to which Moslems turn their faces at prayer*

гибләнүма : *n* *rare* compass *device pointing at Mecca*

гибтә : *n* envy

гида : *n* food, nourishment

гидаландырычы : *a* feeding, feed, nourishing

гидаландырмаг : *v* feed, nourish

гидаланма : *n* nourishment

гидаланмаг : *v* feed *on* , live on, receive nourishment

гидалы : *a* nourishing, nutritious

гидалылыг : *n* nutritiousness

гидасыз : *a* unnourishing, un-nutritious

гиіаби : *a* 1) by default, in absentia *as in judgement by default/ in absentia;* correspondence *as in correspondence course external as in external student; one who is registered in college but studies independently adv* 2) by correspondence

гиіабичи : *n* external student, student taking correspondence course

гиіам : *n* insurrection, mutiny, revolt, rebellion

гиіамәт : *n* 1) end of the world, doomsday, judgement day *Arabic lit. resurrection a* 2) terrific!, marvellous!, great!

гиіамчы : *n* rebel, mutineer

гиіафә, гиіафәт : *n* physiognomy, face; appearance, outward appearance, exterior, look, aspect, mien

гиііә : *n* whooping, scream, shout

гиімә : *n* ground meat

гиімәкеш : *n* kitchen knife, chopper

гиімәт : *n* 1) price, cost 2) value, valuation 3) mark, grade (in courses, studies) 4) estimation

гиімәтгоіан : *n* appraiser, price-fixer, valuer, estimator

гиімәтләндирилмәк : *pass* be priced, evaluated, appraised, appreciated, estimated

гиімәтләндирмәк : *v* value, evaluate, appraise, fix the price of, estimate, appreciate

гиімәтләшмәк : *v* ask the price of; come to an agreement about the price

гиімәтли : *a* valuable, precious

гиімәтсиз : *a* 1) worthless, of no value 2) cheap

гиімәтсизлик : *n* insignificance, valuelessness

гираәт : *n* reading

гираәтхана : *n* reading room

гисас : *n* vengeance

гисим : *n* share, portion

гисим-гисим : *adv* in parts/portions, piecemeal

гисмән : *adv* partly, partially, in part, by degrees

гисмәт : *n* 1) part, portion, share, apportionment 2) fate, lot, predestination, predetermination *math* 3) quotient

гит'ә : *n* 1) continent, mainland *a* 2) continental, mainland

гиша : *n anat* membrane

гывраг : *a* 1) adroit, lively, alert, chipper, active 2) hale and hearty, healthy

гывраглашмаг : *v* 1) become proficient, get the hang of, become/get good at 2) become/grow hale and hearty/healthy 3) get better, recover, get well

гывраглыг : *n* liveliness, jauntiness, chipperness, nimbleness, robustness, heartiness

гыврыг : *a* see **гыврым**

гыврыла-гыврыла : *a* extremely winding *road* ; very curly, all in curls

гыврылмаг : *v* 1) writhe, squirm, scrunch down, huddle up, roll up 2) coil, wriggle 3) curl, wave

гыврылтма : *n* waving, curling

гыврылтмаг : *v* wave, curl, frizzle

гыврым : *a* 1) curly, curly-headed 2) twisted, curled, frizzled, crimped *n* 3) lock, curl

гыврым-гыврым : *a* strongly twisting/winding together, extremely curly, all in curls

гыврыхмаг : *v* 1) writhe, squirm 2) fidget, move restlessly

гыҹ : camel, sheep, and goat dung

гыҹылдамаг : *v* 1) utter a squeak/chirp, laugh *of a child* 2) lisp *specifically, to have difficulty pronouncing the Azerbaijani and Russian /r/ phoneme*

гыҹылты : *n* squeak, chirp, loud laughter *a child*

гыҹылчым : *n* spark

гыҹылчымланмаг : *v* sparkle, scintillate

гыҹылчымлы : *a* sparkling, scintillating

гыҹылчымсачан : *n* see **гортөкан**

гыҹылчымсыз : *a* sparkless

гыҹырдаг : *n anat* 1) cartilage, gristle *a* 2) cartilaginous, gristly

гыҹырдаглы : *a* cartilaginous, rather gristly, on the gristly side

гыҹламаг : *v* defecate, drop dung *of camels, sheep and goats*

гыдыг : *n* tickling

гыдыглама : *n* tickling

гыдыгламаг : *v* tickle

гыдыгланмаг : *v* be subject to tickling

гыдыглашмаг : *v* tickle one another

гыдылбурун : *a* snub-nosed

гыжгыжы : *n zool* click-beetle, elater *Elateridae*

гыжылдамаг : *v* flow violently/noisily

гыжылты : *n* noise/sound of swiftly flowing water

гыжов : *n* violent/storm-tossed flow of a river

гыжhагыж : *n* violent/storm-tossed, noisy flow of water

гыз : *n* 1) girl, little girl, lass, young woman, lady 2) daughter 3) virgin 4) *often used as a familiar address to any woman, especially by other women*

гызабахма : bride-show *the prospect whereby the bridal prospect meets her prospective parents'-in-law* and is *'looked over' by them*

гызардылмаг : *v* 1) be roasted, browned *meat* ; be flushed, reddened *fig* 2) be ashamed

гызарыб-бозармаг : *v* 1) redden, turn red, flush 2) turn/grow pale 3) change countenance 4) be ashamed *of*

гызарма : *v* fr. **гызармаг**

гызармаг : *v* 1) redden, turn red, flush 2) roast, broil, brown *of* 3) be ashamed *of*

гызартдаг : *a* brown, browned, crisp; reddish

газартдырмаг : *caus of* **гызартмаг**

гызарты : *n* 1) redness, red spot, high color, flush 2) glow

гызартма : *n* 1) roast meat *vn* 2) of **гызартмаг**

гызартмаг : *v* 1) roast, broil, brown, bake 2) make nice and brown *fig* 3) give a good scolding, dress down

гызбәјәнмә : *n* see **гызбахма**

гызгушу : *n zool* lapwing, peewit *Vanellus vanellus* , a plover-like Old World bird

гызғын : *a* 1) hot; warm 2) ardent, passionate 3) intense *adv* 4) hotly, warmly *n* 5) climax, highest point

гызғынлыг : *n* 1) heat, quick/hot temper, fury, rage, white-rage 2) enthusiasm, exhortation, passion, excitement

гызғынча, гызғынчасына : *adv* hotly, furiously, passionately, intensely

гыздырылмаг : *v* 1) get warm 2) get warmed up/heated up, be heated

гыздырычы : *n* heating-man *worker responsible for heating s.t.* ; heater *appliance a* 2) heating

гыздырма : *v* 1) from **гыздырмаг** *med* 2) high temperature, temperature 3) malaria, fever 4) burning, heating

гыздырмаг : *v* 1) heat, warm, warm up, heat up, preheat *med* 2) have a temperature 3) have a fever, be ill with malaria

гыздырмалы : *n* 1) one suffering from malaria, malarial patient *a* 2) malarial, febrile

гыздыртмаг : *v* request/ have s.o. heat *up* , warm *up* , preheat s.t.

гызыл : *n* 1) gold *a* 2) gold, golden 3) red

гызылағач : *n bot* 1) alder, alder tree *Alnus L a* 2) alder

гызылағачлыг : *n* alder thickets

гызылазар : *n med* scarlet fever

гызылахтаран : *n* gold-prospector

гызылбалыг : *n zool* salmon

гызылбаш : *n bot* 1) aspen mushroom *Boletus rufus a* 2) red-headed, ruddy-headed 3) Shiite Moslem *colloquial slightly obsolete*

гызылбоз : *a* reddish-grey

гызылгаз : *n zool* flamingo

гызылганадлы : *a ornit* red-winged

гызылгујруг : *n zool* song-bird of the thrush family, having a reddish-brown tail

гызылгуш : *n* falcon, hawk

гызылы : *a* golden, gold-colored, gold, aureous

гызылјел : *n med* see **машара**

гызылкүл : *n bot* rose *Rosa L*

гызыллы : *a* gold-bearing, auriferous

гызылсач, гызылсачлы : *a* golden-haired, reddish-golden haired

гызылсығырчын : *n zool* see **гыларгушу**

гызылча : *n med* measles, rubeola

гызылчалы : *a* ill with measles, suffering from measles

гызынма : *v* fr. **гызынмаг**

гызынмаг : *pass* be heated *up* , be warmed *up*

гызырғаланмаг : *v* 1) feel sorry for s.o, for s.t. 2) stint, grudge, be sparing

газыхмаг : *v* become passionate

гызышган : *a* 1) quick-tempered, hot-tempered, vehement, impassioned 2) reckless, excitable

гызышганлыг : *n* 1) passion, fervor, 2) quick/hot temper 3) ardor, excitement

гызышдыра-гызышдыра : *adv* 1) warming up, stirring up, rousing 2) inciting, instigating, egging on

гызышдырмаг : *v* 1) warm *up,* heat *up* 2) incite, stir up, rouse, egg on , instigate 3) excite, vex, irritate

гызышма : *v* 1) from **гызышмаг** 2) excitement, passion

гызышмаг : *v intr* 1) warm up, get warm 2) get excited, angry 3) fly into a temper, lose control of o.s., rage, bluster, blow up 4) become provoked, become furious, get mad

гызлаpгушу : *n zool* bee-eater *any of a number of brightly-colored insectivorous birds of the family Meropidae, order Corasiiformes;* the most common European representative is Merops-apiaster

гызлыг : *n* 1) step-daughter 2) girlhood; virginity

гызма : *n* 1) heating *up* , warming *up met* 2) annealing *v* 3) from **гызмаг**

гызмаг : *v* 1) warm o.s., get warm 2) get angry, be irritated 3) become excited 4) rely upon, trust in

гызмамазлыг : *n* distrustfulness

гызмар : *a* heated, incandescent, burning-hot

гызчыг, гызчығаз : *n* 1) little daughter, girlie 2) young thing, kid, slip of a girl

гыј : *n* see **гијјә**

гыјгач : *a* 1) slanting, oblique, crooked, awry *adv* 2) sideways, obliquely aslant, asquint, askance *n* 3) triangular corner plate/connection plate/gusset plate

гыјгачы : *a* 1) slanting, oblique, crooked, awry 2) sideways, obliquely, atilt, slantwise

гыјгачламаг : *v* fold or cut material/paper etc. on the bias

гыјыг : *n* large needle *sail, matting, sacking a* 2) screwed up, closed tight *i.e. eyes*

гыјмаг : *v* 1) not spare, not begrudge, not stint 2) permit o.s. to do s.t. in relation to s.o. else 3) screw up/ close tight *eyes*

гыл : *n* 1) bristle, hair *horse's, goat's* 2) coarse wool

гылаф : *n* case, étui *for small articles*

гылыг : *n* 1) easy disposition 2) disposition, temper

гылыгланмаг : *v* fawn upon s.o., make up to/ingratiate o.s. with s.o., curry favor with s.o., worm o.s. into s.o.'s confidence

гылыглы : *a* affable, friendly, easy to get on with

гылыгсыз : *a* unfriendly, unwinsome, hard to get along with

гылыгсызлыг : *n* unfriendliness, unsociability, quarrelsome disposition, unaccommodating nature

гылынч : *n* sable, cavalry sword, sword

гылынчламаг : *v* cut/slash with a sable/sword

гыллы : *a* hairy, bristly

гылмаг : *v* make, do, accomplish, perform

гылча : *n* leg, foot

гылчасыәјри : *a* bow-legged

гылчыг : *n bot* 1) tendril, spike, hairlike outgrowth, awn *corn, grain, grass etc.* 2) barb, burr 3) small bone *fish, bird*

гылчыглы : *a bot* 1) having many tendrils, awns, hairlike growths *n* 2) meat having many small bones *fish, fowl*

гымыз : *n* koumiss *a drink made of fermented camel's, goat's or cow's milk*

гымылданмаг : *v* move, stir

гымылданмадан : *adv* motionless

гымылдашмаг : *v* move together with s.o. else

гымышмаг : *v* see **күлүмсәмәк, күлүмсүнмәк**

гымров : *n* handbell, cymbal

гын : *n* 1) sheath *sword, dagger* 2) case *for small objects* 3) external plate, tortoise shell *bot* 4) pod

гынама : *n* reproach, censure, blame

гынамаг : *v* reproach, censure, blame

гынанмаг : *v intr* be blamed/censured, be subject to reproach

гынчанмаг : *v* flirt *with* , be affected, attitudinize, give o.s. airs

гыпгырмызы : *a* red-faced, with flush cheeks

гыр : *n geol* 1) kir *solidified petroleum* , a type of asphalt *a* 2) grey; swarthy, dark-complexioned 3) see **шивә**

гыраг : *n* 1) edge *of a table, board, book etc* 2) shore, bank, coast *a* 2) strange, non-familiar 3) additional *income*

гырагдакы : *a* extreme

гырбасан : *n* see **гырчы**

гырбиширән : *n* kir *solidified petroleum* boiler *agent. This material is widely used in Azerbaijan for waterproofing roofs*

гыргырама : *a* too salty, over-salted

гырговул : *n* 1) pheasant *a* 2) pheasant['s]

гырғы : *n* 1) hawk *a* 2) hawk, hawk-like, accipitral

гырғыз : *n* 1) Kirghiz *man a* 2) Kirghiz

гырғызыстан : *n* Kirghizia

гырғызча : *adv* in Kirghiz *language*

гырғын : *n* 1) slaughter, butchery, carnage, massacre, bloodshed 2) *vet med* epizootic, murrain, cattle plague

гырдашыјан : *n* one who transports and delivers kir *solidified petroleum*

гырды-гачды : *a* unreliable, unsteady, inconstant, changeable

гырдырмаг : *caus of* **гырмаг**

гырдырнаг : *a* tenacious

гырыг : *a* 1) smashed, broken *n* 2) scrap, fragment[s], bit

гырыг-гырыг : *adv* 1) in pieces, in bits 2) curtly, abruptly 3) into smithereens *a* 4) broken, interrupted

гырыг-гуруг : *n* bits, pieces, fragments

гырыглыг : *n* abruptness, curtness

гырылдама : *v* fr. **гырылдамаг**

гырылдамаг : *v* call *cranes*

гырылма : *v* fr. **гырылдамаг**

гырылмаг : *v intr* break, smash 2) become detached, break off, come away 3) die, die out, die off, become extinct *singly or en masse* 4) be cut down, felled *of a forest*

гырым : *n* disposition, mood

гырынты : *n* 1) fragments, bits, pieces, scraps 2) scrap, debris

гырычы : *n* 1) destroyer, exterminator *in a general sense* 2) fighter aircraft 3) tank-killer 4) fast naval vessel, patrol boat

гырыш : *n* wrinkle, crease

гырыш-гырыш : *a* wrinkled, puckered

гырышдырмаг : *v* 1) wrinkle, crease 2) rumple, crumple 3) knead, mash

гырышыг : *n* 1) wrinkles, folds, pleats 2) see **гырышмыш**

гырышыглыг : *n geol* folding

гырышмаг : *v* knit o.'s brow, screw up o.'s face

гырышмал : *n* rascal, scoundrel

гырышмыш : *a* 1) wrinkled, puckered 2) rumpled, crumpled, crushed

гырјыған : *n* kir *solidified petroleum* collector

гырламаг : *v* cover/coat with kir *solidified petroleum*

гырланмаг : *v pass* be covered/coated with kir *solidified petroleum*

гырлатдырмаг : *caus of* **гырламаг**

гырма : *v* fr. **гырмаг**

гырмаг : *v* 1) break, smash 2) fell, cut down, hew, hack, chop 3) tear, tear asunder 4) destroy, annihilate, exterminate 5) beat down, kill

гырманч : *n* lash, whip, switch, knout

гырманчламаг : *v* whip, lash, slash with a knout, scourge

гырмызы : *a* red

гырмызы турп : *n* radish

гырмызыдәрили : *a* redskin *pertaining to Native Americans*

гырмызыдодаг : *a* red-lipped

гырмызыјанаг : *a* rosy-cheeked

гырмызылашмаг : *v* see **гызармаг**

гырмызылыг : *n* redness, red spot, high color, blush, flush

гырмызымтыл, гырмызымтраг, гырмызытәһәр *a* reddish, shot with red

гырмызытүклү : *a* red-feathered *bird*

гырмызыча : *a* 1) nice little, pretty little, fine *adv* 2) nicely, prettily *fig* 2) brazenly, *over* familiarly, impudently

гыров : *n* hoar-frost, rime

гырпылмаг : *pass* be plucked, picked/cut *plants*

гырпым : *n* moment, instant, the twinkling of an eye, a flash

гырпмаг : *v* 1) blink, wink 2) pluck, pick *i.e. flowers* 3) clip, cut, trim, prune; tear off/away *plants*

гыр-сагтыз : *n* 1) pitch, pine-tar *a fig* 2) importunate, nagging, persistent, boring, bothersome

гырсалан : *n* see **гырчы**

гырсатан : *n* kir-vendor/seller/merchant *kir is a naturally occuring solidified petroleum used for caulking roofs etc in Transcaucasian region*

гырт-гырт : *n onomatopoetic* cluck-cluck *the clucking sound made by a chicken sitting on eggs*

гыртдатмаг : *v* hold back, take a little s.t. for o.s. *cheat a bit on what is due*

гыртыг : *n* little piece

гыртыг-гыртыг : *adv* bit by bit

гыртылдамаг : *v* see **гыртламаг**

гыртылты : *n onomatopoetic* the clucking sound made by a sitting hen

гыртлаг : *n anat* 1) larynx *a* 2) laryngeal

гыртлагүстү : *a anat* epiglottal

гыртламаг : *v* cluck *the particular sound made by a sitting hen*

гырх : *num* 1) forty 2) a forty day period after a death *marked by certain traditional religious rites in Moslem countries*

гырхајаг : *n zool* centipede *Class Chilapoda*

гырхдырмаг : *v* request that/make s.o. shave

гырхиллик : *n* 1) forty years, fortieth anniversary, fortieth birthday *a* 2) forty-year, of forty years, forty year old

гырхыг : *a* shaven, shaved

гырхылмаг : *v intr* shave, have a shave, be shaved

гырхын : *n* 1) sheep-shearing 2) shearing *sheep*

гырхынты : *n* hair-cutting, shearing, clipping

гырхычы : *n* sheep-shearer

гырхынчы : *a* fortieth

гырхјарпаг : *a bot* double *having two sets of petals*

гырхкүнлүк : *a* 1) forty-days', forty-day, of forty days *n* 2) forty day period

гырхлыг : *n* shears for sheep-shearing

гырхма : *v* fr. **гырхмаг**

гырхмаг : *v* shave

гырһагыр : *n* brutal destruction/extermination

гырчы : *n* kir *solidified petroleum* specialist/worker *kir is used as a waterproofing agent for caulking roofs etc*

гырчыл : *a* see **чал**

гырчын : *n* pleat, tuck, accordion pleats

гырчынламаг : *v* pleat, make accordion pleats *in*

гырчынлы : *a* pleated, goffered, accordion-pleated

гыса : *a* 1) short, concise, not long, not tall *adv* 2) shortly

гысааjаглы : *a* short-legged

гысабармаг : *a* short-fingered

гысабығ : *a* short-whiskered, short-moustached

гысабој, гысабојлу : *a* 1) undersized, stunted *n* 2) short person, shorty, shrimp

гысабојун : *a* short-necked

гысабујнуз : *a* short-horned

гысаганад, гысаганадлы : *a* short-winged

гысагујруг : *a* short-tailed

гысадалғалы : *a* short-wave

гысадишли : *a* short-toothed

гысаjаллы : *a* short-maned

гысаjунлу : *a* short-wooled

гысалыг : *n* 1) shortness *length, time* 2) shortness *height*

гысалма : *v* fr. **гысалмаг**

гысалмаг : *v intr* become/get/grow short, shorten 2) grow short, shorten

гысалтдырмаг : *caus of* **гысалтмаг**

гысалтмаг : *v* 1) shorten 2) curtail, shorten, abbreviate

гысамүддәтли : *a* short-term, of short duration

гысасы : *adv* in short, in a word, to make a long story short

гысатүклү : *a* see **гысаjунлу**

гысафокуслу : *a* short-focus, close-up

гысача : *a dim* 1) short-little *adv* 2) briefly, in brief, succinctly 3) not long

гысачыг : *a dim* 1) extremely short, short-little 2) extremely low, not very high, not very tall

гысганма : *v* fr. **гысганмаг**

гысганмаг : *v intr* be jealous

гысганч : *a* 1) jealous *n* 2) jealous man

гысганчлыг : *n* jealousy

гысгач : *n zool* 1) earwig *family Forficulidae* , an insect 2) clamp, clip, cramp *iron*

гысгы : *n* pressure, thrust, stress, push

гысгырмаг, гысгыртмаг : *v* set *a dog on* , stir up *against* , set *against s.o.*

гысыг : *a* see **гысабојун**

гысылмаг : *v* 1) be pressed *into, against* be pressed *down* , be flattened *against*, be driven/rammed/hammered *into*, be squeezed/compressed 2) be shy *about*, be embarrassed, confused

гысым : *n* see **нөв**

гысыр : *a* 1) barren, dry, sterile, fruitless *n* 2) barren cow

гысырламаг : *v* be barren, sterile *a cow*

гысырлыг : *n* barrenness, sterility, dryness *cow*

гысмаг : *v* press, put pressure on, squeeze

гыснамаг : *v* 1) drive on, speed on, hurry 2) press, oppress, keep down

гыснатдырмаг, гыснатмаг, гыснашдырмаг *caus of* **гыснамаг**

гысраг : *a* barren, sterile *domestic animal*

гыст : *n* part, portion

гыст-гыст : *adv* in parts, part/portion by part/portion

гыт : *a* insufficient, inadequate

гытыготу : *n bot* 1) horse radish *Cochlearia armoracea a* 2) horse radish

гытлашмаг : *v* become rare/hard to find/scarce/in short supply

гытлыг : *n* 1) lack, shortage, deficiency 2) poor harvest, crop failure 3) famine

гыф : *n* funnel

гыфаохшар : *a* funnel-shaped

гыфвары : *a* see **гыфаохшар**

гыфыл : *n* lock *device for securing a door*

гыфыллама : *v* fr. **гыфылламаг**

гыфылламаг : *v* lock, lock up, bolt, bar

гыфылланмаг : *pass* be locked, locked up, bolted, barred

гыфыллатдырмаг, гыфыллатмаг : *caus of* **гыфылламаг**

гыфыллы : *a* locked *door, box etc*

гыфышмаг : *v* rot, turn, go sour

гыхмыг : *n* fragment, particle, bit, grain, chip, sliver

гыч : *n* leg, limb

гыча : *n* see **дилим**

гыч : *n med* 1) numbness *of the extremeties* 2) convulsion

гычамаг : *v* clench *the teeth*

гычанмаг : *v* raise o.'s hand *against s.o.*., threaten s.o.

гычгырма : *n* fermentation, turning sour

гычгырмаг : *v* 1) become pickled, be made sour 2) ferment, sour, go sour, turn sour

гычгыртмаг : *v* pickle, make sour

гычыг : *n* 1) irritation 2) teasing 3) arousal of envy/jealousy

гычыгландырычы : *n* 1) irritant *a* 2) irritable

гычыгландырмаг : *v* arouse, provoke, irritate

гычыгланмаг : *pass* be irritated

гычымаг : *v* show/bare o.'s teeth

гычырдатмаг : *v* 1) grit/grind/gnash o.'s teeth 2) make a click with o.s teeth, have o.'s teeth chattering

гычырты : *n* gritting, grinding sound; gnashing of teeth

гычлыг̀ : *n* see **гыч**

гыш : *n* 1) winter *a* 2) winter, wintry

гышгырыг : *n* see **гычырты**

гышгырыгчы : *n* 1) shouter, brawler, rowdy *a* 2) loud, clamorous

гышгырышмаг : *v* shout all together

гышгырма : *n* exclamation, cry, shout

гышгырмаг : *v* cry out, shout, give a shout, utter a shriek

гышгырты : *n* cry, shout

гышгыртмаг : *caus of* **гышгырмаг**

гышлаг : *n* 1) winter hut/cabin; winter quarters 2) winter pasturage

гышлагчы : *n* winterer *one who for some special purpose stays in winter quarters*

гышлама : *n* wintering, winter stay

гышламаг : *v* winter, winter over, pass/spend the winter

гышлыг : *a* winter, intended for winter

глисерин : *n* 1) glycerin, glycerol *a* 2) glycerin

гобу : *n* sloping gully, dry river bed, shallow valley, dry gulch

гобур : *n* holster

гов : *n* tinder, punk *dry material used for starting a fire*

гова : *n* see **бадја**

говаг : *n* dandruff

говға : *n* fight, brawl, argument, row, shouting, uproar, abuse, discord

говғачы : *n* pugnacious fellow, bully, brawler, trouble-maker

говду-гачды : running away, fleeing *surrepticiously*

говдуртмаг : *v* request/compel s.o. to drive *out* /send away/ dismiss

говзамаг : *v* lift, raise up, lift up a little

говламаг : *v* see **говмаг** 1)

говланмаг : *v* see **говулмаг**

говлатмаг : *v* see **говдуртмаг**

говлуг : *n* folder, file-folder

говма : *n* 1) banishment, expulsion, exile *v* 2) from **говмаг**

говмаг : *v* 1) banish, exile, expel, drive out 2) jump, hop, rush off at a gallop, gallop away 3) pursue s.o.

говра : *n* file

говрулмаг : *v* 1) fry, roast, broil 2) writhe, squirm 3) worry deeply *about* , be very troubled *about*

говсара : *n* basket, bast-basket

говуг : *n* 1) bubble 2) bladder

говугсуз : *a zool* bladderless

говугчуг : *n* phial, vial

говулмаг : *pass* be exiled, expelled, banished, driven out, dismissed

говун : *n* 1) melon *a* 2) melon

говурға : *n* see **горға**

говурма : *n* 1) kavurma *grilled meat* 2) grilling, frying

говурмаг : *v* roast, grill, fry

говурмачы : *n* kavurma-chef, grill-cook

говуртдурмаг, говуртмаг : *v* request/order/compel s.o. to grill, roast, fry

говут : *n* ground roast wheat or peas flavored with powdered sugar *a delicacy*

говушдурмаг : *v* pour together, combine

говушдуртмаг : *v* request/order/compel s.o. to pour together, combine

говушма : *n* pouring together, combining, uniting

говушмаг : *v* gather/come together, unite, join, flow together

говушуг : *a* 1) closed up, densely packed, intertwined, melded, fused *adv* 2) together

говушуглуг : *n* 1) state of being closed up/a closed system 2) coalescence, fusion, unification

говһагов : *n* hurry, rushing

говшаг : *n* junction

гоғал : *n* gog̃al *a kind of cookie*

гоғлу-моғлу : *n* gogol-mogol *beaten-up egg yolks with sugar; Ukrainian dish*

годуг : *n* foal/young of an ass

годуглуг : *n* the lock-up, slammer *colloq. for 'jail'*

гоз : *n* 1) walnut *a* 2) walnut

гоза : *n* *bot* 1) pine-cone 2) cotton boll

гозаламаг : *v* be covered with bolls *of cotton*

гозбел : *n* 1) hunchback *adv* 2) hunch-backed

гозла, гозлу : *n* coachman's seat

гозлуг : *n* 1) filbert *tree* , European hazelnut tree *Coryllus avellana* 2) place having a dense growth of hazelnut trees

гозсындыран : *n* nutcracker *for cracking walnuts*

гозшәкилли : *a* walnut-shaped

гој : *part* let. . .

гојма : *v* 1) from **гојмаг** *n* 2) clubbing, pooling *describes the action of a number of people pooling resources or money in order to achieve a common goal*

гојмаг : *v* 1) lay down, put down, place, set 2) adjust, put in 3) mount, install 4) leave *behind* 5) allow, permit, let 6) give leave *to do s.t.*, authorize

гојуб-гачмаг : *v* make off, run, take to o.'s heels, bolt leave, move away from *someplace*

гојуб-кетмәк : *v* leave,go away, depart, move away from *someplace*

гојулмаг : *pass* 1) be placed/put/set 2) be given leave *to do s.t.*, be authorized/permitted

гојулуш : *n* 1) laying *bricks, masonry, stonework* , placement 2) erection, raising, arrangement

гојун : *n* 1) sheep, ewe 2) embrace; *fig* 3) bosom *a* 4) sheep['s]

гојунбахан : *n* sheep-breeder

гојунбоған : *n* *bot* loosestrife *Lysimachia vulgaris*

гојунгырхан : *n* sheep-shearer

гојунгулағы : *n* *bot* forget-me-not *Myosotis*

гојунешшәји : *n* stupid, uncouth young person, a lout

гојунотаран : *n* shepherd

гојунчу : *n* 1) sheep-breeder

гојунчулуг : *n* 1) sheep-breeding *a attrib* sheep-breeding

гол : *n* 1) arm 2) branch, bough 3) tributary *of river* *tech* 4) lever, crank etc., balance arm/beam *scales* , rocker arm etc 5) sleeve *clothing* 6) signature 7) finger-board *guitar, other stringed instruments*

гол гојмаг : *v* 1) give one's agreement 2) sign, put signature

гол чәкмәк : *v* put signature, sign

гола кирмәк : *v* take by the hand

голдан тутмаг : *v* help, assist

голај : *a* easy, simple, comfortable

голајланмаг : *v* threaten, raise o.'s hand threateningly, wave/swing/brandish arms

голатма : *n* overarm stroke *in swimming*

голач : *n* see **гулач**

голбаг : *n* see **виләрзик**

голбојун : *adv* with arms around each other, in an embrace

гол-будаг, гол-ганад : *n* branching, ramification, branching out

гол-будаглы : *a* see **голлу-будаглы**

гол-гола : *adv* with arms linked, arm-in-arm

голлу-будаглы : *a* 1) branching, branchy *bot* 2) ramose

голсуз : *a* 1) armless 2) sleeveless *n* 3) sleeveless garment *jacket, blouse, sweater*

голтуг : *n* 1) arm-pits, under-arm *fig* 2) protection, patronage, bosom

голтуғағачы : *n* 1) crutch *fig* 2) support, helper

голтугалты : *n* 1) arm-pit, the hollow under the arm 2) gusset *in the underside of sleeve*, wedge *a* 3) auxillary

голтугламаг : *v* take s.o.'s arm, take s.o. by the arm, link arms *fig* 2) flatter

голтуглу : *a* equipped with elbow-rests or handrails *furniture, stairways etc*

голтугчу : *n* *obs* peddler

голчаг : *n* 1) muff, oversleeve, armlet *obs* 2) couter *elbow piece for a suit of armor*

голчомаг : *n* *hist* 1) kulak *in the former Soviet Union an ideological cliche for a prosperous peasant who employed labor and opposed the collectivization of farm-land* 2) see **голчу**

голчомаглыг : *n* *hist* *coll* 1) the kulaks 2) violence, coercion *a* 3) kulak

гом : *n* see **топа**

гонаг : *n* 1) visitor, guest *a* 2) guest *attrib*

гонаглыг : *n* 1) entertainment, treating *to* 2) formal dinner party, banquet; evening party

гонагпәрәст, гонагсевән : *a* 1) hospitable *n* 2) hospitable person

гонагпәрәстлик, гонагсевәнлик : *n* hospitality

гонагсевмәз : *a* inhospitable

гонагсевмәмәзлик : *n* inhospitality

гонагчы : *n* lodger, guest

гонагчанлы,гонагчыл : *a* hospitable

гондара : *n* shoes

гондарылмаг : *v* 1) be written, composed, made up, be fabricated, contrived 2) be put *into*, be introduced *into text*, be adapted/ established/set up

гондарма : *n* 1) invention, fiction, fabrication 2) inserting/including (into, in); adjusting, regulaating, establishing *a* 3) false, fictitious 4) inserted

гондармаг : *v* 1) compose, dream up, think up, invent 2) put *into*, insert, fit *to*, adapt *to*, install

гондола : *n* gondola

гондолачы : *n* gondolier

гондурмаг : *v* land, set down

гонма : *v* fr. **гонмаг**

гонмаг : *v* sit *down*, land *birds*; settle *dust*

гонур : *a* brown, dark-brown

гонурлашмаг : *v* grow brown

гоншу : *n* 1) neighbor *a* 2) neighboring, adjacent, adjoining

гоншулашмаг : *v* be in the vicinity *of*, become/come to be a neighbor *of*

гоншулуг : *n* neighborhood, vicinity

гоншулугда : *adv* in the neighborhood/vicinity

гоншучасына : *adv* as a neighbor, in a neighborly way

гопараг : *adv* quickly, swiftly

гопардылмаг : *pass* be cut off *from*, be taken off, be broken off *from*

гопармаг, гопартмаг : *v* tear, tear off/away, unstick, pull out, break off

гопмаг : *pass* 1) be torn off/away, be/get unstuck, be pulled out, be broken off 2) get irritated 3) start suddenly, rise up suddenly, break out *fire*

гопуг : *n* tearing off, break-away, split

гопча : *n* see **илмә-дујмә**

гор : *n* little grains of hot coal in ashes; sparks in ashes

гора : *n* unripe/green grapes

гор-годуг : *n* kiddies *scornful*

горға : *n* roast wheat, or corn

горланмаг : *v* sparkle, scintillate

гортөкән : *n* hearth which is throwing sparks

горуг : *n* preserve, reserve, restricted area of forest-land/pasture-land

горугчу : *n* watchman

горугчулуг : *n* profession of watchman charged with guarding pasture-land, forest, or orchards

горујучу : *n* see **горучу**

горумаг : *v* take care of, guard, protect, watch

горунмаг : *v* be careful, be on guard against, be guarded against, beware of, protect o.s. against

горучу : *n* 1) watchman, guard *a* 2) protecting, guarding, preventive

горхаг : *a* 1) shy, timid, timorous, faint-hearted, craven 2) irresolute, indecisive *n* 3) coward

горхаглыг : *n* 1) shyness, timidity, faint-heartedness, cowardice 2) indecision

горха-горха : *adv* shyly, timidly, timorously

горхагчасына : *adv* 1) indecisively, irresolutely 2) in a cowardly manner

горхачаг : *a* see **горхаг**

горхмаг : *v* be afraid of, fear, be scared, dread, get cold feet

горхмаз : *a* 1) see **горхубилмəз** 2) *male first name*

горху : *n* fear, fright, dread, angst

горхубилмəз : *a* fearless, intrepid

горхудулмаг : *pass* be frightened/scared

горхузмаг : *v* see **горхутмаг**

горхулу : *a* menacing, terrible, fear-inspiring

горхулуг : *n* 1) danger, peril, dangerous situation 2) scarecrow, a fright

горхунч : *a* terrible, terrifying, frightful, perilous

горхусуз : *a* 1) fearless 2) harmless, safe

горхусузлуг : *n* 1) fearlessness 2) safety, security

горхутмаг : *v* frighten, scare, intimidate

готаз : *n* pompon, rosette, tassel *decoration on caps and slippers*

готазлы : *a* tassled, with pompons/rosettes

готман : *n* shock, stook *hay, grain*

готур : *n med vet* 1) scabies, mange, the itch *a* 2) mangy, infected with scabies

готурламаг, готурлашмаг : *v* grow bald *as a result of a skin disease*

готурлуг : *n* see **готур** 1)

гохарча : *n* 1) *zool* 1) polecat *European carnivore, genus Mustela, related to the weasel, noted by an offensive odor given off when frightened or alarmed a* 2) polecat

гоху : *n* 1) scent, aroma 2) stink, bad smell

гохуламаг : *v* smell, sniff *at* , sniff around

гохулашмаг : *v* sniff at one another *animals*

гохулу : *a* 1) odorous 2) stinking, fetid

гохумаг : *v* emit an unpleasant odor, stink, smell bad

гохусуз : *a* odorless

гохутмаг : *v* 1) emit an unpleasant odor, stink 2) become foul, rotten, go bad, decay

гоһум : *n* relative, kinsman/kinswoman

гоһумбаз : *a* extremely partial *to* /protective of o.'s relatives

гоһумбазлыг : *n* attachment to family; nepotism, favoritism based on kinship

гоһум-гардаш, гоһум-əграба : *n* relatives, relations, kinsfolk

гоһумлашмаг : *v* become a relative

гоһумлуг : *n* 1) relationship, kinship *a* 2) related *to*

гоһумсуз : *a* without relations, without kin

гоһумчанлы : *a* loving o.s relatives, having close ties to family and kin

гоч : *n* 1) ram 2) see **гочаг**

гочаг : *a* 1) daring, brave, dashing, foolhardy, reckless n 2) dare-devil, brave spirit

гочагланмаг, гочаглашмаг : *v* grow/become brave/daring/courageous; summon up courage

гочаглыг : *n* bravery, courage, valor

гочагчасына : *adv* bravely, valiantly, courageously

гочу : *n* 1) gang-leader, robber chief 2) professional assassin/hit-man, cut-throat

гоча : *n* 1) old man, aged man *a* 2) old 3) decrepit

гочаіемиши : *n bot* bearberry *Arctostaphylos uva ursi*

гочалыг : *n* old age

гочалмаг : *v* grow old, age, advance in years

гочалтмаг : *caus of* **гочалмаг**

гочаман : *a* 1) aged, advanced in years, venerable 2) veteran

гочасаіаг, гочасаіағы : *adv* in the manner of a very old person, as one in his/her dotage

гоша : *a* 1) paired, forming a pair 2) adjoining, contiguous

гошабуінуз : *a zool* two-horned

гоша-гоша : *adv* in pairs, two and/by two

гошаламаг, гошалатмаг, гошалашдырмаг *v* 1) double 2) couple, pair

гошалашмаг : *v* become paired

гошалүлə : *a* 1) double-barreled *n* 2) double-barreled gun

гошачылыг : *n*) holding more than one office, wearing two hats

гошашдырмаг : *v* combine

гошгу : *n* 1) harness, gear *a* 2) draught

гошдурмаг, гошдуртмаг : *v* request that/make s.o. harness/put into harness

гошма : *v* 1) from **гошмаг** *n* 2) hitching/hooking *up* 3) verse form in paired rhymes *gram* 4) postposition 5) affix

гошмаг : *v* 1) harness 2) join, hook up, link 3) compose

гошулмаг : *pass* 1) be harnessed *to* 2) be joined *to together* , be linked 3) associate/consort *with* , get in contact *with*, have to do *with* 4) be attached

гошун : *n* 1) army, forces; horde *a* 2) army, military

гошункешлик : *n* military campaign/march

гошучу : *n* coupler

гөвр : *n* inflammation; swelling

гөвс : *n* 1) bow *astron* Sagittarius *a* 2) attrib. of 1) arc

гөвси-гүзеһ : *n* rainbow

гөнчә : *n* 1) bud 2) Gönça *female first name*

гөт : *n* *vulgar* ass, buttocks; idiot, dummy

гөтверән : *vulgar* 1) homosexual male 2) *expletive expressing extreme contempt on the part of the speaker*

грамматик : *a* grammatical

граммафон : *n* 1) gramophone *a* 2) gramophone

гран : *n* kran *Persian silver coin*

граф : *n* 1) count, earl *title of nobility* *a* 2) attrib. of 1)

графика : *n* script, writing system

графин : *n* carafe

графлыг : *n* earldom; county

грим : *n* make-up; grease-paint

гримләмә : *v* fr. **гримләмәк**

гримләмәк : *v* make up, apply make-up

гримләнмә : *n* making up, applying make-up/grease-paint

гримләнмәк : *v* make o.s. up

гримләтдирмәк, гримләтмәк : *caus of* **гримләмәк**

гримчи : *n* make-up man/woman/person

грип : *n* 1) influenza, flu, grippe *a* 2) influenza, flu

грипли : *a* influenza, flu

грифел : *n* 1) slate-pencil *a* 2) attrib. of 1)

груп : *n* 1) group, unit *a* 2) group, organization

груплашдырылмаг : *v* be grouped, form groups

груплашдырма : *n* grouping, classification

груплашдырмаг : *v* group, classify

груплашма : *n* grouping, classification

груплашмаг : *v* group, form groups

групчу : *n* group leader, one who forms and leads groups

групчулуг : *n* clannishness, clique formation

гу : *n* 1) swan *a* 2) attrib. of 1)

гугту : *n* see **гуғу**

гугтулдамаг : *v* *cry* cuckoo

гугтулугу : *n* cock-a-doodle-doo

гуғу : *n* 1) cuckoo *a* 2) cuckoo's

гуғулдамаг : *v* coo

гуғуоту : *n* *bot* German catchfly *Lychnis viscaria*, a meadow grass

гуда : *n* parent of a child's spouse

гудуз : *a* 1) rabid, mad *fig* 2) infuriated, wild, violent

гудузлашмаг : *v* 1) become rabid, mad 2) become/get furious, make a row, start a row

гудузлуг : *n* 1) hydrophobia, rabies 2) fury, rage

гудузоту : *n* *bot* spurry *Spergula* Annual plant

гудузчасына : *adv* rabidly

гудурған : *a* 1) rabid, wild, violent, unbridled, frenzied, infuriated 2) arrogant, insolent, conceited

гудурғанлыг : *n* 1) disorderly conduct, unruly behavior 2) insolence, arrogance, conceit, self-conceit

гудурмаг : *v* 1) become rabid, rage, be furious *fig* 2) grow arrogant/ insolent, become impudent

гудуртмаг : *caus of* **гудурмаг**

гузаг : *n* *zool* a species of mute swan *Cygnus olor*

гузғун : *n* 1) lammergeyer *vulture* 2) hawk

гузғунгылынчы : *n* *bot* sword lily *Gladiolus* , a bulbous plant

гузеј : *n* 1) northern, shaded side; north 2) damp locality

гузу : *n* lamb

гузугулағы : *n* *bot* sorrel, dock *Rumex*

гузукөбәләји : *n* *bot* morel *Morchela esculenta* , a mushroom

гузуламаг : *v* lamb, yean

гузуотаран : *n* lamb shepherd

гујламаг : *v* 1) dig in/into, plant, fill up *a hole in the Earth* bury in earth 2) inter

гујланмаг : *pass* be buried in the ground

гујлатдырмаг, гујлатмаг : *caus of* **гујламаг**

гујмаг : *n* sweet, farinaceous Kasha with meat

гујруг : *n* 1) tail 2) fat tail of certain breeds of sheep; the fat derived from the tail, used for various domestic purposes 3) *coll* long waiting-line

гујругалты : *n* see **гушун**

гујругламаг : *v* 1) catch by the tail *fig* 2) catch s.o.

гујруглу : *a* tailed, having a tail

гујругсуз : *a* tailless

гујругчулуг : *n polit hist lit* 'tailism', *abstract term coined by Lenin to describe the intellectual state of those who couldn't change as quickly as the tactics of the Bolshevik party*

гујругүстү : *a* supracaudal *located above the tail*

гујруғукәсик : *a* dock-tailed, tailless

гују : *n* 1) well 2) bore, bore-hole, bore-well *a* 3) attrib. of 1)

гујугазан : *n* well-digger, well-borer

гул : *n* 1) slave *a* 2) servile, slavish

гулаг : *n* 1) ear *a* 2) aural

гулаг асмаг : *v* listen

гулаг кәсмәк : *v* cheat, swindle

гулагалты : *n* see **гулагјастығы**

гулагбалынчы, гулагбалышы : *n* see **гулагјастығы**

гулагбатыран, гулагбатырычы : *a* 1) deafening *adv* 2) deafeningly

гулагбурмасы : *n* box on the ear, hiding, thrashing; scolding, dressing down, punishment

гулагјастығы : *n* small pillow

гулагламаг : *v* 1) grab by the ear *fig* 2) hold s.o. fast, not permitting them to slip out of o.'s grasp

гулаглы : *a* eared, having ears

гулаглыг : *n* 1) tell-tale, tattle-tale, snitcher, stool-pigeon, informer 2) ear-phones

гулагсыз : *a* earless

гулағакирән : *a* see **гысач**

гулағыағыр : *a* hard of hearing

гулағыкәсик : *a* crop-eared

гулан : *n* see **гулун**

гуланчар : *n* asparagus *Asparagus officinalis*

гулач : *n* 1) swing of the arm 2) unit of measurement equal to the distance from the arm with fingers extended to the head

гулачламаг : *v* 1) measure with a swing of the arm *fig* 2) walk quickly, walk a distance quickly

гулдар : *n* slave-owner, slave-holder

гулдарлыг : *n* slave-holding, slave-owning *a* 2) slave-owning, slave-holding

гулдур : *n* 1) robber, brigand, bandit, gunman *a* 2) robber, bandit

гулдурлуг : *n* robbery, banditry, brigandage

гулдурчасына : *adv* in the manner of robbers, thugs

гуледичи : *a* enslaving, oppressing, enthralling

гулјабаны : *n* monster; marvel, wonder

гуллаб : *n* inhaling, drag, puff *while smoking*

гуллуг : *n* 1) service 2) good turn 3) command, injunction; order, instruction, assignment 4) slavery, thralldom, servitude, bondage 5) looking after, nursing, caring for *patients, children etc*

гуллугкөстәрән : *a* 1) obliging, helpful, obsequious, anxious to help *n* 2) toady, bootlicker

гуллугкөстәрәнлик, гуллугкөстәричилик *n* 1) helpfullness, obligingness 2) toadying, bootlicking, grovelling

гуллугпәрәст : *a* subservient, servile, obsequious

гуллугпәрәстлик : *n* subservience, obsequiousness

гуллугчу : *n* 1) employee, office-worker 2) servant, domestic, help, housemaid

гуллугчулуг : *n* profession of servant, domestic

гулп : *n* handle *of pot, kettle, pan, tray etc.* grip, shaft

гулплу : *a* provided with a handle/grip/knob/shaft

гулун : *n* colt, foal *less than one year old*

гулунч : *n* pain in the back from cold/chill; muscle-pain under the shoulder-blade

гулунчан : *n bot* galanga, galangal, China root *ALpina officinarum*, herbaceous perennial

гулчасына : *adv* servиley, slavishly, subserviently

гум : *n* 1) sand *adv* 2) sandy

гумар : *n* gumar *card game for money*

гумарбаз : *n* card-player, gambler, card-shark

гумархана : *n* 1) gambling-house 2) den *of thieves etc*

гумаш : *n* 1) cloth *a* 2) tightly-woven *of cloth*

гумбара : *n mil* grenade

гумгума : *n* flask, water-bottle

гумдашы : *n* sandstone *depositional rock*

гумәләјән : *n* worker engaged in sifting sand

гумлама : *v* fr. **гумламаг**

гумламаг : *v* cover, strew with sand

гумлу : *a* 1) containing sand, sandy 2) gritty, gravelly

гумлуг : *n* 1) sandy terrain *a* 2) sandy

гумрал : *a* light-brown, blond

гумру : *n zool* turtle-dove *Streptopelia turtur*

гумсал : *n* sandy locale, sandy shore/bank

гумсаллыг : *n* locale abounding in sand

гундаг : *n* 1) swaddling clothes; child wrapped in swaddling clothes 2) rifle-stock, rifle-butt *the entire wooden part of a firearm*

гундагбағы : *n* swaddling bands, swaddling clothes

гундаглы : *a* equipped with a stock/butt *firearm*

гундагсыз : *a* without wooden stock *firearm*

гундуз : *n* 1) beaver *fam Castoridae a* 2) beaver

гунч : *n* 1) top *of a boot* 2) handle *of s.t.*

гупгуру : *a* dried out, parched

гурабиjә : *n* almond pastry

гураг : *a* arid, beset with drought *month, year*

гураглыг : *n* 1) drought, rainless period *a* 2) arid, dry, beset by drought

гурама : *a* 1) patch-work, composed of patches *quilt cover*

гуран : *n* the Koran *sacred Moslem book*

гуращдырычы : *n* assembler, rigger, fitter

гуращдырма : *n* 1) union, conjunction, combination; combining 2) assembly *of machines* 3) invention, fiction, fantasy *a* 4) assembly, assembling

гуращдырмаг : *v* 1) combine, arrange the parts *of* , put together 2) gather *together* , assemble *a machine* 3) invent, compose

гурбаға : *n* 1) frog *a* 2) batrachian, frog['s]

гурбағакөз : *a* goggle-eyed, pop-eyed, having bulging eyes

гурбан : *n* 1) offering; sacrifice 2) victim

гурбанкаh : *n sacrificial* altar, place of sacrificial offering

гурбанлыг : *n* 1) sacrificial offering, oblation 2) sacrificial animal

гур-гур : *onomatopoetic* : **гур-гур еләмәк етмәк** *v* gurgle

гургут : *n* dishwater, slops *any cloudy unpleasant looking liquid*

гурғу : *n* apparatus, installation, facility

гурғушун : *n* 1) lead *Pb metal a* 2) lead, leaden

гурд : *n* 1) wolf *a* 2) wolf['s], lupine n 3) worm a 4) vermicular

гурдаjағы : *n bot* club moss *Lycopodium*

гурдаламаг : *v* 1) stir, move 2) pick *at* s.t. 3) stir *tea*

гурдаланмаг : *v* 1) dig, delve *into* 2) fidget, move restlessly

гурдбасан : *n* wolfhound

гурдкөкү : *n bot* aconite, monkshood *Aconitum* , a medicinal plant the extract of whose roots is used as a sedative

гурдламаг : *v* become worm-eaten

гурдлу : *a* 1) worm-eaten, wormy *a* 2) envious

гурдлулуг : *n* 1) worm-eaten state 2) envy

гурдуртмаг : *caus of* **гурмаг**

гурма : *n* 1) construction, structure, building up, building 2) factory, plant *a* 3) factory, plant

гурмаг : *v* 1) build, construct, erect, install 2) pitch 3) wind *watch, toy etc.*

гурна : *n* tap, stop-cock, faucet

гурс : *a* compact, dense; massive

гурсаг : *n zool* abomasum *part of the stomach of a ruminant*

гурсал : *n* mandrell, spindle, core, made from melted lead

гуртарачаг : *n* end, termination, limit

гуртарычы : *n* 1) savior, rescuer *a* 2) rescue, saving

гуртармаг : *v* 1) end, terminate 2) complete, conclude 3) save from, deliver, liberate 4) come to s.o.'s help/aid/assistance 5) save, rescue

гуртармаз : *a* inexhaustible, never-ending, never-ceasing, endless

гуртдамаг : *v* see **гурдаламаг**

гуртулмаг : *v* free o.s., extricate o.s., disengage o.s., save o.s., escape, rid o.s. *of* , shake off

гуртулуш : *n* liberation, rescue, deliverance

гуртум : *n* drink, mouthful, sip *liquids*

гуртум-гуртум : *adv* in mouthfuls, sip-by-sip

гуртумламаг : *v* gulp, drink in sips/mouthfuls

гуру : *n* 1) dry-land, continent, land *a* 2) dry *adv* 3) dryly

гуру-бош : *a* 1) naked, bare; empty *fig* 2) groundless, baseless, unsubstantiated, unfounded

гуругурбағасы : *n zool* toad

гуру-гуру : *adv* 1) dryly 2) without grounds/proof, groundlessly, baselessly

гурудан-гуруја : *adv* in vain, to no purpose, for nothing

гурудулмаг : *v* be dried out, get dried, be subject to/exposed to drying

гурудучу : *a* 1) drying out, drying up, withering *n* 2) drier, dessiccator

гуруламаг : *v* wipe dry

гуруланмаг : *pass* be wiped dry

гурулдамаг : *v* 1) croak 2) mutter; bubble, seethe 3) coo

гурулдашмаг : *v* croak *about large number of frogs together*

гурулма : *v* fr. **гурулмаг**

гурулмаг : *pass* 1) be built/erected/constructed 2) be wound up *clock mechanism*

гурултај : *n* congress, conference, convention

гурулту : *n* 1) croaking 2) grumbling

гурулуг : *n* 1) dryness, aridity 2) leanness, thinness

гурулуш : *n* 1) system 2) construction, structure, layout 3) composition, arrangement

гурум : *n* 1) soot, carbon deposit 2) cobweb/spiderweb

гурумаг : *v* 1) dry, get dried, dry out 2) run dry, dry up 3) become emaciated/thin/wasted, grow thin

гурумлу : *a* 1) slender, slim, stately 2) soot-covered; covered with cobwebs/spiderwebs

гурумсаг : *a* 1) dishonorable *n* 2) scoundrel, rogue 3) procurer, pander, pimp

гурумсаглыг : *n* 1) dishonor, disgrace 2) procuration, pandering, pimping

гурунмаг : *v* wipe/dry o.s., wipe o.s. dry, dry o.s.

гурутдурмаг : *v* request/order/make s.o. dry s.t.

гурутәһәр : *a* 1) dryish, on the dry side 2) lean, meagre

гурутма : *n* 1) drying (out) *a* 2) drying

гурутмаг : *v* dry, dry out, dry up, sun-dry, dry-cure

гурутмалыг : *a* set asside/designated for sun-drying/dry-curing *fruits/ vegetables/meat/ fish etc*

гуручу : *n* builder, creator

гуручулуг : *n* 1) construction, building 2) creator

гуруш : *n* *obs* half-kopeck piece

гурчаланмаг : *v* see **гурчухмаг**

гурчухмаг : *v* 1) stir, move, move restlessly, move about, fidget, toss and turn 2) somersault

гуршаг : *n* 1) sash, girdle, belt 2) hoop, cartridge clip, grasp *compass of both arms* , girth *geog* 3) zone, region 4) rainbow

гуршагламаг : *v* 1) seize s.o. by the belt 2) surround, encircle

гуршагтутма : *n* see **куләшмә**

гурашмаг : *v* put a belt on s.o., gird; engirdle, encircle

гуршанмаг : *v* 1) gird o.s. *with* , girt o.s., put on a belt *fig* 2) give o.s. up to, abandon o.s. to s.t., become keen on s.t., join in/take part in s.t., undertake s.t.

гуршун : *n* see **гурғушун**

гусдурмаг : *v* compel/make vomit, evoke/cause vomiting

гусдурмаоту : *n* *bot* ipecac *Psychotria Ipecacuanha* plant, used as an emetic

гусдуручу : *a* 1) emetic, vomitive *n* 2) emetic *substance*

гусма : *n* 1) vomiting, retching, puking *a* 2) vomitive, emetic

гусмаг : *v* vomit, puke, upchuck, spew

гусунту : *n* vomit, puke

гутаб : *n* gutab *very thin meat pasties*

гутабсатан : *n* gutab seller

гутан : *n* *zool* pelican

гуту : *n* 1) box, small box, case *a* 2) attrib of 1)

гучаг : *n* 1) embrace 2) armful 3) the grasp/compass of both arms

гучаг-гучаг : *adv* by armfuls

гучаг-гучаға : *adv* embracing

гучагламаг : *v* 1) hug, embrace, take/fold in o.'s arms 2) clasp, encompass with outstretched arms

гучаглашмаг : *v* embrace/hug one another

гучамаг, гучмаг, гучумаг : *v* see **гучагламаг**

гуш : *n* 1) bird *a* 2) avian, bird['s]

гушабахан : *n* poultry-man, poultry-woman

гушбаз : *n* bird-fancier *usually pigeons and raptorial birds such as falcons*

гушбашы : *n* snow-flakes

гушгун : *n* tailstrap, a harness-element *a strap with an aperture through which the* *horse's tail is passed in order to keep the saddle from creeping forward*

гушгунламаг : *v* put on the tailstrap *harness element see above*

гушәппәји : *n bot* shepherd's purse *Castella bursa pastoris*

гушјејән : *n zool* 1) avivore *bird which kills other birds for food, carnivorous bird a* 2) avivorous *referring to birds which kill other birds for food*

гушсатан : *n* poultryman, poultry-butcher

гуштәрәси : *n bot* thlaspi, pennycress, fanweed *Thlaspe arvense* , poisonous herbaceous field plant

гушхана : *n* 1) chicken-house, chicken-run 2) dove-cot, pigeon-loft

гушчу : *n* poultry farmer/breeder, bird fancier

гушчулуг : *n* 1) poultry-farming/breeding *a* 2) poultry farming/breeding

гушчуғаз : *n dim* little bird, birdie

гүббә : *n* cupola, dome, vault, canopy

гүббәли : *a* domed, vaulted, canopieds

гүввә : *n* see **гүввәт**

гүввәт : *n* 1) power, strength, force, might, energy *math* 2) exponent, index, power

гүввәтверичи, гүввәтләндиричи : *n* intensifier, booster, amplifier

гүввәтләндирмә : *n* strengthening, intensification, amplification *radio, electricity etc.*

гүввәтләндирмәк : *v* strengthen, intensify, boost, amplify

гүввәтләндиртмәк : *caus of* **гүввәтләнмәк**

гүввәтләнмә : *v* fr. **гүввәтләнмәк**

гүввәтләнмәк : *v* become/get strong/powerful

гүввәтли : *a* 1) strong, powerful, intense 2) stalwart, hefty

гүввәтлилик : *n* power, strength, force

гүввәтөлчән : *n* dynamometer

гүввәтсиз : *a* weak, powerless, feeble

гүввәтсизлик : *n* weakness, feebleness, powerlessness

гүдрәт : *n* might, power, force, strength

гүдрәтли : *a* mighty, strong, powerful

гүдс : *n* Jerusalem

гүлбә : *n* small, wretched house, hovel

гүллә : *n* tower

гүрбәт : *n* 1) stay/sojourn abroad, wandering in foreign lands 2) foreign/strange land

гүррәләнмәк : *v* 1) be proud of, take pride in 2) boast, swagger, throw o.'s weight around

гүррәли : *a* proud, haughty, arrogant, conceited, presumptious, smug

гүруб : *n* setting *of the sun*

гүруг : *n* foal, colt *up to six months old*

гүрур : *n* 1) pride, stateliness, majesty 2) haughtiness, arrogance, self-satisfaction, conceit

гүрурла : *adv* proudly

гүрурланмаг : *adv* 1) become proud, haughty, grow arrogant 2) be proud of, take pride in

гүрурлу : *a* arrogant, insolent, conceited, proud, haughty, boastful

гүрурлулуг : *n* see **гүрур**

гүссә : *n* melancholy, sorrow, grief, woe, "weltschmertz"

гүссәләндиричи : *a* distressing, doleful, mournful

гүссәләндирмәк : *v* sadden, grieve, pain, distress, bring on grief, sorrow

гүссәләнмәк : *v* be sad, be melancholy, grieve *about* , mourn *over*, sorrow

гүссәли : *a* sad, melancholy, mournful, doleful

гүссәсиз : *a* carefree, untroubled, untouched by sorrow

гүсур : *n* 1) defect, deficiency, blemish, flaw 2) fault, guilt, blame

гүсурлу : *a* 1) flawed, defective 2) guilty, culpable

гүсурлулуг : *n* state/condition of being defective/incomplete/flawed

гүсурсуз : *a* 1) irreproachable, impeccable, blameless *adv* irreproachably, impeccably, blamelessly

гүсурсузлуг : *n* blamelessness, faultlessness, irreproachability

гүтб : *n* pole, terminal

Д

д : sixth letter of the Azerbaijani alphabet

да : *part* and, right, well, even, also, as well; *also emphatic particle*

дабаг : *n vet* hoof and mouth disease

дабан : *n* 1) heel 2) heel *of footwear*

дабаналты : *n* heel *of footwear*

дабанбалығы : *n zool* crucian, a species of carp

дабанбасма : *adv* immediately after, on the heels of

дабандалы : *n* back, counter *of shoes*

дабандашы : *n* pumice stone *for smoothing the heels while bathing*

дабанлы : *a* heeled, supplied/provided with a heel

дабанлыг : *n tech* 1) footstep bearing, bearing *for vertical axis* 2) suitable/good for heels *i.e. material*

дабансыз : *a* heelless, having no heel

даббағ : 1) tanner, currier, leather-dresser 2) furrier, fur-dresser

даббағлыг : *n* 1) tanning, tanning trade, leather-dressing trade/business 2) furriers trade, fur-dressing trade

даббағхана : *n* tannery, tanyard, leather-dressing plant

дава : *n* healing, curing substance; panacea

дава : *n* 1) fight, brawl, row, scuffle, quarrel 2) war, campaign

дава-далаш : *n* see **дава-шава**

дава-дәрман : *n coll* drugs, medications

давакар : *n* pugnacious, quarrelsome fellow, brawler, bully; belligerent person

давакарлыг : *n* pugnacity, rowdyism; belligerence

давалы : *a* 1) questionable, disputable 2) noisy, scandalous, provoking 3) having medication against itself

давам : *n* 1) firmness, steadfastness, steadiness, stability, self-control 2) durability, strength 3) extension, continuation

даваметдиричи : *n* see **давамчы**

давамлы : *a* 1) durable, strong 2) protracted, continued

давамлылыг : *n* 1) durability, strength 2) *powers of* endurance, staying power 3) duration, length

давамсыз : *a* 1) instable, impermanent, lacking endurance 2) flimsy, perishable, friable, fragile

давамсызлыг : *n* 1) instability, impermanence, lack of endurance 2) flimsiness, perishability, friability, fragility :

давамчы : *n polit* one who continues, a continuer, one who carries on ideals, ideological theories *often rendered as follower; i.e. ' one who promotes the ideas of Lenin*

давар : *n coll* sheep and goats

дават : *n* inkstand

давачы, давачыл : *n* see **давакар**

давачат : *n* medicaments

дава-шава : *n* fight, brawl, row, disagreement, falling-out

давла : *n* 1) bridge *support for the string of a bowed instrument* 2) blind made of canvas stretched on a frame *used in pheasant hunting*

давраныш : *n* address to s.o., relationship; behavior; manner, conduct

давранмаг : *v* 1) treat s.o., appeal to s.o., behave 2) use, utilize *in a certain manner*

давул : *n* see **дәф**

дағ : *n* 1) mountain *a* 2) mountain, mountainous *n* 3) burn, brand *made with hot iron a* 4) hot, scalding, boiling

дағар, дағарчыг : *n* knapsack

дағгочу : *n zool* mouflon *wild sheep*

дағдаған : *n bot* hackberry *Celtis*

дағдиби : *n* foothills, country at foot of mountain

дағәтәји : *n* foot hill, lower slope[s]

дағыдылма : *n* 1) spreading about, scattering, dispersion 2) destruction, ravages, devastation 3) squandering

дағыдылмаг : *pass* 1) be spread about, scattered, dispersed 2) be destroyed, ravaged, devastated 3) be squandered

дағыдылмаз : *a* indestructible, unbreakable

дағыдычы : *a* 1) devastating 2) ruinous, destructive

дағылышмаг : *v* see **дағылмаг**

дағылма : *v* fr. **дағылмаг**

дағылмаг : *v* 1) be pulled/torn down/destroyed 2) disperse, break up, separate 3) spread out, stretch out 4) spill, overflow 5) wear out

дағыныг : *a* 1) sparse, scarce; separate, uncoordinated, scattered, spread out 2) disorderly, confused

дағыныглыг : *n* sparseness, dispersedness, separateness, uncoordinatedness

дағынты : *n* rubble; devastations; ruins; economic chaos

дағыстан : *n* 1) Dagestan *a* 2) Dagestanian

дағыстанлы : *n* a Dagestanian, resident of Dagestan

дағытдырмаг : *caus of* **дағытмаг**

дағытмаг : *v* 1) smash up/destroy/devastate 2) throw about, scatter, disperse, spread out, throw left and right 3) wear out,wear to rags, get tattered, tear 4) drive away, break up 5) squander 6) spill, pour out

дағкечиси : *n zool* Caucasian goat

дағламаг : *v* 1) effect/cause profound, unforgettable grief/misfortune/injury 2) cauterize, sear with a hot iron

дағлы : *n* mountaineer

дағлыг : *n* 1) mountainous terrain, upland, high country, highlands *a* 2) mountainous, upland

дағсаггызы : *n bot* tau saghya *Scorzonera tau-saghyz, a rubber-bearing plant*

дағсичовулу : *n zool* 1) hamster *a small burrowing rodent a* 2) hamster

дағтәрхуну : *n bot* tansy *Tanasetum vulgare*

дад : *n* 1) taste, sense of taste 2) help, assistance 3) complaint; call for help

дадамал : *a* getting into the habit of doing s.t.; taking to, conceiving a liking for s.t.

дад-аман : *n* 1) see **дад** 3) *in comb :* **дад-аман еләмәк** *етмәк* beseech, beg for help, mercy

даданаг : *a* see **дадамал**

дадандырмаг : *v* accustom, train; give one an impulse to, make keen on

даданыг : *a* see **дадамал**

даданмаг : *v* get into the habit of doing s.t.; take to, conceive a liking for s.t.

дадаш : *n* older brother *respectful address; Dadaş, male first name*

дад-бидад : *n* noise, shout, cry, scream for help, complaint

даддырмаг : *v* see **дадыздырмаг**

дадыздырмаг, дадызмаг : *v* have a taste, taste *food*

дадыхмаг : *v* lose flavor, have an aftertaste / funny/bitter taste *because of long storage*

дадландырмаг : *v* make tasty, impart a pleasing taste to s.t.

дадлы : *a* tasty, dainty *of a dish* , delicious

дадлылыг : *n* pleasant taste, deliciousness

дадмаг : *v* taste, check the taste

дадсыз : *a* tasteless, unflavored, flat, insipid

дад-фәрјад : *n* moan, groan, cry, shout for help

даз : *n* bald spot/patch

дазбаш : *a* bald, bald-headed

дазланмаг, дазлашмаг : *v* grow/get bald

даим, даима : *adv* constantly, continually, always

даими : *a* 1) constant, continual, lifelong 2) chronic

даимлик : *n* constancy, permanency, eternity

даир : *postp* 1) relating to s.t. 2) concerning, about, relative to

даирә : *n* 1) circle, circumference 2) district *administrative* 3) see **гавал**

даирәви : *a* round, circular

даирәчик : *n* circle, group

дај : *n* see **дајча**

дајаг : *n* 1) stand, prop *fig* 2) support, bulwark, protection, defense

дајаглы : *a* supported, protected, propped up, undergirded

дајаглыг : *a* supporting

дајагсыз : *a* unsupported, without support/undergirding

дајаз : *a* 1) shallow, shoal, small *fig* 2) superficial, perfunctory, petty, trivial

дајазландырмаг : *v* make small, shallow

дајазланмаг : *v* become small, shallow

дајазлатмаг : *v* see **дајазландырмаг**

дајазлашмаг : *v* see **дајазландырмаг**

дајазлыг : *n* shoal, shallow water

дајазча : *a* see **дајаз**

дајама : *v* from **дајамаг**

дајамаг : *v* 1) lean/rest/put against 2) prop up, place under

дајаначаг : *n* 1) prop, support, underpinning 2) stop *bus, train, tram*

дајандырылмаз : *a* 1) irrepressible 2) unceasing, ceaseless 3) unchecked, unrestrained

дајандырма : *n* 1) stopping, stoppage 2) halt, suspension, cessation, discontinuance

дајандырмаг : *v* 1) stop, call a halt to, suspend 2) cease, discontinue, put an end to

дајаныглы : *a* 1) firm, stable, hardy, enduring 2) consistent, steady

дајаныгсыз : *a* 1) unstable, not persistent, not hardy, not enduring 2) lacking self-control, unrestrained

дајанма : *v* fr. **дајанмаг**

дајанмаг : *v* 1) stop, come to a stop/ halt, stand still, pause 2) stand 3) lean against/on, rest against, set against 4) hold, hold on to, stick to, hold o.'s ground, endure 5) bear, endure

дајанмадан : *adv* 1) immediately, at once 2) continuously, unceasingly, ceaselessly

дајә : *n* nanny, nurse-maid

дајы : *n* uncle *mothers' brother; also the form of address to an older man used both with the first name and without it*

дајыарвады : *n* aunt by marriage *wife of a maternal uncle*

дајыгызы : *n* first cousin *daughter of a maternal uncle*

дајыдосту : *n* see **дајыарвады**

дајынәвәси : *n* second cousin *grandchild of a maternal uncle*

дајыоғлу : *n* first cousin *son of a maternal uncle*

дајлаг : *n* see **дајча**

дајча : *n* colt, foal *from six months up to four years*

дал : *n* 1) back *of a human, animal or chair* 2) back part, back *also a* 3) reverse side, verso 4) rear *also a*

дала : *adv* back, backwards

далаг : *n* *anat* spleen

далајан : *a* burning

даламаг : *v* sting *nettles* 2) bite, be given to biting

далан : *n* 1) passage, vaulted passage 2) blind alley; dead end street

даландар : *n* janitor

даландарлыг : *n* the occupation of janitor

далашган : *n* pugnacious fellow, bully, brawler

далашганлыг : *n* pugnacity, brawling; bullying

далащдырмаг : *v* cause to quarrel compel to fight, cause to fight

далашма : *n* fight, scuffle, quarrel

далашмаг : *v* fight *with* , bicker, quarrel, abuse one another

далбадал : *adv* one after another, running *as in three days 'running'* in succession, continuously

далға : *n* wave

далғавары : *a* wavy, undulatory, undulating

далғагыран : *n* breakwater

далғадөјән : *n* surf, breakers

далғаландырмаг : *v* 1) stir up, disturb, agitate *the surface of water* 2) blow about

далғаланма : *n* 1) agitation, choppiness, roughness *water* 2) swaying, surging *troops, people* 3) blowing about, flapping

далғаланмаг : *v* 1) be stirred up, agitated, rise, heave, rage, storm *waves* 2) heave, sway, flutter, fly

далғалы : *a* wavy, undulant

далғаөлчән : *n* *rad* wave-meter

далғын : *a* 1) thoughtful, pensive, dreamy, rapt *adv* 2) thoughtfully, pensively, raptly

далғынлыг : *n* meditation, thoughtful mood, reverie, concentration

далғыч : *n* 1) diver *a* 2) diving

далда : *n* 1) secret, secluded refuge, secluded or protected place 2) shelter, cover, ambush *adv* 3) behind; inside-out

далдабучаг : *n* remote/God-forsaken/solitary region, back-of-beyond, remote place, Podunk junction

далдаламаг : *v* 1) conceal, hide, secrete 2) set aside, save *money*

далдаланачаг : *n* 1) shelter, refuge, haven 2) see **далда** 1), 2)

далдаландырмаг : *v* shelter, give refuge

далдаланмаг : *v* take shelter, take cover, make use of [a] shelter

дал-далы : *adv* back, backwards

далдалыг : *n* 1) object behind which one can find shelter/protection, a shelter *mil* 2) screen, covering force

далдан : *adv* behind, from behind

далдырмаг : *v* be plunged/lost/buried *in thought, meditation*

далы : *n* 1) continuation 2) the other side, reverse, verso

далынча : *prep* behind, following, immediately after

далысы : *n* see **далы** 1)

далмаг : *v* 1) be plunged/lost/buried *in thought, meditation* 2) plunge into, be utterly engrossed *in some occupation, endeavor*

дам : *n* 1) roof, roofing, flat roof 2) shanty, hovel, dug-out, earth-house 3) cattle-barn/shed, cow-barn, sheep-shed *fig* 4) lock-up, slammer, jail

дам сачағы : *n* eaves

дама : *n* 1) square, check 2) checkers *board game* 3) king *in checkers*

дамаг : *n* *anat* 1) palate *fig* 2) good humor, excellent mood *vet* 3) lampas *a decease of horses, inflammation of the palate* *a* *anat* 4) palatine, palatal

дамаглы : *n* 1) jovial/cheery/merry fellow *a* 2) merry, jolly, cheerful

дама-дама : *a* checked, checkered

дама-дама : *adv* dripping, dribbling with drops

дамазлыг : *n* thoroughbred/ pure-blooded animal selected for breeding *cattle*

дамар : *n* vein, blood-vessel, artery

дамар-дамар : *a* veinous

дамарыбош : *a* soft, yielding, pliable, pliant, weak-willed, easily influenced

дамарлы : *a* see **дамар-дамар**

дамарчыг : *n* secondary vein

дамба : *n* levee

дамбул : *n* see **кавалы**

дамға : *n* 1) brand, stamp 2) rubber-stamp

дамғавуран : *n* stamper *person charged with using stamping or postmarking device*

дамғаламаг : *v* stamp, place a stamp on *using a rubber stamp or other device* brand, mark

дамғаланмаг : *v* undergo branding, stamping, be branded, stamped

дамғалатдырмаг, дамғалатмаг : *caus of* **дамғаламаг**

дамғалы : *a* stamped, branded, having a stamp, a brand

дамғачы : *n* see **дамғавуран**

дамдабача : *n* bogey-man *used to frighten children*

дамдандүшмә : *adv* off-handedly, off the cuff, inopportunely, ineptly

дам-даш : *n* structure, building, dwelling, habitation

дамызмаг, дамыздырмаг : *v* drop, let fall a drop, drip

дамјолу : *n* attic

дамла : *n* see **дамчы**

дамламаг : *v* put in jail, jail, lock up in a jail, arrest

дамланмаг : *pass* be arrested, be put in jail

дамлатдырмаг : *v* ask/make/ compel to arrest s.o.

дамлатмаг : *v* see **дамлатдырмаг**

даммаг : *v* drop, drip, dribble

дамчы : *n* drop, droplet

дамчы-дамчы : *adv* drop by drop, in drops/driblets

дамчыламаг : *v* drizzle, fall in drops, drop, drip, dribble

дамчылатмаг : *v* 1) drop, let a drop fall 2) pour in drops, dribble

дамчысалан : *n* pipette/pipet

дан : *n* daybreak, dawn

дана : *n* heifer, bull-calf *two-year old*

данабаш : *n* dim-wit, blockhead, idiot

данадиши : *n zool* mole-cricket *Gryllotalpa a garden pest, burrowing cricket whose front legs are large and mole-like*

данакеш : *n* player making the next to the last move

даналыг : *n* 1) see **пәјә** *fig* 2) prison, jail

данаотаран : *n* herdsman *tending a herd of young cattle*

данг : *intj* boom!, bang!

дангылдамаг : *v* ring/jingle; make ring/jingle

дангылдатмаг : *v* ring, clang; make ring, clang

дангылты : *n* peal, ringing, clanging

дангыр : *n* bald spot/patch

данә : *n* seed, *little* piece of something

данимарка : *n* 1) Denmark *a* 2) Danish

данимаркалы : *n* Dane

даньшган : *n* 1) talker, chatterer, chatterbox *a* 2) garrulous, gabby, talkative, loquacious

даньшганлыг : *n* talkativeness, loquacity, loquaciousness, garrulousness

даньшдырмаг : *v* 1) cause/compel/make to talk *for any reason, benign or malignant* 2) interrogate

даньшыг : *n* 1) talking, speaking, speech, talks, conversations 2) persuasion, terms *of an agreement*, agreement, understanding 3) rumor, hearsay

даньшыгсыз : *adv* unconditional, unreserved, indisputably, unquestionably

даньшма : *v* fr. **даньшмаг**

даньшмаг : *v* speak, talk, discuss, converse 2) arrange things, arrange *with* , come to an agreement

даньшмамазлыг : *n* taciturnity, reticence

данлаг : *n* reproach, reproof, censure, blame, scolding

данламаг : *v* reprove, reproach, rebuke

данланмаг : *v* be subject to reproach, be rebuked/reproved

данланч : *n* scapegoat *one subject to constant reproaches*

данлатмаг : *caus of* **данланмаг**

данма : *n* denial, disavowal

данмаг : *v* deny, gainsay, refuse to admit

дар : *a* narrow, cramped

дараба : *n* board fence/barrier

дара-бара : *n* quarrel, discord, strife, hullabaloo

дараг : *n text* 1) comb 2) combing machine 3) cartridge clip

дараггајыран : *n* master craftsman/comb-maker

дарагчы : *n text* comber, carder

дарајы : *n* fine silk cloth

даралма : *n* 1) narrowing, constriction *med* 2) stenosis *narrowing of organs of the body*

даралмаг : *v intr* 1) narrow, get/grow narrow *fig* 2) be sparing *of* , scant, skimp, stint, begrudge

даралтмаг : *v* narrow, make narrow

дарама : *n* combing/brushing s.o.'s hair, combing/carding

дарамаг : *v* comb, card *wool, linen* ; do/brush/comb s.o.'s hair

даранмаг : *v* do/comb o.'s hair

даратдырмаг, даратмаг : *caus of* **дарамаг**

дарашмаг : *v* see **дарышмаг**

дарбалаг : *n* drawers *a somewhat baggy type of woman's undergarment*

дарваза : *n* very wide gate

дарға : *n* 1) chief steward, property manager employed by a land-owner *hist* 2) bailiff

дар-дүдүк : *a* too tight and short *clothing*

дардүшүнчәли : *a* 1) *intellectually* backward, narrow-minded *n* 2) *intellectually* backward, narrow-minded person

дардүшүнчәлилик : *n intellectual* backwardness, narrow-mindedness

дары : *n bot* 1) millet *Panicum miliaceum* *a* 2) millet

дарысгал : *a* narrow, on the narrow side, cramped, restricted

дарысгаллыг : *n* narrowness, tightness

дарыхдырычы : *a* dull, boring, tedious, tiresome, depressing

дарыхдырмаг : *v* 1) put restraint on, get rid of 2) irritate, annoy, bore 3) cause to long for

дарыхма : *v* fr. **дарыхмаг**

дарыхмаг : *v* be bored, be depressed/melancholical 2) be worried, uneasy 3) long for, crave for

дарышдырмаг : *caus of* **дарышмаг**

дарышлыг : *n* see **дарысгаллыг**

дарышмаг : *v* 1) crawl away *insects* 2) swarm over, crawl all over s.t. edible in a great mass *i.e. ants upon s.t. sweet*

даркешлик : *n* narrowness, tightness

даркөз : *a* stingy, miserly; greedy *for gain*

дарлыг : *n* 1) narrowness, tightness 2) straitened circumstances, need

дармадағын : *adv in combinations* utterly, completely : **дармадағын еләмәк** ***етмәк*** destroy completely/utterly

дартајчы : *n hist* oil-bailer *worker engaged in manual drawing oil out of an open well in pre-technological times*

дартәһәр : *a* rather narrow, narrowish, on the tight side

дартылы : *a* tight, stretched out

дартылмаг : *v* 1) twitch; pull out 2) pump, wring out

дартынмаг : *v* 1) be jerked back, be withdrawn

дартынч : *a* 1) tight, taut, stretched *adv* 2) tightly, tautly

дартышдырмаг : *v* stretch, drag out, draw/pull apart, pull in all directions

дартышма : *v* fr. **дартышмаг**

дартышмаг : *v* 1) pull one another *fig* 2) quarrel with each other, be at war/loggerheads with one another

дартма : *v* fr. **дартмаг**

дартмаг : *v* 1) pull, pull off, draw 2) rock, shake 3) draw out, stretch

дарфикирли : *a* see **дардүшүнчәли**

дархәтли : *a* narrow-gauge

дарчын : *n* cinnamon

дарчыны : *a* brown

дарча : *a* a bit narrow

дастан : *n* epos, legend 2) epic, ballad, story, tale, fable *a* 3) epic, legendary

дахил : *n* 1) inside, interior, inner part *a* 2) going in, entering in, starting, forthcoming

дахил едилмәк : *v* be included

дахил еләмәк : *v* include, introduce

дахили : *a* internal, inner

дахыл : *n* 1) cash-desk, cash-register 2) money-box, money drawer, till

дахылдар : *n* cashier

дахма : *n* shanty, hovel, cabin, shack

даһа : *part* 1) still, yet 2) already 3) no more 4) part of a comparative construction close in meaning to an English 'even more than that' *precedes the adjective*

даһи : *n* 1) genius *a* 2) brilliant, gifted, intellectually superior, genius-level

даһијанә : *a* 1) intellectually-gifted, intellectually superior, genius-level, brilliant *adv* 2) brilliantly

даhилик : *n* genius, brilliance *intellectual, artistic*

даhичэсинэ : *adv* brilliantly, in a genius-like manner

даш : *n* 1) stone *a* 2) stone, stoney

дашадөјэн : *n zool* wagtail *genus Motacilla* , a small singing bird

дашакирэн : *n* hermit, anchorite, recluse

дашакирэнлик : *n* a hermit's life, an anchorite's life

дашармуду : *n* dašarmudu, a late-ripening, firm variety of pear which can be kept through the winter

дашаh : *n vulg* penis

дашбадам : *n* dašbadam, a hard-shelled almond

дашбаш : *n iron* dishonest, illegal income, or profit

дашбашчы : *n* person engaged in dishonest deals/transactions

дашверэн : *n* supplier of stones for construction

дашгалаг : *in combn* **дашгалаг елэмэк етмэк** throw stones *at s.o.*

даш-гаш : *n* precious stones

дашгын, дашгынлыг : *n* flood, inundation, high-water, flash-flood

дашгыран : *n* 1) stone-crusher *agent* 2) stone-crusher *machine*

дашговуну : *n bot* cantaloupe, a variety of muskmelon *Cucumis melo cantalupensis*

дашдырмаг : *v* see **дашырмаг**

дашдөшэјэн : *n* pavement layer *worker who lays pavement*

дашдуз : *n* rock salt

дашыјычы : *n* 1) carter, carrier 2) porter

дашыма : *n* conveyance, transportation, transference

дашымаг : *v* carry, convey, transport, transfer

дашындырмаг : *v* 1) make change his/her mind/decision 2) move *from one place to another*

дашынмаг : *v* 1) emigrate, resettle 2) be carried away

дашырмаг, дашыртмаг : *v* pour somewhere else *from A.to B.,* decant, pour over the edge

дашытдырмаг, дашытмаг : *caus of* **дашымаг**

дашјонан : *n* stonecutter, mason

дашка : *n* 1) two-wheeled cart 2) wheelbarrow, hand-cart

дашкэнд : *n* Tashkent *capital of the Uzbek Republic*

дашкэсэн : *n* see **дашгыран**

дашламаг : *v* 1) pave with stones 2) throw, cast stones

дашлатмаг : *caus of* **дашламаг**

дашлашма : *n* 1) fossilization, petrification 2) throwing one stone after another

дашлашмаг : *v* 1) turn to stone, petrify 2) throw one stone after another

дашлы : *a* containing stones, stone

дашлыг : *n* 1) stoney/rocky terrain *a* 2) stoney, rocky

дашма : *v* 1) from **дашмаг** *n* 2) rice pilaff

дашмаг : *v* 1) overflow, go over the banks *body of water* 2) boil over, flow from one place to another, flow over the edge

дашмишарлајан : *n* stone-cutter, quarry-man

дашнаг : *n* dašnak *member of the worldwide Armenian nationalist political party*

дашүрэкли : *a* heartless, hard-hearted, pitiless, implacable

дашүрэклилик : *n* hard-heartedness, heartlessness

дашчы : *n* mason, stonemason, stone-cutter

дашчыхаран : *n* see **дашгыран** 1)

двојној : *a Ru* double

дворјан : *n* 1) nobleman *a* 2) noble

дворјанлыг : *n* nobility

девирмэк : *v* 1) overturn, topple over 2) overthrow, throw down

деврилиш, деврилмэ : *n* overthrow, overturn subversion, revolution

деврилмэз : *a* stable, not susceptible to revolution/overthrow/subversion

деврилмэк : *pass* be overthrown, toppled, subverted

деди-году : *n* gossip, calumny, scandal, whispering

деди-годучу : *n* gossip, scandal-monger, slanderer

деди-годучулуг : *n* malicious gossip

дедикчэ : *adv* enough, quite, fully, utterly, in the highest degree

дедиртмэк : *v* ask/have//insist/compel s.o. to speak/talk

дејэ : *adv part* 1) having said that, being based *on* , originating *from conj* 2) in order to, so that

дејәк ки : *intro wd* let us suppose/assume/say that

дејәсән : *intro wd* it seems that. . ., as if/though,

дејил : *neg* not, is not

дејилиш : *n* pronunciation, accent *of speech*

дејилмәк : *v* 1) report oneself 2) be spoken pronounced 3) be named/called

дејилми : *expr* isn't that so?

дејиндирмәк : *v* make s.o. grumble, be peevish

дејинкән : *n* 1) grumbler *a* 2) peevish, cantankerous, grumbling

дејинкәнлик : *n* peevishness, cantankerousness, grumbling

дејинмә : *v* fr. **дејинмәк**

дејинмәк : *v* grumble, be peevish/cantankerous

дејичилик : *n* denunciation of, information against, informing, ratting, squealing

дејишдирмәк : *v* 1) make s.o. have angry words *with* / exchange angry words *with* , make s.o. argue with 2) make/compel to compete in the improvisation of verses and song *among ashugs, traditional narrators*

дејишмә : *n* 1) wrangling, squabbling 2) competition in improvising verses and songs *among ashugs, traditional narrators*

дејишмәк : *v* 1) wrangle, squabble 2) compete in the improvisation of verses and songs *among ashugs, traditional narrators*

дејр : *n* chapel

декабрь : *n* December

декада : *n* ten-day period

декан : *n* dean *head of a faculty*

деканлыг : *n* 1) deanship *administration of dean* 2) the duties of a dean 3) Dean's office

декламасија : *n* 1) recitation, declamation *a* 2) declamatory

декорасија : *n* 1) scenery *stage* 2) decor

декоратив : *a* decorative

демагог : *n* demagogue

демагоглуг : *n* demagogy

демагогчасына : *adv* in a demagogic, rabble-rousing manner

демәјәсән : *expr* it turns out to be/is found to be/proves to be

демәк : *v* 1) speak, talk, say 2) name, call, designate 3) articulate, pronounce *intro-wd* 4) so, consequently

демәли : *intro-wd* see **демәк** 4)

деми : *n* tube

демократ : *n* Democrat

демократизм : *n* democratism, democracy

демократија : *n* democracy

демократик : *a* democratic

демократлашдырмаг : *v* democratize

депутат : *n* deputy *elected member of a parliament*

депутатлыг : *n* rank and duties of a deputy

десантчы : *n* paratrooper

деһли : *n* Delhi *capital of India*

дешдирмәк, дешдиртмәк : *v* ask/compel s.o. to pierce/ puncture/ prick/ perforate /make a hole in

дешик : *n* 1) hole, opening, puncture, slit 2) den, lair *a* 3) worn through, full of holes

дешикачан : *n* 1) drill operator 2) punch, perforator

дешикачма : *n* boring, drilling, piercing

дешик-дешик : *a* 1) worn through; full of/pierced with holes 2) porous, spongy

дешикли : *a* worn through, having a hole, punctured

дешилмәк : *v* 1) pierce, puncture, perforate, make a hole in 2) wear through 3) burst, break, come to a head *carbuncle*

дешичи : *n* 1) driller, drill-operator *a* 2) drilling

дешмә : *n* drilling; making a hole in, perforating, punching

дешмәк : *v* 1) make a hole/holes in, chisel *through* , pierce, puncture, drill through 2) lance, cut open *carbuncle, boil*

дә : *part* see **да**

дәб : *n* 1) fashion, vogue 2) custom[s], morals and manners, tradition

дәббә : *n* 1) pretext/excuse for breaking off a deal which is already in progress 2) hernia *scrotal*

дәббәләмәк : *v* seize upon some dubious excuse to back out of a deal, back out of/refuse to conclude a deal/transaction

дәббәчи : *n* person backing out of a deal on some specious excuse

дәббәчилик : *n* tendency to "welsh", to back out of a deal on some excuse or other

дәбдәбә : *n* luxury, splendor, pomp, magnificence, ceremony, solemnity

дәбдәбәли : *a* ceremonial, splendid, luxuriant, ornate

дәбәрдилмәк, дәбәрилмәк : *v* get moving

дәбәрмәк : *v intr* make a move, get going, advance

дәбәртмәк : *v* move, budge

дәбилгә : *n* helmet

дәвә : *n* 1) camel *a* 2) camel['s]

дәвәгырхан : *n* camel-shearer

дәвәгулағы : *n bot* sea lavender, marsh rosemary *Statice* , a perennial grass indigenous to Transcaucasus and Turkestan, out of which brooms are made

дәвәгушу : *n zool* 1) ostrich *a* 2) ostrich

дәвәдабаны : *n bot* coltsfoot *Tussilago farfara*

дәвәдәлләји : *n zool* praying mantis *Mantodea*

дәвәјуну : *n* camel wool

дә'вәт : *n* invitation; call *to a meeting or party*

дәвәтиканы : *n bot* see **гангал**

дә'вәтнамә : *n* invitation card, printed invitation

дәвәчи : *n* camel herder

дәггүлбаб : *n* knocker *on a gate*

дәгиг : *a* 1) delicate, slender, thin 2) exact, punctual *adv* 3) exactly, precisely, punctually

дәгигә : *n* minute

дәгигәбашы : *adv* minute by minute

дәгигәбәдәгигә : *adv* every minute

дәгигәлик : *a* minute *second part of complex adjectives , such as 'twenty one'*

дәгигләшдирилмәк : *v* become/be defined more accurately

дәгигләшдирмә : *n* more precise/more accurate definition

дәгигләшдирмәк : *v* specify, make more exact, define more exactly

дәгиглик : *n* exactness, precision

дәдә : *n* father

дәдә-баба : *n* forefathers, fathers and grandfathers

дәдә-бабадан : *adv* from ancestral times, long ago

дәдәлик : *n* 1) stepfather 2) the paternal relationship

дәзкаһ : *n* 1) machine 2) joiner's/carpenter's bench 3) counter

дәзкаһалты : *n* space under a workbench

дәзкаһсазлајан : *n* mill-wright *specialist in repair and adjustment of machines used in factories*

дәзкаһчы : *n* machine-operator

дәјанәт : *n* tenacity, steadfastness

дәјанәтли : *a* tenacious, steadfast

дәјанәтлилик : *n* see **дәјанәт**

дәјанәтсиз : *a* 1) unstable, unpersistant *n* 2) unreliable person

дәјә : *n* shanty, hovel; tabernacle

дәјәнәк : *n* cudgel

дәјәр : *n* cost, price, value

дәјәр-дәјмәзинә : *adv* for nothing, free, cheaply

дәјәрли : *a* 1) valuable 2) sensible, worthy, worthwhile 3) qualitative

дәјәрсиз : *a* 1) worthless 2) good-for-nothing, unfit, trifling

дәјәрсизлик : *n* 1) valuelessness 2) unfitness, uselessness, unsuitableness, insignificance

дәјирман : *n* 1) mill *a* 2) mill, milling

дәјирмандашы : *n* millstone

дәјирманлыг : *n* grain set aside for milling

дәјирманчы : *n* miller

дәјирманчылыг : *n* miller's profession, milling

дәјирми : *a* round

дәјирмиләмәк : *v* see **дәјирмиләтмәк**

дәјирмиләнмәк : *v* get/become round

дәјирмиләтмәк, дәјирмиләшдирмәк *v* round, make round

дәјирмиләшмәк : *v* see **дәјирмиләнмәк**

дәјирмилик : *n* roundness

дәјирмисифәт : *a* curvilinear

дәјирмисов, дәјирмитәһәр : *a* somewhat rounded

дәјирмичә : *a* a bit rounded

дәјишдирилмәк : *v* cause to be changed

дәјишдиричи : *n elect* switch

дәјишдирмә : *n* 1) exchange, substitution 2) renewal, alteration, modification

дәјишдирмәк : *v* 1) exchange, replace, substitute 2) do anew, refashion 3) alter, change, modify

дәјишәк : *n* 1) underclothes 2) change *of linen*

дәјишәклик : *a* earmarked/suitable for linens *cloth*

дәјишәктикән : *n* seamstress

дәјишән : *a phys* 1) variable, varying, fluctuating, alternating *other meanings on this theme*

дәјишик : *a* entangled, confused, mixed-up, muddled, exchanged/substituted by mistake

дәјишиклик : *n* 1) change, alteration 2) break, breaking

дәјишилән : *a* changing, changeable, varying, unstable

дәјишилмә : *n* change, alteration, modification

дәјишилмәз : *a* constant, changeless, immutabled, unaltered

дәјишилмәк : *v* 1) alter, regenerate 2) exchange *accidentally* , change 3) switch *over to other work*

дәјишкән : *a* changeable, changeful, inconstant

дәјишкәнлик : *n* vicissitude, changeableness, mutability, inconstancy

дәјишмә : *n* 1) exchange, interchange 2) alteration *gram* 3) conjugation

дәјишмәк : *v* change, exchange, alter *gram* 2) conjugate

дәјјус : *n* cuckold

дәјмәдүшәр : *n* 1) touchy person *a* 2) touchy, quick to take offense

дәјмәдүшәрлик : *n* touchiness, susceptibility to offense

дәјмәз : *intj* Don't mention it! Not at all! You're welcome! *response to 'thank you'*

дәјмәк : *v* 1) touch, brush against 2) hit, strike *against* 3) ripen 4) call on, come to see, look in on

дәлдирмәк, дәлдиртмәк : *caus of* **дәлмәк**

дәлә : *n zool* squirrel

дәләгарын : *a* 1) voracious, gluttonous, insatiable *n* 2) glutton

дәләгарынлыг : *n* gluttony, piggishness

дәләдуз : *n* swindler, scoundrel

дәләдузлуг : *n* fraud, swindle

дәләдузчасына : *adv in a* fraudulent, crooked way

дәләмә : *n* soft cheese *cheese which has not yet become firm*

дәли : *a* 1) demented, mentally ill, insane, crazy, touched *n* 2) lunatic, mad person 3) madcap 4) fool

дәлибаш : *a* 1) violent, wild, furious *n* 2) madcap, dare-devil

дәлибашлыг : *n* violence, wildness, fury

дәлибәнк : *n bot* thornapple, Locoweed Datura stramonium

дәлибөјүрткән : *n bot* blackberry, bramble *Rubus*

дәлиганлы : *n* 1) dare-devil, bold spirit, dashing fellow 2) young lad *a* 3) fervent, ardent

дәлиганлылыг : *n* fervor, ardence

дәли-диванә : *a* see **диванә**

дәли-долу : *a* smart, sharp

дәлик : *n* 1) hole, aperture, chink, slit, gap *a* 2) worn through

дәлик-дешик : *n coll* holes, slits

дәлик-дәлик : *a* full of holes, completely worn out

дәлил : *n* 1) reason, motive 2) proof

дәлилик : *n* insanity, mental illness, lunacy

дәлилсиз : *a* unfounded, unsupported by evidence

дәлилсизлик : *n* prooflessness

дәлинмәк : *v* see **дешилмәк**

дәлиоту : *n bot* sedge *Carex caespitoza*

дәлисов : *a* half-witted, unbalanced, crazy

дәлисовлуг : *n* half-wittedness, lunacy, looniness

дәлихана : *n* insane asylum, hospital for the mentally ill

дәличәсинә : *adv* insanely, crazily

дәллал : *n* broker, go-between

дәллаллыг : *n* 1) brokerage, mediation 2) fee, honorarium, recompense for mediation

дәлләк : *n* 1) barber 2) masseur *in a bath-house* 3) swindler, fleecer

дәлләклик : *n* 1) job/profession of barber/masseur *fig* 2) characteristics of a swindler

дәлләкхана : *n* barbershop

дәлмә : *n* punching *holes* , piercing, perforating

дәлмә-дешик : *n coll* 1) holes and crevices *a* 2) full of holes

дәлмәк : *v* 1) pierce, drill 2) perforate 3) puncture, make a hole in

дәм : *n* 1) fumes 2) brewing *tea* 3) moment, instant

дәмадәм, дәмбәдәм : *adv* every minute, continuously, constantly

дәмдәмәки : *a* 1) unsteady, changeable, thoughtless, frivolous 2) giddy person, flibbertigibbet

дәмдәмәкилик : *n* 1) inconstancy, frivolousness 2) foppery 3) snobbery

дәмәшг : *n* Damascus *capital of Syria*

дәмир : *n* 1) iron *a* 2) iron, ferrous

дәмирағач : *n bot* iron tree *a tree of the Gynera Sideroxilon*

дәмир-бетон : *n* 1) reinforced concrete, ferro-concrete *a* 2) reinforced concrete, ferro-concrete

дәмирдашыјан : *n* iron-carrier/transporter

дәмирдоғрајан : *n* iron cutter

дәмирјајан : *n* iron roller

дәмирјол : *a* railroad

дәмирјолчу : *n* railroad worker

дәмирчи : *n* blacksmith

дәмирчилик : *n* blacksmith's trade

дәмирчихана : *n* smithy, forge, blacksmith's shop

дәмјә : *a* unirrigated, dry-farm

дәмкеш : *n* part of the samovar above its chimney or flue upon which the tea-pot rests and where it is kept heated while the tea brews

дәмләмәк : *v* 1) make, brew *tea* 2) steam *rice pilaf*

дәмләнмәк : *v intr pass* 1) brew, be brewed *tea* 2) steam, be steamed/steaming *rice pilaf*

дәмләтмәк : *caus of* **дәмләмәк**

дәмров : *n med* herpes *viral skin desease*

дән : *n* 1) grain 2) chicken-feed

дәндә : *n* spoke *wheel*

дән-дән : *a* 1) granular *adv* 2) grain by grain

дәндәнә : *n tech* cog wheel, toothed wheel 2) tooth; cog, lug

дәндәнәли : *a* 1) toothed, geared, cogged; 2) notched, jagged

дәнә : *n* 1) thing, piece *counting classifier for inanimate objects* 2) seed, kernel

дәнәвәр : *a* granular

дәнә-дәнә : *adv* by the piece

дәнәләмәк : *v* husk/pod/shell *corn, oeas, nuts etc* , remove the chaff *from grain*

дәнләтдирмәк : *v* 1) ask/make s.o. to husk/pod/shell *corn, peas, nuts etc.* 2) ask/make s.o. to remove the chaff *from grain*

дәнәләтмәк *see* **дәнәләтдирмәк**

дәни : *a* see **әдна**

дәниз : *n* 1) sea *a* 2) sea, maritime

дәнизгарангушу : *n zool* phaeton, a tropical sea bird *genus Phaetontidae*

дәнизоту : *n bot* see **чығ**

дәнизпәриси : *n* Siren *sea nymph*

дәнизпишији : *n zool* sea bear, fur seal

дәнизчи : *n* 1) sailor, seaman *a* 2) sailor['s], seaman['s]

дәнизчилик : *n* 1) navigation, seafaring *a* 2) navigational, nautical, seafaring

дәнилик : *n* see **әдналыг**

дәнјејән : *a zool* granivorous

дәнк, дәнкәсәр : *adjective in combinations* : **дәнк** ***дәнкәсәр*** **етмәк** ***еләмәк*** annoy s.o. by constant chattering, talk nonsense, weary s.o. with idle or loud talk, shouting

дәнкил-дүнкүл : *a* 1) sparse, scattered *adv* 2) sparsely, infrequently/ sporadically occurring

дәнләмәк : *v* peck, peck up kernels *poultry*

дәнли : *a* cereal, grain

дәнлик : *n* crop, craw *poultry* 2) poultry-feed *grain* 2) grain piled up for milling 4) seed grain

дәнсиз : *a* having no kernels *of a head of corn or grain*

дәрбәдәр : *n obs* wanderer

дәрбәнд : *n geog* 1) anticline, ravine 2) Derbent *port-city in Dagestan, about 150 miles north of Baku*

дәрбәст : *a* fenced in, isolated *e.g. house*

дәрбәчә : *n* door, *wicket* gate

дәрвиш : *n* dervish *wandering anchorite, member of any of a number of Moslem orders dedicated to poverty and chastity*

дәрд : *n* grief, sorrow, anguish

дәрд-гәм : *n* see **дәрд-гәм**

дәрдәчәр : *a* 1) ailing, sickly, unwell *n* 2) poor devil

дәрдирмәк : *v* request that/make s.o. gather/pluck *fruit , berries, flowers*

дәрди-сәр : *n* trouble, efforts, cares, concerns

дәрдләндирмәк : *v* distress, grieve s.o.

дәрдләнмәк : *v* grieve *about, over* mourn *over* , sorrow *over*

дәрдләшмә : *n* mutual condolences on one-another's grief, sorrow

дәрдләшмәк : *v* mutually confide/unburden one another's grief

дәрдли : *a* 1) hapless, ill-starred, burdened down with sorrow 2) sickly, ailing

дәрдлилик : *n* sorrow, sorrowful state

дәрдсиз, дәрдсиз-гәмсиз : *a* 1) light-hearted, carefree *adv* 2) light-heartedly, unconcernedly

дәрә : *n* ravine, gully, valley, gorge

дәрәбәји : *n* feudal lord

дәрәбәјлик : *n* feudalism

дәрәлик : *n* terrain broken by ravines, gullies

дәрә-тәпә : *n* hilly, rugged country

дәрәчә : *n* 1) grade, rank 2) degree 3) category, class

дәрәчәсиз : *a* having no title or degree; unclassified

дәрз : *n* sheaf

дәрзбағлајан : *n agric* binder *a machine that cuts and ties grain* 2) sheaf-binder *agent*

дәрзи : *n* tailor, dressmaker

дәрзилик : *n* tailoring trade, dressmaking trade

дәрзихана : *n* tailor-shop

дәри : *n* 1) skin *human* 2) hide *animal*

дәриалты : *a* subcutaneous

дәриашылајан : *n* tanner

дәрибичән : *n* leather-cutter

дәрибојајан : *n* leather-dyer

дәригашыјан : *n* hide-cleaners *worker who cleans the inner side of hides from bits of flesh etc.*

дәригурудан : *n* leather-dryer

дәридузлајан : *n* hide-salter *worker in a tannery*

дәриисладан : *n* tannery worker engaged in soaking hides

дәријамајан : *n* leather-repair person

дәријыған : *n* leather/hide collector

дәријујан : *n* leather/hide washer/cleaner *agent*

дәрилмәк : *v* be harvested, gathered, plucked, picked *fruits, flowers*

дәрин : *a* 1) deep *adv* 2) deeply

дәриндүшүнчәли : *a* profound, thoughtful

дәринләтмәк, дәринләшдирмәк : *v* 1) deepen, become deeper 2) aggravate

дәринләшдиртмәк : *caus of* **дәринләшдирмәк**

дәринләшмәк : *v* deepen, become deeper

дәринлик : *n* 1) depth, profondity *a* 2) deep

дәринфикирли : *a* profound, thoughtful

дәринфикирлилик : *n* profundity, insight, depth of thought

дәрисаггову : *n vet* strangles *contagious disease*

дәрисечән : *n* hide-grader, leather-grader *agent*

дәрисигара : *a* black, black-skinned

дәрисојан : *n* skinner *one engaged in skinning hides, firs from dead animals*

дәричи : *n* see **даббағ**

дәрја : *n* sea, ocean

дәрјаз : *n* scythe

дәрк : *in v-cmp* : **дәрк еләмәк *етмәк*** 1) get to know 2) get it, get the point 3) understand, grasp, take in, comprehend

дәркәнар : *n* instructions *in a document*

дәрман : *n* remedy, medicine, medicament, pill

дәрмангајыран : *n* pharmacist

дәрманламаг : *v* treat with a disinfectant solution, disinfect

дәрманланмаг : *pass* be treated with a disinfectant solution, be disinfected

дәрманлатдырмаг, дәрманлатмаг : *v* ask/make s.o. disinfect/ treat with a disinfectant solution

дәрмәк : *v* pick, pluck, gather *fruits, berries, flowers*

дәрнәк : *n* circle, study group

дәрнәкчилик : *n* clannishness

дәрракә : *n* consciousness, perception, intelligence, realization

дәрракәли : *a* conscious, perceptive, understanding, intelligent

дәрракәсиз : *a* imperceptive, lacking understanding, unintelligent

дәрракәсизлик : *n* thoughtlessness, lack of receptivity, slow-wittedness, stupidity

дәрс : *n* 1) lesson 2) subject *of study* , discipline

дәрслик : *n* textbook, manual

дәрһал : *adv* immediately, at once, without delay

дәрч : *in comb* : **дәрч еләмәк *етмәк*** seal, stamp *with a seal*

дәсмал : *n* handkerchief

дәсмалламаг : *v* wipe with a handkerchief

дәсмаллыг : *a* handkerchief *attrib*

дәст : *n* 1) pair *of clothing* 2) set

дәставүз : *n* proof, argument

дәстана : *n* see **фәтир**

дәст-дәст : *adv* in sets

дәстә : *n* 1) bouquet, bunch 2) group, detachment/column 3) hilt, handle 4) pile, stack 5) troupe, company *of actors*

дәстәбаз : *n* person inclined to clannishness, cliquishness

дәстәбазлыг : *n* lobbyism; clannishness

дәстәбашы : *n* group leader

дәстәбашылыг : *n* role/activity of a group leader

дәстә-дәстә : *adv* 1) in bunches/bouquets 2) in groups/ detachments/columns 3) in piles/stacks

дәстәк : *n* 1) handle, hilt 2) strut, brace 3) receiver *telephone* 4) cuff

дәстәкли : *a* see **дәстәли**

дәстәләмәк : *v* 1) form into a group, gather into a single whole 2) compose a bouquet

дәстәли : *a* having a handle/haft/hilt

дәстәмаз : *n* ritual ablution before public worship *Moslem*

дәстәрхан : *see* **сүфрә**

дәстәфәрман : *n* errand boy

дәсткаh : *n* 1) luxury, decoration *mus* 2) set of musical instruments 3) appliance, apparatus

дәсткаhлы : *a* luxurious, splendid, magnificent, well-furnished/decorated

дәстләшдирмәк : *v* bring up to strength, equip fully

дәстпәрвәрдә : *n* pupil, foster child

дәстур : *n* 1) formula, prescription 2) instruction

дәстхәт : *n* handwriting

дәсхош : *n* celebration *on making a good bargain*

дәф : *n* 1) drum 2) see **гавал** 3) repulse, repelling, beating off *an onslaught/attack*

дәф етмәк : *n* repulse, repel, beat off

дәфгајыран : *n* master drum-maker

дәфә : *n* times *as in multiplied by*

дәфәләрлә, дәфәләрчә : *adv* repeatedly, time and time again, many times

дәфинә : *n* buried treasure

дәфн : *n* 1) funeral *a* 2) funeral, funereal

дәфнә : *n* *bot* laurel *Laurus*

дәфтәр : *n* notebook

дәфтәрхана : *n* 1) stationery *a* 2) stationery

дәфтәрханачы : *n* clerk

дәфтәрханачылыг : *n* red-tape

дәфтәрчә : *n* exercise-book, copy-book, blank writing-book

дәфчалан, дәфчи : *n* drummer, percussionist

дәхи : *conj* also, as well, too

дәхли : *in compounds* : **дәхли олмаг** touch, concern, have to do with, relate to

дәhә : *n* strip/zone/area between two irrigation ditches/canals

дәhләмәк : *v* urge on, drive *beast of burden, draft animal*

дәhлиз : *n* outer entrance hall, ante-room, vestibule

дәhмәрләмәк : *v* urge on, say "come on"

дәhнә : *n* 1) dam, weir 2) floodgate 3) bridle

дәhрә : *n* 1) large garden knife; peat cutter 2) large kitchen knife for chopping/mincing meat, chopper

дәhшәт : *n* fear, fright, terror; nightmare

дәhшәтләндирмәк : *v* 1) frighten, scare, terrify, horrify, terrorize

дәhшәтләнмәк : *v* be afraid of, fear, give way to fear

дәhшәтли : *a* 1) terrible, frightful, horrible *adv* 2) terribly, horribly, terrifyingly

дәч : *a* full to the brim/edge, overfilled

дәчәл : *n* 1) rake, scapegrace, mischief-maker, prankster *a* 2) playful, lively, capricious

дәчәлләшмәк : *v* become mischievous/playful, be naughty, play tricks

дәчәллик : *n* prank, trick, naughtiness

дәчлә : *n* Tigris *river in Mesopotamia*

дәччал : *n* *relig* 1) Evil personified *in Moslem religious tradition an anti-Mohammed who will come mounted on an ass before the end of the world; analogue of Antichrist* *ext* 2) an iniquitious, wicked, despicable person

ди : *intj* Well! Right! *used in prompting to some action*

диагонал : *n* 1) diagonal *a* diagonal

диаграм : *n* graph, chart, diagram

диалект : *n* 1) dialect *a* 2) dialectal, dialect

диалектик : *a* *philos* dialectical

диалектика : *n* *philos* dialectics

диалектоложи : *a* *ling* dialectological *pertaining to dialectology*

диалектоложи : *n* *ling* dialectology

диаметрал : *a* 1) diameter, diametric *adv* 2) diametrically

диб : *n* 1) bottom 2) depth, root, basis *of a matter, a problem, a question*

диб-дәһнә : *n* see **диб** 2)

дибәк : *n* 1) wooden mallet 2) mortar *ceramic or stone vessel used for grinding substances*

дибибиз : *a* having a pointed *acutely angled* bottom

дибијасты : *a* flat-bottomed

дибсиз : *a* 1) bottomless 2) very deep

дибчәк : *n* flower-pot

дибчик : *n* rifle-butt, rifle-stock

див : *n* 1) monster, giant *fig* 2) person of huge strength, and build

диван : *n* 1) court, law-court 2) punishment, reprisal 4) divan, sofa, settee *obs* 5) collection of poetical works

диванә : *a* 1) mad, crazy, insane *n* 2) insane /mentally ill, person, lunatic

диванәлик : *n* insanity, mental illness

диванәчәсинә : *adv* foolishly, crazily, wildly

диванхана : *n obs* 1) court, court-house, courtroom 2) trial 3) office, bureau *premises of a government operation*

дивар : *n* 1) wall, partition *a* 2) wall, partition

диваркағызлајан : *n* upholsterer

дигт : *n* see **вәрәм**

диггәт : *n* 1) attention 2) carefulness, diligence

диггәтәлајиг, диггәтәшајан : *a* notable, noteworthy, remarkable, worthy of attention

диггәтлә : *adv* attentively, carefully

диггәтли : *a* 1) attentive, careful 2) prompt, punctual 3) cautious *adv* attentively, carefully, cautiously

диггәтлилик : *n* 1) attentiveness, carefullness, keenness of observation 2) promptness, punctuality

диггәтсиз : *a* 1) inattentive, distracted, negligent *adv* inattentively, distractedly, negligently

диггәтсизлик : *n* inattention, carelessness, absent-mindedness

диггәтсизчәсинә : *adv* inattentively, thoughtlessly

диггәтчил : *a* attentive, careful, particular

дидактик : *a* didactic

дидәркин : *n* 1) see **авара** 2) **дидәркин салмаг** be expelled, kicked out

дидик, дидик-дидик : *a* rent, torn, ragged, ripped to pieces

дидикләмәк : *v* see **дидмәк** 1), 2)

дидилмәк : *v* 1) be torn up, become frayed, torn, ragged be torn to small pieces 2) ravel, come to pieces 3) wear out

дидишдирмәк *v* see **дидмәк**

дидишмә : n friction, disorder, discord bickering, disagreement, dissention

дидишмәк : *v* fight, squabble

дидишмәсалан : *n* squabbler; provoker

дидмә : *n* pulling/picking at, torment, tearing up

дидмәк : *v* pinch, tweak, tear off little pieces 2) tear to pieces 3) fray, wear 4) pull, scratch

диета : *n Ru* diet

диз : *n* 1) knee *a* 2) knee

дизбәдиз, диз-дизә : *adv* eye to eye, face to face

дизин-дизин : *adv* on all fours, on hands and knees

дизкин : *n* see **чилов**

дизлик : *n* shorts, knee-length pants

дијар : *n* country, land, region

дијирләмәк, дијирләндирмәк : *v* drive, bowl along

дијирләнмәк : *v* roll, rush off, take off *straight ahead*

дијирләтмәк : *v* see **дијирләмәк**

дијирчәк : *n* 1) caster *small swivelling wheel on legs of furniture* 2) scooter *text* 3) bobbin spindle

дијирчәкли : *a* roller : **дијирчәкли јастыг** *tech* roller bearing

дик : *a* 1) vertical, perpendicular 2) elevated, high, lofty 3) steep 4) ascent, rise *adv* 5) erect, upright

дикбаш : *a* 1) defiant, stubborn, disobedient 2) proud, arrogant, overbearing, not amenable to persuasion

дикбашлыг : *n* 1) recalcitrance 2) pride, arrogance, haughtiness

дикбурун : *a* 1) long-narrow-nosed *person* 2) long-narrow toed *Turkish slipper* 3) see **фындыгбурун**

дикгулаг : *a* pointy-eared

дикдабан : *a* high-heeled

дик-дик : *in combs* : **дик-дик бахмаг** look defiantly/ proudly/ haughtily/ condescendingly

дикдир : *n* slope, ascent, steep slope

дикәлмәк : *v* rise, tower *above* 2) assume a vertical position 3) half rise *to greet s.o.*

дикәлтмәк : *v* raise, lift *a little, slightly* impart a vertical position *to* , erect, hoist

дикинә : *adv* upright, on end, erect

дикләнмәк : *v* ascend to a height, rise, climb up a hill

диклик : *n* high/steep terrain

диксија : *n* articulation, enunciation

диксиндирмәк : *v* scare, frighten away

диксинмәк : *v* 1) be frightened *by* , be startled *at* , shudder/start back/recoil from an unexpected encounter with s.t. 2) shrink *from s.t.*, experience repulsion *to s.t.*

диктатор : *n* 1) dictator *a* 2) dictatorial

диктаторлуг : *n* dictatorship

диктә : *n* dictation

дикәр : *a* other, different

дил : *n* 1) tongue, language 2) key *of piano, typewriter tech* 3) latch; catch, pawl *geol* 5) spit *small point of land running into the sea*

дил вермәк : *v* promise

дил јетирмәк : *v* solicitate

дил төкмәк : *v* butter up

дилдән дүшмәк : *v* get exhausted, fatigued

дилә тутмаг : *v* expostulate

дилавәр : *a* 1) voluble, talkative, eloquent, skilful/clever in discourse 2) smart, sharp, dashing, gallant

дилавәрлик : *n* 1) eloquence, gift of speech, ability to speak well 2) courage, bravery, valor

дилавәрчәсинә : *adv* 1) volubly, eloquently 2) courageously, bravely, valorously

дилазар : *a* speaking with malice, calumniating o.'s colleagues

дилалты : *a* sublingual

дилбәр : *n poetic* 1) sweetheart, charmer 2) Dilbar *feminine first name*

дилбилмәз : *a* muddle-headed, stupid, slow-witted *lit. 'one who does not understand the language'*

дилбир : *a* 1) unanimous, united *with* , at one *with* *n* 2) like-minded person, person of like mind, person holding the same views

дилбирлик : *n* harmony/conformity/identity of ideas/opinions, agreement, solidarity

диләк : *n* wish, desire, request

диләмәк : *v* wish, desire, request

диләнмәк : *v* beg, go begging, request alms

диләнчи : *n* beggar, pauper

диләнчилик : *n* begging

диләнчипајы : *n* alms, handout, dole

дилиачы : *a* see **ачыдил**

дилик : *n colloq* stripe

дилик-дилик : *adv* 1) in scallops *a* 2) scalloped, saw-edged

диликли : *a* tooth-edged, scalloped, corrugated, rippled

диликөдәк : *a* exposed, unmasked, guilty *of*

дилим : *n* slice, round *bread, melon, cucumber*

дилим-дилим : *adv* rounds/slices

дилимләмәк : *v* cut into slices/rounds/slice up, cut up

дилимләнмәк : *v pass* be cut into slices/rounds, be sliced up, be cut up

дилиширин : *a* 1) honey-tongued *n* 3) stammerer, stuttering

дилкир : *a* see **дилхор**

дилләндирмәк : *v* 1) compel/make to speak/answer, draw into conversation 2) interrogate, question, examine

дилләнмәк : *v* begin to speak *after a silent period*

дилләшмәк : *v* 1) quarrel *with,* argue *with,* abuse one another

дилли, дилли-ағызлы, : *a* see **'дилли-дилавәр'**

дилли-дилавәр : *a* glib-tongued, talkative

диллилик : *n* volubility, talkativeness, loquaciousness

дилманч : *n* translator, interpreter

дилоту : *in combinations* : **дилоту јемәк** be restless, fidgety; speak incessantly

дилөнү : *a ling* velarised

дилсиз : *a* taciturn, silent

дилсиз-ағызсыз : *a* unreciprocated, without a murmur, uncomplaining, submissive

дилсизлик : *n* 1) speechlessness, muteness, dumbness *fig* 2) silent acceptance of reproaches/demands

дилтутулмасы : *n med* aphasia *partial or total loss of power of articulate speech*

дилучу : *n* 1) *ling* apical, apico-dental *articulated with the apex of the tongue touching or approaching the upper teeth* *adv* 2) in passing, casually

дилхор : *a* sad, downcast, depressed

дилхорлуг : *n* 1) depression, blues, grief, distress 2) tedium, boredom

дилхорчу : *a* 1) boring, tiresome, irksome, annoying *n* 2) bore

дилхорчулуг : *n* see **дилхорлуг**

дилхош : *a* merry, jolly, joyful

дилхошлуг : *n* courtesy, compliment

дилчә : *n* *tech* detent, arresting device, stop

дилчәк : *n* *anat* 1) uvula *tech* 2) button, push-button, knob

дилчи : *n* linguist

дилчилик : *n* linguistics

дилчавабы : *a* 1) oral, verbal, vocal *adv* 2) orally, verbally, by word of mouth, aloud

дилшүнас : *n* see **дилчи**

дилшүнаслыг : *n* see **дилчилик**

димдик : *n* *zool* beak, bill

димдик : *adv* 1) at attention, at full height 2) on end, upright, erect

димдикбурун : *a* aquiline-nosed, eagle-beaked

димдикләмәк : *v* peck

димдири : *a* very lively, very smart/bright

дин : *n* religion

динамик : *a* dynamic

динамика : *n* dynamics

динамомашин : *n* *elec* dynamo

диндар : *a* see **динчи**

диндарлыг : *n* see **динчилик**

диндаш : *n* 1) co-religionist *one belonging to the same religious faith* *a* 2) sharing the same religion

диндашлыг : *n* commonality of religion *condition of belonging to the same religion*

диндирмә : *n* interrogation, examination, inquiry

диндирмәк : *v* begin to speak *with* , summon for a talk, conversation 2) interrogate

дини : *a* religious

диниш : *n* squared beam, squared timber

динк : *n* sheller, hulling mill, rice-hulling mill

динки : *n* see **тинк, тинки**

динкилдәмәк : *v* 1) jump up, jump/bob up and down 2) shake, tremble, rock/reel in place

динкилдәтмәк : *v* 1) make/compel to jump, jump up *and down* 2) make/compel to shake/tremble 3) make/compel to dance

динкилти : *n* 1) rocking, swing, jumping up and down 2) shaking, trembling, dancing

динкиш : *a* 1) frivolous *n* 2) giddy person

динкчи : *n* thresher

динләјә-динләјә : *adv* listening, harking *to*

динләјичи : *n* listener

динләјиш, динләмә : *n* hearing, audition, listening

динләмәк : *v* hear, listen

динләнилмәк : *pass* be heard

динләнмәк : *pass* be heard

динмәз : *a* 1) taciturn, tacit, silent *adv* 2) silently, tacitly, without a word

динмәз-данышмаз : *a* see **дилсиз-ағызсыз**

динмәз-сөјләмәз : *a* see **дилсиз-ағызсыз**

динмәзлик : *n* see **динмәмәзлик**

динмәзчә : *adv* silently, tacitly, without a word, implicitly

динмәк : *v* say, utter

динмәмәзлик : *n* taciturnity, reticence

динсиз : *n* atheist, unbeliever

динсизлик : *n* atheism, unbelief

динсизчә, динсизчәсинә : *adv* heartlessly, mercilessly

динчи : *n* believer, religious advocate

динчилик : *n* religiousness, piety

динч : *a* 1) quiet, calm, tranquil, peaceful *adv* 2) quietly, peacefully, tranquilly

динчәлиш, динчәлмә : *n* rest, respite, breathing-spell

динчәлмәз : *a* restless, fidgety, uneasy

динчәлмәк : *v* 1) rest, pause for breath, take a short rest 2) calm/quiet/settle down, resign o.s.

динчәлтмәк : *v* calm, quiet, sooth

динчләшдирмәк : *v* pacify, quiet

динчләшмәк : *v* grow quiet

динчлик : *n* 1) rest, peace, calm 2) short rest, break, breathing spell

диншунаслыг : *n* theology, the study of religion

дипдири : *a* 1) alive, quite alive 2) not quite cooked *cereals*

дипломатија : *n* diplomacy

дипломатик : *a* 1) diplomatic *adv* 2) diplomatically

дипломатлыг : *n* tactfulness

дипломлу : *a* possessing a diploma, granted a diploma

дипломсуз : *a* not having a diploma

дир-диррик : *n* 1) house with a lot of land attached to it 2) utensils

директив : *n* 1) instructions *written, published* *a* 2) instructional

директор : *n* director, boss, headmaster, principal

директорлуг : *n* 1) post and duties of a director 2) board of directors, management

дирәк : *n* post, pillar, log, beam, girder 2) prop, support

дирәмәк : *v* rest/set/put/place against, prop up

дирәнмәк : *v* 1) be placed against, be propped, supported 2) insist on, demand persistently 3) persist

дири : *a* 1) alive, living; energetic, vivacious 2) hard, firm, incompletely cooked *of cereal, rice*

дирибаш : *a* lively, animated, brisk, smart, agile, resourceful, adroit

дирибашлыг : *n* liveliness, animation, agility, resourcefulness, adroitness

дири-дири : *adv* alive

дирижор : *n* conductor *orchestra*

дирижорлуг : *n* directorship *orchestra*

дирилдичи : *a* life-giving, vivifying

дирилик : *n* life, existence, being; vivacity

дирилмә : *n* resurrection, reanimation, revival, return to life

дирилмәк : *v* return to life, revive; take heart

дирилтмәк : *v* raise from the dead, revive, resuscitate, return to life, animate

диринкә : *n* light/simple dance music

дирисојан : *n* 1) knacker *one who butchers and skins old or disabled animals* *fig* 2) cruel person

диррик : *n* garden

диррикчи : *n* gardener

диррикчилик : *n* market-gardening truck-gardening

дирсәк : *n* 1) elbow 2) bend, curve *of a river* *tech* 3) arm, bracket

дирсәкләмәк : *v* 1) elbow, poke with the elbow 2) rest the elbows *on*

дирсәкләнмәк : *v* lean o.'s elbows on

дирсәкли : *a* *tech* elbow[ed], knee-like, geniculate

дирчәлмә : *n* reanimation, reviving, revival, rebirth

дирчәлиш : *n* reanimation, revival, rebirth, resurrection

дирчәлмәк : *v* 1) revive, reanimate 2) become animated, liven up, become frisky 3) get better, recover, summon up energy, get stronger

дирчәлтмәк : *v* 1) enliven, animate 2) invigorate, give strength, further/be conducive to recovery

диссертасија : *n* 1) thesis, dissertation *a* 2) thesis, dissertational

диссимилјасија : *n* dissimilation

дитдили : *n* gnat, mosquito

диш : *n* 1) tooth *tech* 2) cog, lug 3) dental, tooth

дишбатан : *a* vulnerable

дишбатмаз : *a* invulnerable

диш-диш : *a* 1) toothed, cogged, notched, jagged *n* 2) notch, jag

дишәбәнзәр : *a* tooth-like, odontoid

дишәдәјәр : *a* edible

дишәмәк : *v* 1) replace the milk teeth 2) serrate, notch, sharpen the teeth of a saw, serrations of a millstone etc

диши : *n* female *animal*

дишичик : *n* *bot* pistil

дишлә : *n* pole, beam

дишләк, дишләк-дишләк : *n* 1) bite, sting *a* 2) bitten, stung

дишләмә : *v* 1) from **дишләмәк** *adv* 2) **дишләмә чај** unsweetened tea drunk while holding a piece of loaf sugar in o.'s mouth

дишләмәк : *v* bite, sting

дишли : *a* 1) toothed, cogged, having cogs/lugs *fig* 2) large-toothed

дишсиз : *a* 1) toothless *zool* 2) edentate, edentulous

дишчәкән : *n* *colloq* dentist

дыбыр : *n* young goat *older than two years*

дығ : *n* see **вәрәм**

дыға : *n* *slightly perjorative* Armenian

дығырламаг : *v* see **дијирләмәк**

дызылдамаг : *v* hum, buzz, drone

дызылты : *n* humming, buzzing, droning

дызыхгулу : **дызыхгулуја дәм вәрмәк** see **дызыхмаг**

дызыхмаг : *v* make off, run away *from* , try to get out of s.t.

дызман : *n* sheep, ram *older than five years*

дылғыр : *a* 1) useless, good-for nothing *n* 2) ragamuffin, ragged fellow, riff-raff

дымыг : *n* sheep with very short ears, and a heavy, fatty tail

дымырчыг : *n* hillock

дымырчыг-дымырчыг : *a* rough, knobby, knobbly, pock-marked

дымырчыглы : *a* see **дымырчыг-дымырчыг**

дынгылдамаг : *v* jingle, rattle, clank

дынгылдатмаг : *v* 1) ring. clang 2) make a jingling sound on s.t. 3) rattle

дынгылы : *a* small, little, diminutive, tiny, wee

дынгылты : *n* 1) peal, ringing, clanging 2) jingling

дыппылы : *a* see **дынгылы**

дырмаламаг : *v* see **чырмагламаг**

дырманмаг, дармашмаг : *v* climb *up* , clamber *up* , scramble *up*

дырмыг : *n* rake

дырмыгламаг : *v* 1) rake up, gather together by raking 2) harrow, scrape with a harrow

дырмыгчы : *n* excavator, excavating machine, shoveler *machine*

дырнаг : *n* 1) finger-nail, toenail, claw 2) hoof 3) inverted comma, quotation mark

дырнагламаг : *v* pick at, scratch with a *finger* nail

дырнаглы : *a* 1) hooved, having a hoof, ungulate 2) tenacious, able to hold on

дырнагшәкилли, дырнағаохшар : *-a* fingernail-shaped

дышары : *a* external, outward

дов : **дов кәлмәк** frighten, scare

довға : *n* dovğa *soup with rice and vegetables in sour milk*

довдаг : *n* *zool* bustard *Otididae* , a bird

довтәләб : *a* 1) warlike, belligerent 2) arousing, provoking *n* 3) lover, fan *of s.t.*

довшан : *n* 1) hare, rabbit *a* 2) hare['s], rabbit's

довшандодаг : *n* hare-lip *a congenital fissure of the upper lip*

довшанјатышы : *n* hare's lair

доггаз : *n* wicket-gate

доггуз : *num* nine

доггузајлыг : *a* nine-month

доггуз-доггуз : *adv* in nines, in groups of nine

доггузиллик : *a* nine-year *lasting/ continuing for nine years*

доггузјашлы : *a* nine-year old

доггузкүнлүк : *a* ten-day *lasting/continuing for ten days*

доггузлуг : *num* 1) nine 2) nine *in cards*

доггузмәртәбә : *a* ten-story

доггузрәгәмли : *math* nine-digit

доггузсинифли : *a* ninth-grade *of class in school*

доггузунчу : *a* *num* ninth

доггузча : *num* nine in all, a total of nine; only nine, just nine

доғанаг : *n* 1) kind of hook *used to tighten the loop or knot* 2) hide-scraper

доғар : *a* fruitful, fecund, bearing young *of a domestic animal*

доғма : *v* 1) from **доғмаг** 2) childbearing, procreation *a* 3) own *by blood relation in the direct line*

доғмаг : *v* 1) bear, give birth; calve, foal, lamb 2) rise *sun, moon* 3) arise, be born, come into existence/being

доғрама : *vn* 1) from **доғрамаг** 2) okroshka *cold Russian kvass soup with chopped vegetables and meat*

доғрамаг : *v* 1) chop 2) crumble, chop into pieces

доғрамач : *n* see **доғрама** 2)

доғрам-доғрам : *a* all cut up/cut to pieces

доғранмаг : *v* 1) be chopped into very small pieces 2) be crumbled

доғратдырмаг, доғратмаг : *caus* of **доғрамаг**

доғру : *a* 1) faithful, true, straightforward, open-hearted 2) right, veritable, real, trustworthy *postp* 3) to. . ., on the road/way to. . . *n* 4) truth

доғру чыхмаг : *v* turn to be true

доғрудан : *adv* really/really and truly, indeed, in truth

доғрудан-доғруја *adv* 1) frankly, directly 2) truth to say, to tell the truth

доғруданмы : *adv* really? Is it possible?

доғрујабәнзәр, доғрујаохшар : *a* very probable, likely, seeming to be true

доғрулмаг : *v* 1) justify o.s., turn out to be right/that o. is right 2) become straight, make straight, straighten

доғрултмаг : *v* justify, prove the value of

доғрулуг : *n* 1) honesty, integrity, correctness, straightforwardness 2) truth 3) plain dealing

доғрулугсевэн : *a* truth-loving

доғрулугсевэнлик : *n* love of truth

доғрусу : *intrd wd* to tell you the truth, indeed, really

доғручу : *a* truthful, veracious, upright

доғручулуг : *n* truthfulness, veracity, uprightness

доғруча : *adv* truthfully, uprightly

доғуб-төрэмэк : *v* procreate, give birth, bring into the world, breed, spawn

доғуздурмаг : *v* assist during parturition/birth/labor

доғулмаг : *v* 1) be born, come into being 2) come into the world, come into existence, arise

доғулуш : *n* 1) birth 2) birth rate 3) appearance, origin, beginnings

доғум : *n* 1) childbirth, lying-in *a* 2) delivery, lying-in, maternity

доғурмаг : *v* see **доғуздурмаг**

дод : *in combs* : **дод вермэк** pull the wool over s.o.'s eyes, deceive with empty promises

додаг : *n* 1) lips *a* 2) labial

додагвары : *a* in the form of lips, shaped like lips

додагланма : *n ling* labialization

додагланмајан : *a* lipless, thin-lipped

додағыјоғун : *a* thick-lipped

додағысаллаг : *a* see **лөкдодаг**

доду : *n* Christmas carol

дозангурду : *n* bombardier beetle *Brachinus tscherniki, that, upon irritation, releases an acrid liquid*

дојдурма : *n* satiation, satiety

дојдурмаг : *v* feed *to satiation*, satiate, sate *with*

дојмаг : *v* eat o.'s fill, eat plenty *of*, be full, be sated

дојмаз : *a* insatiable, greedy, grasping

дојмамазлыг : *n* greed, insatiability, avidity *for*

дојуздурмаг : *v* see **дојурмаг**

дојумлу : *a* satisfied, replete, full

дојумлуг : *a* relating to a quantity of food sufficient to satisfy the appetite/hunger *tummy filling*

дојунча : *adv* to o.'s heart's content, in plenty, in abundance

дојурмаг : *v* feed to repletion/to satiety, satiate *with*, sate *with*

доклад : *n Ru* report

доктор : *n* 1) physician 2) doctor *of any discipline*

докторлуг : *n* 1) doctorate, the rank, title, profession of a doctoral science 2) medical profession *a* 2) doctoral

дол : *n* 1) leather bucket/pail 2) water-carrier

долаб : *n* 1) dodge; slyness 2) closet 3) winch

долабча : *n* bedside-table

долаг : *n* 1) puttees 2) foot-windings *worn instead of socks or stockings*

долајы : *a* 1) roundabout, indirect 2) curly, frizzy 3) zig-zag

долама : *n* 1) winding, entwining 2) zig-zag *med* 3) whitlow, felon *suppurating/ purulent inflammation of the finger* *a* 4) screw-shaped, spiral 5) roundabout, detour,

доламаг : *v* 1) wind *around*, entwine, twine *around*, wrap *up* *fig* 2) fool, make a fool of, pull the wool over the eyes *of*

доланачаг : *n* 1) life, existence 2) way of life

доланбач : *n* 1) labyrinth *a* 2) roundabout, devious, winding, labyrinthine

доландырычы : *n* 1) shady dealer, swindler, crook 2) blackmailer

доландырычылыг : *n* 1) fraud, swindle, shady transaction 2) blackmail

доландырмаг : *v* 1) turn *round and round*, drive/lead, direct *around* 2) protect/take care of, support, give subsistence *to* 3) govern/ drive/ steer/ direct/manage/superintend

доланыш, доланышыг : *n* see **доланачаг**

доланма : *v* fr. **доланмаг**

доланмаг : *v intr* turn round, revolve, rotate 2) go around, bypass, try to get around 3) walk up and down, go for a stroll, promenade 4) live, get along, get on *with* 5) treat *s.o.*

долаша : *n zool* daw, jackdaw *Corvus monedula*, bird

долашдырмаг : *v* 1) entangle, tangle, muddle up, confuse 2) bewilder, confuse *s.o.*

долашыг : *a* 1) entangled, tangled, muddled up, confused 2) unclear, misunderstood, not properly understood, confusing *adv* 3) confusedly, incomprehensibly

долашыглыг : *n* confusion, muddle, mess

долашмаг : *v* 1) get tangled, become muddled/confused, find o.s. in difficulties 2) ramble, roam, stroll

долғун : *a* 1) full 2) thick, dense; portly, burly *fig* 3) rich *in content* , substantial, valuable

долғунлашмаг : *v* grow stout, put on weight

долғунлуг : *n* stoutness, corpulence, fatness, portliness

долдурма : *v* 1) from **долдурмаг** 2) stuffed, packed

долдурмаг : *v* 1) fill 2) stuff, pack *into* 3) load, charge 4) fill *cavities in teeth* 5) fulfill *a plan*

долдуртмаг : *caus of* **долдурмаг**

долдурулмаг : *pass* 1) be filled 2) be packed, stuffed 3) be loaded, charged 4) be filled *cavities in teeth* 5) be fulfilled *i.e. plan*

доллар : *n* dollar

долма : *v* 1) from **долмаг** 2) dolma *grape leaves stuffed with ground meat and rice*

долмаг : *v* 1) fill *with* , fill up *with* 2) pack into, become packed into, stuff into, become stuffed into 3) be filled *i.e. cavities in teeth*

долу : *a* 1) full, filled, well-packed, stuffed 2) loaded, charged 3) hail, sleet, heavy shower

долувурма : *n* damage done by hail

долугијмәтли : *a* of full value, valuable

долудөјмә : *n* damage done by hail

долулуг : *n* stoutness, corpulence

долусифәт : *a* full-faced, round-faced

долухмаг, долухсунмаг : *v* be felt deeply, be experienced profoundly, be deeply touched, be moved to tears

долушмаг : *v* rush into, push a way through, shoulder o.'s way through *of a crowd of people trying to get somewhere*

долча : *n* can, jug

домба, домбаг : *a* 1) protuberant, bulging, convex 2) *adv* in relief, prominently

домбакөз : *a* goggle-eyed, pop-eyed, with bulging eyes

домбалаг : *n* somersault

домбалан : *n* truffle *genus Tuber* , a fleshy underground mushroom prized as a food delicacy

домбаланкөз : *a* see **домбакөз**

домбалмаг : *v* 1) be bent, become bent/crooked, twist 2) swell, become swollen, be inflated, distend

домбалтмаг : *v* bend, twist

дон : *n* 1) clothes, clothing 2) frost *a* 3) frozen, congealed

донанма : *n* fleet

донгабел : *a* see **донгар**

донгар : *a* 1) crooked, bent, hunched, stooped *n* 2) hump

донгарбурун : *a* hook-nosed

донгарланмаг : *v* become crooked, be bent, bend, become warped

донгарлатмаг, донгарлашдырмаг : *v* bend over, make hunched; warp

донгарлашмаг : *v* become warped/bent/curved

донгарлыг : *n* round-shoulderedness, condition/state of being stooped

донгулданма : *n* muttering, grumbling

донгулданмаг : *v* mutter, mumble, grumble

дондурма : *n* 1) ice-cream 2) freezing, congealing, congelation *a* 3) frozen *attrib* 4) pertaining to land ploughed in the autumn for spring sowing

дондурмаг : *v* freeze, ice up

дондурмасатан, дондурмачы : *n* ice-cream vendor

дондуручу : *a* refrigeratory, cooling, chilling, icy

донкихотлуг : *n* quixoticism *state of having high but impractical sentiments*

донлуг : *n* 1) salary, pay 2) wardrobe, material for clothing

донма : *n* freezing

донмаг : *v* 1) freeze, be frozen, turn to ice, ice up 2) grow numb, stiffen *from cold*

донос : *n Ru* secret information *provided to an intelligence service, police, etc about an individual*

донуб-галмаг : *v* freeze into immobility, be petrified *from surprise, fear etc.*

донуг : *a* 1) frozen, very cold 2) taken aback, puzzled 3) dull, lustreless; frosted *glass*

донуз : *n* pig, swine

донузабахан : *n* swine-herd

донузотаран : *n* swine-herd

донузсахлајан, донузчу : *n* pig-breeder

донузчулуг : *n* pig-breeding

донухмаг : *v* 1) grow dumb 2) be stunned, struck with surprise, be dumbfounded, be perplexed, be taken aback

допдолу : *a* overfilled, overcrowded, packed *so that no one else can get in*

допуск : *n Ru* security clearance *of a certain level*

дор, дорағачы : *n* mast

досент : *n* senior lecturer, assistant professor

досентлик : *n* senior-lectureship, assistant professorship

дост : *n* 1) friend, pal, buddy *a* 2) friendly, amicable

дост-ашна : *n* friends, pals, buddies

достбазлыг : *n* favoritism *towards one's friends in an economic sense; steering into jobs etc.*

достјана : *adv* see **достчасына**

достлашмаг : *v* make friends *with* , become friends

достлуг : *n* 1) friendship *a* 2) friendly

достчасына : *adv* in a friendly way/ fashion, amicably

дохсан : *num* ninety

дохсанынчы : *num* ninetieth

дохсанјашлы : *a* of ninety-years, ninety-year, ninety-year-old

дошаб : *n* došab *boiled juice of grapes and other fruits*

дәв : *n* see **див**

дөвләт : *n* 1) state 2) wealth, fortune *a* 3) state, governmental

дөвләтәзидд : *a* anti-State

дөвләти : *a* State *pertaining to a sovereign state*

дөвләтиндән : *expr* Thanks to you / due to you

дөвләтләндирмәк : *v* make richer, enrich

дөвләтләнмә : *n* enrichment

дөвләтләнмәк : *v* grow rich

дөвләтли : *a* rich, well-to-do, well-off, prosperous

дөвләтлилик : *n* prosperity, wealth

дөвләтпәрәст : *n* 1) cupidity, self-interest 2) profit-seeker, mercenary-minded person 3) statist, person loving the government

дөвр : *n* 1) period, time, epoch, era 2) cycle, revolution 3) circle, perimeter 4) circulation 5) stage

дөвран : *n* 1) circulation 2) time, period, era

дөврә : *n* 1) perimeter, circle *phys* 2) circuit 3) cycle 4) deep dish

дөврәләмә : *n* encirclement

дөврәләмәк : *v* encircle, surround

дөври : *a* 1) periodical 2) circulating, circulatory

дөвријјә : *n* 1) turn, revolution, circulation 2) circulating

дөзмәк : *v* suffer, endure, bear, stand, withstand

дөзүлмәз : *a* unbearable, intolerable, unendurable

дөзүм : *n* stability, endurance, staying-power, tolerance

дөзүмлү : *a* of great endurance, steadfast, forbearing, patient

дөзүмлүлүк : *n* stamina, endurance

дөзүмсүз : *a* 1) not hardy, unstable 2) impatient, lacking self control

дөзүмсүзлүк : *n* impatience; lack of self-control

дөјдүрмәк, дөјдүртмәк : *caus of* **дөјмәк**

дөјәнәк : *n* corn, callosity

дөјәч : *n* rammer, tamper, tamping iron *tool for working the earth*

дөјәчләмәк : *v* 1) beat, pound 2) beat around, ram, tamp, smooth down, make even

дөјмәк : *v* 1) beat unmercifully, flog, strike 2) knock, rap *on,* bang *on* 3) forge, hammer 4) pound, thresh

дөјүлмәк : *pass* 1) be beaten unmercifully, flogged, thrashed 2) be pounded thoroughly, be chopped up, be threshed *grain* 3) be hammered out 4) be pounded/beaten

дөјүм : *n* threshing

дөјүнмә : *n* beating, pulsation *i.e. heart, pulse*

дөјүнмәк : *v* 1) beat, pulsate *heart, pulse* 2) make sharp convulsive movements with the entire body *i.e. as in struggling*

дөјүш : *n* 1) battle, combat 2) fight

дөјүшдүрмәк : *v* make/compel to fight with one another *i.e. fighting cocks, rams and other animals*

дөјүшкән : *a* 1) martial, warlike, bellicose, fighting *n* 2) pugnacious fellow, one who is spoiling for a fight

дөјүшмәк : *v* fight *with, against* join battle

дөјүшчү : *n* fighting man, warrior, fighter

дөл : *n* 1) race, breed, species 2) litter, offspring 3) breeding season *period during which domestic animals are receptive to impregnation*

дөлләндирмәк : *v* impregnate, fecundate

дөлләнмә : *n* impregnation, fecundation

дөлләнмәк : *v intr* be impregnated, propagate itself, multiply, breed

дөллүк : *a* pedigreed, thoroughbred

дөндәрилмәк : *pass* be displaced, removed, turned over, overturned, toppled

дөндәрмә : *n* 1) turning, displacement, removal 2) directing *towards*

дөндәрмәк : *v* 1) turn, swing, twist off, turn back 2) turn *towards* , direct, steer; change *into* 3) upset, overturn

дөнә-дөнә : *adv* repeatedly, time and time again, more than once

дөнкә : *n* 1) side-street, alley 2) turn/curve/bend in a road/street 3) winding

дөнмә : *v* fr. **дөнмәк**

дөнмәдән : *adv* irrevocably

дөнмәз : *a* 1) unflinching, steady, irrevocable, persistent *adv* 2) unflinchingly, steadily, irrevocably, persistently

дөнмәк : *v* 1) come back, return 2) change *into* , turn *into* 3) turn, turn around, turn from, swing, be reversed 4) go back on *one's word* , disavow *o.s own convictions* 5) turn over, capsize

дөнмәксизин : *adv* irrevocably, finally

дөнүк : *a* 1) changeable, unreliable, fickle, inconstant *n* 2) traitor, betrayer, turncoat

дөнүклүк : *n* 1) treachery, betrayal, perfidy 2) apostasy, recreancy

дөнүм : *n* 1) turning, bend 2) return 3) alternation

дөнүш : *n* 1) return, return trip 2) sudden change, crisis 3) turnaround of things

дөрд : *num* four

дөрдадамлыг : *a* 1) four-person, for four persons 2) four-seat, four-place

дөрдаjаг : *adv* at a gallop, at full gallop

дөрдаjаглы : *a* 1) four-legged *n* 2) grill for preparing food on an open fire

дөрдаjлыг : *a* of four months, four-month *of a period*

дөрдатомлу : *a* tetra-atomic

дөрдбармаг : *a zool* tetradactylous *four digited*

дөрдбучаг : *n* quadrangle

дөрдбучаглы : *a* quadrangular

дөрдгат : *a* four-ply *made with four layers*

дөрд-дөрд : *adv* four each, by fours

дөрдәлли : *adv* very tightly, very firmly, doubly tight

дөрдәм : *adv* at a gallop, at full/top speed

дөрдиллик : *a* 1) four-year *n* 2) fourth anniversary, four years/ four-year period

дөрдjарпаг : *a bot* four-leaved

дөрдjаш, дөрдjашар, дөрдjашлы : *a* four-year

дөрдjерли : *a* four-seat; with four places

дөрдкүнч : *n* quadrangle, square

дөрдкүнчлү : *a* quadrangular

дөрдкүнлүк : *a* four-day

дөрдләмә : *a* dividing into four parts

дөрдләчәкли : *a bot* tetrapetalous *having four petals*

дөрдлүк : *num* four, a four

дөрдлүкдә : *adv* four together

дөрдмәртәбә, дөрдмәртәбәли : *a* four-story

дөрднала : *adv* at full/top speed

дөрдпәрдәли : *a* four-act

дөрдрәгәмли : *a math* four-digit

дөрдсаатлыг : *a* four-hour, of four hours duration

дөрдсәсли : *a mus* four-part

дөрдсимли : *a mus* four-stringed

дөрдсинифли : *a* fourth-grade *of a school/a student*

дөрдтарлалы : *a agr* four-field

дөрдтелли : *a* see **дөрдсимли**

дөрдтәкәрли : *a* four-wheel[ed]

дөрдтәрәфли : *a* quadrilateral, four-sided

дөрдүнчү : *a* fourth

дөрдүнчүсү : *introd-wd* 1) fourthly *i.e. in enumerating points* 2) fourth, the fourth of these *in writing or speaking of a number of items*

дөрдфаизли : *a* four-percent

дөрдһечалы : *a gram* four-syllable

дөрдһәдли : *a* four-membered, four-period

дөрдчә : *num* four in all, only four

дөрдчәркәли : *a* four-row

дөш : *n* 1) breast 2) slope *of a mountain*

дөшдән : *adv* impromptu

дөш-дөшә : *adv* hand to hand, one against the other

дөшәjатан : *a* 1) attractive, alluring, inviting 2) piquant, savory 3) that which was to o.'s taste

дөшәк : *n* mattress

дөшәкағы : *n* sheet, bed-sheet

дөшәкчә : *n dim* small mattress, pallet

дөшәмә : *v* 1) fr. **дөшәмәк** 2) floor 3) roadway, paved roadway 4) flooring, planking 5) bedding; litter *for cattle*

дөшәмәјујан : *n* charwoman; cleaner

дөшәмәк : *v* 1) spread, lay *bedding, flooring, litter, carpet etc* spread out, lay under, stretch under 2) furnish, decorate, arrange *a room* 3) pave 4) beat, beat up, thrash

дөшәмәсилән : *n* floor polisher

дөшәнәкли : *a* decorated, furnished

дөшәнәчәк : *n* 1) bedding, flooring, planking, decking 2) everything that is spread on the floor in order to arrange a room in Eastern fashion *rugs, cushions, carpets, mats etc*

дөшәнмәк : *v* 1) be spread, scattered under, be spread out *bedding etc* 2) pave, be paved 3) lie on o.'s back

дөшәтдирмәк, дөшәтмәк : *caus of* **дөшәмәк**

дөшлүк : *n* apron, pinafore, bib

дөшлүклү : *a* in an apron, aproned, wearing a bib

дөшүачыг : *a* bare-breasted; bare-chested

дөшүгара : *a* black-breasted

дөшүзәиф : *a* weak-chested *prone to pulmonary diseases*

дөшүјасты : *a* flat-chested

драм : *n* 1) drama *a* 2) dramatic

драматик : *a* dramatic

драматуржи : *n* dramaturgic

драматуркија : *n* dramaturgy *dramatic composition/theory*

дуа : *n* prayer

дуаку, дуачы : *n* one who prays

дуваг : *n* veil

дуда : *n* soot

дудкеш : *n* chimney, smoke-stack

дудман : *n* 1) hearth, home 2) family, kin, clan 3) generation

дуел : *n* duel

дуелчи : *n* dueller, duellist

дуз : *n* salt

дузаг : *n* snare, trap

дузгабы : *n* salt cellar

дузгыран : *n* salt-miner *one engaged in breaking up pieces of rock salt obtained from the open salt pits*

duздашыјан : *n* salt carrier/driver/transporter

дузлаг : *n* salt deposit, salt mines

дузлајычы : *n* salter, pickler

дузлама : *n* salting, pickling, curing

дузламаг : *v* salt, pickle, cure

дузланмаг : *pass* be salted/pickled/cured

дузлатдырмаг : *caus of* **дузламаг**

дузлатмаг : *caus of* **дузламаг**

дузлу : *a* 1) salted, pickled, cured *fig* 2) nice, pleasant, likeable

дузлулуг : *n* 1) saltiness, salinity *fig* 2) niceness, pleasantness, likeableness, attractiveness

дузлуча : *a* see **дузлу**

дузсуз : *a* 1) insipid, unflavored, unsalted *fig* unpleasant, not nice

дузсузлуг : *n* insufficient salt, absence/lack of salt

дузхана : *n* salt-works

дузчөрәк : *n* bread-and-salt, hospitality

дузчулуг : *n* salt production

дујғу : *n* 1) scent, flair, sense, feeling, sensation 2) conjecture, surmise, mother-wit, sharpness, keenness of wit

дујғулу : *a* 1) sensitive 2) keen/quick-witted

дујғусуз : *a* 1) insensible, insensitive 2) dull-witted

дујғусузлуг : *n* 1) absence of flair, sense, feeling 2) dull-wittedness

дујма : *v* fr. **дујмаг**

дујмаг : *v* 1) feel, have a sensation, become aware of 2) sense 3) guess

дујуг : *a* keen, sharp, alert *quick to react to a given action/event*

дујулмаг : *v* be observed, make itself felt, be foreseen

дул : *n* widow, widower

дуллуг : *n* widowhood, widowerhood

дулус : *n* potter, ceramist

дулусхана : *n* pottery *workshop/ factory where pottery and ceramic ware are produced*

дулусчу : *n* see **дулус**

дулусчулуг : *n* pottery/ceramics business/trade

думан : *n* fog, mist, haze

думанланмаг : *v* be fog-covered, grow foggy/misty/hazy

думанлы : *a* foggy, misty, hazy

думанлыг, думанлылыг : *n* fogginess, mistiness, haziness

думансыз : *a* clear *skies without clouds, fog, mist, haze*

думдуру : *a* completely transparent

дурачаг : *n* stop, stopping place

дурбин : *n* binocular[s}, spy-glass, telescope

дурғу : *n* pause, stop

дурғузмаг : *v* awaken *from sleep*, get s.o. up

дурғун : *a* 1) standing, stand-up 2) still, standing, not flowing *water*

дурғунлуг : *n* 1) stagnation 2) flabbiness, sluggishness, languor, inertness, passivity

дурдурмаг : *v* stop, halt, make/compel to stop

дурмаг : *v* 1) stand *be on the feet, motionless, in a vertical position* 2) stop, come to a stop 3) get up, rise

дурмагсызын, дурмадан : *adv* unceasingly, ceaselessly, constantly

дурна : *n zool* crane *family Gruidae*

дуру : *a* 1) liquid, watery, thin 2) clear, not turbid

дуруланмаг, дурулашмаг : *v* 1) become clear/transparent 2) dilute, thin 3) clear up, become cleared up *i.e. sky*

дурулмаг : *v* see **дуруланмаг, дурулашмаг**

дурултмаг : *v* 1) allow to settle *sediment* , make transparent/clear 2) dilute, thin out

дурулуг : *n* 1) liquid condition 2) clarity, transparency, purity

дурум : *n* stability, stableness

дурумлу : *a* 1) stable, firm, steadfast, able to stand firm for a long time 2) filling, satisfying *of food*

дурумсуз : *a* 1) unstable, not lasting 2) not filling, unsatisfying *of food*

дурухмаг : *v* 1) look down, cast down o.'s eyes, become confused, stop short *in confusion*, stumble, halt 2) be puzzled/bewildered 3) waver, hesitate, be undecisive

дуруш : *n* 1) carriage, bearing, attitude 2) stop, halt

дустаг : *n* prisoner, arrestee, detainee

дустаглыг : *n* confinement, detention, arrest

дустагхана : *n* prison, jail, penitentiary

душ : *n* shower *in a bathroom*

дүбарә : n 1) two dots on both the bones cast in *nard* game *adv* 2) for the second time, again

дүдәмә : *n* cur, mongrel

дүдкеш : *n* chimney

дүдүк : *n* pipe, reed-pipe, fife, flute

дүдүкчалан, дүдүкчү : *n* piper, fife-player, flutist

дүдүш : *n* penis *juvenile speech*

дүз : *a* 1) correct, right 2) honest 3) exact, precise 4) flat, even *adv* 5) straight 6) honestly 7) precisely 8) correctly *n* 9) plain, steppe

дүзбучаг : *n* rectangle

дүзбучаглы : *a* rectangular

дүзвуран, дүзгаравуллаjан : *n* sniper

дүзгәлбли : *a* straightforward, frank

дүзгәлблилик : *n* straightforwardness, frankness

дүз-дүзүнә : *adv* frankly, openly

дүздүрмәк, дүздүртмәк : *caus of* **дүзмәк**

дүзәлдилмәз : *a* faulty, out of order, irreparable, irremediable

дүзәлдилмәк : *v* 1) be straightened 2) be corrected, be touched up, retouched 3) be patched up, put in order, fixed 4) be put together

дүзәлиш : *n* 1) repair[ing], mend[ing] 2) correction, amending/amendments

дүзәлишмә : *n* 1) agreement, compact, pact, treaty 2) transaction, deal, scheme 3) making amendments, corrections

дүзәлишмәк : *v* make arrangements *with s.o. about s.t.*, reach an agreement

дүзәлмәк : *v* 1) be : repaired/mended/set straight/put right/regulated 2) be : straightened, unbent/flattened out 3) be put in order

дүзәлтдирмәк : *caus of* **дүзәлтмәк**

дүзәлтмә : *n* 1) correction 2) straightening out, unbending, flattening out 3) adjusting, putting right, regulating 4) putting together 5) fixing up 6) idea, invention 7) conjecture *a gram* 8) derivative

дүзәлтмәк : *v* 1) correct, proof-read 2) straighten out, even out, unbend, flatten 3) adjust, put right, regulate 4) mend, repair 5) put together, arrange 6) eliminate errors 7) think up, invent, contrive 8) form, model, mold

дүзән, дүзәнкаһ, дүзәнлик : *n* 1) plain, flat area *a* 2) plain

дүзкү : *n* formation, structure, order

дүзкүн : *a* 1) right, true 2) truthful, veracious, honest, straightforward 3) in good repair

дузкүнләшдирмәк : *v* correct, make correct/accurate

дузкүнлүк : *n* 1) straightforwardness, uprightness, veracity 2) correctness

дузләмәк : *v* smooth, level, make even

дузләндиричи : *n elect* rectifier

дузләндирмә : *n* smoothing, levelling; rectifying

дузләндирмәк : *v* even, level, smooth out; rectify

дузләнмәк, дузләшмәк : *pass* be made smooth, level; be rectified

дузлүк : *n* faithfulness, honesty, conscientiousness, straightforwardness, plain-dealing

дузмә : *n* 1) stringing, threading 2) placing, arranging

дузмәк : *v* 1) thread, string 2) place, arrange, lay out, draw up, form up, line up *typ* 3) compose

дузнәгулу : *adv* straight, directly, frankly, openly

дузүлмәк : *v* 1) be threaded, strung 2) be lined up, be arranged, organized

дузүлү : *a* 1) threaded, strung 2) placed, arranged

дузүлүш : *n* 1) disposition, arrangement, placement, order

дузүм : *n* line, row, formation

дузүнә : *adv* direct[ly], openly

дузүчү : *n typ* compositor, type-setter

дузхәтли : *a* rectilinear

дузчә : *adv* see **дузнәгулу**

дузчызыглы : *a* see **дузхәтли**

дүјә : *n* heifer

дүјәлик : *n* see **кәлик**

дүјәчә : *n* heifer *in a water-buffalo herd*

дүјмә : *n* 1) button *bot* 2) bud 3) press-button

дүјмәк : *v* knot, tie in a knot

дүјмәләмәк : *v* button up, fasten, do up

дүјмәләнмәк : *v* be buttoned up

дүјмәли : *a* 1) buttoned *up* 2) equipped with buttons 3) budded, having buds

дүјү : *n* 1) rice *a* 2) rice

дүјүн : *n* 1) knot 2) knot *in a beam, a board*

дүјүн-дүјүн : *a* see **дүјүнлү**

дүјүнләмәк : *v* tie a knot, knot

дүјүнләнмәк : *v* be tied with a knot

дүјүнлү : *a* knotted *cord/rope/string* ; knotty *lumber*

дүјүнчә : *n dim* small knot

дүкан : *n* shop, small store

дүканчы : *n* shop-keeper

дүкчә : *n* hank of yarn *wound on a spindle*

дүлкәр : *n* carpenter

дүлкәрлик : *n* profession of carpenter

дүлкәрхана : *n* carpenter shop

дүмбәк : *n* 1) drum *a* 2) drum['s]

дүмбәкгајыран : *n* master drum-maker

дүмбәкчалан, дүмбәкчи : *n* drummer, tympanist

дүмбүридә : *a* dock-tailed, short-tailed

дүмгара : *a* deeply black *usually of the eyes*

дүмдүз : *a* 1) completely straight/flat/level 2) exact, precise *adv* 3) straight, at attention

дүмәләнмәк : *v* delay, dally, spend too much time over

дүмсүк : *n* kick, hit, jab

дүмсүкләмәк : *v* 1) kick 2) push, shove 3) poke, jab

дүмүк : *n* amusement, diversion, pastime *any occupation with which one can kill the time*

дүнән : *n* yesterday

дүнәнки : *a* yesterday's, of yesterday

дүнја : *n* 1) world *a* 2) world['s]

дүнја-аләм : *n* the whole world, everything

дүнјабахышы : *n* world outlook, Weltanschauung, *one's* philosophy

дүнјакир : *a* 1) greedy, grasping, miserly *n* 2) miser, skinflint

дүнјакөрмүш : *a* worldly-wise, having broad life-experience, experienced

дүнјакөрүшү : *n* world outlook, Weltanschauung, *one's* philosophy

дүнјасында : *adv* 1) never 2) Not for the world! Not on your life!

дүнјәви : *a* secular, temporal, worldly

дүпдүз, дүппәдүз : *a* see **дүмдүз**

дүрәк : *n* see **мәләз**

дүрмәк : *n* 1) sheaf, bunch 2) durmak *a kind of a sandwich made of lavaş (a thin flat bread), butter and cheese folded into a tube*

дүрмәкләмәк : *v* roll food up in a tube of bread

дүрр : *n* 1) pearls *fig* 2) precious stones

дүртәләмәк : *v* see **дүртмәк**

дүртмә : *n* 1) shoving/pushing *in, into* 2) hit/jab/prod

дүртмәк : *v* stick/shove *into* , shove/push *into*, push/cram *into*

дүртмәләмәк : *v* 1) shove, push 2) strike by poking/jabbing

дүртүлмәк : *v* 1) thrust/stick shove s.t. into, cram s.t. into 2) shove/elbow o.'s way through 3) plunge into *i.e. crowd*

дүртүшдүрмәк : *v* see **дүрмәк**

дүрүст : *a* 1) correct, right, true, truthful, veracious, exact, authentic *adv* 2) correctly, rightly, truly, exactly, authentically

дүрүстләшдирмәк : *v* make more exact/precise/accurate

дүрүстлүк : *n* correctness, exactness, accuracy

дүсәр : *n* pick, pick-axe, mattock

дүстур : *n* formula

дүчар : *a* subject to/ open to the influence of *s.t.*

дүшбәрә : *n* duşbane *meat dumplings or soup with them*

дүшәнбә : *n* Monday

дүшәринә : *a* at random, anyhow, any old way

дүшәркә : *n* camp *temporary, overnight*, bivouac, halt, stopping place, nomad encampment

дүшкүн : *a* 1) depressed, downhearted 2) weak, lacking strength 3) having an inclination towards s.t. 4) elderly, on life's downward path

дүшкүнлүк : *n* 1) depression 2) inclination towards s.t. 3) old age

дүшмә : *n* 1) fall, falling, lowering 2) dismounting, climbing down, getting/coming off 3) going off 4) getting, getting into

дүшмәк : *v* 1) fall 2) descend, go/come down 3) get, get into

дүшмән : *n* 1) enemy, foe *a* 2) enemy, hostile

дүшмәнлик, дүшмәнчилик : *n* hostility, animosity

дүшмәнчәсинә : *n adv* hostile, with enmity, with animosity

дүшүк : *a* 1) aborted, miscarried *n med* 2) miscarriage, abortion

дүшүндүрмәк : *v* make/compel s.o. to think about s.t., worry, cause anxiety, alarm

дүшүнмә : *n* 1) thinking, thought 2) reflection 3) consideration

дүшүнмәдән : *adv* rashly, thoughtlessly

дүшүнмәк : *v* think, consider, reflect, meditate

дүшүнүб-дашынмаг : *v* think over

дүшүнүлмәк : *pass* be thought over/planned/conceived

дүшүнүш : *n* thinking, thought, reflection, consideration

дүшүнчә : *n* 1) reason, intellect, consciousness, thought 2) dream, day/waking dream, dreaming

дүшүнчәли : *a* 1) conscious 2) thoughtful, given to reflection

дүшүнчәлилик : *n* 1) consciousness 2) intelligence, perception

дүшүнчәсиз : *a* 1) unconscious, instinctive 2) slow-witted *adv* 3) unconsciously, instinctively

дүшүнчәсизлиик : *n* 1) unconsciousness 2) slow-wittedness

дүшүрдүлмәк : *v* 1) decline, be reduced 2) get out of, get off, alight from, disembark 3) be removed, dismissed *at s.o.'s request/order*

дүшүрмә : *n* 1) taking down, dismissal 2) alighting, disembarking, getting out/off of 3) coming down

дүшүрмәк, дүшүртмәк : *v* 1) overthrow, depose 2) remove, lower 3) help down, set down, put off *passenger*

дүшүрүлмәк : *v* 1) be overthrown/deposed 2) be removed, be lowered, be helped down/set down/put off *passenger*

е

е : the seventh letter of the Azerbaijani alphabet

ев : *n* 1) home, house, household *a* 2) hose, home, domestic

евдар : *a* 1) thrifty, economical *n* 2) family man, family woman, good house-keeper

евдарлыг : *n* state/condition of being skilful and successful in maintaining a home/household, uxoriousness

евдә : *adv* at home, home

евенк : *n* Evenk *a people of Eastern Siberia*

ев-ешик : *n coll* 1) home, household and family 2) household effects; utensils, goods and chattels

евләндирмәк : *v* marry *to* , wed *to about men*

евләнмә : *n* marriage *of a man*

евләнмәк : *v* marry, get married *to about men*

евли : *a* married *of men*

евли-ешикли : *a* 1) having a family 2) *adv* with the whole family/whole household

евлилик : *n* state/condition of having a family, the married condition

евсиз : *a* homeless

евсиз-ешиксиз : *a* homeless, shelterless, without a roof over o.'s head

евсизлик : *n* homeless condition, the state of a person without a roof over his head

евчијәз, евчик : *n dim* house

е'дам : *n* capital punishment

едиләмәк : *v* 1) lament/mourn for a deceased person 2) stroke/soothe a cow who is withholding her milk

едилмәк : *pass* be done/effected/accomplished

е'зам : *in combs* starting, setting out : **е'зам етдирмәк** send on an official journey, detach, post *to a new assignment/ job*

е'замиј̌јәт : *n* official journey, business trip

еј : *intj* Hey! Say!, Look here! *used to get the attention of s.o.*

еј̌бәчәр : *n* 1) freak, monster, degenerate, ugly mug *a* 2) ugly

еј̌бәчәрләндирмәк : *v* disfigure, make look ugly

еј̌бәчәрләнмәк, еј̌бәчәрләшмәк : *v* become ugly/deformed/misshapen

еј̌бәчәрлик : *n* ugliness, deformity, abnormality

еј̌ван : *n* porch; balcony

еј̌ваh : *intj* Alas!

еј̌зән : *adv* completely, entirely

еј̌иб : *n* 1) shame, disgrace, infamy 2) flaw, defect, harm; **еј̌би јохдур**–it does not matter

еј̌ибләмәк : *v* 1) shame, put to shame, make blush *with shame*, admonish

еј̌ибли : *a* 1) shameful, disgraceful 2) defective, flawed, harmful

еј̌ибсиз : *a* flawless, impeccable, defect-free

еј̌ибсизлик : *n* flawlessness, absence of defects

еј̌мә : *n* skin-container filled with sour clotted-milk

еј̌нәк : *n* glasses, eyeglasses

еј̌нәкли : *a* bespectacled, wearing eyeglasses

еј̌нәкчи : *n* optician

еј̌нән : *adv* exactly, word for word, literally

еј̌ни : *a* identical, one and the same, the same

еј̌ниј̌јәт : *n* identicalness

еј̌ниләшдирилмәк : *pass* be made identical; be made the same; be perceived as being the same

еј̌ниләшдирмәк : *v* make identical, make the same

еј̌нилик : *n* see **еј̌ниј̌јәт**

еј̌hам : *n* hint, allusion

еј̌hана : *conj* if, in the event that, if *contrary to expectations*

еј̌ш : *n* drinking bout, binge, carousal

еј̌ш-ишрәт : *n obs* revelry, debauch

екран : *n* screen

екскаватор : *n* excavator, digger *machine*

екскаваторчу : *n* excavator-operator, digger-operator

екссентрик : *n* 1) *tech* eccentric *a machine element for converting rotary into reciprocating motion, consisting of a disk attached off-center to a driving shaft and able to revolve freely within a fixed collar or strap connected with a rod* *a* 2) eccentric *not having a common center, opposed to concentric*

ел : *n* 1) tribe, society, people, folk 2) country, nation

е'лан : *n* announcement, advertisement

еластик : *adv* elastic, flexible, resilient

еластиклик : *n* elasticity, flexibility, resiliency

елат : *n* nationality, people *Arabic plural of ел*

елгован : *n* cold wind and rain of mountain origin *this annual phenomenon formerly compelled nomadic herdsmen to descend from the mountains for winter quarters*

електрик : *n* 1) electricity *a* 2) electrical

електрикләмәк, електрикләндирмәк *v* electrify, electrize

електрикләшдирилмә : *n* electrification

електрикләшдирилмәк : *pass* be electrified

електрикләшдирмә : *n* electrification

електрикләшдирмәк : *v* electrify

електрикчәкән : *n* electrician

електрокимја : *n* electro-chemistry

електромагнит : *n* 1) electromagnet *a* 2) electromagnetic

електротехник : *n* 1) electrotechnician, electrician 2) electrical engineer

елемент : *n* element

елә : *pro* 1) so, such 2) namely, to wit 3) well, then

еләләри : *pro plu* such *ones*

еләмәк : *v* 1) do, accomplish, perform, produce 2) employed as an auxiliary in forming compound verbs *mostly formed from the nouns of Arabic and Persian origin*

еләси : *pro* such

еләчә : *adv* 1) that's the way, that's right, thus, in exactly this way 2) simply

еллик : *a* 1) general, common, public, popular, people's, national, social 2) special

елликлә : *adv* see **елликчә**

елликләшдирмә : *n* socialization, collectivization

елликләшдирмәк : *v* socialize, collectivize

елликчә : *adv* with the backing/support of the whole nation/world/society

елм : *n* science

елми : *a* 1) scientific 2) learned

елми-бәјан : *n* rhetoric

елми-илаһи : *n* theology

елми-кәф : *n* chiromancy, palm-reading

елмли : *a* educated, learnt

елмсиз : *a* uneducated

елмсизлик : *n* lack of education, ignorance; lack of scientific approach

елоғлу : *n* fellow-countryman/ townsman/ villager

елти : *n* brother-in-law's wife

елчи : *n* 1) matchmaker 2) ambassador; envoy, emissary

елчилик : *n* 1) embassy 2) match-making

елчары : *adv* publicly, openly

е'мал : *n* process[ing], operation, manufacture

е'малатхана : *n* workshop

ембриоложи : *a* embryological

ембриолокија : *n* embryology

емпириокритисизм : *n Ru* emperio-criticism *Soviet coined term for the reactionary subjective-idealistic philosophic theory of the early 20th century*

емулсија : *n* emulsion *a liquid mixture in which a fatty or resinous substance is suspended in minute globules*

ен : *n* width, breadth

ендирилмәк : *pass* 1) be lowered, thrown down, reduced

ендирмә : *n* 1) lowering, reduction 2) deposing, dethronement

ендирмәк : *v* 1) lower, draw down 2) take away, lower, reduce 3) overthrow

ендиртмәк : *caus of* **ендирмәк**

енержи : *n* energy

енеркетик : *n* specialist in energetics *power-engineering*

енеркетик : *a* energetics, power-engineering

енеркетика : *n* energetics *power engineering*

енинә : *adv* broadwise, across, crosswise

енинә-бојуна, енинә-узунуна : *adv* far and wide

ениш : *n* descent, slope, incline

ениш-јохуш : *n* uneven surface

енишли : *a* sloping, slanting

енли : *a* broad, wide

енлијарпаг : *a bot* broad-leafed

енликүрәк : *a* broad-shouldered

енлисифәт : *a* broad-faced

енличә : *a* quite wide

енмә : *v fr.* **енмәк**

енмәк : *v* go/come down, descend, bring down, lower

енсиз : *a* narrow

енсизлик : *n* narrowness

енсизчә : *a* rather narrow, narrow-ish

енсиклопедија : *n* 1) encyclopedia 2) encyclopedic

енсиклопедик : *a* encyclopedic

енсиклопедист : *n* encyclopedist *writer for, or compiler of an encyclopedia*

ентомоложи : *a* entomological

ентомологија : *n* entomology

епиграм : *n* epigram

епик : *a* epic

епители : *n* epithelium *outer layer of the skin*

ер : *adv* early

ера : *n* era

еркәк : *n* male *of animals*

еркәкләнмәк : *v* 1) grow up, be grown up, come to man's estate, mature *fig* 2) get on one's high horse, swagger, boast

еркәкчик : *n bot* stamen

еркәкчиксиз : *a bot* pistillate, having no stamens

еркән : *adv* early, early in the morning; a bit earlier

еркәч : *n* lead-goat *of a herd*

ермәни : *n* 1) an Armenian *a* 2) Armenian

ермәнистан : *n* Armenia

ермәничә : *adv* in Armenian *language*

ертә : *adv* early

ескадра : *n nav* squadron

ескадрилја : *n air* squadron

естон : *n* an Estonian

естонија : *n* 1) Estonia *a* 2) Estonian

естонијалы : *n* see **естон**

естонча : *adv* in Estonian *language*

етажерка : *n* etagere, an ornamental stand with shelves, a whatnot *for books or small objects*

етдирмәк : *v* cause to make, cause to do

е'тибар : *n* 1) faith, trust, confidence 2) authority 3) trustworthiness, reliability 4) *male first name*

е'тибарән : *postp* beginning with

е'тибарлы : *a* 1) loyal, trustworthy 2) reliable, authoritative 3) enjoying/deserving of trust

е'тибарлылыг : *n* 1) reliability, trustworthiness 2) solidity, strength 3) dependability, unfailingness, unfailing nature

е'тибарнамә : *n* warrant, power-of-attorney

е'тибарсыз : *a* 1) unreliable 2) unworthy of trust/reliance, undependable 3) precarious, insecure, unstable

е'тибарсызлыг : *n* 1) unreliability, undependability 2) untrustworthiness

е'тибарсызчасына : *adv* with distrust, distrustfully, mistrustfully

е'тигад : *n* faith, belief; conviction

е'тигадлы : *a* believing, convinced, persuaded

е'тигадсыз : *a* unbelieving, without convictions

е'тигадсызлыг : *n* unbelief, disbelief, absence of convictions

е'тимад : *n* trust, confidence, certitude

е'тимадлы : *a* reliable, trustworthy

е'тимаднамә : *n* 1) letters of credence, credentials 2) letter of credit

е'тимадсыз : *a* 1) unreliable 2) unworthy of trust, untrustworthy

е'тимадсызлыг : *n* 1) unreliability 2) untrustworthiness

етимолоҝија : *n* etymology

е'тина : *n* attention, mindfulness, regard

е'тинасыз : *a* 1) inattentive, neglectful, disregardful *adv* 2) inattentively, neglectfully, disregardfully

е'тинасызлыг : *n* inattentiveness, disregard, neglect

е'тираз : *n* objection

е'тираф : *n* recognition

етмәк : *v* see **еләмәк**

етнограф : *n* ethnographer, social anthropologist

етнографија : *n* ethnography, social anthropology

етноложи : *a* ethnological

етнолоҝија : *n* ethnology

етүд : *n art* 1) study *sketch to be used for a projected future work mus* 2) étude *composition expressly made for practice/exercise in some particular aspect of instrumental playing*

ефир : *n* 1) ether *a* 2) ether, etherial

еффект : *n* effect

еффектив : *a* effective, efficacious

еффектли : *a* effective, efficacious

еффектлилик : *n* effectiveness, efficaciousness

еһ : *intj* expresses a feeling of pity, regret, disappointment, anxiety, reproach, or even admiration, depending on the circumstances

еһкам : *n* dogma

еһкамчылыг : *n* dogmatism

еһмал, еһмаллы : *adv* carefully, quietly, cautiously, noiselessly

еһмаллыча, еһмалча : *adv* prudently, with a bit of care/caution

еһсан : *n* 1) good deed, alms, charity 2) funeral repast; food served at the funeral repast

еһтизаз : *n* oscillation, vibration, trembling

еһтијат : *n* 1) prudence, care, caution, precaution 2) misgiving, apprehension 3) reserve, stores, stock *a* 4) reserve, spare

еһтијаткар : *a* see **еһтијатлы**

еһтијаткаранә : *adv* with prudence, foresightedly, cautiously

еһтијаткарлыг : *n* see **еһтијатлылыг**

еһтијаткарлыгла : *adv* with care, with foresight, guardedly

еһтијатла : *adv* see **еһтијаткарлыгла**

еһтијатлы : *a* 1) careful, discreet, prudent 2) thrifty, economical, provident *adv* 3) carefully

еһтијатлылыг : *n* prudence, care, caution, discretion

еһтијатсыз : *a* 1) imprudent, incautious 2) without reserve stock *food, other needful things* *adv* 3) too self-confident 4) imprudently, incautiously

еһтијатсызлыг : *n* imprudence, rashness, improvidence

еһтијатсызчасына : *adv* see **еһтијатсыз** 3)

еһтијач : *n* need, want, necessity

еһтијачлы : *a* needy, indigent, poor

еһтијатсыз : *a* not in need, in easy circumstances, well off, in good shape

еһтикар : *n* speculation, profiteering, "cornering the market"

еһтикарчы : *n* speculator, profiteer

еһтимал : *n* 1) probability 2) supposition, assumption, hypothesis 3) probably, possibly

еһтималчы : *n* Probabilist, follower of the doctrine, proposed originally by the Skeptics that since certainty is impossible, probability suffices to govern faith and practice

еһтималчылыг : *n* Probabilism *Philosophical tenet of Sceptics*

еһтирам : *n* awe, adoration

еһтирамла : *adv* with due awe, adoration

еһтирамлы : *a* paying the due honor, awe

еһтирамсыз : *a* without due owe, adoration

еһтирамсызчасына : *adv* without due awe, adoration

еһтирас : *n* passion, lust, desire, concupiscence

еһтираслы : *a* passionate, lustful

еһтирассыз : *a* passionless, impassive, frigid

еһтирассызлыг : *n* impassivity, frigidity

еһтишам : *n* glory, pomp, splendor, grandeur

е'чазкар : *n* wonder-worker, miracle-man, thaumaturge

еш : *n* pair, buddie, partner

ешг : *n* love

ешгбазлыг : *n* philandering, womanizing, making love without serious intentions *used of a man*

ешдирмәк, ешдиртмәк : *caus of* **ешмәк**

ешәләмәк : *v* 1) peck, pick *at*, dig, burrow 2) rummage, delve *into*, look for

ешәләнмәк : *v* 1) dig, rummage *in* 2) be occupied with s.t. requiring painstaking, long efforts 3) toss and turn *in bed* 4) lie about, be scattered all over

ешәнәк : *n* 1) place which has been dug up, in which the soil has been disturbed 2) place where things have been displaced, and scattered around in disorder

ешидилмәк : *pass* be heard, be audible

ешик : *n* 1) exterior portion, or outside of s.t. 2) yard, courtyard, area outside of premises

ешилмәк : *pass* 1) be dug up 2) be twisted, rolled *of thread/rope*

ешитдирмәк : *caus of* **ешитмәк**

ешитмәк : *v* hear, hear about

ешмә : *n* 1) twisting, winding *around*, rolling *up* *a* 2) twisted, wound *around*, rolled *up*

ешмәк : *v* 1) dig, dig out, burrow 2) twist, twirl, wind around *thread, rope*

ешшәк : *n* donkey; *also a very popular expletive*

ешшәкарысы : *n* hornet; wasp

Ә

ә : 1) eighth letter of Azerbaijani alphabet 2) *intj* hey!

әбәдән : *adv* never, at all

әбәди : *a* 1) everlasting, eternal *adv* 2) eternally, forever, forevermore

әбәдијјәт : *n* eternity

әбәдиләшдирилмәк : *v* be eternalized, be immortalized, be perpetuated

әбәдиләшдирмә : *n* eternalization, immortalization, perpetuation

әбәдиләшдирмәк : *v* eternalize, immortalize, perpetuate

әбәдиләшмәк : *v* be eternalized, be immortalized, be perpetuated

әбәдилик : *n* 1) eternity *adv* 2) forever

әбәс : *a* 1) vain, unnecessary, useless, futile, unavailing *adv* 2) for nothing, to no purpose, vainly, in vain *n* 3) absurdity, nonsense, trifles

әбәчә : *see* **мамача**

әбкәрдан : *n* ladle

әбләг : *a* piebald *of a horse's coat*

әбләһ : *n* 1) idiot, imbecile *a* 2) scatter-brained

әбләһанә : *see* **әбләһчәсинә**

əбləhчəсинə : *adv* idiotically, foolishly

əбləhлик : *n* folly; idiocy; extreme light-mindedness

əбləhчəсинə : *adv* stupidly, like a fool, idiotically; very light-mindedly

əбүлhөвл : *n* sphinx

əввəл : 1) *adv* at first, earlier, before, previously, in the beginning, formerly 2) *n* beginning

əввəла : *see* **əввəлəн**

əввəл-ахыр : *adv* 1) sooner or later; finally, at last, after all, ultimately 2) in all, only

əввəлдəн : *adv* 1) at first, at the beginning 2) earlier, formerly, previously, in the past, long ago 3) in advance, beforehand

əввəлəн : *adv* firstly, in the first place, first of all

əввəли : *n* beginning *of s.t.* **əввəлинчи** : *a* first, beginning, initial

əввəлки : *a* previous, preceding, former

əввəллəр, əввəллəрдə : *adv* in former times; in the past, formerly, previously

əввəлчə : *adv* at first; in the beginning, before, formerly, previously

əввəлчəдəн : *adv* beforehand, in advance

əвəз : *n* 1) substitute, substitution, change, replacement 2) retribution, requital, repayment 3) compensation

əвəзедичи : *a* substitutive, compensatory, retributive

əвəзəмəк : *v* waddle *of a person*

əвəзиндə : *adv* instead of, in return [for], in exchange for

əвəзинə : *adv* for, instead of, in place of, in exchange for

əвəзлик : *n* *gram* pronoun

əвəзсиз : *a* irreplaceable

əвəзсизлик : *n* irreplaceability

əвəлик : *n* *bot* sorrel *plant of genus Rumex*

əгиг : *n* *min* agate *semiprecious stone*

əгидə : *n* belief, persuasion, conviction, opinion, view, idea

əгидəли : *a* convinced, confirmed, persuaded, ideological, committed to philosophical principles

əгидəсиз : *a* devoid of principles and ideals, having no principles or ideals, not having one's own convictions/beliefs or opinion

əгли : *a* mental, intellectual

əгрəб : 1) *zool* scorpion 2) hand *of a watch/clock* , needle, pointer, arrow *of measuring instruments*

əда : *n* 1) manner, way 2) affectation, swagger 3) payment

əдабаз : 1) *n* person with affected ways, person with bad manners 2) *a* affected

əдабазлыг : *n* affectation, putting on airs

əдавəт : *n* dissension, discord, enmity, hostility, animosity, spite, malice

əдавəтли : *a* hostile, inimical, nourishing spite/malice

əдаланмаг : *v* put on airs or affectations

əдалəт : *n* 1) justice; fairness, impartiality 2) *male first name*

əдалəтли : *a* fair, just; impartial

əдалəтсиз : *a* unfair, unjust, partial

əдалəтсизлик : *n* injustice, unfairness, partiality

əдалəтсизчəсинə : *adv* unjustly, unfairly, with partiality, with prejudice

əдалы : see **əдабаз**

əдвə, əдвиjjат, əдвиjjə : *n* spice

əдə : *intj* Hey!, Hey, you!, Listen! *impolite form of address often used simply to express strong emotions*

əдəб, əдəб-əркан : *n* 1) civility, courtesy, politeness, correctness, courtliness, good manners 2) tact

əдəб-əрканлы : see **əдəбли**

əдəби : 1) *a* literary 2) *adv* in a literary manner

əдəбиjjат : *n* literature

əдəбиjjатчы : *n* man of letters, writer

əдəбиjjатшүнас : *n* specialist in study of literature

əдəбиjjатшүнаслыг : *n* study of literature

əдəбкөзлəмəз : *a* frivolous, *unduly* familiar

əдəблəнмəк : *v* become well-mannered, become educated

əдəбли : *a* gentleman-like *or lady-like*, civil, courteous, with good manners, polite, proper, tactful

əдəблилик : *n* good breeding, good manners, civility, courtesy, politeness

əдəбсиз : 1) *a* impolite, discourteous, uncivil, tactless, ill-bred, bad-mannered 2) *n* shameless fellow, boor

əдəбсизлик : *n* ill breeding, bad manners, impoliteness, incivility, discourtesy, tactlessness

əдəбсизчəсинə : *adv* discourteously, uncivilly, impolitely

əдəд : *n* 1) number 2) piece, thing, item

әдәди : *a* 1) numerical 2) piece, by the piece

әдән : *n geog* Aden *port*

әдәсә : *n* lens

әдиб : *n* man of letters, writer

әдиблик : *n* literary activity; profession of writer

әдирнә : *n geog* Edirne *in Turkish Thrace; ancient name Adrianople*

әдл : see **әдаләт**

әдлиjjә : *n* justice

әдна : 1) *a* vile, loathsome, vulgar, low, base, mean 2) *n* scoundrel

әдналыг : *n* meanness, baseness, pettiness, abomination, mean/dirty trick, vile thing

әждәһа : *n* 1) dragon 2) chimera, myth

әза : *n* mourning

әзаб : *n* 1) torture, torment, pangs, oppression, suffering 2) anguish, agony

әзабверичи, әзаблы : *a* poignant, exhausting, painful, distressing, agonizing

әзбәр : *adv* by heart; to a high degree *about knowledge*

әзбәрләмә : *n* learning by heart/rote, repeating over and over again, cramming

әзбәрләмәк : *v* learn by rote/heart, cramming

әзбәрләнмәк : *v* be learned by rote/heart

әзбәрләтдирмәк, әзбәрләтмәк : *caus of* **әзбәрләмәк**

әзбәрчи : *n* crammer, grind

әзваj : *n bot* aloe

әздирмәк : 1) *caus of* **әзмәк** 2) indulge, pamper, coddle, spoil

әзәлә : 1) *n* muscle 2) *a* muscle, muscular

әзәләли : *a* brawny, muscular

әзәмәт : *n* 1) greatness, grandeur, splendor, magnificence 2) importance, pompousness

әзәмәтлә : *adv* grandly, majestically

әзәмәтли : *a* grand, majestic, stately, grandiose, monumental

әзәмәтлилик : *n* majesty, grandeur, stateliness, grandiosity

әзиз : *a* 1) dear, darling, honey 2) revered 3) spoiled *in combinations about a child* 4) Aziz *male first name; the female variant is* Әзизә Aziza

әзизләмәк : *v* show kindness toward, indulge, pamper, coddle, cherish, care for, take tender care *of* ; caress, prize; fondle

әзизләнмәк : *v* be pampered, be coddled, be caressed; be fondled

әзизләшмәк : *v* become dear *to*

әзизчиjәз, әзизчик : *n* my dear, sweetheart, darling, honey

әзиjjәт : *n* torture, torment, suffering, trouble, anxiety

әзиjjәтли : *a* agonizing, poignant, distressing, difficult, troublesome

әзиjjәтсиз : 1) *a* inoffensive 2) *a* painless 3) *a* not difficult 4) *adv* painlessly, without difficulty

әзик : 1) *a* crumpled, crushed 2) *n* injury, bruise, contusion

әзик-әзик : *a* crumpled, absolutely crushed

әзикләмәк : see **әзмәк**

әзилиб-бүзүлмә : *n* self-conscious, unnatural coquettishness *of a woman*

әзилиб-бүзүлмәк : *v* behave affectedly, flirt, behave with false modesty

әзилмәк : *v* 1) be crumpled, be rumpled 2) be crushed, be squashed 3) be beaten 4) be oppressed, be conquered, be defeated, be staggered 5) *fig* pose, put on airs, behave affectedly, behave with false modesty

әзиник : see **әзик**

әзичи : *a* exhausting, crushing

әзишдирилмәк : *caus of* **әзишдирмәк**

әзишдирмә : *vn from* **әзишдирмәк**

әзишдирмәк : *v* 1) crumple with force, mash 2) beat, beat unmercifully, beat up, thrash

әзкил : *n bot* medlar *fruit bearing bush or small tree and its fruit*

әзкиллик : *n* place planted with medlars

әзкин : *a* 1) sluggish, listless, tired, weary 2) beaten, crushed, crumpled

әзкиниш : *n* poseur, affected person

әзкинлик : *n* tiredness, sluggishness, lethargy

әзм : *n* resoluteness, will, persistence

әзмә : 1) *vn from* **әзмәк** 2) *n* puree

әзмә-бүзмә : 1) *n* poseur, affected person, coquette, flirt 2) *a* affected, pretentious

әзмәк : *v* 1) crumple, rumple 2) crush 3) beat unmercifully, beat up 4) break, smash

әзмкар : *a* persistent, resolute

әзраил : *n* 1) Azrail *according to Moslem belief* angel of death 2) death

әjал : see **арвад** (1)

әjаләт : 1) *n* province 2) *a* provincial

әјалəтчилик : *n* provincialism

әјан : *a* obvious, apparent, evident, clear, well known

ә'јан : *n* aristocrat, noble

әјани : 1) *a* graphic, visual 2) *a* evident, obvious 3) *adv* graphically, visually, obviously, evidently

әјанилик : *n* obviousness, graphic nature

ә'јар : *n* 1) assay *of precious metals* 2) measure, standard

әјдәм : *n* slope, incline, declivity

әјдәмли : *a* sloping, inclined

әјдәмлилик : see **әјдәм**

әјдирмәк : *caus of* **әјмәк**

әјдиртмәк : *caus of* **әјмәк**

әјә : *n* file *the tool*

әјәр-әскик : *n* shortages, deficits, defects, imperfections

әјилмә : *n* 1) bending, sloping, bowing 2) curve, warp, warping, list

әјилмәз : *a* inflexible; non-bending

әјилмәзлик : *n* inflexibility; *fig* sense of honor

әјилмәк : *v intr* 1) stoop, bend, bend down, bow 2) be bent, be bowed down, become crooked; become bent 3) warp, be warped 4) list

әјин : *n* 1) body of a person 2) apparel

әјинти : *n* bend, curve

әјирдәк : *n* kind of pastry similar to chowmein noodles

әјирилмәк : *v* be spun

әјиричи : *n* spinner

әјирмәк : *v tr* spin

әјиртдирмәк : *caus of* **әјирмәк**

әјјам : *n poetic* days, times

әјјаш : *n* reveler, carouser, drunkard, rascal

әјјашлыг : *n* drunkenness, hard drinking, revelry

әјләмәк : *v tr* stop; detain, delay, hold back

әјләндиричи : *a* entertaining, diverting, amusing

әјләндирмә : *n* 1) entertainment, amusement, diversion 2) stopping

әјләндирмәк : *v* 1) amuse, entertain, divert 2) stop

әјләнмәк : *v intj* 1) stop 2) have a good time, entertain oneself, amuse oneself, enjoy oneself

әјләнчә : *n* 1) amusement, fun, entertainment 2) entertaining/amusing things, toy

әјләнчәли : *a* amusing, entertaining

әјләшдирмәк : *v* cause or make to sit down

әјләшмәк : *v* sit down, take a seat

әјмә : *n* 1) bend, curve 2) arch

әјмәк : *v tr* bend, curve, twist, warp, bow, incline, tilt

әјри : *a* 1) crooked, bent *adv* 2) crookedly *n fig* 3) cheat, swindler *a fig* 4) dishonest *n* 5) crooked line

әјрибојун : *a* 1) with a crooked neck *n* 2) crooked neck

әјрибурун : *a* crooked-nosed, with a crooked nose

әјридиш : *a* crooked-toothed, with crooked teeth

әјри-әјри : see **әјри** (1, 2)

әјрилик : *n* 1) crookedness, curvature *fig* 2) dishonesty, falsehood

әјрилмәк : *v* bend *intr* , be crooked

әјрим : *n* bend, curve, turn

әјрим-үјрүм : see **әјри-үјрү**

әјрипача : *a* bow-legged, bandy-legged

әјрипәнчә : *a* pigeon-toed

әјрисинә : *adv* slantwise, obliquely, aslant

әјри-үјрү : *a* 1) curving, twisting, winding, meandering, sinuous, tortuous, zigzag *adv* 2) crookedly, zigzag, in a zigzag manner *a* 3) uneven, rough

әјричизкили : *a* curvilinear

әкдирмәк : *caus of* **әкмәк**

әкәбә : Aqaba *Jordan port on the Red Sea*

әкәч : *a* hardened, inveterate, big, strong, grown-up

әкәчлик : *n* hardened nature or quality, inveterate nature or quality

әкиз : *n* twins

әкизтај : *n* twin *one of a pair of twins*

әкили : *a* sown

әкилмәк : *v* 1) be sown, be planted 2) make off, run away, slip away, leave unnoticed; take to one's heels

әкин : 1) *n* sowing 2) *a* sowing

әкинәбахан : *n* field patroller

әкинчи : *n* plowman, tiller

әкинчилик : *n* plowing, tillage

әклил : *n* wreath, garland, crown

әкмә : 1) *n* sowing 2) *n* planting 3) *a* sown, planted *as opposed to growing wild*

әкмәк : *v* 1) sow 2) plant 3) get rid *of s.o.*, send *s.o.* packing, send *s.o.* off somewhere under some pretext, separate *oneself* from someone

әкс : *n* 1) portrait, likeness, picture, image *n* 2) reflection *n* 3) the reverse, the opposite *in meaning* *prep* 4) against *a* 5) counter, contrary

әксәрән : *adv* mainly, chiefly, for the most part, in most cases, mostly

әксәријјәт : *n* majority, the greater/most part *of*

әкс-зәрбә : *n* counterblow, counteroffensive, counterstrike

әксингилаб : *n* counterrevolution

әксингилаби : *a* counterrevolutionary

әксингилабчы : *n* counterrevolutionary

әксинә : *adv* opposite, inside out, back to front, in defiance *of*

әкс-кәшфијјат : *n* counterintelligence

әкс-кәшфијјатчы : *n* counterintelligence agent

әкс-сәда : *n* echo

әкс-тә'сир : *n* counteraction, opposition, counter-influence

әкс-һүчум : *n* counterattack, counteroffensive

әкәр : *conj* if

әл : *n* 1) hand *a* 2) hand, manual

әл вурмаг : *v* 1) touch 2) applaud

әл еләмәк : *v* 1) make a sign 2) wave one's hand

әл кәздирмәк : *v* rummage

әл сахламаг : *v* refrain from s.t.

әл тутмаг : *v* lend money; support materially

әл чәкмәк : *v* give up; refuse, reject

әли кәтирмәк : *v* to be lucky *especially in a game*

ә'ла : *a* 1) excellent, perfect, outstanding, splendid *adv* 2) excellently, splendidly

әлавә : *n* 1) addition, supplement 2) additional, any further *prep* 3) above, beyond, besides *adv* 4) in addition, to boot, additionally *a* 5) side, collateral

әлагә : *n* 1) contact, dealings, intercourse, connection, communication 2) relation, relationship, links

әлагәдар : *a* 1) having a relationship *with s.t.*, having a connection *with s.t.*, tied/connected *to*, privy *to*, participating/involved *in* *conj* 2) concerning, in this connection

әлагәләндирмәк : *v* tie together, bind, tie up; encourage to maintain relationship

әлагәли : see **әлагәдар**

әлагәсиз : *a* not having ties or bonds, not having a relationship with, not having a connection with; unintelligible *about speech*

әлагәсизлик : *n* lack or absence of ties or bonds, alienation, isolation, detachment; lack of intelligibility

әл-ајаг : *n* limbs, extremities

әлалты : *n* 1) apprentice, assistant, subordinate 2) the first player in a game of cards

әламәт : *n* sign, index, omen, presage, portent, symbol, emblem

әламәтдар : *a* significant, revealing, symbolic

ә'лаһәзрәт : *n* 1) His/Your Majesty *a* 2) highest, royal, imperial

әлаһиддә : *a* 1) separate, isolated 2) special

ә'лачы : *n* excellent person, outstanding person; honor student *in a secondary school*

әлач : *n* 1) remedy, means, way, method, way out 2) treatment, cure

әлачсыз : *a* 1) incurable, helpless, hopeless 2) desperate

әлачсызлыг : *n* hopelessness, helplessness; lack of remedies; incurability

әлбәәл : *adv* 1) personally 2) instantly

әлбәјаха : **әлбәјаха вурушма** (**дөјүш**) hand-to-hand fighting

әлбәт : *adv* probably, must be

әлбәттә : *adv* 1) of course, certainly, undoubtedly 2) without fail, absolutely, unconditionally

әлбәһәл : *adv* immediately, at once, instantly

әлбир : *adv* 1) hand in hand, together, amicably, in a friendly manner/ fashion *a* 2) friendly, amicable, united with, in full agreement with *n* 3) accomplice, confederate, like-minded person

әлбирлик : *n* unity, solidarity

әлборчу : *n* a small sum of money lent for a brief period

әлван : *a* colored, multicolored, motley, variegated

әлванлыг : *n* diversity of colors, variegation

әлверишли : *a* comfortable, convenient, suitable for, fit for, favorable

әлвериш(ли)лик : *n* comfort, convenience, suitability, fitness

әлвида : *n* 1) farewell, parting *a* 2) farewell, parting *intj* 3) goodbye!, farewell!

әлгәрәз : *intj* in short, in a word, to make a long story short

әл-гол : **әл-гол өлчмәк** to threaten or menace by gesturing with one's hands or arms

әлдәгаjырма : *a* 1) home-made 2) unreliable

әлдәjирманы : see **киркирә**

әлдән : *adv* 1) for a quick profit, for a quick buck lit : *"off o.'s hand"*. This term is derived from Russian "**с рук [сбыть]**" lit : "palm/push off on/dump *s.t.* on *s.o.*/get off *o.'s* hands". *Soviet term referring to the sale, at a grossly inflated price by individual speculators , of scarce commodities not available at any price in state stores* 2) on purpose, deliberately, intentionally *in a negative sense*

әлејкәссалам, әлејкүмәссәлам : *intj* hello!, how do you do! *return greeting*

әлејhгаз : *n* gas mask

әлејhдар : *n* opponent

әлејhинә : *prep* against, opposite

әләк : *n* sieve, sifter

әләкјамаjан : *n* mender of sieves/sifters

әләксатан : *n* vendor of sieves/sifters

әләктохуjан : *n* weaver of sieves/sifters

әләкчи : *n* person engaged in weaving sieves/sifters

әләкчилик : *n* occupation of a weaver of sieves/sifters

әл-әл, баш-баш : *adv* in equal amounts, in equal proportions

әл-әлә : *adv* hand in hand

әләлхүсус : *adv* especially, particularly, in particular

әләм : *n* 1) melancholy, sadness, sorrow, grief 2) gonfalon, standard

әләмдар : *n* gonfalonier, standard bearer

әләмә : *vn from* **әләмәк**

әләмәк : *v* sift

әләмли : *a* melancholy, sad, sorrowful, mournful

әләни : *adv* 1) frankly, candidly, openly 2) evidently, obviously, publicly, in public

әләнилэшдирмәк : *v* promulgate, publish, proclaim

әләнмәк : *v* 1) be sifted *intr* 2) pour, run out, fall *in a large amount*

әләсалма : *n* letting down, mockery, humiliation; no end of trouble, troublesome and protracted matter

әләтдирмәк, әләтмәк : *caus of* **әләмәк**

әлиағыр : *n* 1) man with a heavy hand; man whose blows are powerful and painful 2) man with a heavy hand that brings misfortune

әлиачыг : *a* generous

әлиачыглыг : *n* generosity

әлиашағы : *n* impoverished man; man who is in difficult straits

әлибош : *adv* 1) with empty hands, with one's bare hands, without anything 2) with nothing to do

әлиәjри : *n* pilferer, thief

әлиәjрилик : *n* 1) inclination toward thievery, cleptomania 2) dishonesty

әлиjалын : *a* unarmed

әлиjүнкүл : *n* lucky person

әлик : *zool* roe deer

әликәтирән : *a* lucky, bringing luck; successful

әлил : *n* 1) invalid, crippled, handicapped *a* 2) maimed, disabled, mutilated

әлиллик : *n* disablement, infirmity, disability, crippled, handicapped nature

әлиндән : *prep* 1) because of, on account of, owing to, in consequence of 2) because of a multitude/great number *of*

әлисилаhлы : *a* with weapon in hand, armed

әлиузун : *n* 1) person with long arms 2) pilferer, petty thief 3) influential person

әлиузунлуг : *n* inclination toward thievery; habit of taking without permission; klepto-mania

әлиф : see **әлиф jағы**

әлифба : *n* 1) alphabet 2) primer, book of ABC's

әлифбасыз : *a* unwritten; having no alphabet

әлиф jағы : drying oil

әлjазма : *n* manuscript

әлкимjа : *n* alchemy

әлкимjачы : *n* alchemist

әлламә : *n* 1) wise man, sage *a* 2) omniscient *n* 3) know-it-all

әлламәлик : *n* *iron* philosophizing

әлләмә : *n* touching, feeling, palpating; gropping, feeling up, roughly hugging

әлләмәк : *v* 1) touch with the hand, feel 2) grope, feel up, hug roughly

әлләниб-әлләшдирилмәк : *v* be felt, be palpated

әлләшдирмәк : *v* fumble about *in s.t.*, rummage about *in s.t.*

әлләшмә : *n* 1) trouble 2) importunity 3) fuss, bustle, bother

әлләшмәк : *v* 1) try, try hard, make efforts, strive to obtain 2) toil, labor, work hard *at* , sweat *over*, work diligently, take trouble 3) spend much time *with s.t.*, mess about *with s.t.*, bother *with s.t.*, busy oneself *with s.t.*, delve *into s.t.*, putter about *with/ in s.t.*

әлли : *num* fifty

әлли-ајаглы : *a* 1) agile, nimble, lively, active *adv* 2) without leaving a trace, totally

әлли-әлли : *adv* fifty each, in groups of fifty

әллииллик : *n* 1) fiftieth anniversary, fiftieth birthday, *period of* fifty years *a* 2) fifty-year, of fifty years

әллијашлы : *a* fifty-years old, of fifty years

әллилик, әллиманатлыг : *n* fifty-ruble bill/note

әллинчи : *a* fiftieth

әлөјрәнчәји : *n* experimental work, work undertaken for the first time without having prior experience

әлсиз : *a* handless, armless; helpless

әлсиз-ајагсыз : *a* helpless, disabled; totally crippled, handicapped

әлүзјујан : *n* washstand

әлүзсилән : see **мәһрәба**

әлүстү : *adv* quickly, instantly, in a hurry, in a slapdash manner, carelessly, offhand, in a jiffy, right now, at once, immediately, in a flash

әлфәчин : *n* pointer, bookmark

әлчалма : *n* clapping, applause

әлчатмаз : *a* inaccessible, unattainable, unavailable

әлчатмамазлыг : *n* unavailability, inaccessibility, unattainability

әлчим : *n* flax or hemp tow, combings

әлчәзаир : *geog* Algeria, Algiers

әлчәк : *n* glove; mitten

әлчәкбичән : *n* glove cutter *one who cuts material for making gloves*

әлчәклик : *n* material suitable for making gloves

әлчәктикән : *n* glover, glovemaker

әманәт : *n* 1) thing given for storage or temporary use 2) hostage 3) *a* savings *bank or account*

әманәтчи : *n* 1) one who takes *s.t.* for storage, keeper, custodian 2) depositor *of a savings bank*

әмәзәк : *n* 1) wishy-washy person *a* 2) frail, puny

әмәк : *n* 1) labor, work, toil *a* 2) labor, working

әмәкдар : *a* deserved, well-deserved; celebrated; honored *title of honor in the former USSR*

әмәкдаш : *n* colleague, fellow-worker; employee *of an office*

әмәкдашлыг : *n* cooperation, mutual assistance, collaboration

әмәкөмәчи : *n* *bot* mallow

әмәнкөмәчикүлү : *n* *bot* mallow clusters

әмәкһагты : *n* wages, pay

әмәкчи : *n* 1) worker, laborer *a* 2) labor, laboring, work, working

әмәл : *n* 1) work, operation 2) action, act, deed

әмәлә : see **фәһлә**

әмәли : *a* practical, business, businesslike

әмәлијјат : *n* 1) operation 2) action; transaction; activity; act

әмәлисалеһ : *n* just/righteous man

әмәлли, әмәлли-башлы, әмәлличә : *a* 1) decent, respectable, honest, good *adv* 2) well, thoroughly, properly

әмзик : *n* 1) nipple, teat 2) nipple *on a baby's botttle* , *baby's* pacifier

әмзикли : *n* 1) baby in arms, baby, infant 2) woman with a baby in arms

әми : *n* uncle *on the father's side*

әмиарвады : see **әмидосту**

әмигызы : *n* cousin, daughter of an uncle *on the father's side*

әмидосту : *n* aunt, wife of an uncle *on the father's side*

әмиздирилмәк : *v* nurse, be fed at the breast, feed at the breast

әмиздирмә : *n* nursing, breast-feeding

әмиздирмәк : *v* feed with milk, nurse, suckle, breast-feed

әмиздиртмәк : *v* ask or compel someone to breast-feed/nurse/suckle

әмилмәк : *v* be sucked/ dry

әмин : *a* 1) reliable, dependable, trustworthy 2) assured, confident, sure 3) quiet, even-tempered, composed

әмин-аманлыг : *n* safety, security, tranquility, confidence, assurance

әминәвәси : *n* second cousin *on father's side*

әминлик : *n* confidence, being sure, assurance

әмиоғлу : *n* uncle's son *on father's side*

әмир : *n* emir

әмиушағы : *n* cousins *brother's children*

әмишмәк : *v* suck milk all together

әмкәк : *n* crown, top of the head

әмлак : *n* 1) property *a* 2) property

әмлик : *n* milk-fed lamb *or calf*

әмма : *n* but, doubt, difficulty, impediment

әммагоjан : *a* carping, captious, creating unnecessary problems

әммалы : *a* doubtful, questionable

әммамә : *n* turban

әммамәгоjан, әммамәли : *n* turban-wearer

әммә : *n* sucking *with the lips*

әммәк : *v* suck with the lips

әмниjjәт : *n* security, safety, tranquility, calm,

әмр : *n* order, command, injunction

әмрнамә : *n* directions, instructions, order *in written form*

әмсал : *n* coefficient

әмтиә : *n* goods

әмтиәгаблаjан : *n* packer of goods

әмтиәшүнас : *n* commodity researcher/expert

әмтиәшүнаслыг : *n* commodity research

әмуд : *n* mace, cudgel

әмуди : *a* perpendicular

әмчәк : *n* udder, teat, nipple

ән : *part* most *in superlative degree of adjectives*

әнбәр : *n* 1) ambergris 2) aroma, fragrance, perfume

әнбәрбу : *n* kind of rice

әнбәриjjә : *n bot* sundew *bog plant*

әнбур : *n* pliers

әндазә : *n* 1) measure, size, dimensions 2) cut *the style in which the garment is cut* 3) border, boundary, frontier, bound, limit

әндазәли : *a* 1) proportionate, commensurate, symmetric[al] 2) correct, right

әндазәсиз : *a* ungainly, awkward, clumsy, disproportionate, asymmetric[al]

әндам : *n* figure, build

әндамлы : *n* person with slender/slim/well-proportioned figure/build, person with a stately figure, person with a stout/portly figure

әндәрилмәк : *v* 1) run/flow/pour/spill out *completely intr* 2) overturn, tip over, capsize, be overturned, be tipped over

әндәрмәк : *v intr* 1) pour out, gush out, spout *tr* 2) pour out, empty, spill *tr* 3) overturn, tip over, overthrow

ән'әнә : *n* tradition

ән'әнәви : *a* traditional

ән'әнәпәрәст, ән'әнәчи : *n* traditionalist

ән'әнәчилик : *n* faithfulness to traditions

әнк : *n* lower jaw

әнкәл : *n* 1) hindrance, obstruction, 2) obstacle, impediment, stumbling block

әнкәлли : *a* attended by obstacles or bad luck

әнкәлсиз : *a* 1) unimpeded, free *adv* 2) without difficulty/hindrance, without obstacles/obstruction, freely

әнкәч : *n* floodgate

әнкибош : *n* talker, windbag

әнкинар : *n bot* artichoke

әнлик : *n* rouge

әнлик-киршан : **әнлик-киршан вурмаг** to make up one's face, to powder oneself, to powder one's face

әнликли : *a* rouged, made up

әнтәр : *n* 1) *zool* baboon *fig* 2) ugly

әнтигә : *a* 1) antique *n* 2) rarity, curiosity, curio, rare thing *a* 3) rare, interesting

әнтигәчи : *n* antiquary *collector, custodian or vendor of rare objects*

әнчам : *n* 1) end, ending, outcome, conclusion, result 2) means, ways of assistance

әнчир : *n bot* fig

әппәк : see **чөрәк**

әпримәк : *v* go bad, go/turn sour, rot *as a result of being exposed to too humid air*

әпримиш : *a* rotten

әр : *n* 1) husband *a* 2) manly, courageous, brave

әрази : *n* 1) territory *a* 2) territorial

әр-арвад : *n* husband and wife, spouses

әр-арвадлы : *adv* altogether *about a family*

ә'раф : *n relig* Purgatory

әрбаб : *n* master

әргүвани : *a obs.* crimson, scarlet

әрдәм : see **тагәт**

әрәб : *n* 1) Arab *a* 2) Arabian, Arabic, Arab

әрәбдовшаны : *n zool* jerboa *a rodent*

әрәбизм : *n* Arabism

әрәбистан : *n* 1) Arabia 2) Arab world *as opposed to Iran and Turkic-speaking countries*

әрәбчә : *adv* in Arabic

әрәмик : *n* barren draft animal

әрән : *n* man, wise man, sage

әрәфә : *n* eve

әрз : *n* 1) *obs* Earth 2) *obs* latitude 3) application; complaint

әрзаг : *n* provisions, foodstuffs, victuals

әрзиндә : *prep* during, throughout, in the span *of*, for *a period of time*

әрз-һал : see **әризә**

әридилмәк : *v* 1) melt, fuse 2) dissolve

әридичи : *n* 1) founder, smelter, furnace operator *n* 2) solvent *a* 3) melting, smelting

әризә : *n* application, petition; memorandum

әризәбаз : *n* person prone to complaints and litigation

әризәбазлыг : *n* being prone to complaints and litigation

әризәјазан : *n* engaged in writing applications, complaints

әризәчи : *n* petitioner, applicant

әријән, әријичи : *a* fusible

әрик : *n* apricot *a* apricot

әриклик : *n* area planted with apricot trees

әримә : *n* 1) fusion, melting, liquifaction 2) thaw, thawing, solution, dissolving

әримәзлик : *n* see **әримәмәзлик**

әримәк : *n* 1) thaw, dissolve, be dissolved 2) melt, fuse *fig* 3) be ashamed *of*

әримәмәзлик : *n* insolubility

әриник : *a* 1) thawed, melted 2) dissolved, liquefied, in a liquid state

әринкән, әринчәк : *n* lazy person, idler

әринмә : *vn* from **әринмәк**

әринмәк : *pass* 1) be fused, melted 2) be lazy, be too lazy *to*

әринмиш : *a* thawed, melted, molten, fused

әринти : *n met* alloy

әринчәклик : *n* laziness, idleness, indolence

әритдирмәк : *v* make/cause to melt/melt down/fuse/dissolve

әритмәк : *v* melt, melt down, fuse, dissolve

әриш : *n tex* warp

әришлик : *n tex* material suitable for, or earmarked for the warp of cloth

әриштә : *n* 1) noodles *a* 2) noodle

әрк : *n* famialiarity, unceremoniousness, level of acquaintance

әркән : *n* virgin, bride, marriageable young woman

әрклә : *adv* in a familiar manner, familiarly

әркөјүн : *n* 1) pet, milksop a 2) spoiled, indulged

әркөјүнләшмәк : *v* become spoiled/indulged

әркөјүнлүк : *n* spoiling, overindulgence

әрли : *a* 1) married *about a woman n* 2) married woman

әрли-арвадлы : *adv* as husband and wife together *fig* 2) as an entire family

әрлик : *n* 1) matrimony, conjugality, wedlock, marital relations 2) see **әркән**

әрмәған : *n obs* 1) message 2) dedication

әров : *n* 1) scraps of soap 2) slops, waste-water

әрп : *n* thin coating, film

әррә : *n* see ’**мишар**’

әррәчи : *n* see ’**мишарчы**’

әрсиз : *a* unmarried woman, husbandless

әрсин : *n* scraper for dough

әрсинләмәк : *v* scrape dough with a scraper

әруз : *n* prosodic measure based on syllabic length

әсарәт : *n* 1) slavery, bondage, servitude 2) captivity

әсас : *n* 1) basis, foundation, base *a* 2) fundamental, basic, essential

әсасән : *adv* basically, in principle

әсасландырмаг : *v* be grounded on, be based on, conform with/to

әсасланмаг : *v* 1) be based upon 2) allude to, cite, be supported by

әсаслы : *a* well-grounded, well-founded, fundamental

әсаслыча : *adv* thoroughly

әсаснамә : *n* thesis, principal proposition, principles, maxims

әсассыз : *a* baseless, unfounded, groundless

әсассызлыг : *n* groundlessness, baselessness

әсатир : *n* 1) myth, legend 2) mythology

әсатири : *a* mythic, mythological, legendary

әсдирмәк : *v* shake, sway, rock

әсәб : *n* nerve

әсәби : *a* 1) nervous, neural; irritable, short of temper *adv* 2) nervously

әсәбиләшдирмәк : *v* irritate, annoy, agitate

әсәбиләшмәк : *v* become nervous, feel nervous, get irritated/annoyed

әсәбилик : *n* nervousness, irritability

әсә-әсә : *adv* convulsively, in spasms, trembling, shaking

әсәјән : *a* shaking

әсәр : *n* 1) work, production, labor, composition 2) sign, indication, trace 3) activity, influence

әсәрли : *a* see **тә'сирли**

әсил : *a* noble, well-born

әсилзадә : *n* aristocrat

әсил-көк : *n* 1) generation 2) dynasty

әсиллик : *n* nobility, nobleness

әсилсиз : *a* 1) false, fictitious 2) of humble birth

әсим-әсим : *adv* **әсим-әсим әсмәк** tremble violently, shake, quiver

әсир : *n* 1) prisoner, captive *obs* 2) slave

әсиредичи : *a* 1) enslaving 2) fettering, shackling, one-sided

әсиркәмәк : *v* decline, reject, be grudging with

әсирлик : *n* 1) captivity, imprisonment 2) the position or state of a prisoner

әскик : *a* 1) incomplete, insufficient, inadequate 2) less *n* 3) lack, deficiency, deficit, shortage

әскиклик : *n* 1) lack, deficiency, shortage, insufficiency 2) baseness, abasement

әскилә-әскилә : *adv* 1) diminishing, lessening 2) abasing

әскилмә : *vn* from **әскилмәк**

әскилмәк : *v* 1) diminish, decrease 2) abase *o.s.*

әскилтмәк : *v* 1) diminish, lessen, reduce 2) abase, humble

әскәр : *n* soldier

әскәри : *a* 1) military, martial, army *n* 2) special variety of grape

әскәрлик : *n* military service

әскәрчәсинә : *adv* in the manner of a soldier, in a soldierly way

әски : *n* 1) rag, swaddle *a* 2) old, archaic

әскиләшмәк : *v* become decrepit, fall into decay

әскинас : *n* 1) bank note 2) paper money/currency

әски-пүскү, әски-үскү : *n* rags, trash, junk

әскичи : *n* rag merchant, old clothes dealer

әсл : *n* 1) essence, main point, principal basis 2) original copy, original *a* 3) real, genuine, true

әсла : *adv* 1) by no means, not at all 2) not in any way, never, under no circumstances 3) not in the least, not a bit 4) quite, completely, absolutely

әслән : *adv* in substance, on the whole, in the main, basically, in general

әсли : *a* *gram* 1) basic, root, primary 2) original, initial

әслиндә : *adv* 1) indeed, actually, in actuality, in fact 2) in the original 3) in substance, substantially

әсмә : *n* 1) whiff, puff, breath, blowing of wind 2) vibration, trembling, shaking, quivering

әсмәк : *v* 1) blow, waft *of wind* 2) vibrate, quiver, tremble, shake *fig* 3) take care of

әсмәр : *n* 1) dark-skinned, sunburnt 2) Asmar *feminine first name*

әсмәшал : *n* bengaline, a corded silk, or rayon fabric of fine weave

әсна : *n* moment, instant

әснасында : *postp* during, for, throughout

әснаф : *n* 1) artisan, handicraftsman

әснәк : *n* *anat* 1) pharynx 2) yawning, yawn

әснәмә : *n* see **әснәк** 2)

әснәмәк : *v* yawn

әснәшмәк : *v* yawn repeatedly and altogether

әспәрәк : *n* *bot* mignonette *Reseda*

әср : *n* epoch, age, era; century

әсрар : *n* secret, mystery

әсрарәнкиз : *a* mysterious, enigmatic, secret, magical

әсрләрчә : *adv* for ages

әсрлик : *a* century, century-long

әт : *n* 1) meat *a* 2) meat *n* 3) pulp, flesh

әталәт : *n* laziness, apathy, sluggishness

әтганад : *n* see **јараса**

әтдашыјан : *n* meat-distributor, one who transports meat

әтәк : *n* 1) skirt, tail of a garment, flap, hem 2) foot of a mountain

әтәк-әтәк : *adv* 1) with full hems/skirts *num-indef* 2) much, plenty of

әтәкләмәк : *v* 1) seize/catch by the edge/hem of s.o.'s garment 2) fan a fire with the hem of a garment

әтәкләнмәк : *pass* be grabbed/seized/caught by the hem of o's garment

әтиачы : *n* irritable, acrimonious, unpleasant person, faultfinder

әтир : *n* 1) smell, odor, aroma 2) perfume, scent, fragrance

әтирләмәк : *v* dab/spray/splash scent on

әтирләнмәк : *v--intr* put scent on o.s., use scent

әтирли : *a* sweet-scented, aromatic, fragrant, perfumed

әтиршаһ : *n bot* geranium, stork's-bill *Pelargonium*

әтјејән : *a* carnivorous, flesh-eating

әтләнмәк : *v* become fleshy, put on flesh, grow, stout, put on weight, grow fat

әтли : *a* 1) meat 2) fleshy, stout, fat

әтлик : cattle intended for slaughter

әтли-чанлы : *a* plump, stout

әтраф : *n* 1) place, parts, suburbs, environs *anat* 2) extremities, limbs

әтрафында : *prep* around

әтрафлы : *a* 1) detailed, minute, thorough, many-sided, comprehensive *adv* 2) thoroughly, comprehensively, minutely, many-sidedly

әтрафлыча : *adv* see **әтрафлы**

әтрәнки : *a* flesh-colored

әтриjјат : *n* perfumes

әтриjјатчы : *n* perfumer *occupation*

әтсиз : *a* 1) meatless, without meat 2) lean, thin, skinny

әттар : *n* 1) perfume-merchant 2) dealer in chemical preparations, dyestuffs etc *British, dry-salter*

әтчәкән : *n* meat-chopper, meat-grinder

әтчәбала : *n* fledgling, nestling, chick

әфв : *n* pardon, forgiveness

әфган : *n* 1) Afghan *a* 2) Afghan

әфганыстан : *n* Afghanistan

әфәл : *a* 1) dull, untalented *n* 2) irresolute person, a mumbler

әф'и : *n zool* boa constrictor *Constrictor constrictor*

әфкари-үмумиjјә : *n* public opinion

әфлатун : *n* Plato *Greek philosopher, 428-347 BCE*

әфсанә : *n* 1) myth, legend, fable, popular belief 2) cock-and-bull story, fabrication, invention

әфсанәви : *a* legendary, mythological

әфсун : *n* see **овсун**

әфсус : *intj* 1) Pity! Too bad! Alas! 2) *adv* unfortunately

әхбар : *n* news, tidings, information

әхлаг : *n* 1) morality, ethics 2) conduct, behavior

әхлаги : *a* moral, ethical

әхлаглы : *a* well-behaved, well-brought-up, courteous; keeping high moral standards

әхлагсыз : *a* debauched, dissolute, licentious, immoral, badly behaved

әхлагсызлыг : *n* immorality, licentiousness, debauchery, lechery

әхлагсызчасына : *adv* dissolutely, in a debauched manner, licentiously

әһ : *intj* Oh! The hell with him!

әһали : *n* 1) inhabitants, residents 2) population

әһалисиз : *a* uninhabited

әһалисизлик : *n* condition/state of being uninhabited

әһатә : *n* 1) encirclement *mil* 2) flanking movement, pincer-movement

әһатәли : *a* comprehensive

әһвал : *n* 1) state of health 2) mood, disposition 3) state, status, condition, position

әһвалат : *n* event, incident, case, circumstance

әһвали-руһиjјә : *n* spirit, mood, humor

әһваллашмаг : *v* say how do you do *to*, greet, hail

әһд : *n* vow, promise, agreement

әһди-әтиг : *n* the Old Testament

әһди-чәдид : *n* the New Testament

әһднамә : *n* obligation, commitment *in written form*

әһд-пејман : *n* see **әһд**

әһәмиjјәт : *n* 1) significance, meaning, sense 2) importance, significance

әһәмиjјәтли : *a* important, significant, deserving of attention

әһәмиjјәтсиз : *a* unimportant, insignificant

əhəмијјəтсизлик : *n* unimportance, insignificance

əhəнк : *n* lime

əhəнкјандыран : master lime-calciner

əhəнкләмәк : *v* white-wash

əhəнкләнмәк : *v* be white-washed/covered with white-wash

əhəнклəтдирмəк : *v* cause or request that s.t. be white-washed/covered with white-wash

əhəнкли : *a* lime, calcareous, calciferous, calcium, white-wash

əhəнксөндүрəн : *n* expert lime-slaker

əhкам : *n relig* 1) dogmas, tenets 2) commandments, precepts

əhл : *n* resident

əhл-əјал : *n* family members; dependents

əhли : *n* tamed, domesticated animal

əhли-кеф : *n* carouser; party-animal

əhлилəшдирмəк : *v tr* tame, domesticate

əhлилəшмəк : *v intr* become tamed, domesticated

əhли-сəлиб : *n* crusader

əhли-хибрə : *n* professional, expert, specialist

əhсəн : *interj* Good! Well done!

ə'чаз : *n* magic; fabulous

ə'чазкар : *n* magician, sorcerer

əчаиб : *a* 1) astonishing, wonderful 2) strange, odd fellow

əчаиблик : *n* extreme oddity, eccentricity

əчдад : *n* ancestors

əчəб : *intj adv* 1) terrific! wonderful! 2) *used to give an additional emotional or ironic hue to a question, sometimes to make the question sound more rhetorical*

əчəл : *n* the appointed hour of death; death

əчəлə : *adv* in a rush, hastily

əчəл-мајаллаг : *n* accidental, unexpected death

əчəрли : *n* brand-new *about clothes*

əчзачы : *n* pharmacist

əчзаhана : *n* drugstore, pharmacy

əчзачылыг : *n* pharmaceutics; running pharmacy or drugstore

əчлаф : *n* scoundrel, rascal, villain

əчлафлыг : *n* action of a scoundrel, rascal, villain; being a scoundrel, rascal, villain

əчнəби : 1) *a* foreign 2) *n* foreigner

əчр : *n* compensation, payment, wage

əчузə : *n* witch

əшја : *n* things, stuff, belongings

əшјаји-дəлил : *n* material evidence

əшрəфи : *n* pure gold

Ж

ж : ninth letter of Azerbaijani alphabet

жавел : **жавел сују** Javel water, liquid bleach

жакет : *n* cardigan-sweater

жалə : *n* dew

жандарм : *n* 1) gendarme *a* 2) pertaining to gendarmes

жанр : *n* genre

желатин : *n* 1) gelatin *a* 2) gelatin[ous]

женшен : *n bot* ginseng, root of life

жəнк : *n* 1) verdigris *n* 2) cupric oxide 3) see **пахыр**

журнал : *n* 1) magazine, journal *a* 2) magazine, journal

журналист : *n* journalist

журналистика : *n Ru* journalism

жүри : *n* jury *group of judges, or committee to select winners and award prizes*

З

з : tenth letter of Azerbaijani alphabet

забастовка : *n Ru* strike *action taken by workers against an employer*

забит : *n* 1) officer *a* 2) officer, officer's

забитə : *n* discipline, order, strictness

забитəли : *a* strict, severe, exacting

забитəлилик : *n* strictness, severity, exactingness

забитлик : *n* 1) officer's rank 2) the officers 3) occupation of an officer

завал : *n* troubles, misfortunes, grieves, woes

заваллы : *n* poor fellow, poor thing, unfortunate creature

завијə : *n* corner, nook; viewpoint

завијəнишин : *n* hermit, recluse, ascetic

завмаг : *n Ru* store manager

завод : *n* 1) plant, factory, works *a* 2) pertaining to plant/factory/works

загавгазија : *n* Transcaucasus

заҝ : *n* 1) vitriol, ferrous sulfate, zink sulfate 2) metallic luster/glitter

заға : *n* hole, burrow, den, lair

зағара : *n* worn or bare spot on fur

зағлама : *n* oxidation *surface oxidation of metals to impart a luster or gloss to them*

зағламаг : *v* blue, subject to oxide treatment, oxidize

зағланмаг : *v* be oxidized

зағлатдырмаг, зағлатмаг : *caus of* **зағламаг**

зағлы : *a* blued, subjected to oxide treatment

зағча : *n zool* jackdaw

зад : *n* 1) thing *pro* 2) something, anything *intr.* 3) now... *used when one has forgotten a word or a name* 4) *used after other words with the meaning close to 'stuff like that'*

задә : *word added to names to form some family names*

задәкан : *n* 1) aristocracy *a* 2) aristocratic

задәканлыг : *n* aristocratic nature or quality

задәканчасына : *adv* in an aristocratic manner, aristocratically

зажигалка : *n Ru* cigarette lighter

зај, заје : *a* spoiled, wasted

зал : *n* hall, gathering place for a number of people

залым : *a* 1) cruel, brutal, inhuman, merciless, pitiless, ruthless, heartless, hardhearted *n* 2) torturer, oppressor, despot, tyrant *colloq* 3) buddy. pal *used ironically*

залыманә : see **залымчасына**

залымлыг : *n* cruelty, brutality, inhumanity, despotism, tyranny

залымчасына : *adv* cruelly, brutally, despotically, tyrannically

заман : *n* 1) time 2) period, epoch, era, age

замин : *n* guarantor, sponsor, co-signer one who vouches for another

заминлик : *n* 1) bail, surety, co-signing, statement vouching for another person, reference 2) guarantee

занбаг : *n* 1) tulip *a* 2) tulip

заправка : *n Ru* gas station *lit. refuelling*

зар : *n* weeping, moan, groan, sobbing

зарафат : *n* joke, jest, prank

зарафатјана : *adv* jokingly

зарафатла : *adv* in jest, jokingly, for fun, facetiously

зарафатлашма : *vn from* **зарафатлашмаг**

зарафатлашмаг : *v* joke back and forth with s.o., jest, exchange witticisms

зарафатсыз : *adv* joking aside, no kidding

зарафатчы : *n* joker, jester, wag, amusing person

зарафатчылыг : *n* jocularity, facetiousness, buffoonery

зарафатча : see **зарафатјана**

зарафатчыл : see **зарафатчы**

зар-зар : *adv* uncontrollably *about sobbing*

зарылдама : *vn from* **зарылдамаг**

зарылдамаг : *v* moan, groan, sigh

зарылты : *n* moan, groan, moaning

зарыма : *vn from* **зарымаг**

зарымаг : *v* 1) whine, moan, languish 2) entreat, beg, implore, beseech

зат : *n* 1) person, personage 2) nature, temperament, disposition 3) essence

зат-алиләри : *n* His Excellency *title*

затән : *intj* as a matter of fact, practically speaking

зат-нәчабәтләри : *n* His Highness *title*

зат-һәшәмәтләри : *n* His Majesty *title*

заһид : *a* 1) devout, pious *n* 2) ascetic, anchorite, hermit

заһир : *n* 1) exterior *a* 2) evident, manifest, clear, obvious

заһирдә : *adv* outwardly

заһирән : *adv* in appearance, by outward appearance

заһири : *a* visible, outward, external

заһы : *n* woman in childbirth, women who has just given birth

заһылыг : *n* state of being in childbirth or just having given birth

зебр : *n zool* zebra

зејтун : *n* 1) olive *a* 2) olive

зеһ : *n* 1) stripe, border 2) edging, piping

зеһин : *n* 1) receptivity, perception, comprehension, intuition, instinct 2) memory 3) mind, intellect

зеһинли : *a* 1) able, capable, receptive, quick on the uptake 2) possessing a good memory 3) intelligent

зеһинлилик : *n* ability, aptitude, receptivity

зеһинсиз : *a* obtuse, stupid, of limited ability

зеhинсизлик : *n* obtuseness, stupidity, inability, lack of receptivity

зеhли : *a* 1) striped 2) having edging or piping

зеhнән : *adv* mentally, intellectually

зеhни : *a* mental, intellectual

зеhниачыг : *a* 1) receptive, quick on the uptake, able, capable 2) quick-witted, sharp, bright

зеhниjjат : *n* world outlook, weltanshauung; mentality

зәбәрчәд : *n min* topaz

зәбт : *n* seizure, capture, usurpation, expropriation, confiscation

зәбур : *n* 1) plaster *cloth with a medical compound* 2) Book of Psalms

зәввар : *n* pilgrim; person on a tour

зәвзәк : *a* 1) talkative, garrulous *n* 2) talker, chatterbox, windbag, phrasemonger

зәвзәклик : *n* talkativeness, garrulity, idle talk, twaddle, talking profusely

зәвзәмәк : *v* chatter, prattle, talk nonsense

зәвзәтмәк : *v* give cause to chatter or prattle or twaddle

зәггум : *a* very bitter, most bitter

зәггумланмаг : *v* gorge, guzzle

зәдә : *n* flaw, defect, damage, injury, bruise, contusion, trauma

зәдәләмә : *vn from* **зәдәләмәк**

зәдәләмәк : *v* damage, injure, inflict damage

зәдәләнмә : *n* damage, injury

зәдәләнмәк : *v* be damaged, be injured, be beaten, be spoiled

зәдәли : *a* damaged, injured, having a flaw/defect

зәдәсиз : *a* unharmed, safe, undamaged

зәиф : *a* 1) weak, feeble *a* 2) sickly, puny, cachectic *a* 3) frail *adv* 4) weakly, feebly

зәифләмәк : *v* weaken *intr* grow feeble, grow weak[er], grow sickly, get/grow or become thin/emaciated, become exhausted

зәифләндирмәк : *v tr* weaken, exhaust, wear out, enfeeble

зәифләнмәк : see **зәифләмәк**

зәифләтдирмәк : *caus of* **зәифләтмәк**

зәифләтмәк : see **зәифләндирмәк**

зәифләшдирмәк : *v-tr* weaken

зәифләшдиртмәк : *caus of* **зәифләшдирмәк**

зәифлик : *n* 1) weakness, feebleness, exhaustion, emaciation 2) frailty, debility

зәj : *n chem* alum

зәjәрәк : *n* linseeds, flaxseeds

зәjләмә : *n* aluming, treating with alum

зәjләмәк : *v* alum, treat with alum

зәjләтдирмәк, зәjләтмәк : *caus of* **зәjләмәк**

зәjлик : *n* place where alum is mined/extracted

зәка, зәкавәт : *n* 1) mind, intellect, endowments, natural gifts, talent 2) good sense, judiciousness 3) perspicacity, keen-wittedness, quick-wittedness

зәкавәтли, зәкалы : *a* intelligent, keen-witted, quick on the uptake, talented, sharp, bright, reasonable

зәкасыз : *a* untalented, ungifted, slow-witted

зәкасызлыг : *n* lack of natural talent, slow-wittedness

зәкат : *n relig* Sayyid tithe

зәки : see **зәкавәтли, зәкалы**

зәлаләт : see **зәлиллик**

зәлзәлә : *n* earthquake

зәли : *n* leech

зәлил : *a* 1) humble, meek, pitiful, pitiable, oppressed, depressed, unfortunate *n* 2) sufferer

зәлиллик : *n* 1) humility, depression, extreme need 2) misfortune

зәллә : *n* miser, skinflint, penny pincher

зәманә : *n* time, age, century, epoch, era

зәманәт : *n* bail, surety, guarantee, reference

зәманәтли : *a* warranty

зәми : *n* 1) field, cornfield 2) plantation

зәмин, зәминә : *n* 1) ground, basis; soil, earth 2) background 3) zamin *male first name,* zàmina *female first name*

зәмhәрир : *n* extreme cold

зәнанә : *a* female, woman's/women's, lady's/ladies'

зәнбил : *n* big basket

зәнбилтохуjан, зәнбилhөрән : *n* basket weaver

зәнбилчи : *n* basket maker

зәнбирәк : *n* spring *in mechanism*

зәнәки : *n* a meddlesome husband *man who meddles into household matters of women*

зәнк : *n* bell

зәнкуран : see **зәнкчалан**

зәнкәл : see **гунч**

зәнкин : *n* 1) rich person *a* 2) rich, wealthy 3) richly

зәнкинләмәк : see **зәнкинләшмәк**

зәнкинләшдирмәк : *v* enrich

зәнкинләшдиртмәк : *caus of* **зәнкинләшмәк**

зәнкинләшмә : *vn from* **зәнкинләшмәк**

зәнкинләшмәк : *v* grow rich, enrich oneself

зәнкинлик : *n* riches, wealth

зәнкулә : *n* trill, warble, modulations

зәнкчалан : *n* bell ringer

зәнкчичәји : *n bot* bluebell

зәнн : *n* opinion, supposition, assumption, conjecture, surmise

зәнчәфил : *n* white ginger

зәнчәфрә : *n min* cinnabar, vermilion

зәнчи : *n* 1) black person, Negro *a* 2) black, Negro

зәнчир : *n* 1) chain 2) *fig* fetters

зәнчирә : *n* braid *ornamentation for women's dresses*

зәнчирләмәк : *v* chain, put into chains

зәнчирләнмәк : *v* be chained, be put into chains

зәнчирләтдирмәк, зәнчирләтмәк : *caus of* **зәнчирләмәк**

зәнчирли : *a* 1) chained 2) chain

зәнчироту : *n bot* dandelion

зәр : *n* 1) gold, gilt, gilding 2) die *in a game akin to backgammon*

зәравәнд : *n bot* aristolochia *poisonous decorative plant*

зәрбасан : *n typ* gilder

зәрбаф : *n* master of gold embroidery

зәрбафлы : *a* gold-embroidery

зәрбафлыг : *n* gold-embroidery trade/handicraft

зәрбә : *n* blow, shock, kick

зәрбәли : *a* shock, striking

зәрбәчи : *n* shock-worker, pace-setting worker, one who or that which strikes

зәрбәчилик : *n* shock work, shock-worker movement *in the former Soviet Union*

зәрбүлмәсәл : *n* proverb, saying

зәрхана : *n* mint

зәрвараг : *n* gold foil

зәрвуран : *n* gilder *person engaged in gilding*

зәрд : see **сарыкөјнәк**

зәрдаб : *n med* serum, serous liquid

зәрдаблы : *a* serous

зәрдә : see **јеркөкү**

зәрдәпәр : *n zool* shiner *kind of fish with red fins*

зәрдүшт : *n* Zoroaster *founder of religion of fire-worshippers; also used as the male first name*

зәрдүшти : *n* fire-worshipping, Zoroastrianism, Parsism

зәрдүштилик : *n* Parsism, Zoroastrianism

зәрәр : *n* 1) harm, damage, injury 2) loss 3) important matter *in some colloquial expressions*

зәрәрверичи : *n* pest, economic saboteur *in the Soviet Union*

зәрәрдидә : *n* victim

зәрәрли : *a* harmful, injurious, deleterious, unprofitable

зәрәрсиз : *a* 1) harmless, innocuous, without loss *adv* 2) harmlessly, innocuously, without loss

зәрәрсизлик : *n* harmlessness, innocuousness

зәрәрсизләшдирмәк : *v* render harmless, make innocuous, neutralize

зәрәрсизләшмәк : *v* be rendered harmless, be made innocuous, be neutralized

зәрәрсизчә : *adv* harmlessly, innocuously, without loss

зәрзәми : *n* basement, cellar

зәринч : *n bot* barberry

зәриф : *a* delicate, elegant, graceful, refined, subtle

зәрифјунлу : *a* fine-fleeced, fine-wool

зәрифләшдирмәк : *v* make elegant, make refined, make delicate

зәрифлик : *n* delicateness, refinement, elegance

зәркәр : *n* jeweler, goldsmith

зәркәрлик : *n* 1) jeweler's art 2) jeweler's occupation

зәрләмәк : *v* gild

зәрли : *a* gilded

зәррә : *n* grain, grain of sand, speck of dust

зәррәбин : *n* 1) microscope 2) magnifying glass

зәрурәт : *n* 1) necessity, need 2) inevitability

зəрури : *a* 1) necessary, indispensable, obligatory, compulsory 2) inevitable

зəрурилик : see **зəрурəт**

зəрф : *n* 1) envelope *gram* 2) adverb 3) vessel

зəрфлик : *n gram* adverbial modifier

зəрхара : *n* brocade

зəфəр : *n* 1) victory, triumph *a* 2) victorious, triumphant, triumphal

зə'фəран : *n bot* saffron

зəфəрли : *a* victorious, triumphant

зəhəндə : *a* rude, obtrusive, boring *about a person*

зəhəр : *n* poison; *also used as an expletive*

зəhəрлəјичи : *a* 1) poisonous *n* 2) poisoner *a* 3) caustic, biting

зəhəрлəмəк : *v* 1) poison 2) speak sarcastically or maliciously, make malicious or spiteful or venomous remarks, be malicious/spiteful

зəhəрлəнмə : *n* poisoning

зəhəрлəнмəк : *v* be poisoned, poison oneself

зəhəрли : *a* 1) poisonous, venomous, toxic 2) stinging, caustic, biting

зəhəрлилик : *n* toxicity

зəhəрсиз : *a* nonpoisonous, nontoxic

зəhлə : *n* aversion, repugnance, hatred, disgust, loathing

зəhлəапаран, зəhлəкар, зəhлəтөкəн : *a* 1) boring, tiresome, irksome, tedious, unbearable, intolerable *n* 2) pest, nuisance, bore

зəhлəтөкəнлик : *n* quality or state of being a pest/nuisance/bore, importunity

зəhм : *n* fear, fright, terror, horror, threat, menace

зəhмəт : *n* 1) labor, toil, work 2) trouble

зəhмəтапаран : *a* 1) laborious, labor-intensive 2) taking the trouble of doing something

зəhмəткеш : *n* 1) worker, toiler *a* 2) working, labor

зəhмəтли : *a* difficult, laborious, labor-intensive, troublesome, burdensome

зəhмəтсевəн : *a* industrious, hard-working

зəhмəтсиз : *adv* 1) without difficulty, easily *a* 2) easy, not difficult, not arduous

зəhмəтсизчə : *adv* without any difficulty, quite easily

зəhмли : *a* terrible, frightful, fearful, dreadful, terrifying, horrifying

зəhримар : *n* 1) snake venom 2) *used as an oath or swearword*

зəhримарланмаг : *v* gorge, guzzle, choke down

зибил : *n* 1) garbage, trash, litter, junk, sweepings, rubbish *a* 2) good-for-nothing, worthless 3) nonsense 4) stuff

зибиллəмəк, зибиллəндирмəк : *v* litter, scatter rubbish

зибиллəнмə : *n* littering

зибиллəнмəк : *v* be littered

зибиллəтмəк : see **зибиллəмəк, зибиллəндирмəк**

зибилли : *a* litter, trash, littered

зибиллик : *n* trash dump, scrap heap

зибилчи : *n* garbage collector, refuse collector

зивана : *n tech* 1) groove, rabbet 2) tenon, tongue

зивилдаг : *n* 1) smooth, slippery place 2) skating rink

зидд : *a* 1) opposite, contrary, contradictory, conflicting *n* 2) antagonist *postp* 3) *corresponds to the English prefixes anti-, un-, non- etc.*

зиддијјəт : *n* 1) contradiction 2) antagonism 3) contrast

зиддијјəтли : *a* contradictory, conflicting, antagonistic

зиддинə : *prep* opposite, counter to

зидлик : see **зиддијјəт**

зија : *n* 1) light, beam, ray, luster, brilliance, radiance 2) brains, intellect

зијадбалығы : *n zool* omul *fish of salmon family*

зијалы : *n* 1) intellectual *a* 2) intellectual, educated, enlightened

зијалылыг : *n* intelligence

зијан : see **зəрəр**

зијанверичи : *n* wrecker, economic saboteur *one who harms production, government plans etc*

зијанкар : see **зијанчы**

зијанкарлыг : see **зијанчылыг**

зијанлы : see **зəрəрли**

зијансыз : see **зəрəрсиз**

зијанчы : *a* 1) causing harm, harmful, pernicious *n* 2) wrecker, economic saboteur *one who harms production or government programs etc.*

зијанчылыг : *n* economic or social wrecking or sabotage

зијарәт : *n* 1) visit 2) worship of sacred places, pilgrimage *except Mecca*

зијарәткаһ : *n* sanctuary; place of worship or pilgrimage; shrine

зијафәт : *n* feast, banquet, ceremonial dinner

зијил : *n* wart

зијилли : *a* covered with warts, warty

зил : *n* 1) high voice, treble 2) high notes 3) guano, birds' droppings 4) *in combination with adjectives intensifies the quality*

зилгә'дә : *n* Zilqada (eleven month of the traditional lunar calendar)

зиләф : *a* 1) importunate, nagging *n* 2) bore, obsessive, obtrusive person

зиләфлик : *n* importunity, obtrusiveness, boringness

зилләмәк : **көзләрини зилләмәк** stare *at*, fix one's eyes *on*

зилләт : *n* extreme need, destitution, poverty, depression

зилләтмәк, зилләшдирмәк : *v tr* shift to high tonality

зилһиччә : *n* Zilhicca *last month of the traditional lunar calendar*

зина : *n* fornication, adultery

зиндан : *n* 1) anvil 2) dungeon

зиндәканлыг : *n* life

зинә : see **сучуг**

зинәт : *n* attire, apparel, ornament, decoration

зинәтләндирмәк : *v* decorate, ornament, adorn

зинәтләнмәк : *v* dress oneself up, adorn oneself, be adorned/decorated

зинәтли : *a* smart, well-dressed, decorated, adorned

зинкилдәмәк : *v* whine, whimper, yelp *about a dog*

зинкилдәтмәк : *caus. of* **зинкилдәмәк**

зинкилти : *n* yelp, yelping

зинһар : *used with a number of words referring to desperation, unbearability*: **зинһаркалмак** give way to despair; exhaust o.'s patience

зинч : *n* dulcimer

зира : see **чүнки**

зираб : see **ајагјолу**

зирвә : *n* top, peak *of a mountain*

зиреһ : *n* armor

зиреһдешән : *a* armor-piercing

зиреһләмәк : *v* cover with armor, armor

зиреһләнмәк : *v* be covered with armor, be armored

зиреһли : *a* armored, ironclad

зирә : *n bot* caraway *herb whose seeds are used as spice*

зирәк : *a* 1) adroit, dexterous, deft, bright, smart, sharp, nimble, wily, fidgety, spry *a* 2) keen-witted, quick on the uptake *adv* 3) smartly, adroitly, nimbly

зирәкләнмәк, зирәкләшмәк : *v* 1) become adroit/dexterous/deft 2) become resourceful/keen-witted

зирәклик : *n* 1) adroitness, dexterity, deftness, nimbleness, agility 2) keen-wittedness

зир-зәбәр : *adv* 1) upside-down 2) utterly

зирзәми : *n* cellar, dungeon; basement

зиринчәк : see **зиләф**

зифт : *n* 1) resin 2) pitch *boiled resin*

зыгты : *n* miser, skinflint, penny-pincher, greedy person

зыгтылдамаг : *v* whine, whimper, moan, groan

зыгтылты : *n* moan, groan, whimper, moaning, whimpering

зығ : *n* slush, mire, muck, mud

зығ-зығ : *n* 1) crybaby *a* 2) tiresome, irksome

зығылдамаг : *v* squeak, cheep, peep, squeal, screech, yelp

зығылдатмаг : *caus of* **зығылдамаг**

зығылдашмаг : *v* squeak, cheep, peep, squeal, screech, yelp *by many together*

зығылты : *n* squeal, screech, yelp, peep, chirp, squeak, cheep, child's crying

зылх : *n* beet

зымба : *n* punch *tool*

зынг : *n* 1) guano 2) ding *imitation of the sound of a bell*

зынг-зынг : *n* ding-ding *imitation of the sound of a bell*

зынгылдамаг : *v* ring, jingle

зынгылдатмаг : *v* clink s.t., jingle s.t.

зынгылты : *n* peal, ringing, clanging, clang, clank

зынгыров : *n* handbell

зындыг : *n* 1) atheist *n* 2) miser, skinflint 3) see **зәһләапаран, зәһләкар, зәһләтөкән**

зыппылты : *n* commotion, flurry, bustle, turmoil

зыр-зыр : *n* 1) crybaby, sniveller *a* 2) whining

зырылдамаг : *v* to weep/cry shrilly

зырылдатмаг : *caus of* **зырылдамаг**

зырылты : *n* shrill weeping/crying

зырных : *n* orpiment, arsenic trisulfide

зырпы : *a* 1) stalwart, hefty, robust, muscular *n* 2) ugly, misshapen thing

зырпылашмаг : *v* become strong[er], put on weight, grow stout

зыррама : *n* 1) fool, dunce, idiot, imbecile, blockhead *a* 2) stupid, muddle-headed *n* 3) a very crude, strong and stupid person, flatfoot *n* 4) uncouth boor

зоғ : *n* *bot* shoot, sprout, sucker

зоғал : *n* 1) *bot* Cornelian cherry *a* 2) Cornelian cherry

зоғаллыг : *n* Cornelian cherry grove *place abounding in Cornelian cherry bushes*

зоғламаг : *v* shoot, sprout

зод : *n* temper, tempering, hardening *of metal*

зодламаг : *v* temper, harden *metal*

зодланмаг : *v* be tempered/hardened

зодлу : *a* 1) tempered, hardened *about metal* *fig* 2) strict, tough, demanding

зол, золаг : *n* stripe

золаг-золаг : *adv* in stripes

золагламаг : *v* stripe

золагланмаг : *v* be striped

золаглы : *a* striped

зол-зол : see **золаг-золаг**

золлаг : *n* smooth and slippery place; slide *on a hill*

золламаг : *v* throw, fling

зона : *n* zone

зонтик : *n* *Ru* umbrella

зоолог : *n* zoologist

зоolожи : *a* zoological

зоолокија : *n* zoology

зоопалеонтолокија : *n* zoopaleontology

зоотехник : *n* livestock expert/specialist

зоотехники : *a* zootechnic, livestock *pertaining to livestock expertise*

зопа : *n* club, cudgel

зор : *a* 1) strong *n* 2) intensification, coercion, pressure, force *a* 3) difficult, hard 4) force, violence

зоракы : *adv* 1) by force, forcibly *a* 2) forcible

зоракылыг : *n* violence, coercion

зорба : *a* stalwart, bulky, stocky, thickset, robust

зорбазорлуг : *n* tyranny, violence, brute force

зорбалашмаг : *v* grow strong[er], become big/large, become muscular/robust

зорбалыг : *n* hugeness, enormity

зорла : *adv* by force, forcibly, by compulsion, against one's will

зорлама : *n* 1) violence, coercion 2) rape, violation

зорламаг : *v* 1) force, coerce, compel by force, exert pressure 2) rape, violate

зорлу : *a* strong, powerful

зорлулуг : *n* strength

зорхана : *n* *obs* place for athletic exercise

зөвг : *n* 1) taste *artistic* 2) bliss, enjoyment, delight 3) pleasure, fun

зөвглəнмəк : *v* enjoy oneself, obtain pleasure

зөвглү : *a* 1) pleasing, providing pleasure 2) good/pleasant tasting

зөвг-сəфа : see **зөвг**

зөвгсүз : *a* 1) unpleasant 2) tasteless, not having asthetic taste

зөвгсүзлүк : *n* bad taste, lack of taste

зөкəм : *n* cold in the head

зөһрə : *n* *astron* Venus *of Arabic tradition*

зөһрəви : *a* *med* venereal

зубул : *n* punch

зурна : *n* *mus* zurna *wind instrument*

зурначалан : *n* musician who plays the zurna

зурначы : *n* 1) see **зурначалан** *fig* 2) windbag, babbler, talker, chatterbox

зурначылыг : *n* occupation of musician who plays the zurna

зүј : *n* second part *accompanying on a wind instrument*

зүјтутан : *n* accompanist on a wind instrument

зүјүлдəмəк : *v* slip, slide

зүјчү : see **зүјтутан**

зүлал : *n* albumen, protein

зүлали : *a* albuminous, proteinous

зүлм : *n* oppression, tyranny

зүлмәт : *n* dark, darkness, gloom

зүлмкар : *n* oppressor, despot, tyrant

зүлмкарлыг : *n* oppression, despotism

зүлф : *n* hair, locks, curls

зүмзүмә : *n* humming

зүмрә : *n* 1) estate, class 2) group 3) galaxy, brilliant assemblage

зүмрүд : *n* 1) emerald *a* 2) emerald

зүрафә : *n* *zool* giraffe

зүһәл : *n* Saturn *the planet*

зүһур : *n* appearance

И

и : Eleventh letter of Azerbaijani alphabet

ианә : *n* donation, monetary aid

ибадәт : *n* 1) divine service, public worship, public prayer, praying, pilgrimage 2) worship

ибадәткар : *n* pilgrim *person who travels to some sacred place from religious motives*

ибадәтkaһ : *n* chapel, temple, shrine

ибадәтхана : *n* temple, shrine, house of prayer, place of worship

ибарә : *n* phrase, expression, figure of speech

ибарәбаз : *n* one who speaks in high-flown language, one who uses high-flown, grandiloquent words and phrases, phrasemaker *one using empty or meaningless phrases*, phrasemonger, *poseur*

ибарәбазлыг : *n* empty phrasemaking, phrasemongering, passion for using pretentious, high-flown words and expressions

ибарәли : *n* grandiloquence, love of flowery language, pretentious, high-flown style of speech

ибарәпәрдаз : see **ибарәбаз**

ибарәпәрдазлыг : see **ибарәбазлыг**

ибарәт : *a* consisting of/made up of/composed of s.t.,

иблис : *n* 1) devil, Satan, demon *fig* 2) cunning person, intriguer, plotter, finagler

иблисанә, иблисчәсинә : *adv* devilishly

ибраһим : *n* Abraham

ибрә : *n* pestle *used with a mortar*

ибрәт : *n* lesson *for edification,* instructive example

ибрәтамиз, ибрәтләндиричи, ибрәтли : *a* instructive, edifying, didactic

ибтида : *n* beginning

ибтидаи : *a* 1) beginning, initial 2) elementary 3) primeval, primordial; primitive

ибтидаилик : *n* 1) beginning stage, primary nature 2) primitive state, primitiveness

игамәткаһ : *n* 1) stop 2) residence *the official quarters of a high official*

игбал : *n* fate, destiny, a person's lot in life

игдам, игдамат : *n* undertaking[s], initiatives

иглим : *n* 1) climate *a* 2) climatic

играр : *n* 1) acknowledgement, assertion confirmation 2) corroboration 3) evidence, testimony

игтибас : *n* borrowing, extract, quotation, citation

игтидар : *n* 1) strength, force, might, power 2) ability

игтидарлы : *a* 1) strong, powerful, mighty 2) able, capable, skillful

игтидарсыз : *a* 1) feeble, powerless, weak 2) incapable, unskillful

игтидарсызлыг : *n* 1) feebleness, impotence, weakness 2) inability, helplessness

игтисад : *n* see **игтисадиј̄јат**

игтисади : *a* economic

игтисадиј̄јат : *n* economics, economy

игтисадиј̄јатчы, игтисадчы : *n* economist

иғтишаш : *n* troubles, turmoil, chaos, upheaval

иғтишашлы : *a* troubled

иғтишашсалан, иғтишашчы : *n* troublemaker, rabble-rouser

идарә : *n* 1) office, directorate, institution, department 2) governing, government

идарәедән : *n* manager

идарәедилән : *a* being managed

идарәләрарасы : *a* interdepartmental

идарәетмә : *n* management *process*

идбар : n 1) monster, monstrosity, freak *of nature* a *a* 2) hideous, deformed

идбарлыг : *n* deformity, abnormality

иддиа : *n* 1) claim 2) action, suit 3) haughtiness, conceit, self-importance, arrogance, pride

иддиа сатмаг : *n* be boastful; be arrogant

иддиаланмаг : *v* claim to be something, be proud, be haughty, display conceit, imagine/fancy oneself as...

иддиалы : n 1) person with great pretensions/claims 2) conceited, proud, haughty

иддиасыз : *a* 1) not having pretensions, unpretentious 2) modest

иддиачы : *n* pretender, claimant, plaintiff, petitioner

идеал : *n* 1) ideal *a* 2) ideal

идеаллашдырма : *n* idealization

идеаллашдырмаг : *v* idealize

идеоложи : *a* ideological

идеолокија : *n* ideology

идеја : *n* *Ru* idea

идиом : *n* idiom, idiomatic expression

идиоматик : *a* idiomatic

идман : *n* 1) sport[s] *a* 2) sport, sporting, athletic

идманчы : *n* sportsman, athlete

идрак : *n* 1) cognition, understanding, intellect 2) perception, conscience

идраклы : *a* 1) receptive, quick on the uptake, keen, sharp, comprehending 2) reasonable, wise, judicious, conscientious

идраксыз : *a* 1) unreceptive, slow-witted 2) irresponsible, unwise, foolish

идхал, идхалат : *n* import[s], importation

из : *n* 1) track, trace, footprint 2) imprint

из аздырмаг : *v* give deceptive information, lead astray

изафи : *a* superfluous, excessive, surplus

изаһ : *n* explanation, detailed account, interpretation

изаһат : *n* explanation, interpretation, account

изаһедилмəз : *a* inexplicable

изаһедичи : *a* explanatory

изаһлы : *a* explanatory, with explanation/interpretation

издиһам : *n* crowd, throng, mob, mass of people

издиһамлы : *a* populous, crowded, of great numbers *often used contemptuously*

иззəт : *n* 1) honor, dignity 2) Izzat *feminine first name*

иззəти-нəфс : *n* self-esteem, self-respect

иззəтли : *a* honest

изин : *n* permission, authorization

изинсиз : *adv* 1) without permission, without authorization; willfully *a* 2) unauthorized, prohibited, banned, illicit

измир : *n* 1) Izmir *Smyrna -- city in Turkey* *a* 2) Izmir

излəмə : *n* shadowing, tracking, following, pursuit; attentive watching, observation

излəмəк : *v* 1) follow in *s.o.'s* footsteps 2) track, shadow, pursue

излəтдирмəк, излəтмəк : *caus* of **излəмəк**

изолə : **изолə елəмəк (етмəк)** insulate

изолəедичи : *a* insulating

изолјасија : *n* insulation

изсиз : *a* 1) without leaving a trace/clue *adv* 2) without leaving a trace/clue

изтаныјан : *n* tracker, pathfinder

изтираб : *n* 1) agitation, confusion, alarm, trouble 2) torment, suffering

изтираблы : *a* alarming, agonizing, causing suffering

из-тоз : *adv* *in v-cmp* **изи-тозу јоха чыхмаг (чох олмаг)** vanish without a trace

изһар : *n* 1) showing, manifestation, display 2) utterance

иј : *n* 1) smell, odor, scent 2) spindle

ијдə : *n* *bot* 1) oleaster, wild olive *Eliagnus* a 2) oleaster

ијдəлик : *n* place overgrown with oleaster , oleaster grove

ијимəк : *v* see **ијлəнмəк**

ијирми : *num* twenty

ијирмигəпиклик : *n* 20-kopeck coin *no longer extant*

ијирми-ијирми : *adv* twenty each, twenty at a time, in twenties

ијирмииллик : *n* 1) twentieth anniversary, twentieth birthday, twenty years *a* 2) twenty-year, of twenty years

ијирмикүнлүк : *n* 1) period of twenty days *a* 2) twenty-day, of twenty days

ијирминчи : *a* twentieth

ијитмəк : *v* stink *of*, reek *of*, make a stench

ијлəмəк : *v* smell, smell at

ијлəнмəк : *v* become saturated with an unpleasant odor, become foul/rotten, stink

ијлəтмəк : *v* 1) stink *of* , reek *of* 2) let out an unpleasant odor

ијлəшмəк : *v* sniff at each other

ијли : *a* 1) having an odor 2) odorous 3) stinking, fetid

ијлилик : *n* strong smell, strong odor

ијнə : *n* 1) needle 2) sting, injection 3) prickle, spike, thorn

ијнəгабы, ијнəдан : *n* box for needles, needle case, needle cushion

иjнəjарпаг : *n* needle[s] *of a conifer*

иjнəjарпаглы : *a* coniferous

иjнəлəмəк : *v* pierce/puncture/prick *with a needle*

иjнəли : *a* prickly, covered with needles

иjрəндирмəк : *v* give rise to/evoke disgust or loathing, sicken

иjрəнмəк : *v* feel disgust *or* loathing, be squeamish *about*, loathe, have a repugnance *to*

иjрəнч : *a* 1) disgusting, despicable, loathsome, sickening, revolting, offensive, repulsive *a* 2) dirty, unscrupulous *adv* 3) in a disgusting way/manner, disgustingly

иjрəнчлик : *n* loathsomeness, repulsiveness

иjсиз : *a* 1) without smell/odor, not having an odor 2) not strong-smelling

икəн : *adv* while being, while

ики : *num* two

икиағызлы : *a* 1) double-edged 2) with two blades 3) two-mouthed *of an impoverished family with two dependents*

икиадамлыг : *a* two-seater, two-place, for two

икиаjаглы : *a* two-legged, bipedal

икиаjлыг : *a* two-month

икиарвадлылыг : *n* bigamy

икиаршынлыг : *a* two-arshin

икиатлы : *a* two-horse

икиатомлу : *a* two-atom

икибаша : *adv* both ways, there and back

икибашлы : *a* 1) two-headed 2) two-sided, with two sides, double-sided, bilateral

икибир : *adv* in twos, in pairs, two by two

икиганадлы : *a* 1) two-winged, dipterous 2) of two folds/flaps/leaves *e.g. a folding door*

икигат : 1) *a* double, twofold 2) *adv* in two layers

икигəпиклик : *a* 1) two-kopeck 2) two kopeck's worth of

икигиjмəтли : *a* two-digit

икидекадлыг : *a* 1) of two ten-day periods *adv* 2) for two ten-day periods

икидилли : *a* bilingual

икидиллилик : *n* bilingualism

икидырнаглы : *a* *zool* cloven-hoofed

икидорлу : *a* two-masted

икиелементли : *a* two-element, of two elements

икиəлли : *adv* with two hands/arms, firmly

ики-ики : *adv* in twos, in pairs, two by two

икииллик : *a* two-year, of two years, biennial

икиjанлы : *a* two-sided, double-sided, bilateral

икиjаш, икиjашар, икиjашлы : *a* 1) two-year-old 2) two-year

икиjелкəнли : *a* two-sail, with two sails

икиjерли : *a* two-seater, two-place, for two

икикаваһынлы : *a* two-share, two bladed *plow*

икикөзлү : *a* two-eyed

икикүвəнли : *at* two-humped, double-humped *of* Bactrian *camels*

икикүнлүк : *a* two-day, of two days

икилаjлы : *a* two-layer, double-layer, of two layers

икилəмə : *n* 1) doubling 2) division into two

икилəмəк : *v* 1) double 2) divide into two

икилəнмə : *n* division into two

икилəнмəк : *v-intr* 1) divide into two, be divided into two *bot* 2) bifurcate

икилəпəли : *a* *bot* dicotyledonous

икилəшмəк : *v* *intr* double, couple; be paired

икили : *a* 1) dual *adv* 2) two together

икили-башлы : *adv* it is all the same, it makes no difference, one way or another, anyway

икилик : n 1) two, the number two; the name of anything consisting of two units, or designated by the number two a 2) consisting of two parts

икиликдə : *adv* two together

икимə'налы : *a* 1) ambiguous, of double entendre *adv* 2) ambiguously, with double entendre

икимə'налылыг : *n* ambiguity, double entendre

икимəртəбə, икимəртəбəли : *a* two-storey

икинөвбəли : *a* two-shift

икинчи : *a* second

икинчилик : *n* second place, second degree

икиохлу : *a* two-axled, biaxial

икипалаталы : *a* two-chamber, bicameral

икипəрдəли : *a* two-act

икирəгəмли : *math* *a* two-digit

икирəнк, икирəнкли : *a* two-color[ed], of two colors

икиси : *n* two of them

икисилиндрли : *a* two-cylinder

икисимли : *a mus* two-string[ed]

икитаjлы : *a* of two folds/flaps/leaves *e.g. a folding door*

икитарлалы : *n* two-field crop rotation

икителли : see **икисимли**

икитәкәрли : *a* two-wheel[ed]

икитәрәфли : *a* 1) two-sided, double-sided, bilateral 2) mutual

икитирәлик : *n* 1) duality 2) discord, dissension, a split into two camps, schism

икиүзвлү : *a math* binomial

икиүзлү : *a* 1) hypocritical, two-faced, insincere, duplicitous 2) double-faced *of material* 3) dihedral *n* 4) hypocrite, double-dealer; sanctimonious person

икиүзлүлүк : *n* hypocrisy, duplicity, double dealing, sanctimony

икиүзлүчәсинә : *adv* hypocritically, in a duplicitous manner, sanctimoiously

икифазалы : *a* two-phase

икиһакимиjjәтлилик : *n* diarchy, dual power

икиһечалы : *a gram* two-syllable, disyllabic

икиһәдли : *math n* 1) binomial *sum or difference of two algebraic expressions a* 2) two-digit

икиһәфтәлик : n 1 bi-weekly, semi-weekly, periodical issued every two weeks a 2) two-week, bi-weekly, semi-weekly

икиһөкумәтлилик : *n* see **икиһакимиjjәтлилик**

икиһүркүчлү : *a* see **икикүвәнли**

икичархлы : *a* two-wheel[ed]

икичанлы : *a* pregnant

икичанлылыг : *n* pregnancy

икичә : *num* two, two in all, only two

икичәркәли : *a* two-row, double-row, two-series

икичилдлик : *n* two-volume work/set

икичинсли : 1) *a* bisexual 2) *n bot* gynandria, gynandry

икичинслилик : *n* bisexuality

икишаһылыг : *n* ten-kopeck coin *no longer extant*

икмал : *n* 1) perfection, improvement 2) completion, finishing 3) addition, replenishment, reinforcement

икраһ : *n* aversion, disgust, loathing, antipathy

иксир : *n* elixir

икид : *a* 1) brave, daring, courageous, valiant, heroic *n* 2) man of courage, daring/bold fellow, daredevil

икидjана : *adv* see **икидчәсинә**

икидләнмәк, икидләшмәк : *v* become braver, become manly, become courageous, become brave

икидлик : *n* 1) bravery, courage, valor, daring 2) feat, exploit, heroic deed

икидчәсинә : *adv* dashingly, bravely, courageously, heroically, like a man

ил : *n* year

илан : n *zool* 1) snake a 2) snake, snake-like

иланбалығы : *n zool* 1) eel, a teleost fish Order *Apodes* 2) lamprey, an eel-like carnivorous cyclostome, *Petromyzon* and related genera

иланjолу : n 1 zigzag, bend, crook a 2) zigzag

иланоjнадан : *n* snake charmer

иланпәрәст : *n* snake worshipper

иланпәрәстлик : *n* snake worship

илаһә : *n* goddess

илаһи : *n* God

илаһиjjат : *n* theology

илашыры : *adv* every other year, once in two years

илбәил : *adv* from year to year, yearly, annually, every year

илбиз : *n zool* snail

илбизшәкилли : *a* 1) spiral, helical 2) conchoidal

илгар : *n* word, vow, promise

илғым : *n* haze, mirage

илдән-илә : *adv* from year to year

илдырым : *n* lightning

илдөнүму : *n* anniversary

илә : *postp* with, together with

илик : *n* [bone] marrow

иликли : *a* containing marrow

илишдирилмәк : *v* be hitched *to,* be hooked *on to* , be attached *to,* be pinned *to,* be nailed *to*

илишдирмә : n 1 hitching *to,* hooking *on to* 2) *vn fr.* **илишдирмәк**

илишдирмәк : *v* 1) hitch *to* , hook *to* , catch *on,* apply *to* , fasten *fig* 2) strike, hit, strike forcefully, bang

илишик : *a* 1) coupled, hooked up, connected *n* 2) tangle, obstacle, impediment

илишкән : *a* tenacious, clinging, clutching, gripping

илишкәнлик : *n* tenacity

илишмәк : *v* 1) catch *on,* stick *to*, cling *to* 2) be caught (in) 3) get tangled, become entangled, become enmeshed *in*

илыг : *a* lukewarm, tepid

илыгландырмаг : *v* make warm

илыгланмаг : *v* see **илыглашмаг**

илыглатмаг, илыглашдырмаг : *v* see **илыгландырмаг**

илыглашмаг : *v* become warm, get warm

илјуминатор : *n* *Ru* porthole

илк : *a* first, primary, initial, preliminary

илкин : *a* original, primary

илкинди : *n* late afternoon, *period immediately preceding evening*

илкинлик : *n* primacy, primary nature

илкәк : *n* loop

илкәкләмәк : *v* tie a loop

илкәкләнмәк : *v* be tied in/with a loop

илкәкли : *a* tied in/with a loop

иллаһ : *adv* especially

илләрлә, илләрчә : *adv* for years, for years on end, for many years

илләт : *n* 1) sickness, disease, illness, ailment 2) defect, shortcoming 3) cause, reason

илләтли : *a* 1) sick, ailing 2) having a defect/shortcoming, defective

иллик : *a* yearly, annual

илменит : *n* *min* ilmenite

илмә : *n* loop

илмә-дүјмә : *n* fastening, clasp, buckle

илмәк : *n* knot

илмәкләмәк : *v* tie in/with a knot *or* loop

илмәкләнмәк : *v* be tied in/with a knot *or* loop

илмәкли : *a* 1) with knots, with loops 2) tied in/with a knot *or* loop

илтизам : *n* obligation, commitment

илтизамнамә : *n* written pledge, signed statement

илтимас : *n* request

илтифат : *n* 1) goodwill, kindness, benevolence, courtesy, favor, favorable disposition 2) esteem, respect 3) friendly reception

илтифаткар, илтифатлы : *a* amiable, affable, friendly, favorable, benevolent, gracious

илтифаткарлыг, илтифатлылыг : *n* benevolence, favor, goodwill, courtesy, kindness

илтифатсыз : *a* unfavorable, ill-disposed, ungracious, discourteous, unfriendly

илтифатсызлыг : *n* unfavorable attitude, unfriendliness, unfriendly reception

илтиһаб : *n* 1) inflammation *a* 2) inflammatory

илхы : *n* 1) herd *a* 2) herd

илхыотаран : *n* herder, herdsman

илхычы : *n* herder, herdsman

илһаг : *n* annexation, incorporation

илһам : *n* inspiration, revelation

илһамверичи : *n* 1) inspirer *a* 2) inspiring

илһамландырмаг : *v* inspire

илһамланмаг : *v* be/feel inspired

имални : *n* enema

имам : *n* 1) imam *one who carries on Mohammed's cause* 2) Moslem religious leader 3) Any leader *in Azerbaijan*

иман : *n* 1) belief, faith 2) creed

иман кәтирмәк : *v* believe *in religious sense*

иманлы : *n* husband, better-half

имансыз : *a* impious, profane

имарат : *n* precious ornament worn next to the skin

имарәт : *n* 1) palace, castle 2) mansion

имдад : *n* help, assistance

имәкләмә : *vn* *fr.* **имәкләмәк**

имәкләмәк : *v* creep/crawl on all fours

имәчи : *n* 1) unpaid volunteer *hist* 2) *participant in a "subbotnik", or" holiday of Communist labor " usually held on the eve of Soviet holidays*

имза : *n* signature

имзаламаг : *v-tr* put one's signature *to* , sign

имзаланмаг : *v-intr* be signed, sign one's name, subscribe

имзалатдырмаг, имзалатмаг : *v* cause to be signed

имзалы : *a* with a signature, signed

имзасыз : *a* without signature, anonymous

имкан : *n* possibility, opportunity

имкансыз : *a* 1) not having the opportunity 2) impossible, impracticable, unfeasible 3) not having the means *or* resources

имкансызлыг : *n* lack of opportunity, impossibility, unfeasibility, impracticality

имла : *n* 1) dictation 2) spelling, orthography

имлачы : *n* 1) orthographer 2) one engaged in dictating text etc

империализм : *n* imperialism

империализмәзидд : *a* anti-imperialistic

империалист : *n* 1) imperialist *a* 2) imperialist[ic]

империја : *n Ru* empire

имтаһан : *n* 1) examination, test, trial a 2) examination, test, trial

имтијаз : *n* 1) advantage, preference, privilege 2) concession

имтијазлы : *a* privileged, preferential, favorable

имтијазчы : *n* concessionaire

имтина : *n* 1) refusal 2) abstention

инаг : *n* false croup *illness*

инад : *a* 1) stubborn, obstinate, intractable, willful, uncompromising, unyielding *n* 2) stubbornness, obstinacy, pertinacity, unyieldingness 3) see **инадкар, инадчы, инадчыл**

инадкар, инадчы, инадчыл : *n* 1) stubborn/obstinate person *a* 2) stubborn, obstinate

инадкарлыг : *n* see **инадчыллыг**

инадлы : 1) *a* stubborn, obstinate, persistent 2) *adv* stubbornly, obstinately, persistently

инадчыллыг : *n* stubbornness, obstinacy, pertinacity, persistence, unyieldingness

инам : *n* belief, confidence, trust, faith

инамлы : *a* trusting, trustful

инамсыз : *a* distrustful

инамсызлыг : *n* disbelief, lack of faith; distrustfulness

инандырылмаг : *v* be persuaded/convinced, be assured

инандырычы : *a* convincing, persuasive

инандырычылыг : *n* persuasiveness

инандырма : *n* assurance, assertion, aspiration to convince/persuade *s.o.*

инандырмаг : *v* assure, convince, persuade, make *s.o.* change *his/her* mind

инанылмаз : *a* 1) incredible, unbelievable, inconceivable, improbable, unlikely *adv* 2) incredibly, unbelievably, inconceivably, improbably

инанма : *n* see **инам**

инанмаг : *v* 1) believe, trust 2) be convinced, be persuaded, make sure/certain 3) confide *in,* rely *on*

инанмаз : *a* distrustful

инанмалы : *a* trustworthy

инанмамазлыг : *n* disbelief; distrustfulness

ингилаб : *n* revolution

ингилаби : *a* revolutionary

ингилабчы : *n* revolutionary

инди : *adv* now, at present

индијәдәк : *adv* up to now, up to this time

индики : *a* present, present-day, current

индилик : *adv* for the present, for the time being, in the meantime

индичә : *adv* now, right now, just now, this very minute, recently

индуксија : *n* 1) induction *a* 2) induction

инәјәбахан : *n* dairy worker *worker who tends cows*

инәк : *n* 1) cow *a* 2) cow, cow's

инәксаған : *n* milkmaid, dairymaid

инәксахлајан : *n* see **инәјәбахан**

инзибати : *a* administrative

инзибатчы : *n* administrator

ин'икас : *n* 1) reflection *the action* 2) reflection *the image*, echo

инилдәмәк : *v* whine, whimper, complain, languish, moan, groan

инилти : *n* 1) moan, groan, moaning, groaning, whining, whimpering 2) languishing

инишил : *n* 1) the year before last *adv* 2) in the year before last

инкар : *n* denial, disavowal

инкишаф : *n* development, progress, growth, flourishing, expansion

инкишафлы : *a* developed, highly developed

инкишафсыз : *a* undeveloped, backward, retarded

инкишафсызлыг : *n* lack of development, backwardness, retardation

инкилис : *n* 1) Englishman *a* 2) English

инкилисләшдирмәк : *v* Anglicize

инкилиспәрәст : *n* Anglophile

инкилисчә : *adv* in English, in the English language

инкилтәрә : *n* England

инләмәк : *v* 1) whine, languish, moan, groan 2) suffer

иннаб : *n* *bot* jujube, any of a genus *Zyzyphas* of Old World trees and shrubs of the buckthorn family, especially *Z. Jujuba*, also called *Christ's Thorn*

инсан : *n* man, person

инсанаохшар : *a* anthropomorphous, anthropoid

инсандангачан : *n* unsociable person, misanthrope

инсани : *a* 1) human, humane *adv* 2) humanely

инсаниҹҹәт : *n* 1) humanity, humaneness 2) mankind

инсаниҹҹәтли : *a* humane

инсаниҹҹәтсиз : *a* inhuman, inhumane; coarse, rough, rude

инсаниҹҹәтсизлик : *n* inhumanity; coarseness, roughness, rudeness

инсанкириз : *n* see **инсандангачан**

инсанлыг : *n* see **инсаниҹҹәт**

инсанпәрвәр : *a* 1) philanthropic, humane *n* 2) humanitarian

инсанпәрвәрлик : *n* philanthropy, love of fellow men, humanism

инсанпәрвәрчәсинә : *adv* philanthropically, humanely

инсансевән : *a* see **инсанпәрвәр**

инсансевмәз : *n* man-hater, hater of mankind, misanthrope, misanthropist

инсанчасына : *adv* humanely, in a human way

инсаф : *n* 1) conscience, justice, fairness 2) humanity, humaneness, charity, mercy, pity

инсафа кәлмәк : *v* pity/be sorry for *s.o.*

инсафән : *adv* judging by conscience, according to one's conscience

инсафлы : *a* conscientious, honest; just, fair, merciful, kind, gracious

инсафлылыг : *n* 1) justice, fairness, humanity, humaneness 2) state, feeling *or* show of compassion *or* pity

инсафсыз : *a* 1) without conscience, unscrupulous 2) unfair, unjust, lacking in conscientiousness 3) cruel, brutal, callous, heartless, pitiless, merciless, ruthless, unmerciful

инсафсызлыг : *n* 1) lack of conscience, unscrupulousness 2) unfairness, unjustness 3) inhumanity, ruthlessness, cruelty, brutality

инсафсызча, инсафсызчасына : *adv* 1) without conscience, unscrupulously 2) unfairly, unjustly 3) inhumanely, pitilessly, mercilessly, ruthlessly, cruelly, brutally, unmercifully

институт : *n* institute

инс-чинс : *n* not a single person, not a soul

интәһа : *n* end, limit

интәһасыз : *a* 1) endless, unlimited, boundless, infinite *adv* 2) endlessly, infinitely, without limit

интибаһ : *n* Renaissance

интибаһнамә : *n* leaflet

интигам : *n* vengeance, revenge, retribution

интигамчы : *n* avenger, revenge-seeker, revanchist

интизам : *n* 1) order 2) discipline

интизама салмаг : *v* introduce discipline, put in order

интизамлы : *a* disciplined

интизамлылыг : *n* state *or* quality of discipline

интизамсыз : *a* undisciplined, outrageous, disorganized

интизамсызлыг : *n* 1) lack of discipline 2) outrage 3) disorganization, disorder

интизар : *n* expectation

интизар чәкмәк : *v* expect , anticipate

интишар : *n* dissemination, diffusion, spreading

информасија : *n* information

инһисар : *n* monopoly

инһисарчы : *n* 1) monopolist *a* 2) monopolistic

инҹә : *a* 1) thin, slender, slim, slight, fine 2) delicate, refined, graceful 3) small, miniature *ling* 4) soft *palatalized*

инҹәбел : *a* having a slim waist, slim-waisted

инҹәвара, инҹәвары : *intj* incidentally, fortunately, luckily, it's good that...

инҹәдән-инҹәјә : *adv* minutely, down to the fine points, in fine detail, in a very detailed manner, in detail

инҹәләтдирмәк : *caus* of **инҹәләтмәк**

инҹәләтмәк : *v* see **инҹәләшдирмәк**

инҹәләшдирмәк : *v* make thinner, make finer, make more delicate

инҹәләшмә : *n* *ling* palatalization

инҹәләшмәк : *v* see **инҹәлмәк**

инчəлик : *n* 1) thinness, slimness, slenderness, fineness 2) refinement, delicacy

инчəлмəк : *v* get/become thin, become emaciated

инчəсəнəт : *n* art, fine art

инчəhиссли : *a* sentimental, excessively sensitive

инчи : *n* 1) pearl[s] *a* 2) pearl

инчидилмəк : *v* be hurt, be offended

инчидичи : *a* agonizing, excruciating, anguished

инчик : *a* 1) tortured, weary, worn out 2) hurt, offended

инчиклик : *n* offense, injury, wrong

инчикүлү : *n bot* 1) lily of the valley *Corvallaria majalis* *a* 2) lily of the valley *attrib of 1)*

инчил : *n* the Gospel

инчимəк : *v* 1) take offense, be offended 2) be tormented, torment oneself, suffer

инчитмəк : *v* 1) inflict pain 2) torment 3) offend, hurt 4) worry, disturb, trouble; harass

инчичичəjи : *n bot* see **инчикүлү**

инчишмəк : *v* be offended at one another, be mutually offended

инша : *n* composition, work

иншаат : *n* 1) building, structure 2) building, constructing, construction *a* 3) building, construction

иншаатчы : *n* builder

иншаллаh : *intj* God willing, with God's help

ип : *n* cord, rope, string, twine

ипə jатыртмаг : *v - tr* tame, calm down, pacify

ипини чəкмəк : *v* call to order, silence, snub

ипачан : *n* one who unwinds yarn *male or female*

ипбоjаjан : *n* dyer of yarn

ипəjатмаз : *a* indomitable, persistent, stubborn, unyielding, tenacious

ипəjат(ма)мазлыг : *n* indomitableness

ипəк : *n* 1) silk *a* 2) silk

ипəкачан : *n* 1) silk-reeler *agent* *a* 2) silk-reeling

ипəкбиширəн : *n* master silk-boiler

ипəкгурду : *n* silkworm

ипəкдидəн : *n* silk-skein plucker

ипəкисладан : *n* worker engaged in soaking silk, silk soaker-reeler

ипəкли : *a* possessing/owning silk

ипəкчи : *n* silkworm breeder, sericulturist

ипəкчилик : *n* 1) silkworm breeding, sericulture *a* 2) pertaining to silkworm breeding, pertaining to sericulture

ипләмə : *n* see **дəли**

иплик : *n* 1) cotton thread *or* yarn *a* 2) cotton

ипликли : *a* 1) half-cotton 2) made of thread

ираг : *adv* 1) in the distance, at a distance 2) far off, far away *n* 3) Iraq *a* 4) Iraqi

ираг олсун : *intj* God forbid!

ираглашмаг : *v* keep away *from* move off/away *from*

ираглыг : *n* distance, remoteness

ирад : *n* 1) defect, flaw 2) mockery

ирадə : *n* 1) will 2) desire, wish

ирадəли : *a* resolute, enterprising, strong-willed, determined

ирадəсиз : *a* weak-willed, irresolute, without strength of character

ирадəсизлик : *n* lack of will, weak will, lack of resolve, weakness of character

иради : *a* strong-willed

ирадтутан, ирадчы : *a* captious, fault-finding, nagging

иран : 1) Iran *a* 2) Iranian

иранлы : *n* a Persian, an Iranian

ирг : *n* race

ирги : *a* racial

иргчи : *n* racist

иргчилик : *n* racism

ирəли : *adv* 1) forward 2) in front, ahead

ирəлидə : *adv* 1) in front, ahead 2) henceforth, in the future

ирəлидəн : *adv* 1) at/from the front 2) beforehand

ирəли-кери : *adv* backward and forward, back and forth, to and fro

ирəлилəjиш, ирəлилəмə : *n* 1) movement forward 2) progress

ирəлилəмəк : *v* 1) go forward, move forward 2) progress, make progress *intr* 3) advance, push forward

ирəлилəтмəк : *v-tr* push forward, advance, put forward, move/push on

ирәличәкилмиш : *a* 1) advanced, promoted *n* 2) person promoted *to an administrative post*

ирәличә, ирәличәдән : *adv* in advance, beforehand

ири : *a* large, big, huge, voluminous, bulky

ирибаш, ирибашлы : *a* large-headed, with a large head, macrocephalic

ирибурун : *a* big-nosed, with a big/large nose

иридиум : *n chem* iridium

иридиш : *a* large-toothed, with large teeth

иридырнаглы : *a* large-hoofed, with large hoofs

ириjанаг : *a* large-cheeked, with large cheeks

ириjарпаг : *a* large-leafed, with large leaves

ирикөз : *a* big-eyed, large-eyed, with big/large eyes

ириләнмәк, ириләшмәк : *v-intr* 1) grow , grow up 2) become big/large/tall

ирилик : *n* 1) portliness, burliness 2) size

ирили-хырдалы : *adv* 1) both the big and the little, large and small together 2) from the small to the large

ирин : *n* pus; boil, abscess

иринләмә : *n* festering, abscess

иринләмәк, иринләнмәк : *v* fester

иринли : *a* festering, purulent

иринлик : *n* abscess, ulcer

иричичәкли : *a* large-blossomed, with large flowers/blossoms

иричә : *a* quite large/big, voluminous, bulky

иришмәк : *v* grin

ирмәк : *n* small bran

ирпәшмә : *n* goose bumps

ирс : *n* inheritance, legacy, heritage

ирсән : *adv* by inheritance

ирси : *a* hereditary, inherited

ирсиjjәт : *n* heredity

иртича : *n* reaction

иртичачы : *n agent* 1) reactionary *a* 2) reactionary

иртмәк : *n* rump of a bird

иса : *n* Jesus

исбат : *n* proof, evidence, argument

исбатлы : *a* demonstrative, conclusive

исбатсыз : *a* unsubstantiated, unproven

исвеч : n 1) Sweden a 2) Swedish

исвечли : *n* Swede

исвечрә : n 1) Switzerland a 2) Swiss

исвеччә : *adv* in Swedish, in the Swedish language

исә : *conj* and, but

исим : *n* 1) name *gram* 2) noun

исиндирмәк : *v-tr* warm, heat, warm/heat up

исиндиртмәк : *caus* of **исиндирмәк**

исинишмәк : *v-intr* 1) grow/get warm *many people together* 2) get accustomed/used *to*, accustom oneself *to*, make oneself familiar *with*, adapt *to*

исинмәк : *v-intr* warm oneself, get warm

иситмә : *n* 1) fever, malaria 2) *vn fr.* **иситмәк**

иситмәк : *v* 1) be ill with malaria *tr* 2) warm, heat, warm up

иситмәли : *a* malarial

искәлә : *n* port, dock, pier, wharf

искәндәриjjә : *n* Alexandria *Egypt*

искәнә : *n* chisel, gouge

искәнчәби : *n* Iskandjebi refreshing drink containing honey, vinegar and water

ислаг : *a* wet, damp, humid, moist, soaked

ислаглыг : *n* moisture, dampness, wetness, humidity

исладылмаг : *pass* be wet/moistened/soaked

ислам : *n* 1) Islam, Mohammedanism *a* 2) Islamic, Moslem, Muslim, Mohammedan

исламлыг, исламчылыг : *n* Islamism, adherence to Islam

исланмаг : *v-intr* get wet, soak, be wet through, be soaked, get soaked, get drenched

ислатдырмаг : *caus* of **ислатмаг**

ислатмаг : *v-tr* soak, steep, wet slightly, dampen, wet thoroughly, moisten

ислаһ : *n* 1) improvement *a* 2) quiet, mild-mannered, obedient 3) correctional, corrective

ислаһат : *n* reform

ислаһатчы : *n* reformer

ислаһатчылыг : *n* reformism

ислаһедилмәз : *a* incorrigible

ислаһедилмәзлик : *n* incorrigibility

ислаһедичи : *a* correctional, corrective

ислаһхана : *n* correctional home, reformatory

ислыг : *n* see **фит**

исмарламаг : *v* see **тапшырмаг**

исмәт : *n* irreproáchability, chastity, modesty

исмәтли : *a* irreproachable, pure, chaste, shy, bashful, modest

исмәтсиз : *n* shameless person

исмәтсизлик : *n* shamelessness, undue familiarity, forwardness

исмәтсизчәсинә : *adv* shamelessly, with undue familiarity; without shame/shyness

исми-шәб : *n* password

иснад : **иснад еләмәк (етмәк)** 1) support/corroborate one's words with a document 2) attribute s.t. to s.o.

испанаг : *n bot* spinach

испанија : n 1) Spain a 2) Spanish

испанијалы : *n* a Spaniard

испанча : *adv* in Spanish, in the Spanish language

исраил : *n* Israel

исраили, исраилли : *n* an Israeli

исрал : *n* see **анаша**

исрар : *n* 1) insisting *on s.t.*, insistence *on s.t.* 2) persistence, perseverance

исраф : *n* waste, wastefulness, extravagance

исрафчы : *n* embezzler, squanderer, spendthrift, wastrel

исрафчылыг : *n* extravagance, squandering, dissipation, overindulgence, excess

иссиз : *a* deserted, desert, uninhabited

исте'дад : *n* cabability, ability, talent, gift

исте'дадлы : *a* capable, able, talented, gifted

исте'дадлылыг : *n* capability, ability, quality *or* state of being gifted/talented

исте'дадсыз : *a* incapable, ungifted, untalented

исте'дадсызлыг : *n* incapability, lack of talent

исте'фа : *n* retirement, resignation

исте'фалы : *a* retired

истеһза : *n* mockery, ridicule, derision, irony

истеһзалы : *a* ironic[al]

истеһкам : *n* fortification, stronghold, fortress, bastion, fort

истеһлак : *n* 1) consumption *a* 2) consumption

истеһлакчы : *n* consumer

истеһсал : n 1) manufacture, making, production *n* 2) mining, extraction *a* 3) production

истеһсал еләмәк : *v* 1) produce, manufacture 2) extract

истеһсалат : *n* 1) production facility, enterprise *a* 2) production

истеһсалчы : *n* producer

истәдикчә : *adv* in abundance, to one's heart's content, more than enough, as much as one wants

истәк : *n* 1) desire, wish 2) love, affection

истәкли : *a* 1) loved, beloved, darling, favorite *n* 2) pet, favorite

истәмә : *n* 1) desire *vn* 2) *from* **истәмәк**

истәмәдән : *adv* involuntarily, against one's will, unwillingly, reluctantly

истәмәк : *v* 1) want, desire, wish 2) request, ask for 3) need, require

истәнилмәк, истәнмәк : *pass* 1) be desirable 2) be needed, be required 3) be loved

истәр : *conj* though

истәр-истәмәз : *adv* unwillingly, reluctantly, like it or not, willy-nilly

истәтдирмәк, истәтмәк : *caus* of **истәмәк**

исти : *a* 1) warm 2) hot *n* 3) heat, fever *adv* 4) warmly, hotly

истиарә : *n* metaphor

истибдад : *n* despotism, tyranny, oppression, yoke

истигамәт : *n* direction

истигамәтверичи : *a* guiding, leading

истигамәтләндиричи : *a* see **истигамәтверичи**

истигамәтләндирмәк : *v* direct

истиганлы : *a* cordial, sympathetic, responsive, affable, friendly, amiable

истиганлылыг : *n* cordiality, sympathy, responsiveness, affability

истиглалијјәт : *n* independence, self-dependence

истиграз : *n* loan

истида : *n* see **хаһиш**

исти-исти : *adv* 1) while it is hot 2) without putting it off

истикечирән : *a* heat-conducting

истикечирмә : *n* heat/thermal conductivity

истила : *n* capture, usurpation, subdual, subjugation, occupation

истилаһ : *n* 1) term, terminology *a* 2) terminological

истилачы : *n* invader, usurper, subjugator

истиләндирмәк : *v-tr* warm, heat

истиләндиртмәк : *caus* of **истиләндирмәк**

истиләнмәк : *v-intr* warm up, get/become warm, warm oneself

истиләтмәк : *v* see **истиләндирмәк**

истиләшмәк : *v-intr* warm up, get warm, become warmer

истилик : *n* 1) warmth, heat 2) fever

истинад : *n* support, reference

истинадән : *adv* based on, supported

истинадкаһ : *n* fulcrum, foothold, strong point

истинаф : *n* appeal

истинтаг : *n* 1) interrogation, inquiry, investigation *a* 2) investigation, investigatory

истиот : *n* 1) pepper *a* 2) pepper

истиотгабы : *n* pepper shaker, pepperbox

истиотламаг : *v* pepper

истиотлу : *a* with pepper, pepper

истираһәт : *n* rest, relaxation

истираһәтчи : *n* one who is resting/relaxing, one who is on vacation

истираһәтчил : *n* 1) sybarite a 2) idle

истираһәтчиллик : *n* sybaritism, sybaritic life, idleness

истиридјә : *n zool* oyster

истисга : *n med* dropsy *an abnormal accumulation of serous fluid*

истисмар : *n* 1) exploitation, operation a 2) operation[al], operating

истисмар еләмәк : *v* 1) exploit 2) operate

истисмарчы : *n* exploiter

истисна : *n* exclusion, exception

истиснасыз : *adv* without exception

истифадә : *n* use, deriving benefit *from*

истифадәләнмәк : *v* make use *of* , use, utilize, avail oneself of

истичә : *a* lukewarm, tepid

истридија : *n zool* oyster

исфаһан : *n* 1) Isfahan *city in Iran* *a* 2) of *or* pertaining to Isfahan

исфәндан : *n bot* maple *tree Acer*

исһал : *n* diarrhea, stomach upset

исһала дүшмәк : *v* suffer from diarrhea

ит : *n* 1) dog *a* 2) dog

итә дөнмәк : *v* be angry, irritated

итаәт : *n* obedience, submission, subjection, subordination, submissiveness

итаәткар : *a* see **итаәтли**

итаәткарлыг : *n* see **итаәтлилик**

итаәтли : *a* obedient, subordinate, submissive

итаәтлилик : *n* submissiveness, obedience

итаәтсиз : *a* disobedient, insubordinate, recalcitrant, unruly

итаәтсизлик : *n* disobedience, insubordination, recalcitrance

итаәтчи : *a* see **итаәткар**

италија : *n* 1) Italy *a* 2) Italian

италијалы : *n* an Italian

италјан : *n* 1) see **Италијалы** *a* 2) Italian

италјанча : *adv* in Italian, in the Italian language

итбаз : *n* 1) huntsman in charge of a pack of Russian wolfhounds 2) hunter who hunts with Russian wolfhounds

ит-бат : **ит-бата дүшмәк, ит-бат олмаг** *v* disappear to somewhere unknown

итбурну : *n bot* see **һәмәрсин**

итдирсәји : *n* sty *swelling of the sebaceous gland on the eyelid*

итәбахан : *n* huntsman *person in charge of hounds*

итәләјичи : *a* repulsive

итәләмә : *a* repulsing

итәләмәк : *v* push, push away, repel, repulse

итәләнмәк : *v -intr* push away *from*, be pushed away, be repulsed

итәләшмә : *n* crush *pushing and shoving*, crowd

итәләшмәк : *v* push *one another*

ити : *a* 1) sharp, acute, keen 2) fluent 3) quick *adv* 4) quickly 5) fluently

итиахан : *a* swift-flowing, fleeting, transient

итибучаглы : *a* acute, acute-angled

итидимдик : *a* sharp-beaked, sharp-billed

итидиш : *a* sharp-toothed

итијарпаг : *a* sharp-leaved

итик : *n* see **итки**

итикедән : *a* swift-footed, fast, high-speed

итикөз, итикөзлү : *a* sharp-sighted, sharp-eyed

итикөзлүк, итикөзлүлүк : *n* keen vision, vigilance

итикөрән : *a* see **итикөз, итикөзлү**

итиләләк : *a* sharp-feathered

итиләмәк : *v* sharpen, whet

итиләнмәк : *pass* be sharpened

итиләтдирмәк, итиләтмәк : *caus* of **итиләмәк**

итиләшдирмәк : *v* make sharper

итиләшмәк : *v* become acute, become sharp/pointed

итилик : *n* 1) sharpness, acuteness 2) speed, quickness

итилмәк : *v* tidy up, clean up

итипәрли : *a* sharp-bladed

итирилмәк : *v -intr* get lost, be lost

итирмәк : *v* lose, be deprived *of s.t.*, forfeit *s.t.*

итиучлу : *a* pointed, sharp, acute, acicular, tapered

итичә : *adv* sharply, keenly

итки : *n* loss, losses; waste

иткин : *a* disappeared, vanished

иткин салмаг : *v* drive away, kick out, exile

итләшмәк : *v* fight, quarrel

итмәк : *v* get lost, disappear, vanish

итөјрәдән : *n* dog-trainer

иттифаг : *n* 1) union, alliance 2) accord, unanimity 3) occurrence, occasion, chance

иттифагән : *adv* by chance

иттиһад : *n* association, society, union

иттиһадчы : *n* unionist, ideologist/visionary of unity

иттиһам : *n* charge, accusation

иттиһамнамә : *n* indictment, bill of indictment

иттиһамчы : *n* accuser, prosecutor

иттиһаф : *n* dedication

иттутан : *n* dogcatcher

итһаф : *n* dedication

ифа : *n* performance, execution, fulfillment

ифа еләмәк : *v* perform, execute, fulfil, complete

ифадә : *n* 1) expression 2) style 3) phrase, saying 4) statement, account 5) deposition *before an investigator*, testimony *in court*

ифадәли : *a* expressive

ифадәлилик : *n* expressiveness

ифадәсиз : *a* inexpressive

ифадәсизлик : *n* inexpressiveness

ифачы : *n* performer, executor

ифлас : *n* crash, bankruptcy, insolvency

ифлич : *n* paralysis

ифраз : *n* secretion, excretion, separation

ифразат : *n* 1) excretion 2) secretion 3) excrement, feces

ифрат : *adv* 1) too, excessively, super-, over-, extremely, arch-; ultra *a* 2) extreme

ифратчы : *n* one who loves the extreme

ифратчылыг : *n* passion for extremes

ифритә : *n* witch, hag

ифтира : *n* slander, calumny, malicious gossip

ифтирачы : *n* slanderer, spreader of malicious gossip

ифтирачылыг : *n* slander[ing], spreading of malicious gossip

ифтихар : *n* pride, honor, fame, reputation

ифтихарла : *adv* proudly, with conscious self-respect

ифша : *n* disclosure, exposure

ихлас : *n* sincerity, devotion, candor, frankness, goodwill

ихлас көстәрмәк : *v* show reverence, respect, devotion

ихласкар : *a* awesome, reverential

ихрач : *n* export

ихрачат : *n* export goods, exports

ихтијар : *n* 1) will, right, authority, power 2) permission, authorization

ихтијарсыз : *adv* 1) involuntarily *a* 2) involuntary, without rights *adv* 3) without permission

ихтијарсызлыг : *n* absence of rights, state of possessing no rights

ихтилал : *n* rebellion, revolution, uprising

ихтилаф : *n* disagreement, discord, dissension, misunderstanding, conflict, incident

ихтилафлы : *a* disputable, debatable, at issue

ихтира : *n* 1) invention 2) idea, concoction

ихтирачы : *n* inventor

ихтирачылыг : *n* 1) invention, development of inventions 2) inventiveness, ingenuity

ихтисар : *n* abbreviation, shortening

ихтисас : *n* specialty, profession, qualification

ихтисасландырмаг : *v* make specialized, assign a specialty *to*

ихтисасланмаг : *v* specialize *in*

ихтисаслашдырмаг : *v* see **ихтисасландырмаг**

ихтисаслы : *a* having a specialty *or* rofession, having qualification[s]

ихтисассыз : *a* not having a specialty *or* profession, unqualified

ич : *n* 1) interior, interior part 2) internal organs, pluck, entrails, offal 3) core, pith, heart, nucleus 4) *pertaining to food* stuffing, filling

ич еләмәк : *v* peel, hull, shell

ичалат : *n* see **ич** (2)

ичдирмәк : *v* see **ичиртмәк**

ичәри : *a/adv* 1) in, into, inside *n* 2) inner side *a* 3) inner, internal, interior

ичибош : *a* hollow, empty

ичилмәк : *pass* be drunk up, be drunk to the last drop

ичим, ичимлик : *n* dose *of liquid medicine etc sufficient for one administration*

ичин-ичин : *v* **ичин-ичин ағламаг** sob

ичиртдирмәк : *v* let someone drink, force someone to drink, give someone something to drink

ичиртмәк : *v* let drink, give *s.t.* to drink; force to drink

ички : *n* drink, beverage, alcoholic drinks

ичкибазлыг : *n* alcohol addiction

ичмәк : *v* 1) drink, drink up 2) sup *eat a liquid with a spoon*

ичмәли : *a* 1) potable, drinking, suitable for drinking 2) delicious *drink*

ич-үз : *n* 1) internal aspect, hidden aspect *of a matter or question* 2) underlying reason, essence *of a matter*

ичад : *n* invention

ичазә : *n* permission, authorization

ичазәли : *a* 1) permitted, allowed, authorized *adv* 2) with permission

ичазәсиз : *adv* 1) without permission *a* 2) unauthorized

ичарә : *n* 1) rent, rental, lease *a* 2) rent, rental, lease

ичарәдар : *n* leaseholder, lessee, tenant

ичарәләмәк : *v* lease, have/hold on lease, rent

ичарәһагты : *n* rent, rental, rent payment

ичарәчи : *n* see **ичарәдар**

ичбар : *n* compulsion, constraint, coercion

ичбари : *a* obligatory, compulsory, forced

ичлас : *n* meeting, conference, session, sitting

ичласчы : *n* representative, participant in a meeting, conference, session

ичма : *n* 1) community, commune *a* 2) communal, common

ичмал : *n* 1) sketch, essay, survey, review 2) summary, report

ичмалчы : *n* commentator, reviewer

ичра : *n* putting in motion, fulfilling, fulfillment, implementation, implementing, carrying out, executing, execution, performing, performance

ичраедичи : *n* see **ичрачы**

ичраиjjә : *a* executive

ичраjи-тә'сир : *n* influence

ичрачы : *n* executor, performer

ичрәт : *n* 1) retribution, requital 2) reward, recompense, compensation, remuneration

ичтимаи : *a* public, social

ичтимаиjjат : *n* social sciences, sociology

ичтимаиjjатчы : *n* social scientist, sociologist

ичтимаиjjәт : *n* the community, the public, public organizations

ичтимаиләшдирилмәк : *v* be socialized, be collectivized

ичтимаиләшдирилмиш : *a* socialized, collectivized

ичтимаиләшдирмә : *n* socialization, collectivization

ичтимаиләшдирмәк : *v-tr* socialize, collectivize

ичтимаиләшмәк : *v* become common *or* public *of property*, be socialized, be collectivized

ичтиһад : *n* scientific training

иш : *n* 1) work, job, business, affair, matter, deed, act, occupation, pursuit, employment 2) undertaking, enterprise, venture

иш кәсмәк : *v* sentence, condemn

иш көрмәк : *v* work, do business; be fit/fitting/suitable; settle *a matter/deal*

ишә дүшмәк : *v* 1) begin to work/act 2) get into trouble

ишә салмаг : *v* 1) start *e.g. an engine* 2) get *s.o.* into trouble

иши кәтирмәк : *v* be lucky, be in luck

ишаранты : *n* barely visible *dim* light, ray of light *in clouds* twinkling, glimmer, flash

ишарә : *n* 1) signal 2) sign, mark 3) hint

ишарәләмә : *n* designation, marking

ишарәләмәк : *v* note, mark

ишарәләнмәк : *pass* be designated, be marked

ишарәт : *n* 1) mark, note 2) label, signature

ишарәчи : *n* signalman, bugler, signal-bugler

ишармаг : *v* 1) shine weakly, glimmer, twinkle 2) appear through, be seen/visible through

ишарты : *n* see **ишаранты**

ишбачаран : *a* able, skillful, active, energetic

ишбөлән : *n* job assignment person/functionary, work assignment person/functionary

ишвә : *n* coquetry, flirting, affectation

ишвәбаз, ишвәкар, ишвәли : *n* 1) coquette, flirt 2) coquettish, affected

ишвәбазлыг, ишвәкарлыг : *n* coquetry, flirting, affectation

ишғал : *n* occupation *of territory, of a building*, capture, seizure

ишғалчы : *n* invader, usurper, occupier

ишғалчылыг : *n* aggressive nature *or* character

ишәјарајан, ишәјарар, ишәјарарлы : *a* 1) fit for work, suitable 2) acceptable

ишәмәк : *n* 1) urine 2) *v* urinate

ишыг : *n* 1) light *a* 2) light, bright, illuminated

ишыгтошан : *n* switch

ишыгдангорхма : *n* photophobia

ишыгландырмаг : *v* illuminate, light up

ишыгланма : *n* 1) lighting 2) dawn, daybreak

ишыгланмаг : *v-intr* 1) shine, brighten 2) dawn, break *of day or daylight*

ишыглатмаг : *v* see **ишыгландырмаг**

ишыглы : *a* 1) illuminated, with light 2) light, bright

ишыглыг : *n* 1) brightness, light 2) window, small window *fig* 3) bright world, better world

ишыгсачан : *a* shining

ишыгсыз : *a* not having light; without light, without illumination, dark

ишыгсызлыг : *n* absence of light; lack of illumination

ишылдагум : *n zool* firefly *fam. Lampyridae*

ишылдамаг : *v* shine, sparkle, glitter, beam

ишылдатмаг : *v* add luster *to* , shed luster *on*

ишылты : *n* luster, brilliance, gleam, sheen, radiance, glitter, sparkle

ишкил : *n* 1) hook 2) ruse, trick, subterfuge 3) snag, impediment, difficulty

ишкилләмәк : *v* close with a hook, hook

ишкилли : *a* 1) hooked, closed with a hook 2) suspicious, cunning, sly 3) difficult

ишкәнә : *n* broth, clear soup, boullion

ишкәнчә : *n* torture, torment

ишкүзар : *a* efficient, businesslike, enterprising

ишкүзарлыг : *n* efficiency, businesslike character, enterprise *state or quality,* resourcefulness

иш-күч : *n* matters, business

ишләдилмәк : *v* be used, be employed

ишләк : *a* 1) efficient, businesslike, able-bodied, industrious, hardworking 2) worker's 3) busy *of a road or street* 4) in good repair, in good working order *of machinery or equipment*

ишләмә : 1) *vn fr.* **ишләмәк** 2) manual labor, handwork 3) decoration, ornament, embroidery 4) working, processing, treatment, exploitation, cultivation

ишләмәк : *v* 1) work, operate, run, act, function 2) process, treat, exploit 3) penetrate, pierce, influence 4) ply, run *between* 5) have diarrhea

ишләнмә : *n* processing, treatment

ишләнмәк : *v* 1) be processed, be treated, be worked, be exploited, be cultivated, be developed 2) be in operation, be in use, be in circulation

ишләтдирмәк : *caus* of **ишләмәк**

ишләтмә : 1) *vn* from **ишләмәк** *a* 2) laxative

ишләтмәк : *v* 1) compel to work, give work *to*, give a job *to* 2) put in action, put in motion, put into circulation, exploit, work, run 3) spend, expend, use, consume 4) have diarrhea

ишсевән : *a* industrious, hardworking

ишсиз : *a* unemployed; without business, without work, without a job

ишсиз-күчсүз : *adv* without any business at all, without any work/job at all, idly

ишсизлик : *n* 1) unemployment 2) idleness

ишсиз-пешәсиз : *adv* see **ишсиз-күчсүз**

иштаһа : *n* appetite

иштаһаачан : *a* whetting the appetite, appetizing

иштаhаланмаг : *v* show/manifest/display a desire *or* appetite *for*

иштаhалы : *a* having an appetite

иштаhасыз : *a* 1) without appetite *adv* 2) reluctantly, unwillingly *i.e. to eat . . .,*

иштаhасызлыг : *n* lack of appetite

иштирак : *n* participation, collaboration

иштирак еләмәк : *v* participate, take part in, be involved in

иштиракчы : *n* participant

ишчи : *n* worker

ишчил : *a* 1) efficient, businesslike 2) hard worker

ишчиллик : *n* businesslike character, efficiency

j

j : thirteenth letter of Azerbaijani alphabet

ja : *conj* or

jaба : *n* pitchfork

jaбагуjруг : *n* see **гарангуш**

jaбаны : *a* desert, deserted, uninhabited, wild

jaбанчы : a 1) somebody else's, alien, stranger *to s.t.* 2) *n* stranger, alien

jaбы : *n* bad horse

jaва : *a* 1) dissipated, dissolute, licentious, lecherous, debauched, indecent, obscene *n* 2) debauchee, profligate, lecher, dissolute/licentious person; trollop, strumpet, streetwalker, woman of easy virtue *a* 3) bad, unfit

jaвалыг : *n* dissipation, debauchery, lechery, depravity, lasciviousness

jaван : n 1) dry food, cold food a 2) lean

jaванлыг : *n* 1) everything that is eaten with bread; food 2) dairy products 3) absence of fat

jaваш : *a* 1) quiet, gentle, slow, unhurried *adv* 2) quietly, gently, slowly

jaвашыма : *n* quieting/calming down, slowing down

jaвашымаг : *v-intr* 1) calm down, quiet down 2) become pacified

jaвашытмаг : *v-tr* 1) quiet, slow down 2) pacify

jaваш-jaваш : *adv* gradually, little by little, by easy stages, slowly

jaвашламаг, jaвашландырмаг : *v* slow one's stride, reduce speed

jaвашлыг : *n* slowness, sluggishness, caution

jaваштәрпәнән : *a* sluggish, slow

jaвашча : *adv* slowly, cautiously, gently; stealthily

jaвашча-jaвашча : *adv* see **jaваш-jaваш**

jaгут : *n* 1) ruby, sapphire *a* 2) ruby, sapphire

jaғ : *n* butter, oil, fat

jaғар : *n* see **jaғыш**

jaғгабы, jaғдан : *n* 1) butter dish, oilcan 2) lamp's reservoir with flammable liquid *kerosene, etc.*

jaғдырмаг : *v* 1) cause rain *or* snow fig 2) produce something in abundance for sale 3) cover, strew *with*

jaғы : *n* enemy, foe

jaғылыг : *n* enmity, hostility, animosity

jaғынлыг : *n* raininess, abundance of precipitation

jaғынты : *n* atmospheric precipitation

jaғыоту : *n bot* willow herb *Epilobium, used to make tea or a tea additive*

jaғыр : *n vet -med* abrasion, excoriatioon *or* wound caused by the rubbing of the harness on the back of draft or pack animals

jaғыш : *n* 1) rain *a* 2) rain

jaғышлы : *a* rainy *day, month*

jaғышлыг : *n* rainy weather

jaғышөлчән : *n* rain gauge

jaғышсыз : *a* without rain, rainless

jaғышсызлыг : *n* dry spell, dry weather

jaғ-jaванлыг : *n* butter and dairy products

jaғлаjычы : *n* greaser, lubricator, oiler

jaғлама : *n* buttering, greasing, lubricating, oiling

jaғламаг : *v* butter, grease, oil, lubricate

jaғландырмаг : *caus* of **jaғланмаг** 2), 3)

jaғланмаг : *v* 1) be buttered *or* oiled, be smeared with butter *or* oil 2) grow fat/plump, grow stout, put on weight *fig* 3) make a fortune, become rich, grow rich

jaғлатдырмаг, jaғлатмаг : *caus* of **jaғламаг**

jaғлы : *a* 1) greasy, oily, buttery 2) rich, short *in ref. to cake, pastry, etc* 3) smeared with oil/butter/grease 4) rich, wealthy, well-to-do

jaғлылыг : *n* 1) greasiness, fatness 2) butteriness, oiliness

jaғма : *n* fall

jaғмаг : *v* 1) fall *re atmospheric precipitation* 2) pour down from above

jaғмур : *n* rain

jaғмурлу : *a* rainy

jaғмурлуг : *n* 1) abundance of rain 2) raincoat

jaғмурөлчән : *n* see **jaғышөлчән**

jaғмурсуз : *a* dry, without rain

jaғмурсузлуг : *n* dry spell, dry weather, dryness, drought

jaғсатан : *n* seller of butter *or* oil

jaғсыз : *a* lean, without fat

јад : *a* 1) somebody else's, another's, strange, alien, unknown, unfamiliar, foreign *n* 2) stranger, alien *n* 3) memory, recollection, reminiscence

јад еләмәк : *v* recall, recollect

јаддан чыхармаг : *v* forget

јадасалма : *n* reminder

јадданчыхмаз : *a* unforgettable, retained eternally in one's memory

јаддаш : *n* memory

јаддашлы : *a* having a retentive memory

јаддашсыз : *a* forgetful, absent-minded

јаддашсызлыг : *n* 1) forgetfulness, absent-mindedness *med* 2) amnesia, loss of memory

јаделли : *n* 1) stranger, foreigner, alien *a* 2) strange, foreign, alien

јадикар : *n* 1) memory, keepsake, souvenir 2) *adv* as a keepsake/souvenir, for remembrance

јадикарлыг : *adv* as a keepsake/souvenir, for remembrance

јадырғамаг : *v* get out of the habit (of), break oneself of the habit *of*, lose the habit *of*, forget how *to*, lose the art of

jаз : *n* 1) spring *a* 2) spring

jазбөҹәји : *n zool* Mayfly *amphibious insect*

jаздырмаг, јаздыртмаг : *caus* of **jазмаг**

jазы : *n* 1) writing, script 2) inscription 3) written language 4) handwriting

jазыг : *a* 1) poor, pitiful, pitiable *n* 2) poor thing 3) *a* inoffensive, harmless

jазығы қалмак : *v* pity/feel sorry for *s.o.*

jазыг-јазыг : *adv* sorrowfully, mournfully, plaintively

jазыгчасына : *adv* entreatingly

jазыгчығаз : *a* somewhat poor

jазылы : *a* 1) noted in writing, having an inscription 2) written *adv* 3) in writing, in written form

jазылыш : *n* writing, method of writing

jазылмаг : *pass* be written, be written down, be recorded

jазысыз : *a* unwritten

jазычы : *n* 1) writer, author *a* 2) writer's, author's

jазышма : *n* correspondence

jазышмаг : *v* correspond with one another, exchange correspondence, carry on correspondence

jазлыг : *a* 1) spring *of the season of the year*, vernal 2) spring *of crops*

jазмаг : *v* write, write down, record

jaj : *n* 1) summer *a* 2) summer *n* 3) spring *watch spring, automotive spring, etc.* 4) *n* bow*weapon*, bow string 5) *n* bow *for stringed instruments*

jaja : *sdv* on foot, afoot

jajar : *a* foot, pedestrian

jajғын : *a* diffuse, diffused

jajдырмаг : *caus* of **jajмаг**

jajылан : *a* diffuse, diffused

jajылма : *vn* from **jajылмаг**

jajылмаг : *v-intr* 1) spread 2) be spread [out], be laid *out* , be dispersed, be scattered, disperse, scatter 3) run *of ink* 4) be rolled out, be rolled, be spread flat with a roller

jajынбалығы : *n zool* burbot, also called eel-pout, cusk, lawyer, ling *Lota lota fresh-water fish*

jajындырмаг : *v* 1) distract, divert *attention* 2) show *s. o.* the door, send *s. o.* on his way 3) remove inconspicuously, *v-tr* hide, conceal

jajынмаг : *v* 1) be distracted, divert one's attention 2) slip away, make off, take to one's heels, run away

jajычы : *n* person engaged in rolling out *dough*

jajла : *n* 1) territory where nomads roam; summer pasture *geog* 2) plateau, tableland

jajлаг : *n* 1) country cottage, summer cottage, place in the country 2) mountain plateau

jajлагламаг, jajлагланмаг, jajламаг : *v* spend the summer at a summer cottage, in the mountains, or in cool places

jajлатмаг : *caus* of **jajламаг**

jajлы : *a tech* equipped with a spring

jajлыг : *n* 1) head kerchief, headscarf 2) see **дәсмал**

jajлым : *n* 1) volley, salvo 2) night pasturage of livestock

jajлымламаг : *v* lead livestock to night pasturage

jajлымлатмаг : *caus* of **jajлымламаг**

jajма : *n* 1) spread, spreading, diffusion, dissemination, expansion, broadening 2) rolling out *dough*

jajмаг : *v* 1) spread, diffuse, disseminate 2) expand, broaden, disperse, scatter, lay out, spread out 3) roll, roll out *dough*

jajханмаг : *v* waddle

jал : *n* 1) mane 2) mash *food for livestock* 3) slope, pass

jалаг : *n* 1) toady, bootlicker *a* 2) having a weakness for food *or* delicacies, insatiable 3) depression dug in the ground where food for dogs is thrown or poured

jалаглыг : *n* 1) sponging 2) gourmandism, hearty interest in food

jалагчы : *n* see **jалаг** 1)

jаламаг : *v* lick, lick clean, lick all over

jалан : *n* 1) lie, fib *a* 2) false, lying, mendacious

jалан сатмаг : *v* lie/tell lies

jаландан : *adv* 1) falsely, affectedly, hypocritically 2) purposely, on purpose, for fun

jаланмаг : *v* be licked, be licked all over, be licked clean

jалан-палан : *n* lies, fibs, cock-and-bull stories

jалансыз : *a* without lies, without deceit

jаланчы : *n* 1) liar, fibber *a* 2) imaginary, sham, false, fake, fictitious

jаланчыбүлбүл : *n* *zool* siskin, *Fringilla spinus , small, seed-eating bird of the finch family*

jаланчылыг : *n* mendacity, falsity, falsehood, habit of lying

jалатдырмаг, jалатмаг : *caus* of **jаламаг**

jалвара-jалвара : *adv* entreatingly, imploringly, with entreaties

jалварыш : *n* entreaty, supplication, incessant begging

jалвар-jапыш, jалвар-jахар : *n* entreaty, supplication, insistent *or* persistent request

jалварма : *n* entreaty, supplication, request

jалвармаг, jалварыб-сытгымаг, jалварыб-jахармаг : *v* entreat, implore, supplicate, beg, pray for

jалгыз : *a* 1) alone, single, lonely, solitary *adv* 2) lonely, by oneself

jалгызлыг : *n* loneliness, solitude, seclusion

jалгызча : *a* absolutely alone, quite alone

jалгузаг : *n* lone wolf

jалыгушу : *n* *zool* swift, any of several swallow-like birds of the family *Apodidae*

jалыкөдәк : *a* short-maned

jалын : *a* bare, naked

jалынаjаг : *a* see **ajaгjалын**

jалынгат : *a* 1) single 2) unlined, without lining *of clothing*

jалламаг : *v* feed a dog with swill/mash

jаллы : *n* 1) line-dance (designation of a dance in which the dancers stand in a line and do what the leader does, as in follow-the-leader) *a* 2) long-maned, with a long mane

jаллыкедән : *n* leader in a line dance; see **jаллы**

jалман : *n* horse's mane

jалманмаг : *v* suck up to *s. o.* lick *s. o.'s* boots

jалныз : *adv* 1) only, exclusively, solely 2) see **jалгыз**

jалнызлыг : *n* see **jалгызлыг**

jалнызча : *a* see **jалгызча**

jалсыз : *a* maneless, without mane

jалтаг : *n* 1) flatterer, stooge, toady, bootlicker, groveller *a* 2) servile, obsequious

jалтагланмаг : *v* flatter, fawn *on*, suck up *to*, lick the boots *of*, curry favor *with*, try to ingratiate oneself *with*, play up *to*, toady *to*

jалтаглыг : *n* flattery, servility, toadying, bootlicking, obsequiousness

jалтагчасына : *adv* 1)in a servile *or* fawning manner *a* 2) servile, fawning

jалхана-jалхана : *adv* in a waddling manner *walking*

jалханмаг : *v* waddle

jалхы : *adv* only, merely

jалчын : *a* steep, sheer, vertical

jам : *n* interest[s]

jамаг : *n* patch

jамаглы : *a* patched

jамагчы : *n* patcher

jамамаг : *v* repair, patch

jаман : *a* 1) bad, nasty, rotten 2) wicked, malicious, scathing, biting 3) passionate, ardent 4) mischievous, naughty, reckless, foolhardy 5) very strong 6) malignant *of a tumor*

jаман дeмәк : *v* curse, swear at, abuse, revile *s.o.*

jаман-jахшы : *adv* with difficulty, by the skin of one's teeth

jаманламаг : *v* criticize severely, swear *at*, defame, revile, say spiteful things

jаманлыг : *n* evil, harm, evil deed

jаманмаг : *v* be repaired, be fixed, be patched *up*

jаматдырмаг, jаматмаг : *caus* of **jамамаг**

jамач : *n* slope, mountain slope

jамjасты : *a* perfectly flat

jамjашыл : *a* perfectly green

jамсылама : *n* imitating, copying, aping, mimicking, mimicry, imitation

jамсыламаг : *v* imitate, make faces, copy *s. o.*, ape, mimic

jамсылатмаг : *caus* of **jамсыламаг**

jан : *n* 1) side *e.g. of the body* , flank *a* 2) side, lateral *n* 3) side *in a general sense adv* 4) aslant, tilted to one side *prep* 5) near, at, by

jан дишлә : *n* shaft *one of the two round shafts attached to the front axle of a carriage or cart, and to which a horse is harnessed*

jан көрүнүш : *n* profile

jанаг : *n* cheek

jанағыjекә : *a* fat-cheeked

jана-jана : **jана-jана галмаг** *v-cmp* feel bitterness/sorrow/grief*because of a wrong, misfortune, or failure*

jанакы : *adv* 1) sideways 2) aslant, tilted to one side

jанар : *a* 1) combustible, inflammable 2) burning

jанардағ : *n* volcano

jаначаг : *n* fuel

jанашдырмаг : *v -intr* 1) half-rise, *v-tr* 2) move nearer, move *up to*

jанашы : *adv* next to, side by side, adjacently

jанашыг : *a* adjacent, adjoining, contiguous

jанашыглыг : *n* contiguity

jанашылмаз : *a* unapproachable, inaccessible

jанашма : *n* 1) approach 2) mooring

jанашмаг : *v* 1) approach, come up to, draw near 2) sail up to, moor to the shore

jанбаjан : *adv* side by side

jанбыз : *n* upper thigh *in man and analogous region in animals*

jанвар : *n Ru* January

jанғы : *n* 1) thirst 2) burning

jанғын : *n* 1) fire, conflagration *a* 2) fire

jанғынсөндүрән : *n* 1) fireman *a* 2) fire

jандан : *adv* on/from one side, at the side

jандыран : *n* 1) arsonist *fig* 2) instigator

jандырыб-jахмаг : *v* 1) burn badly *fig* 2) cause *s. o.* moral pain *or* severe suffering; offend

jандырылмаг : *v* 1) be burned down, catch fire *intr* 2) burn

jандырычы : *a* caustic, pungent, burning

jандырычылыг : *n* causticity, corrosiveness

jандырма : *n* burning, lighting, igniting, burning out; heating

jандырмаг : *v* 1) burn *down/up,* set fire to, light, burn out, kindle, smoke, heat, melt *fig* 2) cause moral suffering

jандыртмаг : *caus* of **jандырмаг**

jаныб-jахылмаг : *v* feel *or* suffer strong moral pain *or* hurt, experience moral suffering

jаныг : *n* 1) cinder[s], snuff, or charred portion of a candlewick, burned/singed/scorched area *a* 2) burned, burnt, scorched

jаныглы : *a* 1) spiteful, embittered, resentful *a* 2) complaining, of complaint, mournful *adv* 3) in a complaining *or* mournful manner

jаныглы-jаныглы : *adv* mournfully, sorrowfully, bitterly

jаныгмаг : *v* regret bitterly, grieve

jанылма : *vn fr.* **jанылмаг**

jанылмаг : *v* be mistaken, make a mistake, be muddled, err

jанылтмаг : *v* bewilder, confuse

jанылтмач : *n* tongue twister

jанына : *adv* to someone *or* something

jанына дүшмәк : *v* join, accompany *s.o.*

jанында : *prep* 1) by, by the side of, close by, near, at *adv* 2) in someone's presence

jанындан : *adv* 1) from someone *or* something 2) past, by

jанынча : *adv* 1) with oneself 2) lengthwise 3) next to someone, side by side with someone

jан-jана : *adv* next to, side by side, near, close by, adjacent to

jан-jөрә : *prep* 1) round, around 2) *n* vicinity, the surrounding area, surroundings

jанламаг : *v* approach, draw near *to*, come up *to*

јанлыш : *n* 1) mistake, error, miss, slip *a* 2) incorrect, wrong, erroneous, mistaken

јанлышлыг : *n* incorrectness, wrongness

јанлышсыз : *a* 1) unerring, faultless *adv* 2) unerringly, faultlessly

јанлышсызлыг : *n* faultlessness, correctness

јанма : *vn fr.* **јанмаг**

јанмаг : *v* 1) burn, burn down/out, be inflamed/afire/aflame *with*, blaze up *with* 2) be overdone 3) become tanned/sunburnt, catch fire 4) burn out *or* fade *because of drought* 5) burn out/through fig 6) suffer, be distressed

јанмаз, јанмајан : *a* incombustible, fireproof

јанпөртү : *adv* 1) sideways 2) slantwise, aslant, obliquely

јансыз : *a* sideless, without side[s]

јанчаг : *n* 1) seat, seating *anat* 2) buttocks *a* 2) sciatic

јаншаг : *n* see **зәвзәк**

јапағы : *n* wool of the spring shearing

јапалаг : *n zool* eagle owl, large predatory Old World owl *Bubo bubo*

јапыг : *a* flat, flattened

јапыгмаг : *v* be flattened, become flat, become compressed/packed

јапыған : *a* plastic

јапылмаг : *v* be stuck together for baking *or* drying *of bread, pressed dung used for fuel*

јапынчы : *n* long cloak *or* mantle of felt

јапынчылы : *a* in a long cloak of felt, dressed in a long cloak of felt

јапынчылыг : *n* material suited *or* intended for a long cloak

јапышган : *n* 1) glue *a* 2) sticky, adhesive

јапышганламаг : *v* smear with glue

јапышганлы : *a* 1) sticky 2) glued together, pasted together

јапышганлыг : *n* stickiness, adhesiveness, viscosity, viscidity

јапышдыран : *n* gluer, one who glues

јапышдырылмаг : *v* be glued/pasted *on, to*

јапышдырма : *n* pasting *in/on,* a paste-in, label

јапышдырмаг : *v* 1) glue, paste, paste *or* glue to/on/in, stick *to/on* 2) solder *on*, braze *to*

јапышдыртмаг : *caus* of **јапышдырмаг**

јапышыг : *a* 1) glued to, stuck to, pasted to, attached to *a* 2) adjacent, adjoining, contiguous *n* 3) liking

јапышыглы : *a* likable, nice, pretty

јапышыгсыз : *a* unlikable, unpleasant

јапышмаг : *v-intr* 1) stick *to*, adhere *to*, be glued/pasted *to*, stick together 2) hold, catch hold *of*, grab, grasp, seize 3) begin, start, set *to s.t.*

јапма : *n* 1) modeling *a* 2) modeled *a* 3) false, dummy, mock

јапмаг : *v* model

јапон : *n* 1) Japanese *a* 2) Japanese

јапонча : *adv* in Japanese, in the Japanese language

јар : *n* 1) friend, comrade 2) sweetheart 3) beloved friend of either sex 4) help

јара : *n* wound, scratch, abrasion, injury, trauma, sore, ulcer

јараг : *n* weapon[s], arm[s]

јарагландырмаг : *v* arm, equip *with a weapon*

јарагланмаг : *v* arm oneself, equip oneself *with a weapon*

јараглы : *a* armed, equipped *with a weapon*

јарагсыз : *a* unarmed

јарадан : *n* creator, maker

јарадылыш : *n* 1) creation, creating 2) nature

јарадылмаг : *v* be created

јарадычы : *n* 1) creator *a* 2) creative

јарадычылыг : *n* 1) creative work *a* 2) creative

јаралама : *n* wounding, wound, injury

јараламаг, јараландырмаг : *v* 1) wound, injure, inflict a wound/injury *fig* 2) sting, shock

јараланабилән : *a* vulnerable

јараланмаг : *v* be wounded/injured

јараланмаз : *a* invulnerable

јаралы : *a* wounded, injured

јаралы-хоралы : *a* all covered with wounds/injuries/sores

јарамаг : *v* be fit *for*, be suitable, be useful, fit, suit, become

јарамаз : *a* 1) unsuitable, unfit, good-for-nothing, useless, worthless 2) bad, playful, mischievous

јарамазлыг : *n* 1) unfitness, unsuitability, uselessness 2) prank

јаран : *n bot* see **этиршаһ**

јаранмаг : *v* 1) be created, arise, be conceived, be born *fig* 2) please, play up to, curry favor *with* , try to ingratiate oneself *with* , oblige

јарарлы : *a* fit, suitable, worthwhile, reasonable

јарарлыг : *n* fitness, suitability, usefulness

јарарсыз : *a* unfit, unsuitable, useless, good-for-nothing

јарарсызлыг : *n* unfitness, unsuitability, uselessness

јараса : *n zool* bat *order Chiroptera*

јаратма : *n* creation, creating

јаратмаг : *v* create, engender

јаращдырылмаг : *v* be fitted *to,* be adapted *to/for*, be adorned, be beautified, be decorated, be ornamented

јаращдырмаг : *v* fit *to*, adjust *to*, adapt *to/for*, adorn, beautify, decorate, ornament

јарашыг : *n* beauty, decoration, adornment

јарашыға миндирмәк : *v* ornament, decorate

јарашыглы : *a* beautiful, elegant, comely

јарашыглылыг : *n* beauty, elegance, comeliness

јарашыгсыз : *a* ugly, plain, not beautiful, unsuitable, unfit

јарашыгсызлыг : *n* uncomeliness

јарашмаг : *v* become, befit, suit,

јарашмаз, јарашмајан : *a* unseemly, improper, unbecoming, unsuitable, indecent, obscene

јарған : *n* precipice, ravine, gully, narrow gorge, hollow, depression

јардарлыг : *n* metayage, a kind of land rental *in return for half the crop*

јардым : *n* help, assistance, backing, support, reinforcement

јардым көстәрмәк : *v* help; provide assistance

јардымсыз : *a* helpless

јардымсызлыг : *n* helplessness

јардымчы : *a* 1) helping; assisting 2) auxiliary, subsidiary

јардырмаг, јардыртмаг : *caus* of **јармаг**

јары : *n* half

јарыбајары : *adv* in two, half and half

јарыг : *n* slit, scar, cleft, crevice, fissure, cut, breach, gap

јарыг-јарыг : *a* ribbed

јары-јары : *adv* in half

јары-јарымчыг : *a* see **јарымчыг** 1), 2)

јарыламаг : *v* achieve half, reach half *of s.t.*

јарыланмаг : *v* become half as much, lose half

јарылатмаг : *caus* of **јарыламаг**

јарылыг : *n* metayage, a kind of land rental *in return for half the crop*

јарылма : *vn fr.* **јарылмаг**

јарылмаг : *v-intr* 1) be cut, split, crack 2) be broken through, break *of a front in wartime* 3) be dissected *of a corpse*

јарым : *n* half

јарымаг : *v* be satisfied, be contented, be well provided for

јарымағ : *a* half-white

јарымада : *n* peninsula

јарымастар : *n* hidden motive, underlying reason

јарымач : *a* half-starved

јарымведрә : *n* half a bucket *of some liquid*

јарымверстлик : *a* half-verst *measure of distance*

јарымвәһши : *a* half-wild

јарымгапалы : *a* half-closed

јарымгаранлыг : *n* 1) semidarkness *a* 2) scantily lit, poorly illuminated

јарымгарын : *adv* not quite full/satisfied *in reference to food*

јарымдағылмыш : *a* tumbledown, dilapidated, half-demolished, partially collapsed

јарымдаирә : *n* semicircle

јарымдөврә : *n* half-turn

јарымзарафат : *n* a story or anecdote told half jokingly, but with serious intent

јарымиллик : *a* 1) half-yearly, semiannual 2) *n* half-year

јарымипәк : *n* silk-mixture *silk combined with another fiber*

јарым-јамалаг : *adv* haphazardly, carelessly, in a slapdash manner, just barely

јарымјун : *a* half-wool

јарымјухулу : *a* half asleep, dozing

јарымкар : *a* half-deaf, hard of hearing

јарымкефли : *a* half-drunk

јарымкәтан : *a* half-linen

јарымкөлкә : *n* penumbra

јарымкөчәри : *a* seminomadic

јарымкүрә : *n* hemisphere

јарымкүрк : *n* sheepskin jacket, short sheepskin coat

јарымкејинмиш : *a* half-dressed, half-naked

јарымкирдә : *a* semicircular

јарымкүнлүк : *a* half-day

јарымламаг : *v* complete half a job, reach a halfway point

јарымлатдырмаг, јарымлатмаг : *caus* of **јарымламаг**

јарыммә'мулат : *n* semifinished product

јарыммүстәмләкә : *n* semicolonial territory

јарымох : *n* semiaxis

јарымөртүлү : *a* half-closed

јарымпалто : *n* short coat

јарымрәсми : *a* 1) semiofficial *adv* 2) semiofficially

јарымсаатлыг : *a* 1) half-hour *adv* 2) for a half hour

јарымсаваддлы : *a* semiliterate

јарымсәрхош : *a* half-drunk

јарымсәһра : *n* semidesert

јарымсојунмуш : *a* half-undressed, half-dressed

јарымсөкүлмүш : *a* tumbledown, dilapidated, half-demolished, partially collapsed; half-dismantled, half-ripped-open

јарымстансија : *n* flag station, way-station *of a railroad*, substation

јарымтон : *n* half tone

јарымһәрби : *a* semimilitary

јарымчеврә : *n* semicircle

јарымчыг : *a* 1) unfinished 2) incomplete, partial, halved, half-and-half *n* 3) premature infant, "preemie"

јарымчыглыг : *n* half-way policy, unfinished state, incomplete state, incompleteness

јарымчылыг : *n* see **јарымчыг** (2)

јарымчылпаг : *a* half-naked, seminude

јарымча : *n* half

јарымчан : *a* neither alive nor dead; half-alive, half-dead, fatal, mortal, deadly, more dead than alive

јарымчидди : *adv* half-seriously, half in jest

јарымшәффаф : *a* semitransparent, translucent

јарысы : *n* half

јарытма : *n* satisfaction

јарытмаг : *v* satisfy, please, oblige

јарытмаз : *a* 1) unsatisfactory 2) unskillful, incapable *adv* 3) unsatisfactorily

јарыш : *n* competition, contest, tournament

јарышмаг : *v* compete

јарышчы : *n* competitor, contender

јар-јолдаш : *n* comrades, friends, pals

јарма : 1) *vn* from **јармаг** *n* 2) groats, grits *a* 3) split, cleaved, chopped, cut *n med* 4) dissection; lancing *a boil*

јармаг : *v* 1) chop, cut, cleave, split, crack 2) break through, tear med 3) operate, lance *a boil*, dissect *a corpse*

јарпаг : *n* leaf

јарпагјејән : *n zool* leaf beetle *Donacia*

јарпагланмаг : *v* turn green, begin to leaf, be covered with leaves *of trees*

јарпаглы : *a* 1) covered with leaves 2) deciduous

јарпагсыз : *a* leafless, bare (of leaves)

јарпагшәкилли : *a* leaf-like, leaf-shaped, foliate[d]

јарпағытүклү : *a* with pilose leaves

јарпызчүчүсү : *n zool* glow-worm, firefly *family Lampyridae*

јарсыз-јолдашсыз : *a* friendless; single, solitary, lonely

јас : *n* mourning

јасавул : *n* 1) local constable 2) Cossack captain

јасәмән : *n* 1) lilac *Syringa vulgaris a* 2) lilac

јасәмәнлик : *n* place overgrown with lilacs

јасламаг : *v-tr* land, bring in/down to land

јасланмаг : *v-intr* land, touch down

јаслы : *a* 1) in mourning, observing mourning rites 2) mourning

јассар : *n* 1) irresponsible person, irresolute person, weak-willed person *a* 2) awkward, clumsy, slow, sluggish

јассарлыг : *n* awkwardness, clumsiness, sluggishness, clumsiness

јасты : *a* flat

јастыбалабан : *n* fife, pipe *musical instrument*

јастыбујнуз : *a* flat-horned

јастыбурун : *n* 1) person with a flat nose *a* 2) flat-nosed, broad-nosed

јастыг : *n* 1) pillow, cushion *tech* 2) bearing, bushing

јастыгламаг : *v* lull

јастыглы : *a* 1) with a pillow *or* cushion *tech* 2) bearing, bushing

јастыглыг : *a* suitable for use as a pillow *or* cushion

јастыгујруг : *a* flat-tailed

јастыгүзү : *n* pillow case

јастыдабан : *a* with low heels *shoes*

јастыдиб, јастыдибли : *a* flat-bottomed

јастыдимдик : *a* flat-beaked, flat-billed

јастыјапалаг : *a* stocky, squat, "built close to the ground"

јастылама : *n* flattening

јастыламаг : *v* make flat, flatten

јастыланмаг : *v* 1) become flat *intr* 2) flatten

јастылатдырмаг : *caus* of **јастыламаг**

јастылатмаг : *v* see **јастыламаг**

јастылыг : *n* flattened state

јастысына : *adv* flat, prone

јатаб : *n* halting place, stage *sending prisoners from one prison to another under escort*

јатаг : *n* 1) bed *geol* 2) bed, deposit *tech* 3) bearing, bushing 4) barn, shed 5) sheep pen 6) vagina

јатагхана : *n* dormitory, hostel

јатаған : *n* 1) sleepyhead *a* 2) sleepy, drowsy

јатағанлыг : *n* sleepiness, drowsiness

јаталаг : *n* typhus

јаталаглы : *a* typhoid, typhus

јатыг : *a* 1) concave, bent in, pressed in, flattened 2) inclined, sloping, slanted 3) precipitated, settled, deposited

јатыгбурун : *n* person with a flattened nose

јатыглыг : *n* concavity, hollowness, state of being pressed in, flattened state

јатыздырмаг : *v* see **јатыртмаг**

јатылы : *a* in a lying position, in a sleeping condition

јатым : *n* see **хов**

јатырылмаг : *v* be suppressed, be pacified

јатырычы : *a* drowsy, soporific

јатыртмаг : *v-tr* 1) lay down to sleep; lull to sleep 2) suppress; pacify, calm 3) try to persuade, try to win over 4) appease, soothe

јатыш : *n* habit of lying down to sleep in some specific position

јатышмаг : *v* sleep together *or* at the same time *of a large number of people*

јатма : *vn fr.* **јатмаг**

јатмаг : *v* 1) sleep 2) settle *of dust,* settle *to the bottom* intr 3) decline

јафәс : *n* 1) Japhet *the third and younger son of Noah a ling* 2) Japhetic

јафәсиләр : *n* speakers of Japhetic languages. *Japhetic refers to a now-discredited linguistic category devised by the Russian Marxist linguistic theoretician Nikolaj Yavovlevich Marr who believed that the Indo-European and Ural-Altaic language groups were a single unitary entity*

јаха : *n* collar

јахасы гуртармаг : *v* be freed

јахасыны таныма : *v* pester *so..* with constant requests; get into the habit of *s.t.*

јахагуртаран : *a* evasive, shifty

јахалама : 1) *vn fr.* **јахаламаг** 2) rinse, rinsing, gargling

јахаламаг : *v* 1) seize, grab, grasp, catch, detain, comprehend *v-intr* 2) stick, adhere, not get loose 3) rinse

јахаланмаг : *pass* 1) be seized, be grabbed, be grasped, be caught, be detained 2) gargle, be rinsed, be rinsed out

јахалы : *a* with collar

јахалыг : *a* for a collar; suitable for a collar

јаханты : *n* liquid left after rinsing

јахармаг : *v* pray for forgiveness

јахасыачыг : *adv* unbuttoned

јахдан : *n* box; box covered with leather

јахдырылмаг : *v* be oiled/greased/lubricated

јахдырмаг, јахдыртмаг : *caus* of **јахмаг**

јахы : *n* ointment, liniment, putty

јахылмаг : *pass* be oiled/greased/lubricated, be puttied

јахын : *a* 1) near, close, neighboring *adv* 2) nearly, roughly, approximately, about 3) welcome, well-received, received with pleasure

јахында : *adv* near at hand, close by, nearby, not far off

јахындакы : *a* neighboring, nearby

јахындан : *adv* 1) nearby, near at hand, close by, not far off, not far away 2) in the near/immediate future 3) not long ago, recently, lately, the other day

јахынында : *adv* 1) nearby, close by *prep* 2) by, near, by the side *of s.t.*

јахынкөрән : *a* nearsighted, myopic

јахынларда : *adv* 1) in the near/immediate future 2) not far off

јахынлашдырылмаг : *v* be drawn near[er], be drawn together, converge, be moved up *to*

јахынлашдырмаг : *v-tr* bring near[er], bring together, move up *to*

јахынлашма : *n* drawing near[er], approaching, drawing together, convergence, rapprochement

јахынлашмаг : *v-intr* draw near[er], draw together, converge, approach, move up *to*

јахынлыг : *n* 1) nearness, closeness, proximity, drawing together, convergence, rapprochement 2) close acquaintanceship, kinship, relationship

јахынлыгда : *adv* see **јахында**

јахма : *vn* from **јахмаг**

јахмаг : *v* smear *with* , spread *with*

јахмач : *n* sandwich

јахуд : *conj* or

јахшы : *a* 1) good, kind 2) *adv* well, all right, okay

јахшы олмаг : *v* recover from an illness, get well

јахшы-јахшы : *adv* see **јахшыча**

јахшыландырмаг, јахшылатмаг : *v* see **јахшылашдырмаг**

јахшылашдырма : *n* improvement

јахшылашдырмаг : *v-tr* improve

јахшылашмаг : *v-intr* improve, grow prettier, get better, recover

јахшылыг : *n* good, kindness, goodness, virtue, good deed

јахшыча : *adv* thoroughly, properly

јаш : *n* 1) age, years, year *a* 2) wet, moist, damp, humid

јаша : *intj* Bravo!, I wish you long life!, I wish you health!

јашајыш : *n* life, way/mode of life

јашама : *n* existence, life

јашамаг : *v* 1) live, exist 2) dwell, inhabit

јашармаг : *v-intr* become wet, fill with tears, shed a few tears

јашасын : *intj* Long live...!

јашатмаг : *v* 1) let *s.o.* live, safeguard *s.o.'s* life 2) immortalize, perpetuate

јашыд : *n* person of the same age

јашыл : *a* green

јашылаjаг : *n* *zool* ruff, an Old World sandpiper *Philomachus pugnax* . The male has an erectile frill of elongated feathers about the neck in the breeding season

јашылбаш : *n* *zool* drake

јашыл-боз : *a* gray-green

јашылымсов, јашылымтыл, јашылымтраг : *a* see **јашылтәһәр**

јашылкөз : *a* green-eyed

јашылландырылма, јашыллашдырылма : *n* planting of greenery, planting of trees and gardens

јашылландырылмаг,јашыллашдырылмаг : *v* be planted with greenery, be planted with trees and gardens

јашылландырмаг, јашыллашдырмаг : *v* make green, plant with trees and gardens

јашылланмаг : *v* see **јашыллашмаг**

јашыллашдырма : *n* planting of greenery, planting of trees and gardens

јашыллашдырмаг : *v* plant trees and gardens, cover with greenery

јашыллашмаг : *v* turn green, be covered with greenery

јашыллыг : *n* greenery, vegetation

јашыл-сары : *a* greenish-yellow

јашылтәһәр, јашылымсов : *a* greenish

јашындырмаг : *caus* of **јашынмаг**

јашынмаг : *v* cover the face *so that strange men do not see a woman's face*

јашламаг : *v* wet, make wet, make moist

јашландырмаг : *v-tr* moisten, make damp

јашланмаг : *v-intr* become moist/damp

јашлатдырмаг, јашлатмаг : *caus* of **јашламаг**

јашлы : *a* elderly, getting on, adult

јашлыг : *n* humidity, moisture, dampness, wetness

јашмаг : *n* yaşmak, face covering of women in the East

једди : *num* seven

једдиајлыг : *a* seven-month, of seven months

једдиаршынлыг : *a* seven-arshin, of seven arshins (arshin = 28 inches)

једдибашлы : *a* seven-headed

јнддибучаг : *n* heptagon

једдибучаглы : *a* heptagonal

једдивершоклуг : *a* seven-vershok, of seven vershoks (vershok = 1.75 inches)

једдигардаш : *n* *astron* Pleiades

једдигатлы : *a* 1) sevenfold, septuple, seven-ply 2) see **једдимәртәвә(ли)** *adv* 3) in seven layers

једдигүлләли : *a* seven-towered, having seven towers

једдидәгигәлик : *a* seven-minute, of seven minutes

једдидилли : *a* *mus* with seven keys *keyboard*

једдидүјмәлик : *a* seven-inch, of seven inches

једдијаш, једдијашар, једдијашлы : *a* 1) seven-year, of seven years *n* 2) age of seven

једдииллик : *n* 1) seven-year plan, seven-year school *a* 2) seven-year, of seven years

једди-једди : *adv* seven each, by/in sevens

једдикилограмлыг : *a* seven-kilogram, weighing seven kilograms

једдикилометрлик : *a* seven-kilometer, seven kilometer distance

једдикирвәнкәлик : *a* seven-pound, weighing seven pounds

једдикүнлүк : *n* 1) seven-day period 2) seven-day, of seven days

једдиләмәк : *v -tr* 1) increase sevenfold, *intr* 2) recur seven times, be repeated seven times

једдилик : *n* *num* seven, a group or set of seven, something designated by the number seven

једдиметрлик : *a* seven-meter, seven meters long/high/wide

једдимәртәбә(ли) : *a* seven-story, seven-stories-high *building*

једдинчи : *ord* seventh

једдипудлуг : *a* seven-pood, weighing seven poods *1 pood = 36 pounds*

једдирәгәмли : *a* *math* seven-digit, consisting of seven digits

једдисаатлыг : *n* 1) seven-hour period *a* 2) seven-hour, seven hour-long

једдисанијәлик : *a* seven-second, seven second-long

једдисимли : *a* *mus* seven-string, seven stringed *instrument*

једдисинифли : *a* seven-grade, seven-year, consisting of seven grades/years, pertaining to the seventh grade/year *ref to school*

једдичә : *adv* seven in all

једдичилдли : *a* seven-volume, consisting of seven volumes

једдичилдлик : *n* a work/collection/set of seven volumes

једәк : *n* 1) leading an animal by rein 2) towline, towrope

једәкләмә : *vn* 1) *from* **једәкләмәк** *n* 2) towing

једәкләмәк : *v* 1) lead by a rein 2) tow

једәкләнмәк : *pass* 1) be led by a rein 2) be towed

једәкчи : *a* leading on a rein, taking in tow

једиздирмәк, једиртдирмәк : *v* see **једир(т)мәк**

једир(т)мә : *vn* from **једир(т)мәк**

једир(т)мәк : *v* 1) feed 2) rub in ointment, liniment or liquid

језнә : *n* brother-in-law *sister's husband*

јејәчәк : *n* food, provisions, foodstuffs, food products

јејиб-ичмәк : *v* 1) eat, dine well 2) enjoy one's life

јејилмә : *n* 1) eating up/away 2) damaging by grazing (or) trampling 3) erosion

јејилмәк : *v* 1) be eaten *up/away* 2) be worn away by grazing or trampling 3) be rubbed away, be worn through

јејин, јејин-јејин : 1) *adv* quickly, fast, at an accelerated rate, swiftly, hastily a 2) quick, rapid

јејинләмәк : *v* go faster, accelerate one's pace

јејинләтмәк, јејинләшдирмәк : *v-tr* accelerate, speed up

јејинлик : *n* quickness, rapidity, speed, velocity

јејинти : *n* 1) food, provisions, foodstuffs, food products 2) leftovers, leavings

јејитмә : *n* *med* gangrene

јејичи : *n* 1) mouth to feed 2) glutton *a* 3) gluttonous, voracious, insatiable

јејичилик : *n* gluttony, voraciousness, insatiability

јекаһәнк : *a* monotonous

јекдил : *a* 1) friendly, amicable, harmonious, unanimous *adv* 2) amicably, together, unanimously

јекдиллик : *n* unanimity, solidarity

јекдилликлә : *adv* unanimously

јекә : *a* large, big, enormous, huge

јекәағыз : *a* wide mouthed

јекәбаш : a 1) large-headed, having a large head *n* 2) person with a large head *a* *fig* 3) emptyheaded, thick-skulled, dull-witted *n* 4) blockhead, bungler, lout, loafer

јекәбашлыг : *n* bungling

јекәбығ : *a* 1) big moustached *n* 2) man with a big moustache

јекәбоғаз : *a* see **јекәгарын** 2)

јекәбујнуз : *a* large-horned, with large horn[s]

јекәбурун : *n* 1) person with a big nose *a* 2) big-nosed

јекәганад : *a* winged

јекәгарын : *a* 1) big-bellied, pot-bellied 2) gluttonous, voracious *n* 3) glutton

јекәгујруг : *a* having a tail, tailed, caudate

јекәгулаг : *a* lop-eared, big-eared

јекәдиш : *a* large-toothed

јекәдырнаг : *a* large-hoofed

јекәдодаг : *a* 1) thick-lipped *n* 2) mumbler

јекәдөш : *a* big-bosomed, broad-chested

јекәјанаг : *a* fat-cheeked

јекәләнмәк : *v* 1) see **јекәлмәк** 2) put on airs

јекәлик : *n* size, large stature

јекәлмәк : *v* grow, grow up, become large

јекәпәр : *a* stocky, robust, big, stout, tall, stalwart

јекәсаггал : *n* 1) bearded man *a* 2) bearded

јекәхана : *a* 1) swaggering, conceited, haughty, arrogant 2) *n* braggart, boaster

јекәханаланмаг : *v* swagger, put on airs

јекәханалыг : *n* swagger, conceit; arrogance, snobbishness

јекнәсәг : *a* 1) uniform, alike, monotonous *adv* 2) uniformly, monotonously

јекнәсәглик : *n* uniformity, monotony

јекпарә : *a* whole, of one piece, monolithic

јекрәнк : *a* 1) of one color, monochromatic 2) alike, monotonous

јекрәнклик : *n* 1) monochromatic state/condition 2) similarity, uniformity

јекун : *n* sum, total, result

јекунлашдырылмаг : *v* 1) be added up *intr* 2) add up *to*

јекунлашдырмаг : *v-tr* add up, sum up, total up

јекшәнбә : Sunday

јеканә : *a* 1) sole, only 2) *adv* solely

јел : *n* 1) wind *med* 2) rheumatism

јелбејин : *a* 1) frivolous, empty-headed 2) *n* frivolous person, empty-headed person

јелбејинлик : *n* frivolity, empty-headedness

јелбејинчәсинә : *adv* flippantly, frivolously

јелгован : *n* weather vane

јелдәјирманы : *n* windmill

јелән : *n* wide border *carpet or rug*

јелин : *n* udder

јелкә : *n* forelock *of a horse*

јелкән : *n* sail

јелкәнли : *a* sail, sailing

јелкәнсиз : *a* without sail[s]

јелкәнтикән, јелкәнчи : *n* sailmaker

јелләмәк : *v-tr* 1) winnow, fan, disperse 2) shake, wave, flap

јелләндирмәк : *v-tr* shake, rock, swing

јелләнмәк : *v-intr* 1) flutter, fly, be blown out, be fanned 2) shake, rock, swing

јелләнчәк : *n* swing *suspended seat for swinging*

јелләтмә : *vn fr.* **јелләтмәк**

јелләтмәк : *v-tr* 1) blow *s.t.* about 2) rock, shake, swing

јелли : *a* 1) windy 2) passionate, fiery *adv* 3) quickly, rapidly

јелпәнәк : *n* see **хијар**

јелпик : *n* fan

јелпиквары : *a* see **јелпикшәкилли**

јелпикләмәк : *v* fan

јелпикләтдирмәк, јелпикләтмәк : *caus* of **јелпикләмәк**

јелпикшәкилли : *a* fan-shaped

јелчәкән : *n* draft, current of air

јем : *n* 1) feed, forage, fodder *a* 2) pertaining to feed, forage or fodder

јем-алаф : *a* grain fodder, forage

јембасдыран : *n agric* silo packer

јембасдырма : *n agric* ensiling

јемә : *vn* from **јемәк**

јемәк : *v* 1) eat 2) etch, eat away, carry away, wash away 3) appropriate *n* 4) eating; nourishment, food, dish

јемәкпајлајан : *n* waiter

јемәкхана : *n* dining hall, dining room

јемәли : *a* 1) edible *n* 2) something edible, something tasty or delicious

јемиш : *n* 1) melon 2) fruits

јемишан : *n bot* hawthorn

јемләјичи : *a* fattening

јемләмә : *n* feeding

јемләмәк : *v* feed, give fodder *to*

јемләнмәк : *v* be fed, obtain fodder *animals*

jемлик : *a* fodder

jемсиз : *a* without fodder

jемһазырлаjан : *n* procurement agent for fodder

jенә : *adv* again, once more

jени : *a* new, fresh

jенидән : *adv* anew, afresh, again, all over again, from the start

jенидәнгурма : *n* *polit* perestroika

jенијетмә : *n* adolescent, teenager

jенијетмә : *n* juvenile, teenager, youth

jениләмә : *n* renewal, revival

jениләмәк, jениләндирмәк : *v* renew, renovate

jениләнмә : *n* renewal, renovation

jениләнмәк : *v* see **jениләшмәк**

jениләщдиричи : *n* restorer

jениләщдирмәк : see **jениләмәк**

jениләшмәк : *v* be renewed, be renovated, be restored

jенилик : *n* news; novelty, innovation

jениликчи : *n* innovator

jениликчилик : *n* innovating, innovation

jенилмәз : *a* indestructible, invincible, insurmountable, rebellious, unshakable, unbending

jенилмәзлик : *n* indestructibility, invincibility

jенитөрәмә : *n* new formation

jеничә : *adv* just now, recently

jенкә : *n* woman who accompanies the bride to the bridegroom's home

jенкәч : *n* *zool* crab

jер : *n* 1) earth, ground, soil 2) place 3) bed 4) kitty, stake, bet *gambling* 5) packing, tare

jер сүрмәк : *v* plow, turn up the soil

jеринә jетирмәк : *v* 1) deliver 2) fulfil, accomplish

jерини тутмаг : *v* replace

jералмасы : *n* *bot* 1) Jerusalem artichoke *Helianthus tuberosus* 2) potatoes

jералты : *a* 1) underground, subterranean, subsoil *n* 2) cave

jербәjер : *adv* thoroughly, in detail

jергазан : *n* 1) excavator 2) dredge

jердәjишщдирмә, jердәjишмә : *n* 1) transfer, movement, rearrangement 2) transplanting 3) castling *chess*

jерәбахан : *n* 1) meek person, timid person *a* 2) reserved, reticent, secretive, sly

jеридилмәк : *v* be advanced *idea or work*

jерик : *n* pregnant woman's whim *craving for pickles etc. during pregnancy*

jерикләмәк : *v* enter/begin the period of pregnancy when a woman gets a craving for pickles etc.

jеримә : *n* walking

jеримәк : *v* walk, step

jериндә : *adv* 1) on the spot, in place 2) appropriately, deservedly

jеринә : *prep* for, instead of, in place of

jеритдирмәк : *caus* of **jеримәк**

jеритмә : *vn* from **jеритмәк**

jеритмәк : *v* 1) compel to walk, put in motion 2) move or push (up or forward) 3) advance *idea or work*

jериш : *n* motion, walking, walk, gait, step, tread, procession, marching

jеркөкү : *n* 1) carrot[s] *a* 2) carrot

jерләщдирилмәк : *pass* 1) be placed, be accommodated 2) be settled, be put up in some place

jерләщдирмә : *n* 1) placing, placement, accommodation, lodging, settling 2) laying, packing up, stowing

jерләщдирмәк : *v* 1) place, put, accommodate, put into, lay, pack up, stow 2) settle, put up *somewhere*

jерләщдиртмәк : *caus* of **jерләщдирмәк**

jерләшмә : *vn* from **jерләшмәк**

jерләшмәк : *v* 1) be put/placed/accommodated, be put in, *v-intr* 2) go/fit in, be packed up, be stowed *v-ntr* 2) settle be settled, settle down, get settled *somewhere,* make oneself comfortable

jерли : *a* 1) local, native, indigenous *of people* 2) appropriate *adv* 3) appropriately

jерли-дибли : *adv* 1) entirely, totally; without leaving a trace 2) flatly, pointblank

jерли-jатаглы, jерли-jериндә : *adv* in detail, with all details, minutely, in a proper fashion

jерлик : *n* background

jерлиләщдирмә : *n* localization *organizing local institutions so that work is performed by representatives of the local native population*

jерлиләщдирмәк : *v* localize *organize local institutions so that work is performed by representatives of the local population*

jерлилик : *n* localistic tendencies

jерөлчән : *n* surveyor

јерпулу : *n* pay for an overnight stay

јерсиз : *a* 1) inappropriate 2) lacking a place of one's own, lacking a roof over one's head, homeless 3) landless *adv* 4) inappropriately, out of place

јерсиз-јурдсуз : *a* lacking a roof over one's head, homeless

јерсизлик : *n* 1) lack of land 2) irrelevance

јерсичаны : *n* zool shrew *fam Soricidae*

јерүстү : *a* ground, above-ground

јерфындығы : *n* *bot* peanut

јес-јекә : *a* tremendous, huge, tall, stalwart, grown-up, adult

јетәр : *a* 1) sufficient, enough *adv* 2) fully, rather, quite, sufficiently, enough *pred* 3) That's enough

јетик : *a* inquisitive, curious

јетиклик : *n* inquisitiveness, intellectual curiosity

јетим : *n* orphan

јетим-јесир : *n* orphan

јетимлик : *n* orphanhood

јетимхана : *n* orphanage, children's home

јетимчә : *n* *dim* orphan

јетимчәсинә : *adv* like an orphan, orphan-like

јетирмә : *vn* *fr.* **јетирмәк**

јетирмәк : *v* 1) catch up *with* , overtake 2) have time, be in time

јетишдирмә : *n* 1) rearing, raising, bringing up, breeding, cultivating, cultivation 2) pupil

јетишдирмәк : *v* breed, raise, rear, bring up, grow, cultivate

јетишкән : *a* mature *of a person*

јетишкәнлик : *n* maturity

јетишмәк : *v* 1) mature, ripen 2) reach, overtake, arrive in time 3) grow up 4) suffice 5) be sufficient, be enough

јетишмәмиш : *a* unripe, immature

јетишмиш : *a* mature, ripe

јеткин : *a* mature, full-fledged

јеткинләшмә : *n* forming, formation, ripening, maturing

јеткинләшмәк : *v* be formed, intr form, ripen, mature

јеткинлик : *n* ripeness, maturity

јетмәк : *v* 1) be sufficient, be enough 2) suffice 3) reach

јетмиш : *num* seventy

јетмишиллик : *n* 1) seventieth anniversary, seventieth birthday 2) seventy-year, of seventy years

јетмишинчи : *a* seventieth

јетмишјашлы : *a* seventy-year, of seventy years

јеһаје : *n* 1) continuous eating 2) misappropriation and disposal for personal gain of public property 3) bribery, bribe-taking

јешик : *n* box

јешикдашыјан : *n* carrier of boxes

јәгин : *adv* certainly, for sure, probably

јәгин еләмәк : *v* make sure, make certain of

јәгинләшмәк : *v* become reliable, become indubitable, become unquestionable

јәгинлик : *n* authenticity

јәмән : *n* 1) Yemen *a* 2) Yemenite

јәмчи : *n* see **чарвадар**

јә'ни : *adv* so, that is, consequently

јәһәр : *n* saddle

јәһәралты : *n* 1) bellyband/girth 2) saddlecloth *a* 3) pertaining to a bellyband/girth 4) pertaining to a saddlecloth

јәһәрбурун : *n* saddle-nosed person

јәһәргајыран : *n* see **сәррач**

јәһәр-әсбаб : *n* harness with breech-band *but without collar*

јәһәрләмәк : *v* saddle

јәһәрләнмәк : *pass* be saddled

јәһәрләтдирмәк, јәһәрләтмәк : *caus* of **јәһәрләмәк**

јәһәрли : *a* saddled

јәһуди : *n* 1) Jew *a* 2) Jewish

јәһудиләшмәк : *v* become familiar with Jews and Jewish ways

јәһудилик : *n* Judaism

јәһудипәрвәр, јәһудипәрәст : *n* Judaeophile

јәһудичә : *adv* in Hebrew

јәшәм : *n* *min* jasper *an opaque, usually red, brown, or yellow variety of quartzquartz*

јәшим : *n* *min* nephrite *a very hard, compact, white to dark green mineral formerly worn as a remedy for diseases of the kidney*

јив : *n* thread, threading

јивачан : *n* *tech* tap *tool for cutting a screw thread*

јивли : *a* threaded

јијә : *n* owner, proprietor

јиједәнмәк : *v* take possession *of*, appropriate

јијәли : *a* having an owner or proprietor, owned

јијәлик : *n* ownership, proprietorship, possession

јијәликләнмәк : *v* see **јијәләнмәк**

јијәсиз : *a* not having an owner, neglected, homeless, ownerless; nobody's

јығдырмаг, јығдыртмаг : *caus* of **јығмаг**

јығылыш : *n* set, collection, assembly

јығылышмаг : *v* see **јығышмаг**

јығылма : *n* 1) accumulating, piling up, accumulation, gathering 2) contraction, shrinkage

јығылмаг : *v-intr* 1) gather, collect, pile up 2) contract 3) shrink

јығым : *n* accumulation

јығыначаг : *n* see **јығнаг**

јығын : *n* 1) pile, heap 2) harvest 3) crowd, throng, gathering 4) mass, great number/amount *of*

јығын-јығын : *adv* in heaps, in piles, in a mass

јығынты : *n* 1) *s. t.* collected from leavings, waste or discards 2) alluvium

јығынчаг : *n* 1) meeting, assembly 2) gathering

јығычы : *n* collector, gatherer, collector *device*

јығышдырылмаг : *pass* be collected, be gathered in

јығышдырычы : *n* picker, packer

јығышдырмаг : *v* collect, gather, gather in, tidy up, put in order, stow, stack

јығышдыртмаг : *caus* of **јығышдырмаг**

јығышма : 1) *vn fr.* **јығышмаг** *n* 2) shrinkage *of cloth*

јығышмаг : *v-intr* 1) gather, collect, come together, accumulate, pile up 2) be packed up, be stowed, intr pack up 3) prepare or get ready for a journey

јығма : *n* 1) collection, collecting, accumulating, accumulation 2) recruiting, recruitment 3) clubbing, pooling *a* 4) picked, selected

јығмаг : *v* 1) collect, gather, accumulate 2) recruit

јығнаг : *n* assemblage, mob, gathering, crowd

јығчам : *a* 1) compressed, abbreviated, laconic, compact; portable *adv* 2) in a condensed/compressed form, in an abbreviated form, concisely, briefly

јығчамлыг : *n* 1) compactness, portability 2) brevity, conciseness

јыпранмаг : *v-intr* wear out

јырғалама : *n* rocking, swinging, swaying

јырғаламаг, јырғаландырмаг : *v-tr* rock, swing

јырғаланмаг : *v-intr* rock, sway, swing

јырғанмаг : *v* see **јырғаланмаг**

јыр-јығыш : *n* tidying up

јыртыг : *a* 1) torn, worn, ragged, torn to shreds, worn through *n* 2) hole, tear, slit *med* 3) hernia

јыртыг-дешик : *n* holes

јыртыг-јамаг : *n* mending *shoes, clothes*

јыртыг-јыртыг : *adv* covered with holes, in rags

јыртыглыг : *n* shabbiness, threadbare state

јыртылма : *n* wear, wear and tear, deterioration

јыртылмаг : *v-intr* tear, wear out, wear through

јыртычы : *n* 1) predator, beast/bird of prey *a* 2) predatory 3) bloodthirsty

јыртычылашмаг : *v* become brutalized

јыртычылыг : *n* brutality, beastiality, predatoriness, rapaciousness, bloodthirstiness

јыртычычасына : *adv* 1) brutally, beastially, predatorily, rapaciously 2) fiercely, ferociously

јыртмаг : *v-tr* 1) wear out 2) tear, tear up

јыхдырмаг, јыхдыртмаг : *caus* of **јыхмаг**

јыхыг : *a* collapsed, caved in, ruined, demolished, destroyed, tumbled down

јыхылмаг : *v* 1) fall, fall down, tumble down, be knocked down 2) collapse

јыхылмаз : *a* indestructible

јыхычы : *a* destructive, shattering, crushing

јыхма : *n* 1) demolition, destruction, knocking down 2) overthrow

јыхмаг : *v* 1) bring down, overcome, subdue, knock down/over 2) demolish, destroy, ruin 3) overthrow

јовуг : *a* 1) near, close adv 2) near, close by

јовуглашмаг : *v-intr* draw near[er], come together

јовуглуг : *n* nearness, closeness, proximity

јовушдурмаг : *v* bring nearer to oneself

јовушмаг : *v* get used *to s.t.,* accustom oneself *to s.t.*

јовшан : *n bot* wormwood *Artemisia* bitter, aromatic herb of the composite family

јовшанлыг : *n* place overgrown with wormwood

јоғун : *a* 1) stout, thick 2) full 3) coarse, rough 4) slow-witted, dull; muddle-headed, stupid

јоғунбалдыр : *a* thick-calved, piano-legged person

јоғундимдик : *a* thick-billed, thick-beaked

јоғундодаг : *a* thick-lipped

јоғунланмаг : *v* 1) put on weight, grow stout/fat

јоғунлатдырмаг : *caus* of **јоғунлатмаг**

јоғунлатмаг : *v* 1) make thick, thicken (tr), make thicker 2) speak or sing in a deep voice

јоғунлашмаг : *v* see **јоғунланмаг**

јоғунлуг : *n* 1) thickness, stoutness, corpulence, plumpness 2) roughness, coarseness, crudity

јоғурд : *n* see **гатыг**

јоғурмаг : *v* knead (dough)

јоғуртдурмаг : *caus* of **јоғурмаг**

јоғуртмаг : *v* ask or compel to knead

јоғурулмаг : *v* be kneaded

јод : *n* 1) iodine *a* 2) iodine, *higher or -ic* iodide

јодламаг : *v* paint with iodine, apply iodine *to*

јодлу : *a lower or -ous* iodide

јоздурмаг, јоздуртмаг : *caus* of **јозмаг**

јозма : *n* interpreting, interpretation, explaining

јозмаг : *v* interpret, explain in one's own way

јол : *n* 1) road, way 2) entry, entrance, exit 3) way, means, manner, method 4) time 5) orientation, direction, conviction, persuasion

јол адамы : *n* traveller

јол ајрычы : *n* crossroad, intersection

јол апармаг : *v* get along *with s.o*

јола дүшмәк : *v* start, set out *of travel, a trip, journey, tour*

јола кәтирмәк : *v* persuade, induce to, talk into

јола салмаг : *v* see off, send off

јолдан чыхартмаг : *v* set on, instigate

јолајахын : *a* compliant, tractable, complaisant

јолајахынлыг : *n* compliancy, tractability, complaisance

јолајыран : *n* switchman *railroad*

јолајырычы : *n* crossroads, crossing

јолајовмаз : v see **јолакәлмәз**

јолакедән : *a* sociable, easy to get along with

јолакедәнлик : *n* sociability, easy disposition

јолакетмәз : *a* unsociable, hard to get along with

јолакетмә(мә)злик : *n* unsociability, orneriness, quarrelsome disposition

јолакәлән : *a* compliant, tractable, complaisant

јолакәлмәз : *a* intractable, inflexible, indomitable

јолбасан : *n* roller for tamping a road or highway

јолбилән : *n* experienced person, one who knows all the ins and outs, one who knows his way around

јолверилмәз : *a* inadmissible, impermissible, intolerable

јолданчыхаран : *n* seducer

јолданчыхарычы : *a* seductive, seducing

јолдаш : *n* 1) comrade *n* 2) fellow traveler, associate, accomplice, confederate *a* 3) comradely, friendly *n fig* 4) husband or wife

јолдашлашмаг : *v* become a comrade *of* make friends *with*

јолдашлыг : *n* comradeship, friendly relationship, complicity

јолдашчасына : *adv* in a comradely manner

јолдәјишән : *n* switchman *railroad*

јолдөшәјән : *n* road worker

јолдурмаг, јолдуртмаг : *caus* of **јолмаг**

јол-јол : *a* striped

јолкәсән : *n* brigand, robber, burglar

јолкәсәнлик : *n* robbery, brigandage, burglary

јолкөстәрән : *n* guide

јолкөстәричи : *n* see **јолкөстәрән**

јоллама : *n* sending

јолламаг : *v* send

јолланмаг : *v* 1) be sent 2) set out *for,* head *for,* make one's way *to/toward*

јоллатдырмаг, јоллатмаг : *caus* of **јолламаг**

јоллашмаг : *v* come to an agreement or understanding, come to terms, agree on a price

јоллуг : *a* on/along a route/way/road

јолмаг : *v* pull out, tear out, pluck

јолсуз : *a* 1) without a road, not having a road *fig* 2) without convictions/beliefs, dissipated, dissolute, licentious, unbelieving

јолсузлуг : *n* lack of roads, *season of* impassable roads

јолуг : *a* plucked

јолуг-молуг : *n* ragamuffin, ragged fellow, tramp, vagabond, hobo

јолунда : *prep* for, for the sake of, to please

јолунмаг : *pass* be plucked

јолухдурмаг : *v* infect

јолухдуручу : *n* 1) infector *a carrier of pathogenic organisms* *a* 2) infectious, contagious

јолухма : *n* 1) contagion, infection *a* 2) contagious, infectious 3) visiting, calling on, coming to see *s.o.*

јолухмаг : *v* 1) call on, visit, come to see *pass* 2) be transmitted, be passed on (about an infection)

јолухучу : *a* contagious, infectious

јолүстү : *adv* on the road, en route, in passing, on the way

јолхәрчи : *n* traveling expenses

јолчу : *n* 1) traveler, passenger 2) beggar

јолчулуг : *n* begging, beggary, penury

јонгар : *n* shavings, chips, filings, sawdust

јондурмаг, јондуртмаг : *caus* of **јонмаг**

јонма : *n* hewing, cutting, planing, shaving

јонмаг : *v* 1) hew, cut, plane, shave, sharpen 2) facet

јонталамаг : *v* hew, cut, plane, shave *in a hurry/slapdash manner*

јонулмаг : *pass* be planed, be shaved, be hewed, be cut

јонурча : *n* *bot* smut disease of cereal grains caused by a fungus, one of the *Ustiliginales*

јонучу : *n* planer

јонча : *n* *bot* 1) clover *Trifolium* , *perennial fodder grass* *a* 2) clover

јончалыг : *n* place overgrown or sown with clover

јорға : *n* amble, pace *horse's gait in which the two feet on one side are lifted alternately with the two on the other side*

јорғаламаг : *v* walk quickly

јорғалатмаг : *caus* of **јорғаламаг**

јорған : *n* quilt

јорғанағы : *n* quilt cover/slip

јорған-дөшәк : *n* 1) bed *a* 2) bed

јорғанлыг : *a* suitable/intended for a quilt

јорғансырыјан, јорғантикән : *n* quilter

јорғанүзү : *n* outside/right side of a quilt

јорғанча : *n* small quilt

јорғун : *a* tired, weary, fatigued

јорғун-јорғун : *adv* in a tired/fatigued manner, wearily

јорғунлуг : *n* tiredness, weariness, fatigue

јорма : *vn fr.* **јормаг**

јормаг : *v-tr* 1) tire, wear out, fatigue, overtire, exhaust, drive to exhaustion 2) pester, bother, bore *with*

јорнуг : *v* see **јорғун**

јортаған : *n* trotter

јорта-јорта : *adv* at a trot

јортдурмаг : *caus* of **јортмаг**

јортма : *n* trot, trotting race

јортмаг : *v* trot

јорулма : *n* exhaustion

јорулмаг : *v-intr* tire, get tired/fatigued, become exhausted

јорулмагсызын, јорулмадан : *adv* 1) tirelessly, untiringly, indefatigably 2) restlessly

јорулмаз : *a* 1) tireless, indefatigable 2) restless, fidgety

јорулма(ма)злыг : *n* 1) indefatigability 2) restlessness

јоручу : *a* tedious, exhausting, tiresome, annoying

јосун : *n* *bot* alga, seaweed

јосунлуг : *n* place covered with algae

јох : *adv* 1) no, not *a* 2) nonexistent, absent

јох еләмәк : *v* destroy, annihilate

јоха чыхмаг : *v* get lost, disappear

јохлајычы : *a* 1) verifying, checking *n* 2) tester 3) inspector

јохлама : *n* 1) check, test, trial; examination *a* 2) verifying, checking; test, trial *n* 3) inspection

јохламаг : *v* 1) check, verify, examine 2) inspect 3) subject to testing/trials 4) touch, feel *with the fingers*

јохланыш : see **јохлама**

јохланмаг : *v* 1) be checked, be verified 2) undergo tests/trials

јохлатдырмаг, јохлатмаг : *caus* of **јохламаг**

јохлуг : *n* 1) nonexistence, absence 2) emptiness

јохса : *conj* or, otherwise, or else

јохсул : *a* 1) indigent, of modest means, needy, poor 2) scanty, meager *n* 3) poor man

јохсуллашмаг : *v* become/grow poorer

јохсуллуг : *n* poverty, need

јохуш : *n* 1) rise, slope 2) height

јохушлу : *a* having a slope/rise

јохушлуг : *n* 1) road with a rise/slope 2) height, high place

јөн : *n* front side, face 2) direction

јөндәм : *n* 1) appearance, look[s] 2) comfort, convenience, opportunity

јөндәмсиз : *a* 1) ugly, ungainly, formless, shapeless, of unpleasant appearance 2) awkward, lumbering, clumsy 3) uncomfortable *n* 4) ugly mug, repulsive face

јөндәмсизлик : *n* 1) clumsiness, awkwardness 2) inconvenience, discomfort

јөнәлдилмәк : *v* head *for*, make one's way *to/toward/into*, direct one's steps *to, toward, into*

јөнәлдичи : *a* guiding, guide

јөнәлмә : *vn fr.* **јөнәлмәк**

јөнәлмәк : *v* 1) head *for*, make one's way *o/toward/into* direct one's steps *totoward/into*, turn in the direction *of* 2) appeal *to*, address

јөнәлтмә : *n* turning, laying, training

јөнәлтмәк : *v* direct, turn, lay, aim

јөнлү : *a* fit, valid, good, useful

јөнлүк : **јөнлүк һал** *gram* dative case

јөнсүз : *a* unfit, useless, unserviceable

јөнсүзлүк : *n* unfitness, uselessness, unserviceability

јубадылмаг : *v* be delayed, be detained, be slowed

јубадылмаз : *a* pressing, urgent, immediate

јубандырылмаг : *v* see **јубадылмаг**

јубандырмаг : see **јубатмаг**

јубанма : *n* delay, dragging out, slowing down, lateness

јубанмаг : *v* be delayed, loiter, linger, be late, be overdue

јубанмадан : *adv* immediately, without delay, urgently

јубатма : *n* delay, procrastination

јубатмаг : *v-intr* 1) linger, be slow *v-tr* 2) delay, detain

јубилеј : *n* 1) anniversary, jubilee *a* 2) anniversary, jubilee

јубилјар : *n* person or institution whose anniversary/jubilee is being celebrated

јубка : *n Ru* skirt

јува : *n* 1) nest 2) burrow, hole, lair, den

јуваг : *n anat* alveolus *air cell of the lungs*

јуваглыг : *n* alveoli *sockets in which the teeth are set*

јуварлаг : *a* round, rounded

јуварлагландырма : *n* rounding off

јуварлагландырмаг, јуварлаглашдырмаг : *v-tr* 1) roll 2) round off

јуварланмаг : *v-intr* 1) roll 2) be rounded off

јуварлатмаг : *v* see **јуварлагландырмаг**

јувасыз : *a* nestless, without a nest

јудуртмаг : *caus* of **јумаг**

јујулма : *n* 1) washing *geol* 2) erosion *wearing away of earth's surface*

јујулмаг : *pass* 1)be washed *intr 2)* wash *of clothes*

јујундурмаг : *v* bathe, give a bath

јујунма : *n* bathing, washing

јујунмаг : *v-intr* 1) wash , wash oneself, bathe, take a bath

јукакир : *n* Yukaghir *a virtually extinct Paleo-Asiatic tribe of Eastern Siberia*

јулаф : *n* 1) oats; oat flour *a* 2) pertaining to oat flour or oats

јулғун : *n bot* tamarisk

јума : *n* washing, laundering, wash

јумаг : *v* 1) wash, launder *n* 2) ball, lump, skein, hank

јумагламаг : *v-tr* wind into a ball

јумагланмаг : *v-intr* wind into a ball, be wound into a ball

јумаламаг : *v-tr* roll, roll up

јумаланмаг : *v* somersault, turn a somersault, roll topsyturvy

јумалатмаг : *v-tr* roll up, roll

јумарламаг, јумбаламаг : *v* see **јумаламаг**

јумбаланмаг : *v* see **јумаланмаг**

јумбалатмаг : *v* see **јумалатмаг**

јумдурмаг, јумдуртмаг : *caus* of **јуммаг**

јумма : *n* closing

јуммаг : *v-tr* close

јумру : *a* 1) round, spherical, ball-shaped *n bot* 2) tuber

јумруг : *n* 1) fist 2) blow with the fist, punch

јумругламаг : *v* hit with the fists, punch

јумруглашма : *n* fist fight, fisticuffs

јумруглашмаг : *v* hit one another with the fists, box

јумруламаг, јумруландырмаг : *v* make round, round off

јумруланмаг : *v* be made round, be rounded off

јумрулатмаг : *v* see **јумруламаг**

јумрулашмаг : *v* see **јумруланмаг**

јумрулуг : *n* round form or shape, roundness

јумрусифәт : *a* round-faced

јумруча : *a* slightly round, rotund

јумулмаг : *v-intr* close, be closed

јумулу : *a* closed

јумурта : *n* 1) egg *a* 2) egg

јумуртавары, јумуртајаохшар : *v* see **јумурташәкилли**

јумурталыг : *n anat;* 1) ovary *bot* 2) germ, ovary

јумуртачыг : *n* 1) little egg *anat* 2) testicle

јумурташәкилли : *a* egg-shaped, oviform, ovoid, oval

јумуртламаг : *v* lay eggs

јумуртлатмаг : *caus* of **јумуртламаг**

јумшаг : *a* 1) soft 2) gentle, mild *adv* 3) softly, gently

јумшагбәдәнли : *a* flabby, soft-bodied

јумшагдәрили : *a* soft-skinned,

јумшагјарпаглы : *a* soft-leaved

јумшагјунлу : *a* soft-haired, soft-furred

јумшагләләкли : *a* soft-feathered

јумшаглыг : *n* 1) softness 2) gentleness, mildness, gentle/mild disposition

јумшаглыгла : *adv* softly, gently

јумшагхасијјәт, јумшагхасијјәтли : *a* complaisant, obliging, of mild/gentle disposition

јумшагхасијјәтлилик : *a* not malicious, complaisant, obliging

јумшагча : *adv dim/affec* 1) softly *a* 2) soft

јумшалдылмаг : *v-intr* break up, become loose *of soil*

јумшалдычы : *a* softening

јумшалма : *n* softening

јумшалмаг : *v-intr* 1) soften become soft 2) become moderate/temperate

јумшалтмаг : *v-tr* 1) soften 2) calm 3) try to persuade

јун : *n* 1) wool *a* 2) woolen, wool

јунабәнзәјән : *a* resembling wool, wool-like

јунан : *n* 1) Greek *a* 2) Greek, Grecian

јунаныстан : *n* Greece

јунанпәрәст : *n* Hellenophile

јунанча : *adv* in Greek, in the Greek language

јун дарағы : *n* wool carding machine

јундарајан : *n* wool comber/carder *agent*

јундидән : *n* wool-scutcher

јунәјирән : *n* wool-spinner

јунјыған : *n* gatherer/collector of wool

јунусбалығы : *n zool* dolphin, *fam. Delphinidae, marine mammal*

јункер : *n* 1) cadet *student in a military school in tsarist Russia and Germany* 2) son of a nobleman or aristocratic landowner

јункерлик : *n collect* cadets or sons of noblemen or aristocratic landowners

јунлу : *a* woolly, fleecy

јунсуз : *a* without wool, hairless *of animals*

јунтаныјан : *n* wool-expert

јунугара : *a* black-furred, black-haired *of animals*

јунукөдәк : *a* short-haired *of animals*

јупјумру, јупјумруча : *a* roundish, spherical, spheroidal, globular

јурд : *n* 1) hearth, dwelling, shelter, house, home, roof 2) native land, homeland, motherland, fatherland, birthplace

јурд салмаг : *v* settle

јурдсуз : *a* 1) homeless, without a roof over one's head, shelterless *n* 2) homeless person

јурдсуз-јувасыз : *n* 1) wanderer 2) see **јурдсуз**

јурдсузлуг : *n* homelessness, lack of shelter

јуха : *n* 1) thinly rolled out unleavened bread *a fig* 2) thin, delicate

јухары : *n* 1) top, upper part *a* 2) upper 3) senior *prep* 4) over

јухарыда : *adv* above

јухарыдакы : *a* located above

јухарыдан : *adv* 1) from above *fig* 2) condescendingly, in a haughty manner

јухарыја : *adv* up, upward

јухарыкы : *a* upper

јуху : *n* 1) sleep 2) dream

јухујозан : *n* 1) soothsayer; interpreter of dreams 2) augur, prophet, soothsayer

јухукәтирән : *a* soporific, sleeping *of a substance intended to induce sleep*

јухукөрмә : *n* dream

јухулама : *vn fr.* **јухуламаг**

јухуламаг : *v* fall asleep, drop off to sleep, sleep

јухулу : *a* sleepy, drowsy, half-asleep

јухулу-јухулу : *adv* while only half-awake, while in a sleepy state

јухусуз : *a* 1) sleepless *adv* 2) without sleep

јухусузлуг : *n* sleeplessness, insomnia

јухучул : *n* 1) sleepyhead *a* 2) sleepy, drowsy

јухучуллуг : *n* sleepiness, drowsiness

јүз : *num* hundred

јүзбашы : *n* 1) village elder *mil* 2) captain

јүзиллик : *n* 1) century *a* 2) centenary, centennial

јүз-јүз : *adv* by/in hundreds

јүзлүк, јүзманатлыг : *n* a hundred rubles, hundred-ruble note

јүзүнчү : *a* hundredth

јүјән : *n* 1) bridle *a* 2) pertaining to bridle[s]

јүјәнләмәк : *v-tr* 1) bridle, put a bridle *on* 2) bridle *control by means of a bridle*

јүјәнләтдирмәк, јүјәнләтмәк : *caus* of **јүјәнләмәк**

јүјәнли : *a* 1) with bridle *of a horse* 2) bridled

јүјәнсиз : *a* 1) without bridle *of a horse* 2) unbridled

јүјүрә-јүјүрә : *adv* at a run, running

јүјүрәк : *a* 1) quick, running well *adv* 2) at a run, running, quickly

јүјүрмә : *n* 1) run, running start/approach 2) *vn fr.* **јүјүрмәк**

јүјүрмәк : *v* run, scatter *of a group of people*

јүјүртдүрмәк, јүјүртмәк : *caus* of **јүјүрмәк**

јүјүрүб-јортмаг : *v* tire oneself out by running, have had one's fill of running

јүјүрүш : *n* run, race

јүјүрүшмә : *n* running about

јүјүрүшмәк : *v* run in stages, break up one's running into definite periods

јүк : *n* 1) load, burden, pack, baggage, luggage *phys* 2) charge *a* 3) pack

јүкдашыјан : *n* porter, carrier

јүккөндәрән : *n* shipper

јүкләјичи : *n* loader, stevedore

јүкләмә : *n* 1) loading 2) burdening

јүкләмәк : *v* 1) load 2) burden

јүкләнмәк : *pass* be loaded, be burdened

јүкләтмәк, јүкләтдирмәк : *caus* of **јүкләмәк**

јүклү : *a* loaded

јүксәк : *a* 1) high *adv* 2) high *a* 3) loud *of a voice*

јүксәлик : *n* height; loftiness; elevation

јүксәкволтлу : *a* high-voltage

јүксәклик : *n* 1) height, altitude *vertical distance or elevation* 2) height *a high place*

јүксәкликөлчән : *n* altimeter

јүксәкмәһсуллу : *a* 1) highly productive 2) high-yield *of crops*

јүксәлән : *a* ascending, rising

јүксәлиш, јүксәлмә : *n* 1) rise, ascent 2) growth, increase

јүксәлмәк : *v-intr* rise, ascend, climb

јүксәлтмә : *n* rise, raising, rising

јүксәлтмәк : *v* 1) raise, elevate 2) erect 3) extol, praise

јүксүз : *a* without load, unloaded

јүмн : *n* sign, indication, omen

јүмнлү : *n* good omen

јүнкүл : *a* 1) light, of light weight 2) easy, not difficult *fig* 3) frivolous,

light-minded

јүнкүлвары : *adv* 1) slightly *a* 2) slight, very light

јүнкүлләдән, јүнкүлләдичи : *a* facilitating, easing, alleviating, relieving

јүнкүлләнмәк : *v-intr* 1) be relieved, find relief, become easier/lighter 2) be freed from work or a load 3) feel relief after an illness

јүнкүлләтмәк : *v* lighten, lessen the weight of, unload

јүнкүлләшдиричи : *a* softening, mollifying, alleviating, allaying, assuaging, mitigating

јүнкүлләшдирмәк : *v* see **јүнкүлләтмәк**

јүнкүлләшмәк : *v* see **јүнкүлләнмәк**

јүнкүллүк : *n* 1) lightness 2) easiness *fig* 3) lack of seriousness, light-mindedness, frivolity

јүнкүлтәбиәт : *a* see **јүнкүлхасиј̃јәт**

јүнкүлтәһәр : *a* somewhat light, lightish

јүнкүлхасијјәт : *a* not serious, not sedate, frivolous, light-minded, imprudent

јүнкүлчә : *adv* slightly

јүпјүнкүл : *a* very light

јүрүш : *n* 1) motion, gait, walk, step 2) march, campaign, offensive, attack

К

к : fourteenth letter of the Azerbaijani alphabet

каб : *n* rocky precipice

кабаб : *n* kebab, shashlik, barbecued meat

кабаблыг : *a* prepared for barbecuing *meat*

кабабчы : *n* kebab-cook , kebab-seller

кабардин : *n* Kabardian/Kabard *a member of the Kabardian ethnic group, a Circassian people of the North Caucasus*

кабардинчә : *adv* in the Kabardian language

кабел : *n* cable; cable communications system

кабелчи : *n* cable-worker; cable network maintenance worker

кабил : *n* Kabul *capital of Afghanistan*

кабина : *n* 1) cabin 2) chamber 3) driver's cab 4) cockpit *aircraft*

кабинет : *n Ru private* office

кабус : *n* ghost, spirit, phantom

кагэбэшник : *n derog Ru* KGB officer or agent

кағыз : *n* paper; letter ; document; securities, valuables; *a* paper, made of paper

кағызбадам : *n* thin-skinned variety of almonds

кағызгајырма : *n* paper-manufacturing industry

кағызгатлајан : *typ* folder *agent and machine*

кағызкәсән : *n* paper-cutter

кағыз-куғуз : *n* piles of paper; petty, unimportant correspondence and notes *ironic*

кағызламаг : v glue, stick paper on s.t.

кағызланмаг : *pass* be glued on, be stuck on *of paper*

кағызлатдырмаг, кағызлатмаг : *v* cause s.o. to glue or stick paper on s.t.

кағызлашмаг : *v* exchange letters, correspondence

кағызпајлајан : *n* errand person; mailman *rare*

кағызсыз : *a* undocumented, having no paper[s] or document

кағызчәкән : *n* wallpaper hanger

кағызчылыг : *n* 1) paper-manufacturing *a* 2) pertaining to paper-manufacturing *n* 3) red tape, procrastination

кадмиум : *n* cadmium

казак : *n* 1) Cossack *a* 2) Cossack

каинат : *n* Cosmos, the Universe

какао : *n* 1) cocoa *a* 2) cocoa

кал : *a* 1) unripened, green 2) undeveloped; immature; oppressed 3) mildly mentally retarded

калағајы : *n* woman's fine silk traditional head-kerchief

калан : *a* 1) rich, having a lot of money *n colloq* 2) a lot of something

калафа : *n* 1) ruins 2) large aperture, large pit

калафлыг : *n* ruins, ruined/demolished area

калиум : *n chem* potassium

калиум-карбонат : *n* potash *potassium hydroxide*

калка : *n* tracing cloth, tracing paper

каллајы : *n* the furthermost room *in a hotel*

каллыг : *n* 1) unripeness, immaturity *fig* 2) mental retardation, dullness, stupidity

калсит : *n* calcite *naturally-occurring calcium carbonate*

калсиум : *n* calcium

кам : *n* 1) dream, wish, desire 2) intention, purpose 3) pleasure, enjoyment

кам алмаг : *v* enjoy to the full; rejoice; esp. *take malicious delight in another's misfortune*

камал : *n* 1) perfection, completeness, maturity 2) brilliant education; intellect, brains, talent 2) emphatic word which strengthens the meaning of that which follows, usually another word, somewhat like English *very*

камалланмаг : *v* become intellectually mature, perfect

камаллы : *a* clever, intellectual, enlightened, educated

камаллылыг : *n* intellectual maturity, perfection

каман : *n* 1) bow *the weapon, fr. Persian* 2) bow-string *mus* 3) bow *for a stringed instrument*

каманлы : *a* 1) bow *pertaining to, or like a bow*

каманча : *n* kamança *Azerbaijani and Persian stringed instrument played with a bow somewhat like a violin*

каманчагајыран : *n* kamança-maker

каманчачалан, каманчалан, каманчачы : *n* kamança-player

камера : *n* 1) solitary-confinement cell *in prison* 1) chamber 3) inner tube *a* 4) chamber *concert*

камерајамајан : *n* vulcanizer

камил : *v* 1) perfect, complete, accomplished, thorough, full 2) knowing no failures, defeats, drawbacks;

камилләшмәк : *v* 1) become complete/perfect/accomplished 2) attain a state of knowing no failures/defeats/setbacks/drawbacks

камиллик : *n* perfection, maturity, completeness

канарја : *n zool* canary, a small finch *Serenus canarius*

кандар : *n* threshold, doorway

каникулы : *n Ru* vacation

канкан : *n* well-digger

капитал : *n* capital; property, assets

капитализм : *n* capitalism

капиталист : *n* capitalist, entrepreneur

капиталлашдырма : *n* transformation of money into capital *Marxist*

капиталлашдырмаг : *v* transform money into capital

капитан : *n* captain

капсул : *n* 1) capsule 2) percussion-cap

кар : *n* 1) work, job, business, occupation, profession *obs* 2) influence *a* 3) deaf

каракәлән : *a* useful, necessary

каракәлмәз : *a* unnecessary, vain, good for nothing

карандаш : *n Ru* pencil

карасты : *n* 1) tool 2) weapon, arms *a* 3) tool/instrument

карбон : *n* carbon

карбоһидрокен : *n chem* hydrocarbon

карбоһидрат : *n chem* carbohydrate

карбүратор : *n* carburator

карбүраторчу : *n* carburator specialist

карван : *n* caravan *of camels*

карванбашы : *n* caravan leader

карвангыран : *n astron* Venus *planet*

карвансара : *n* caravansary, inn; *originally an inn enclosing a court for sheltering caravans in the Near East*

карвансарачы : *n* inn-keeper

карванчы : *n* caravan leader

карел : *n* Karelian , a native of the Karelian Autonomous Republic

карета : *n* carriage, hansom

карикатура : *n* caricature, cartoon

карикатурачы : *n* cartoonist

карыхдырычы : *a* embarrassing, taking aback

карыхдырмаг : *v* embarrass, confuse, take aback *s.o.*

карыхмаг : *v* get completely embarrassed, confused, taken aback, shocked

карјера : *n Ru* career

каркүн : *n* busy, industrious person

каркүнлүк : *n* business-like character/nature, industry, diligence, efficiency

каркаһ : *n* weaving frame; loom, shuttle

каркәр : *n* apprentice junior-worker-employee

каркүзар : *n* chief clerk

каркүзарлыг : *n* 1) position/occupation of a chief clerk 2) help, assistance

кар-лал : *a* deaf-and-dumb

карлашма : *a* becoming deaf

карлашмаг : v become deaf, lose hearing

карлы : *a* 1) necessary, fitting, useful 2) able, skilful *adv* 3) heartily, well-and-truly

карлыг : *n* deafness

карсазлыг : *n* assistance, help

карсала : *a* 1) hard-of-hearing *fig* 2) indifferent, deaf *to other people's grievances*

карсыз : *a* useless, unnecessary, unsuitable, good for nothing

карсызлыг : *n* 1) unfitness, unsuitability 2) uselessness

карт : *n* playing cards

карт басмаг : *v* shuffle cards

картәһәр : *a* slightly deaf

картограф : *n* cartographer

картографија : *n* cartography

картографик : *a* cartographic

картотека : *n* card index

картоф : *n* 1) potatoes *a* 2) potato

картофәкән : *a* *agric* potato-planter *agent/machine*

картофјыған : *n* potato-picking combine, potato-digger *machine*

картофлу : *n* 1) potatoes *a* 2) potato

картошка : *n* *Ru* potatoes

кархана : *n* factory, plant

кас : *a* dull, lustreless

каса : *n* 1) cup, basin *a* 2) cup, basin

касад : *a* 1) scanty, poor *n* 2) sluggishness/stagnation in commerce, drop in sales

касадлыг : *a* see **касад**

касајаохшар : *a* cup-shaped

касајарпаг : *n* *bot* sepal

касамас(т) : *n* yogurt *rare*

касачыг : *n* *bot* calyx *outermost series of leaflike parts of a flower*

касачыгсыз : *a* *bot* achlamydeous *having no calyx or corolla*

касыб : *a* poor, impoverished

касыбјана : *a* in modest circumstances, not rich

касыблашдырмаг : *v* impoverish s.o.

касыблашмаг : *v* become poor/impoverished

касыблыг : *n* poverty, indigence, need, want

касыбчылыг : *n* 1) poverty *econ* 2) the poverty level

касны : *n* *bot* 1) chicory *Cichorium* *a* 2) chicory

касса : *n* cash-register

катиб : *n* secretary *male*

катибә : *n* secretary *female*

катиблик : *n* 1) occupation of secretary, post/job/duties of secretary 2) secretariat

катта : *n* village chief

каучук : *n* 1) caoutchouc, crude rubber 2) rubber

каучуклу : *a* rubber

кафедра : *n* *Ru* chair, professorship

кафи : *a* 1) satisfactory, tolerable *adv* 2) satisfactorily, enough

кафилик : *n* sufficiency, satisfaction

кафир : *n* non-Moslem, non-believer *esp a Christain*, apostate, giaour

кафирлик : *n* unbelief, adherence to a religion other than Islam, atheism

кафирчәсинә : *adv* sacrilegiously, in an un-Godly manner, in a cruel, brutal way

кафтар : *n* *zool* 1) hyena; witch 2) decrepit, senile old man 3) witch

кафтаркус : *n* nasty and dirty old man

кафтарла(ш)маг : *v* grow old and cantankerous

кафтарлыг : *n* decrepitude, senile infirmity, cantankerous old age

кафур : *n* camphor

каһа : *n* cave

каһал : *a* lazy, inert

каһалыг : *n* area rich in caves *mountains*

каһин : *n* *hist* Jewish priest; ancient Egyptian priest

каһинлик : *n* *hist* priesthood *of a Jewish/ancient Egyptian priest*

каһы : *n* *bot* lettuce

каһыл : *a* sluggish, slow to start, inert, lazy

каһылланмаг, каһыллашмаг : *v* become lazy, inert, unenthusiastic

каһыллыг : *n* laziness, inertness, lack of enthusiasm

каш, каш ки : *conj* If only. . ., Would that. . . I wish that... *something would happen*

кашанә : *n* palace, castle, luxurious residence

кашы : *n* 1) glazed bricks, tiles 2) enamelware

квадрат : *n* square

квадрилјон : *n* quadrillion, 1,000,000,000,000,000) *one followed by fifteen zeros*

кварс : *n* *min* quartz

кварсит : *n* *min* quartzite a massive metamorphic rock formed by the hardening of sandstone through the deposition of quartz around each grain

квас : *n* kvass, a Russian fermented drink resembling sour beer maade of rye, barley etc

квит : *a* quits *on even terms by payment or retaliation*

квитләшмәк : *v* be quits

кеј : *a* 1) insensitive, cold, stuporous, benumbed 2) unable to grasp *facts, ideas* , stupid, dull

кејидичи : *a* person administering anesthesia, anesthetist

кејикмәк *v* 1) become motionless, be frozen in o.'s tracks; 2) lose consciousness, lose track of things, be in a stupor

кејимәк : *v* 1) become motionless, lose the ability to move 2) lose consciousness, lose track of things, be in a stupor

кејитмә : *n* anesthetizing, admministering anesthesia

кејитмәк, кејләтмәк, кејләшдирмәк : *v* 1) make s.o. sluggish/inert/senseless/without feeling 2) put under anesthesia, anesthetize

кејләшмәк : *v* 1) become numb, lose the ability to move 2) lose consciousness, lose track of things, be in a stupor

кејлик : *n* 1) diffusion, dispersion, dissipation 2) absent-mindedness, distraction

кејтәс : *n astron* Cetus *the Whale, a constellation visible in autumn and early winter*

кејфијјәт : *n* 1) quality; property 2) state, status, situation

кејфијјәтәбахан : *n* quality-controller, quality-control specialist

кејфијјәтли : *a* 1) qualitative 2) high-quality

кејфијјәтсиз : *a* low-quality, poor-quality

кеф : *n* 1) mood, humor, internal-disposition 2) health

кеф чәкмәк : *v* have fun, enjoy one's life

кефи позулмаг : *v* get upset

кефинәгулу : *n* ladies' man, philanderer, playboy

кефләндиричи : *a* intoxicating, stupifying

кефләндирмәк : *v* 1) make *s.o.* drunk, intoxicated; *also fig*

кефләнмә : *n* 1) becoming drunk, intoxicated *fig* 2) falling into a state of delirious enjoyment/ecstasy

кефләнмәк : *v* 1)become drunk/intoxicated *fig* 2) fall into a state of delirious enjoyment/ecstasy

кефли : *n* 1) drunk, tipsy, tight *fig* 2) dizzy with pleasure, ecstatic

кефли-кефли : *a* dead drunk

кефлилик : *n* drunkenness, intoxication

кефсиз : *n* indisposition, queasiness, discomfort

кефсизләмәк : *v* become indisposed/unwell, feel ill, not be o.s.

кефсизлик : *n* indisposition, slight illness

кефчи, кефчил : *n* 1) debauchee, profligate, bon-vivant

кечә : *n* 1) large piece of thickfelt *a* 2) tousled, dishevelled *hair*

кечәбичән : *n* felt-cutter

кечәл : *a* 1) bald-headed *n* 2) tetter, mange, scab 2) lousy creature/fellow

кечәл кәркәс : *n zool* griffon vulture *Gyps fulvus*

кечәллик : *n* 1) baldness 2) mange, scab

кечән : *a* 1) past, last 2) former, preceding

кечәсатан : *n* 1) felt merchant, feltmonger

кечәтәпән, кечәчи : *n* feltmaker

кечәчилик : *n* occupation of feltmaker

кечәхана : *n* felt-fulling shop

кечи : *n* goat

кечид : *n* 1) transition, passage 2) passing, crossing, pass 3) ford *a* 4) transitional

кечиәмчәји : *n* brand of grapes white *with elongated berries*

кечилиш : *n* passing, passage

кечилмәз : *a* 1) impassable 2) unpardonable

кечилмәзлик : *n* impassability

кечинмәк : *v* 1) live, exist 2) get along with *s.o.*

кечиотаран : *n* goat herd

кечирдилмәк, кечирилмәк : *v* 1) take trouble over s/t., toil and moil to do s.t. 2) mess about, muck about, play about 3) be conducted, led, taken

кечиричи : *n phys* conductor

кечиричилик : *n phys* conductability

кечир(т)мә : *n* 1) causing to pass; 2) putting on, sticking on 3) transferring; shifting 4) holding, taking 5) suffering, undergoing

кечир(т)мәк : *v* 1) cause to pass 2) cause to put on, stick on 3) cause to transfer,shift 4) cause to hold, take 5) cause to make true 6) cause to suffer, undergo

кечичи : *a* 1) transient, transitory, temporary 2) brought forward, carried over 3) contagious

кечмә : *vn fr.* **кечмәк**

кечмәк : *v* 1) cross; move *to another place*;, transfer, get to, go to, switch to 2) enter, join, affiliate with 3) change 4) get busy 5) pass to, occupy; 6) be over, be later than 7) spend *time* 8) last; have, *be in as a step* *in o.'s career;* 9) be held, be gone; take *a course* 10) overrun; fly over 11) be picked up from, inherited 12) influence, have an impact on s.o. 13) pass *succesfully* 14) forgive *unkind actions* 15) pass *as a result of a vote* 15) be useful)

кечмиш : *a* 1) past *in various senses* , former, preceding *n* 2) the past

кечмишдә : *adv* in the past, in previous times

кешик : *n* 1) guard, watch 2) guarding, protection

кешикчи : *n* 1) guardhouse, check-point sentry-box, outpost, security detachment

кешикчихана : *n* 1) sentry, guard, watchman *a* 2) guard, watch

кешиш : *n* priest *christian*

кешниш : *n keşniş Bifora radians* umbelliferous plant, evil-smelling, but edible

кә'бә : *n* Kaaba, the Muslim shrine at Mecca, enclosing a sacred black stone supposedly given to Abraham by the angel Gabriel, and toward which worshippers face while praying

кәбин : *n* 1) Muslim marriage contract *sometimes temporary*; see also **сиғә** 2) formal Muslim marriage ceremony

кәбинкәсмә : *n* Muslim marriage ceremony

кәбинли : *a* 1) having a marriage contract 2) legal *spouse*

кәбинсиз : *a* 1) without a concluded/signed/valid marriage contract 2) invalid *marriage*

кәвәл : *a* fragile, weak, frail

кәвәр : *n bot* leek *Allium porrum*

кәдәр : *n* torture, suffering, sorrow, grief

кәдәрләндиричи : *a* distressing, painful

кәдәрләндирмәк : *v* bring sorrow, grieve, distress, pain

кәдәрләнмәк : *v* grieve for, be distressed, be sad, mourn

кәдәрли : *a* sad, sorrowful, suffering

кәдәрсиз : *a* without sorrow, free from suffering

кәкә : *n* stammerer, stutterer

кәкәләмә : *n* stammering, stuttering

кәкәләмәк : *v* stammer, stutter

кәкәләнмәк : *v* swagger, strut

кәкәлик : *n* stammering

кәкил : *n* forelock, topknot; crest *rooster's*

кәкилли : *a* wearing a topknot *hair*, crested *rooster*

кәклик : *n zool* partridge

кәкликоту : *n bot* summer savory *Satureia hortensis,* an herb

кәков : *n* stammerer

кәковлуг : *n* stammering

кәкоту : *n bot* summer savory *Satureia hortensis,* an herb

кәл : *n* water buffalo

кәлам : *n* word, saying

кәлбәтин : *n* pliers

кәлә : *n* 1) bull, ox *fig* 2) big fellow, stud *of a man*

кәләдуран : *n* three year old female water buffalo

кәләз : *n zool* pangolin, or scaly ant-eater *genus Manis* a heavily armored edentate mammal of Asia and Africa

кәләк : *n* cheating, trickery, dirty tricks, fraud, deception

кәләјә дүшмәк : *v* get cheated, fall into a trap, be placed in an unpleasant situation

кәләкбаз : *n* 1) cheat, swindler 2) crafty, sly person

кәләкбазлыг : *n* 1) cheating, swindling, defrauding 2) cunning, guile

кәләк-күләк : *n* tricks, ruses, guile, dodges

кәлә-көтүр : *a* 1) uneven *of a surface* 2) rough, rugged

кәлә-көтүрләшдирмәк : *v* 1) make uneven 2) make rough, make rugged

кәлә-көтүрләшмәк : *v* become uneven/rough/rugged

кәлә-көтүрлүк : *n* unevenness, roughness, ruggedness

кәләксиз : *a* ingenuous, artless, unsophisstocated, simple-hearted

кәләкчи : *n* 1) cheat, swindler 2) sly, cunning person

кәләм : *n* 1) cabbage *a* 2) cabbage

кәләмдолмасы : *n* "golubtsy" *stuffed cabbage roll*

кәләф : *n* 1) lock *hair* , strand *rope/cable* 2) ball *of thread* ; knot,tangle

кәләфачан : *n* reel, reeling frame *device for winding thread/yarn*

кәләфләмәк : *v* wind, reel *thread*

кәләфләнмәк : *pass* be wound. reeled

кәләфчә : *n* skein, hank, coil

кәлик : *n* unripe melon, cantaloup

кәлин : *n* hornless ram

кәлкүттә : *n* Calcutta *city in India*

кәллә : *n* head, skull

кәлләкөз : *n* 1) Cyclops , a mythical one-eyed giant *a fig* 2) wrathful, mad, infuriated

кәлләләмәк : *v* butt, strike with the head or horns

кәлләләшмәк : *v* butt, strike with the head or horns

кәлләли : *a* brainy, intellectual

кәллә-мајаллаг : *a* upside down, topsy-turvy

кәллә-пача : *n* khash , jellied meat

кәлләпәз : *n* khash merchant, khash maker-vendor

кәлмә : *n* word

кәлтән : *n* lump/clot/lump of earth

кәлтәнли : *a* lumpy, clotty, clumpy

кәлчә : *n* baby water-buffalo

кәм : *a* 1) a little, a bit, few 2) in short supply, insufficient 3) bad, rude, unpleasant 4) low *n* 5) shortage, deficiency in payment or supply, short weight, undersized object etc *prep* 6) without

кәмағыл : *a* mildly mentally retarded

кәмағыллыг : *n* slight mental retardation

кәме'тигад : *a* lacking faith;/conviction, sceptical

кәме'тигадлыг : *n* lack of faith, scepticism

кәмәнд : *n* lasso

кәмәр : *n* 1) belt; *tech* 2) ring, band *metal*

кәмәрә : *n* beam

кәмәрләмәк : *v* 1) gird, engirdle *fig* 2) surround, encircle

кәмәрләнмәк : *pass* 1) be girded, engirdled be surrounded 2) be surrounded, encircled

кәмәрчин : *n* child's dress

кәмијјәт : *n* 1) quantity, number *math* 2) magnitude, value

кәмилтифат : *a* 1) discourteous, unfriendly, ungracious *n* 2) discourteousness, unfriendliness

кәм-кәсир : *n* 1) shortage, deficit 2) drawback, shortfall, incompleteness

кәммәһәл : *a* neglectful, indifferent

кәммәһәллик : *n* negligence, indifference

кәмсавад : *a* semi-literate

кәмсәр : *a* mildly mentally retarded

кәмсик : *n* piece of rope, leash

кәмсикләмәк : *v* 1) leash, keep/put on a leash *fig* 2) force/compel to do o.s will

кәмһөвсәлә : *a* 1) impatient 2) intolerant, quick-tempered

кәмчик : *n* 1) shortage, deficit 2) shortfall, state of lacking part of what is necesssary for completeness, incomplete state

кәнар : *n* 1) shore, coast 2) side, edge, brink, margin *a* 3) provincial, backwater; marginal 4) strange, alien, foreign 5) last *in a line* , extreme

кәнарә : *n* 1) edge, corner, border, side 2) marginal note *in a book* 3) frame 4) embroidery, 5) side carpet

кәнаф : *n* kenaf, a variety of flax plant *Linum usitatissimum*

кәнд : *n* village

кәнд тәсәррүфаты : *n* agriculture

кәндарасы : *a* rural *ref to open country between villages*

кәнди : *n* granary

кәндир : *n* rope

кәндирбаз : *n* 1) tight rope walker *fig* 2) somnambulist

кәндирбазлыг : *n* 1) tight rope walking *fig* 2) somnambulism

кәндистан : *n* 1) the country, countryside, rural area 2) country bumpkin

кәндли : *n* 1) peasant, fellow-villager *a* 2) peasant, village, rural

кәндлиләшмәк : *v* 1) become a rural resident, become a peasant, get used to/learn to put up with country life

кәндли-мәндли : *n* bumpkins, rubes, hicks

кәндличәсинә : *adv* in a countrified way, in a boorish manner

кәндхуда : *n* traditional village chief

кәндчи : *n* peasant

кәндчик, кәндчијәз : *n* tiny little village

кәнзик : *n* *anat* nasopharynx

кәниз : *n* 1) maid, female-servant *hist* 2) slave, bondwoman 3) odalisque *harem slave*

кәпәји : *a* friable, crumbly

кәпәк : *n* 1) bran, siftings 2) dandruff

кәпәкли : *a* 1) with/of bran 2) dandruffy

кәпәнәк : *n* butterfly, moth

кәпәнәкгурду : *n* *zool* tape-worm *Class Cestoda*

кәпәнәкқүлү : *n* *bot* 1) pansy/heartsease *Viola tricolor* 2) cow-wheat *Melampyrum nemorosum*

кәпиткә : *n* caulker's chisel, caulking-gun

кәпиткәләмәк : *v* caulk

кәрамәт : *n* mercy, lavishness, generosity, magnanimity

кәрамәтли : *a* merciful, lavish, generous, magnanimous

кәрбалаjы : honorary title bestowed on those who have made a pilgrimage to the tomb of Imam Hussein, grandson of Mohammed in Kerbala, Iran, the Holy City of the Shiites

кәрди : *n* 1) variety of non-freestone peach 2) bed *in a garden*

кәрә : *n* 1) fresh, unsalted butter 2) short-eared ram 3) boy with a shaved head

кәрәвиз : *n bot* celery *Apium graveolens*

кәрәм : *n* 1) see **кәрамәт** *slang* 2) skinhead

кәрәми : *n* karami *one of the melodies of the Azerbaijani aşug-folk narrators*

кәрән : *n* log

кәрәнаj : *n mus* Persian pipe of ancient lineage

кәрәнти : *n* scythe

кәрәнтиләмәк : *v* scythe

кәрәнтиләнмәк : *pass* be scythed

кәрәчи : *n* 1) barge 2) conveyance, vehicle

кәркәс : *n zool* griffon, a vulture *Gyps fulvus*

кәрки : *n* adze

кәркиләмәк : *v* 1) work on with an adze *cut, hew; trim* 2) work with a mattock *the earth*

кәркиләтдирмәк : *v* cause s.o. to work on with an adze *cut, hew; trim* 2) cause s.o. to work with a mattock *the earth*

кәркинчәк : *n zool* merlin, European blackbird

кәркәдан : *n* rhinoceros

кәрпич : *n* brick

кәрпичбиширән : *n* brick-maker

кәрпичи : *n* brick-colored

кәрпичкәсән : *n* brick-maker

кәрпиччи : *n* brick-maker

кәрпиччилик : *n* brick-manufacturing

кәррә : *n* 1) time 2) shaven-headed boy *a* 3) fresh-butter *of unprocessed butter sold directly by the producer, and used only adjectivally. › Persian kara = butter*

кәрт : *n* incision, notch

кәртәнкәлә : *n zool* lizard

кәрти : *a* not fresh, stale

кәртик : *n* mark, incision, notch

кәртикләмәк, кәртләмәк : *v* make an incision, mark *s.t.*

кәс : *n* person, individual, someone

кәсаләт : *n* 1) reluctance *to act* 2) passivity, inertness 3) indolence

кәсаләтли : *a* 1) reluctant 2) passive, inert 3) indolent

кәсафәт : *n* uncleanness, dirtiness, depravity

кәсб : *n* 1) livelihood, business, trade 2) acquisition *of property etc*

кәсбкар : *n* 1) profession, occupation 2) professional, business person, working person

кәсдирмәк, кәсдиртмәк : *caus* of **кәсмәк**

кәсә : *n* the shortest/nearest way/road

кәсәjән : *n zool* rodents

кәсәк : *n* clump of dry soil/clay

кәсәкли : *a* clumpy

кәсәклик : *n* area abounding in dry clumps of earth/clay

кәсән : *n geom* secant

кәсәр : *n* 1) cutting instrument 2) edged tool *hatchet/axe* 3) sharpness 4) influence , operation, activity

кәсәрли : *a* 1) sharp 2) accurate *of weapons fig* 3) weighty, efficacious, convincing

кәсәрсиз : *a* 1) inaccurate, dull *fig* 2) unconvincing, trivial

кәсәсинә : *adv* 1) so as to cross s.o.'s path 2) in the shortest way, shortest route

кәсик : *a* 1) cut, incised 2) reduced, shortened 3) torn *clothing* 4) discontinuous, abrupt 5) unattended *n* 6) cutting, cut, sharp piece/ fragment 7) leak 8) strip/allotment *land*

кәсик-кәсик : *adv* 1) quietly, patiently, *a* 2) jerky, abrupt 3) broken, interrupted, intermittent 4) ribbed

кәсик-кусук : *n* 1) fragment, piece, 2) cut fabric, remnants, scraps *cloth*

кәсилишмәк : *v* 1) settle/pay off an account 2) make final arrangements, come to an understanding

кәсилмәк : *pass* 1) be cut off, chopped off 2) be circumcised 3) be broken off, severed 4) be sentenced *to juridical punishment* 5) be robbed, have something stolen 6) be deprived, bereft of s.t. *v-intr* 7) finish, calm down, pacify 8) fail an examination

кәсим, кәсилиш : *n* 1) cutting, cut 2) cross-section, model; *a* 2) appointed, allotted, funded 3) decided on

кәсинти : *n* see **кәсик-кусук** 1)

кәсир : *n* 1) shortage, deficiency, insufficiency, hiatus, lacuna 2) breakthrough 3) harm, damage, injury *math* 4) fraction

кәсирли : *a* 1) defective, substandard *math* 2) fractional 3) having a remainder 4) incomplete

кәсирсиз : *a* 1) having no defects/shortcomings *math* 2) without a remainder

кәсичи : *n* 1) cutter, cutting instrument *a* 2) cutting, capable of cutting *of an instrument/tool*

кәсишмәк : *v -intr* intersect, cross

кәски : *n tech* 1) cutter, cutting tool *anat* 2) incisor *tooth*

кәскин : *n* 1) sharp, penetrating 2) strong, influential 3) quite-visible; 4) heavy, tough; tense *of a situation* 5) rude, crude, rough, abrupt 6) sensitive 7) direct, unhesitating *adv* 8) sharply, penetratingly

кәскинләтмәк, кәскинләшдирмәк : *v-intr* 1) intensify, become intense/tense *trans* 2) aggravate, worsen

кәскинләшмәк : *v* 1) sharpen 2) become tenser/more strained *of relations*

кәскинлик : *n* sharpness, harshness, abruptness; 2) tenseness, aggravation, exacerbation

кәсмә : *vn* fr. **кәсмәк**

кәсмәк : *v* 1) cut, cut off; circumcise separate 2) slay, kill, cut down, wound, stab 3) interrupt, give a curt answer to 4) curtail, reduce, shorten 5) bar, block the way, fence off, surround with 6) stop, calm down, pacify7) finish, accomplish 7) fail, flunk *an exam*

кәсмик : *n* 1) unsalted cottage cheese

кәтан : *n bot* flax *Linum usitatissimum*

кәтангушу : *n zool* linnet, fringilline songbird *Carduelis cannabina*

кәтанјыған : *n* flax-picking machine

кәтә : *n* meat and vegetable pie/pasty

кәтил : *n* chair, stool

кәтмән : *n agric* 1) ketmen, a tool used in Central Asia to earth up crops during the growing season 2) hoe, mattock

кәтмәнләмәк : v work/earth up crops with a ketmen/hoe/mattock

кәтхуда : *n* village chief

кәф : *n* foam, froth, scum

кәфән : *n* shroud, cerement

кәфәнләмәк : *v* wrap in a shroud *a corpse*

кәфәнли : *a* wrapped in a shroud

кәфәнлик : *n* cloth/material for a shroud

кәфәнсиз : *a* without a shroud *of a corpse*

кәфкир : *n* 1) perforated spoon, straining spoon 2) ladle, strainer, skimmer 3) pendulum *clock*

кәфләмә : *n* medicinal powder

кәфләмәк : *v* take medicine in powdered form

кәфләнмәк : *v* 1) be covered with foam/froth *during cooking* 2) boil, boil up

кәфрәм : *n* inner case *of a pillow or cushion*

кәфрәмлик : *n* pillow case fabric

кәһәр : *a* 1) bay *horse color* *n* 2) light-chestnut horse

кәһилдәмәк : *v* be short of breath, wheeze, gasp

кәһкәшан : *n astron* Milky Way

кәһраба : *n* 1) amber *a* 2) amber

кәһриз : *n* drain, sewer, underground water-conduit

кәчап : *n* ketchup

кәч : *a* crooked, curved

кәчавә : *n* palanquin, *type of covered litter used to transport dignitaries in the Orient*

кәч-кәч : *adv* obliquely, slantwise

кәчлик : *n* 1) crookedness, curvature 2) obstinacy

кәшкүл : *n* cup suspended from a chain and carried by dervishes

кәшмир : *n* cashmere *a fine cloth made of the wool of Cashmere goats*

кәшф : *n* discovery, finding out

кәшфијјат : *n* 1) intelligence, reconnaisance *a* 2) intelligence

кәшфијјатчы : *n* intelligence officer, scout

ки : *conj* 1) that 2) in order to, in order that

кибр : *n* arrogance, haughtiness

кибрә : *n* hangnail

кибрит : *n* match *for fire*

кибрләнмәк : *v* be haughty, arrogant

кибрли : *a* arrogant, haughty

кикирткә : *n* gum, resin

кил : *n* keel

килид : *n* lock

килидләмәк : *v* lock

килидләнмәк : *pass* be locked

килидләтдирмәк, килидләтмәк : *v* cause s.o. to lock

килидли : *a* locked

килим : *n* *kilim* , a type of pileless, tapestry-woven carpet

килимтохујан : *n* *kilim* carpet-weaver

килкә : *n* combings, tow, bits of rag

килкәләшдирмәк : *v-trans* rumple, ruffle

килкәләшмәк : *pass* be tousled/disheveled/rumpled *e.g. hair/clothing*

килкәшик : *a* rumpled, ruffled, messy

кило : *n* kilogram

киловат : *n* kilowatt

киловат-саат : *n* kilowatt-hour

килограм : *n* kilogram

килограмлыг : *a* weighing a kilogram

километр : *n* kilometer

километрлик : *a* kilometer

килсә : *n* church, cathedral

килка : *n* *Ru* spiced sprats

ким : *pro* who, whoever

ким сә : *pro* somebody, someone

кими : *pro* 1) whom *prep* 2) like, as 3) until 4) as soon as

кимин, киминки : *pro* whose

кимја : *n* chemistry

кимјакәр : *n* 1) chemist *hist* 2) alchemist

кимјалашдыран : *n* 1) agricultural chemist 2) industrial chemist

кимјалашдырылмаг : *v* be introduced into manufacturing *of chemical processes*

кимјалашдырма : *n* chemicalization *e.g. introduction of chemical fertilizers into agriculture*

кимјалашдырмаг : *v* introduce chemicals into manufacturing and agriculture

кимјачы : *v* chemist

кимјәви : *a* 1) chemical *adv* 2) chemically

кимсә : *pro* 1) no one, nobody 2) someone, somebody

кимсәнә : *n* 1) person, individual *pro* 2) someone, somebody 3) see **кимсә** 1)

кимсәсиз : *a* lonely, solitary, in oblivion, forgotten and abandoned by everybody

кимсәсизлик : *n* loneliness

кимсиз : *a* see **кимсәсиз**

кин : *n* hatred, spite

кинајә : *n* 1) hint 2) allegory 3) irony *expressed in Aesopian language*

кинајәли : *a* containing a hint 2) allegorical 3) ironic

киндар : *a* see **кинли**

кинә : *n* 1) quinine *a* 2) quinine

кинли : *a* 1) spiteful, vindictive *n* 2) spiteful, vindictive person

кинлилик : *n* bitterness, animosity, rancor

кино : *n* cinema, film, movie[s]

кинолашдырылмаг : *v* develop a network of movie-theaters

кинолашдырма : *n* development of a network of movie-theaters

кинолашдырмаг : *v* create a network of movie-theaters

кинсиз : *a* 1) good-natured, good-hearted *n* 2) good-natured, good-hearted person

кинсизлик : *n* good-heartedness

кип : *a* 1) thick, compact 2) close, hermetic, sealed 3) firm, solid *fig* 4) familiar, thick, close *to one another* *adv* 5) closely, tightly, hermetically

кипләнмәк, кипләшмәк : *v* 1) become thicker 2) concentrate, move closer together 3) become solid, firm, strengthened

кипчәк : *tech* stuffing-box, packing gland

кир : *n* dirt

кирвә : *n* 1) godparent *person who holds an infant during circumcision* *colloq* 2) Hey, friend! Hey, buddy!

кирвәчијәз, кирвәчик : *n* *colloq* buddy, friend, guy

кирә : *n* 1) rent, lease 2) rental payment 3) carting, carrying on horse-drawn wagons

кирәдар : *n* see **кирәнишин**

кирәкеш : *n* 1) carter 2) see **кирәчи**

кирәкешлик : *n* 1) carting, carrying on horse-drawn wagon 1) carter's profession/business

кирәмит : *n* 1) tile *a* 2) tile, tiling

кирәмитбиширән : *n* master tile-maker

кирәнишин : *n* renter, tenant

кирәчи : *n* 1) tenant 2) one who rents s.t. out

кирәч : *n* 1) alabaster 1) gypsum, plaster

кирәчләмәк : *v* 1) cover with alabaster 2) plaster

кирил : *a* Cyril

киримәк : *v* 1) become silent, fall silent 2) quiet down, calm down 3) cease weeping/speaking/crying out

киритмәк : *v* 1) calm, calm down, quiet, sooth 2) compel to cease weeping/speaking/crying out

кириш : *n* bow-string *of sheep-gut, or goat-gut*

киришчи : *n* master rope-maker/ bow-string maker

киркирә : *n* hand-mill

кирләмәк, кирләндирмәк : *v* dirty, stain, soil

кирләнмәк : *v* become dirty, stained, soil o.s.

кирләтмәк : *v* make s.t. dirty, stained, soiled

кирли : *a* dirty

кирпи : *n* *zool* hedgehog, *fam. Erinaceidae*

кирпик : *n* eye-lashes

кирпикли : *a* eyelashed, having eyelashes

кирс : *n* 1) scar, cicatrice 2) crease on a carpet or fabric

киртик : *n* sliver of soap

киршан : *n* face powder

киршанламаг : *v* powder o.'s face

киршанланмаг : *pass* be powdered *the face*

киршә : *n* sled, sledge, sleigh

киршәбағлајан, киршәгајыран : *n* sled-maker

кисә : *n* 1) bag, sack 2) tobacco pouch 3) rubbing-glove *for rubbing down the body in a bath-house*

кисәји : *n* muslin

кисәләмәк : *v* rub down the body with a rubbing-glove

кисәләнмәк : *pass* be rubbed with a rubbing-glove

кисәләтмәк : *caus* of **кисәләмәк**

кисәли : *a* having a bag/sack

кисәтохујан : *n* bag/sack-maker

кисәчәкән, кисәчи : *n* rubber *employee of an Azerbaijani bath-house*

кисиб : *n* 1) trophy *fig* 2) spoils, captured war materiel

китаб : *n* book

китабалты : *n* 1) desk, stand 2) control-panel

китабә : *n* 1) epitaph, insciption on a grave-stone 2) grave-stone

китабијјат : *n* bibliography

китабсатан : *n* book-seller

китабсевән : *n* bibliophile

китабхана : *n* library

китабханачы : *n* librarian

китабханачылыг : *n* library-science, the profession of librarian

китабча : *n* booklet, pamphlet, brochure

китабчы : *n* scribe

китабшүнас : *n* bibliologist

китабшүнаслыг : *n* bibliology

китрә : *n* gum, resin

китрәли : *a* gummy, resinous

киф : *n* mold *fungus growth*

кифајәт : *a* 1) enough, sufficient, in satisfactory quantity *adv* 2) satisfactorily, sufficiently

кифајәтләндиричи : *a* enough, satisfactory, sufficient

кифајәтләндирмәк : *v* satisfy *demands/requirements*

кифајәтләнмәк : *pass* be satisfied

кифајәтсизлик : *a* insufficiency; shortage

кифир : *a* 1) dirty, ugly *n* 2) ugly person

кифирләнмәк, кифирләшмәк : *v* grow ugly, become dirty; lose one's looks *of a woman*

кифләнмә : *n* growing moldy, putrifaction

кифләнмәк : *v* grow moldy/musty, become covered with mold

кифли : *a* moldy, musty

кичик : *a* little, small

кичикләнмәк, кичикләтмәк : *v* grow smaller, decrease, shrink 2) flatter 3) humiliate o.s., abase o.s. before other's

кичикләтдирмәк : *v* cause to grow smaller, decrease, shrink

кичиклик : *a* 1) small/little/diminutive *n* 2) childhood 3) insignificance, wretchedness

кичикликдән : *adv* since childhood, ever since one was a child

кичиктәһәр : *a* a bit too small, not quite enough, not very much

кичилдилмәк : *v* be reduced, decrease, lessen *in size/height*

кичилдичи : *a* diminishing

кичилмәк : *v* 1) decrease, reduce, shrink *fig* 2) humble o.s.

кичилтмә : *n* reduction, diminution

кичилтмәк : *v* decrease, reduce *size/height*

кичичик : *a* very little, small, tiny

киш : intj shoo! *e.g. used in driving away poultry*

киши : *n* 1) man, adult male *colloq* 2) husband 3) person, individual *fig* 4) courageous, valiant, brave, decent *added to given names of older men as a sign of respect*

кишиләнмәк : *v* 1) grow up quickly, come early to maturity *fig* 2) swagger, boast

кишиләшмә : *n* maturing, becoming a grown man, reaching puberty/manhood

кишиләшмәк : *v* 1) mature, become a grown man, reach puberty/manhood

кишилик : *n* 1) courage, honor, manliness 2) maturity, manhood *a* 3) brave, courageous

кишинјов : *n* Kishinev *capital of the Moldavian Republic*

кишичијәз, кишичик : *n* unmanly fellow

кишләмәк : *v* shoo hens away

кишмиш : *n* raisins

кишнәмә : *n* neighing

кишнәмәк : *v* neigh

кишнәшмәк : *v* neigh simultaneously *of many horses*

кларнет : *n* *mus* clarinet

кларнетчалан, кларнетчи : *n* *mus* clarinetist

классик : *n* 1) classical author 2) classicist

классик : *a* classical

классисизм : *n* classicism

клиник : *a* clinical

клиника : *n* clinic

клише : *n* cliche; pattern

кнјаз : *n* *hist* *R* 1) prince *a* 2) princely

кнјазлыг : *n* *hist* 1) reign 2) principality

кнопка : *n* *Ru* button *of a device or appliance*

кобалт : *n* *chem* 1) cobalt *a* 2) cobalt

кобуд : *a* 1) rude, discourteous, crude, uncouth 2) tasteless, crudely constructed *adv* 3) crudely, discourteously

кобудлашмаг : *v* become rude, crude, rough, uncouth

кобудлуг : *n* rudeness, discourtesy

кобудчасына : *adv* rudely. crudely, toughly

ков : *a* taken into consideration/account

ковлу : *a* hot-tempered, irascible, easily infuriated

коғуш : *n* hollow, cavity *in a tree trunk*

коғушланмаг : *v* form a hollow/cavity *n a tree trunk*

коғушлу : *a* hollow, having a hollow *tree trunk*

код : *n* code

козал, козар : *n* gleanings *of grain*

кокс : *n* coke

кокслашдырмаг : *v* *tech* coke

кокслашмаг : *v--intr* coke

кол : *n* bush

кола : *a* muley, butt-headed, hornless *of a cow*

колаз : *n* dug-out *canoe*

колазчы : *n* paddler *dug-out canoe*

колбаса : *n* sausage

кол-кос : *n* brushwood, undergrowth, tall weeds

кол-кослу : *a* overgrown with brush/tall weeds

кол-кослуг : *n* area of thick brush, undergrowth, tall weeds

колланмаг : *v* be overgrown with brush undergrowth, tall weeds

коллексија : *n* collection

коллексијачы : *n* collector

коллектив : *n* *hist* 1) collective 2) staff *a* 2) staff, collective

коллективләшдирилмәк : *v* *hist* be collectivized

коллективләш(дир)мә : *n* *hist* collectivization

коллективләшдирмәк : *v* *hist* collectivize

коллективләшмәк : *v* *hist* collectivize

коллективчи : *n* *hist* collectivist

коллекија : *n* board, collegium

коллуг : *n* thicket, area overgrown with brush

колпан : *a* 1) fluffy, downy 2) branchy, twiggy 3) lushly overgrown

колхоз : *n* *hist* 1) kolkhoz *a* 2) kolkhoz

колхозчу : *n* *hist* kolkhoz worker

кома : *n* 1) clump; pile 2) hut, log-cabin

кома-кома : *a* clumpy, clumped, in clods

комаламаг : *v* pile up, earth up, gather into piles

комаланмаг : *v* be piled up, pile one on top of the other

команда : *n* 1) team, crew 2) command

командан : *n* commander

ком473анланлыг : *n* command, command group

командир : *n* 1) commander *a* 2) commander's

командировка : *n Ru* business trip

комачыг : *n* 1) little hut, little log-house, shack, hovel 2) little clump, little pile

комбајн : *n agric* combine

комбајнчы : *n agric* combine-operator

комбинезон : *n* coveralls

комедија : *n* 1) comedy *a* 2) comic

комедијачы : *n* comic actor

комедијачылыг : *n* 1) profession of comic actor *fig* 2) fooling around

комета : *n astron comet*

комик : *a* comic, comical, funny

комисјон : *n* commission store

комисјончу : *n* commission store employee; employee working on commission

комиссар : *n* commissar

комиссарлыг : *n* 1) commissariat 1) the position of commissar

комитә : *n* committee

коммуна : *n* commune

коммунал : *a* communal, municipal

коммунизм : *n* communism

коммунист : *n* 1) communist *a* 2) communist, communistic

коммунистчәсинә : *adv* in a Communistic manner

компјүтер : *n* computer

комплект : *n* complete set

комплектләшдирмә : *n* staffing, bringing up to strength, recruit

комплектләшдирмәк : *v* staff, bring up to strength, man recruit,

комплектләшдиртмәк : *caus* of **комплектләшдирмәк**

композисија : *n* 1) composition *in various senses* 2) theory of composition

компрессор : *n tech med* compressor

компрессорчу : *n* compressor-operator

компул : *a* downy, fluffy

комсомол : *n hist* Komsomol *the Young Communist League in the former Soviet Union*

комсомолчу : *n* Komsomol member

конгрес : *n* congress

кондуктор : *n* conductor *bus, streetcar*

кондукторлуг : *n* job of conductor

коњјак : *n* cognac, brandy

конкрет : *a* 1) concrete, specific *adv* 2) concretely, specifically

конкретлик : *n* concreteness, specificity

консерв : *n* 1) canned food *a* 2) canned

консерт : *n* concert

конструктор : *n Ru* designer

консул : *n* consul

консуллуг : *n* 1) profession of consul 2) consulate, consulate office

консулхана : *n* consulate

континент : *n* continent

континентал : *a* continental

контингент : *n* 1) contingent 2) quota, share

контор : *n* office

контрол : *n* 1) control, checking, inspection 2) monitoring, supervision observation

контролјор : *n* 1) controller, inspector, supervisor 2) monitor, attendant

контроллуг : *n* 1) responsibilities of a supervisor 2) occupation of a supervisor/inspector/monitor

контролсуз : without control/restrictions, monitoring, supervision

контролчу : *n* see **контролјор**

конус : *n geom* cone

конусвары, конусшәкилли : *a* cone-shaped, conical

конфедерасија : *n* confederation

конфет : *n* candy

конфранс : *n* conference

кооперасија : *n* 1) cooperation 2) cooperative *society* 3) partnership

кооператив : *n* 1) cooperative *society* 2) partnership; joint venture;

кооперативләшдирмәк : *v* compel to form into cooperatives

кооперативләшмәк : *v* become formed into cooperatives

кооперативчи : *n* member of a cooperative or partnership

копјор : *n* pile driver

коппуш : *a* plump, chubby

кор : *a* blind

кора : *n* dull nail

коразеһин : *a* dull, stupid, lacking in mental acuity

коразеhинлик : *n* 1) incapability 2) dullness, stupidity, lack of mental acuity

корамал : *n zool* grass-snake

корбучаглы : *a* obtuse-angled

кореја : *n* 1) Korea *a* 2) Korean

корејалы : *n* Korean

корејача : *adv* in Korean *language*

коричневый : *a colloq Ru lit."brown" used in reference to the far right wing of the political spectrum*

кор-корана : *adv* blindly, without thinking, without due consideration

корламаг : *v* 1) break; spoil; damage; injure; 2) squander

корланмаг : *pass* 1) be broken; be spoilt; be injured 2) be squandered

корлуг : *n* 1) blindness *fig* 2) need; shortage; insufficient quantity 3) shortsightedness

корнет : *n mus* 1) cornet *hist mil* 2) cornet

корнетчалан : *n mus* 1) cornetist

корпут : *n* ram/beetlehead of a pile-driver

корт : *a* blunt *e. g. knife/saw-blade*

корталма : *n* becoming blunt

корталмаг : *v* become/grow blunt

корталтмаг : *v* blunt, dull

кортәбии : *a* spontaneous

кортланмаг, **кортлашмаг** : *v* see **корталмаг**

коруш : *a* 1) weak-sighted, having poor sight *n zool* 2) mole *fam. Talpidae*

корчасына : *adv* see **кор-корана**

кос : *n* ball *for games*

коса : *a* 1) sparse *hair/beard* *n* 2) man whose beard is sparse

коса-коса : *n* buffoon, clown

косала : *n* dressed goatskin

косалашмаг : *v* grow sparse *of hair/beard*

косалыг : *n* sparseness *of hair/beard*

космогонија : *n astron* cosmogony

космографија : *n astron geol geog* cosmography

космодром : *n* Space-flight Launch Center

космологија : *n astron* cosmology

костјол : *n* Roman Catholic parish church

костјум : *n* dress, clothes, suit

костјумлуг : *n* 1) material suitable/earmarked for suits/costumes *a* 2) suit, costume

котан : *n* plough

котанчы : *n* ploughman

коттеч : *n* cottage

котул : *a* rude; awkward, clumsy

көбә : *n* 1) embroidery 2) edging, trim, border, hem

көбәләмәк : *v* 1) embroider 2) hem, attach border-trim/hemming material

көбәли : *a* 1) embroidered 2) hemmed, having border-trim/edging

көбәр : *n geog* plateau

көврәк : *a* fragile; frangible

көврәклик : *n* 1) fragility; brittle, delicate *fig* 2) soft-heartedness

көврәлмәк : *v* 1) become fragile/brittle/delicate *fig* 2) be easily moved to tears

көвшәк : *a* fragile, frail

көвшән : *n* 1) thatch, straw 2) plantation, large farm

көвшәнлик : *n* stubble

көз : *n* ember

көзә : *n* brook, creek, rivulet

көзәрдилмәк : *v* be scorching, be brought to incandescence/white heat

көзәрмәк : *v* 1) heat to a very high temperature, bring to white heat 2) twinkle, gleam, give out a glimmer of light

көзәртмә : *vn tech* incandescence

көзәртмәк : *v tech* heat, incandesce

көјнәк : *n* 1) shirt, blouse 2) case for musical instruments *tech* 2) protective layer 3) inner layer of a cocoon *sericulture*

көјнәклик : *n* 1) shirt material, material suitable for sewing shirts *a* 2) shirt, shirting

көјнәкчәк : *a* 1) shirtless, unshirted *adv* 2) while shirtless, unshirted

көк : *n* 1) root; carrot *math* 2) radical 3) stitch *a* 4) fat *coll* 5) adjectival emphasizer of words which follow *mus* 6) tuned

көк еләмәк : *v* tune *a musical instrument*

көкә : *n* small loaf of home-baked bread

көкәлмә : *vn* putting on weight

көкәлмәк : *v* put on weight

көкәлтмәк : *v-tr* 1) fatten 2) tease, tantalize

көкләјичи : *n mus* tuner

көкләмә : *n* tuning

көкләмәк : *v-tr* 1) tune, tune up; set for usage 2) quilt

көкләнмә : *vn* fr. **көкләнмәк**

көкләнмәк : *v-intr* 1) be tuned; be adjusted 2) be quilted 3) take root, become firmly established, be well-grounded

көклләтмәк : *caus* of **көкләмәк**

көкләшдирмәк : *v* 1) strengthen, reinforce, make fast 2) put on a solid basis/foundation

көкләшмәк : *v-intr* 1) become/grow fat 2) put down roots, settle somewhere

көклү : *a* 1) rooted, having a root 2) big, strong 3) having an extended family

көклүк : *n* 1) fatness, stoutness, plumpness 2) nutritional state 3) plantation of carrots

көкс : *n* 1) chest, breast *fig* 2) heart

көксүз : *a* rootless

көкүмејвәли : *n* root-crop, root-plant

көлә : *n* slave

көләлик : *n* 1) slavery, servitude *fig* 2) severe oppression

көлкә : *n* shade, shadow; reflection

көлкәләмәк : *v* 1) shade *fig* 2) conceal

көлкәләндирмә : *v* 1) shading *fig* 2) shielding, concealing

көлкәләндирмәк : *v* 1) place in the shade, shade 2) overshadow

көлкәләнмәк : *v* 1) sit in the shade 2) take shelter in the shade; hide in the shade *fig* 3) be in a bad temper, be out of sorts

көлкәли : *a* 1) shadowy; shady *fig* 2) suspicious; upset; gloomy

көлкәлик : *n* 1) shade; shadow; shady place/area 2) s.t. used to produce shade

көлкәсиз : *a* 1) unshaded, shadeless *fig* 2) person incapable of doing good/giving assistance

көмбә : *n* 1) large loaf of bread *fig* 2) big klutz, fat slob

көмәк : *n* help, aid, assistance, support

көмәккешлик : *n* mutual assistance, effecting work by joint effort

көмәкләшмәк : *v* assist mutually, help one other mutually

көмәкли : *adv* having another person to give support, mutually helping each other

көмәклик : *n* assistance, help, helping, aid

көмәксиз : *a* helpless

көмәксизлик : *n* helplessness

көмәкчи : *n* 1) helper; assistant; deputy *a* 2) auxiliary, subsidiary

көмүр : *n* coal, charcoal

көмүргазыјан : *n* coal-miner

көмүрјандыран : *n* furnace-man

көмүрләшдирмә : *vn* carbonization, charring

көмүрләшдирмәк : *v* carbonize, char

көмүрләшмәк : *v-intr* carbonize

көмүрлүк : *n* coalbin

көмүрсатан, көмүрчү : coal-vendor/merchant

көмүрчүлүк : profession of coal-vendor/merchant

көндәлән, көндәләнинә : *a* 1) diametrical, cross-cut, transverse *adv* 2) slantwise, aslant, across

көнлүачыг : *a* merry, jolly, open-hearted, cordial

көнтөј : *a* rude, crude; rough

көнтөјләшмәк : *v* become rude, crude; become awkward

көнтөјлүк : *n* rudeness, crudeness; roughness; clumsiness

көнүл : *n* *lit* heart

көнүлачан : *a* gratifying, pleasurable, very nice

көнүллү : *a* 1) voluntary 2) cordial *n* 3) volunteer

көнүллүлүк : *n* 1) voluntaryism 2) cordiality, warmth

көнүлсевән : *a* lovely, dear to one's heart, desirable *n* 2) the beloved, the person dear to one's heart

көнүлсүз : *a* 1) non-voluntary, compulsory 2) heartless *adv* 3) reluctantly, unwillingly

көнүлсүзлүк : *n* 1) non-voluntariness, compulsoriness, unwillingness 2) heartlessness;

көп : *n* 1) swelling; plumpness 2) inflation *stomach* *a* 3) swollen; plump

көпәк : *n* *pej* dog; bitch

көпәкбалығы : *n* *zool* shark

көпәшик : *n* blister; bump

көпәшмәк : *v* appear, pop up *of a blister*

көпкәр : *n* *zool* chamois *Rupicapra rupicapra*

көпмәк : *v* 1) become erect; raise up 2) pop up *of a blister*; swell,swell up

көпүк : *n* foam

көпүкләмәк : *v* foam

көпүкләндирмәк : *v* cover s.t. with foam

көпүкләнмәк : *intr-v* foam

көпүклү : *a* foamy

көпүксүз : *a* flat, foamless, having no foam

көпүрмәк : *v* 1) swell, become inflamed *fig* 2) get irritated, get annoyed

көпүртмәк : *v* blow up, inflate, cause to swell

көрәмәз : *n* köramaz *mixture of yogurt and milk, a common food of nomadic herdsmen*

көрпә : *a* 1) fresh-cut *of fruit/vegetables n* 2) nursling, tiny breast-fed infant

көрпәлик : *n* infancy, babyhood

көрпәчијәз, көрпәчик : *n dim* little baby

көрпү : *n* bridge

көрпүчүк : *n dim* little bridge

көрүк : *n* blacksmith's bellows

көрүкбасан : *n* see **көрүкчү**

көрүкләмәк : *v* pump air with a bellows

көрүкләнмәк : *pass* be pumped *of air in a bellows*

көрүклү : *a* equipped with a bellows

көрүкчү : *n* blacksmith's bellows operator

көрүкчүлүк : *n* job of a blacksmith's forge-worker

көрфәз : *n geog* bay

көсөв : *n* 1) smut, *disease of cereal plants esp wheat caused by a fungus of the order Ustiliginales* 2) charred fire-wood

көстәбәк : *n zool* mole *fam Talpidae*

көтәк : *n* beating, flogging, slapping

көтәкләмәк : *v* beat, slap

көтәкләнмәк : *v-intr* be beaten, hit, slapped

көтәкләтмәк : *caus* of **көтәкләмәк**

көтү : *a* mean, spiteful; wicked

көтүк : *n* 1) tree-stump, block 2) head of a clan

көтүкчә : *n* great great grandson

көһлән : *n* gelding, castrated stallion

көһнә : *a* 1) old, olden, ancient *not used for persons* 2) second-hand

көһнә-күрүш : *a* old clothes, rubbish, trash, junk

көһнәлик : *n* decrepitude, antiquity, out-datedness, old-fangledness

көһнәлмә : *v* becoming old, wearing out

көһнәлмәк : *v* become old, wear out

көһнәлтмәк : *v* make look old[er], wear out, wear into rags

көһнә-мөһнә : *n* junk, garbage

көһнәпәрәст : *n* retrograde person, reactionary/conservative person

көһнәпәрәстлик : *n* 1) conservatism, reactionary nature 2) rut, routine

көһнәсајаг : *adv* 1) in an old-fashioned/obsolete way *a* 2) old-fashioned, obsolete

көһнәфүруш, көһнәчи : *n* junk-dealer, old clothes-dealer

көһнәчилик : *n* see **көһнәпәрәстлик**

көч : *n* 1) nomadic tribe's/ nomadic people's territory 2) temporary campsite, nomadic encampment

көчәбә : *a* 1) nomadic 2) wandering, nomadic existence

көчәри : *a* nomadic

көчәрилик : *n* nomadic life-style

көчмәк : *v* be a nomad , wander, roam from place to place

көчүрдүлмәк : *v* be displaced, resettled; evacuated

көчүрмә : *v* 1) resettlement; moving to another place *a* 2) mobile, travelling

көчүрмәк, көчүртмәк : *v* resettle; move to another place

көчүрүлмәк : *v* see **көчүрдүлмәк**

көшәк : *n* camel-calf

көшк : *n* 1) kiosk 2) castle, palace 3) gazebo, pergola

крал : *n* king

кралича : *n* queen

краллыг : *n* kingdom

кран : *n Ru* faucet

краска : *n Ru* dye; paint

кремл : *n* Kremlin

кресло : *n Ru* armchair

криминал : *a* criminal

криминалист : *n leg* criminalist, specialist in criminal law

криминалистика : *n science of* crime detection

кристал : *n* crystal

кристаллашдырмаг : *v* crystallize

кристаллашма : *n* crystallization

кристаллашмаг : *v-intr* crystallize

кристаллик : *n* crystallization

кристаллыг : *a* crystal, crystalline

крым : *n* Crimea

кроват : *n* *Ru* bed

крупоз : *a* *med* croupous, relating to, or similar to croup

куду : *n* pumpkin

кузә : *n* jug, pitcher

кузәчилик : *n* the potter's trade

кузов : *n* *Ru* truckbed

кукла : *n* doll; puppet

кула : *n* piece of firewood

кулачок : *n* *Ru* cam

култиватор : *n* *agr* cultivator *machine*

кулуар : *n* lobby *in Parliament, also fig*

кум : *n* 1) beehive *a* 2) beehive

курјер : *n* messenger, courier

купалник : *n* *Ru* woman's bathing suit

курс : *n* *Ru* course *for study*

курс : *n* *fin* *Ru* exchange, rate of exchange

кустар : *n* handicraftsman

кустарлыг : *n* handicraft

кут : *n* clump

кут-кут : *a* 1) clumpy *adv* 2) in clumps

куфи : *n* 1) Kufic *ancient Arabic script* *a* 2) Kufic

куфлан : *n* carrousel, merry-go-round

күбар : *n* 1) nobleman, aristocrat *a* 2) aristocratic; refined 3) arrogant, haughty

күбарлыг : *n* aristocracy, nobility

күвән : *n* hump of a camel

күдурәт : *n* 1) displeasure, vexation, aversion, disgust 2) sorrow, grief

күдурәтләнмәк : *v* be irritated/annoyed/vexed

күз : *n* sheep-fold, cattle-pen

күј : *n* 1) noise 2) noisy squabble/quarrel

күјә душмәк : *v* make a fuss

күј-гарачы : *n* see **күјчү**

күј-кәләк : *n* 1) meamingless noise/shouting/racket 2) mess, disorder

күј-кәләкчи : *n* 1) alarmist, panic-monger, scare-monger, noisy person

күјләмәк : *v* spread a rumor, exaggerate

күјүл : *n* 1) swarm *insects* 2) school *fish*

күјчү : *n* alarmist; braggart; one inclined to exaggerations,

күјчүлүк : *n* alarmism, trouble-making

күкнар : *n* fir-tree

күкнарлыг : *n* fir-grove, fir-plantation

күкрәмә : *n* hot temper, irascibility, irascibleness

күкрәмәк : *v* be angry, be irascible, flare up

күкү : *n* omelet with greens/vegetables

күкүрд : *n* 1) sulphur *a* 2) sulphurous

күкүрдләмәк : *v* dust with sulphur *plants*

күкүрдлү : *a* sulphurous

күл : *n* ashes

күлафирәнки : *n* 1) gazebo, open summer house 2) covered balcony constructed so that the railing is flush with the outer wall of a building, the floor being part of an apartment and closed off from the living space by a glass-windowed door

күлбаш : *a* 1) unlucky *n* 2) unlucky person; good-for-nothing; wretch

күлбә : *n* ash-pit *of furnace/stove*

күлгабы : *n* ash-tray

күләк : *n* wind

күләкдөјән : *n* windward side, side exposed to wind/weather

күләкли : *a* windy

күләксиз : *a* windless

күләчә : *n* woman's sleeveless jacket *usually padded or fur-lined*

күләш : *n* 1) straw, thatch; *a* 2) straw, thatch

күлләнмәк : *v* 1) stroll idly, hang around, fool around, mooch around 2) spread ashes; become ashes *fig* 3) become shambles;

күлли : *adv* 1) much, many, a lot of *a* 2) considerable, sizeable, numerous

күллијјат : *n* collected works *of a specific author*

күлрәнки : *a* ash, ash-colored

күлүнк : *n* pick, pickaxe

күлүнкләмәк : *v* dig with a pickaxe

күлфәт : *n* family

күлфәтли : *a* family, domestic, familial

күлфәтсиз : *a* without a family, single

күлхан : *n* stoke-hole, stoke-hold

күлханчы : *n* stoker, fireman

күлчә : *n* ore

күм : *n* silkworm

күмхана : *n* silkworm garden *installation where silkworms and their eggs are bred, incubated, fed, and raised*

күндә : *n* 1) ball of dough 2) stocks *for criminals* *hist* 3) executioner's block

күндәачан : *n* rolling-pin

күндәләмәк : *v* 1) make a ball of dough 2) put into stocks *a criminal*

күндәләтмәк : *v* 1) *caus* of **күндәләмәк**

күндәтутан : *n* dough-roller *agent*

күндүр : *n* incense

күнә : *n* wider end of an egg

күнч : *n* corner

күнчүт : *n bot* sesame *Sesamum indicum*

күп : *n* 1) big clay jug 2) butt-stock 3) blunt side of an axe 4) fetters lock *med* 5) cup *a glass used in cupping*

күпә : *n* 1) bud 2) earthenware pot

күпәкирән гары : *n* wicked witch *in folk-tales*

күпәчичәји : *n bot* fuchsia *a plant of the evening-primrose family*

күпәштә : *n* side *of vessel*

күр : *n* 1) Kura *the largest river in the Transcaucasus* 2) fidgety, noisy child *a* 3) nagging; quarrelsome, cantankerous 4) lazy, inert 5) clean, transparent *of water*

күрд : *n* 1) Kurd *a* 2) Kurdish

күрдү : *n* woman's fur-lined, padded jacket

күрдчә : *a* in Kurdish

күрд-шаһназ : *n Kurd-şahnaz title of a mugam traditional Azerbaijani melody*

күрә : *n* 1) *in combination* **күрреји-әрз** the terrestrial sphere *populated portion of the earth* 2) kitchen stove/oven

күрәви : *a* spherical, spheroidal

күрәк : *n* 1) spade, shovel 2) oar *anat* 3) back 4) shoulder-blade

күрәк чәзасы : *n* penal servitude

күрәкән : *n* son-in-law

күрәкли : *a* broad-backed *person*

күрәкчи : *n* rower, oarsman

күрәмәк : *v* dig out with a spade or shovel; uproot *s.t.*

күрән : *a* red-haired *person*

күрәтдирмәк : *v* cause someone to shovel up *s.t.*

күрәчи : *n* forge worker; furnace worker

күрәчик : *n dim* little ball

күрәшәкилли : *a* spherical, spheroidal, globular

күрк : *n* fur-coat; lambskin/shearling coat

күрклү : *a* wearing a fur-coat/lambskin/shearling coat

күрктикән, күркчү : *n* furrier, fur-dresser

күркүр : *n zool* kite *Falconidae sp.*

күрреји-әрз : *n* earth, world

күрсәк : *n zool* heat, oestrus

күрсү : *n* 1) chair, stool 2) rostrum

күрт : *n* sitting on eggs, hatching *of birds*

күрү : *n* caviar

күрүлү : *a* caviar

күрүмәк : *v* spade up, shovel up

күрүнмәк : *v* be spaded up, shoveled up, moved away, cleaned

күрүнтү : *n* remains, scrapings

күрүшмә : *n* embryo in an egg

күсдүмкүлү : *n bot* mimosa

күсдүрмәк : *v* 1) cause a quarrel 2) insult

күсәјән : *a* 1) easily offended/insulted 2) quarrelsome

күскү : *n* break-up *between parties formerly friendly*

күскүнлүк : *n* touchiness, susceptibility to offense

күсмә : *v* 1) misunderstanding, disagreement 2) quarrel; hostility

күсмәк : *v* quarrel; cease speaking to one another

күстаһ : *a* 1) rude, boorish, insolent 2) uneducated

күстаһлыг : *a* 1) rudeness, boorishness, insolence 2) lack of decency or respect

күсү : *n* quarrel, disagreement, dissention

күсүлү : *a* offended, insulted , not speaking to s.o.

күсүлүлүк : *n* state of not talking to one other, state of permanent enmity

күсүшмә : *v* quarreling

күсүшмәк : *v* quarrel, fall out, fail to come to an understanding *with s.o.*

күт : *a* 1) blunt, not sharp 2) stupid *n* 3) dull, stupid person 4) under-baked flatbread

күтбејин, күтбејинли : *a* stupid, dumb

күтбејинли(ли)к : *n* stupidity, dumbness

күтбучаглы : *a geom* obtuse-angled

күтлә : *n* mass

күтләви : *a* mass, popular

күтләвиләшдирмәк : *v* give *s.t.* a mass character, popularize *Communist jargon*

күтләвилик : *n* mass character of *s.t. Communist jargon*

күтләнмәк : *v* see **күтләшмәк**

күтләшдирмәк : *v* 1) blunt 2) thicken, condense, conceentrate

күтләшдиртмәк : *v caus of* **күтләшдирмәк**

күтләшмәк : *v* 1) become blunt 2) become thick/ccondensed/concentrated

күтлүк : *n* 1) bluntness 2) dumbness, slowness on the uptake; lack of talent

күтүм : *n* kütüm *species of scaleless, smooth-skinned fish indigenous to the southern area of the Caspian Sea*

күф, күфлән : *n* swing

күфр : *n* sacrilege

күфтә : *n* meat- balls

күчә : *n* 1) street; outside *a* 2) street

күчүк : *n* 1) puppy 2) cub, whelp *wild animals fig* 3) kid

күчүкләмәк : *v* 1) pup 2) whelp, cub*wild animals fig* 3) have a baby

күчүкләнмәк : *v* 1) be born *of a wild animal colloq* 2) butter up, lick s.o.'s boots, suck up to

К

к : fifteenth letter of the Azerbaijani alphabet

кавалы : *n* plum

кавалылыг : *n* plum-tree orchard

каваһын : *n* ploughshare

каллаһ : *n* buffalo herd

кап : *n* talk, conversation

каһ : *adv* 1) sometimes 2) either. . . or

каһданбир : *adv* sometimes, from time to time

каһ-каһ : *adv* ssometimes, from time to time

каһкир : *a* 1) obstinate; capricious; restive *horse*

каһкирләнмәк, каһкирләшмәк : *v* become/begin to be obstinate, become capricious; grow restive *horse*

каһкирлик : *n* obstinacy; capriciousness; restiveness

каһлы : *a* greatly creased *clothes*

кедә-кедә : *adv* en route, on one's way

кедиш : *n* 1) going away, departure 2) riding; walking, strolling; moving 3) process, course 4) move *in chess, checkers etc* 5) run, distance, haul *of a motor vehicle*

кедиш-кәлиш : *n* 1) relations, dealings, ties 2) walking, strolling; hanging around

кејдирмәк : *v* 1) cause *s.o.* to get dressed 2) put on clothes

кејилмәк : *v* 1) be dressed, be put on, worn 2) be set, put on its place

кејим : *n* clothes

кејимли : *a* dressed; wearing clothes

кејимли-кечимли : *a* 1) beautifully dressed, 2) elegant, smart

кејиндириб-кечиндирмәк : *v* dress *s.o.* up

кејиндирмәк : *v* 1) dress s.o. 2) adorn, dress out *s.t.*

кејиндиртмәк : *v* cause *s.o.* to dress *s.o. else* up

кејинәчәк : *n* dress, clothes, garb, attire

кејиниб-кечинмәк : *v* be dolled up/beautifully dressed

кејиникли : *a* beautifully/smartly dressed, dolled up

кејинмәк : *v* get dressed, put on one's clothes

кејмәк : *v* 1) put on; get dressed; cover the top of something n 2) clothes

кематит : *n* hematitis *iron-mining*

кен : *a* 1) wide, broad; spacious *a* 2) unrestrained, free 3) cold, alienated *of personal relations n* 4) gene *adv* 5) broadly, widely; spaciously ; at a distance

кен-бол : *a* spacious, roomy, ample

кен-боллуг : *n* 1) breadth; spaciousness 2) expanse, wide open spaces

кенерал : *n mil* 1) general *a* 2) general['s]

кенераллыг : *n* rank of general, generalship

кенератор : *n tech* generator

кенетик : *a* 1) genetic, inborn, innate *n* 2) geneticist

кенәлмәк : *v* broaden, widen

кенәлтдирмәк : *caus* of **кенәлтмәк**

кенәлтмәк : *v* broaden, widen, make wide

кениш : *a* 1) broad, wide 2) spacious, free *adv* 3) broadly, widely

кенишләдилмәк : *v* be broadened, be widened

кенишләндирмә : *n* broadening, widening

кенишләндирмәк : *v-tr* broaden, widen, expand

кенишләндиртмәк : *caus* of **кенишләндирмәк**

кенишләнмәк : *v* broaden, widen, expand

кенишлик : *n* expanse width, breadth

кентәһәр : *a* slightly too wide, slightly too broad, a bit wide, a bit broad

кенуја : *n* 1) Genoa *a* 2) Genoese

кеодезија : *n math* geodesy

кеодинамика : *n geol phys* geodynamics

кеокимја : *n geol* geochemistry

кеолог : *n geol* geologist

кеоложи : *a geol* geological

кеолокија : *n geol* geology

кеотектоника : *n geol* geotectonics

кеофизика : *n geol* geophysics

керб : *n* 1) arms, coat of arms 2) insignia, emblem of a *state/government, organisation*

кери : 1) *adv* back[wards] *n* 2) bottom, back part *of s.t.* n 2) result, that which follows as consequence *a* 3) backward, retarded

кери дөнмәк : *v* return, get back

кери дүшмәк : *v* lag behind

керидә : *adv* behind *of place, position*

керидән : *adv* from behind, from the rear

керијә : *adv* back, in the rear *direction*

керијәбахан : *a* retrospective

кери-кери : *adv* backwards, backing up *i.e. vehicle/person,*

кериләмәк : *v* go back, retreat; lag behind;

керилик : *n* backwardness, retardation

керисиндә : *adv* behind, beyond *of place*

керчәк : *a* 1) fair, just 2) true, authentic, actual *adv* 3) truly; actually 2) seriously, in earnest

керчәкдән : *adv* truly, seriously, in earnest

керчәкләнмәк : *v* be true, be fair

керчәклик : *n* 1) truth, veracity 2) authenticity, trustworthiness 3) actuality, reality

кетдикчә : *adv* gradually, still further, further and further

кет-кедә : *adv exp* the further. . . the more/the greater

кет-кәл : *n* 1) relations/intercourse/dealings, personal relations; vissiting, visit 2) traffic 3) *coll* procrastination, the run around, red tape

кетмәк : *v* 1) go, walk; get to; ride to 2) pass on, pass, depart, go away 3) be necessary 4) be on 5) lead to

кеч : *adv* 1) late *a* 2) late

кечганан : *a* dull, slow-witted, dim-witted

кечә : *n* 1) night *a* nocturnal, night

кечәгушу : *n* 1) owl *a fig* 2) sleepless

кечәјары : *n* midnight

кечәкәпәнәји : *n zool* nocturnal butterfly

кечә-күндүз : *n* 24 hour period

кечәләмәк : *v* spend the night, stay overnight

кечәләтмәк : *v* cause someone to spend the night, stay overnight

кечәлик : *n* days' worth, for. . . days : used after cardinal numbers in such expressions as **беш кечәлик ишим галыр** "I've got 5 days worth of work left" I've got work for 5 days left

кечәли-күндүзлү : *adv* 24 hours a day, daily and nightly

кечикдирмәк : *v* make s.o. be late 2) be slow in 3) keep back, retard, postpone, delay, put off

кечикмә : *vn* lateness, delay, hold-up

кечикмәз : *a* pressing, urgent, top-priority

кечикмәк : *v* 1) be late 2) be slow in, lag

кечјетишән : *a* late, late-ripening

кеч-тез : *adv* sooner or later

кәбә : *n* traditional Azerbaijani carpet, long and narrow and usually laid down along a wall

кәбәрмәк : *v* die, fall over dead *of animals*

кәбәтохујан : *n* carpet-weaver

кәбәчилик : *n* carpet-weaving

кәвәзә : *n* chatter-box, windbag

кәвәзәлик : *n* talkativeness, garrulity, volubleness

кәвәләмәк : *v* 1) chew 2) eat without appetite

кәвәнк : *n geol* tufa

кәда : *n hist* 1) serf, bondsman *fig pejor* 2) lackey, servile person

кәдә : *n* 1) boy *hist* 2) slave, bondsman, servant

кәдәк : *n* hem *of a skirt*

кәз : *n* 1) time 2) incision/cut/mark/notch *on a tree-trunk* 3) nougat

кәздәк : *n* col, saddle-shaped hollow at the crest a mountain

кәздирмәк : *v* give a ride, take s.o. *by vehicle*

кәзәјән : *a* 1) hare-brained, gadabout, wolfish *in dealing with women* 2) playboy, rolling-stone

кәзәл : *n* 1) purple dye *extracted from pomegranate rind* 2) pomegranate *in some dialects*

кәзән : *a* 1) wandering, roving 2) trampish, easy-going *of a woman* 3) contagious *of illnesses*

кәзәнти : *a* 1) fidgety *n* 2) a fidget

кәзәрки : *a* movable, portable

кәзинә-кәзинә : *v-adv* walking around, strolling around, hanging around

кәзинмәк : *v* walk around, stroll around, hang around

кәзинти : *n* 1) walk, stroll, promenade 2) outdoor festival

кәзиш : *n* 1) gait, manner of walking 2) beat, round *doctor/postman/guard*

кәзишмә : *vn* walking around, strolling around, hanging around

кәзишмәк : *v* 1) walk, stroll, go; travel; 2) rummage 2) hang around with *s.o.*. 3) have fun 4) pass through 5) show up, appear

кәзмәк : *v* 1) walk, stroll, go; travel 2) travel all over, travel over, traverse 3) go for a drive

кәјирмә : *n* belch, belching, burping eructation

кәјирмәк : *v* belch, burp

кәјирти : *n* belch, burp

кәл : *exp* 1) Come and. . . 2) Let's . . . *do s.t.*

кәлди-кедәр : *exp* extremely transient, temporary/ephemeral; Here today and gone tomorrow

кәлән : *a* 1) future, forthcoming *n* 2) future

кәләчәк : *a* 1) following, next 2) guest, newcomer

кәлиб-чыхмаг : *v* arrive, appear, show up

кәлин : *n* 1) fiancѐe; bride 2) daughter-in-law

кәлинчә : *adv* as far as *s.t.* is concerned

кәлинчик : *n* 1) puppet, doll *zool* 2) weasel *genus Mustela*

кәлир : *n* income, revenue

кәлирли : *a* profitable, income-generating

кәлирлилик : *n* profitability

кәлирсиз : *a* unprofitable, not income-generating

кәлирсизлик : *n* unprofitability

кәлир-чыхар : *n* profit and expences, debit and credit

кәлиш : *n* 1) coming, arrival *theater* 2) scene; entrance

кәлиш-кедиш : *n* 1) walking, going to and fro 2) interpersonal relations

кәл-кет : *n* see **кет-кәл**

кәлмә : *vn* fr. **кәлмәк**

кәлмәк : *v* 1) arrive 2) appear, arrise, spring up, come 3) obey, report 4) seem 5) act *v-intr* 6) weigh

кәлмәмәзлик : *n* non-attendance *at*

кәм : n 1) sieve n 2) bit *part of harness*

кәмалмасы : *n* paradise apple, *Malus sylvestris paradisiaca,* a dwarf variety of the common apple used for graft-stock

кәми : *n* 1) ship; steamer; boat *a* 2) ship['s]; steamer['s]; boat['s]

кәмигајыран : *n* ship-builder

кәмигајырма : *n* ship-building

кәмиринти : *n* butt, end, stump *of s.t.*

кәмиричи : *n zool* rodent

кәмиришмәк : *v* 1) gnaw each other, bite one another, fight *animals fig* 2) fight, quarrel

кәмирмәк : *v* gnaw; bite

кәмирчәк : *n anat* cartilage, gristle

кәмичи : *n* 1) navigator 2) sailor 3) ship owner

кәмичилик : *n* 1) seafaring 2) navigation

кәмищдирмәк : *v-tr* unhood and slip a hawk, release a hunting hawk *falconry*

кәмишмәк : *v* circle, or "wait on" while hunting for prey *of raptorial birds*

кәндалаш : *n bot* elderberry *Sambucus*

кәнә : *n zool* tick, mite

кәнәзә : *n bot* stinging nettle *Urtica*

кәнәкәрчәк : *n bot* castor-oil plant *Ricinus communis*

кәнәшмәк : *v-intr* consult, check *with s.o.*

кәнзик : *n anat* nasopharynx

кәнч : *a* young

кәнчләшдирмәк : *v* rejuvenate

кәнчләшмәк : *v* grow young again

кәнчлик : *n* 1) youth, youthfulness 2) young people, youngsters

кәнччәсинә : *adv* in a youthful manner, youthfully

кәр : *conj obs* if

кәрдәк : n curtain/screen traditionally placed before a bride's bed

кәрдән : *n* neck

кәрдәнбәнд : *n* necklace

кәрәк : *a* 1) necessary, needed *pred* 2) have to

кәрәкли : *a* necessary, suitable

кәрәклилик : *n* necessity, vital nature *of s.t.*

кәрәксиз : *a* 1) unnecessary, unneeded 2) unsuitable

кәрәксизлик : *n* uselessness, worthlessness

кәрилә : *a* spread wide, spread apart, opened wide

кәрилмә : *v* spreading apart, spreading wide

кәрилмәк : *v* spread apart, spread wide; bulge aside

кәркин : *a* 1) tense, intense 2) intensive *adv* 3) tensely, in a forced manner

кәркинләнмәк, кәркинләшмәк : *v* become strained, become tense

кәркинләшдирмәк : *v-tr* complicate, aggravate, worsen

кәркинлик : *n* tension; aggravation, aggravated situation

кәрмә : *n* 1) pulling on s.t., straining 2) spreading wide, sspreading apart 3) cattle-dung bricks *used as fuel*

кәрмәк : v 1) bulge; bulge o.'s eyes out in staring 2) spread wide *n* 3) special variety of melon

кәрмәшов : n 1) snowball tree, guelder-rose *Viburnum opulis* *a* 2) guelder-rose

кәрнәшмәк : *v* stretch oneself

кәрчәк : *n* *bot* castor-oil plant *Ricinus communi*

кәтирилмәк : *v* be brought, fetched, delivered

кәтиричи : *a* 1) purveyor 2) delivery-man 3) pedlar

кәтирмә : *vn* 1) of **кәтирмәк** *a geol* 2) alluvial, drift

кәтирмәк : *v* 1) bring, fetch 2) deliver 3) achieve

кәтиртдирмәк, кәтиртмәк : *caus* of **кәтирмәк**

кәч : *n* 1) plaster made up of gypsum and clay 2) putty

кизилдәмә, кизилти : *n* the creeps, goose-pimples *involuntary chills caused by fear, apprehension etc*

кизилдәмәк : *v* 1) cause a stitch *i.e. in the side* 2) give/cause colic pains

кизләдилмәк : *v* be hidden, concealed

кизләдичи : *n* concealer, harborer

кизләдичилик : *n* concealment

кизләмәк : *v* conceal, hide

кизләнгач : *n* hide-and-seek

кизләнә-кизләнә : *adv* stealthily

кизләнмәк : *v* be hidden, be concealed

кизләнпач : *n* hide-and-seek

кизләтдирмәк : *caus* of **кизләтмәк**

кизләтмәк : *v-tr* hide, conceal s.t.

кизли(н) : *a* 1) secret; mysterious 2) illegal, conspiratorial 3) intimate *adv* 4) secretly; incognito

кизли(н)говушма : *n* *bot* cryptogamy

кизли(н)лик : *n* 1) secrecy; security *of an illegal operation* 2) illegality 3) intimacy

кизлинч : *n* *mil* 1) cover, escort 2) underground work; hiding place *a* 3) secret, concealed, hidden *adv* 4) secretly

кизли(н)чә : *adv* secretly

кијәв : *n* son-in-law

киковун : *n* gadfly

кил : *n* 1) clay *a* 2) clay

килабы : *n* special type of alkali-rich clay used for laundering clothes and shampooing the hair

килавар : *n* southern hot and humid wind *in Baku, and the south-western Caspian Sea area*

килас : *n* 1) sweet cherry *a* 2) sweet-cherry

килдани : *n* *hist* Chaldean *a representative of the race that conquered and ruled Babylon* *a* 2) Chaldean

килди : *n* *hist* 1) guild 2) class, order *of merchants in Czarist Russia*

килеј, килеј-кузар : *n* 1) gripe, expression of dissatisfaction 2) complaints behind s.o.'s back

килејләнмәк : *v* gripe; grumble; complain; express dissatisfaction

килејли : *a* grumbling, dissatisfied, inclined to permanent complaints

килә : *n* 1) berry 2) droplet

киләк : *n* Gilyak member of a small nation in the north of Iran, and in Azerbaijan on the Iranian border

киләләмәк : *v* strip grapes from the bunch

киләләнмәк : *v* be stripped *of a bunch of grapes)*

киләмејвә : *n* 1) berry *a* 2) berry

киләнар : *n* sour cherry

киләнарлыг : *n* sour cherry orchard

килиз : *n* 1) cartridge-case, shell-casing 2) cigarette-wrapper

килјотин : *n* guillotine

килкилə : *n* hoopla *game*

килләндирмәк, килләтмәк : *v-tr* roll, move smth by rolling

килләнмәк : *v-intr* roll

килли : *a* clayey, argillaceous

киллик : *n* argillaceous area, area rich in clay

килмөhрә : *a* adobe

килторпаг : *n chem* alumina, aluminum oxide

кимназија : *n* gymnasium

кимрик : *a* grainy

кинеколог : *n* gynecologist

кинеколожи : *a* gynecological

кинеколокија : *n* gynecology

киперстен : *n min* hypersthene, *a pyroxene*

кипс : *n* 1) gypsum, plaster of Paris *a* 2) gypsum, plaster of Paris

кипсләмәк : *v* plaster, cover something with plaster

кипсләтдирмәк, кипсләтмәк : *v caus* of **кипсләмәк**

кир : *n* 1) power, strength 2) difficult/critical/tough situation *a* 3) tart, sharp, astringent

кирвәнкә : *n* the girvenk is equivalent to the *funt*, or pound, an old Russian unit of weight equal to 409.5 grams,

кирвәнкәлик : *a* weighing one girvenk

кирдаб : *n* whirlpool, eddy

кирдә : *a* rounded, roundish

кирдәағыз : *a* round-mouthed

кирдәләмәк, кирдәләндирмәк : *v* make round, round off

кирдәләндиртмәк : *caus* of **кирдәләмәк**

кирдәләнмәк : *v* become round/rounded

кирдәләтмәк, кирдәләшдирмәк : *v* see **кирдәләмәк**

кирдәлик : *n* sphericity, globularity

кирдәсифәт : *a* round-faced

кирдәчә : *a dim* round, round-shaped

кирдин : *n* log, billet

кирдирмәк : *v* 1) make *s.o.* put *s.t.* in/push *s.t.* in, cause *s.t.* to enter

кирeh : *n* vershok 1.75 inches *old Russian linear unit*

кирәвә : *n* 1) favorable opportunity, good chance 2) secret place; ambush; tracing, tracking, spotting

кирәвәләмәк : *v* 1) seize an opportunity, find an appropriate moment catch s.o. at the right time 2) capitalize on something 3) gain momentum

киринти : *n* hollow *place*, concavity

киринтили : *a* hollow, concave

киринти-чыхынты : *n* 1) hollows, uneven surface, ccnvolutions 2) warts and bumps

киринти-чыхынтылы : *a* uneven *surface*

кирифтар : *a* subject to *s.t.*, prone to *s.t.*

кириш : *n* 1) entrance, doorway 2) foreword, preface

кирищдирмәк, кирищдиртмәк : *v caus* of **киришмәк**

киришмә : *vn* fr. **киришмәк**

киришмәк : *v* start doing *s.t.*, get to some business

кирки : *n* colic, pains in the stomach

кирләмәк : *v* 1) attach o.s. to s.o., keep following s.o. around, harrass s.o. 2) put s.o. in a diffficult position

кирләнмәк : *v* 1) stray, err 2) loiter, dawdle 3) live, dwell 4) get along, take a temporary job just to earn a living wage

кирмә : 1) *vn fr.* **кирмәк** 2) entering, coming 3) bushy area

кирмәк : *v* 1) enter, come in, step/drop in 2) fit *into s.t.* 3) begin, start 4) pull over *i.e. a blanket* 5) reach, attain *some age*

киров : *n* 1) deposit, pledge pawned/mortgaged property 2) hostage

кирс : *n* dumpling *Azerbaijani style*

китара : *n* guitar

китарачалан : *n* guitarist

кич : *n* fool, idiot, dullard

кичбәсәр : *a* foolish, idiotic, dim-witted

кичбәсәрлик : *n* foolishness, idiocy, craziness

кичәлләндиричи : *a* overwhelming, stunning, breath-taking, stupendous

кичәлләндирмәк : *v* 1) cause giddiness, vertigo *fig* 2) cause the head to spin

кичәлләнмәк : *v* whirl/spin around *of the head*

кичәлмәк : *v* experience vertigo, feel giddy/unwell

кичәлтмәк : *v* see **кичәлләндирмәк**

кичик : *n* 1) see **кичишмә** *a fig* 2) foolish, idiotic, crazy, dim-witted

кичимәк : *v* play the fool; fool around

кичиткән : *n* nettle

кичиткәнанасы : *n* dead-nettle

кичиткәнли : *a bot* nettle *Urtica*

кичишмә : *n* itch, itching

кичишмәк : *v* itch

кичкаһ : *n anat* temple

кич-кич : *adv* foolishly, idiotically

кичләшмәк : *v* become foolish, crazy, idiotic, silly

кичлик : *n* idiocy, foolishness, crazyness, silliness

киш : *n* canvas

ковур : *n* giaour *non-Moslem*

код : *n* barrel,tun

кодгаjыран : *n* cooper

комбул : *n 1)* plump/fat/heavy-set man *a* 2) plump, fat, heavy-set

коп : *n* bragging, boasting

копа басмаг : *v* praise falsely

копламаг : *v* brag, boast

копчу : *n* braggart, boaster

копчулуг : *n* bragging, boasting

кор : *n* grave

корбакор : *n derog* food for the worms

корбиз : *a* powerful; strong

корда : *n* curved sword; broadsword

кордах, кордаһ : *n* virgin land

корешән : *n zool* 1) hyena *fig* 2) mean person

көбәк : *n* navel

көбәкпулу : *n* baby-present

көбәксапы : *n* umbilical cord, navel string

көбәксиз : *n* without a navel

көбәләк : *n* 1) mushroom *a* 2) mushroom-like, fungous, fungoid

көбәләквары : *a* mushroom-shaped

көвдә : *n anat* 1) body, torso *bot* 2) trunk *tree tech* 3) framework, hull

көвдәли : *a* big, huge

көвдәсиз : *a bot* 1) aculescent, having no trunk/stem *or apparently so*

көвшәjән : *n zool* 1) ruminant *a* 2) ruminant

көвшәк : *n zool* 1) ruminant 2) jaw *of ruminants*

көвшәмә : *vn* chewing, masticating

көвшәмәк : *v* chew, masticate

көдәк : *a* 1) short *adv* 2) shortly

көдәкбармаг : *a* short-fingered, stubby-fingered

көдәкбоj : *a* short, short-statured

көдәкбоjун : *a* short-necked

көдәкбуjнуз : *a* short-horned

көдәкганад : *a* short-winged

көдәкгуjруг : *a* short-tailed

көдәкдил : *a* short-tongued

көдәкдиш : *a* short-toothed

көдәкjунлу : *a* short-wooled

көдәклик : *n* briefness, shortness

көдәкөмүр : *n* not very long *of time*

көдәкөмүрлүк : *n* short life, short duration, ephemerality

көдәкпача : *a* short-legged

көдәксач : *a* short-haired

көдәкчә : *n* short sheepskin coat

көдәкчә : *adv* briefly, shortly

көдәлмә : *v* shortening

көдәлмәк : *v* shorten

көдәлтдирмәк : *caus* of **көдәлмәк**

көдәлтмәк : *v-tr* shorten, make short

көдән : *n* stomach, belly

көдәчик : *a dim* 1) rather short *in stature* 2) quite short, rather short *clothing etc*

көз : *n* 1) eye 2) aperture 3) source *of a stream* 4) pan *of scales* 5) eye *of needle*

көз ачмаг : *v* get a break

көз вериб ишыг вермәмәк : *v* harrass, chase around *s.o.*

көз вурмаг : *v* wink

көз гапағы : *n* eyelid

көз дәjмәк : *v* put an evil eye on, give the evil eye to

көз jашы : *n* tear

көз тикмәк : *v* stare at *s.o.*

көзә дәjмәк : *v* show up, be noticed

көзү су ичмәмәк : *v* distrust, dislike

көзағартмасы : *n* glare, angry look

көзаjдынлығы : *n* congratulation

көj гуршағы : *n* rainbow

көj даш : *n* blue vitriol, copper sulfate

көj jагут : *n* sapphire

көзалты : *adv* 1) secretly, without reporting *n* 2) marital prospect

көзгамашдырычы : *a* blinding, dazzling

көз-гаш : *n* eyes and brows

көз-гулаг : *n* eyes and ears

көздәјмә : *n* evil eye

көзәјары : *adv* by eye, by eyeball guess, approximately

көзәјичи : *n* darning needle

көзәк : *n* rope, tow-rope, cable

көзәкөрүнмәз : *a* 1) invisible *n* 2) invisible being

көзәл : *a* beautiful, pretty, good-looking, nice-looking

көзәлданышан : *a* eloquent person; skilled orator

көзәлләмә : *n* verse form in praise of feminine beauty

көзәлләнмәк : *v* become beautiful/pretty

көзәлләтмәк, көзәлләшдирмәк : *v* make pretty/handsome/beautiful/good-looking

көзәлләшдиртмәк : *caus* of **көзәлләшмәк**

көзәлләшмәк : *v* become beautiful, pretty, handsome, good-looking

көзәллик : *n* beauty, prettiness

көзәлчә : *a* 1) rather beautiful, quite pretty *adv* 2) good, well, very nice

көзәлчәсинә : *adv* beautifully

көзәм : *n* sheep's wool sheared at the end of summer

көзәмә : *v* darning

көзәмәк : *v* darn

көзәнәк : *n* knitting, embroidery

көзәнмәк : *v* be darned

көзәтләмә : *n* 1) guarding, attendance 2) expectation, waiting

көзәтләмәк : *v* 1) guard, attend 2) expect, await

көзәтчи : *n* 1) guard, sentry, watchman, patrol 2) observer; witness

көзәтчилик : *n* watching, guarding, oversight; observation

көзәчарпан : *a* noticeable, visible

көз-көз : *a* porous, spongy

көзкөрәси : *adv* openly, noticeably; obviously

көзләмә : *v* 1) waiting, awaiting, expectation 2) guarding 3) observation, observance

көзләмәк : *v* 1) wait, expect 2) guard, attend 3) observe

көзләнилмәдән : *a* suddenly, unexpectedly

көзләнилмәз, көзләнмәз : *a* sudden, unexpected

көзләнилмәзлик : *n* suddenness, unexpectedness

көзләнмәјән : *a* sudden, unexpected

көзләнмәк : *v* 1) be awaited, be expected 2) be guarded 3) be observed

көзләнмәксизин : *a* suddenly, unexpectedly

көзләтдирмәк : *caus* of **көзләмәк**

көзләтмәк : *v* make s.o. expect/guard/obsserve

көзләшмәк : *v* exchange glances, look at one other

көзлү : *a* 1) having eyes 2) having drawers, compartments, shelves

көзлүк : *n* 1) eye-glasses 2) small ventilating-window

көзлүклү : *a* 1) wearing eye-glasses 2) having a small window used for ventilation

көзлүкчү : *n* oculist; optician

көзмунчуғу : *n* amulet

көзоту : n bot eyebright *Euphrasia officinalis*

көзсәјримәси : *n* tic

көзсүз : *a* eyeless

көзучу : *adv* superficially

көзүачыг : *a* vigilant; farsighted, perspicacious

көзүачыглыг : *n* vigilance; perspicacity; farsightedness

көзүач : *a* greedy

көзүачлыг : *n* greed, covetousness

көзүбағлы : *a* with one's eyes closed; unaware, retarded, short-sighted

көзүбағлыча : *adv* blindly, without consideration, on the off-chance

көзүгыпыг : *n* 1) blind-man's buff *game* 2) conjuror, sleight-of-hand artist

көзүдојмаз : *a* greedy, insatiable

көзүити : *a* sharp-sighted; vigilant

көзүјашлы : *a* with tears in one's eyes, constantly grieving *for s.o.*

көзүјашлылыг : *n* tearfulness, weeping

көзүјумулу : *a* see **көзүбағлы**

көзүмчыхды : *n* oppression, persecution

көзүтох : *a* generous, moderate, temperate

көзүтохлуг : *n* generosity, moderation, temperance

көзчүк : *n dim* 1) eye 2) peep-hole *bot* 3) pansy *Viola tricolor hortensis*

көј : *n* 1) sky, heavens 2) bruise 3) miser, skinflint *a* 4) miserly, tight-fisted 5) *dark* blue; green, unripe

көјганад : *a* dove-color/dark blue-winged

көјдәндүшмә : *a* 1) out-of-the-blue, fallen from the sky *fig* unexpected *in a pleasant sense*

көјәм : *n* 1) blackthorn, sloe, wild plum tree *Prunus spinosa a* 2) sloe, blackthorn, wild plum

көјәрмәк : *v* 1) become blue; get a bruise; display/show blue 2) turn/come up green *of spring plants* 3) happen, come to life

көјәртә : *n* deck

көјәртәсиз : *a* undecked

көјәрти : *n* green plants, vegetation

көјәртисатан : *n* see **көјсатан**

көјәртмәк : *v* 1) grow, emerge 2) make s.t. blue; paint s.t. blue

көјәрчин : *n* 1) pigeon; dove *a* 2) dove-like, pigeon

көјәрчиноту : *n bot* verbena *herb*

көјәрчинсахлајан : *n* 1) pigeon-fancier 2) pigeon breeder

көјкөз, көјкөзлү : *a* blue-eyed

көј-көјәрти : *n* edible greens, green vegetables

көјлүк : *n* 1) blue color, bluish tint 2) green plants, greens, vegetation 3) bruise, contusion 4) miserliness

көјнәдичи : *a med* formicative, causing strong itching

көјнәдичилик : *a med* formication, property of evoking/causing strong itching,

көјнәмә : *vn* 1) fr. **көјнәмәк** 2) moaning, whining, sobbing 3) itch, ache 4) blowing *on the surface of a liquid*

көјнәмәк : *v* 1) itch 2) ache 3) sob quietly, moan, whine 4) blow *on the surface of a liquid*

көјнәтмәк : *caus* 1) of **көјнәмәк** 2) bother, worry, give trouble *to s.o.*

көјөскүрәк : *n med* whooping-cough, pertussis

көјрүш : *n bot* ash-tree *Fraxinus*

көјсатан : *n* green-grocer, produce merchant

көјумсов, көјумтраг, көјумтул : *a* blueish

көјүш : *n* see **көјшүк**

көјчәк : *a* pretty, beautiful

көјчәкләнмәк, көјчәкләшмәк : *v* become beautiful/pretty

көјчәклик : *n* beauty, prettiness, grace

көјчәчичәк : *n bot* 1) cornflower *Centaurea cyanus* 2) Jacob's ladder *Polemonium ceruleum med* 3) cyanosis

көјшәк : *a* ruminant

көјшүк : *n* cud

көл : *n* 1) lake 2) medallion *a* 3) lake, lacustrine

көлләндирмәк : *v* make a pond or an artificial lake

көлләнмәк : *v* grow into a lake/pool/puddle

көллүк : *n* lake region

көлмә : *n* small pond

көлмәчә : *n* puddle, pool, pond

көлмәч : *n* small puddle

көлшүнаслыг : *n* lymnology *lake science*

көмкөј : *a* dark- blue

көмрүк : *n* 1) duty, customs a 2) dutiable

көмрүксүз : *a* non-dutiable, not subject to the imposition of duty

көмрүкхана : *n* customs office, custom-house

көн : *n* cow-hide

көнбичән : *n* leather-cutter

көндәрилмә : *n* sending, submitting

көндәрилмәк : *v* be sent, mailed

көндәрмә : *n* 1) sending, mailing 2) parcel sent by mail

көндәрмәк : *v* 1) send; submit 2) dispatch s.o.

көндәртдирмәк, көндәртмәк : *caus* of **көндәрмәк**

көндоғрајан : *n* leather-cutter

көнисладан : *n* leather-soaker

көнүгалын : *a* 1) thick-skinned 2) slow thinker, dumb person

көрдүрмәк : *v-tr* make someone do s.t.

көрә : *prep* because of; due to; according to

көркәм : *n* 1) sight, aspect 2) face, appearance 2) shape, configuration

көркәмли : *a* 1) noticeable, visible 2) having an imposing look, appearance; 3) outstanding, famous

көркәмлилик : *n* imposing appearance, imposingness, presence

көркәмсиз : *a* unsightly, uncomely, plain-looking

көрмә : *vn* 1) fr. **көрмәк** 2) seeing; sight

көрмәдән : *adv* 1) in one's absence 2) by correspondence course, externallly

көрмәк : *v* 1) see 2) do *some kind of work*

көрмәли : *a* worthy of attention, worth mentioning, interesting

көрмәмиш : *a* greedy

көрсәнмәк, көрукмәк : *v* see **көрүнмәк**

көрүлмәк : *v* be done, be made, be executed *of work*

көрүм-бахым : *n* material support/assistance

көрүнмә : *n* appearing, showing up

көрүнмәдән : *adv* unnoticeably

көрүнмәз : *a* invisible

көрүнмәк : *v* 1) show up, become visible 2) seem 3) be visible, clear, obvious

көрүнүр, көрүнүр ки : *adv* it is evident that. . . it is probable that. . ., one must suppose. . ., apparently

көрүнүш : *n* sight, appearance

көрүш : *n* 1) meeting, date, appointment 2) opinion, point of view

көрүшмә : *v* see **көрүш** 1)

көрүшмәк : *v* 1) see, meet *s.o.* 2) talk to *s.o.* 3) greet s.o.

көрүшүк : *n* see **көрүш**

көстәрилмә : *n* show, demonstration

көстәрилмәк : *v* be shown, indicated, demonstrated

көстәричи : *n* 1) indicator 2) index

көстәриш : *n* order, direction

көстәрмәк : *v* 1) show, demonstrate, exhibit 2) show, present 3) exert influence , make effort *many other such combinations*

көтүр-гој : *n* considerations, pros and cons

көтүр-гој еләмәк : *v* consider *some opportunities*

көтүрә : *adv* 1) one by one, altogether 2) on a fixed price basis *of a contract*

көтүрәчилик : *n* fixed-priced work

көтүркә : *n mil* sword-belt

көтүрмәк : *v* 1) take, get 2) borrow, acquire *a habit, experience* 3) pick up *a skill/knowledge* 4) raise, elevate, lift 5) bear, endure

көтүртдүрмәк, көтүртмәк : *v caus* of **көтүрмәк**

көтүрүлмәк : *pass* 1) be taken, be gotten 2) be acquired, borrowed *of a skill, experience* 3) be picked up *of a skill/knowledge* 4) be raised/elevated 5) be endured/borne

көтүрүм : *n colloq* paralysis

көтүрүмлү : *a* 1) receptive, impressionable 2) susceptible

куја : *conj* 1) as if, as though *intj* 2) I say!

кумбулдамаг : *v* thump, bang *i.e. on the floor*

кумбулдатмаг : *v-tr* cause to thump *s.t. i.e. on the floor*

кумбулту : *n* crash, din; rattle

купамаг : *v* strike a hard blow

куппулту : *n* sound of a fist landing a blow

купсамаг : *v* hit, strike, thump

кур : *a* 1) strong, powerful 2) loud *voice* 3) luxuriant, succulent, closely packed *of vegetation* 4) splendid; magnificent 5) populous

курламаг : *v* see **курулдамаг**

курлуг : *n* loudness

курраһ : *n* 1) gushing out, spouting, spurting 2) coming in masses

курулдамаг : *v* 1) rumble, roar, burst out, crash out

курулдатмаг : *v caus* of **курулдамаг**

курулту : *n* rumble, roar, thunder, crash

курултулу : *a* roaring, rumbling, booming, noisy

курултучу : *a* 1) rumbling, roaring *n* 2) braggart, boaster

курһакур : *a* 1) unrelenting, deafening din/thunder *adv* 2) very loudly i

куршад : *n* downpour, pouring rain with thunder and lightening

кушә : *n* 1) corner; nook *a* 2) corner

кушәбәнд : *n* iron bracket

кушәнишин : *n* ascetic *person*

кушәнишинлик : *n* asceticism

күбрә : *n agr* fertilization

күбрәләмә : *n agr* fertilization

күбрәләмәк : *v agr* fertilize

күбрәләнмәк : *v agr* be fertilized

күбрәләтдирмәк, күбрәләтмәк : *caus* of **күбрәләмәк**

күбрәлик : *a* earmarked for/designated for fertilization

күвә : *n zool* clothes-moth

күвәнмәк : *v* 1) rely on *s.o./s.t.* 2) be proud, boastful

күвәч : *n* clay pot

күдаз : *n* 1) victim 2) ruin, destruction, death

күдә, күдәбој : *a* short *of a person*

күдмә : *n* spying, overhearing, eavesdropping, shadowing

күдмәк : *v* 1) lie in wait for, entrap, spy on overhear, eavesdrop on, shadow *s.o.* 2) guard; observe

күдүк : *n* shadowing, tailing

күдүкчү : *n* shadow, tail *person responsible for keeping track of the movememts of another*

күзәм : *n* sheep's wool of the autumn shearing

күзәр : *n* occasional visit to some place

күзәран : *n* 1) life, existence, way of life 2) earning one's living, living standard

күзәранлы : *a* prosperous, affluent

күзәранлыг : *n* means of subsistence, daily bread

күзәркаһ : *n* way, road, route

күзәшт : *n* 1) rebate, discount, concession; 2) compromise 3) condescension, 4) forgiving

күзкү : *n* looking-glass, mirror

күзкүгајыран : *n* mirror-master, mirror-maker

күзкүлү : *a* mirror

күзкүчү : *n* master mirror-maker

күзкүчүлүк : *n* manufacturing of mirrors, mirror production

күзлүк : *n* winter-sowing

күјүм : *n* güjüm, large copper jug, with neck and handle for transportation on the shoulder

күл : *n* 1) flower 2) rose 3) ornament, pattern, design

күлаб : *n* rose water

күлабдан : *n* vial for rose-water

күлабпуш : *n* vial for rose-water

күлбаз : *n* flower-fancier, flower-lover

күлбәсәр : *n* early cucumber

күлгабы : *n* flower-vase

күлдан : *n* flower-pot, flower-vase

күлдүрмәк : *v* make someone laugh, evoke laughter/a smile

күлдүрүчү : *a* 1) laughable 2) absurd, ridiculous

күләбәтин : *n* gold thread, silver thread

күләјән : *n* 1) idle laugher *zool* 2) golden-eye *Clangula bucephala,* a large diving duck

күлә-күлә : *adv* laughingly, smilingly

күләрүзлү : *a* welcoming, affable, cordial, friendly

күләш : *a* affable, friendly, full of *joie de vivre*

күләшдирмәк, күләшдиртмәк : *v caus* of **күләшмәк**

күләшлик : *n* affability, friendliness, *joie de vivre*

күләшмә : *n* wrestling

күләшмәк : *v* wrestle

күләшчи : *n* wrestler

күлзар, күлзарлыг : *n* 1) flower-bed 2) Güzlar *popular feminine name*

күллә : *n* bullet

күллә атмаг : *v* shoot

күлләбаран : *n* fierce gunfire; shooting to death

күлләләмә : *n* execution by gunfire/shooting

күлләләмәк : *v* shoot , shoot to kill

күлләлә(н)мә : *n* execution by gunfire/shooting

күлләләнмәк : *v* be shot to death

күлләләтдирмәк, күлләләтмәк : *v caus* of **күлләләмәк**

күлләмәк : *v* begin to flower/blossom 2) grow moldy/musty, become covered with mold

күлләсиз : *a* 1) blank, not loaded/charged *n* 2) blank cartridge

күллү : *a* 1) colored, flowered *n* 2) ornamented, decorated

күллүк : *n* flower-bed

күллү-чичәкли : *a* flower-covered, flower-strewn

күлмәк : *v* 1) laugh, burst out laughing 2) jeer at, ridicule, mock

күлмәли : *a* 1) funny, droll, laughable *adv* 2) funnily, laughably, amusingly, comically

күлмәхмәр : *n* panne-satin *dress material*

күлмых : *n* small nails

күлсатан : *n* florist, flower-seller

күлү : *a* scarlet, red

күлүл : *n bot* adonis, false hellebore *Adonis vernalis*

күлүмсәмә : *n* smile; smiling

күлүмсәмәк, күлүмсәнмәк : *v* smile, smile upon

күлүнч : *a* 1) funny; ridiculous, ludicrous *n* 2) mockery; laughing-stock, butt *adv* 3) funnily

күлүстан : *n* 1) flower garden, rose garden *fig* 2) paradise

күлүш : *n* laughter 2) way of laughing

күлүшдүрмәк : *v* cause a lot of people to laugh

күлүшмә : *n* general laughter

күлүшмәк : *v* laugh *many people together*

күлхәтми : *n bot* 1) mallow *Malva* , hollyhock 2) marshmallow *Althea*

күлчү : *n* 1) florist, flower-seller 2) flower-grower, floriculturist

күлчүлүк : *n* flower-growing, floriculture

күлшән : *n* flower-bed

күман : *n* 1) supposition, surmise 2) suspicion 3) hope

күмраһ : *a* bright, sharp, adroit, quick, hale and hearty

күмраһланмаг, күмраһлашмаг : *v* become adroit, quick

күмраһлыг : *n* excellent health, hale and hearty state ; good spirits/humor

күмүш : *n* 1) silver *a* 2) silver

күмүшләмәк : *v* silver, silver-plate

күмүшләтдирмәк, күмүшләтмәк : *v caus* of **күмүшләмәк**

күмүшлү : *a* silver-plated, decorated with silver

күмүшү : *a* silvery, silver-colored

күн : *n* 1) day 2) sun

күн ағламаг : *v* think of one's future

күнаһ : *n* fault, guilt, sin, transgression

күнаһкар : *n relig* 1) sinner; guilty person *a* 2) sinful, guilty

күнаһсыз : *a relig* 1) sinless; innocent; guiltless *adv* 2) sinlessly, guiltlessly

күнаһсызлыг : *n* 1) sinlessness; innocence 2) blamelessness, guiltlessness

күнаһсызчасына : *adv* innocently, without a trace of guilt

күнашыры : *adv* once in two days

күнбатан : *n* west

күнбәд, күнбәз : *n* dome; arch

күнбәкүн : *adv* daily; day after day

күндә : *adv* every day, daily

күндәлик : *a* 1) daily, constantly, routinely 2) ordinary, everday, routine *n* 3) agenda, daily routine; vital questions 4) diary, journal

күндән-күнә : *adv* day by day

күндоған : *n* east

күндүз : *n* 1) daytime, afternoon 2 adv in the afternoon

күнеј : *n* sunny side, sunny place

күнејли : *a* 1) located on the sunny side *n* 2) Oriental, resident of the Orient

күнәбахан : *n* sun-flower *Helianthus annuus*

күнәвәр : *n* sunny side

күнәмузд : *a* 1) daily, by the day *of pay* *adv* 2) by the day *of pay* *n* 3) dayworker *one paid by the day*

күнәмуздчулуг : *n* work paid by the day, day labor

күнәш : *n* sun

күнәшли : *a* sunny

күнјә : *n* 1) set-square; *tech* angle-iron, corner iron *geod.* 2) cross-staff *instrument for erecting a perpendicular*

күнкөрмүш : *a* 1) experienced, worldly-wise *n* 2) experienced/worldly-wise person

күн-күзәран : *n* life, existence

күн-күндән : *adv* every day, from day to day

күн-күнә : *a* 1) azure *n* 2) azure

күнләрчә : *adv* for days on end

күнлүк : *a* 1) one-day *n* 2) umbrella 3) peaked cap

күнорта : *n* 1) midday, noon *a* 2) midday, noon

күнү : *n* new wife *as opposed to a previous one*

күнүгара : *a* unhappy, unlucky, unfortunate

күнүгаралыг : *n* unhappiness, an unhappy, ill-starred life

күнүлүк : *n* relations between the various wives of one husband *in a polygamous marriage*

күнһесабы : *adv* on daily basis

күнчичәји : *n bot* heliotrop *Heliotropium*

күнчыхан : *n* east

күрз : *n mil hist* mace

күрзә : *n* 1) viper 2) dumplings

күруһ : *n* crowd, gang

күрчү : *n* 1) Georgian *person* *a* 2) Georgian

күрчүстан : *n* 1) Georgia *country* *a* 2) Georgian

күрчүчә : *adv* in Georgian *language*

күч : *n* 1) power; strength 2) force; violence

күч етмәк : *v* force; rape

күчү чатмаг : *v* cope *with s. t.*

күч-бәлә : *adv* hardly, scarcely, with great difficulty

күчдәндүшмә : *n* prostration

күчәһдирмәк : *v* *caus* of **күчәнмәк**

күчәнмә : *n* strain

күчәнмәк : *v* strain oneself

күчләндиричи : *n* amplifier

күчләндирмә : *n* amplification

күчләндирмәк : *v* 1) make stronger 2) amplify

күчләндиртмәк : *caus* of **күчләндирмәк**

күчләнмәк : *v* make stronger, become stronger

күчлү : *a* powerful, strong, mighty

күчлүлүк : *n* power, strength, force, might

күчөлчән : *n* dynamometer

күчсүз : *a* powerless, weak

күчсүзлүк : *n* powerlessness, weakness

күчүрләмә : *v* 1) violence 2) rape

күчүрләмәк : *v* 1) overpower 2) rape

күшад : *a* cosy, comfortable, spacious

Л

л : sixteenth letter of the Azerbaijani alphabet

лабораторија : *n* laboratory

лабүд : *a* 1) unavoidable, inescapable *adv* 2) see **лабүддән**

лабүддән : *adv* inavoidably, unescapably

лабүдлүк : *n* inevitability, unavoidability

лаваш : *n* Lavaş *Transcaucasian home-made bread baked from thin dough*

лаваша : *n* 1) jam made of sour fruits 2) pastille made of this jam 3) restraining bridle *used on a skittish horse during shoeing*

лавашгулаг : *a* lop-eared

лавта : *n* obstetrical forceps

лаггылдама : *n* gurgling

лаггылдамаг : *v* gurgle

лаггылдатмаг : *caus* 1) of **лаггылдамаг** 2) lap *up of animals*

лаггылты : *n* careless chattering, chit-chat

лагејд : *a* 1) careless, negligent indifferent *adv* 2) indifferently, carelessly, negligently

лагејдлик : *n* carelessness, negligence, indifference

лаг : *n* mockery, irony

лағагојма : *n* mockery, mocking, scoffing

лағар : *n* *agric* furrow

лағбаз : *n* mocker, scoffer, scorner, ridiculer

лағым : *n* *mil* 1) sapping, undermining 2) underground channel 3) sewage system

лағымчы : *n* *mil* 1) sapper 2) mine-layer 3) tunnel construction worker, *fig* underminer, plotter

лағлағы : *n* idle talker, chatter-box

лағлағылыг : *n* idle talk, chit-chat

лазым : *a* needed, due, necessary

лазыми : *a* necessary, needed

лазымынча : *adv* in a normal, appropriate way, manner, *comme-il-faut*

лазымлы : *a* needed, necessary

лазымсыз : *a* unneeded, unnecessary

лај : *n* layer

лајәншуур : *adv* mechanically

лајиг : *a* 1) worthy; worth *attention etc* 2) respectable, decent

лајигинчә : *adv* properly, in a proper way, as it should be

лајигли : *a* worthy; worth *attention etc*

лајигсиз : *a* indecent, undue, unworthy

лајиһә : *n* project, design, scheme

лајиһәчи : *n* designer, architect

лајла : *n* 1) lullaby 2) singing lullabies

лај-лај : *adv* in layers

лајлама : *n* layering, putting down layers

лајламаг : *v* layer, install layers, place in layers

лајланмаг : *v* be put/place/install in layers

лајлатдырмаг : *caus* of **лајламаг**

лајлатмаг : *v* make/oblige *s.o.* to put/place/install *s.t.* in layers

лајлы : *a* laminated, laminar, stratified, layered

лак : *n* 1) lacquer, varnish *a* 2) lacquer[ed], varnish[ed]

лакеј : *n* 1) man-servant *fig* 1) lackey, flunkey

лакејлик : *n* 1) servant's occupation/mentality *fig* 1) servility, flunkyism; toadyism

лакејчәсинә : *adv* servilely, obsequiously, fawningly

лакин : *conj* but, however

лакламаг : *v* lacquer, varnish

лакчәкән : *n* lacquerer, varnisher

лал : *a* 1) dumb, mute; quiet, noiseless *adv* 2) quietly, noiselessly

лалдили : *n* chirology, dactylology *study of the hand*

лалән *bot* : 1) tulip 2) poppy *Papaver* 3) Lalen *common feminine name*

laләзар : *n* flower-bed

лалыг : *a* overripe

лалыгламаг : *v* overripe

лалыглыг : *n* overripeness

лал-кар : *a* 1) deaf and dumb 2) silent, taciturn *adv* 1) silently, in complete silence

лаллашмаг : *v* 1) become mute 2) grow/become numb

лаллыг : *n* 1) muteness 2) numbness

ламәзһәб : *n* atheist, non-believer; godless/sacriligeous person

ламәһала : *n* stone, brick, clay fence

лампа : *n* lamp

лап : *adv* quite, at all, completely

лапдан,лаппадан : *adv* without any visible reason; suddenly, out of the blue

лапчын : *n* soft leather shoe

лапчынчы : *n* soft leather shoe-maker

лары : *n* a breed of large long-necked chickens

латајыр : *a* cynical, obscene, baudy

латајырчы : *n* cynic

латајырчылыг : *n* cynicism

латвија : *n* Latvia

латвијалы : *n* Latvian

латынча : *adv* in Latin

латыш : *n* Latvian

лат-лүт : *n* 1) round, flat stone 2) naked person 3) poor man

лах : *a* 1) loose, shaky, unsteady, hanging loosely 2) rotten, spoiled

лахлама : *n* swaying, loosening

лахламаг : *v* be loosened, be shaky/not firmly seated

лахлатмаг : *v* loosen *s.t.*

лахлыг : *n* looseness, unreliability

лахта : *n* clot, coagulation

лахталанма : *n* thickening, clotting, coagulation; curdling

лахталанмаг : *v* thicken, coagulate, clot; curdle

лахта-лахта : *adv* in clots, in curdles

лачын : *n zool* white falcon

лачивәрд : *n* 1) azure, light blue color *a* 2) azure, light blue

лачивәрди : *a* azure, light-blue

лејлач : *n* 1) inveterate hunter 2) devoted fan *sports*

лејләк : *n* 1) stork *a* 2) stork

лејсан : *n* 1) April showers 2) heavy shower, downpour, cloudburdt

лејтенант : *n* lieutenant

ленинчи : *n* 1) Leninist *a* 2) Leninistic

лент : *n* 1) ribbon, band 2) tape

лепрозори : *n* leprosarium, hospital for lepers *sufferers from Hansen's disease*

леһим : *n* solder; brazing solder

леһимләмә : *v* brazing; soldering

леһимләмәк : *v* braze, solder

леһимләнмәк : *pass* be brazed, be soldered

леһимләтдирмәк, леһимләтмәк : *caus* of **леһимләнмәк**

леһимли : *a* soldered, brazed

леһимсиз : *a* unsoldered, unbrazed

леһимчи : *n* solderer, brazer

леһинә : *postp* for, in favor *of s.o.*

леһмә : *n* slush, liquid mud

леш : *n* carrion, carcass, dead animals

лешјејән : *n zool* 1) vulture, carrion eagle 2) carrion crow

ләббадә : *n* 1) cloak, gown, robe 2) loose overall; cassock

ләбләби : *n* fried peas; fried beets

ләвазим, ләвазимат *n* belongings

ләвәнки : *n* kind of a fish dish

ләгәб : *n* nickname; pseudonym

ләғв : *n* abolition, voiding

ләззәт : *n* 1) taste 2) pleasure, amusement

ләззәт чәкмәк : *v* have fun; enjoy *s.t.*

ләззәтверичи : *n* tasty; pleasant, amusing

ләззәтләндирмәк : *v* make something tasty, pleasant, amusing; impart taste, pleasure, amusement

ләззәтләнмәк : *v* become tasty, pleasant, amusing

ләззәтли : *a* tasty, pleasant, amusing

ләззәтсиз : *a* 1) tasteless, insipid 2) distasteful, unpleasant

ләзиз : *a* tasty, pleasant, amusing

лэзки : *n* Lezghins *a people of north-eastern Azerbaijan and southern Dagestan*

лэзкиhэнки : *n* Lezghin folk dance

лэзкичэ : *adv* in the Lezghin language

лэjагэт : *n* merit, desert 2) decency, politeness, good manners 3) capacity, suitability, fitness

лэjагэтли : *a* 1) decent 2) polite 3) suitable

лэjагэтсиз : *a* 1) indecent 2) impolite

лэjагэтсизлик : *n* 1) indecency 2) impoliteness

лэjэн : *n* basin, tub

лэjэнчэ : *n dim* basin, tub

лэк : *n* 1) garden-bed 2) flower-bed

лэкэ : *n* 1) spot, stain *fig* 2) shame, disgrace

лэкэлэмэк : *v* 1) spot, stain *fig* 2) disgrace, defame, discredit, blacken the character/name *of s.o.*

лэкэлэндирмэк : *v* see **лэкэлэмэк**

лэкэлэнмэк : *v* 1) be spotted, stained *fig* 2) be shamed, compromised, have o.'s name blackened

лэкэли : *a* 1) covered with spots, stained *fig* 2) shamed, disgraced, discredited, blackened in name

лэкэрсиз : *a* ill-favored, unattractive, unprepossessing

лэкэсиз : *a* 1) spotless, stainless *fig* 2) pure, sinless, irreproachable

лэкэсизлик : *n* blamelessness, irreproachability,sinlessness

лэк-лэк : *adv* in rows, in beds *of a garden*

лэ'л : *n* ruby

лэлэ : *n* tutor

лэлэк : *n* 1) feather[s] 2) flight-feather *strong, stiff feather from the tail or wing* 3) full-fledging, plumage

лэлэклэнмэк : *v* 1) become fully fledged *fig* 2) become independent

лэлэкли : *a* 1) fledged, feathered *n* 2) bird

лэлэксиз : *a* featherless, unfledged

лэлэ-кирjан : *a* homeless, shelterless, neglected

лэлэш : *n your* obedient servant *of oneself; ironically polite*

лэлик : *n* begging, entreating

лэлимэк : *v* beg, entreat *i.e. tearfully*

лэлитмэк : *caus* of **лэлимэк**

лэлөjүн : *a* greedy; covetous

лэ'л-чаваhир : *n* 1) object of great value 2) precious stones

лэмэ : *n* shelf

лэмпэ : *n* ceiling

лэмс : *a* sluggish, phlegmatic

лэ'нэт : *n* damnation, anathema

лэ'нэтлэмэк : *v* damn

лэ'нэтлик : *a* damned, cursed

лэнк : *a* 1) slow 2) heavy 3) lame

лэнкэр : *n* 1) burden, ballast, heavy weight 2) balancing-pole used by tightrope-walkers

лэнкэрлэнмэк : *v* balance oneself, pitch and roll

лэнкэрли : *a* 1) balancing 2) heavy, weighty

лэнкимэ : *n* slowing down, deceleration, delay

лэнкимэдэн : *adv* immediately, without delay

лэнкимэк : *v* 1) slow down; delay 2) be late/tardy

лэнкитмэк : *v-tr* slow down, delay, retard

лэнклик : *n* slowness, sluggishness, unhurriedness

лэпэ : *n* 1) wave *bot* 2) seed of a dicotyledonous plant *walnut, almond etc*

лэпэдөjэн : *n* surf

лэпэлэмэк : *v* crack, husk, hull, shell

лэпэлэнмэ : *v* 1) cracking, husking, hulling, shelling 2) surging, swelling *of the sea*

лэпэлэнмэк : *v* 1) be cracked, be husked, be hulled, be shelled 2) be agitated/choppy, rippled *of the sea*

лэпэли : *a* 1) wavy 2) having a seed/kernel

лэпик : *n* smooth and flat stone

лэпир : *n* footprint

лэрзэ : *n* trembling, shaking, tremor

лэркэ : n *bot* vetchling, a leguminous plant *Lathyrus*

лэт : *a* 1) grumbling, peevish 2) sluggish, inert, indifferent

лэтафэт : *n* tenderness; grace, elegancy

лэтафэтли, лэтиф : *a* tender; gracious, elegant

лэтиф : *a* agreeable, delightful, charming, pleasant

лэтифэ : *n* joke, humorous story; anecdote

лэтлэшмэк : *v* become fat/flabby/paunchy

лэтлик : *n* flabbiness, paunchiness; sluggishness

ləhзə : *n* moment, instant, wink of time, twinkling of an eye

ləhləmək : *v* puff; be short of breath

ləhн : *n* tone, intonation

ləhчə : *n* dialect; accent

ləчək : *n* 1) kerchief *bot* 2) petal

ləчəкли : *a* *bot* petalous, petalled

ləчəксиз : *a* apetalous

ləчəр : *n* *pej* cantankerous, quarrelsome woman

ləч : *n* hater, enemy, archfiend

ləчləшмək : *v* hate each other, have mutual hostility towards one another

ləчлик : *n* dislike, hatred, hostility

либас : *n* clothes

либерал : *n* 1) liberal *a* 2) liberal

либераллашмаг : *v* become a liberal

либераллыг : *n* liberal views

лидер : *n* *Ru* leader

лил : *n* 1) silt; slime, ooze 2) blueing

лилləмək : *v* 1) silt; cover with slime, ooze 2) blue *clothes*

лилləнмək : *v* 1) be silted; be covered with slime, ooze 2) be blued *fig* 3) remain for a long time in the same place

лилləтмək : *caus* of **лилləмək**

лиман : *n* 1) port, bay; harbor *a* 2) port, bay; harbor

лимон : *n* 1) lemon *a* 2) lemon, lemony

лимонлу : *a* with lemon

лимфа : *n* lymph

лимфатик : *a* lymphatic

линк : *n* 1) crow, crow-bar 2) lever

линкləмək : *v* lift, pick up something with a crow-bar

линотип : *n* 1) linotype *a* 2) linotype

линотипчи : *n* lynotypist, linotype machine operator

лирə : *n* lire; pound *monetary unit of Italy,Turkey, Egypt*

литва : *n* 1) Lithuania *a* 2) Lithuanian

литвалы : *n* Lithuanian

литвача : *adv* in Lithuanian *language*

литиум : *n* *chem* lithium

литолоkиja : *n* lithology *science of the structure and composition of rocks*

литосфер : *n* 1) lithosphere *a* 2) lithospheric

лиф : *n* *anat* 1) fiber 2) wisp 3) filament

лифə : *n* belt of a skirt or pants

лифəли : *a* having a rolled edge through which a belt, or cord may be pulled *of garments*

лифли : *a* 1) filamentous *anat* 2) fibrous

лифт : *n* elevator

лифтчи : *n* elevator attendant/operator

лифчик : *n* *Ru* brassiere

личим : *n* shabby looking, shabby appearance

лjук : *n* hatch

лыгга : *n* slush, liquid mud

лыгтылты : *n* plopping, splashing *of water*

лығ : *n* slush, liquid mud

лыға : *n* dregs *of society*

лығырса : *n* incompletely baked bread

лыртлашмаг : *v* become porous

лобjа : *n* beans

ловға : *a* haughty, arrogant; boastful

ловғаланмаг : *v* be haughty, arrogant; be boastful

ловғалашмаг : *v* become haughty, arrogant; become boastful

ловғалыг : *n* haughtiness, arrogance; boastfulness

логгулдамаг : *v* bubble; boil; gurgle

логгулдатмаг : *v* lap

логгулту : *n* bubbling; boiling, gurgling

ломба : *n* liquid clump; loose clump

лопа : *n* flakes *snow or cereal*

лопабығ : *a* 1) large-moustached *n* 2) a man with big moustaches

лопуг : *n* finger tap on the pushed out/blown out cheek

лору : *a* vulgar, popular ; vernacular *of speech*

лоту : *n* *colloq* 1) person belonging to the fringes of the criminal world, shady individual 2) guy, man *general term for a male person*

лоту-бамбылы : *n* 1) fop, coxcomb *fig* 2) old fox

лотубечə : *a* 1) prompt, active, lively *n iron* 2) wise guy

лотулуг : *n* crookedness, petty thievery

лоту-поту : *n* crooks, thieves

лош : *a* 1) fat and flabby, sluggish, inert 2) baggy *n zool* 3) turkey

ләвбәр : *n* 1) anchor *a* 2) anchor

ләвбәр атмаг : *v* cast an anchor

ләвhә : *n* 1) board; plate 2) sign-board, advertisement *sign* 3) picture

ләвhәјазан : *n* 1) painter *artist*

ләвhәчик : *n dim* 1) picture 2) board 3) plate

ләкдодаг : *a* thick-lipped person

ләккүлдәмәк : *v* 1) miss a beat *of the heart* 2) miss a step *of a horse* 3)) have a throbbing pain

ләкләмә : *n* gallop *of a camel*

ләкләмәк : *v* gallop *of a camel*

ләкүд : *n* underboiled/incompletely cooked rice

ләhран : *n* virgin land, virgin soil

ләhрәм : *n* 1) race-horse *a* 2) race-horse

луғаб : *n* mucus; slime

луғаблы : *a* mucous; slimy

луғаблылыг : *n* mucosity; sliminess

луғәт : *n* 1) dictionary *a* 2) dictionary, lexicographic

луғәтчи : *n* lexicographer, dictionary compiler

луғәтчилик : *n* lexicography

луғәтчә : *n* pocket dictionary

лүзум : *n* need, necessity

лүзумлу : *a* necessary, needed, requisite

лүзумсуз : *a* unnecessary, unneeded, not required

лүзумсузлуг : *n* superfluity, lack of necessity

лүл, лүл-гәнбәр : *a* dead-drunk, sloppy-drunk

лүлә : *n* 1) muzzle *of a gun*; orifice 2) jet 3) icicle 4) faucet, spout 5) tube; tubular object

лүләјигырыг : *a* broken spouted *of a tea kettle*

лүләк : *n* faucet; nose/spout *of some object*

лүләкабаб : *n* barbecued ground meat *cooked on a skewer*

лүләләмәк : *v* wrap s.t. into a tubular shape

лүләмаја : *n* 1) soft-shelled egg laid prematurely by a hen 2) healed wound

лүлләнмәк : *v* drink o.s. dead-drunk

лүмә, лүмәк : *a* 1) dock-tailed, bob-tailed 2) acaudal, tailless *of birds*

лүт : *a* 1) naked, stark-naked, undressed 2) impoverished *n* 3) poor man, pauper

лүтеран : *n* 1) Lutheran *a* 2) Lutheran

лүтеранлыг : *n relig* Lutheranism

лүтләндирмә : *n* 1) denudation 2) baring, uncovering

лүтләндирмәк : *v* 1) denudate 2) strip bare *fig* lose everything one has

лүтләнмәк, лүтләшмәк : *v* denude; undress oneself completely

лүтлүк : *n* 1) nakedness 2) extreme poverty

лүт-мәдәрзад, лүт-үрјан : *adv* quite naked, nude, buck-naked

лүтф : *n* favor, service, merciful kindness

лүтфән : *expr* Do me a favor, Be so kind as to. . .

лүтфкар : *a* merciful; courteous, polite

лүтфкарлыг : *n* courteousness *towards s.o.*

М

м : seventeenth letter of the Azerbayjani alphabet

маариф : *n* education, learning, enlightenment

маарифләндирмәк : *v* educate s.o.

маарифләнмәк : v get/become educated

маарифпәрвәр : *n* 1) educator, enlightener *a* 2) educational

маарифчи : *n* educator, educationalist

мааш : *n* salary, wage

маашла : *adv* on salary

маашсыз : *adv* without salary, unpaid

мави : *a* light-blue

мавијәчалан : *a* light-blueish

магас : *n* railroad switch

магасчы : *n* switchman *railroad*

маггаш : *n* pincers, nippers, forceps

магнезиум : *n chem* magnesium

магнит : *n* magnet

магнитафон : *n Ru* tape-recorder

магнитләндирмәк : *v* magnetize

магнитләнмәк, магнитләшмәк : *v-intr* get/become magnetized

магнитлик : *n* magnetic property

магнитсизләшдирмәк : *v* demagnetize

мағаза : *n* 1) store, shop *a* 2) store, shop

мағазачы : *n* store-keeper, shop-keeper

мағара : *n* 1) cave *a* 1) cave

мағул : *exp* Well, to be sure !

мадам ки : *conj* since, seeing that

маддә : *n* 1) matter substance; essence 2) article, item; clause, paragraph, point

маддәбамаддә, маддә-маддә : *adv* 1) by paragraphs, paragraph-by-paragraph; clause-by-clause

мадди : *n* material, substantial, substantive physical

маддилик : *n* palpability, palpableness, substantiality

мадәршаһлыг : *n* matriarchy

мадјан : *n* mare

мажор : *mus* 1) major key *a* 2) major-key

мазаг : *n* 1) joke 2) flirtation

мазаглашмаг : *v* 1) joke, kid, fool around 2) flirt

мазғал : *n* *mil* embrasure, firing port, loop-hole *in a fortress wall*

мазы : *n* 1) oak gall, oak apple, gallnut *round lesion caused on an oak tree by an insectt* 2) ball *used in games* 3) coniferous tree

мазы-мазы : *n* ballgame

мазут : *n* 1) black oil, petroleum residue; fuel oil

мазутламаг : *v* oil/grease with black oil, petroleum residue

мазутланмаг : *v* be greased/coated/daubed with black oil

мазутлу : *a* coated/daubed with black oil

маил : *a* 1) inclined to, disposed to 2) sloping, slanting, inclined 3) favorable, gracious

маиллик : *n* 1) slope, incline, declivity 2) tendency, proclivity, penchant

мај : *n* 1) May *month* *a* 2) May

маја : *n* 1) leaven, yeast; ferment 2) embryo *fig* 2) foundation,basis; 3) she-camel

мајабаш : *adv* neither profit nor losses

мајак : *n* *Ru* light-house

мајалама : *n* leavening, fermenting

мајаламаг : *v* leaven, ferment

мајаландырма : *n* impregnation, fertilization, conception

мајаландырмаг : *v* 1) impregnate, fertilize 2) conceive

мајаллаг : *n* somersault

мајаллаг ашмаг : *v* somersault

мајбөчәји : *n* *zool* 1) wingless beetle *Meloe*

маје : *n* 1) liquid *a* 2) liquid

мајеләшдирмәк : *v* 1) dilute, thin 2) liquify, turn to liquid

мајеләшмә : *n* liquifaction,transition into a liquid state

мајеләшмәк : *v-intr liquify,* become liquid

мајәһтач : *n* kitchen utensils, domestic equipment

мајка : *n* *Ru* T-shirt; undershirt

мајмаг : *n* 1) milksop 2) slow-witted person, scatter-brained person 3) kneading trough *a* 4) sluggish, slow, slow-witted

мајмаглыг : *n* 1) clumsiness, awkwardness, 2) sluggishness, slowness of wit 3) milksop-ishness

мајор : *n* *mil* major

макара : *n* reel, coil; bobbin *in sewing/knitting/weaving machines*

макарон : *n* 1) macaroni *a* 2) macaroni

македонија : *n* 1) Macedonia *a* 2) Macedonian

македонијалы : *n* Macedonian

макина : *n* typewriter

макиначы : *n* typist

макиначылыг : *n* typing, work/occupation of a typist

магистрал : *n* main highway; railroad trunk line

мал : *n* 1) goods; property 2) wealth, substance; estate 3) livestock *fig* 4) silly/stupid/dull person

мала : *n* 1) plaster, stucco 2) plaster grinder *device* 3) latch 3) harrow

мала чәкмәк : *v* 1) plaster 2) harrow

малај : *n* 1) lad, young fellow, guy 2) Malayan

малајыран : *n* sorter; distributor

малакан : *n* the Molokane, a Russian Christian sect. Several dozen villages in Azerbaijan are inhabited by its adherents

малакеш : *n* plasterer

малакешлик : *n* profession of plasterer

малаламаг : *v* 1) harrow 2) plaster, apply plaster

малаланмаг : *pass* 1) be harrowed 2) be plastered

малалатдырмаг, малалатмаг : *caus* of **малаламаг**

малачәкән, малачы : *n* plasterer

малбаш : *a* 1) stupid, dull, idiotic *n* 2) big-headed perosn

малбашлыг : *n* silliness, stupidity

мал-гара, мал-давар : *n* livestock; cattle

малдар : *n* cattle-breeder

малдарлыг : *n* cattle-breeding, cattle-raising

малдили : *n* *bot* cactus

малиjjә : *n* 1) finances *a* 2) financial

малиjjәт : *n* value, price

малиjjәчи : *n* financier

малик : *n* 1) owner, possessor *a* 2) owning, possessing

маликанә : *n* 1) farmstead, estate, real property *hist* 2) feudal estate

мал-микнәт, мал-мүлк : *n* property, assets, estate

малотаран : *n* herdsman

малсыз : *a* propertyless, owning no goods, having no livestock

малхулjа : *n* melancholy, depression

малхулjалы : *a* melancholy, depressed

малхулjачы : *n* melancholic *person*

малчибини : *n* *zool* horsefly *Tabanidae*

малчанлы : *n* careful, thrifty owner *of property*

мама : *n* *med* 1) midwife 2) mama 3) see **биби**

мамалыг : *n* obstetrics, midwifery

мамача : *n* midwife

мамачалыг : *n* profession of midwife

мамыр : *n* *bot* moss

мамырлы : *n* mossy

ман : *a* unacceptable, impermissible; shameful

манат : 1) manat *basic monetary unit of Azerbaijan* 2) ruble

манатлыг : *n* 1) one manat bill 2) one ruble bill

манга : *n* 1) link *of a chain* 2) group, team

мангабашы : *n* chief of a group/team

мангал : *n* brazier, hearth

манган : *n* *chem* manganese

манго : *n* mango

мангур, мангыр : *n* half-kopek piece

мандолина : *n* *mus* mandolin

мандолиначалан : *n* mandolin-player

мане : *n* 1) obstacle, interference *a* 2) interfering, obstructing

маневр : *n* maneuver

манеә : *n* obstacle, nuisance

манеәли : *adv* obstructively, interferingly

манеәлик : *n* obstacles, impediments, nuisances

манеәсиз : *a* 1) clear, unimpeded *adv* 2) unimpededly

манечилик : *n* obstacles, impediments nuisances

манжет : *n* cuff

манивела : *n* 1) crank, lever

маникүр : *n* manicure

маникүрчү : *n* manicurist

мантар : *n* cork

манчанаг : *n* 1) winch for raising water from a well; shadoof, or counterpoised sweep used for that purpose *hist* 2) catapult *device for hurling stones*

мараг : *n* interest, curiosity

марагландырмаг : *v* cause/arouse interest or curiosity

марагланмаг : *n* be interested, be curious

мараглы : *a* 1) interesting, abssorbing *adv* 2) interestingly, abssorbingly

марагсыз : *a* 1) uninteresting, holding no interest 2) indifferent, non-participatory *adv* 3) uninterestingly, boringly, tediously

марал : *n* *zool* deer, fallow-deer

маргарин : *n* margarine

мари : Mari *a people of the middle Volga region*

маричә : *adv* in Mari *language*

марыг : *n* 1) ambush 2) pursuit

марыт : *n* point *of a dog*

марытламаг : *v* 1) set on a point *of a dog* 2) follow, shadow

марка : *n* 1) postage stamp 2) mark, brand

маркаламаг : *v* 1) mark 2) stick postage stamps on

маркалы : *a* stamped

маркасыз : *a* unstamped

марксизм : *n* Marxism

марксист : *n* 1) Marxist *a* 2) Marxist

марксистчәсинә : *adv* in a Marxist way/manner

марн : *n* *geol* dense siliceous clay

марс : *n* *astron* 1) Mars *planet* 2) Mars : double game loss *in dominos*

март : *n* *Ru* March

мартыгушу : *n zool* kingfisher *fam. Alcedinidae*

марч : *n* smacking kiss, loud, juicy kiss

марчмарч : *n* protracted smacking/loud,juicy kisses

марчылдатмаг : *v* 1) give a smacking/loud, juicy kiss 2) smack the lips *while eating*

марчылты : *n* 1) smacking/loud,juicy kiss, smacking/loud,juicy kissing 2) smacking the lips while eating

маршал : *n mil* 1) marshal *a* 2) marshal['s]

маршаллыг : *n mil* rank of marchal

масаж : *n* 1) massage *a* 2) massage

масажламаг : *v* massage

масажчы : *n* masseur, masseuse

масгара : *n* 1) joke, fun 2) parody

масгарачы : *n* 1) joker, prankster, clown 2) parodist

масыра : *n* spool, bobbin

маска : *n* mask

маскаламаг : *v* 1) mask 2) disguise, camouflage

маскаланмаг : *pass* 1) be masked 2) be disguised, be camouflaged

маскалы : *a* 1) masked 2) disguised camouflaged

масон : *n* 1) mason, freemason *a* 2) masonic

масонлуг : *n* masonry, freemasonry

мат : *n* mate, a check-mate *chess*

матаһ : *n* dainty, delicacy, jewel, rarity, *Equivalent to " my darling ", often ironic ; fr. Persian, lit. goods, things, property*

мат галмаг : *v* be amazed, astounded, shocked

матгаб : *n* drill; gimlet, auger

материализм : *n* materialism

материалист : *n* materialist

материалистчәсинә : *adv* materialistically

матәм : *n* 1) mourning *a* 2) mourning

мат-мат : *adv* in surprise, in astonishment

мат-мәәттәл : *adv* 1) in a state of bewilderment/perplexity 2) in a helpless state

матра : *n* flask; waterbottle, canteen

матрис : *n* matrix

матрос : *n* 1) sailor *a* 2) sailor['s]

матрослуг : *n* profession of sailor

матросчасына : *adv* in a sailor's/seaman-like manner

мафар : *n* opportunity; possibility

мафә : *n* 2) hearse 2) catafalque, bier

маһал : *a* 1) impossible *n* 2) region, province; county

маһач-гала : *n* Makhach-Kala *capital of Dagestan, on the western coast of the Caspian Sea*

маһиjjәт : *n* essence, nature, spirit

маһиjjәтчә : *adv* in essence, really and truly, virtually, essentially

маһиjjәт е'тибары илә : *adv* in essence, really and truly, virtually, essentially

маһир : *a* skilful, adroit, gifted, talented

маһиранә : *adv* skillfully, adroitly

маһирләшмәк : *v* become skillful, become gifted, talented

маһирлик : *n* talent, giftedness, natural endowments, virtuosity

маһлыч : *n* ginned cotton

маһмыз : *n* 1) spur *bot* 2) nectary *spur-like projection of a corolla or calyx*

маһмызламаг : *v* set spurs; spur

маһмызлы : *a* equipped with spurs

маһны : *n* song

маһраса : *n* 1) monk *a* 2) monk's, monkish

маһуд : *n* 1) cloth, broadcloth *a* 2) cloth, broadcloth

маһур : *n mus* a middle-eastern classical melody

мач : *n* kiss

мача : *n* 1) shank-meat 2) shank (of dressed beef)

мач : *n* shaft of a wooden plough

мачал : *n* 1) opportunity (as determined by time) 2) leisure, rest

мачалсызлыг : *n* lack of free time

мачар : *n* 1) Hungarian, Magyar *a* 2) Hungarian, Magyar

мачарыстан : *n* Hungary

мачарча : *adv* in Hungarian *language*

мачәра : *n* 1) adventure, escapade, occurence 2) event, happening; occasion

мачәрачы : *n pej* adventurer

мачкир : *n* ploughman

мачуна : *n* winch; windlass

маша : *n* pliers; pincers

машаллаһ : *exp* Thank God!; Cross your fingers! May you be preserved from the evil eye! *lit. in Arabic: "How great is God"*

машара : *n* erysipelas, St. Anthony's fire, staphyllococcus infection

машинист : *n* locomotive-engineer

машинистлик : *n* profession of locomotive-engineer

машын : *n* 1) machine 2) car, automobile *a* 3) machine, mechanical

машынгајыран : *n* 1) machine-constructor, mechanical engineer *a* 2) machine-construction, mechanical engineering

машынгајырма : *n* machine-construction, mechanical engineering

машынгуращдыран : *n* automobile assembly-line worker

машынлащдырылмаг : *pass* be mechanized

машынлащдырма : *n* mechanization

машынлащдырмаг : *v* mechanize *i.e. transform a manual process to a machine operation*

машынсазлајан : *n* machine fitter, machine repairman

МДБ : *n* CIS

мебел : *n Ru* 1) furniture *a* 2) furniture

мабелгајыран : *n* furniture-maker

мебелли : *a* furnished

мебелчи : *n* furniture-maker

медал : *n* 1) medal *a* 2) medal

медалјон : *n* medallion

медаллы : *a* 1) decorated *awarded a medal* *n* 2) medalist

медиан : *n geom* median

между прочим : *intro-wd Ru* by the way

меј : *n* wine

ме'јар : *n* criterion

мејвә : *n* 1) fruit *a* 2) fruit

мејвәгурудан : *n* 1) fruit-dryer *person* 2) fruit-dryer *device*

мејвәјыған : *n* fruit-picker

мејвәкөк : *n* root, plant with edible roots

мејвәли : *a* fruit-bearing, fruitful

мејвәлик : *n* fruit-orchard

мејвәлилик : *n* fruitfulness

мејвәсатан : *n* fruit merchant; fruit salesman

мејвәсиз : *a* unfruitful, fruitless, sterile, barren

мејвә-тәрәвәз : *n* 1) fruits and vegetables *a* 2) fruit-and-vegetable

мејвәчи : *n* fruit-grower

мејвәчилик : *n* fruit-growing

мејвәчат : *n* fruits and berries

мејдан : *n* 1) square, plaza 2) arena 3) battlefield

мејдана кәлмәк : *v* appear; come *from a certain source*

мејдана кәтирмәк : *v* create, form, bring to life

мејданча : *n* playground

мејзар : *n* apron

мејит : *n* 1) corpse, cadaver, dead body *a* 2) corpse-like, cadaveric

мејит намазы : *n* dirge, funeral service

мејитхана : *n* morgue

мејл : *n* 1) slope, declivity 2) inclination; trend, tilt towards, tendency

мејлли : *a* inclined to, disposed to

мејлсиз : *a* 1) stubborn, persistent 2) unwilling, disinclined, reluctant

мејлсизлик : *n* 1) aversion, reluctance, disinclination 2) unwillingness

мејмун : *n* monkey; ape

мејмунабәнзәр : *a* simian, ape-like

мејмунлуг : *n* aping, imitating s.o., grimacing, making faces

мејмунојнадан : *n* 1) aper, imitator 2) person who keeps laughing at/poking fun at others

мејмунсифәт : *a* 1) ugly *n* 2) ugly person

мејмунчуг : *n* lock-pick; master-key, skeleton-key

мејнә : *n* grape-vine

мејнәгурду : *n zool* phylloxera *insect attacking grape vines*

мејнәлик : *n* vineyard

мејрулу : *n* bunch of grapes with small, underdeveloped berries

мејхана : *n* 1) dukhan *Caucasian inn* 2) chastushka, couplet, a two-line rhymed poem or ditty on a topical or humorous theme

мејханачы : *n* inn-keeper; bar-tender

мејхош : *a* sweet-sour

мексика : *n* 1) Mexico *a* 2) Mexican

мексикалы : *n* a Mexican

мелодрам : *n* melodrama

ме'мар : *n* architect

ме'марлыг : *n* 1) architecture *a* 2) architectural

меншевик : *n* Menshevik *member of the conservative wing of the Social-Democratic Party in pre-revolutionary Russia*

меншевиклик : *n* Menshevism *affiliation to the conservative wing of the pre-revolutionary Russian Social-Democratic Party*

ме'рач : *n relig* Ascension *the bodily ascent of Jesus into Heaven after the resurrection*

меркел : *n geol* marl *mineral deposit which serves as the raaw material for cement*

местком : *n Ru* local trade union committee *at a Soviet enterprise or organization*

метал : *n* 1) metal *a* 2) metallic

металəридəн : *a* metal-smelting

металкəсəн : *n* metal-cutter

металлашдырмаг : *v* metallize, coat with metal

металлуржи : *a* metallurgical

металлуркија : *n* metallurgy

метеор : *n* meteor

метеороложи : *a* meteorological

метеоролокија : *n* meteorology

метод : *n* method

методик : *a* methodical

методоложи : *a* methodological

методолокија : *n* methodology

методсуз : *a* unmethodical

метр : *n* 1) meter *a* 2) metric

метроложи : *a* metrological

метролокија : *n* metrology *the science treating of weights and measures*

механик : *n* mechanic

механика : *n* mechanics

механики : *a* mechanical

механиклəшдирилмəк : *v* be mechanized

механиклəшдирмə : *n* mechanization, automation

механиклəшдирмəк : *v* mechanize

механиклəшмəк : *v* become mechanized, automated

меһ : *n* light wind, breeze

меһвəр : *n* 1) axle *a* 2) axle, axial

меһдизм : *n* Mahdism *expectation of the coming of the twelveth, and last Imam as a predecessor of the Holy Prophet*

меһдијун : *n* Mahdists *Moslems who expect the imminent coming of the Mahdi*

меһман : *n* guest

меһманхана : *n* hotel

меһманханачы : *n* owner of a hotel

меһр : *n hist* ransom paid by the husband-to-be for his bride

меһраб : *n* altar

меһрибан : a 1) kind, affectionate 2) friendly; courteous *adv* 3) affectionately in a friendly way; courteously 3) Mehriban *feminine given name*

меһрибанлашмаг : *v* become friendly, affectionate

меһрибанлыг : *n* friendliness, affectionateness

меһрибан-меһрибан : *adv* friendly, affectionately

меһрибанчылыг : *n* see **меһрибанлыг**

меһрибанча, меһрибанчасына : *adv* see **меһрибан-меһрибан**

меһтəр : *n* groom, stable-man

меһтəрбашы : *n* chief groom, chief stable-man

меһтəрлик : *n* occupation, duties of chief groom or chief stable-man

меш : *n* game-player who makes the first move

мешарды : *n* game-player who makes the second move

мешг : *n* 1) exercise, training, rehearsal 2) written exercise

мешə : *n* 1) forest, wood *a* 2) forest, woodland

мешəалмасы : *n* wild apple

мешəбəји : *n* forestry officer/forest warden/forester

мешəбəјилик : *n* 1) occupation of forester/forestry officer/forest warden 2) forest sector for which a forester has responsibility

мешəгыран : *n* wood- cutter

мешəлəндирмəк : *n* plant forests, engage in afforestation

мешəлик : *n* wooded area

мешəсалма : *n* afforestation

мешəсиз : *a* unforested

мешəсизлик : *n* unforested area

мешəторагајы : *n zool* woodlark *Lululla arborea*

мешəхорузу : *n zool* woodgrouse, or capercaillie *Tetrao urogallus*

мешәчи : *n* forestry specialist/sylviculturist; graduate of a Forestry Institute

мешәчилик : *n* afforestation, sylviculture

мешә-чөл : *n geog* forest-steppe *transitional-zone from forest to steppes*

мешәчик : *n* small wood, copse, grove

мешәчүллүтү : *n* woodcock *Scolopax rusticola*

мешин : *n* soft leather

мешшан : *n hist* 1) petty bourgeois, member of a class of small merchants and traders in pre-revolutionary Russia 2) philistine, hypocrite, narrow-minded person *a* 3) petty bourgois, philistine, hypocrital, narrow-minded

мешшанлыг : *n hist* 1) petty bourgeoisie, class of small merchants and traders in pre-revolutionary Russia 2) philistinism; narrow-mindedness, hypocrisy

мешшанчасына : *adv* hypocritically; narrow-mindedly

мәбадә : *adv* in no way, under no circumstances

мә'бәд : *n* temple, shrine; place of worship

мәбләғ : *n* sum of money

мәвачиб : *n* salary

мәгалә : *n* article *in a newspaper, magazine*

мәгам : *n* the right moment

мәгбәрә : *n* mausoleum; burial vault, crypt

мәгбул : *a* acceptable; permissible; sound, valid *argument,proof, evidence etc*

мәгәд : *n anat* anus

мәгсәд : *n* 1) purpose; aim, target, objective 2) intention

мәгсәдәујғун : *a* 1) reasonable, sound, sensibly *adv* 2) reasonably, sensibly

мәгсәди : *a* destined, having a special purpose

мәгсәдсиз : *a* 1) aimless *adv* 2) aimlessly

мәғз : *n* 1) seed/pit/kernel of a fruit; pulp of fruit under the skin/rind *fig* 2) core, essence

мәғлуб : *a* defeated

мәғлубедилмәз : *a* invincible, unconquerable

мәғлубедилмәзлик : *n* invincibility

мәғлубијјәт : *n* defeat

мәғмун : *a* 1) deceived, cheated, made a fool of 2) deprived, bereft

мәғриб : *n* 1) west 2) the Maghrib *western part of North Africa*

мәғрур : *a* 1) proud, haughty, arrogant 2) ambitious *adv* 3) proudly, haughtily, arrogantly 4) ambitiously

мәғруранә : *adv* 1) proudly, haughtily, arrogantly 2) ambitiously

мәғрурijјәт : *n* 1) pride, haughtiness, arrogance 2) ambition

мәғрурланмаг : *v* 1) be proud, be haughty, be arrogant 2) be ambitious

мәғрурлуг : *n* 1) pride, haughtiness, hauteur arrogance 2) ambition

мәдахил : *n* income, revenue; profit

мәдахилли : *a* profitable

мәддаһ : *n* panegyrist, eulogist flatterer, booster

мә'дә : *n* 1) stomach; abdomen *a* 2) gastric, abdominal

мәдәд : *n* help, aid, assistance

мә'дән : *n* 1) ore; mineral 2) mine, pit

мәдәни : *a* cultural; civilized

мәдәнијјәт : *n* culture; civilization

мәдәнијјәтјајан : *n* civilizer

мәдәнијјәтсиз : *a* uncultured, uncivilized, backward

мәдәнијјәтсизлик : *n* 1) uncultured ways; low level of civilization 3) bad manners, boorishness

мәдәниләшдирмәк : *v* enlighten, educate, civilize

мәдәниләшмәк : *v* become enlightened, educated, civilized

мә'дәнчилик : *n* mining

мә'дәчик : *n zool* ventricle, chamber, cavity

мәдинә : *n* Medina *city in Arabia; site of the grave of the Prophet Muhammed*

мәдрәсә : *n* madrassah *Moslem religious school*

мәдһ : *n* praise, eulogy

мәдһијјә, мәдһнамә : *n* ode, panegyric, eulogistic verses *intended to be chanted*

мәәттәл : *a* 1) expecting, expectant, waiting, hesitant 2) astonished, surprised 3) idle, at liberty *involuntarily n* 4) surprise, astonishment

мәзар : *n* 1) grave; tomb *a* grave; tomb, cinerary, sepulchral

мәзарлыг : *n* cemetery

мәзарханлыг : *n* funeral prayer, requiem

мәзач : *n* 1) nature, character, temperament 2) quality, property, attribute

мәздәки : *n* a Zoroastrian

мəздəкилик : *n* Zoroastrianism

мəзə : *n* 1) snack; 2) dessert 2) fun, joke

мəзəли : *a* 1) funny, humorous *n* 2) joker, buffoon, comedian, comical fellow

мəзəлилик : *n* the comic element; humor

мəзəммəт : *n* reproach, reprimand

мəзəммəтлəмəк : *v* reproach, reprimand

мəзəммəтлəнмəк : *v* be subjected to reproach, receive a reprimand

мəзəммəтли : *a* reproachful, expressing reproach/ a reprimand

мəзəннə : *n* market price

мəзиjjəт : *n* merit, advantage

мəзкур : *a* above-mentioned, aforesaid

мəзлəмəк : *v* 1) eat, eat up *fig* 2) acquire *s.t.*

мəзлум : *a* 1) oppressed, humiliated, offended, insulted 2) meek, timid; gentle; humble

мəзлуманə : *adv* meekly, timidly

мəзлумлуг : *n* 1) oppression, humiliation, degradation martyrdom 2) meekness, timidity, humility, gentleness

мəзлум-мəзлум, мəзлумчасына : *adv* 1) meekly, timidly, humbly 2) imploringly 3) excruciatingly

мəзмун : *a* content; plot *in fiction*

мəзмунлу : *a* 1) pithy, rich in content, interesting *adv* 2) pithily, interestingly

мəзмунлулуг : *n* pithiness, richness of content

мəзмунсуз : *a* jejune, poor in content

мəзмунсузлуг : *n* poverty of content

мəзмунча : *adv* essentially

мə'зун : *n* 1) person on leave, vacationer; 2) graduate

мə'зуниjjəт : *n* leave, vacation

мə'зуниjjəтчи : *n* person on leave, vacationer

мə'зур : *a* forgivable

мəзһəб : *n relig* 1) faith, belief, creed, religion denomination 2) sect

мəзһəбсиз : *n* 1) atheist; non-believer 2) heretic

мəзһəкə : *n* 1) joke, anecdote 2) comedy

мəзһəкəли : *a* 1) joking, humorous 2) anecdotal, comic, comical

мəзһəкəнəвис : *n* comedic-playwright

мəзһəкəчи : *n* joker; wit, comical fellow

мəзһəкəчилик : *n* clowning, clownery

мəиjjəт : *n* suite, retinue *accompanying s.o.*

мəишəт : *n* 1) everyday life, routine 2) economic conditions

мə'јус : *a* upset, disappointed

мə'јусанə : *adv* disappointedly, gloomily

мə'јуслуг : *n* depression, blues; disappointment

мə'јус-мə'јус : *adv* disappointedly, gloomily

мəкан : *n* 1) place, locality 2) dwelling, shelter, housing 3) space, expanse

мəкə : *n* 1) corn *a* 2) corn

мəкəнəк : *n* birching, beating

мəкик : *n* shuttle *on a machine loom*

мəкикгајыран, мəкикчи : *n* master shuttle-maker

мəккилти : *n* bleating *of goats*

мəкр : *n* slyness; shrewdness, trickery, treacherousness

мəкрли : *a* sly, cunning; treacherous

мəктəб : *n* 1) school; educational institution *a* 2) educational, pedagogical, school

мəктəбдəнкəнар : *a* out-of-school, extracurricular *activities*

мəктəбјаны : *a adjoining a* school *i.e. of a plot cultivated by students*

мəктəбјашлы : *a* school age *of a child*

мəктəбли : *n* pupil, student

мəктуб : *n* letter

мəктублашма : *n* exchange of letters, correspondence

мəктублашмаг : *v* exchange letters, correspond

мə'кулат : *n* food, comestibles, provisions

мəкəр : *qw* Isn't it that. . . .? Do you. . . *etc* really. . . ?

мəкəш : *n* curdled milk

мəлаикə : *n relig* 1) angel; handsome man/beautiful woman

мəлаһəт : *n* 1) beauty; charm; 2) grace 3) Malahat *feminine first name*

мəлаһəтли : *a* beautiful, charming, graceful

мəлејкə : *n* 1) angel 2) queen

мəлəз : *n* person of mixed ancestry

мəлəзлəшдирмə : *n* hybridization

мəлəк : *n* angel

мəлəкмəнзəр : *a* 1) angelic in appearance *n* 2) handsome man; beautiful woman

мəлəкə : *n* queen

мәләкоту : *n bot* angelica *Angelica archangelica*

мәләксурәт : *a* angelic in appearance

мәләмә : *n* bleating

мәләмәк : *v* bleat

мәләтмәк : *caus* of **мәләмәк**

мәләфә : *n* bed-sheet

мәләшмә : *n* bleating of many she-goats/sheep jointly

мәләшмәк : *v* bleat of many she-goats/sheep jointly

мәлик : *n* king, tsar, monarch

мә'лул : *a* sad, gloomy

мә'лул-мә'лул : *adv* sadly, gloomily

мә'лум : *a* 1) known, understood, apprehended *math* 2) datum

мә'лумат : *n* 1) news; information 2) report; message 3) learning

мә'луматлы : *a* 1) informed, knowledgeable, aware 2) erudite, educated 3) bookish

мә'луматсыз : *a* 1) ignorant; unaware *n* 2) ignoramus

мә'луматфүруш : *n* pedant

мә'луматфүрушлуг : *n* pedantry

мәл'ун : *a* 1) damned, cursed ; vicious *n* 2) rascal, scoundrel, scumbag

мәлһәм : *n* ointment

мәмә : *n* 1) breast; nipple 2) udder

мәмәлиләр : *n zool* mammals

мәмәсиз : *a zool* monotreme *the lowest order of mammals Monotremata , i.e. the oviparous duckbills and echidnas, lacking true teeth, nipples, and having a cloaca*

мәмләкәт : *n* country, state, government

мәмлү : *a* overfilled

мәмнун : *a* 1) sufficient, satisfactory 2) thankful, grateful

мәмнунијјәт : *n* 1) satisfaction 2) gratitude, thankfulness

мәмнунијјәтлә : *adv* with pleasure *polite response*

мәмнунлуг : *n* see **мәмнунијјәт**

мә'мулат : *n* manufactured product

мә'мур : *n* 1) official, functionary *pej* 2) bureaucrat *a* 3) bureaucratic

мә'муријјә : *n* mission

мән : *pro* I

мә'на : *n* 1) meaning, sense, purport, point 2) thought, idea

мә'налы : *a* 1) meaningful 2) significant

мә'налылыг : *n* significance

мә'насыз : *a* 1) senseless, meaningless *adv* 2) senselessly, meaninglessly

мә'насызлыг : *n* nonsense, absurdity

мә'насызчасына : *adv* absurdly, ridiculously

мәнафе : *n* interest, profit; benefit

мә'нача : *adv* by definition

мәнбә : *n* beginning; source; origin

мәндулә : *n* nankeen *textile*

мә'нәви : *a* spiritual, moral

мә'нәвијјат : *n* spirituality

мәнәм-мәнәмлик : *n* self-aggrandizement; blowing one's own horn

мәнзәрә : *n* 1) view, panorama, landscape 2) picture

мәнзәрәли : *n* picturesque, pleasing to the eye

мәнзил : *n* 1) lodging, accomodation, house, housing, quarters, apartment; 2) passage, run, stage, day's journey 3) temporary camp, stopping/halting place, 2) range *ballistics*

мәнзилкаһ : *n* see **мәнзил** 3)

мәнзум : *a* poetic

мәнзумә : *n* poem, verse

мә'ни : *n* see **мә'на**

мә'нидар : *a* see **мә'налы**

мәним, мәнимки : *pro* my; mine

мәнимсәмә : *n* 1) appropriation, acquissition 2) mastering, assimilation

мәнимсәмәк : *v* 1) acquire, appropriate 2) master, assimilate, become familiar with

мәнкәнә : *n* vice *tool*

мәнкирләмәк : *v* not let something go, not let s.t. get out of o.'s hands 2) become the owner of s.t.

мәнлик : self-esteem, personal dignity, self-awareness, "me-ness" of a person

мәнсәб : *n* 1) rank, office, post, position 2) career 2) mouth *of a river*

мәнсәбпәрәст : *n* careerist; power-hungry/power-oriented person

мәнсәбпәрәстлик : *n* love of power, lust for power

мәнсиз : *pro* without me

мәнсил : *n* nagger, egger-on

мәнсуб : *a* belonging to, being a part of, affiliated with

мәнсублуг, мәнсубиј̇јәт : *n* 1) relation, affiliation, membership, connection 2) kinshship tie

мәнсур : *a* prosaic

мәнтәгә : *n* 1) point 2) unit 3) block 4) station; location

мәнтиг : *n* logic

мәнтиги : *a* logical

мәнтигли : *a* 1) logical 2) convincing

мәнтиглилик : *n* logicality

мәнтигсиз : *a* illogical

мәнтигсизлик : *n* illogicality, lack of logic

мәнфәәт : *n* profit, interest; benefit

мәнфәәтбәрдар : *n* 1) profit *a* 2) profit-making, profitable interest-generating

мәнфәәтдар : *n* materially interested person

мәнфәәткүдән : *n* profiteer, profit-oriented businessman, money-grabber,

мәнфәәтли : *a* profitable, useful

мәнфәәтлилик : *n* profitability, usefulness

мәнфәәтпәрәст : *n* profiteer, money-grabber, covetous person, person concerned only with self-advantage

мәнфәәтпәрәстлик : *n* excessive profiteering, money-grabbing, covetousness

мәнфәәтпәрәстчәсинә : *adv* covetously, self-seekingly, in a mercenary-minded manner

мәнфәәтсиз : *a* unprofitable

мәнфәәтсизлик : *n* unprofitability

мәнфәз : *n* electrical outlet

мәнфи : *a* 1) negative *adv* 2) negatively

мәнфилик : *n* negativity, negativeness

мәнфур : *a* unpleasant, antipathetic scorned, accursed, nasty, mean

мәнһус : *a* damned, scorned, vile, foul, mean

мәнчә : *exp* "1n my opinion. . . .", "To my mind. . . .", "I believe that.. . . "

мәншә : *n* 1) origin, source, beginning 2) genesis

мәракеш : *n* 1) Morocco, *a* 2) Moroccan

мәракешли : *n* resident of Morocco

мәрам : *n* 1) wish, desire 2) purpose, aim, intention

мәрамнамә : *n* program

мәрасим : *n* ritual, ceremony

мәрд : *a* 1) courageous, brave, valiant 2) generous, magnanimous

мәрданә : *adv* courageously, bravely and sincerely, like a man

мәрдимазар : *a* 1) pernicious, noxious 2) inflicting suffering

мәрдимазарлыг : *n* 1) perniciousness, noxiousness 2) malignancy, malevolence, well-spring of suffering

мәрдлик : *n* 1) courage, valor, bravery 2) magnanimity

мәрд-мәрданә : *adv* 1) courageously, bravely, valiantly 2) magnanimously

мәрдчәсинә : *adv* courageously, bravely, valiantly

мәрәз : *n* 1) leash 2) disease 3) clothes-line

мә'рәкә : *n* 1) noise, row, racket; mess 2) crowd, throng; assembly

мә'рәкәчи : *n* brawler, trouble-maker, rowdy

мәрз : *n* 1) boundary-strip *between two land-plots* *a* 2) boundary

мәрзләмәк : *v* establish/lay-out boundaries

мә'рифәт : *n* 1) knowledge, cognition, understanding 2) courtesy, politeness, good manners , tact

мә'рифәтләнмәк : *v* become courteous/polite/well-mannered, acquire good manners

мә'рифәтли : *a* courteous, polite, well-mannered

мә'рифәтлилик : *n* courtesy, politeness, good manners, tactfulness

мә'рифәтсиз : *a* 1) crude, uneducated, ill-mannered *n* 2) crude, uneducated, ill-mannered person

мә'рифәтсизлик : *n* lack of education, crudity, impoliteness, diacourtesy, bad manners

мәрјәмгурду : *n* *zool* wood-louse

мәркәз : *n* center

мәркәздәнгачан, мәркәздәнгачма : *a* centrifugal

мәркәзәгачан : *a* centripetal

мәркәзи : *a* central

мәркәзиј̇јәт : *n* centralism, centrism

мәркәзиј̇јәтчи : *n* centralist, centrist

мәркәзиј̇јәтчилик : *n* see **мәркәзиј̇јәт**

мәркәзләшдирилмәк : *v* be centralized

мәркәзләшдирмәк : *v* centralize, concentrate

мәркәзләшмә : *n* centralization, concentration

мәркәзләшмәк : *v* become centralized, concentrated

мәркәзчи : *n* centrist, centralist

мәркәзчилик : *n* centralism, centrism

мәркүмүш : *n chem* 1) arsenic *a* 2) arsenious

мәрмәр : *n* 1) marble *a* 2) marble

мәрми : *n* shell, cartridge

мәррих : *n astron* Mars

мәрсијә : *n* elegy

мәрсијәхан : *n* elegy-reciter

мәрсин : *n* whortleberry, bilberry, European blueberry *Vaccinium myrtillus*

мәртәбә : *n* 1) floor *geol* 2) stage, layer 3) degree, rank, office 4) grade, level, category

мәртуб : *a* 1) cheerful, brisk 2) slender, well- proportioned, stately

мә'руз : *a* liable *to*, susceptible *to*, prone *to*

мә'рузә : *n* 1) report *oral* 2) lecture

мә'рузәчи : *n* 1) one who makes a report 2) speaker, lecturer

мәрһәба : *exp* Well done!; Good !

мәрһәлә : *n* stage, phase

мәрһәм : *n med* medicinal ointment

мәрһәмәт : *n* 1) mercy, magnanimity, good-heartedness 2) condescension

мәрһәмәтә кәтирмәк : *v* propitiate, soften *s.o.'s* heart

мәрһәмәткар, **мәрһәмәтли** : *a* 1) merciful, generous, good-hearted, magnanimous 2) condescending,

мәрһәмәтсиз : *a* 1) cruel, brutal, unmerciful *adv* 2) cruelly, brutally, unmercifully

мәрһәмәтсизлик : *n* cruelty, brutality, unmercifulness

мәрһум : *n* 1) deceased, departed, *the* late *man a* 2) *also adjectival*

мәрһумә : *n* 1) deceased, departed, *the* late *woman a* 2) *also adjectival*

мәрч : *n* bet, wager

мәрчан : *n* 1) coral *a* 2) coral

мәрчангулу : *n* coral-shell

мәрчаны : *n bot* cranberry *Oxycoccus palustris*

мәрчәк : *n* ear-lobe

мәрчи, **мәрчимәк** : *n* 1) lentil *Lens esculenta a* 2) lentil

мәрчләшмәк : *v* bet, wager

мәс : *n* slippers, flip-flops *typical of the Caucasus and Crimea*

мәсамә : *n* pores

мәсамәли : *a* porous

мәсамәлилик : *n* porousness

мәсариф : *n* expenses, expenditures

мәсафә : *n* distance, interval

мәсафәөлчән : *n* range-finder

мәсдәр : *n gram* infinitive, indefinite verb form

мәсәл : *n* 1) saying, proverb 2) parable, example, fable

мәсәлә : *n math* 1) problem,task 2) question, issue, matter

мәсәлән : *adv* for example

мәсиһ : *n relig* Messiah

мәскән : *n* house, dwelling, premises, place of residence

мәскун : *a* inhabited, populated

мәсләк : *n* 1) idea, conviction 2) trend *a* 2) expressing an idea or ideas

мәсләкдаш : *n* like-minded person

мәсләксиз : *a* devoid of ideas/principles/convictions

мәсләксизлик : *n* lack of ideas/principles/convictions

мәсләһәт : *n* advice, consultation

мәсләһәт көрмәк : *v* advise

мәсләһәтләшмә : *n* meeting, consultation, gathering

мәсләһәтләшмәк : *v* consult together, confer about

мәсләһәтхана : *n* 1) advice bureau *i.e. legal etc.* 2) clinic *i.e. children's, prenatal etc*

мәсләһәтчи : *n* advisor, consultant, tutor *in higher educational institution*

мәснәви : *n* distich, couplet

мәсрәф : *n* 1) expenditure, expense *a* 2) suitable, fitting

мәст : *a* 1) drunk, intoxicated *n* 2) a drunk, an intoxicated person

мәстедичи : *a* intoxicating

мәстәки : *n* wood-polish

мәстлик : *n* drunkenness, intoxication

мәс'уд : *a* lucky, happy

мәс'ул : *a* responsible

мәс'улијјәт : *n* responsibility

мәс'улијјәтли : *a* responsible

мәс'улијјәтсиз : *a* irresponsible

мәс'улијјәтсизлик : *n* irresponsibility

мәс'улијјәтсизчәсинә : *adv* irresponsibly, carelessly

мә'сум : *a* 1) pure, chaste 2) innocent; sinless

мә'сумлуг : *n* 1) purity, chastity 2) innocence, sinlessness

мәсхәрә : *n* see **масгара**

мәсхәрәчи : *n* see **масгарачи**

мәсчид : *n* mosque

мәт : *n* thick mass, clot; lees

мәтанәт : *n* steadfastness, staunchness, stability

мәтанәтли : *a* steadfast, staunch, stable, courageous

мәтанәтсиз : *a* weak, vacillating, unreliable

мәтбәә : *n* printing-house/office, press

мәтбәх : *n* 1) kitchen *a* 2) kitchen

мәтбәхгурду : *n zool* cockroach *fam. Blattidae*

мәтбу : *a* printing, press

мәтбуат : *n* press, media

мәтбуатчы : *n* journalist, press employee, media representative

мәтин : *a* steadfast, staunch, unshakeable

мәтинлик : *n* see **мәтанәт**

мәтләб : *n* 1) essense, heart of the matter/question/issue 2) demand, request 3) intention, objective 4) matter, substance, subject, topic

мәтләшдирмәк : *v* thicken *a liquid*

мәтләшдиртмәк : *v-tr* cause someone to thicken *a liquid*

мәтләшмәк : *v* thicken, become thick *of liquids*

мәтн : *n* text

мәтни : *a* textual

мәтншүнас : *n* textual critic

мәтншүнаслыг : *n* textual criticism, textual study

мәфкурә : *n* ideology

мәфкурәви : *a* ideological, expressing an idea or ideas

мәфрәш : *n* large sack for transportation and storage of carpets and bedclothes

мәфтил : *n* wire

мәфтилгајыран : *n* wire-maker

мәфтилли : *a* wire

мәфтилсиз : *a* wireless

мәфтун : *a* 1) charmed, carried away, in love *n* 2) admirer,worshipper

мәфтунедичи : *a* charming, captivating

мәфтунлуг : *n* charm, infatuation, fascination; adoration,

мәфһум : *n* concept, notion, idea

мәхарич : *n* expenditure, waste

мә'хәз : *n* source *of a scientific, literary work, or a quotation,*

мәхлуг : *a* 1) created, made *n* 2) creation, work 2) people, the masses

мәхлугат : *n* created beings, creatures

мәхмәр : *n* 1) velvet *a* 2) velvet

мәхмәрәк : *n med* German measles *rubella*

мәхмәри : *a* velvet-like

мәхрәч : *n ling* 1) articulation *math* 2) denominator

мәхсус : *a* 1) special 2) characteristic, peculiar *to*, proper *to* 3) specially designated for s.o./s.t.

мәхсусән : *adv* deliberately, purposely consciously, premeditatedly

мәхсуси : *a* 1) special, peculiar 2) belonging to *s.o.*

мәхсусијјәт : *n* peculiarity, specific feature

мәхфи : *a* 1) secret *adv* 2) secretly

мәһарәт : *n* 1) mastery, skill, skillfullness, dexterity 2) talent, giftedness

мәһарәтлә : *adv* skilfully, artistically, masterfully

мәһарәтли : *a* 1) talented, gifted 2) skilful, masterly

мәһарәтлилик : *n* giftednes, talent, viruosity

мәһарәтсиз : *a* ungifted, untalented, unskilful

мәһбуб : *a* 1) in love *n* 2) lover

мәһбубә : *n* sweetheart, lover, mistress

мәһбус : *n* 1) arrestee; prisoner, prison-inmate *a* 2) under arrest, arrested, detained

мәһв : *n* annihilation, destruction, ruin

мәһведичи : *a* ruinous, destructive, pernicious

мәһдуд : *a* limited

мәһдудијјәт : *n* limitation, limitedness

мәһдудланмаг : *v* be limited

мәһдудлашдырмаг : *v-tr* limit

мәһдудлашма : *n* limitation

мәһдудлашмаг : *v* limit

мәһдудлуг : *n* 1) limitedness 2) enclosedness; reticence, reserve

мәһәббәт : *n* love, affection

мәһәббәтли : *a* loving, affectionate, devoted

мәһәббәтчичәји : *n bot* mignonette *Reseda*

мәһәк, мәһәкдашы : *n* touchstone *fine-grained stone used to test fineness of gold and silver by streaking*

мәһәл : *n* importance, attention *used only in combinations*

мәһәл гојмамаг : *v* neglect, ignore

мәһәлл : *n* area, neighborhood

мәһәллә : *n* area, neighborhood, quarter, community

мәһәлли : *a* local, communal, territorial

мәһәррәм : *n* Muharram *first month of the Islamic lunar year*

мәһәччәр : *n* banister, handrail

мәһз : *adv* namely, to wit, only, solely

мәһзун : *a* 1) gloomy, sad *adv* 2) gloomily, sadly

мәһзун-мәһзун : *adv* sadly, sorrowfully, gloomily

мәһкәмә : *n* 1) court; trial *a* 2) court, trial

мәһкум : *a* 1) sentenced, convicted, condemned 2) doomed, destined

мәһкумлуг : *n* doom

мәһлул : *n* solution

мәһлулгарышдыран : *n* blender

мәһрәба : *n* towel

мәһрәк : *n astron* orbit

мәһрәм : *a* 1) intimate, one's own *n* 2) close relative

мәһрәманә : *adv* intimately, confidentially

мәһрум : *a* deprived, impoverished

мәһрумиjjәт,мәһрумлуг : *n* deprivation

мәһсул : *n* 1) harvest 2) product 2) bag, catch *fish, game*

мәһсулдар : *a* 1) fruitful 2) productive

мәһсулдарлашдырма : *n* impregnation, fecundation

мәһсулдарлашдырмаг : *n* impregnate, fertilize, fecundate

мәһсулдарлыг : *n* 1) level *of yield of crops*, fertility; 2) procductivity

мәһсуллу : *a* fertile, productive

мәһсуллулуг : *n* see **мәһсулдарлыг**

мәһсулсуз : *a* infertile; unfruitlful unproductive

мәһсулсузлуг : *n* 1) poor harvest, crop failure 2) low productivity

мәһтаб : *n* moonlight, lunar radiance

мәһчуб : *n* see **утанчаг**

мәһшәр : *n relig* Doomsday, Judgement Day

мәчаз : *n* metaphore, figurative expression

мәчази : *a* metaphorical, figurative, extended *meaning/usage*

мәчазилик : *n* figurativeness metaphorical imagery

мәчбур : *a* forced, compelled

мәчбурән : *adv* by force, compulsorily

мәчбури : *a* compulsory, obligatory

мәчбуриjjәт : *n* compulsion, necessity

мәчбурилик : *n* obligatoriness, binding force

мәчәллә : *n* code *of laws* , regulations

мәчлис : *n* 1) Majlis, parliament 2) meeting, conference, gathering, assembly 3) society, association, company 4) scene *theatrical*

мәчлиси-мүәссисан : *n polit* Constituent Assembly

мәчмәји : *n* round copper tray

мәчму : *pro* 1) all *n* 2) everything, totality, sum, sum total

мәчмуә : *n* 1) magazine 2) collection *of stories, articles etc*

мәчнун : *n* 1) see **дәли** 2) mad/crazy with love/infatuation

мәчра : *n* river-bed

мә'чун : *n* 1) sweets in spread or paste form 2) sweets *in general*

мәчуси : *n* magician, wizard

мәчусилик : *n* magic, sorcery

мәчһул : *a* 1) unknown, not experienced previously *gram* 2) passive *n math* 3) unknown quantity

мәччани : *a* see **пулсуз**

мәшвәрәт : *n* consultation, advice

мәшг : *n* practice; practicing

мәшғәлә : *n* lesson, session

мәшғул : *a* busy, occupied *with work, business*

мәшғулиjjәт : *n* 1) occupation, pursuit 2) diversion, way of spending o.'s time, preoccupation

мәшәггәт : *n* difficulties, hardships, sufferings, torments/tortures

мәшәггәтли : *a* difficult, hard, painful, burdensome

мәшәди : *n relig* 1) Meşadi *title given to those who have made a pilgrimage to the city of Meshkhed in Iran, site of the tomb of Imam Reza, a religious figure honored by*

Shiite Muslims 2) Meşadi masculine first name

мәш'әл : *n* 1) torch *a* 2) torch

мәшриг : *n rare* East

мәшрут : *a* see **шәрти**

мәшрутә : *a* 1) constitutional *n* 2) constitution

мәшрутәли : *a* constitutional

мәшрутәчи : *n* proponent/supporter of a constitution, constitutionalist

мәшрутәчилик : *n* constitutionalism

мә'шуг : *n* 1) lover; beloved man *a* 2) beloved; in love

мә'шугә : *n* 1) sweetheart, girlfriend 2) mistress; concubine

мәш'ум : *a* sinister, fatal

мәшһур : *a* famous, well known, popular

мәшһурлашмаг : *v* become famous, well known, popular

мәшһурлуг : *n* fame, popularity

мәшшатә : *n* a woman who adorns the bride before sending her off to the bridegroom

мига : *n geol* see **гарғазлу**

мигдар : *n* quantity, dose

мигдарча : *adv* quantitatively

мигјас : *n* scale; scope

мидија : *n hist* 1) Medea *ancient country in SW Asia, corresponding to NW Iran a* 2) Medean

миз : *n* table

мизан : *n* 1) measure 2) balance

мизан-тәрәзи : *n relig* Purgatory

мизган : *n* see **гармон**

мизраб : *n mus* plectrum

мизраг : *n* dart, javelin

мијана : *a* 1) average, indifferent, passable 2) object of average size and quality

мијанпур : *n* stuffed dried fruit

мијанчы : *n* go-between, mediator

мијанчылыг : *n* mediation

мијов : *n* mew, meow *crying sound made by a cat*

мијовламаг : *v* mew, meow

мијовулту : *n* mewing, meowing

микнәт : *elev* property

микроб : *n* microbe, germ

микробиоложи : *a* microbiological

микробиолокија : *n* microbiology

микробсузлашдырма : *n* sterilization

микробсузлашдырмаг : *v* sterilize

микрометрлик : *a* micrometer *pertaining to the use of a micrometer*

микроскоп : *n* microscope

микроскопик : *a* microscopic

микдан : *n* inn

мил : *n* 1) spoke 2) shaft 3) master-key, skeleton key, pass-key 4) rod 5) mile

милади : *n* Christian system of chronology *lit: pertaining to the birth of Christ*

миләмил : *a* striped

милис : *n* 1) police, police force *a* 2) police

милисионер : *n* policeman, police officer

милјард : *num* billion

милјардчы : *n* multi-millionaire

милјон : *num* million

милјонер : *n Ru* millionaire

милјончу : *n* millionaire

милләмә : *adv* headlong

милләнмәк : *v* 1) fly up, soar *av* 2) dive

милләт : *n* 1) nation 2) nationality *in various senses. The term refers not to the state, but to the particular national groups which compose it*

милләтпәрәст, милләтчи : *n* 1) nationalist 2) chauvinist

милләтчилик : *n* 1) nationalism 2) chauvinism

милли : *n* national, ethnic

миллијјәт : *n* nationality *in various senses. The term refers not to the state, but to the particular national groups which compose it*

миллиләшдирилмәк : *v* be nationalized

миллиләшдирмә : *n* nationalization

миллиләшдирмәк : *v* nationalize

мил-мил : *a* striped

милчә : *n tech* 1) drum, roller, pulley, sheave 2) knitting-needle

милчәк : *n zool* fly

милчәкгыран : n *bot* fly-agaric *Amanita muscaria, mushroom*

милчәкгован : *n* 1) fly-swatter 2) fan

милчәкјејән : n *zool* fly-catcher *fam Muscicapidae, passerine bird*

мимик : *a* mimic

мимика : *n* mimicry

мин : *num* thousand

мина : *n* enamel

мина : *n mil* mine

минаатан : *n mil* mortar

миналамаг : *v* enamel

миналамаг : *v* mine, lay mines

миналанмаг : *pass* be mined

миналы : *a* enameled

минарә : *n* minaret *tower from which the muezzin calls Mulim faithful to prayer*

минасыз : *a* unenameled

миначичәји : *n bot* verbena, vervain *an herb*

миначы : *n mil* 1) mine specialist, specialist in mines, mine-clearing and demolition *a* 2) adjectival application of 1)

миначат : *n relig* mullah's call notifying the faithful that s.o. has died

минбашы : *n hist mil* commander of a military unit consisting of one-thousand warriors in ancient times

минбәр : *n* preacher's pulpit in a mosque

минвал : *n* see **тәһәр**

миндәбир : *num* one thousandth

миндилли : *a n* liar

миндирмәк : *v-tr* offer a seat, seat s.o. *on a vehicle or any other means of transportation*

минерал : *n* 1) mineral *a* 2) mineral

минераллашма : *n* mineralization

минераложи : *a* minerological

минералокија : *n* minerology

минәк : *n* 1) animal trained to carry a rider 2) saddle-horse

миник : *n* 1) rider, horseman 2) passenger 3) carriage

миниллик : *n* 1) millenium *a* 2) millenary

минимал : *a* minimal

минимум : *n* minimum

мининчи : *ord* thousandth

миничи : *n* rider, horseman

миничилик : *n* equestrianism, horseback-riding

минкәрләмәк : *v* see **јахалмаг**

минләрчә : *adv* in thousands

минмәк : *v* get in/on, take a seat *on a horse/ship/train etc*

мин-мин : *adv* in thousands

миннәт : *n* 1) request, petitioning, entreaty 2) favor,service, good turn/deed, 3) gratitude, thanks, thankfulness

миннәт гојмаг : *v* reproach in ingratitude

миннәт чәкмәк : *v* be indebted

миннәтдар : *a* thankful, grateful

миннәтдарлыг : *n* thankfulness, gratitude

миннәтчи : *n* 1) intercessor, mediator 2) solicitor; attorney

миномјот : *n Ru* mortar

миолокија : *n anat* myology *study of muscles*

мираб : *n* water-distributor, water-master *person in charge of the orderly distribution of water from irrigation canals in Near Eastern villages)*

мираблыг : *n* position, occupation of water-distributor, water-master. See **мираб**

мирас : *n* inheritance, heritage

мират : *n* clothes left by a dead person

мирвары : *n* 1) pearl *a* 2) pearl

миргәзәб : *n* see **чәллад**

мирзә : *n* 1) traditional address to a professional, an academic, or middle-rank official 2) clerk; secretary, teacher 3) Mirza, title of nobility; when used before the surname, it signifies "Prince."

мирзәји : *n* the Mirzayi, an Azerbaijani folk dance

мири : *a* 1) fiscal 2) of State, of Treasury

мис : *n* 1) copper *a* 2) copper

мисал : *n* 1) example; precedent; sample 2) likeness, similarity

мисғал : *n* zolotnik *old Russian measure of weight equal to 4.25 grams*

мисәридән : *a* copper-smelting

мисил : *n* resemblance, likeness, similarity

мисилсиз : *a* unexampled, matchless, unprecedented

мисилсизлик : *adv* unbelievably, incomparably, unprecedentedly

мисир : *n* 1) Egypt *a* 2) Egyptian

мисирли : *n* an Egyptian

мисиршүнас : *n* Egyptologist

мисиршүнаслыг : *n* Egyptology

мисјонер : *n* 1) missionary *a* 2) missionary

мискин : *a* poor, poverty-stricken, impoverished, helpless

мискинләшмәк : *v* become poor/impoverished/helpless

мискинлик : *n* poverty, wretchedness, helplessness

мискәр : *n* copper-smith *esp. one specializing in copper vessels*

мискәрлик : *n* occupation of a copper-smith *esp. one specializing in copper vessels*

мисмар : *n* nail

мисмарламаг : *v* nail, drive nails

мисра : *n* hemistich *half a line of verse*

миттал : *n* calico

митил : *n* 1) inner part of a case for bed-clothes 2) blanket 3) good-for nothing fellow *a* 4) old, worn out

митил-шитил : *n* house belongings

митинг : *n* *Ru* meeting

михәји : *a* brown

михәк : *n* cloves

михи : *n* 1) cuneiform *a* 2) cuneiform

мичәткән : *n* bed-curtain

мишар : *n* saw

мишарағзы, мишаркәпәји : *n* sawdust

мишарбалығы : *n* *zool* saw-fish *genus Pristis*

мишарламаг : *v* saw, saw in two, saw up

мишарланмаг : *v* be sawed/sawn

мишарлатдырмаг, мишарлатмаг : *v* cause to saw

мишарчы : *n* sawyer

мишарчылыг : *n* occupation of a sawyer

мығмыға : *n* *zool* midge, gnat *small insect*

мызы : *a* 1) slow-moving 2) gloomy, unfriendly, bleak 3) captious

мызылда(н)маг : *v* mumble

мызылыг : *n* 1) sluggishness, tardiness 2) captiousness

мызмыз(ы) : *a* 1) speaking in a nasal manner 2) tiresome, importunate

мырыг : *n* 1) hare-lipped person 2) person with a missing front tooth

мырылдама : *n* see **мырылты**

мырылдамаг : *v* grumble, growl, mutter

мырылданмаг : *v* grumble, mutter, mumble

мырылты : *n* grumbling, mumbling

мырт : *n* idle talk *used only in combinations*: **мырт вурмаг** have a chat with, idly bat the breeze with s.o. *of two persons*

мыртда(н)маг : *v* grumble, mumble, mutter

мыртылдамаг : *v* murmur, mutter *rebelliously*

мысылдамаг : *v* see **фысылдамаг**

мысмырыг : *n* frown-faced state, *only in combinations*

мысмырығыны салламаг (төкмәк) *v* frown, knit o.'s brows, purse/pout the lips

мысмырыглы : *a* gloomy, sullen, sombre, dismal

мых : *n* 1) nail 2) peg

мыхгајыран : *n* blacksmith specializing in nail-making

мыхлама : *n* nailing, driving nails, hammering in nails

мыхламаг : *v* 1) nail, hammer in nails 2) nail onto s.t.

мыхланмаг : *v* be nailed *onto/into*

мыхлатдырмаг, мыхлатмаг : *caus* of **мыхланмаг**

мыхча : *n* small nail

мыхчаламаг : *v* nail with small nails

мышовул : *n* *zool* weasel *Genus Mustela*

мода : *n* fashion

модабаз : *n* dandy *man* ; clothes-horse *woman*

модел : *n* 1) model; pattern *a* 2) model, pattern

моделгајыран, моделчи : *n* model-maker

модернлашдырмаг : *v* modernize

мозалан : *n* *zool* gadfly

молдаван : *n* 1) a Moldavian *a* Moldavian

молдавија : *n* Moldova

молдавча : *adv* in Moldavian *language*

молекул : *n* molecule

молла : *n* mullah *Moslem clergyman*

моллахана : *n* Moslem religious school

монастыр : *n* 1) monastery *a* 1) monastery

монгол : *n* 1) Mongol, a Mongolian *a* 2) Mongolian

монголустан : *n* Mongolia

монголча : *adv* in Mongolian *language*

монпасы : *n* fruit drops *from French brand-name Mon Pensée*

монтјор : *n* 1) repairman; *a* 2) maintenance

мордва : *n* 1) the Mordva, the Mordvinians *Finno-Ugric people in European Russia* *a* 2) Mordvinian

мордвалы : *n* Mordvinian

мороженое : *n* *Ru* ice-cream

моруг : *n* 1) raspberry *Rubus* *a* 2) raspberry

моруглуг : *n* area rich in raspberry bushes/sown with raspberry bushes

морфоложи : *a* morphological

морфолокиjа : *n* morphology

мотал : *n* sheepskin specially adapted for storing home-made cheese

моталпапаг : *n* 1) man wearing a shaggy sheepskin cap 2) peasant

мотмоту : *n* 1) gooseberry *Ribes grossularia* *a* 2) gooseberry

мотор : *n* 1) motor, engine *a* 2) motor, engine

моторлашдырмаг : *v* motorize

моторлу : *a* equipped with a motor, engine

моторчу : *n* motorist

мотосикл : *n* motorcycle

мөвге : *n mil* 1) position 2) post 3) rank

мөвзү : *n* 1) subject 2) topic, theme 3) plot

мөвсүм : *n* season

мөвсүми : *a* seasonal

мөвсүмлүк : *n* seasonal, for one specific season

мөвүч : *n* raisins

мөвһум : *a* 1) imaginary, fictitious, mythical 2) superstitious 3) fanatical

мөвһумат : *n* 1) superstition 2) fanaticism, bigotry, prejudice

мөвһуматчы : *n* 1) superstitious person 2) fanatic *a* 3) superstitious, fanatical

мөвһуматчылыг : *n* 1) superstitiousness 2) fanaticism

мөвчуд : *a* present; extant, currently available

мөвчудиjjәт : *n phil* Existence, Being, Entity

мө'мин : *a relig* pious, devout

мө'минлик : *n* piety, devotion; righteousness

мө'тәбәр : *a* reliable, trustworthy

мө'тәдил : *a* 1) moderate *chem* 2) neutral

мө'тәдилләшдирмәк : *v* moderate, cause to become moderate

мө'тәдилләшмәк : *v* become moderate

мө'тәдиллик : *n* moderation, moderateness

мө'тәризә : *n* parenthesis

мөһкәм : *a* 1) firm, reliable, stable *adv* 2) firmly, reliably, stably

мөһкәмләндирмәк : *v* strengthen, make firmer

мөһкәмләндиртмәк : *v* cause to strengthen, make firmer

мөһкәмләнмәк : *v* become stronger/firmer/more firmly rooted

мөһкәмләтмәк : *v* see **мөһкәмләндирмәк**

мөһкәмләшдирмәк : *v* see **мөһкәмләндирмәк**

мөһкәмләшмәк : *v* see **мөһкәмләнмәк**

мөһкәмлик : *n* 1) firmness 2) stability, steadiness, endurance, reliability 3) toughness, condition/state of being hardened/tempered

мөһкәм-мөһкәм : *adv* very firmly, very solidly

мөһкәмчә : *adv* firmly, soundly, solidly

мөһләт : *n* term, deadline *time given to fulfil a given task/assignment*

мөһнәт : *n* 1) suffering, trouble 2) hard labor 3) calamity

мөһнәткеш : *a* 1) industrious, diligent 2) living in poverty *n* 3) victim, martyr, sufferer, person with chronic hard-luck

мөһтач : *a* in need, needy, hard-up

мөһтачлыг : *n* need, poverty

мөһтәкир : *n* 1) profiteer, speculator *a* 2) speculatory, profiteering

мөһтәкирлик : *n* speculation, profiteering

мөһтәрәм : *a* respected, honorable *official form of address*

мөһтәшәм : *a* magnificent, grandiose, monumental, majestic, luxurious

мөһүр : *n* seal

мөһүрләмәк : *v* 1) affix a seal 2) seal

мөһүрләнмәк : *v* 1) certify/attest by affixing a seal 2) be sealed

мөһүрлү : *a* 1) having a seal 2) stamped, sealed

мө'чүзә : *n* wonder, miracle

мө'чүзәкар, мө'чүзәкөстәрән : *n* miracle-worker, thaumaturge, thaumaturgist; magician

муғаjат : *n* 1) care for, take care of, guard *s.o.* 2) keep an eye on, look after

муғаjат олмаг : *v* take care *of someone*

муғамат : *n* traditional middle-eastern melodies

мужик : *n* guy, fellow *fr. Russ muzhik= peasant*

мужикчәсинә : *adv* crudely, in a crude way *cnf. Russ muzhik= peasant*

муз : *n bot* pimpinella *Pimpinella saxifraga,* a polyphyllous herbaceous plant

музд : *n* 1) recompense, reimbursement, restitution 2) salary, pay, wages

муздлу : *a* working for hourly/daily/annual wage etc *as opposed to self-employed*

муздур : *n* 1) day-laborer, farm laborer, hired-man/hand *on a farm*; 2) civilian employee *in a military establishment*

муздурлуг : *n* 1) work paid by the day 2) temporary/seasonal farm-work

музеј : *n* 1) museum *a* 2) museum, museum-related

музејшүнас : *n* museologist

музејшүнаслыг : *n* museology *science of museum design, organization and management*

мум : *n* 1) wax *a* 2) wax, waxen

мумија : *n* 1) mummy 2) ferric oxide dye

мумијаламаг : *v* 1) mummify 2) embalm

мумкүн : *n* black day *in one's life*

мумкүнлүк : *adv* for a rainy day, just in case just to be on the safe side

мумламаг : *v* 1) coat with wax 2) wax, polish with wax

мумурган : *n* skin-cream, skin-nourishing cream

мумурганламаг : *v* lubricate, rub with skin-cream

мунчуг : *n* beads

мурад : *n* 1) wish, desire; 2) goal, purpose; intention

мурдар : *a* nasty, dirty, disgusting

мурдарлама : *n* desecration

мурдарламаг : *v* spoil, foul, defile, dirty, mess up; desecrate;

мурдарланмаг : *v* be spoilt, be defiled/dirtied/messed up; be desecrated;

мурдарлыг : *n* untidiness, slovenliness

мурдарчы : *a* 1) untidy, unclean, sloven *n* 2) untidiness, uncleanliness, slovenliness

мурдарчылыг : *n* untidiness, uncleanliness, slovenliness

мурдов : *n* see **зығ**

мусәмма : *n* musamma *a pilaf dressing made of meat and eggplants*

мусиги : *n* 1) music *a* 2) musical

мусигили : *a* musical

мусигичи : *n* musician

мусигишүнас : *n* musicologist

мусигишүнаслыг : *n* musicology

мухтар : *a* autonomous, independent

мухтаријјәт : *n* autonomy

мухтаријјәтли : *a* see **мухтар**

муша : *n* see **һамбал**

мушгурмаг : *v* 1) smack one's lips 2) summon/call by a whistle 3) urge on with a whistle *trained animals*

мушгурт : *n* leftover fodder in mangers

муштулуг : *n* 1) good news 2) traditional reward to the bringer of good news

муштулугламаг : *v* bring good news

муштулугчу : *n* 1) bringer of good news *ext* 2) stormy petrel

мүавин : *n* assistant, deputy *of an official*

мүадил : *a phys* equidimensional, equivalent: *only in combinations*: **мүадил чисимләр** equivalent masses

мүајинә : *n* 1) checkup, inspection; research *leg* 2) hearing, investigation

мүаличә : *n* 1) treatment; healing; medical care *a* 2) treatment, healing, medical care-related

мүаличәхана : *n* 1) clinic, medical center, out-patient department

мүамилә : *n* see **сәләм**

мүамиләчи : *n* see **сәләмхор, сәләмчи**

мүасир : *a* 1) modern, up-to-date *n* 2) contemporary

мүасирләшдирилмәк : *v* modernize

мүасирләшдирмә : *n* modernization

мүасирлик : *n* the present time; contemporaneity

мүаһидә, мүаһидәнамә : *n* agreement, treaty, convention, pact

мүбадилә : *n* 1) exchange *a* 2) exchange, exchange-related

мүбалиғә : *n* exaggeration, hyperbole

мүбалиғәли : *a* exaggerated, blown-up, inflated

мүбалиғәсиз : *a* 1) without exaggeration *adv* understatedly, without exaggeration

мүбалиғәчи : *a* 1) inclined/given to exaggeration *n* 2) person given to exaggeration

мүбарәк : *a* blessed; happy

мүбарәк олсун : *interj* congratulations!

мүбарәкбадлыг : *n* congratulation

мүбариз : *n* 1) fighter, warrior a 2) militant, belligerent

мүбаризә : *n* struggle, fighting

мүбаһисә : *n* argument, discussion, debate

мүбаһисәли : *a* disputable, arguable

мүбаһисәсиз : *a* 1) doubtless, undisputable *adv* 2) doubtlessly, undisputably

мүбаһисәчи : *n* debater, wrangler

мүбтәда : *n gram* subject

мүбтәла : *a* 1) subject/exposed to 2) gripped/racked with, suffering from

мүвази : *a* equiponderant, equally balanced

мүвазинә, мүвазинәт : *n* balance, equilibrium

мүвазинәтли : *a* balanced, even

мүвазинәтлик : *n* 1) balance, evenness 2) sang-froid, composure

мүвафиг : *a* suitable, corresponding, proper

мүвафигәт : *n* suitability, conformity, correspondence

мүвәггәти : *a* 1) temporary *adv* 2) temporarily

мүвәггәтилик : *n* temporality, temporary nature/character

мүвәккил : *n* plenipotentiary; chargě d' affaires

мүвәккиллик : *n* having full power; being authorized; position of a chargě d'affaires

мүвәффәг : *adv* successfully

мүвәффәгијјәт : *n* success

мүвәффәгијјәтлә : *adv* successfully

мүвәффәгијјәтли : *a* successful, lucky

мүвәффәгијјәтлилик : *n* successfulness

мүвәффәгијјәтсиз : *a* unsuccessful

мүвәффәгијјәтсизлик : *n* failure : *lit* unsuccessfulness

мүгабил : *a* 1) against, opposed, contrary *adv* 2) opposite

мүгабилиндә : *postp* in front of, facing, against

мүгабиллик : *n* 1) opposition, contrast 2) opposite, antithesis

мүгавилә, мүгавиләнамә : *n* agreement, contract, pact, treaty

мүгавимәт : *n* resistance

мүгавимәт көстәрмәк : *v* resist

мүгајисә : n 1) comparison a 2) comparative

мүгајисәли : *a* comparative

мүгәвва : *n* stuffed animal; manequin

мүггәддәрат : *n* fate, predestination

мүгәддәс : *n* holy, sacred

мүгәддәслик : *n* holiness, sanctity

мүгәддимә : *n* 1) foreword, preface 2) premise, pre-condition, prerequisite

мүгәссир : *n* guilty

мүгәссирлик : *n* guilt

мүгәшшәр : *n* shelled peas

мүғајир : *a* 1) contradictory 2) disparate, essentially different

мүғәнни : *n* 1) singer *a* 2) singing of , praising in song

мүдавим : *n* 1) listener, hearer, student 2) visitor

мүдафиә : *n* 1) defense, protection *a* 2) defense, defensive, protective

мүдафиәсиз : *a* defenseless

мүдафиәсизлик : *n* defenselessness

мүдафиәчи : *n* defender

мүдахилә : *n* interference, intervention

мүдахиләсиз : *a* 1) non-interventional *adv* free from interference, without interference

мүдахиләсизлик : *n* non-intervention, non-interference

мүдахиләчи : *n polit* interventionist

мүддәа : *n* thesis, proposition

мүддәи : *n* plaintiff

мүддәт : *n* 1) term, period of time 2) time, flow of time, duration of time

мүддәтли : *a* having a definite term/deadline

мүддәтсиз : *a* without time-limit, indefinite

мүдир : *n* manager, directoe, administrator

мүдиријјәт : *n* management, administration, directorship

мүдирлик : *n* position of manager/director/administrator

мүдрик : *a* wise, sage

мүдриклик : *n* wisdom, sagacity

мүдһиш : *a* **дәһшәтли**

мүәззин : *n* see **азанчы**

мүәјјән : *a* definite, concrete, established, specified

мүәјјәнләшдирилмәк : *v* be defined, be specified, be fixed

мүәјјәнләшдирмәк : *v-tr* define, specify

мүәјјәнләшмәк : *v* become definite, concrete, specified

мүәјјәнлик : *n* definiteness, specificity

мүәллим : *n* teacher *male*

мүәллимә : *n* teacher *female*

мүәллимәлик : *n* profession of teacher

мүәллимлик : *n* profession of teacher

мүәллиф : *n* author

мүәллифлик : *n* authorship

мүәмма : *n* riddle, enigma, mystery, inexplicable thing

мүәммалы : *a* mysterious, inexplicable

мүәрриф : reference *person providing reference[s] for s.o.*

мүәррифлик : *n* recommendation, references

мүәссис : *n* see **бани**

мүәссисә : *n* enterprise, organization, establishment, institution

мүждә : *n* see **муштулуг**

мүждәләмәк : *v* see **муштулугламаг**

мүждәчи : *n* see **муштулугчу**

мүзајигә : *n* denying o.s./or s.o. else s.t., being stingy/tight-fisted

мүзајидә : *n* sale, auction

мүзакирә : *n* 1) argument, discussion 2) debate

мүзәффәр : *a* victorious

мүзәффәријјәт : *n* victory

мүзәффәријјәтли : *a* victorious

мүзмин : *a* chronic

мүзүрр : *a* harmful, perilous

мүјәссәр : *a* achievable, attainable, capaable of accomplishment, realizable, feasible

мүкалимә : *n* 1) dialogue 2) debate

мүкафат : *n* prize, reward, material recompense

мүкафатландырмаг : *v* reward, award a prize *to*

мүкафатланмаг : *v* be rewarded, be awarded a prize

мүкафатсыз : *a* 1) unpaid, without reward or compensation *adv* 2) gratuitously, for nothing

мүкәлләфијјәт : *n* obligation, duty

мүкәммәл : *a* perfect, superlative, outstanding, first class

мүкәммәлләшдирилмәк : *v* be perfected, improved

мүкәммәлләшдирмәк : *v-tr* perfect, improve

мүкәммәлләшмәк : *v* become perfect, improved

мүкәммәллик : *n* perfection, excellence

мүлазим : *n* *obs* lieutenant

мүлајим : *a* 1) moderate 2) gentle, mild

мүлајимләшмәк : *v* 1) become moderate 2) become mild/gentle

мүлајимлик : *n* 1) moderation, moderateness, temperance 2) mildness, gentleness

мүлајимчә : *adv* mildly, gently

мүлаһизә : *n* consideration, considered opinion, view

мүлаһизәли : *a* prudent, reasonable

мүлаһизәсиз : *a* imprudent, lacking common sense

мүлаһизәсизлик : *n* imprudence, lack of common ssense

мүлк : *n* 1) property, estate, real estate 2) premises, building

мүлкәдар : *n* landlord, landowner

мүлки : *a* civic, civil

мүлкијјәт : *n* property

мүлкијјәтчи : *n* man of property, owner, proprietor

мүлксүз : *a* propertyless, landless, having no estate *of a nobleman*

мүлһүд : *n* heretic

мүманиәт : *n* obstacle

мүмәссил : *n* representative; envoy, attachě

мүмкүн : *a* 1) possible *adv* 2) possibly

мүмкүнат : *n* opportunity; possibility

мүнагишә : *n* 1) argument, quarrel, conflict 2) debate, discussion;

мүнасиб : *a* appropriate, acceptable; proper, reasonable

мүнасибәт : *n* 1) relations, relationship, kinship 2) case, occasion

мүнасибәтсиз : *a* 1) inappropriate, unacceptable; improper; unreasonable *adv* 2) inappropriately, unacceptably; inopportunely, mal à propos

мүнасибәтсизлик : *n* inappropriateness; unacceptability; impropriety

мүнасиблик : *n* 1) appropriateness, acceptability; propriety, 2) availability

мүнбит : *a* fertile *of soil*

мүнбитлик : *n* fertility

мүндәричат, мүндәричә : *n* table of contents *book*

мүнәччим : *n* 1) astrologist *hist* 2) astrologer

мүнәччимбашы : *n* senior astrologist

мүнзәви : *n* see **дашакирән**

мүнсиф : *n* judge; referee, arbitrator

мунсифлик : *n* judgeship, arbitration

мунтэзэм : *a* 1) regular, systematic; disciplined; well-balanced *adv* 2) regularly, systematically, in a disciplined manner

мунтэзир : *a n* expecting, waiting

мунтэхэбат : *n* 1) selected passaages from literary works 1) chrestomathy, collection *of stories/articles etc*

мурасилат : *n* correspondence

мурачиэт : *n* appeal; address *to s.o.*

мурачиэтнамэ : *n* appeal *written*

мурвэт : *n* compassion; magnanimity

мурвэтли : *a* humane, compassionate, magnanimous

мурвэтсиз : *a* 1) inhumane, brutal, pitiless 2) covetous

мурвэтсизлик : *n* 1) inhumanity, brutality, pitilessness 2) covetousness

мурдэсэнк : *n chem* lead ochre

мурдэшир : *n* ritual corpse-washer

мурэббэ : *n* jam

мурэбби : *n* 1) tutor, home-teacher *male* 2) trustee,

мурэббиjэ : *n* tutor, home-teacher *female* 2) trustee,

мурэббиjэлик : *n* occupation/duties of a home-teacher *female*

мурэббилик : *n* occupation/duties of a home-teacher *male*

мурэккэб : *n* 1) ink a 2) complicated, compound

мурэккэбгабы : *n* ink-pot, ink-well

мурэккэблэщдирмэк : *v-tr* complicate, make complicated

мурэккэблэшмэ : *n* complication

мурэккэблэшмэк : *v* become complicated

мурэккэблик : *n* complication, complexity

мурэссэ : *n* fried eggs

мурэттиб : *n* compositor, type-setter

мурэттиблик : *n* profession compositor,type-setter

мурэттибхана : *n* see **мэтбээ**

мурэххэс : *a* 1) manumitted, freed, released *n* 2) freedman, former slave

мурид : *n* Murid, disciple, devotee *of a spiritual teacher in Islam*

муридизм : *n* Muridism, a conservative spiritual movement in Islam

муркү : *n* napping, dozing

муркүлэмэк : *v* take a nap, doze

муртэд : *n* renegade, apostate

муртэче : *n* 1) reactionary *a* 2) reeactionary

муртлэмэк : *v* gut, clean, disembowel *a fowl*

мурчум : *n* icicle

мусабигэ : *n* competition, match, contest

мусават : *n* Musavat *National-democratic Party of Azerbaijan, lit. equality*

мусави : *n* equal

мусадирэ : *n* confiscation, expropriation

мусаидэ : *n* permission, authorization

мусамирэ : *n* 1) party, evening party, gathering 2) evening

мусафир : *n* 1) traveller 2) guest 3) passenger

мусаһиб : *n* interlocutor

мусаһибэ : *n* conversation; interview

мусбэт : *a* 1) positive , affirmative *adv* 2) positively, affirmatively

мусэддэс : *n* hexameter

мусэллэһ : *a* armed

мусэлман : *n* 1) Moslem, Mohammedan *a* 2) Moslem, Mohammedan

мусэлманчылыг : *n* Mohammedanism, Islam

мусэһһиһ : *n* proof-reader, copy-editor

мусэһһиһлик : *n* profession of proof-reader/copy editor

мусибэт : *n* trouble, misfortunes, grief, woe

мусибэтли : *a* disastrous, calamitous, troublesome, grievous, woeful

мустэбид : *n* despot, tyrant, dictator

мустэбидлик : *n* despotism, tyranny, dictatorship

мустэбидчэсинэ : *adv* tyrannically, despotically

мустэви : *n* 1) flatness, plane *fig* 2) platitude *a* 3) flat, flattened

мустэгил : *a* 1) independent *adv* 2) independently

мустэгиллик : *n* independence

мустэмлэкэ : *n* 1) colony *a* 2) colonial

мустэмлэкэлэщдирмэ : *n* colonization

мустэмлэкэлэщдирмэк : *v* colonize

мустэмлэкэчи : *n* colonizer

мустэмлэкэчилик : *n* colonialism

мустэнтиг : *n* 1) detective; investigator 2) interrogator

мустэнтиглик : *n* occupation/profession of investigator or interrogator

мустәсна : *n* 1) exclusion *a* 2) exclusive, outstanding, unusual

мустәсналыг : *n* exclusiveness, exclusivity

мутабиг : *a* fitting, suitable, proper; corresponding to; conformable to

муталиә : *n* reading

муталиәли : *a* well-read

муталиәчи : *n* person who is fond of reading, book-lover

мутарикә : *n* truce, ceasefire

мутәәссир : *a n* saddened; frustrated

мутәккә : *n* long, cylindrical pillow placed against the wall *Used for support while sitting on the floor*

мутәмади : *a* permanent, constant, incessant

мутәнасиб : *a* proportional, symmetrical, commensurate

мутәнасиблик : *n* proportionality, symmetry, balance

мутәрәгги : *a* progressive, advanced

мутәрәддид : *a* 1) vacillating, hesitant *adv* 2) uncertainly, indecisively

мутәрәддидлик : *n* indecision, indecisiveness, inconstancy, vacillation

мутәрчим : *n* 1) translator, interpreter 2) dragoman *official interpreter/translator employed by consulates in the Middle-East*

мутәрчимлик : *n* profession of translator/interpreter

мутәфәккир : *n* 1) thinker; thoughtful person *a* 2) thoughtful, immersed in thought

мутә'фин : *a* nasty, disgusting, revolting

мутәхәссис : *n* specialist, professional

мутәһәррик : *a* mobile; energetic

мутәшәккил : *a* organized, formed

мутәшәккиллик : *n* organization *in a positive sense*; orderliness

мути : *a* 1) obedient *adv* 2) obediently

мутилик : *n* obedience

мутләг : *a* 1) absolute, unconditional, categorical,sure, certain *adv* 2) unconditionally, categorically; for sure, certainly, undoubtfully, absolutely

мутләгиііәт : *n* monarchy, autocracy, absolutism

мутләгиііәтпәрәст, мутләгиііәтчи : *n* monarchist

мутрүб : *n* 1) transvestite 2) effeminate man *obs* 3) young boy-dancer, dressed in female costume *in Middle East, fr. Arabic "mutrib" = musician, dancer, singer, chanteur/chanteuse*

мүттәсил : *adv* incessantly, constantly

мүттәфиг : *n* 1) allies *a* 2) allied

мүттәһим : *n* defendant, the accused

мүфәссәл : *a* 1) detailed 2) *adv* minutely, in detail

мүфәттиш : *n* inspector

мүфәттишлик : *n* 1) inspection 2) work/job/responsibility of inspector

мүфлис : *a* 1) bankrupt, insolvent, impoverished *n* 2) a bankrupt *one who is judicially declared insolvent*

мүфлислик : *n* bankruptcy, insolvency

мүфрәд : *n gram* singular number

мүфтә : *a* 1) free, gratuitous, cost-free *adv* 2) free of charge, gratis

мүфтәхор : *n* parasite, sponge[r], scrounger, free-loader

мүфтәхорлуг : *n* parasitism, sponging, scrounging, free-loading

мүфти : *n* Mufti *head of the Sunni clergy in a district*

мүхалиф : *a* 1) opposite, contradictory, not in agreement with *n* 2) opposition

мүхалифәт : *n* opposition; contradiction

мүхалифәтчи : *n* member of the opposition

мүхбир : *n* 1) correspondent *a* 2) correspondent['s], journalistic

мүхбирлик : *n* occupation of a correspondent/journalist

мүхәлләфат : *n* household belongings, personal belongings/property, goods and chattels

мүхәммәс : *n* pentameter

мүхәннәс : *a* 1) cowardly *n* 2) coward

мүхәннәт : *n* traitor

мүхтәлиф : *a* various, different, diverse

мүхтәлифлик : *n* variety

мүхтәлифнөвлү : *a* heterogenious, various, diverse

мүхтәлифрә'іли : *a n* differing in opinion; dissident

мүхтәлифрә'іlик : *n* difference, contradiction, differently minded, variety of points of view

мүхтәлифтәрәфли, мүхтәлифчәһәтли : *a* various, divergent

мүхтәсәр : *a* 1) brief, short *adv* 2) briefly, shortly 3) in short, to make a long story short

мүхтәсәрлик : *n* brevity, briefness, shortness

мүхтәсәрчә : *adv* briefly, shortly, in short

мүhазирә : *n* 1) lecture *a* 2) lecture

мүhазирәчи : *n* lecturer

мүhакимә : *n* 1) judgement, 2) law-suit; judicial/court investigation,

мүhакимәли : *a* reasonable, sober-minded

мүhакимәсиз : *a* 1) unreasonable, delirious 2) reckless, fool-hardy

мүhарибә : *n* war

мүhасиб : *n* 1) book-keeper; accountant *a* 2) book-keeping, accountancy

мүhасибат : *n* book-keeping department; accountancy department

мүhасирә : *n* siege, encirculment, blockade

мүhафиз : *n* guard, protection

мүhафизә : *n* *mil* guarding, protection, defence, covering action, cover

мүhафизәкар : *n* 1) conservative *a* 2) conservative

мүhафизәкарлыг : *n* conservatism, Toryism

мүhафизәчи : *n* 1) guard, security officer 2) arm of the law

мүhачир : *n* refugee, resettler, emigrant

мүhачирәт, мүhачирлик : *n* resettlement, emigration

мүhәввәл : *n* *only in comb* **мүhәввәл (етмәк)** : leave up to *s.o.*, place responsibilities on *s.o.*

мүhәндис : *n* 1) engineer a 2) engineer['s], engineering

мүhәндислик : *n* profession of engineer

мүhәррик : *n* motor, engine

мүhәррир : *n* journalist

мүhәррирлик : *n* 1) journalism 2) profession of journalist/correspondent

мүhит : *n* 1) environment, social environment, social atmosphere *ext* 2) atmosphere

мүhүм : *a* important, substantive, vital, urgent

мүhүмлүк : *n* importance, degree of importance vitality, vital nature

мүчавир : *n* devotee, votary living in the immediate vicinity of a mosque

мүчаhид : *n* Islamic fundamentalist fighter

мүчәрраб, мүчәрраб дәрман : *n* panacea

мүчәррәд : *a* abstract

мүчәррәдләшдирмә : *n* making*s.t.* abstract

мүчәррәдләшдирмәк : *v* make *s.t.* abstract

мүчәррәдләшмәк : *v* become abstract

мүчәррәдлик : *n* abstraction

мүчәссәмә : *n* embodiment, incarnation

мүчрү : *n* wooden or plastic case/box

мүчтәhид : *n* higher spiritual authority *of the Shiite Muslims*

мүшавир : *n* consultant, advisor

мүшавирә : *n* meeting, consultation

мүшајиәт : *n* accompaniment, escort, convoy

мүшаhидә : *n* observation, watching

мүшаhидәчи : *n* observer

мүшаhидәчилик : *n* keenness of observation

мүшди : *n* handle of a wooden plough

мүшәмбә : *n* oilcloth

мүшәррәф : *a* 1) honored *n* 2) honored person

мүшк : *n* musk

мүшкүл : *a* hard, difficult, tough

мүшкүлкүша : *a* 1) resolving problems, difficulties *n* 2) problem solver

мүштәрәк : *a* common, collective, joint

мүштәри : *n* 1) customer 2) client *astron* 3) Jupiter *planet*

мүштәрикир : *a* marketable, in demand

мүштүк : *n* cigarette-holder *a* 2) cigarette-holder

Н

н : eighteenth letter of the Azerbaijani alphabet

набат : *n* fruitdrop, hard candy, sugar candy,

набәләд : *a* unfamiliar with, unaccustomed to

набәләдлик : *n* unfamiliarity *with s.t.*

навала : *n* mash, fodder *livestock food*

навалча : *n* rain-spout

навар : *n* camel-saddle

нагабил : *a* 1) unworthy 2) unskilful, clumsy 3) indecent

нагафил : *a* 1) sudden, unexpected *adv* 2) suddenly, unexpectedly, out of the blue

наггабалыг : *n* sheat-fish *Siluris glanis*, a large catfish of the fresh waters of central and Eastern Europe, sometimes weighing as much as 400 pounds

наггал : *a* 1) talkative, garrulous *n* 2) talkative person, chatter-box, motor-mouth

нагалламаг : *v* talk idly, be loquacious, run off at the mouth, prate

нагғаллыг : *n* idle talk, chatter

нагғалхана : *n* a meeting, gathering, establishment etc where endless, fruitless discussions take place in place of work *lit: talk-shop, talk- house*

нагғаш : *n* painter, artist; specialist in decorative art

нагғашкарлыг : *n* painting

нагғашлыг : *n* 1) painting[s]; fresco-painting 2) profession of painter/artist/specialist in decorative art

нагил : *n* electric wire

нагис : *a* 1) defective, incomplete, unfinished; defectiveness, incompleteness, insufficiency *n* 2) shortage, shortfall, inadequacy

наголај : *a* 1) inconvenient, awkward, uncomfortable *adv* 2) inconveniently, awkwardly, uncomfortably

наголајлыг : *n* inconvenience

нағара : *n* nağara, kettle-drum *used in folk-music especially for wedding-parties*

нағарачалан, нағарачы : *n* nağara-player

нағд : *a* 1) cash *adv* 2) in cash *n* 3) amount on hand, cash on hand

нағыл : *n* 1) tale, fairy tale, fable story, narrative *a* 2) fabular, anecdotal, fairy-tale

нағылбаз : *n* 1) story-teller; one who loves stories/tales *fig* 2) windbag; fabricator

нағылдејән : *n* story-teller; folktale-narrator

нағыл-мағыл : *n* tale; story

нағылчы : *n* 1) story-teller, folktale-narrator 2) windbag; fabricator liar

надан : *a* 1) ignorant *n* 2) ignoramus, ignorant person

наданлыг : *n* ignorance; obscurantism

надинч : *n* 1) naughty/mischievous child, rascal *a* 2) naughty, mischievous

надинчлик : *n* naughtiness, mischievousness

надир : *a* 1) rare, exotic *adv* 2) rarely, exotically

надүрүст : *a* 1) sly, arch; roguish, scoundrelly 2) rogue, scoundrel

надүрүстләшмәк : *v* become sly, arch; become roguish

надүрүстлүк : *n* slyness, archness; roguishness

наәлач : *a* 1) in a hopeless, desperate situation, in a situation from which there is no way out *n* 2) helpless person in a situation from which there is no egress/no way out

наәлачлыг : *n* hopelessness, helplessness, situation with no a way out

наәлачлыгдан : *adv* forced by circumstances, no way out

наәһл : *a* 1) incapable, stupid, unreceptive 2) ungenerous

наз : *n* coquetry, affectedness, putting on airs

назбалығы : *n* species of bream Cyprinus nasus, a cyprinoid fish

назбалыш : *n* pillow, cushion

наз-гәмзә : *n* coquetry, affectation

назәнин : *a* 1) coquettish 2) graceful, tender, charming

назик : *a* 1) thin, high-pitched *voice* 2) tender *adv* 2) thinly, highly 3) tenderly

назикгәлбли : *a* soft- hearted

назикдиварлы : *a* thin-walled

назикләнмәк : *v* grow thinner

назикләтмәк, назикләшдирмәк : *v* make thinner

назикләшдиртмәк : *v* *caus* of **назикләшдирмәк**

назикләшмәк : *v* see **назикләтмәк**,

назиклик : *n* 1) thinness, subtlety 2) frailty, delicacy

назикчә : *a* 1) thin *adv* 2) thinly, subtly

назилмәк : *v* see **назикләшмәк**

назилтмәк : *v* make thin, tender, subtle

назим : *n* regulator, controller, governor *device*

назир : *n* minister *chief of a governmental department*

назирлик : *n* ministry *governmental department*

назламаг, назландырмаг : *v* cherish; be affectionate/caring

назланмаг : *v* 1) behave capriciously 2) pose, put on airs, behave affectedly

назлы : *a* 1) capricious; spoiled *child* 2) spoiled child, molly-coddle, sissy

назсатан : *a* 1) coquette, flirtatious, playful woman *n* 2) coquettish

наил : *n* achievement *only in combinations*

наиллијјәт : *n* achievement

наинсаф : *a* conscienceless, unscrupulous, unfair, brutal

наинсафлыг : *n* consciencelessness, unscrupulousness, unfairness; brutality

нај : *a* 1) merry, jovial *n* 2) convivial fellow

накам : *a* not reaching a goal; dissatisfied, disappointed

накладнаја : *n* *Ru* invoice

накаһ, накаһан : *a* 1) unexpected, sudden *adv* 2) unexpectedly, suddenly

накаһани : *a* unexpected, sudden

накаһанилик : *n* suddenness, unexpectedness

нал : *n* 1) horse-shoe 2) stake, picket

налајиг : *a* 1) unfitting, improper, impolite *adv* 2) unfittingly, improperly, impolitely

налајиглик : *n* 1) impropriety, unfitting remark 2) obscene language

налбәнд : *n* blacksmith/horseshoer

налбәндлик : *n* occupation of blacksmith/horse-shoer

налвары : *a* horseshoe-shaped

налә : *n* moan, weeping, sobbing, outburst of tears

налламаг : *v* shoe a horse

наллaнмаг : *v* be shod *of a horse*

наллатдырмаг, наллатмаг : *v* *caus* of **налламаг**

наллы : *a* shod *of a horse*

налча : *n* small horse-shoe

налсыз : *a* unshod *of a horse*

намаз : *n* namaz *Moslem prayer said five times a day*

намдар : *a* famous, popular, well-known

намә : *n* 1) letter 2) written order 3) deed, document, official document

намәгбул : *a* 1) unacceptable, unsuitable, improper, unseemly

намә'лум : *a* unknown

намә'лумлуг : *n* unknowableness

намәрбут : *a* 1) indecent, unworthy *n* 2) action unacceptable to aa respectable person

намәрд : *a* 1) treacherous, mean, base *n* 2) traitor

намәрдлик : *n* treachery; baseness;

намәрдчәсинә : *adv* treacherously, basely

намәһрәм : *a* 1) alien, strange 2) uninitiated, unaware, uninformed

намизәд : *n* 1) candidate 2) engaged *to be married*

намизәдлик : *n* 1) candidacy *in various senses*

намөһкәм : *a* unstable, precarious, unreliable

намөһкәмлик : *n* instability, precariousness, unreliability

намус : *n* sense of honor; honesty

намусуна гысылмаг : *v* refrain *from an action for the sake of one's honor*

намусуна саташмаг : *v* deprive of honor; deprive of moral or physical chastity, rape

намусла : *adv* honestly, conscientiously

намуслу : *a* honest, conscientious

намуслулуг : *n* honesty, sense of honor; conscientiousness

намуссув : *a* dishonest, shameless, conscienceless

намуссузлуг : *n* shamelessness, dishonesty

намуссузчасына : *adv* dishonestly, shamelessly

намүәјјән : *a* indefinite

намүәјјәнлик : *n* vagueness, uncertainty, indefiniteness

намүнасиб : *a* see **мүнасибәтсиз**

намүнасиблик : *n* see **мүнасибәтсизлик**

нанә : *n* *bot* mint *Mentha*

нанәчиб : *a* ignoble; mean; common

наныг : *a* 1) weak; underdeveloped 2) diffuse, scattered, dispersed 3) home-bred *of livestock*

нанкор : *a* ungrateful

нанкорлуг : *n* ungratefulness

нар : *n* 1) pomegranate *a* 2) pomegranate

наразы : *a* dissatisfied

наразылыг : *n* dissatisfaction

нараһат : *a* 1) anxious, uneasy, fussing 2) uncomfortable, inconvenient, troublesome 3) anxiously, fussily

нараһатлыг : *n* 1) worry, anxiety, trouble 2) inconvenience

нарвал : *n* *zool* narwhal *Monodan monocerous a large Arctic cetacean*

нардан : *n* dried pomegranate seeds

нарданча : *n* pomegranate jam

наринки : *n* *bot* tangerine *Citrus reticulata*

нарын : *a* small, fragmented, powdery

нарынламаг : *v* become pulverized/fragmented

нарынланмаг : *v* be fragmented, be pulverized

нарынлатмаг : *v-tr* pulverize, pound, crush, divide into particles

нарынч : *n* *bot* bitter orange *Citrus aurantium*

нарынчы : *a* orange

наркилә : *n* narghile, hookah *Oriental tobacco pipe with a long flexible tube that passes through a water-vessel*

нарлыг : *n* area planted with pomegranate bushes

нарушение : *n Ru* violation; felony

наршәраб : *n* narşarab *pomegranate juice used as a dressing/condiment for food*

наряд : *n Ru* warranty

нас : *n* chewing tobacco

насаз : *n* 1) unhealthy, ill, ailing, unwell 2) disordered, deranged; frustrated

насазламаг : *n* be sick, unwell

насазлыг : *n* 1) indisposition, ailment, malady 2) disorder, derangement

насир : *n* fiction-writer

наснас : *n zool* chimpanzee *Pan troglodytes*

насос : *n* 1) pump *a* 2) pump[ing]

насосламаг : *v* pump *by means of pump*

натамам : *n* incomplete, unfinished

натамамлыг : *n* incompleteness

натараз : *a* 1) clumsy, awkward 2) gigantic

натаразлыг : *n* clumsiness, awkwardness

натаразчасына : *adv* clumsily, awkwardly

натәмиз : *a* 1) unclean, dirty 2) *adv* uncleanly, dirtily

натәмизлик : *n* uncleanliness, impurity

натиг : *n* 1) orator, speaker 2) Natig *common masculine first name*

натиглик : *n* eloquence, oratory

натигчәсинә : *adv* eloquently

натыгбурун : *a n* snub-nosed *of a person*

натриум : *n chem* sodium, Na

натура : *n* see **хасиjjәт**

натурал : *a* natural, real, genuine

натуралист : *n* 1) naturalist 2) naturalist, realist *proponent of the principle of realism/naturalism in literature and art*

натуралистлик : *a* naturalistic

наүмид : *a* hopeless

наүмидлик : *n* hopelessness

наүмидчәсинә : *adv* hopelessly

нахәләф : *a* 1) filialy ungrateful *n* 2) ungrateful son

нахәләфлик : *n* 1) filial ingratitude 2) absence of good qualities

нахыр : *n* cattle herd

нахырчы : *n* 1) cattle-herder 2) see **дәвәдәлләjи**

нахырчылыг : *n* occupation of cattle-herder

нахыш : *n* 1) ornamental design, illustration 2) embroidery

нахышы кәтирмәк : *v* become lucky *finally*

нахышбәнд : *n* see **нахышчы**

нахышламаг : *v* decorate with designs/patterns

нахышланмаг : *v* be decorated with designs/patterns

нахышлатдырмаг, нахышлатмаг : *v caus* of **нахышламаг**

нахышлы : *a* decoraated with patterns/designs, embroidered; patterned, ornamented

нахышчы : *n* master-specialist in ornamental design

нахош : *a* sick, unwell

нахошлама : *n* disease, sickness, illness, malady

нахошламаг : *v* fall sick, fall ill

нахошлатмаг : *v* cause someone to fall ill, be the causse of s.o.'s illness

нахошлуг : *n* disease. sickness, illness, malady

нахүнәк : *n* taking advantage of the good will/generosity/hospitality of another by helping o.s. without invitation or polite request to s.t., *e.g. food, cigarettes*; cadging, sponging, freeloading

нахүнәкчи : *n* petty pilferer, sponge, free-loader, cadger

нахчыван : *n* 1) Nakhichevan *city in the Nakhichevan Autonomous Republic located within the territory of Armenia* *a* 2) Nakhichevan

наһаг : *a* 1) vain *adv* 2) in vain

наһагдан : *adv* unfairly, baselessly

наһамар : *a* uneven, rough

наһамарлыг : *n* unevenness, roughness

наһар : *n* 1) lunch; dinner *a* 2) lunch; dinner

наһарпаjлаjан : *n* waiter *rare*

наһиjә : *n* 1) area, region, territory *med* 2) tractначаг

начаг : *a* see **насаз**

началник : *n Ru* chief, boss, manager, supervisor

начар : *a* 1) helpless, hopeless, in a disasstrous state *adv* 2) involuntarily, against the will

начиз : *a* pitiable, miserable

начаг : *n* pole-axe, hatchet, axe

начинс : *n* ignoble, ungenerous person

начинслик : *n* mean/base/ignoble/dishonest action

нашатыр : *n* ammonium hydroxide, aqueous ammonia

нашир : *n* publisher

нашири-əфкар : *n* organ of the press, a publication

нашы : *a* inexperienced, unsophisticated, lacking expertise; unfamiliar *with*, unaware *of*

нашылыг : *n* lack of expertise; unfamiliarity, unawareness

наштаб : n 1) breakfast *adv* 2) on an empty stomach

наштаблыг : *n* 1) breakfast, mid-morning snack 2) lunch[eon]

нашүкүр : *a* ungrateful; unappreciative

нашүкүрлүк : *n* ungratefulness, ingratitude, unappreciativeness

неј : *n* flute

нејбəт : *a* ugly, nasty, disgusting, offensive

нејзə : *n* broadaxe

нејсан : *n poet* April showers *fr. Arabic/Persian Nisan, a month covering parts of March and April*

нејтрал : *a* 1) neutral *n* 2) neutral

нејтраллашдырмаг : *v-tr* neutralize

нејтраллыг : *n* neutrality

нејчалан, нејчи : *n* flute-player

не'мəт : *n* grace; gift; abundance

нен : *n* Nenets *reindeer-herding people of north-eastern European Russia and Northern Siberia*

нефт : *n* 1) oil *a* 2) oil

нефтајыран : *a* oil-refining *of a plant*

нефтверəн : *a* oil-bearing

нефтдашыјан : *a* oil-tanker, tanker

нефтли : *a* 1) oil, oil-bearing 2) oily, oil-stained

нефтлилик : *n* presence of oil; oil-bearing condition, petroliferous state

нефтөлчəн : *n* oil-gage

нефтсиз : *a* without oil

нефттəмизлəјəн : *a* oil-refining

нефтчи : *n* oil-industry worker, oil-well worker

нефтчыхарма : *a* oil-drilling

неһрə : *n* butter-churn

нечə : *pro* how many ?, how much ?

нечəјə : *pro* how much ? *of a price*

нечəлик : *n* the price charged *lit "how-muchness"*

нечə-нечə : *pro* a lot of, lots of, many *people*

нечəнчи : *pro* which *one* ?

нечəси : *pro* how many of them ?

нечə : *pro* how? ; in what way ?

нечəлик : *n* see **кејфијјəт**

нештəр : *n* 1) scalpel, lancet 2) sting

нештəрлəмəк : *v* lance

нештəрлəнмəк : *v* be lanced

нештəрлəтмəк : *v-tr* cause to lance

нə : *pro* what ?

нə билим : *exp* 1) I do not know 2) I do not care *often used in situations when Europeans simply shrug their shoulders*

нə вар : *exp coll* what's up?

нə вахт : *exp* when? *lit what time?*

нə гəдəр : *exp* how many, how much

нə үстə : *exp* why? *lit What further/in addition?*

нə ки вар : *exp* all, everything

нə үчүн : *exp* why?, what for?

нəбатат : *n* 1) vegetation, verdure, flora 2) botany, the plant world *a* 3) botanical

нəбататчы : *n* botanist

нəбататшүнас : *n* botanist

нəбз : *n* pulse

нəбзөлчəн : *n tech* pulsometer, vacuum pump

нəвазиш : *n* friendliness, affability, cordiality

нəвазишкар : *a* see **нəвазишли**

нəвазишлə : *adv* cordially, affably

нəвазишли : *a* friendly, cordial, affable

нəвə : *n* grandchild *m. & f.*

нəвə-нəтичə : *n* descendants; posterity *lit grandchildren and great-grandchildren*

нəгəрат : *n* 1) part *of a piece of music or a song* 2) refrain *of a song*

нəгл : *n* 1) shifting, transference 2) carrying; delivery; transportation

нəгли : *a gram* narrative *of a sentence*

нəглијјат : *n* vehicles, means of transportation

нәглиј̌атчы : *n* transportation/transport worker

нәгш : *n* 1) see **нахыш** 2) imprint, impress

нәғмә : *n* 1) melody, tune, song 2) singing *as a school subject*

нәдән : *pro* why ?

нәдим : *n* joker, buffoon

нәдимлик : *n* buffoonery

нәдимчәсинә : *adv* buffoonishly

нәдир : *exp* What is it ? What does it mean?

нәдән : *pro* why?

нәдәнсә : *pro* somehow, for no obvious reason, for some reason

нәзакәт : *n* delicacy, politeness, courtesy, tact; correctness

нәзакәтлә : *adv* delicately, politely, courteously; correctly

нәзакәтли : *a* delicate, polite, courteous, correct, tactful

нәзакәтсиз : *a* 1) coarse ,indelicate, impolite, discourteous; 2) incorrect *politically, socially or morally*

нәзакәтсизчәсинә : *adv* coarsly, indelicately, impolitely, discourteously

нәзарәт : *n* control; observation; supervision

нәзарәтсиз : *a* uncontrolled, unmonitored; without observation, unsupervised

нәзарәтсизлик : *n* lack of control/monitoring/supervision; lack of observation

нәзарәтчи : *n* supervisor, monitor

нәзәр : *n* 1) glance; viewpoint 2) attention; consideration 3) the evil eye

нәзәр ј̌етирмәк : *v* observe, watch, follow

нәзәри : *a* theoretical, abstract, notional

нәзәрдә тутмаг : *v* mean

нәзәри-диггәт : *n* attention

нәзәриј̌ј̌ә : *n* theory, doctrine

нәзәриј̌ј̌әчи : *n* theoretician

нәзәринчә : *adv* according to *s.o.'s* opinion

нәзир : *n relig* vow, promise; offering, donation

нәзирә : *n* imitation; modelling after *in poetry*

нәзирәчи : *n* imitator, author of an imitative work *in poetry*

нәзм : *n* poetry; versification

нәинки : *adv* not to speak of . . .

нәлбәки : *n* little saucer

нә'лејн : *n* antiquated variety of woman's shoes having no back/counter

нәм : *a* moist,damp, humid

нәмәкбәһарам : *a* see **нанкор**

нәмәкдан : *n* salt-cellar

нәмәков : *n* salt water

нәмиш : *a* moist, damp, humid

нәмишли : *adv* slightly humid/damp

нәмишлик : *n* 1) humidity; rawness, dampness 2) cloudy/overcast weather 3) damp, moist place

нәмләмәк, нәмләтмәк, нәмләшдирмәк : *v* make something wet/humid/damp

нәмләнмәк : *v* become wet/humid/damp

нәм-нүм : *n* affectation, putting on airs; mincing simpering

нәмов : *a* slightly wet, humid, damp

нәмсевән : n *bot* hydrophyte *aquatic plant*

нәмсиз : *a* dry, arid

нәмчимәк, нәмчиләмәк : *v* begin to sweat/perspire

нәнә : *n* 1) grandmother, granny 2) form of address by a young person to any elderly woman) 3) mother

нәнәчан : *n* grannie *affectionate*

нәнни : *n* 1) cradle 2) hammock

нәр : *n* 1) he-camel *fig* 2) brave person, hero 3) courageous, brave , strong

нәрд : *n* nard, *variety of dominos, popular game in Azerbaijan* . see **нәрдтахта**

нәрдиван : *n* staircase

нәрә : *n zool* sturgeon *fam Acipenseridae*

нә'рә : *n* uproar,whooping; roar[ing], howling

нәрилдәмәк : *v* roar

нәрилдәтмәк : *caus* of **нәрилдәмәк**

нәрилдәшмәк : *v* roar *many together*

нәрилти : *n* 1) roaring 2) crash, din, thunder

нәркиз : *n bot* 1) narcissus 2) Narkiz *a common woman's surname*

нәрмада : *n* fold in assembly *of printed materials*

нәрмәназик : *n* 1) softie, person shirking hard, dirty physical work 2) unhandy person; milksop, drip *a* 2) delicate, effeminate, coddled

нәр-нәр : *intj* hub-bub *mainly in combination* **нәр-нәр нәрилдәмәк** : grumble incessantly

нәрдтахта : *n* nard-board ; see **нәрд**

нәсб : *n* *rare* binding, tying

нәсиб : *n* 1) portion, share, lot 2) predestination, fate, destiny

нәсил : *n* 1) gender 2) posterity, generation

нәсилбәнәсил, нәсләнбәнәсл : *adv* from generation to generation

нәсилсиз : *a* childless

нәсим : *n* light breeze

нәсиһәт : *n* admonition, precept, exhortation

нәср : *n* 1) prose *a* 2) prose, prosaic

нәсрани : *n* 1) Christian *a* 2) Christian

нәсраниjjәт : *n* Christianity

нәстәрән : *n* *bot* nasturtium *Tropaeolum*

нәстури : *n* 1) Nestorian *a* 2) Nestorian

нәстурилик : *n* Nestorianism *Christian community of Iran, Iraq, and Malabar, India*

нәтичә : *n* 1) result 2) conclusion 3) great-grandchild

нәтичә чыхармаг : *v* conclude

нәтичәдә : *n* as a result, finally, in the final analysis

нәтичәләндирмәк : *v* achieve a result

нәтичәләнмәк : *v* 1) have *s.t.* as a result 1) come true, really happen

нәтичәли : *a* effective, successful

нәтичәсиз : *a* 1) ineffective, unsuccessful *adv* 2) ineffectively, unsuccessfully

нәтичәсизлик : *n* ineffectiveness, lack of results, non-success, unfulfillment

нәф : *n* benefit; profit

нәфәр : *n* person, human being, individual

нәфәс : *n* breath, breathing; spirit; sigh

нәфәс алмаг : *v* breathe

нәфәскаһ : *n* see **нәфәслик**

нәфәсли : *a* wind *descriptive for musical instruments*

нәфәслик : *n* 1) air-vent 2) small hinged frame for ventilation in a window, *Russ. fortochka*

нәфәссиз : *a* breathless

нәфинә : *adv* to advantage, to *s.o.'s* good, of benefit

нәфис : *a* subtle, rarified, delicate

нәфислик : *n* subtlety, beauty, delicacy

нәфли : *a* beneficial, useful

нәфс : *n* 1) person, individual, personality, 2) passion, eagerness, desire

нәһаjәт : *n* *rare* 1) end, finish *adv* 2) at last, finally *conj* 3) thus, in this way, so then

нәһаjәтсиз : *a* endless, infinite

нәһаjәтсизлик : *n* endlessness, infinity

нәһв : *n* syntax

нәһви : *a* syntactic

нәһәнк : *n* 1) giant, monster *a* 2) huge, gigantic, colossal

нәһәнклик : *n* giganticness, immensity, hugeness

нәһс : *a* 1) unlucky, luckless; sinister, fateful 2) stubborn

нәчидир : 1) be occupied *with s.t.*, be engaged *in s.t.*, have a particular profession 2) be/serve as *s.t.*

нәчабәт : *n* generosity

нәчә : *pro* in what language?

нәчиб : *a* 1) noble, of noble birth 2) generous, magnanimous

нәчибанә : *adv* see **нәчибчәсинә**

нәчибләшдирмә : *n* ennobling

нәчибләшдирмәк : *v* ennoble

нәчибләшмәк : *v* become ennobled, be ennobled

нәчиблик : *n* generosity, nobleness, magnanimity

нәчибчәсинә : *adv* generously, nobly, magnanimously

нәчис : *n* excrement

нәччар : *n* carpenter

нә'ш : *n* corpse

нәш'ә : *n* 1) tipsiness, slight inebriation, pleasure 2) merriness, elevated mood; good humor

нәш'әбаз : *n* voluptuary, lustful person

нәш'әбазлыг : *n* lust; lustfulness

нәш'әверән, нәш'әверичи : *a* ravishing, entrancing, intoxicating

нәш'әләндирмәк : *v* amuse, entrance, raise the spirits *of s.o.* 2) inebriate, intoxicate, get *s.o.* drunk

нәш'әләнмәк : *v* 1) become jolly/merry 2) become tipsy

нәш'әли : *a* 1) jovial, merry 2) convivial 3) tipsy

нәшр : *n* 1) edition, editing, publishing 2) diffusion, dissemination

нәшр еләмәк : *v* publish

нәшриjjат : *n* 1) publishing-house 2) edition *a* 3) publishing, publisher's

нәшриҹјатчы : *n* publisher

нигаб : *n* veil

нида : *n* 1) exclamation 2) cry *gram* 3) interjection

нидерландиҹа : *n* Netherlands

низам : *n* 1) order, discipline 2) code, regulation 3) dispossition, arrangement *mil* 4) formation, order, line

низама кәтирмәк : *v* regulate, put into order

низами : *a mil* 1) regular 2) drill, pertaining to military drill

низам-интизам : *n* schedule, procedure

низамла : *adv* regularly, directly; in a disciplined manner

низамлајычы : *n* regulating mechanism

низамлы : *a* 1) well-regulated; in good order; 2) disciplined

низамлылыг : *n* regularity, state/degree of discipline

низамнамә : *n* regulations, statute

низамсыз : *a* 1) disorderly 2) irregular *adv* 2 irregularly

низамсызлыг : *n* disorderliness; mess ; chaos

низамчы : *n* regulator *person*

низә : *n* spear, pike, javelin

низәләмәк : *n* wound *s.o.* with a spear

нијә : *pro* why?, what for?

нијјәт : *n* intention

нијјәтсиз : *a* 1) unintentional *adv* 2) unintentionally, without premeditation

никаһ : *n* marriage, marriage ceremony, marriage contract

никаһламаг : *v* marry, perform a marriage ceremony

никбин : *n* 1) optimist *a* 2) optimistic

никбинләшмәк : *v* become an optimist

никбинлик : *n* optimism

никел : *n* 1) nickel *a* 2) nickel

никелләмәк : *v* nickelplate

никаран : *a* worried, agitated, anxious

никаранлыг, **никаранчылыг** : *n* worry, anxiety, troubles

нилуфәр : n *bot* 1) water-lily *Nymphaea* 2) Nilufar *feminine first name*

нимдаш : *a* worn-out, used, second-hand

нимру : *n* eggs fried sunny side up

нимтән : *n* 2) bust, bosom 3) brassiere, bra 1) sleeveless gown *woman's*

нимчә : *n* plate

нисан : *n obs* April

нисбәт : *n* 1) relation, correlation 2) comparison

нисбәтән : *adv* as compared to. . ., in comparison with. . .

нисби : *a* comparative, relative

нисбијјәт : *n* relativity

нисбијјәтсизлик : *n* irrespectivity

нисбилик : *n* relativity

нисјә : *n* purchase or sale with financing/on credit

нискил : *n* dreaming about/longing for *s.o.'s* presence

нитг : *n* 1) speech *the capacity to speak* 2) a speech, an address

нифаг : *n* enmity, hostility

нифрәт : *n* disgust, aversion, antipathy 2) hatred, contempt 3) indignation

нифрәтлә : *adv* 1) disgustedly, with aversion 2) indignantly

нифрәтләндиричи : *a* 1) causing disgust, aversion 2) evoking indignation

нифрәтләнмәк : *v* feel disgust/aversion/hatred

нифрәтли : *a* disgusting, aversive, nasty, terrifying

нифрин : *n* damnation; anathema

ниҹат : *n* salvation, liberation, deliverance

ниҹатверичи : *n* saviour, liberator, deliverer

нишан : *n* 1) sign; marking 2) note 3) badge, emblem 4) target 5) sight *of a weapon* 6) engagement; engagement present

нишан вурмаг : *v* 1) mark *s.t.* 2) wear a badge

нишанбазлыг : *n* formal engagement visit of a fiancě to the bride-to-be's parents' home

нишанә : *n* 1) sign, symbol, symptom 2) target

нишанкаһ : *n* target

нишанлама : *n* 1) engagement 2) marking, designation

нишанламаг : *v* 1) make a note as a reminder, notice 2) betroth to 3) aim at

нишанланма : *n* engagement

нишанланмаг : *n* be noted, be marked/stamped 2) get engaged, be betrothed

нишанлы : *a* 1) marked, noted 2) engaged

нишансыз : *a* unmarked, without marks *referring to school work, papers, examinations*

нишанчы : *n mil* 1) rifleman, sniper, gun-layer *a* 2) rifle, infantry

нишанчылыг : *n* target shooting

нишаста : *n* starch

нишасталамаг : *v* starch

нишасталы : *a* starched

нишастасыз : *a* without starch, unstarched

нырх : *n* rate, price

нырхгојан : *n* rate-fixer

нырхгојма : *n* establishing of a rate *of payment,* rate-fixing

нобар : *n* first fruit appearing in an orchard

нов, новдан : *n* gutter, trough, channel; drain-spout, drain-pipe

новруз : *n* 1) New Year's Day 2) the first day of spring

новрузкүлү : *n* primrose *fam. Primulaceae*

новур : *n* 1) deep furrow 2) groove, slot, rabet *woodworking*

ноғул : *n* noğul *Azerbaijani candy with a rough surface, stuffed with spices or almond paste*

нојабр : *n Ru* November

норвеч : *n* 1) Norway *a* 2) Norwegian

норвечли : *n* a Norwegian

нормал : *a* normal, standard, usual

нормалашдырма : *n* rate setting, rate fixing, standardization

нормалашдырмаг : *v* set/fix rates, standardize

нормаллашдырмаг : *v-tr* normalize

нормаллыг : *n* normality

нота : *n mus* **нота**

нохта : *n* halter

нохталамаг : *v* 1) put a halter on *a horse*; *fig* 2) put a tight rein on *s.o.*, take *s.o.* firmly in hand

нохуд : *n* 1) pea *a* 2) pea

нохудлу : *a* made of peas

noһур : *n* paddle; pond

нөв : *n* 1) kind, type, sort *n gram* 2) voice

нөвбә : *n* 1) line, queue; turn *a regular time or chance in some succession*, period of duty; shift *at a workplace med* 2) bout, fit, attack

нөвбәләнмә : *n* alternation, interchange, rotation

нөвбәләнмәк, нөвбәләшмәк : *v* alternate, take turns

нөвбәли : *a* shift

нөвбәнөв : *a* various, different, assorted, diverse

нөвбәсиз : *adv* out of turn, jumping the queue

нөвбәт : n see **нөвбә**

нөвбәти : *a* next, next in turn

нөвбәтчи : *n* person on duty; person working on some particular shift

нөвбәтчилик : *n* duty, on duty, of-the-watch; shift

нөвһә : *n* Moslem lamentations in verse form on the deaths of martyred saints

нөвһәхан : *n* Növhaxan *Moslem cantor or lector, chanting or reciting lamentations in verse form on the deaths of martyred saints*

нөгсан : *n* defect, flaw, shortage, error, omission

нөгсанлы : *a* having shortages, missing parts; in error ; defective, flawed

нөгсанлылыг : *n* state of imperfection/defectiveness, faultiness, condition of being out-of-order

нөгсансыз : *a* 1) flawless; irreproachable, impeccable *adv* 2) flawlessly, irreproachably, impeccably

нөгсансызлыг : *n* flawlessness, perfection

нөгтеји-нәзәр : *n* point of view, opinion

нөгтә : *n* 1) point 2) spot, dot, period

нөгтәбәнөгтә : *adv* word by word; item by item

нөгтәләмә : *n* making markings

нөгтәләмәк : *v* mark

нөгтәләнмәк : *v* be marked

нөгтәләр : *n* dots, points *in punctuation*

нөгтәли, нөгтә-нөгтә : *a* dotted

нөгтәли веркүл : *n* semicolumn

нөгтәсиз : *a* unpunctuated

нөгтәси-нөгтәсинә : *adv* 1) punctually, on the dot 2) accurately, precisely

нөкәр : *n* servant

нөкәрчилик : *n* domestic service, occupation of servant

нөмрә : *n* ordinal number

нөмрәләмә : *n* numeration, enumeration,

нөмрәләмәк : *v* enumerate

нөмрәләнмәк : *v* be enumerated

нөмрәләтмәк : *v* cause someone to enumerate

нөмрәли : *a* numbered, assigned a specific number; enumerated

нөмрәсиз : *a* unnumbered

нур : *n* light

нурландырмаг : *v* light up, illumine, illuminate

нурланмаг : *v* shine, begin to shine, brighten with light, beam

нурлу : *a* luminous

нуһ : *n* 1) Noah *biblical patriarch* *a* 2) Noah's, Noachian

нуш : *a* pleasant, sweet *of food*

нуши-чан : *exp* bon appĕtit!, Enjoy your meal!

нүвә : *n* 1) kernel, seed 2) nucleus *a* 3) nuclear

нүвәли : *a* 1) having a kernel, a seed 2) nuclear

нүвәсиз : *a* 1) seedless,without a kernel/a nucleus 2) nuclear-free

нүвәчик : *n* *dim* kernel, seed

нүдрәтән : *adv* 1) rarely, seldom, from time to time 2) suddenly, unexpectedly

нүмајәндә : *n* delegate, deputy, representative

нүмајәндәлик : *n* representation, mission

нүмајиш : *n* demonstration, rally, march

нүмајишкаранә : *adv* by means of a demonstratiion, as a deliberate protest

нүмајишчи : *n* demonstrator, marcher

нүмунә : *n* 1) example; pattern 2) sample; specimen

нүмунәви : *a* 1) exemplary; modelsamplary; pattern-like

нүмунәлик : *n* designed as a sample/model/test-piece

нүсхә : *n* 1) copy 2) prescription *fig* 3) a character *person*

нүсхәбәнд : *n* pharmacist, druggist

нүтфә : *n* sperm

нүфуз : *n* 1) influence, prestige 2) authority 3) penetration; perspicacity

нүфуздан салмаг : *v* discredit, disgrace *s.o.*

нүфузедичи : *a* 1) influential 2) penetrating, piercing, perspicacious

нүфузлу : *a* influential, prestigious authoritative

нүфузлулуг : *n* influence, power; authoritativeness

нүфус : *n* people, inhabitants; population

нүчүм : *n* astrology

О

о : nineteenth letter of the Azerbaijani alphabet

о : *pro* he, she, it; that

о бири : *a* other, next

о вахт : *exp* then, in those days *lit: at that time*

о вахтдан бәри : *exp* since, since that time

о гәдәр : *exp* so many/much/long etc. *lit: to that extent*

о чүмләдән : *exp* including *lit: from that group*

оба : *n* farm, farmstead

обашдан : *n* before daybreak, before dawn

обашданлыг : *n* the pre-dawn meal during the Ramadan fast

објед : *n* *Ru* dinner; lunch

објект : *n* 1) object, thing 2) construction, project 3) objective, unit; installation

објектив : *n* 1) objective lens *optics* *a* 2) objective

објективләшдирмәк : *v* regard s.t. as an objective reality

објективлик : *n* *phil* objectivity, objective character, lack of bias

образ : *n* *Ru* image, character, personage

ов : *n* hunt, hunting *for game*

ова : *n* *geog* plain

оваламаг : *v* see **овмаг**

овалыг : *n* *geog* lowland

овгат : *n* 1) times, periods, epochs 2) mood, frame of mind

овгаттәлхлик : *n* 1) frustration, upset/distressed state 2) disappointment; trouble 3) misunderstanding, disagreement

овдан : *n* underground water-reservoir

овдуг : *n* see **ајран**

овдурмаг, овдуртмаг : *caus* of **овмаг**

овлаг : *n* 1) game-rich area, hunting area 2) *s.o.'s* permanent residence, place of *s.o.'s* frequentation, s.o.'s hangout

овламаг : *v* go hunting

овма : *n* 1) massage, rub/rubbing *med* 2) epidemic

овмаг : *v* 1) crumble 2) massage, rub

овсар : *n* camel-halter

овсарламаг : *v* put a halter on/halter a camel

овсарлы : *a* haltered *of a camel*

овсарсыз : *a* unhaltered *of a camel*

овсун, овсунлама : *n* incantation, spell, sorcery, fortune-telling

овсунламаг : *v* bewitch, enchant, lay a spell on

овсунланмаг : *v* be bewitched/enchanted, have a spell put on one

овсунлу : *a* 1) magic[al] 2) charmed, under a spell, bewitched

овсуноту : *n bot* saxifrage *Saxifraga,*

овсунчу : *n* magician, exorcist, sorcerer

овсунчулуг : *n* magic, sorcery

овуг : *a* crumbled

овуг-овуг : *a* crumbled, crushed, fragmented

овулан : *a* friable, crumbly

овулмаг : *v* 1) crumble; 2) be rubbed, massaged

овум : *a* see **овуг**

овундура-овундура : *part* consoling, calming down *s.o.*

овундурма : *n* consolation, calming down

овундурмаг : *v* console, calm down

овундуручу : *a* relieving, consoling

овунмаз : *a* 1) inconsolable *adv* 2) inconsolably

овунту : *n* crumbles, tiny pieces

овутмаг : *v* see **овундурмаг**

овуч : *n* 1) palm *of the hand* 2) handful

овучламаг : *v* gather in handfuls

овучу : *n* masseur, masseuse

овуштурма : *n* 1) crumpling 2) see **овма** 1)

овуштурмаг : *v* 1) crumple 2) see **овмаг** 2)

овуштуртмаг : *caus* of **овуштурмаг**

овуштурулмаг : *v* 1) be crumpled 2) be rubbed, massaged

овушуг : *a* crumpled; crumbled

овхалама : *vn* 1) *fr.* **овхаламаг** 2) massaging, rubbing

овхаламаг : *v* 1) crumble 2) massage, rub

овхам : *a* friable, crumbly; loose

овхамлыг : *n* friability, crumbliness; looseness

овхам-овхам : *a* crushed, crumbled, broken into tiny pieces, smashed to smithereens

овханты : *n* see **овунту**

овчу : *n* hunter

овчубашы : *n* chief-huntsman, jägermeister *pre-revolutionary court rank*

овчулуг : *n* occupation of a professional hunter/huntsman

овчучасына : *adv* in the manner of a hunter

овшүнас : *n* hunting specialist

овшүнаслыг : *n* science/craft of hunting

оғлаг : *n* 1) goat-kid *from six months to a year old astron* 2) Capricorn

оғлан : *n* 1) boy, young man 1) bridegroom

оғланчығаз : *n* little boy

оғраш : *n* 1) pimp, procurer, pander; bastard, scoundrel *a* 2) pimping, procuring, pandering

оғрашлыг : *n* 1) occupation of a pimp *ext* 2) depravity

оғру : *n* 1) thief *a* 2) thief's, thieving

оғру-әјри : *n* thievish people

оғрун-оғрун : *adv* stealthily

оғрунчасына : *adv* stealthily, like a thief

оғул : *n* 1) son *a* 2) filial

оғуллуг : *n* step-son

оғул-ушаг : *n* 1) children; dependents *a* 2) dependent

оғул-ушагсыз : *a* childless

оғулчуг, оғулчуғаз : *n dim* sonny

оғурлама : *vn* fr. **оғурламаг**

оғурламаг : *v* steal

оғурланмаг : *v* be stolen

оғурлатмаг : *v* 1) make theft possible by one's own negligence 2) cause s.o. to steal

оғурлуг : *n* 1) theft, embezzlement 2) stolen property

оғурлугча : *adv* stealthily

од : *n* 1) fire *a* 2) fiery

од вурмаг : *v* put on fire

одадавамлы : *a* fire-proof

од-алов : *n* 1) quick, spry, sharp 2) trouble-maker

одвуран : *n* arsonist, fire-bug

оддаг : *n* see **јанғын**

одејало : *n Ru* blanket

одламаг : *v* burn; set on fire

одланмаг : *v* 1) begin to burn, catch fire *fig* 2) be in a highly indignant state

одлу : *a* fiery, hot

одлуг : *n* 1) fuse, primer 2) fire-chamber; furnace; fire-box

одлу-одлу : *adv* extremely agitated

одонтолокија : *n med* odontology

одпускүрән : *a* fire-spitting

одрәнкли : *a* flame-colored

одсачан : *a* flame-thrower

одсуз : *a* fireless

одун : *n* 1) firewood *a* 2) firewood

одунбөчәји : *n zool* capricorn beetle *Agapanthia dahli*

одунгыран : *n* wood-cutter

одунhазырлајан : *n* firewood-stacker

одунчаг : *n* wood, timber

ојаг : *a* 1) awake; alert 2) cautious, observant, vigilant

ојаглыг : *n* 1) wakefulness 2) alertness, vigilance caution

ојадычы : *a* 1) awakening 2) exciting, arousing

ојандырычы : *n* one who is charged with the wake-up call, one who is responsible for awakening others

ојандырмаг : *v* 1) see **ојатмаг** 2) wake up, awaken

ојаныг : *a* awake, alert

ојаныглыг : *n* 1) wakefulness, alertness; 2) caution, vigilance

ојанма : *n* waking up, awakening

ојанмаг : *v* wake up, awaken

ојанмаз : *a* heavy, deep *of sleep*

ојатмаг : *v* 1) wake up s.o. 2) excite, arouse

ојдуртмаг, **ојдурмаг** : *caus* of **ојмаг**

ојма : *n* 1) digging 2) excavation, pit; rut

ојмаг : *v* 1) dig out, excavate *n* 2) community, commune 3) thimble 4) bush, bushing

ојмадәрән : *n bot* yarrow *Lachillea millefolium*

ојмачы : *n* 1) engraver, carver 2) borer, driller

ојнаг : *a* 1) mobile, nimble, spry 2) fidgety, overvivacious *anat* 2) joint, articulation

ојнагламаг : *v* play, run around

ојнаглашмаг : *v* play around *many together*

ојнаглыг : *n* mobility, nimbleness, spryness, fidgeting, vivacity

ојнагсыз : *a* unjointed, unarticulated

ојнаған : *a* playful

ојнаја-күлә : *adv* playfully

ојнајан : *a* 1) dancing *n* 2) dancer

ојнама : *vn* 1) fr. **ојнамаг** *n* 2) dance 3) game

ојнамаг : *v* 1) play; have fun 2) be carried away by a game 3) dance 4) rock, reel

ојнанмаг : *v* be played; be staged

ојнатмаг : *caus* 1) of **ојнамаг** 2) make s.o. dance 3) make a fool of, deceive 4) shake loose

ојнаш : *n iron* boy-friend

ојнашмаг : *v* play together

ојуг : *n* hollow; groove; gutter

ојуг-ојуг : *a* hollow, hollowed out, very porous; pocked

ојулмаг : *v* 1) be drilled, be dug out; 2) form a hollow, form a groove

ојун : *n* 1) game 2) dance 3) performance *fig* 4) trick, prank

ојунбаз : *n* clown, buffoon

ојунбазлыг : *n* buffoonery

ојун-ојунчаг : *n* trinket, knick-knack

ојунчу : *n* player

ојунчаг : *n* 1) toy 2) butt *target of jokes and ridicule*

ојунчагчы : *n* toy-maker

океан : *n Ru* ocean

оксид : *n chem* oxide

оксидләшдиричи : *n chem* oxidizing agent, oxidizer, acidifier

оксидләшдирмәк : *v* oxidize, acidify

оксикен : *n* 1) oxygen *a* 2) oxygen

октапод : *n zool* octopus

октјабр : *n Ru* October

олан : *ptc* taking place, being, staying *usually after words of Arabic or Persian origin*

ола-ола : *adv--exp* "in the presence of. . ." "given that. . . " "though it's. . . " "still it is. . ." *reduplicated adverbial participle of the verb "олмаг"*

олар : *exp* Is it possible that. . . ? May I . . . ?

олачаг : *n* inevitability

олдугча : *adv* 1) very much, to a great extent 2) extremely

олмаг : *v* 1) be 2) become 3) have 4) happen, take place 5) come 6) be suitable 7) be possible

олмаз : *exp* It is not allowed *lit undoable* . *Usually a request to cease an action*

олмазын : *a* 1) unbelievable, incredible, improbable 2) impermissible, inacceptable

олмаjа : *adv* maybe, perhaps

олмаjа-олмаjа : *exp* 1) locution embodying prohibition, categorical admonition, cautionary advice 2) expression denoting surprise, astonishment etc

олмама : absence

олса-олса : *exp* 1) at best 2) at the outside, at the very most, at the very least *Refers to the extreme nature of a situation*

олсун : *exp* "Let it be so !", I agree !", "I don :t object" "OK!" "All right!"

омба : *n* 1) buttock[s] 2) hip

омбаүстү сарығы : *n* loincloth

он : *num* ten

онадәк : *adv* 1) up to this point, hitherto 2) up to ten

онаjлыг : *n* 1) ten month period *a* 2) ten-month

онбашы : *n* 1) foreman *mil* 2) lance-corporal, private first-class, PFC

онда : *adv* 1) then, and so, in that case 2) he/she/it has

ондакы : *a* 1) located at his/her/its place; belonging to hm/her/it 2) taking place then/there

ондан : *pro* 1) from him/her/it 2) because of that

онjашар : *a* ten year old

онjашлы : *a* ten-year period

ониллик : *n* 1) ten-year period *hist* 2) ten-year school; ten-year education *primary plus secondary*

онкүнлүк : *n* 1) ten-day period *a* 2) ten-day period

онлар : *pro* they; those

онларынкы : *pro* theirs, belonging to them

онларча : *adv* in tens, in groups of ten

онлуг : *n num* 1) ten, quantity of ten 2) ten-ruble bill

онманатлыг : *n* 1) ten-ruble bill *a* 2) ten-ruble bill

онмәртәбә : *a* ten-story, ten-storied *building*

онмәртәбәли : *a* ten-story/storied *building*

он-он : *adv* in/by tens

онрәгәмли : *a math* ten-digit

онсинифли : *a* ten-grade, tenth-grade *relating to school or education*

онсуз : *pro* without it/him/her

онсуз да : *exp* Even without that *usually said when suggesting that an already bad situation, s.o.'s grievances etc. not be aggravated*

онункү : *pro* his; belonging to him

онунла : *pro* with him; with that

онунчу : *num* tenth

онурға : *n* 1) spine; backbone *zool* 2) vertebrate

онурғалы : *a* vertebral

онурғасыз : *a zool* invertebrate

онча : *adv* just ten, only ten

ончилдли : *a* ten-volume, in ten volumes

ончилдлик : *n* ten-volume edition/set

оншаһылыг : *n* fifty kopeks, fifty kopek piece

оптик : *a* optical

оптик : *n* optician

оптика : *n* optics

ора : *adv* there, over there

ора-бура : *adv* here and there

ора-бурада : *adv* see **орада-бурада**

ораг : *n* sickle

орагламаг : *v* sickle, reap with a sickle

орағабәнзәр : *a* sickle-shaped, crescent

орада-бурада : *adv* here and there

орадакы : *a* located, being/staying there

орадан : *adv* from there, thence

орадача : *adv* at the same place *earlier mentioned* 2) ibidem/ibid. *in footnotes*

оралар : *pro* those places

оралы : *n* local resident *of that place*

оранжереjа : *n* 1) greenhouse, hot-house *a* 2) greenhouse, hot-house

орган : *n mus* organ

орд : *n* interior side of cheeks *inside the mouth*

орден : *n Ru* order, decoration

орденли : *a* recipient of a decoration

ординат : *m math* ordinate designation of one of two or three numbers determining the position of a point on a plane

орду : *n* 1) army *a* 2) army

ордукаһ : *n* military camp

орижинал : *n* 1) original *document a* 2) original

орижиналлыг : *n* originality, authenticity

орта : *n* 1) middle *a* 2) middle, average moderate *adv* 3) lit. "satisfactorily" *academic grade corresponding to C in the US*

ортаја атмаг : *v* propose, suggest *a resolution, draft etc.*

ортаја чыхмаг : *v* appear, show up, become noticeable

ортабаб : *n* 1) peasant of average means; any person of average means and position *a* 2) of middle quality, merit or worth 3) of average build and height

ортаг : *n* 1) participant, accomplice; companion *math* 2) common denominator, least common multiple

ортаглы : *a* 1) general, joint, combined, common adv 2) jointly, in shares with another, "clubbing" together

ортаглыг : *n* métayage system *farming in return for a share, usually one half, of the yield* 2) companionship, comradeship

ортада : *adv* in the middle *of*, half way along

ортадакы : *a* 1) average *n* 2) that which is in the middle, ther mean

орталамаг : *v* 1) halve, divide s.t. into halves 2) seize/grab s.o. by the belt

орталыг : *n* middle, nidst

ортанчы : *a* middle, medium

ортанчыл : *a* middle in terms of age

ортасында : *adv* , in the middle of, in the midst of; among, between

оруч : *n* fasting, abstinence

оруч тутмаг : *v* fast

оручлуг : *n* Ramadan, The Month of Fasting

османландырмаг : *v* 1) make fun of, mock 2) question in a roundabout way, pump

османлы : *n* 1) Osmanli Turk *a* 2) Osmanli

остановка : *n* *Ru* stop

от : *n* 1) grass *a* 2) grass

отабәнзәр : *a* grassy, herbaceous

отаг : *n* 1) room *a* 2) room

отагсүпүрән, отагтәмизләјән : *n* charwoman, cleaning woman

от-алаф : *n* weed

отарға : *n* see **отлаг**

отарма : *n* pasturage

отармаг : *v* tend *livestock*, shepherd, pasture, graze

отартмаг : *caus* of **отармаг**

отбичән : *n* 1) mower *agent* 1) hay-mowing machine

отдырмыглајан : *n* pitchfork

отел : *n* see **меһманхана**

отјејән : *a* herbivorous

отјыған : *n* mower *agent*

отлаг : *n* pasture

отлама : *vn* fr. **отламаг**

отламаг : *v* graze, pasture

отланмаг : *v* be trampled down/damaged *of crops, by cattle*

отлатмаг : *v* deliberately cause damage to crops, or pasture by driving cattle on to the land

отлу : *a* abounding in/rich in grass *meadow/field*

отпуск : *n* *Ru* leave, vacation

отставка : *n* *Ru* resignation

отсуз : *a* grassless

отсузлуг : *n* absence of grass; lack of fodder-crops

отуз : *num* thirty

отузкүнлүк : *n* 1) thirty day period *a* 2) thirty-day

отуз-отуз : *adv* by thirty *of groups*

отузунчу : *num* thirtieth

отураг : *a* 1) sitting *place/position* 2) settled *as opposed to nomadic*

отураглыг : *n* settled way of life *as opposed to nomadism*

отурачаг : *n* 1) sitting *geom* 2) base

отурдулмаг : *v* be seated

отурмаг : *v* 1) sit; sit down 2) cost, come to

отуртдурмаг : *caus* of **отурмаг**

отуртмаг : *v* 1) cause to sit *tech* 2) seat, cause to fit into a groove

отуруб-дурмаг : *v* czrry on an acquaintanceship *with s.o.* go around with, hang around with *s.o.*

отурум : *n* one go, one stretch, one sitting, one gulp

отуруш : *n* manner of sitting, manner of sitting down

отуруш-дуруш : *n* manner of behaving

отурушмуш : *a* 1) elderly, getting on *n* 2) elderly person

отчалан : *n* mower *agent*

отчулуг : *n* meadow-cultivation, grass-farming

оф : *intj* Oh!, Ah!, Alas!

ох : *n* 1) arrow 2) axle *intj* 3) see **охај**

охај : *intj* Fine! Great !

охатан : *n* 1) archer *astron* 2) Sagittarius *constellation*

охгабы : *n* quiver

охлов : *n* rolling-pin

охловламаг : *n* roll out dough

охлу кирпи : *n* *zool* porcupine

охранник : *n* *Ru* guard

оху : *n* reading; learning

охудулмаг : *v* 1) learn, be educated 2) read through, peruse

оху-јазы : *n* literacy

охујан : *a* 1) reading ; 2) *a* diligent *n* 3) student 4) singer

охуја-охуја : *adv* 1) reading 2) studying, learning 3) in a sing-song voice *reciting*

охујуб-чыхмаг : *v* read through to the end

охума : *n* 1) reading; reciting 2) singing, chanting

охумаг : *v* 1) read 2) sing 3) learn, study

охумуш : *n* learned, educated, literate

охунаглы : *a* 1) legible, distinct *handwriting* *adv* 2) legibly

охунаглыг : *n* legibility, distinctness *handwriting*

охунмаг : *v* 1) study; learn 2) be read 3) be sung

охунмаз : *a* illegible *handwriting*

охутдурмаг : *caus* of **охумаг**

охутмаг : *v* 1) teach, educate 2) cause to sing

охучу : *n* reader, lector *agent* 1) professional reciter

охшајыш : *n* resemblance, analogy

охшама : *n* 1) see **охшајыш** 2) cherishing, amusing

охшамаг : *v* 1) resemble, look like 2) pet, cherish, amuse 3) grieve for, lament over a dead person with ritual lamentations

охшар : *a* like, resembling, analogical

охшарлыг : *n* see **охшајыш**

охшатма : *n* 1) likening, comparison, imitation 2) assimilation

охшатмаг : *v* make alike, assimilate 2) imitate, compare 3) take one object for another *because of their similarity*

оh : *intj* Oh! Ah!

оhо : *intj* Oho!

очерк : *n* *Ru* feature article *in a newspaper* ; essay

очаг : *n* 1) fire-place 2) dwelling-place, home, hearth-and-home 2) shrine

очаггалајан, очагчы : *n* stoker, furnace-man

очагхана : *n* stokehold

очагчылыг : *n* stoker's or furnace-man's occupation

очығаз : *n* 1) just he/she/it 2) just that much, that much and no more

ө : twentieth letter of the Azerbaijani alphabet

өвкәләмәк : *v* 1) rub; massage 2) crumple

өвкәләнмәк : *v* 1) be rubbed; be massaged 2) be crumpled

өвкәләтмәк : *caus* of **өвкәләмәк**

өвлад : *n* 1) child 2) descendant[s]

өвладсевән : *a* 1) child-loving, philoprogenitive

өвладсыз : *a* childless

өвладсызлыг : *n* childlessness

өврә : *n* *med* lupus *lupus vulgaris*

өд : *n* 1) bile, gall *a* 2) bilious, gall

өддәк : *a* cowardly; timid; meak

өддәклик : *n* cowardice, timidity

өдәјиш : *n* see **өдәниш**

өдәмә : *n* compensation, payment, paying off *a debt*

өдәмәк : *v* 1) satisfy, give satisfaction to 2) carry out, execute 3) compensate, pay, pay off

өдәнилмәк : *v* see **өдәнмәк**

өдәниш : *n* 1) satisfaction 2) execution, fulfilment 3) compensation, payment, paying off *debt*

өдәнмә : *n* payment, remuneration; paying off *debt*

өдәнмәк : *v* 1) get paid, compensated 2) get paid off 3) be fulfilled, executed

өдәтмәк : *caus of* **өдәмәк**

өдлүк : *n* *anat* gall bladder

өдүнч : *n* debt

өз : *pro* 1) self 2) one's own

өзүнә кәлмәк : *v* recover *i.e. after a shock or similar incident*

өзүнү чәкмәк : *v* puff up, be arrogant, haughty

өзбашына : *a* 1) wilful, unbridled, unchecked, self-willed *adv* 2) independently; wilfully, selfishly

өзбашыналыг : *n* arbitrariness, stupid wilfulness

өзбәк : *n* 1) Uzbek *a* 2)

өзбәкистан : *n* Uzbekistan

өзбәкчә : *adv* in Uzbek *language*

өздан : *n* *anat* pancreas

өзәк : *n* 1) cell; foxhole, slit-trench 2) core, nucleus 3) rod; spindle

өзкә : *a* 1) other ; strange 2) stranger

өзкәјерли : *a* see **јаделли**

өзкәләшмәк : *v* become a stranger, become alienated from one's own people

өзкәлик : *n* strangeness, alienism

өзләри : *pro* they themselves

өзләринин, өзләринки : belonging to them

өзләшдирмә : *n* privatization

өзләшдирмәк : *v* privatize

өз-өзлүјүндә : *adv* in and of oneself, by oneself

өз-өзүнә : *adv* to oneself

өзү : *pro* he himself

өзүјазан : *a* self-recording/registering

өзүл : *n* base, basis, foundation

өзүмүзүнкү : *pro* one's *my/your his etc* ; belonging to one *me/you/him, in accordance with the subject ,or object of the sentence or clause*

өзүмүнкү : *pro* mine

өзүндәнкетмә : fainting; hysterics; seizure, epilepsy

өзүндәнчыхма : *n* madness, anger, fury, rage, wrath

өзүнәһаким : *a* restrained, capable of restraining *o.'s* passions

өзүнүалчалтма : *n* self-abasement, self-disparagement, licking s.o.'s boots, sucking up to s.o.

өзүнүбилмәмәзлик : *n* loss of consciousness, fainting

өзүнүгорума : *n* 1) self-preservation 2) self-defence, self-protection

өзүнүидарә : *n* 1) self-government 2) ability to conduct oneself properly in society

өзүнүитирмә : *n* confusion, embarrassment, loss of composure

өзүнүјандырма : *n* self-immolation

өзүнүмүдафиә : *n* self-defence, self-protection

өзүнүнкү : *pro* one's own

өзүнүөјмә : *n* self-advertisement, bragging, arrogance

өзүнүтәнгид : *n* self-criticism *Communist terminology*

өзүнүтә'рифләмә : *n* see **өзүнүөјмә**

өзфәалијјәт : *n* 1) amateur activities *a* 2) amateur

өјәч : *n* three year old sheep or ram

өјлә : *n* see **күнорта**

өјләшмәк : *v* carry a sheep holding it by its hind legs

өјмә : *n* praise; appreciation

өјмәк : *v* praise

өјнә : *n* time, occasion

өјрәдилмәк : *v* 1) be studied 1) be educated

өјрәдилмиш : *a* 1) educated, learned 2) tamed, trained

өјрәнилмәк : *v* be learned, be studied

өјрәнишли : *a* accustomed, used to

өјрәнишмәк : *v* get accustomed, get used to, become attached to

өјрәнмә : *n* 1) study, learning 2) habituation, habitude, familiarization

өјрәнмәк : *v* 1) study, learn 2) find out 3) get used to, become accustomed/habituated 4) become tamed/domesticated/trained

өјрәнмиш : *a* 1) used to, accustomed/habituated 2) learned 3) tamed, trained

өјрәнчә : *n* habit; skill, experience

өјрәнчәли : *a* used to, accustomed, habituated

өјрәтмәк : *v* 1) teach, instruct 2) admonish, exhort 3) instigate, put up to, set on 4) tame, train

өјрәшмәк : *v* get used to, get familiar with, grow accustomed to

өјүд : *n* moral admonition, exhortation

өјүдләмәк : *v* admonish, exhort

өјүдүчү : *n* 1) emetic *a* 2) emetic

өјүмә : *n* sickness, nausea, giddiness, dizziness

өјүмәк : *v* 1) feel sick, be nauseous 2) feel giddy, dizzy

өјүнкән : *a* 1) boastful, bragging *n* 2) braggart, boastful person

өјүнкәнлик : *n* boasting, boastfulness, bragging, braggadocio

өјүнмә : *n* boast, boasting

өјүнмәк : *v* boast, brag, vaunt

өксә : *n bot* mistletoe *Viscum album*

өксүз : *n* see **јетим**

өкүз : *n* 1) bull, bullock *a* 2) bull[s]

өкүзкөзү : *n bot* mountain arnica *Arnica montana*

өкчә : *n* see **даван** 2)

өкеј : *a* step-, non-consanguinely related, not related by blood

өкеј ана : *n* stepmother

өкеј ата : *n* stepfather

өкеј бачы : *n* stepsister

өкеј гардаш : *n* stepbrother

өкеј гыз : *n* stepdaughter

өкеј оғул : *n* stepson

өкејлик : *n* non-consanguinity *position of an unrelated person*

өлдүрмәк : *v* kill

өлдүртмәк : *caus* of **өлдүрмәк**

өлдүрүлмәк : *v* be killed

өлдүрүчү : *a* lethal, fatal, mortal, death-dealing

өлкә : *n* country

өлкәшүнас : *n* specialist in local history and lore

өлкәшүнаслыг : *n* 1) local history and lore *a* 2) regional-historical

өлкүн : *a* 1) numb, half dead, neither dead nor alive, feeble 2) fragile, frail 3) sluggish, torpid, inactive

өлкүнләшмәк : *v* become numb/half dead/neither dead nor alive 2) weaken; become enfeebled/exhausted 3) grow frail,fragile 4) become sluggish; sink into apathy/torpidity/inactivity

өлкүнлүк : *n* 1) fragility, frailty 2) sluggishness, torpidity, apathy, inactivity

өлмәз : *a* immortal

өлмәзлик : *n* immortality

өлмәк : *v* die, expire

өлмүш : *a* dead, deceased, defunct

өлү : *a* 1) dead, lifeless *n* 1) dead person, corpse, the deceased

өлүвај : *a* sluggish, indifferent, torpid, logy

өлүвајлыг : *n* sluggishness, indifference, torpidity, loginess

өлүдәнгорхма, өлүмдәнгорхма : *n* necrophobia, pathological fear of the dead

өлүјандырма : *n* cremation

өлүјарма : *n* necrotomy *the dissection of a dead body*

өлүјујан : *n* ritual corpse-washer

өлүм : *n* 1) death; 2) death rate, mortality

өлүмдәнгорхан : *a* 1) life-loving 2) thanatophobic *fearing death n* 3) thanatophobe *one who fears death*

өлүм-дирим : *adv* somehow or other, with a struggle

өлүмчүл : *a* 1) utterly exhausted , worn out 2) morrtal, deadly

өлүмчүллүк : *n* state of complete exhaustion

өлүнчә : *adv* to death

өлүсојан : *n* marauder, pillager

өлүсојанлыг : *n* pillage, looting

өлүхана : *n* morgue

өлүчәсинә : *adv* like a log *sleeping*

өлүшкәмәк, өлүшкүмәк : *v* fade away

өлчдүрмәк, өлчдүртмәк : *caus* of **өлчмәк**

өлчмә : *n* measuring

өлчмәк : *v* measure

өлчү : *n* 1) measure; size 2) standard, criterion *a* 3) measuring

өлчүб-бичмәк : *v* 1) try on, fit,adapt, adjust, measure 2) think over, consider

өлчүјәкәлмәз : *a* 1) immeasurable 2) huge. tremendous

өлчүлмә : *n* measuring

өлчүлмәз : a 1) immeasurable *adv* 2) immeasurably

өлчүлмәк : *v* be measured

өлчүсүз : *a* immeasurable;, beyond measure, quantitatively indefinite, of indeterminate dimension/magnitude

өмрүндә : *adv* forever, ever, as long as one lives

өмүр : *n* life; lifetime

өмүр сүрмәк : *v* live, dwell, get along

өмүрлүк : *a* 1) life, lifetime *adv* 2) for life, for one's entire life, forever, for eternity

өмүрлүлүк : *n* longevity

өн : *n* 1) front, fore-part; foreground *a* 1) front, anterior

өндәки : *a* front, forward, in front of

өндән : *adv* from the front

өнлүк : *n* apron

өнлүклү : *a* 1) aproned,wearing an apron *n* 2) aproned person, person wearing an apron

өнүндә : *n* front, fore-part, anterior

өнчә : *adv* 1) in front of 2) in advance, well in advance, in good time, beforehand

өпдүрмәк, өпдүртмәк : *v* cause to kiss

өпмәк : *v* kiss

өпүш : *n* kiss

өпүшдүрмәк, өпүшдүртмәк : *v* see **өпдүрмәк, өпдүртмәк**

өпүшмәк : *v* kiss each other

өрдәк : *n* 1) duck *a* 2) duck['s]

өрдәкбурун : *n* *zool* platypus *Ornithorhyncus* , a monotreme

өркән : *n* wide horse tether

өрнәк : *n* sample, example; pattern

өрс : *n* anvil

өрт-басдыр : *n* concealment, harboring

өртдүрмәк : *caus* of **өртмәк**

өртмә : *n* covering

өртмәк : *v* 1) cover 2) close, close up

өртү : *n* see **өртүк**

өртүб-басдырмаг : *v* veil, conceal, cover, cover up

өртүк : *n* cover, spread, cloth

өртүлмәк : *v* be closed, shut, locked up, covered

өртүлү : *a* 1) covered, concealed 2) ambiguous, vague, unclear, fishy

өртүнмәк : *v* cover/wrap/conceal oneself

өрүмчәк : *n* *zool* spider

өрүмчәк пәрдәси : *n* *zool* spider web

өрүш : *n* pasture, meadow

өскүрәк : *n* cough

өскүрмәк : *v* cough

өскүртмәк : *v* cause coughing

өтә : *a* 1) superlative, ssuperb, outstanding *adv* 2) on the other side; at a distance; in the background

өтәки : *a* other, another, different

өтән : *a* 1) last, previous, past 2) outstripping, outdistancing, overrunning

өтәри : *adv* in passing, cursorily, superficially, at a glance

өтәрки : *adv* fleetingly, transiently, in passing

өтәсиндә : *n* behind, beyond

өткәм : *a* haughty, proud, selfish, arrogant

өткәмлик : *n* haughtiness, hauteur, pride, selfishness, arrogance

өткүн : *a* 1) overripe 2) overboiled, overcooked, fried too crisp 3) intolerant

өткүнлүк : *n* overripedness

өтмә : *vn* fr. **өтмәк**

өтмәк : *v* 1) overtake, outrun 2)pass

өтрү : *adv* for the sake of, in order to

өтүб-кечмәк : *v* outrun, pass

өтүрмә : *n* passing, handling over, transmission, communication

өтүрмәк : *v* 1) see off; accompany 2) let go 3) pass over, transmit 4) eat, guzzle, gobble

өтүр-өтүр : *v* *n* passing to one another

өтүрүлмәк : *v* be seen off/escorted/accompanied; be let pass, be allowed to go through

өтүрүчү : *n* guide, escort

өтүшдүрмәк : *v* set in motion a game of racing with one another

өтүшмә : *n* running races, running competition

өтүшмәк : *v* 1) compete to win, outrun 2) make do *with/on* , manage *with/on* 3) become settled/set/arranged/established 4) sing, twitter, chirp *of birds*

өфкә : *n* *anat* lungs

өһдә : *n* duty, debt, obligation

өһдәсиндә олмаг : *v* be dependent/a dependent

өһдәсиндән кәлмәк : *v* be capable *of s.t.*

өһдәчилик : *n* obligation, duty; liability

өч : *n* see **гисас**

өчәшкән : *n* bully, troublemaker, pugnacious/quarrelsome fellow

өчәшкәнлик : *n* irascibility, pugnacity; fault-finding

өчәшмә : *vn* fr. **өчәшмәк**

өчәшмәк : *v* find fault *with* , nag *at* , tease, pick on

өчүл : *n* leader *of a herd/flock*

П

п : twenty-first letter of the Azerbaijani alphabet

павилјон : *n* pavilion

пагғылдамаг : *v* swirl, seethe, boil up

падзәһәр : *n* antidote

падшаһ : *n* king, shah, ruler, monarch

падшаһлыг : *n* 1) reign 2) kingdom

падшаһпәрәст : *n* monarchist, royalist

паз : *n* wedge

пазы : *n* see **зылх**

пазламаг : *v* 1) wedge *fig* 2) swindle, palm s.t. worthless off on s.o.

пај : *n* share, portion

паја : *n* prop, support, base ; pole, pillar

пајаламаг : *v* install supports

пајәндаз : *n* door-mat

пајыз : *n* 1) autumn, fall *a* 2) autumn, fall

пајызбүлбүлү : *n zool* goldfinch *genus Carduelis*

пајызлыг : *a* 1) fall, autumn, counted on for/planned for/expected in autumn/fall 2) winter *crop*

пајлајан : *v* one who distributes, apportions

пајлајычы : *n* 1) distributor *a* 2) distributor, distributive

пајлама : *n* 1) distribution, apportionment 2) delivery *to customers*

пајламаг : *v* 1) distribute, apportion 2) deliver *to customers*

пајланмаг : *v* 1) be distributed, be apportioned 2) be delivered *to customers*

пајлатдырмаг, пајлатмаг : *caus* of **пајламаг**

пајлашдырылмаг : *v* be distributed, be apportioned

пајлашдырма : *n* distribution, allocation, apportionment

пајлашдырмаг : *v* distribute, allocate, apportion

пајлашдыртмаг : *caus* see **пајлатдырмаг, пајлатмаг**

пајлашма : *n* sharing, division, dealing out *among a given group*

пајлашмаг : *v* share, deal out *among a given group*

пај-пај : *n* shares

пај-пүшк : *n* 1) distribution, allotment 2) gift, present

пајтахт : *n* 1) capital *city* *a* 2) capital

пајчы : *n* share-holder

пак : *a* 1) clean, pure; sinless, unspoiled *n relig* 2) ritual ablution prior to conducting divine service

пакет : *n* package *postal* , envelope

пакизә : *a* clean, pure

палаз : *n* see **килим**

палазгулаг : *a* 1) lop-eared 2) *n zool* see **јараса**

палан : *n* 1) pack-saddle 2) cushion, worn as protection on the back by stevedores/cargo-loaders/porters

паландуз : *n* 1) pack-saddlemaker *n* 2) large needle

паландузлуг : *n* occupation of pack-saddlemaker

паланламаг : *v* put on a pack-saddle

паланланмаг : *v* put on a cargo-loader's back-cushion

паланлы : *a* pack-saddled *animal*

палата : *n Ru* chamber

палеонтоложи : *a* paleontological

палеонтолокија : *n* paleontology

палыд : *n bot* 1) oak-tree *a* 2) oak

палыдлыг : *n* oak forest, a wood of oak-trees

палма : *n bot* palm-tree *a* 2) palm

пал-палтар : *n* a great variety of clothing

палтар : *n* 1) clothes, clothing, garb, attire 2) bed clothing

палтарапарма : *n* traditional bringing, and presentation to the bride by the groom, of the bridal costume at her house

палтарасан, палтарасылан : *n* hanger; clothes-rack, stand; hall-stand

палтарбичмә : *n* traditional ceremony of cutting and display of the bride's dress, and the party held on this occasion

палтарјујан : *n* laundress

палтарлыг : *n* material for a dress

палтар-палаз : *n* beddings, linens, carpets and clothing *a collective term for household belongings made of textile material*

палтарсахлајан : *n* cloakroom attendant

палто : *n* overcoat

палтолуг : *n* material for an overcoat

палчыг : *n* slush, dirt, mud, slush

палчыгламаг : *v* coat with clay

палчыглатдырмаг : *caus* of **палчыгламаг**

палчыглатмаг : *caus* of **палчыгламаг**

палчыглы : *a* coated/covered with clay

палчыглыг : *n* muddy morass

памбыг : *n* 1) cotton 2) cotton-wool *bot* 3) cotton plant *a* 4) cotton

памбыгатан : *n* cotton-carder/comber

памбыгјыған : *n* cotton-picker

памбыглы : *a* stuffed/wadded/padded with cotton-wool

памбыгтәмизләјән : *a* cotton-cleaning

памбыгчы : *n* cotton-grower

памбыгчылыг : *n* 1) cotton-growing, cotton-raising *a* 2) cotton-growing

пампаг : *a* 1) clumsy, unskilful *n* 2) coward

пампаглыг : *n* 1) clumsiness, unskilfulness 2) cowardice

панчур : *n* outside shutters

папа : *n* pontiff

папаг : *n* 1) papag, papakha, Caucasian fur hat 2) hat

папаглы : *a* with a papakha or hat on o.'s head

папаглыг : *n* hat-material, material suitable for, or employed in making a papakha, or hat

папагсыз : *a* hatless, bare-headed

папагчы : *n* hatter, hat-maker; milliner

папагчылыг : *n* profession of a hatter/hat-maker/milliner

папирос : *n* cigarette

папиросјандыран : *n* cigarette-lighter

папироссатан, папиросчу : *n* cigarette-merchant; cigarette vendor

пара : *n* half, moiety

паравана : *n* screen

параг : *n* *zool* lap-dog

паразит : *n* 1) parasite *a* 2) parasitic

паразитлик : *n* parasitism

параламаг : *v* 1) bisect, divide into halves 2) divide, tear into pieces, cut into pieces

параланмаг : *v* be divided in half/into two parts

паралел : *n* 1) parallel *a* 2) parallel

паралеллик : *n* parallelism

паралелограм : *n* *geom* parallelogram

пара-пара : *adv* in pieces, in parts

парашүт : *n* 1) parachute *a* 2) parachute

парашүтчү : *n* parachutist

пардаг : *n* polish[ing], gloss, luster

пардагламаг : *v* polish, impart gloss, luster

пардагланмаг : *v* be polished :

пардаглатдырмаг, пардаглатмаг : *caus* of **пардагламаг**

пардаглы : *a* polished, lustrous, glossy

пардагчы : *n* polisher

парылдамаг : *v* shine, glitter

парылдатмаг : *v-tr* polish, impart shine/luster to, shine, cause to glitter

парылты : *n* shining, glittering, twinkling

парк : *n* *Ru* park

парлаг : *a* bright, shining; glittering; twinkling

парлаглыг : *n* brightness, shine; glitter, twinkle

парламаг : *v* see **парылдамаг**

парламент : *n* 1) parliament *a* 2) parliamentary

паровоз : *n* locomotive

паровозсүрән : *n* locomotive engineer

пароход : *n* steam-boat, steamship

пар-пар : *adv* shiningly/glistenly/gleamingly *onomatopoeia*

партапарт : *n* quickened/faster/more frequent firing/shooting

партизан : *n* 1) partisan, guerilla *a* 2) partisan, guerilla

партизанлыг : *n* 1) partisan/guerilla movement 2) guerilla warfare

партија : *n* party *political*

партијалы : *n* party-member

партијалылыг : *n* party-membership

партијасыз : *a* see **битәрәф**

партылдамаг : *v* crack apart, crack up

партылты : *n* cracking, crack, thunder, uproar

партладычы : *n* blaster*agent* , detonation-specialist

партлајан : *a* 1) explosive *gram* 2) labial

партлајычы : *a* explosive

партлајыш : *n* explosion

партлајышлы : *a* *gram* plosive

партлама : *vn* fr. **партламаг**

партламаг : *v* 1) explode, burst out 2) break, split, crack, snap

партлатмаг : *v* explode, blow up

парч : *n* mug; tankard

парча : *n* 1) material, fabric 2) piece, fragment

парчаламаг : *v-tr* tear apart, chop off, break away, fragment

парчаланмаг : *intr* 1) get broken, get smashed 2) tear apart, break away, disintegrate

парча-парча : *adv* in pieces, in clusters; in clots

парча-тикә : *n* scraps, shreds, rags *fabric, material*

парчачы : *n* textile merchant

пас : *n* rust, rustiness, corrosion

пас атмаг : *v* get rusty *literal meaning only*

пахыры ачылмаг : *v* become exposed

пасланмаг : *v* corrode, rust, become rusty

пасланыб-галмаг : *v* 1) become rusty, corrode *as a result of protracted disuse fig* 2) allow o.'s skills to deteriorate *for lack of practice*

пасланмајан : *a* stainless, rustproof *of metals*

паслы : *a* rusty, corroded

паспорт : *n* 1) passport; certificate; title *a* 2) passport, certificate; title

паспортлашдырма : *n* issue of passports, certificates, titles

паспортсуз : *a* having no passports, certificates, titles

пассив : *a* 1) passive *adv* 2) passsively

пассивлик : *n* passivity

пастеризасија : *n* pasteurization

патава : *n* footcloth

патга : *n* treacle

патент : *n* patent

патентли : *a* patented

патентсиз : *a* unpatented

патоложи : *a* pathological

патолокија : *n* pathology

патрон : *n* cartridge

патрондаш : *n* ammunition pouch, bandolier

патронламаг : *v* load, charge *a gun*

патрул : *n* patrol; guards

пахыл : *a* 1) jealous, envious *n* 2) jealous, envious person

пахыллыг : *n* envy, jealousy

пахыр : *n* patina *brownish-green metal oxide film or aerugo that covers ancient bronzes, coins etc*

пахла : *n* 1) bean *a* 2) bean

пахлава : *n* baklava *sweet pastry with almond or nut filling*

пахлагурду : *n zool* bean weevil

пахлалы : *a* bean

пah, пaho : *intj* Here we go! Here is how it works!

пача : *n* leg *the entire leg from hip down*

пачаламаг : *v* 1) grab, seize by the leg 2) tear into two parts

педагог : *n* teacher, tutor, pedagogue

педагожи : *a* pedagogic, pedagogical

педагокика : *n* pedagogy, *science or methods of teaching*

педолокија : *n* paidology/pedology *scientific study of the behavior and development of children*

пези : *n* lanky, stupid person

пејвәнд : *a bot* 1) grafted *med* 2) inoculated *n bot* 4) grafting *med* 5) inoculation

пејвәндләшдирмә : *v bot* grafting

пејвәндләшдирмәк : *v tr bot* graft

пејғәмбәр : *relig* prophet

пејғәмбәрлик : *relig* prophesy

пејғәмбәрчичәји : *n bot* cornflower *Centaurea*

пејғәмбәрчәсинә : *adv* prophetically

пејдәрпеј : *adv* incessantly, continually, unceasingly

пејин : *n* 1) dung *a* 2) dung

пејингурду : *n zool* dung beetle *any of a number of scarabaeid beetles that breed in dung*

пејинләмәк : *v* dung, manure, fertilize the soil with dung

пејинләтдирмәк, пејинләтмәк : *caus* of **пејинләмәк**

пејинлик : *n* dung-hill, manure-pile dung-pit

пејинсиз : *a* without dung

пејк : *n astron* satellite *planet*

пејсәр : *n* back of the head; *med* occiput

пендир : *n* cheese

пендиргајыран, пендиртутан : *n* cheese-maker

пендирхана : *n* cheese-dairy, cheese-store, cheese-monger's

пенчәк : *n* jacket, suit-coat

пенчәр : *n* greens *edible*

перикдирмәк : *v* scare the birds away

перикмәк : *v* be scared away *of birds*

перикеј : *n astron* perigee

перитон : *n* *anat* peritoneum

пероксид : *n* *chem* peroxide

перрон : *n* platform *railroad*

перспектив : *n* 1) perspective *a* 2) perspective

печ : *n* *Ru* 1) stove *Russian style with oven* *a* 2) stove

печгајыран : *n* stove-maker

пешә : *n* profession; occupation; craft

пешәкар : *n* 1) professional *a* 2) professional

пешәкарлыг : *n* craftsmanship; professionalism

пешәки : *adv* in advance, as an advance; as a prepayment

пешин : *n* advance *payment;* prepayment

пешкәш : *n* gift, present *often to an official as a form of bribe*

пешман : *a* 1) remorseful, repentant *n* 2) penitent/contrite/remorseful person

пешман олмаг : *v* be repentant, feel repentance

пешманлыг, **пешманчылыг** : *n* remorse, repentance, contrition, regret

пәдәршаһи : *a* patriarchal

пәдәршаһлыг : *n* patriarchate

пәжмүрдә : *a* 1) sluggish; faded 2) gloomy

пәзәвәнк : *n* see **пези**

пәјә : *n* barn

пәлә : *n* ear-lobe

пәләнк : *n* 1) tiger *a* 2) tiger['s]

пәләсәк : *n* fuss, bustle

пәлмә : *a* unclear, indistinct, foggy, murky

пәлтәк : *n* 1) stammerer, stutterer *a* 2) lisping, speaking thickly

пәлтәкләмәк : *v* stammer, stutter; lisp

пәлтәкләшмәк : *v* begin to stammer/stutter; begin to lisp

пәлтәклик : *n* stammering; lisping, speaking thickly

пәмбәчә : *n* 1) full handful 2) see **гапаз**

пәмбәчәләмәк : *v* grab a full handful

пәнаһ : *n* shelter, asylum, protection

пәндәм : *n* *med* constipation

пәнчә : *n* 1) paw 2) palm with fingers extended 3) foot 4) sole *of the foot*

пәнчәләмәк : *v* grab with all five fingers, grab with a full grip

пәнчәләшмәк : *n* 1) grapple with, come to grips with, seize hold of one another 2) wrestle with, contend with,squabble

пәнчәрә : *n* 1) window *a* 2) window

пәнчур : *n* lamp-shade

пәнчшәнбә : *n* Thursday

пәпә, пәпәш : *n* bread *in baby talk*

пәр : *n* wing; propeller; vane, blade

пәракәндә : *a* 1) scattered around/about; uncoordinated *adv* 2) apiece 3) separately, in disunity

пәракәндәлик : *n* sparseness, scantiness scattered character/nature

пәрваз : *n* 1) cornice, ledge, eaves 2) edging, border, edge-embroidery

пәрванә : *n* 1) nocturnal butterfly 2) flywheel 3) screw, propeller, see **винт**

пәрвәрдикар : *n* God, Lord

пәрвәрдикара : *intj* God ! Oh, my Lord!

пәрвәриш : *n* care, attention, looking after, upbringing

пәргу : *n* 1) down *a* 2) downy

пәрдә : *n* 1) curtain *anat* 2) hymen *anat* 3) tympanum, eardrum membrane; 4) act *theatre*

пәрдәләмәк : *v* curtain, veil

пәрдәләнмәк : *v* be curtained, veiled

пәрдәли : *a* 1) curtained, veiled 2) membranous *fig* 3) unclear, unexplained, dubious

пәрди : *n* see **тир** 1)

пәрәгулаг : *a* see **саллаггулаг**

пәрәк : *n* 1) nostril 2) nose ornament

пәрән-пәрән : *adv* scattering around

пәрәстиш : *n* 1) devotion, worship, adoration, reverence 2) cult, awe

пәрәстишкар : *n* worshipper, adorer

пәри : *n* 1) fairy, angel, nymph

пәри-чаду : *n* evil witch

пәришан : *a* 1) sad, upset, gloomy 2) scattered about 3) disheveled

пәришанлыг : *n* sadness, gloom, unsettled/upset state

пәркар : *n* 1) compass, dividers, calipers *a* 2) skilful 3) in good order

пәрпәр-пәрпәр : *adv* dazzledly, confusedly with spots/stars seemingly before the eyes *onomatopoeic*

пәрпәтөјүн : *n* *bot* see **хвош**

пәрсәнк : *n* 1) ballast 2) crated weight

пәрт : *a* upset, embarrassed, confused

пәртдәкөз : *a* goggle-eyed, bug-eyed

пәртләшмәк : *v* get upset, embarrassed, confused

пәртлик : *n* confusion, embarrassment

пәртов : *a* 1) negligent, inaccurate 2) talking nonsense/drivel; loose-tongued,; dirty-mouthed

пәртовлуг : *n* 1) negligence, inaccuracy 2) lack of restraint in speech, smutty/lewd/dirty-mouthedness

пәрхашлыг : *n* disorder; mess; chaos

пәрчим : *n* 1) rivet, clinch, clincher 2) object jammed/stuck between other objects

пәрчимвуран : *n* riveter

пәрчимләмә : *n* riveting

пәрчимләмәк : *v* rivet, clinch

пәрчимләнмәк : *v* be riveted, be clinched

пәршум : *n* second ploughing

пәс : *n* 1) low voice, alto 2) down-and-outer, pauper, insolvent; pass *decision not to participate in a game sequence*

пәсдән : *adv* quietly, in a low voice, low *of singing*

пәсмәндә : *n* back-inventory, non-marketable goods

пәтә : *n* coupon

пәтәк : *n* beehive

пәтәклик : *n* apiary

пәтәнәк : *n* birds' stomach

пәтәнәсидар : *a* impatient

пәһләван : *n* 1) hero; strong man 2) wrestler

пәһләванлыг : *n* 1) heroism 2) profession of wrestler

пәһләванчасына : *adv* 1) heroically 2) athletically

пәһ-пәһ : *intj* 1) expresses, praise, delight, admiration 2) disapproval *rare*

пәһриз : *n* 1) diet *relig* 2) fast, abstinance

пәшмәк : *n* Azerbaijani sugar-cake

пәшо : *n* urine

пианиночалан : *n* pianist

пиано : *n* piano

пивә : *n* 1) beer *a* 2) beer

пивәгајыран : *n* brewer

пивәхана : *n* tap-room, pub, alehouse

пижам : *n* pajamas

пиј : *n* 1) fat, grease, tallow *a* 2) fatty, greasy, tallowy

пијада : *n* 1) pedestrian 2) pawn *chess* 3) ill-informed person *adv* 4) on foot

пијада гошун : *n* infantry

пијан : *n* drunkard; drunken person

пијалә : *n* 1) goblet 2) beaker, cup *without handles*

пијәбәнзәр : *a* oleaginous, resembling fat/grease

пијәридән : *n* fat-renderer

пијләмәк : *v* grease, coat with grease/tallow

пијләнмә : *n* 1) greasing 2) fattening, putting on weight

пијләнмәк : *v* 1) grease, cover with fat, tallow 2) grow fat, put on weeight

пијли : *a* greasy, fatty, covered with fat/tallow

пијлилик : *n* greasiness, fattiness,

пијсиз : *a* fat-free, non-greasy

пијсуз : *n* torch, oil-lamp; lamp

пилә : *n* raw silk

пиләк : *n* flat button

пиләкләмәк : *v* fasten, button

пиләтә : *n* kerosene-lamp

пиләтәчи : *n* kerosene-lamp repairman

пиллә : *n* stair, step

пилләкән : *n* staircase, stairway; ladder

пилләли : *a* gradual, graduated; stepped, in steps/stages

пиллә-пиллә : a 1) gradual,graduated; in steps/stages *adv* 2) by the staircase, by going up/down stairs *fig* 3) step-by-step; by degrees, gradually

пилпилә : *n* *geol* mud-volcano

пилтә : *n* 1) wick; pilot-light; fuse, slow-match *med* 2) tampon

пинә : *n* 1) leather patch for a shoe, shoe-patch *typog* 2) paste-up, pasting-up; making ready *for the press*

пинәләмәк : *v* repair, patch shoes *typ* 2) paste up; make ready *for the press*

пинәчи : *n* cobbler, shoe-repairman

пинәчилик : *n* profession of cobbler, shoe-repairman

пинти : *a* 1) slovenly, untidy, disorderly; shabby *n* 2) sloven, slob, untidy person; shabby person

пинтиләшмәк : *v* become untidy/slovenly/disorderly; grow shabby

пинтилик : *n* untidiness, slovenliness, shabbiness

пинч : *n* pinj *kind of glue used to put together parts of broken china, pottery and glass dishes*

пионер : *n* 1) pioneer *member of the Pioneer Organization, a youth movement of the Communist Party in the former Soviet Union for children up to the age of fourteen a* 2) pioneer

пионерлик : *n* membership in the Pioneers *children's Communist organization*

пипик : *n zool* comb *of birds*

пир : *n* 1) old man 2) spiritual guide; saint 3) holy place, shrine *graves, villages, etc associated with particular persons of this category*

пирәм : *n* sawdust

пиркешик : *n* salesman *in a larger store*

пирог : *n Ru* pie; cake

пирожна : *n* small cake

пирожок : *n Ru* filled roll *with meat, fish, vegetables etc*

пис : *a* 1) bad, poor *adv* 2 badly, poorly

писикмәк : *v* become cowardly, timid

писләмә : *n* condemnation, censure, conviction

писләмәк : *v* condemn, convict, censure

писләтмәк, писләшдирмәк : *v* worsen, lower the quality

писләшмәк : *v* worsen

63ислик : *n* 1) evil evil action 2) viciousness, depravity; unfitness, unsuitability

писниjjәтли : *a* ill-intended

писниjjәтлилик : *n* ill/bad intentions

пис-пис : *adv* badly, meanly, spitefully

пистон : *n* 1) piston; sucker *of a pump* 2) plunger 3) percussion cap

писфикирли : *a* ill-intentioned person

писхассәли : *a med* malignant

пити : *n* see **бозбаш**

пич : *n* screw; screw propeller

пичини бурмаг : *v* rebuff, snub

пич бағлаjан : *n* screw-driver

пиши : *n* layer-cake

пишик : *n* cat

пишикбаз : *n* cat-fancier

пишикгуjруғу : *n bot* timothy grass *Phleum pratense*

пишикоту : *n bot* valerian *Valeriana officianalis*

пиш-пиш : *intj* kitty-kitty *call for a cat*

пишпиши : *n bot* see **бәлмүшк**

пишраз : *n* early-ripening varietal grape

пишт : *intj* Shoo! *used to drive a cat away*

пиштахта : *n* counter

пjес : *n* play, drama, performance

пыттылдамаг : *v* 1) boil 2) burst into laughter

пыттылты : *n* boiling, bubbling

пырылдамаг : *v* flit, flutter

пырылты : *n* noise produced by fluttering of birds

пырныг : *n* hair standing on end

пырпыз : *a* dishevelled, ruffled, rumpled

пырпызландырмаг : *v* dishevel, make shaggy rumple

пырпызланмаг : *v* become hairy, shaggy; bristle up

пырпызлы : *a* hairy, shaggy

пырпызлылыг : *n* hairiness, shagginess

пыртдағыгыны чыхартмаг : *v* smash s.o.'s skull

пыртдатмаг : *v* see **пыртлатмаг**

пыртламаг : *v* 1) suddenly spring up/show up 2) protrude

пыртлатмаг : *v* squeeze out, to force out

пыртлашдырмаг : *v* 1) get confused 2) ruffle, rumple

пыртлашыг : *a* confused, ruffled, rumpled

пыртлашмаг : *v* get tangled, messed up, rumpled *of thread, hair*

пыспысы : *n zool* dung beetle

пытырган : *n bot* burdock *Arcticum lappa*

пытых : *n* see **тотуг**

пытраг : *n bot* 1) bur, cocklebur, burdock *a* 2) rapid-growing, thick, dense *of fruits*

пычылған : *n med* malanders *disease of horses*

пычылдамаг : *v* 1) whisper 2) prompt

пычылдашмаг : *v* whisper *together*

пычылты : *n* whispering

пычы-пычы : *n* confidential whispering, gossiping

пыч-пыч : *n* whisper, whispering, spreading gossip

планерчи : *n* glider-pilot

планетари : *a astron* planetary

планлашдырылмаг : *v* lay out, plan

планлашдырма : *n* planning, laying out

планлашдырмаг : *v* lay out, plan

планлашдыртмаг : *caus* of **планлашдырмаг**

планлы : *a* systematic, planned

плансыз : *a* 1) unplanned, unsystematic *adv* 2) unsystematically, in an unplanned manner

плансызлыг : *n* planlessness, lack of plan, lack of systematization

планчы : *n* planner *In the former USSR the functionary of an enterprise who was in charge of fitting the assets of the enterprise with the plans and " socialist obligations " imposed by higher level planning organs*

пластик : *a* plastic; flexible

пластилин : *n Ru* plasticine

платин : *n* 1) platinum *a* 2) platinum

плаш : *n Ru* raincoat

пљонка : *n Ru* film

плов : *n* pilaf

пломб : *n* filling *in a tooth*

пломблама : *n* filling *a tooth*

пломбламаг : *v* fill *a tooth*

пљаж : *n Ru* beach

пневматик : *a* pneumatic

повестка : *n Ru* written notice; subpoena

поворот : *n Ru* turn

подагра : *n med Ru* goiter

поднос : *n Ru* tray

подрат : *n* 1) contract *a* 2) contract

подратчы : *n* contractor

подумаешь : *exp Russian. Literally it means "you will think", and is close to an English "my eye!"*

поезд : *n Ru* train

поезија : *n* poetry

позан : *n* 1) violator, law-breaker 2) eraser

позғун : *a* 1) confused, disorderly, disorganized 2) prodigal, dissolute, ungoverned, errant

позғунлашдырмаг : *v tr* 1) disorganize, bring into a disordered state 2) demoralize

позғунлашмаг : *v* 1) be distressed be demoralized 2) be disorganize

позғунлуг : *n* 1) chaos, disorder 2) demoralization, disintegration, turmoil, upheaval

позмаг : *v* 1) upset, demolish, break up 2) violate, spoil 3) cross out, X out

позмагарачы : *n* see **чизмагарачи**

позуг : *a* 1) crossed out 2) lascivious, dissolute *n* 3) debauchĕe

позулма : *n* disintegration, collapse, dissolution

позулмаг : *v* 1) be upset 2) be deeply touched/affected 3) be spoilt 4) be crossed out

позулмаз : *a* 1) inviolable 2) ineradicable, indestructible 3) insoluble

позулушмаг : *v* 1) break up *by mutual effort* 2) disperse 3) annul *i.e. marriage*

позучу : *n* 1) violator, law-breaker 2) looter

полад : *n* 1) steel *a* 2) steel

полиграфија : *n tech* 1) poligraphy, printing trades 2) graphic arts

полиграфик : *a tech* 1) poligraphic, printing-trade related 2) graphic

полис : *n* 1) police officer, policeman *a* 2) police

полјак : *n* Pole

полјакча : *adv* in Polish

полк : *n mil R* regiment

полка : *n Ru* shelf

полковник : *n Ru* colonel

помидор : *n* 1) tomato *a* 2) tomato

помпул : *n* see **кәкил**

попугај : *n zool Ru* parrot

порнографија : *n* pornography

порнографик : *a* pornographic

порсуг : *n zool* badger

порсумаг : *v* 1) become sour 2) get rotten, spoilt, begin to smell *meat* 3) spoil, ger spoilt *fig* 4) fly into a rage, become angry

портағал : *n* 1) orange *a* 2) orange

портмоне : *n* wallet

поса : *n* slag, dross

поса-бетон : *n* slag-concrete *made of cement, slag and sand*

постојанный : *a Ru* permanent, stable, constant

посуда : *n Ru* dishes

пота : *a* 1) plump, chubby *n* 2) bull-calf between 6 months and 1) year old 3) *n* bear-cub

потенсиал : *n* 1) potential *a* 2) potential

пох : *n vulgar* shit, crap

почт : *n* 1) post, mail; post-office, mail-room *a* 2) postal

почталјон : *n* mailman, mail-carrier

почтхана : *n* postal installation *post-office, mail-room*

пөртләдилмәк, пөртләнмәк : *v* fry both sides, get slightly roasted all round/seared; stew

пөртләтмәк : *v* roast, fry, stew

пөртмә : *vn* fr. **пөртмәк**

пөртмәк : *v* 1) flush deeply *fr. heat/shame* 2) sear; stew *fig* 3) burst into a rage, grow angry, flare up

пөртүлмәк : *v* steam, take a steam bath 2) be stewed

пөтәнә : *n* pluck, *animal viscera*

пөһрә : *n* shoot *on a tree*

пөһрәләмәк : *v* develop shoots, put out shoots *tree*

пөһрәлик : *n* underbrush *thicket of bushes and very young trees*

прага : *n* 1) Prague *capital of the Czech Republic* *a* 2) Prague

президент : *n* 1) president *a* 2) presidential, president's

президентлик : *n* presidency

приклад : *n Ru mil* butt, butt-stock

прилавок : *n Ru* counter

принсип : *n* principle; basic rule

принсипиал : *a* 1) based on/guided by principle, principled *adv* 2) on principle; in principle

принсипсиз : *a* unprincipled, unscrupulous, not based or guided by principle, immoral

принсипсизлик : *n* unprincipledness, lack of any principles/moral moral scruples

пристан : *n Ru* pier, dock, wharf

пробка : *n Ru* cork

пробкаачан : *n* cork-screw

проблем : *n* 1) problem *a* 2) problem, problem-related

проблематик : *a* problematic[al], not very probable

проводник : *n Ru* conductor *on a train*

програм : *n* 1) program *a* 2) program

проjексиjа : *n Ru* 1) projection *a* 2) projection, projector

прокол : *n Ru* punch-hole in a driver's record *corresponds to a point in the United States*

прокурор : *n Ru* 1) prosecutor; procurator, investigating magistrate *a* 2) prosecutor['s]

прокурорлуг : *n* 1) prosecutor's office; office of the public prosecutor 2) post/occupation/duties of a prosecutor

прокимназиjа : *n Ru* Progymnasium *the six-year classical secondary school in pre-revolutionary Russia which lacked the highest three grades of the Gymnasium*

пролетар : *n Ru* 1) proletarian *a* 2) proletarian

прописка : *n Ru* residence permit *in the Soviet Union*

пропуск : *n Ru* pass

просес : *n Ru* process

простнь : *n Ru* sheet *bedclothes*

профессор : *n* 1) professor *a* 2) professorial

профессорлуг : *n* 1) professorship, university chair *coll* 2) the professoriate, the professsors collectively

профил : *n* profile

профилактик : *a* prophylactic, preventive; preliminary

психоложи : *a* psychological

психолокиjа : *n* psychology

психофизиолокиjа : *n* psychophysiology *the physiology of mental processes*

публисист : *n* publicist, feature-writer

публисистик : *a* publicistic

пук : *n* empty walnut or almond-shell

пул : *n* 1) money 2) scales *of a fish*

пула дөнмәк : *v* become white-hot

пулакы : *a* 1) greedy *for money*, avaricious, money-grubbing *n* 2) money-grubber

пулакылыг : *n* greed, avarice, money-grubbing

пулемjот : *n* 1) machine-gun *a* 2) machine-gun

пулемjотчу : *n* machine-gunner

пулланмаг : *v* become rich

пуллу : *a* 1) wealthy, rich, affluent 2) requiring payment, paid *zool* 3) scaly, squamose

пулпәрәст : *a* see **пулакы**

пул-пул : *adv* into little pieces, into smithereens

пулсуз : *a* 1) gratuitous,free of charge 2) without money adv 3) free, gratis

пулсузлашмаг : *v* be without money; grow poor, sink into squalor,be/become totally broke

пулсузлуг : *n* poverty, impecuniousness

пуп : *n* *zool* chrysalis, pupa

пуплашмаг : *v* *zool* form/take the form of a chrysalis

пусгу : *n* 1) trap, ambush 2) shadowing, being on the track of

пусма : *n* 1) scheming, intriguing; setting a trap; arranging an ambush; 2) espionage, eavesdropping, interception *of information*

пусмаг : *v* 1) scheme, intrigue; set a trap or an ambush 2) spy on, shadow; eavesdrop, intercept *information*

пута : *n* see **бута**

пуч : *a* 1) empty *n* 2) nothing

пуч еләмәк : *v* destroy, annihilate

пучал : *n* marc, pressings, residue *solid refuse of grapes*

пучлуг : *n* 1) hollow *within fruits which have a pit* 2) insignificance

пүкә : *n* sawdust

пүлүк : *n* *anat* 1) prepuce 2) burning rag used to light a bonfire/campfire

пүпитр : *n* desk, reading-desk, reading-stand

пүрибарә : *a* high-flown, eloquent *of speech*

пүрүзлү : *a* **кәлә-көтүр**

пүрфәнд : *a* 1) adroit, dexterous *n* 2) tricky fellow

пүрчүкмәк : *v* screw up one's eyes

пүскәндә : *n* dried peeled fig

пүскүрмә : *n* eruption; ejaculation

пүскүрмәк : *v* erupt; ejaculate

пүскүртмәк : *v-tr* 1) fend off, beat off, throw back, repel 2) *caus* of erupt

пүскүртү : *n* see **пүскүрмә**

пүсмүрүк : *a* uncomely, plain

пүстә : *n* 1) pistachio *a* 2) pistachio

пүстәгарын : *n* frugal eater, one who "eats like a bird"

пүстәји : *a* pistachio-colored, pistachio-green

пүстәлик : *n* pistachio grove

пүфләмәк : *v* blow, blow out

пүхтә : *a* 1) well-baked 2) experienced, sophisticated

пүхтәләшмәк : *v* become experienced, sophisticated

пүхтәлик : *n* expertise; sophisticatedness

пүшк : *n* 1) lot *that which is used in determining s.t. by chance* *fig* 2) fate, destiny

пүштә : *n* cushion used to support the back

пүштәбәнд : *n* saddle-girth

пјатиминутка : *n* *R* *short meeting of management before the beginning of the working day*

р

р : twenty-second letter of the Azerbaijani alphabet

рабитә : *n* 1) connection, link, bonds, ties 2) communication 3) line of communication

рабитәләндирмәк : *v* connect; contact; communicate

рабитәли : *a* 1) liaison, communication 2) connected, coherent *of speech*

рабитәсиз : *a* 1) disconnected, disjunct, unlinked; incoherent *adv* 2) incoherently, disconnectedly

рабитәсизлик : *n* incoherence; lack of communication links

рабитәчи : *n* *mil* 1) signaller 2) postal and telecommunications worker

равәнд : *n* *bot* rhubarb *Rheum*

рави : *n* narrator

радар : *n* radar

радиасија : *n* *phys* radiation

радио : *n* radio

радиоактив : *a* radioactive

радиоактивлик : *n* radioactivity

радиоалычы : *n* radio-set

радиоверилиши : *n* radio-broadcasting; radio program/transmission

радиогәбуледичи : *n* radio-set, radio-receiver

радиограм : *n* wireless message; radiogram

радиолашдырылмаг : *v* have radio installed, be equipped with radio

радиолашдырма : *n* installation of radio

радиолашдырмаг : *v* install radio *in*, equip with radio

радиолокија : *n* radiology

радиостансија : *n* radio-station

радиотелеграм : *n* radiogram, wireless telegram, message

радиотелеграфчы : *n* radio-telegraph operator

радиум : *n chem* radium

раздевалка : *n Ru* clothing-room, fitting-room

разы : *a* 1) agreed, content, satisfied 2) noble

разы олмаг : *v* agree; be satisfied, happy *with s.t.*

разылашдырылмаг : *v* accord *with*, conform *to*, be in agreemeent, correspond to

разылашдырма : *n* coordination, concordance, agreement

разылашдырмаг : *v* coordinate *with* , come to an agreement *with s.o. about s.t.*

разылашма : *n* agreement, understanding

разылашмаг : *v* agree *with*, consent *to*, concur *with*

разылашмамазлыг : *n* lack of agreement

разылыг : *n* 1) agreement 2) gratitude

разјана : *n bot* anise *Pimpinella anisum*

размер : *n Ru* size *used primarily of clothes*

разрешение : *n Ru* permission, permit, authorization

рајон : *n* 1) district *a* 2) district

рајонлararасы : *a* inter-district

рајонлашдырылмаг : *v* be divided into districts

рајонлашдырылмыш : *a* divided into districts

рајонлашдырма : *n* division into districts

рајонлашдырмаг : *v* divide into districts

ракет : *n* 1) missile; rocket *a* 2) missile; rocket

рам : *a* 1) submissive, obedient 2) tame, domesticated

рамазан : *n* Ramadan, ninth month of the lunar year *Moslem month of fasting*

раст : *adv* 1) directly, straightforwardly 2) accurately *n* 3) *rast a classical Azerbaijani muğam*

расткәлә : *adv* 1) by chance, by accident 2) at random, by guesswork

растлашмаг : *v* meet, come across/encounter one another

раһат : *a* 1) quiet, cosy, comfortable, calm *adv* 2) quietly, cosily, calmly, comfortably 3) *n* quiet, quietness, cosiness, comfort, calm

раһатландырмаг : *v* 1) calm down 2) create a cosy atmosphere

раһатланмаг : *v* have a rest; calm down, compose oneself, find peace

раһатлашдырмаг : *v* calm down, compose oneself, create a calm, quiet atmosphere

раһатлашмаг : *v* compose oneself, calm down, relax

раһатлыг : *n* 1) peace, quiet, tranquillity 2) rest 3) silence, stillness, serenity, comfort

раһат-раһат : *adv* see **раһатча**

раһатсыз : *a* 1) disquieted, worried, uneasy 2) uncomfortable

раһатсызлыг : *n* worry, discomfort 2) ailment, indisposition, state of mental stress

раһатхана : *n* see **ајагјолу**

раһатча : *a* calmly, relaxedly

раһиб : *n relig* monk, priest

раһибә : *n relig* nun

раһиблик : *n relig* 1) monasticism *coll* 2) monks, regular clergy, community of monks or nuns

раһибчәсинә : *adv* monastically, as monks; ascetically

раһламаг : *v* get things ready, bring into order

реаксија : *n chem* reaction

реактив : *chem a* 1) reactive *n* 2) reagent

реал : *a* 1) realistic, true to life *adv* 2 realistically

реализм : *n* realism

реалист : *n* 1) realist *a* 2) realistic

редаксија : *n* 1) editiorial staff, editorial board *a* 2) editorial

редактә : *n* editing, the editorial process

редактор : *n* 1) editor *a* 2) editorial, editor's

редакторлуг : *n* editorship

режиссор : *n* 1) film director a 2) film director['s]

режиссорлуг : *n* film direction

резин : *n* 1) rubber *a* 2) rubber

рејһан : *n bot* sweet basil *Ocimum basilicum*

реквизисија : *n* requisition

реклам : *n* advertisement

рекорд : *n* 1) record *sports a* 2) record *sports*

рекордчу : *n* record-holder, record-breaker, champion

ректификасија : *n math* rectification *adjustment for accurate calculations*

ректор : *n* rector, president, chief officer of a university

ректорлуг : *n* 1) office/rank of university rector; rectorate

релсли : *a* railroad

репетисија : *n* 1) rehearsal *a* 2) rehearsal

репродуксија : *n* reproduction

ресензија : *n* review *of a book*

ресензијачы : *n* reviewer *of a book*

ресепт : *n med* prescription

республикачы : *n* republican

рефлексолокија : *n* reflexology

рәбиүлахир : *n* Rabia II, Second Rabia *fourth month of the Moslem calendar*

рәбиүләввәл : *n* Rabia I, First Rabia *third month of the Moslem calendar*

рәбт : *n* connection, binding, joining, fastening, tying together

рәва : *n* 1) decent; suitable 2) fair

рәвајәт : *n* 1) legend, tale 2) rumor 3) saying

рәван : *a* 1) plane; even; balanced *movement* 2) smooth

рәвач : *a* 1) marketable, salable 2) lively, brisk *economy*

рәгабәт : *n* competition, rivalry

рәггасә : *n* dancer *fem* , ballerina

рәгәм : *n* figure, number, numeral

рәгиб : *n* competitor, rival, foe, antagonist

рәгс : *n* 1) dance, dancing *phys* 2) oscillation *a* 3) dancing, terpsichorian

рәғбәт : *n* sympathy, compassion; goodwill

рәғбәтләндирмәк : attract; win over; encourage

рәғбәтли : *a* attractive, compassionate, sympathetic

рәғбәтлилик : *n* attractiveness, compassion, likeableness

рәғбәтсиз : *a* unattractive, unlikeable, repulsive

рәдд : *n* removal, elimination

рәдд олсун : *exp* down with *s.o. or s.t.*

рәзаләт : *n* see **рәзиллик**

рәзә : *n* hinge

рәзил : *a* 1) vile, base, mean 2) infamous, villainous, disgraceful *n* 2) scoundrel, villain, riff-raff, scum

рәзиллик : *n* meanness, vileness, baseness

рәијјәт : *n* national *a citizen or subject of a country*

рәис : *n* chief, head, president, leader

рәислик : *n coll* leadership, the authorities

рә'ј : *n* opinion, judgement; estimate

рәјасәт : *n* leadership

рәјасәтпәрәст : *a* 1) power-loving, power-seeking ambitious *n* 2) power-lover, control-freak

рәјасәтпәрәстлик : *n* love of power; ambition

рәкик : *n* shortcoming, flaw, defect, drawback

рәмз : *n* 1) symbol, emblem 2) hint, allusion, allegory Aesopian language

рәмл : *n* cabalism *occult system of theosophy*

рәммал : *n* cabbalist

рәндә : *n* plane *tool*

рәндәләмә : *n* planing

рәндәләмәк : *v* plane

рәндәләнмәк : *v* be planed, be shaved

рәндәләтдирмәк, рәндәләтмәк : *caus* of **рәндәләмәк**

рәнк : *n* 1) color 2) rang *tune designed for dancing*

рәнкарәнк, рәнкбәрәнк : *a* multi-colored, particolored variegated

рәнкбәрәнклик : *n* diversity of colors

рәнкидәјишилән : *a* changing color

рәнкләмә : *n* painting; dyeing

рәнкләмәк : *v* paint; dye

рәнкләнмәк : *v* be painted; be dyed

рәнкли : *a* 1) painted; dyed 2) colored

рәнксаз : *n* house-painter

рәнксазлыг : *n* house-painter's profession

рәнксиз : *a* colorless, faded

рәнксизләшдирмә : *n* decolorization, bleaching

рәнксизләшдирмәк : *v* decolorize, bleach

рәнксизлик : *n* colorlessness, achromatism

рәнкчәкән : *n* see **рәнксаз**

рәнкчи : *n* see **рәнксаз**

рәнчбәр : *n* farm-laborer, hired hand, landless peasant

рәнчбәрлик : position/occupation of farm-laborer, hired hand, landless peasant

рәсәдхана : *n* observatory

рәсм : *n* 1) painting, drawing *action* 2) picture, painting, drawing, design

рәсмән : *adv* 1) officially 2) formally

рәсми : *a* 1) official, formal 2) ceremonial, parade *adv* 3) officially, formally

рәсмиііәт : formalities; official character; bureaucratism

рәсмиііәтчи : *n* bureaucrat; official

рәсмиііәтчилик : *n* formalities, red tape; bureaucratism

рәсмиләшдирмәк : *v* make something official, formalize

рәсмиләшмәк : *v* become official, be formalized

рәсм-кечид : *n* parade, inspection, review

рәсм-күшад : *n* official opening-ceremony

рәсмли : *a* illustrative

рәсмхәт : *n* drawing, sketching

рәссам : *n* painter, artist

рәссамлыг : *n* painting; profession of painter/artist

рәф : n 1) shelf 2) removal, clearing taking away 2) abolition, elimination

рәфагәт : *n* friendship

рәфиг : *n* friend *male*

рәфиганә : *adv* amicably, on friendly terms

рәфигә : *n* friend *female*

рәфтар : *n* behavior*towards* , attitude, treatment *of*

рәфтарлы : *a* affable, pleasant, well-mannered, urbane

рәфтарсыз : *a* obnoxious, ill-mannered, uncouth

рәфтарсызлыг : *n* obnoxiousness, uncouthness, crudity

рәхнә : *n* breach, break, gap

рәһбәр : *n* 1) chief, leader 2) guide, mentor

рәһбәрлик : *n* leadership

рәһм : *n* mercy, pity, compassion

рәһмдил : *a* merciful, pitying, compassionate

рәһмдиллик : *n* mercy, compassion, good-heartedness

рәһмәт : *n* grace, commiseration, mercy, pardon

рәһмәт охумаг : *v* pray*for the repose of s. o.'s soul*

рәһмәтлик : *a* 1) deceased, late, of blessed memory *n* 2) the deceased *person*

рәһмли : *a* good-hearted, compassionate

рәһмсиз : *a* heartless, unmerciful, cruel, brutal, pitiless

рәһмсизләшмәк : *v* become brutal/heartless, become embittered/hardened

рәһмсизлик : *n* cruelty, brutality, mercilessness, inhumanity

рәһмсизчә, рәһмсизчәсинә : *adv* unmercifully, heartlessly, brutally, inhumanely

рәһн : *n* deposit, security, down-payment; pawned property

рәҹәб : *n* Rajab, seventh month of the Moslem calendar

рәшадәт : *n* braveness, courage, valor

рәшадәтли : *n* brave, courageous, valiant

рә'шә : *n* cramp, spasm, convulsion

рәшид : *n* brave, courageous, valiant person

рәшт : *n* Resht *city in Iran*

риајәт : *n* observation, observance

риајәткар : *n* 1) keeper, guardian *a* 2) observant; loyal

риајәткарлыг : *n* 1) observance 2) fairness, honesty, loyalty

риггәт : *n* mercy, compassion

риггәтә кәлмәк : *v* be touched, moved

ризә : *a* 1) small, petty *adv* 2) fine, into small particles

ризә-ризә : *adv* into small particles

рија : *n* hypocrisy

ријази : *a* 1) mathematical *adv* 2) mathematically

ријазиііат : *n* mathematics

ријазиііатчы : *n* mathematician

ријакар : *a* 1) hypocritical, two-faced *n* 2) hypocrite

ријакарлыг : *n* hypocrisy, pharisaism

ријакарчасына : *adv* hypocritically

рифаһ : *n* sufficiency, prosperity, well-being, welfare

ричал : *n* jam

рича : *n* request, appeal

ришә : *n* 1) root 2) back, spine *of a book*

ришәләнмәк : *v* put out roots

ришәли : *a* rooted, having roots

ришәсиз : *a* rootless

ришхәнд : *n* mockery, derision, scoffing, sarcasm, irony

ришхәндли : *a* ironic, ironical

ришхәндчи : *n* scoffer, mocker

рол : *n* role

роман : *n* novel

романтик : *a* romantic

романчы : *n* novelist

рота : *n* *mil* company

рөвнəг : *n* 1) decoration; beauty 2) splendor, luxury, magnificence,

рөвнəгли : *a* 1) decorated, beautiful 2) splendid, luxurious

рубəнд : *n* *obs* 1) veil 2) visor

рузгу : *n* whip, switch, lash

рузи : *n* daily bread, subsistence, sustenance

рузкар : *n* life, existence, the way one lives, getting along

рупи : *n* rupi *Indian currency unit*

рус : *a* 1) Russian *n* 2) a Russian

русија : *n* 1) Russia *a* 2) Russian

русијалы : *n* 1) a Russian *a* 2) Russian

русча : *adv* in Russian

руһ : *n* spirit, soul

руһани : *n* 1) spiritual, ecclesiastical, religious *a* 2) cleric, clergyman, priest

руһəн : *adv* spiritually, religiously, psychologically

руһи : *a* spiritual, psychic

руһландыран : *a* inspiring; spiritual, mental

руһландырычы : *n* 1) inspirer, inspiration *person* *a* 2) inspiring

руһландырма : *n* encouragement, reassurance, inspiration

руһландырмаг : *v* inspire, encourage, reassure

руһланма : *n* 1) encouragement, reassurance, inspiration 2) enthusiasm for, zeal for

руһланмаг : *v* be inspired, encouraged, reassured

руһсуз : *a* lifeless, sluggish, apathetic

руһсузлуг : *n* lifelessness, sluggishness, apathy

ручка : *n* *Ru* pen

рүб : *n* 1) fourth, fourth part, quarter 2) block *of buildings* , neighborhood, quarter

рүбаб : *n* lute

рүбабчалан : *n* lutinist, lute-player

рүбаи : *n* quatrain

рүсвај : *n* shame, disgrace, dishonor, loss of face

рүсваједичи : *a* shameful

рүсвајчы : *a* shameful, dishonest, disgraceful

рүсвајчылыг : *n* shame, dishonor

рүсд : *n* sugaring *putting a layer of sugar on pastry*

рүсум : *n* 1) toll, duty, tax *a* 2) toll-/duty-/tax-related

рүсхəт : *n* authorization, permission

рүтбə : *n* title, grade, rank

рүтбəли : *a* titled, possessing high rank/title

рүтбəсиз : *a* untitled , not possessing high rank/grade

рүтубəт : *n* moisture, dampness, humidity

рүтубəтлəнмəк : *v* become moist, damp

рүтубəтли : *a* moist, damp, humid

рүтубəтлилик : *n* moisture, dampness, humidity

рүтубəтсиз : *a* not moist, not damp, dry

рүшвəт : *n* bribe, graft

рүшвəтверəн : *n* bribe-giver

рүшвəтхор : *n* bribe-taker

рүшвəтхорлуг : *n* bribery, graft

рүшвəтчи : *n* see **рүшвəтхор**

рүшејм : *n* embryo

рүшејмсиз : *a* *bot* 1) inembryonate, having no embryo

С

c : twenty-third letter of the Azerbaijani alphabet

саат : *n* 1) hour 2) clock, watch

саатбасаат : *adv* with every passing hour, hourly

саатгабы : *n* watch-case

саатлыг, саатлыға : *n* 1) . . . hours *adv* 2) for . . . hours

саатсаз : *n* watch-maker, horologer/horologist

саатсазлыг : *n* profession of watch-maker, horologer/horologist

сабаһ : *n* 1) morning *adv* 2) tomorrow

сабаһын хејир! *exp* Good morning!

сабаһкы : *a* tomorrow's

сабаһы, сабаһысы : *n* tomorrow

сабаһлыг, сабаһлыға : *adv* for tomorrow

сабаһ-сабаһ : *adv* early in the morning

сабит : *a* immovable, fixed permanent, stationary, constant, invariable, stable,

сабитләшдирмәк : *v* make something immovable, make permanent; make stable

сабитләшмә : *n* stabilization

сабитләшмәк : *v* stabilize

сабитлик : *n* permanence, constancy, stability

сабун : *n* 1) soap *a* 2) soapy

сабунгабы : *n* soap-dish, soap-box

сабунлама : *n* soaping

сабунламаг : *v* soap

сабунланмаг : *v* be soaped

сабунлу : *a* covered with soap

сабунчу : *n* soap-maker, soap-vendor

сабунчулуг : *n* soap-making, soap-manufacture

сава : *a* late *of fruit*

саваб : *a relig* salutary, edifying, pleasing to God

савад : *n* literacy

савадландырмаг : *v* teach literacy

савадланмаг : *v* become literate, learn to be literate

савадлы : *a* literate; educated

савадлылыг : *n* literacy, educational competence

савадсыз : *a* 1) illiterate *adv* 2) in an illiterate manner

савадсызлыг : *n* illiteracy

савадчы : *n* silversmith

савај(ы) : *adv* except, with the exception of

саванд : *a* see **әјә**

саваш : *n* quarrel, squabbling, fighting

савашган : *n* 1) bully, trouble-maker *a* 2) pugnacious, violent

савашганлыг : *n* pugnacity, riotous conduct

саващдырмаг : *v* set at variance with each other

саващдыртмаг : *caus* of **савашмаг**

савашма : *n* see **саваш**

савашмаг : *v* fight, quarrel

саг : *n* trunk *tree*

сагга : *n obs* water-carrier

саггал : *n* beard

саггалланмаг : *v* have o.'s beard grow out, become overgrown with beard

саггаллы : *a* bearded

саггалсыз : *a* beardless

саггыз : *n* chewing-gum

сагго : *n vet* glanders *infectious disease of horses*

сагголу : *a* glanders-infected

саги : *n hist* chief-steward, cup-bearer

сагынараг : *adv* carefully, attentively

сагындырма : *n* warning

сагындырмаг : *v* warn, caution

сагынма : *n* warning; caution

сагынмаг : *v* 1) be alert; be cautious 2) refrain *from*; avoid

сагынмајан : *a* careless; unrestrained, uncontrolled, unbridled

сағ : *a* 1) healthy, well 2) right *direction*)

саға : *adv* to the right

сағалдан : *n* 1) healer *a* 2) healing, curing

сағалдылмаз : *a* incurable

сағалдычы : *a* healing, restorative, curative

сағалма : *n* recovery

сағалмаг : *v* 1) recover, become healthy 2) heal over, cicatrize *wound*

сағалмаз : *a* incurable

сағалмамазлыг : *n* incurability, irremediability

сағалтма : *n* healing, curing

сағалтмаг : *v* heal, cure, make well again

сағанаг : *n* 1) rim 2) frame[s] *eyeglasses*

сағда : *adv* on the right, on the right-hand side

сағдан : *adv* from the right, from the right-hand side

сағдырмаг : *caus* of **сағмаг**

сағдыш : *n* best man

сағылмаг : *v* be milked

сағым : *n* milk-yield

сағымлы : *a* high-milk-yield cow

сағын : *n* see **сағым**

сағынчы : *n* milkmaid, dairywoman, dairyman

сағыр : *a n* minor *in age*

сағычы : *n* see **сағынчы**

сағлам : *n* healthy, strong

сағламдүшүнчәли : see **сағламфикирли**

сағламлащдырма : *vn* fr. **сағламлащдырмаг**

сағламлашдырмаг : *v tr* make healthy; cause to recover

сағламлашма : *vn* fr. **сағламлашмаг**

сағламлашмаг : *v* 1) become healthy/strong 2) recover, recuperate, get well/better

сағламлыг : *n* health, strength; haleness, robust health

сағламфикирли : *a* 1) sensible, judicious *n* 1) sensible/common sense person, person of sound judgement

сағлыг : *n* 1) health, life, well-being, prosperity *adv* 2) a bit to the right

сағма : *n* milking

сағмаг : *v* milk

сағмал : *a* 1) milch, milk, yielding milk *n* 2) milk/milch cow , domestic animal yielding milk *cow, goat, ewe*

сағры : *n* 1) crupper *horse anat* 2) thigh, haunch, buttock[s], seat

сағрылы : *a* wide-beamed *of a person*

сағсаған : *n zool* magpie

сағ-саламат : *a* 1) happy, successsful, safe, unharmed, safe and sound *adv* 2) happily, safely, successfully, o.k.

сағ-саламатлыг : *n* well-being, prosperity

садаг : *n* chain mail, shirt of mail, hauberk

садә : *a* 1) simple, uncomplicated, plain 2) naive, modest 3) involuntary 4) smooth *cloth adv* 5) simply, unpretentiously

садәгәлб, садәдил : *a* simple-hearted, naive, honest

садәгәлблик, садәдиллик : *n* naivity, artlessness, ingenuousness

садәгәлблиликлә, садәдилликлә : *adv* naively, artlessly, ingenuously, honestly

садәләшдирмә : *n* simplification

садәләшдирмәк : *n* simplify

садәләшмәк : *v* become simpler, be simplified

садәлик : *n* simplicity

садәлөвh : *a* naive, credulous, gullible

садәлөвhлүк : *n* naivety, naivitě, gullibility

садәчә : *adv* 1) simply *a* 2) very simple

садәчәсинә : *adv* see **садәчә** 1)

садәүрәкли : *a* **садәгәлб**

садиг : *n* faithful, devoted, steadfast

садиглик : *n* faithfulness, devotion

садылама : *n* enumeration

садыламаг : *v* enumerate

саз : *n* 1) saz, *lute-like instrument similar to a mandolin, but with a longer fretboard* a 2) in good condition 3) well-tuned

сазаг : *n* severe cold, hard frost

сазан : *n zool* 1) carp *Cyprinus carpio a* 2) carp

сазанда, сазәндә : *n* sazandar, folk musician-singer

сазиш : *n* deal, agreement, contract; compromise

сазишкар : *n* compromiser, appeaser, conciliator

сазишчи : *n* compromiser, appeaser, conciliator

сазишчилик : *n* compromise, appeasement

сазлама : *n* regulation, adjustment, tuning

сазламаг : *v* 1) correct, set right 2) regulate, adjust, tune

сазланмаг : *v* be corrected/regulated, be tuned

сазлашдырмаг : *v* see **сазламаг**

сазлашмаг : *v* 1) become better, improve

сазлыг : *n* well-tuned state, good condition, good working order

сазчалан, сазчы : *n* saz player, lutinist

саир(ә) : *a* other, different

саит : *n gram* vowel

саитарасы : *a gram* intervocalic

сај : *n* 1) number, count, quantity *gram* 2) numeral 3) shoal, sand-bar, sand-bank

саја : *a* 1) smooth, even *fig* 2) simple-hearted 3) simpleton

сајаг : *n* manner, method of action

сајғач : *n* meter

сајғы : *n* vigilance, alertness; caution

сајғылы, сајғын : *a* cautious, careful, alert,vigilant

сајғысыз : *a* careless, negligent

сајғысызлыг : *n* 1) carelessness, negligence 2) imprudence, unconcern

сајғысыз-сајғысыз : *adv* carelessly, negligently

сајдырмаг, сајдыртмаг : *caus* of **сајмаг**

сајә : *n* 1) shade 2) defense, protection

сајәндә : *exp* because of you

сајәсиндә : *exp* because of him/her/it

сајыг : *a* alert, cautious, careful

сајыглама : *n* delirium, ravings

сајыгламаг : *v* be delirious, rave

сајыглыг : *n* vigilance, caution

сајылы : *a* counted, computed, calculated; numbered

сајылмаг : *v* be counted/numbered/computed/calculated/considered

сајычы : *n* see **сајчы**

сајлашмаг : *v* become shallow *river, lake*

сајма : *n* 1) counting, numbering, computation, calculation 2) respect, consideration

сајмаг : *v* 1) count, number, calculate 2) take into account, consider; recognize

сајмаз : *a* inattentive, negligent

сајмазјана : *adv* inattentively, negligently, carelessly, indifferently

сајмазлыг : *n* negligence, disrespect, ignoring, disregard, indifference

сајмазчасына : *adv* see **сајмазјана**

сајмамазлыг : *n* see **сајмазлыг**

сајмача : *n* counting *in children's games*

сајрышмаг : *v* twinkle

сајсыз : *a* 1) numberless, countless *adv* 2) without number

сајсыз-һесабсыз : *a* 1) without number, in great numbers *n* 2) numberless multitude, huge quantity

сајтал : *a* 1) huge, enormous 2) large, big, heavy-set *person*

сајчы : *n* census-taker

сајча : *adv* quantitatively, numerically; by number, by quantity

сакин : *n* inhabitant, resident

сакит : *a* 1) quiet, calm, silent, still *adv* 2) quietly, silently, calmly

сакит олмаг : *v* become calm, tranquil

сакитләнмәк : *v* see **сакитләшмәк**

сакитләшдиричи : *a* calming, soothing

сакитләшдирмәк : *v-tr* calm, sooth, quieten, pacify

сакитләшмә : *n* calming, quieting, soothing

сакитләшмәк : *v* calm down, compose o.s., become quiet

сакитлик : *n* 1) quiet, silence, serenity, tranquillity 2) calm, lull *at sea*

сакит-сакит : *adv* quietly, calmly, tranquilly

сакитчә : *adv* quietly, calmly, peacefully

сал : *n* 1) plate, slab *stone* *n* 2) raft *a* 3) massive, monolithic

салам : *n* 1) greeting, salute, salutation 2) Salaam! Hello! *verbal greeting fr. Arabic lit. "peace"*

салам вермәк : *v* greet, say 'hello', make a bow

саламат : *a* 1) healthy, well *adv* 2) all right, happily, safely

саламатлашмаг : *v* say goodbye, take o.'s leave, bid farewell

саламатлыг : *n* health, healthiness, well-being, soundness

саламәлејкүм : *intj* Salaam 'aleyküm *traditional Moslem greeting lit* "May peace be with you."

саламламаг : *v* greet, welcome

саламлашмаг : *v* greet *one another*, pass the time of day *with one another*

салат : *n* salad

салача : *n* stretcher

салдырма : *vn* fr. **салдырмаг**

салдырмаг, салдыртмаг : *caus* 1) of **салмаг** 2) poison 3) fend off, drive off, not permit to take away

салы : *n* see **тәк** 3)

салынмаг : be laid on, be spread out, be covered up, be lowered/inserted/overthrown

салышдырычы : *n* 1) instigator, provocateur *a* 2) inciting,stirring up provocative

салышдырычылыг : *n* instigation, incitement, setting on

салышдырмаг : *v* stir up against one another, set on one another

саллаг : *n* 1) slaughterer *of cattle* *a* 2) suspended/hanging on a scale *so as to be weighed*

саллаггарын : *a* with stomach hanging down, with drooping paunch

саллаггулаг : *a* lop-eared

саллагдодаг : *n* see **ләкдодаг**

саллаглыг : *n* occupation of cattle-slaughterer

саллагхана : *n* slaughter-house, abbatoir

саллама : *vn* fr. **салламаг**

салламаг : *v* lower, let down

саллана-саллана : *adv* pitching and rolling, rocking

салланмаг : *v* hang, suspend

салма : *vn* fr. **салмаг**

салмаг : *v* 1) lower, let down, drop, put, throw, overthrow 2) lay on, spread *i.e. bedclothes/carpet* 3) cover 4) put in, insert

салнамә : *n* annals, chronicle, historical account

салон : *n* hall, salon, reception room

салфет : *n* napkin

салхым : *n* bunch *of grapes*

салчы : *n* rafter, raftsman, ferryman

саман : *n* chaff, straw

саманламаг : *v* 1) cover/spread with straw 2) feed with straw *domestic animals*

саманлыҕ : *n* 1) threshing barn 2) barn/shed for storage of straw/chaff

сами : *n* 1) Semite *a* 2) Semitic .

самит : *n gram* 1) consonant sound/phoneme *a* 2) silent, mute

самолјот : *n Ru* plane, aircraft

самур : *n zool* 1) sable *Martes zibellina,* a carnivore prized for its fur *a* 2) sable

сан : *n* reputation, fame, repute, honor

сан кетмәк : *v* march *as in a military parade*

санамаг : *v* see **сајмаг**

санаторија : *n* sanatorium; health center

санбал : *n* weight, weightiness, heaviness

санбаллы : *a* 1) heavy, weighty 2) monumental

сандал : *n bot* sandalwood, logwood *Haematoxylon campechianum*

сандыг : *n* 1) trunk, box, chest 2) magazine *rifle* 3) cash-desk, till

сандыгхана : *n* cellar, vault, store-room

сандыгча : *n dim* small trunk, box, chest

санијә : *n* second *1/60 of a minute*

санијәөлчән : *n* stopwatch, timing device, timer

сантар : *n* 1) hospital-attendant, medical-orderly *m/f,* junior nurse *a* 2) sanitary, medical

санки : *conj* as if, as though

санлы : *a* honorable

санмаг : *v* 1) suppose, think, consider 2) take as, take for

сансар : *n zool* stone marten, *Martes foina* ; small Old-World animal of the weasel family, prized for its fur, marked in white at the throat and breast

санчаг : *n* pin

санчаглама : *n* pinning, fastening/attaching with a pin

санчагламаг : *v* pin, fasten/attach with a pin

санчан : *a* able/apt/prone to, having the capacity to bite/sting/prick

санчдырмаг : *caus* of **санчмаг**

санчы : *n* sharp pain in the abdomen, gripes, colic

санчыланмаг : *v* feel/experience colic/gripes/sharp pain in the abdomen

санчылы : *a* 1) suffering from chronic abdominal colic 2) in a pierced, penetrated condition

санчылмаг : *v* pierce, stick/thrust/stab *with a pin/knife etc*

санчычы : *a* see **санчан**

санчмаг : *v* 1) stick into *a pin etc* , thrust/stab into,*a knife etc* thrust into, drive into *a stake etc* , stick into *a needle etc* 2) begin to prick, stick into *a needle etc* 3) sting, bite 4) gripe, be splitting/piercing *of a pain*

сап : *n* 1) thread 2) handle, shaft *of a shovel, a pick-axe etc*

сапалаг : *n obs* tax *on bread and other products*

сапаг : *n* see **хыш**

сапанд : *n* 1) sling 2) sling-shot *boy's*

сапгын : *a* 1) lecherous, lascivious dissipated, loose *n* 2) libertine, debauchee, dissolute person

сапгынлыг : *n* lasciviousness, lechery, depravity

сапгынчасына : *adv* lasciviously, lecherously in a depraved manner

сапдырма : *v n* 1) from **сапдырмаг** *adv* 2) discordantly, not to the point, out of place

сапдырмаг : *v* 1) avoiding, finding a way around *a* 2) unequal *adv* 3) discordantly, unequally, not to the point, out of place

сапытмаг : *v* tack, maneuvre

саплаг : *n* 1) handle, haft *biol* 2) stalk, pedicle, pedicel *bot* 3) peduncle 4) base 5) see **сап** 2)

саплаглы : *a* stalky, stalk-like, columnar

сапламаг : *v* 1) thread a needle 2) make a haft/handle *for s.t.* 3) strike with all o.'s might 4) thrust/stick/stab/plunge into *knife/dagger*

саплы : *a* 1) having a handle/haft 2) threaded *needle*

саплыг : *a* material suitable for/earmarked for handles/hafts

саплыча : *n* frying pan

сапма : *n* 1) divergence from the direct route/path, declivity 2) deviation *divergence of a compass needle because of the proximity of an iron mass*

сапмаг : *v* 1) wander, stray, err, be mistaken, diverge, deviate, digress 2) turn from the route/course

сапасағ, сапсағлам : *a* completely healthy, unharmed, safe

сапсары : *a* yellow, quite yellow

сар : *n zool* buzzard

сарағаn : *n bot* smoke tree *Cotinus cogyggria*

сарај : *n* 1) palace, mansion, castle *a* 2) palatial

сaралмаг : *v* 1) turn yellow *fig* 2) turn/grow pale, blanch

сарбан : *n* cameleer, camel driver

сарғы : *n* 1) bandage, dressing 2) coil, winding, twining around

сардина : *n zool* sardine

сары : *a* 1) yellow 2) red, red-haired *postp* 3) to. . ., toward. . ., in the direction of. . .

сарыбаш : *a* yellow-haired, tow-headed, blond

сарыбәниз : *n* see **сарышын**

сарыг : *n* 1) bandage, dressing 2) turban

сары-гырмызы : *a* see **гызартдаг**

сарыглы : *a* 1) wound around the head 2) turbaned *n* 3) one who wears a turban

сарыдөш : *a zool* yellow-breasted *bird*

сарыјағыз, сарыјаныз : *n* see **сарышын**

сарыјычы : *n tex* winder *textile worker engaged in winding thread used in weaving cloth*

сарыкөјнәк : *n zool* oriole fam. *Oriolidae*

сарыкөк : *n* yellow ginger *food flavoring*

сары-күрән : *a* light chestnut *horse's coat*

сарыкилә : *n* variety of white grape with spherical berries

сарылыг : *n* 1) yellowness 2) jaundice, icterus

сарылмаг *v-intr* 1) coil, wind, tie about o.s. 2) be clasped, embraced

сарыма : vn fr. **сарымаг**

сарымаг : *v* 1) dress *a wound*, bandage, bind about, tie up *with* 2) wind, wind up, wind around, twist 3) wrap up *in*, envelop *with fig* 4) dupe, hoax, mock, make fun *of*, deride

сарымсаг : *n* 1) garlic *a* 2) garlic, garlicky

сарымтыл : *a* yellowish

сарынма : *v n* from **сарынмаг**

сарынмаг : *pass* 1) tie s.t. round o.s., be tied/bound/wound around 2) coil around s.t., be coiled around s.t. 3) be wrapped up in s.t., wrap o.s. up in s.t.

сарысач : *a* light brown

сарысәндәл : *n* see **сарыкөјнәк**

сарышын : *n* fair-haired man, man with blond/fair hair

сармаг : *v* see **бүрүмәк**

сармашыг : *n bot* bindweed *Convolvulus*

сармашмаг : *v-intr* 1) coil, wind 2) embrace one other

сарп : *a* steep, inaccessible

сарсаг : *a* 1) stupid, unintelligent, imbecilic 2) fool, dolt, blockhead, ninny

сарсаггулу : *n* fool, dolt, blockhead

сарсагламаг : *v* make a fool of o.s., be foolish, play the fool behave in an odd way,

сарсаглыг : *n* stupidity, imbecility, eccentricity

сарсаг-сарсаг : *adv* stupidly, foolishly

сарсагчасына : *adv* stupidly, idiotically

сарсыдычы : *a* staggering, shattering, crushing

сарсылмаг : *v -intr* shake, be shaken, quake

сарсылмаз : *a* unshakeable, steadfast, indestructable

сарсылмазлыг : *n* stability, unshakability, invincibility

сарсыма : *n* 1) swaying, vacillation, oscillation 2) shock, confusion

сарсымаг : *v-intr* sway, swing, shake

сарсынты : *n* swaying, shaking, oscillation

сарсынтылы : *a* vacillating, jolty, shaking

сарсытмаг : *v-intr* shake, shake *for a while*, shake loose, sway

сатасат : *n* see **сатһасат**

саташган : *n* bully, trouble-maker

саташма : *v n* from **саташмаг**

саташмаг : *n* offend, pester, badger, make fun of, mock at

сатты : *n* see **сатыш**

саттын : *a* 1) selling; treacherous *n* 2) traitor, betrayer

саттынлыг : *n* 1) mercenariness, venality 2) betrayal, treason

сатдырмаг, сатдыртмаг : *caus* of **сатмаг**

сатира : *n* satire

сати'рик : *n* satirist

сатири'к : *a* satirical

сатыл : *n* battered copper pail, copper pail with dented sidesca

сатылма : *vn* from **сатылмаг**

сатылмаг : *v-intr* 1) sell out, sell off, dispose of 2) be bribed, suborned, become a traitor

сатылмаз : *a* not for sale, incorruptible

сатылмалы : *a* to be sold, for sale, subject to sale

сатын : *in comb* **сатын алмаг** : buy, obtain for money

сатыналма : *in comb* **сатыналма гијмәти** : purchase price

сатычы : *n* seller, vendor

сатычылы : *n* occupation/work of a seller/vendor

сатыш : *n* sale, selling

сатлыг : *a* to be sold, for sale, earmarked for sale

сатма : *n* selling, sale

сатмаг : *v* 1) sell *fig* 2) betray

сатрап : *n obs* satrap *Governor of a province in ancient Persia*

сатһасат : *n* brisk, uninterrupted trade/commerce

саф : *a* 1) pure, unalloyed 2) clear, bright, transparent

сафгәлбли : *a* see **сафүрәкли**

сафгәлблилик : *n* see **сафүрәклилик**

сафдил : *a* see **сафүрәкли**

сафдиллидик : *n* see **сафүрәклилик**

сафландырмаг, сафлашдырмаг : *v* purify, distil, refine

сафлашдырычы : *a* purifying, cleansing, refining

сафлашмаг : *v* become pure, clean, transparent

сафлыг : *n* cleanness, clarity, transparency

сафүрәклилик : *a* sincere, open-hearted

саф-чүрүк : *v* sort out, look over, sort and remove defective elements, separate out the bad from the good/spoiled from unspoiled

сахлаjан : *n* keeper, custodian; landlord

сахлама : *v n* from **сахламаг**

сахламаг : *v* 1) keep, preserve, secure, take care of, protect 2) get, retain, set aside, defer 3) hold, contain 4) retain, hold back, conserve

сахланмаг : *v-intr* be on o.'s guard against, beware of, take care, be cautious of

сахланмаз : *a* irrepressible, unrestrained, unchecked

сахлатдырмаг, сахлатмаг : *caus* of **сахламаг**

сахсы : *n* 1) faience, a variety of glazed pottery, usually highly decorated *a* 2) faience

сахта : *a* 1) counterfeit, sham, fake, spurious, not genuine 2) forger, falsifier, counterfeiter

сахтакар : *n* forger, counterfeiter

сахтакарлыг : *n* falsification, forgery, adulteration

сахталашдырма : *n* falsification, forgery, adulteration

сахталашдырмаг : *v* falsify, forge, counterfeit

сахталыг : *n* falsity, falseness, imitation, deception, sham

саһә : *n* 1) area, open place, space 2) sector of land 3) field of activity, sphere of action, walk of life 4) branch, field, province

саһиб : *n* master, boss, owner, proprietor *Arabic: title of respect used for people of rank*

саһиб олмаг : *v* become an owner, a proprietor

саһибкар : *n* master, owner, proprietor

саһибләнмәк : *v* take possession of *s.t.*, own, acquire

саһиблик : *n* ownership, proprietorship

саһибсиз : *a* 1) ownerless 2) homeless, neglected

саһибсизлик : *n* 1) absence of an owner/proprietor 2) homelessness, neglect

саһил : *n* shore, coast

саһман : *n* 1) disposition, arrangement, order 2) convenience, possibility, opportunity

саманламаг : *v* dispose, arrange, put in order

саһманлы : *a* 1) comfortable, handy, convenient 2) well-appointed, put in good order

сач : *n* 1) hair, the hair 2) plait, braid, tresses

сач-саггал ағартмаг : *v* grow old

сачаг : *n* fringe

сачаглы : *a* fringed

сачаг-сачаг : *a* fringed

сачагсыз : *a* unfringed, not having a fringe

сач-бирчәк : *n* ringlets, curls : **сач-бирчәк ағартмаг** 1) grow grey, grow old, age *of a woman fig* 2) have extensive experience of life

сачламаг : *v* seize by the hair *s.o.*

сачланмаг : *v* allow o.'s hair to become overgrown/ become too long

сачлашмаг : *v* seize one another by the hair

сачлы : *a* having long hair, long haired, having long braids

сачма : *vn* 1) see **гырма** *vn* 2) from **сачмаг**

сачмаг : *v* disperse, diffuse, spread

сач-саггал : *n* beard, hair of the beard : **сач-саггал ағартмаг** 1)) grow grey, grow old *of a man fig* 2) have extensive experience in life

сачсыз : *a* hairless

сачшәкилли : *a* hair-like, capillary

сач : *n* sheet-iron disk on which flat-bread is baked

сачајаг : *n* iron pot with legs used for cooking over a fire

светофор : *n Ru* traffic-light

севда : *n* 1) love, passion 2) Sevda *female first name*

севдаја дүшмәк : *v* fall in love *with s.o.* ; become prone to *s.t.* ; become addicted to *s.t.*

севдирмәк : *n* make/cause oneself to fall in love

севилмәјән : *a* unloved

севилмәк : *n* make o.s. love

севим : *n* 1) love, favor i.e. *attitude of friendliness,liking, or approbation* 2) liking *for*, sympathy *with/for*

севимли : *a* 1) nice, sweet, pretty, darling, beloved 2) likeable, attractive, charming

севимлилик : *n* prettiness, charm, fascination, likeableness

севиндиричи : *a* joyous, joyful, glad, pleasant

севиндирмәк : *v* make glad/happy, gladden, bring joy to

севинмәк : *v* be glad/happy, rejoice

севинч : *n* gladness, joy, delight, pleasure

севинчәк, севинчлә : *adv* gladly, joyfully

севинчлы : *a* glad, joyous, joyful, gratifying

севинчсиз : *a* cheerless, dismal, dreary

севишмәк : *v* come to love one another, fall in love with one another

севки : *n* 1) love *a* 2) love, loving, amorous

севкили : *a* 1) dear, loved, beloved *n* 2) sweetheart, pet, favorite

севкисиз : *a* loveless, unloved

севмәк : *v* love, fall in love *with*

севмәли : *a* worthy of love, loveable

сездирмәк : *v* 1) let observe 2) let feel 3) guess in advance, divine, foretell, know

сезиләбилән : *a* foretold, guessed in advance, divined, known

сезилмәк : *v* make itself felt, be felt, be guessed in advance

сезмәк : *v* 1) guess, suspect, be divined/perceived 2) catch *the meaning*, sense, feel

сејван : *n* see **ејван**

сејид : *n relig* title of Mohammed's descendants

сејиз : *n* goat whose function is to walk in front of and lead a flock of sheep

сејлон : *n* 1) Ceylon (island, now Sri Lanka) *a* 2) Ceylonese

сејр : *n* 1) walk, stroll, airing 2) contemplation

сејрәк : *a* 1) sparse, not dense *typ* 2) spaced-out *adv* 3) sparcely, rarely, few and far between

сејрәкдишли : *a* having widely spaced teeth

сејрәкјарпагли : *a* sparse-foliaged

сејрәкләнмәк : *v* see **сејрәлмәк**

сејрәкләщдирмәк : *v* see **сејрәлтмәк**

сејрәкләшмәк : *v* see **сејрәлмәк**

сејрәксачли, сејрәктүклү : having thin/sparse hair

сејрәлмә : *n* thinning out, rarification

сејрәлмәк : *v* become sparse, thin out, get thin, rarify

сејрәлтмәк : *v* thin out, weed out

сејрәнкаһ : *n* 1) area for walks, strolls, promenades 2) spaciousness, space *a* 3) open, wide, broad

сејрчи *a* 1) engaged in strolling, going for a walk *n* 2) observer, spectator, onlooker, contemplator

сејсмолокија : *n* seismology

секаһ : seǧah *a classical Azerbaijanian melody*

сел : *n* 1) torrent *snow, or snow melt-water* 2) freshet, spring flood

селедка : *n Ru* herring

селениум : *n chem* Selenium, a grey, crystalline, non-metallic element of the sulfur group, symbol Se

селик : *n* mucous

селикли : *a* mucous, mucose

селләмә : *adv* in torrents, torrentially, in buckets *rain, flood-waters*

семәнт : *n* 1) cement *a* 2) cement

семәнтләмә : *n* cementing

семәнтләмәк : *v* cement

семәнтләнмиш : *a* cemented

сенат : *n* upper branch of national or state legislative bodies in the United States, Canada, France and other governments

сенз : *n* qualification *for enjoyment of voting and propertyr rights especially in western countries*

сензор : *n* censor

сензура : *n* 1) censorship *a* 2) censorship

сент : *n* cent *U.S. coin*

сентнер : *n* centner *measure of weight = 100 kg*

сентјабр : *n* 1) September *a* 2) September

сержант : *n* sergeant

сех : *n Ru* 1) shop, workshop, department *in a factory* *a* 2) shop-/workshop-/ department-related 3) limited, parochial, narrow

сехыш : *n* thrice-repeated ploughing/tillage of the soil

сеһр : *n* sorcery, spell[s], magic, black magic, witchcraft

сеһрбаз : *n* magician, sorcerer, Magian, magician

сеһрбазлыг : *n* magic, sorcery, witchcraft

сеһрлы : *a* magical, magic, bewitching

сечдыртмәк : *caus* of **сечмәк**

сечилән : *a* 1) having been/chosen/ elected/selected 2) selectee, nominee *n* 3) elect, chosen one ; favorite, darling

сечилмә : *n* election, selection

сечилмәз : *a* misty, foggy, unclear, invisible, unseen

сечилмәк : *v* 1) be selected, chosen, elected, picked out 2) be recognized/discerned, be singled out, be different, differ, be distinguished *by*

сечилмиш : *a* chosen, selected, singled out, picked out

сечичи : *n* voter, elector

сечки : *n* 1) elections *a* 2) electoral, elective

сечкигабағы : *a* pre-election

сечкичи : *n* elector

сечмә : *n* 1) selection *adv* 2) by choice, for choice *a* 3) select[ed], choice, picked

сечмәдән : *adv* pell-mell, in a heap, indiscriminately

сечмәк : *v* 1) choose, select, 2) single out, separate, pick out 3) distinguish, discern

сешәнбә : *n* Tuesday

сәадәт : *n* happiness

сәадәтли : *a* happy

сәба : *n* zephyr, light wind

сәбат : *n* constancy, stability. firmness, perseverance, resoluteness

сәбатла : *adv* steadily, staunchly, persistantly

сәбатлы : *a* constant, firm, stable, resolute, persistant, unwavering

сәбатлылыг : *n* see **сәбат**

сәбатсыз : *a* inconstant, irresolute, wavering, vacillating, changeable

сәбатсызлыг : *n* instability, onconstancy, changeableness

сәбәб : *n* reason, cause, ground, motive

сәбәбиjjәт : *n* causation

сәбәбкар : *n* culprit, perpetrator, instigator

сәбәбкарлыг : *n* causality

сәбәбли : *a* 1) causative, having a cause/reason/basis 2) valid, good, well-grounded, substantial

сәбәблилик : *n* causation, causality, determinant 2) validity

сәбәбсиз : *n* 1) causeless, groundless, motiveless, baseless 2) invalid

сәбәбсизлик : *n* 1) causelessness, motivelessness, groundlessness 2) invalidity

сәбәт : *n* basket

сәбәтә : *n* skeleton, framework

сәбәтчи : *n* basket-maker

сәбзә : *n* sabza a special variety of raisin

сәбзәват : *n* vegetables

сәбзәватчы : *n* greengrocer, vegetable merchant, produce-man

сәбзи : *n* greens, vegetables

сәбзиговурма : *n* sabzigovurma a sauce of meat and vegetables *a condiment for pilaff*

сәбир : *n* patience, toleration

сәбиредилмәз : *a* intolerable, unbearable

сәбирлә : *adv* patiently

сәбирли : *a* patient

сәбирлилик : *n* patience, toleration

сәбирсиз : *a* patience, forbearance

сәбирсизлик : *n* impatience, lack of forbearance

сәбирсизликлә : *adv* impatiently

сәвәләмәк : *v* see **сәвмәк**

сәвиjjә : *n* 1) level *fig* 2) horizon, mental outlook *from Arabic "savviyeh" = equality*

сәвмәк : *v* caress, fondle,

сәгф : *n* ceiling, arch, vault

сәда : *n* 1) sound, voice, echo, response 2) news, rumor

сәдагәт : *n* faithfulness, allegiance, devotion

сәдагәтлә : *adv* faithfully, devotedly, unfailingly

сәдагәтли : *a* faithful, devoted

сәдагәтлилик : *n* see **сәдагәт**

сәдарәт : *n* see **сәдрлик**

сәдд : *n* 1) barrier, impediment, obstacle 2) wall, embankment 3) dam, weir

сәдди-чин : *n* Great Chinese Wall

сәдәгә : *n* alms, charity

сәдәф : *n* 1) mother-of-pearl 2) mother-of-pearl

сәдәфли : *a* decorated/inlaid with mother-of-pearl; made of mother-of-pearl

сәдр : *n* chairman, president

сәдри : *n* sadri a superior variety of rice, in ancient times called "The Khan's rice"

сәдрлик : *n* chairmanship, presidency

сә'j : *n* endeavor, effort, diligence

сәjahәт : *n* journey, travelling

сәjahәтнамә : *n* traveller's notes, book of travels

сәjahәтчи : *n* traveler

сәjөләнмәк : *v* see **сәндәләмәк**

сәjиртмә : *adv* at a gallop/full gallop

сәjиртмәк : *v* gallop, hurry off/go along at a gallop

сәjjар : *a* 1) mobile, moveable, wandering 2) marching, field, in the field

сәjjарә : *n* planet

сәjjah : *n* traveller, wanderer

сә'jлә : *adv* with assiduity, assiduously, diligently, industriously,

painstakingly

сә'jли : *a* assiduous, diligent, industrious, painstakin

сә'jлилилик : *n* application, assiduiity, diligence, painstakingness

сәримә *n* *med* tic, convulsion

сә'jримәк : *v* tremble, shake, shiver, shudder

сә'jришмәк : *v* twinkle, shimmer

сәкдмрмә : *n* ricochet, rebound

сәкдмрмәк : *v* make/cause to jump, bound 2) throw with a rebound *i.e. stone, discus*

сәки : *n* 1) pavement, sidewalk 2) terrace 2) elevated place for sitting; platform, built-in seat along a wall *i.e. in a steam-bath*

сәкил : *n* horse with white hair-color on its lower legs, stockinged horse

сәкилтикә : *n* fatty pieces of meat

сәккиз : *num* eight

сәккизбучаг : *a* octagonal

сәккизмллик : *a* of eight years, eight year; eight-year old

сәккизинчи : *ord* eighth

сәккизлик : *num* an eight

сәккизмәртәбә : *a* eight-story

сәккизрәгәмлм : *a* eight-digit

сәккизсаатлыг : *a* of eight hours, eight-hour

сәккиз-сәккиз : *adv* by eights, in groups of eight

сәккизүзлү : *a* octahedral

сәккизhечалы : *a* eight-ply, eight-layer

сәккизhедли : *a* eight-fold, octuple

сәккизчилдли : *a* eight-atom

сәкмә : *vn* fr. **сәкмәк**

сәкмәк : *v* mince along, walk quickly with short steps

сәксәкә : *n* alarm, anxiety, guarded state, suspiciousness

сәксәкәли : *a* anxious, uneasy, guarded, watchful

сәксән : *num* eighty

сәксәничи : *ord* eightieth

сәксәнмә : *vn* fr. **сәксәнмәк**

сәксәнмәк : *v* start, give a start

сәлаhиjjәт : *n* 1) plenary power 2) competence, authority

сәлаhиjjәтдар : *a* plenipotentiary, competent, enjoying full rights

сәлаhиjjәтли : *a* 1) see **сәлаhиjjәтдар** 2) competent, authoritative

сәлаhиjjәтсиз : *a* not competent, not having full rights or authority

селедка : *n* *Ru* herring dish

сәлә : *a* 1) straw *n* 2) type of cork made of a piece of animal stomach, used to seal jugs in which food products are preserved

сәләпапаг : *a* wearing a straw hat

сәләм : *n* interest *paid on loans, bank deposits etc*

сәләмхор, сәләмчи : *n* usurer

сәләмхорлуг, сәләмчилик : *n* usury

сәләф : *n* forerunner, precursor

сәлиб : *n* 1) cross *a* 2) cross

сәлигә : *n* exactness, thoroughness, neatness, order; good taste

сәлигәли : *a* exact, thorough, neat, orderly ; possessing good taste

сәлигәлилик : *n* exactness, precision, neatness, order

сәлигәличә : *a* 1) see **сәлигәли** 2) very precise, very neat

сәлигәсиз : *a* inexact, imprecise, negligent, slipshod, untidy, tasteless, vulgar

сәлигәсизлик : *n* inexactitude, untidyness, negligence, disorder, lack of taste

сәлис : *a* smooth, flowing

сәлиспилик : *n* smoothness, fluency

сәллими : *adv* idly, with complete unconcern

сәлсәлә : *n* scoop, shovel *miller's*

сәлт : *a* 1) continuous, entire *adv* 2) completely, entirely

сәлтәнәт : *n* 1) supreme authority/power 2) reign, kingdom

сәма : *n* sky, heaven

сәмәнд : *a* dun, isabel, light-brown with black mane and tail , light-bay *color of a horse*

сәмәндәр : *n zool* salamander

сәмәни : *n* 1) malt *grain germinated by soaking and then kiln-dried* 2) wheaten malt pottage *a soup of wheat-malt thickened with flour*

әмәргәнд : *n* Samarkand *city in the Uzbek Republic*

сәмәрә : *n* fruit, result 2) benefit, gain, profit advantage

сәмәрәләшдиричи : *n* efficiency expert , rationalizer *chiefly British,* one who reorganizes an industry according to modern methods aand practices

сәмәрәләшдирмә : *n* 1) rationalization, the reorganization of an industry according to modern methods and practices in order to raise productivity *a* 2) rationalistic[al]

сәмәрәләшдирмәк : *v* rationalize, reorganize an industry along modern methods aand practices in order to raise productivity

сәмәрәләшдиртмәк : *caus* of **сәмәрәләшдирмәк**

сәмәрәләшмәк : *v* become more efficient and productive, become rationalized *an industry*

сәмәрәли : *a* rationalized, productive, efficient, profitably and efficiently organized

сәмәрәлилик : *n* productivity, efficiency *of an industry reorganized along modern lines*

сәмәрәсиз : *a* unrationalized, un productive, inefficient *of an industry lacking modern efficient production organization*

сәмәрәсизлик : *n* absence of rationalization, inefficient, unproductive, unprofitable *of an industry not organized along modern lines based on time and motion studies*

сәмизмәк : *v* see **тосунлашмаг**

сәмими : *a* sincere, candid , cordial

сәмими-гәлбдән : *adv* sincerely, candidly, cordially, warmly

сәмимиј̌ј̌әт : *n* sincerity, candidness, cordiality, personal warmth

сәмимиј̌ј̌әтлә : *adv* sincerely, candidly, from the heart

сәмимилик : *n* see **сәмимиј̌ј̌әт**

сәмт : *n* 1) side 2) direction

сәмти-гәдәм : *n astron* nadir, lowest possible point *opposed to zenith*

сәмтләмә : *n* orientation

сәмтләмәк, сәмтләшдирмәк : *v* orient, orientate

сәмтләшмәк : *v-intr* take o.'s bearings, find o.'s way, orient o.s.

сәмум : *n* simoom *hot, dry desert wind*

сән : *pro* thou/you *2nd pers sing*

сән аллаһ : *expr* for God's sake, *in colloquial speech often used loosely in the milder meaning of "Gosh!", "Holy cow!" etc*

сән демә : *expr* it turns out that....; can you imagine that.....

сәнә гурбан олум : *expr* my dear/darling/ honey *lit. "to you I am offering myself," "I am ready to sacrifice my life for your sake"*

сән'а : *n* Sana *capital of Yemen*

сәнаје : *n* industry

сәнаједәшдирилмәк : *pass* be industrialized

сәнајеләш(дир)мә : *n* industrialization

сәнајеләшдимәк : *v* industrialize

сәндәл : *n bot* 1) logwood *tree Haematoxylon campechianum* 2) sandal *dark red dyestuff derived from logwood and other similar trees*

сәндәләмә : *n* swaying, reeling *on o.'s legs*

сәндәләмәк : *v* sway, reel *on o.'s legs*

сәндәли : *n* see **күрсү**

сәндәрә : *n* shingle

сәнәд : *n* document

сәнәдли : *n* 1) secured/guaranteed document *a* 2) documentary

сәнәдсиз : *a* undocumented

сәнәк : *n* sanak *large jug with a long, narrow neck and a handle*

сәнәм : *n* 1) idol, image of a diety 2) beauty, beautiful woman

сәнәт : *n* 1) art 2) trade, profession, occupation

сәнәткар : *n* 1) artisan, craftsman, handicraftsman 2) skilled master *of a recognized craft*

сәнәткаранә : *adv* skillfully, masterfully, cleverly

сәнәткарлыг : *n* handicraft, trade ; skill, craftsmanship

сәнәтшүнас : *n* art critic, art expert

сәнәтшүнаслыг : *n* study of art, art criticism

сәнынки : *pro poss 2nd pers sing* thine/yours , that which belongs to thee/you

сәнкәр : *n* 1) trench, weapon-pit, emplacement 2) barricade

сәнкәрләнмәк : *v* dig in, dig o.s. in

сәнкимәк : *v* see **јавашымаг**

сәнлик : *a* relating to you, of interest to you *refers to 2nd sing*

сәнтирләмәк : *v* see **сәндәләмәк**

сәнчә : *adv* in your own way, according to you *2nd pers sing*

сәпәләмә : *v n* 1) from **сәпәләмәк** *adv* 2) separately, in disunity, in all directions, helter-skelter

сәпәләмәк : *v* 1) scatter about 2) splash, spray, spill

сәпәләнмәк : *v-intr* scatter/splash/spill

сәпилмәк : *pass* 1) be scattered/strewn about 2) be sown, disseminated

сәпин : *n* sowing

сәпичи : *n* sower

сәпишик : *n* pimple, rash

сәпишмәк : *v* break out in a rash

сәпки : *n* 1) see **сәпишик** 2) style 3) apportionment

сәпмә : *vn* 1) from **сәпмәк** 2) typhus, spotted fever

сәпмәк : *v* 1) sow *with* 2) splash, spatter 3) break out *rash*

сәрасәр : *adv* from start to finish/beginning to end, from head to foot, completely

сәрбаст : *a* 1) free, independent, unrestricted, unconstrained *adv* 2) freely, independently, unrestrictedly, unconstrainedly

сәрбастлик : *n* freedom, liberty, independence

сәрбастчә, сәрбастчәсинә : *adv* 1) completely freely/independently,utterly without restraint 2) simply, without ceremony, without any special considerations

сәрб : *n bot* cypress *Cupressus sempervirens*

сәрбахт : *a* vigilant, watchful

сәрбахтлыг : *n* vigilance, watchfulness

сәрбахтлыгла : *adv* vigilantly, watchfully

сәрбәт : *n* wealth, riches, fortune

сәрбәтләнмәк : *v* grow rich

сәрбәтли : *a* 1) rich *n* 2) rich man

сәргыфыл : *n* compensation

сәрдаба, сәрдабә : *n* tomb, sepulchre, burial-vault, crypt, mausoleum

сәрдар : *n* deputy, govrernor-general

сәрән : *n nav* yard, a slender, tapering bar, set crossways on a mast

сәрәнчам : *n* order, instruction

сәрәнчамчы : *n* manager, administrator

сәрили : *a* 1) spread, spread out 2) stretched out

сәрилмәк : *pass* 1) be spread out 2) be stretched out *for drying* 3) be stretched 4) tumble down, collapse, stretch o.s. out , sprawl prone

сәрин : *n* 1) fresh, cool

сәринләдичи : *a* refreshing, cooling

сәринлә(н)мәк : *v* 1) become cool/fresh 2) refresh o.s., freshen o.s. up

сәринләнмәк : *v-intr* 1) become cool/fresh 2) refresh o.s., freshen o.s. up

сәринләтмәк, сәринләщдирмәк : *v-tr* cool, cool off, chill, freshen, makefresh/cool

сәринләщдиричи : *a* refreshing, cooling

сәринләшмәк : *v-intr* cool down, become fresh/cool, become cooler, freshen up

сәринлик : *n* the cool, coolness, cool weather, freshness, crispness

сәриштә : *n* experience, skill, practice, practical experience, competence

сәриштәли : *a* experienced, versed *in*, experienced *in*, expert, competent, sophisticated

сәриштәсиз : *a* inexperienced, not versed/experienced *in*, incompetent, simple, unsophisticated

сәркеш : see **дикбаш**

сәркәрдә : *n* military leader, commander

сәрки : *n* reproach, reproof, rebuke, reprimand

сәркәрдан : *a* 1) wandering, roaming, having no shelter, homeless, unattended

сәрки : *n* 1) exhibition, display 2) place where fruit is put for being dried

сәркүзәшт : *n* adventure

сәрлөвhә : *n* title, heading, headline

сәрмаjә : *n* fixed capital

сәрмаjәдарлыг : *n* capitalism

сәрмә : *v n* 1) fr. **сәрмәк** 2) galoon, braid

сәрмәк : *v-tr* 1) spread out, lay 2) hang

сәрнич : *n* 1) milk pail 2) copper jug/pitcher with two handles

сәрнишин : *n* 1) passenger a 2) passenger

сәрпмәк : *v-tr* dislocate, put out of joint

сәрпуш : *n* cap, cowl

сәрраст : *a* 1) correct, right, straight, direct, well-aimed, accurate adv 2) directly, straight, accurately, to the point

сәррастлыг : *n* accuracy; correctness

сәрраф : *n* 1) money changer 2) one who understands subtleties 3) competent judge of people

сәррач : *n* harness maker and merchant

сәррачлыг : *n* occupation of a harness/saddle maker

сәрсәм : *a* stunned, stupefied

сәрсәмләмәк : *v* lose one's head, go crazy, be stunned/struck with surprise, be in a state of stupor

сәрсәмлик : *n* stupefaction, stunned surprise

сәрсәри : *n* wanderer, prodigal, vagrant, tramp, hobo

сәрсәрилик : *n* wandering, vagrancy

сәрт : *a* 1) hard, tough, stiff, firm, strong 2) acute, sharp, harsh 3) strict, stern, severe 4) coarse, rough, rude 5) malicious, vicious, wicked, evil *adv* 6) firmly, harshly, sharply, strictly, sternly, severely, roughly, rudely

сәртләшдирмәк : *v-tr* make hard/tough/firm/strong, make sharp/harsh

сәртләшмәк : *v-intr* become hard/tough/firm/strong, become acute, become sharp/harsh; grow stern

сәртлик : *n* 1) hardness 2) acuteness, sharpness, harshness 3) strictness, severity, cruelty, brutality

сәрф : *n* consumption, expense, expenditure, outlay

сәрфә : *n* benefit, profit, gain, use

сәрфәли : *a* advantageous, profitable, useful

сәрфәсиз : *a* disadvantageous, unprofitable

сәрхош : *a* 1) drunk, intoxicated *n* 2) drunk, drunkard

сәрхошлуг : *n* hard drinking, intoxication, drunkenness

сәрhесаб : see **саjыг**

сәрhәд : *n* 1) border, boundary, frontier, limit *a* 2) border, frontier

сәрhәд гојмаг : *v* draw a borderline; *fig* make a clear distinction *between*

сәрф еләмәк : *v* consume

сәс вермәк : *v* 1) answer 2) vote

сәс дүшмәк : *v* spread *about a rumor*

сәрhәдчи : *n* border/frontier guard

сәрчә : *n zool* sparrow

сәс : *n* 1) voice, vote, sound, noise 2) call, cry, shout 3) rumor, hearsay, common talk

сәсбоған : *n* muffler, silencer, damper, damping device

сәсвермә : *n* voting

сәсәгојма, сәсәгојулма : voting, balloting

сәсибатыг : *a* muffled, damped down; soundless, silent

сәсибатмыш : *a* weak-voiced, voiceless, hoarse

сәскечирән : *n* sound conductor

сәскечирмә : *n* sound conductivity

сәс-күј : *n* hubbub, uproar, din, racket, sound of voices

сәс-күј салмаг : *v* make a noise, make a fuss

сәс-күјчүлүк : *n* noisiness

сәсләмәк : *v* call, hail, appeal, hail

сәсләндирмәк : *caus* of **сәсләнмәк**

сәсләнмә : *n* sounding, phonation, vibration, sonorousness

сәсләнмәк : *v* 1) emit a sound, sound, ring, resound 2) answer, respond *to*

сәсләшмәк : *v* call to one another, call one another

сәсли : *a* 1) having a voice in , enfranchised 2) noisy, resounding, sonorous, loud,vocal 3) pertaining to voice/sound

сәс-сәда : *n* rumor, hearsay, common-gossip

сәс-сәмир : *n* sound, noise

сәс-сәмирсиз : *a* 1) mute, soundless *adv* 2) soundlessly

сәссиз : *a* 1) soundless, silent, taciturn, mute, unspoken *gram* 2) consonantal, consonant 3) silent *not moving lips while reading adv* 4) quietly, tacitly, taciturnly, noiselessly

сәссиз-күјсүз, сәссиз-сәмирсиз : *adv* without the slightest sound, silently, quietly

сәссизлик : *n* quiet, silence, hush

сәссизчә : see **сәссиз-күјсүз**

сәстутан : *n* sound locator, sound ranger

сәсучалдан : *n* loudspeaker

сәтәлчәм : *n med* pneumonia

сәтир : *n* line *in a text*

сәтирбашы : *n* 1) indented line 2) indentation, paragraph

сәтирбәсәтир, сәтирһесабы : *adv* line by line

сәтирүстү : *a* superlinear

сәтри : *n* 1) lower-case type *a* 2) literal, word for word

сәтһ : *n* surface

сәтһи : *a* 1) surface, superficial *adv* 2) superficially

сәф : *n* row, line, formation, file, rank

сәфа : *n* 1) pleasure, joy, gladness, enjoyment, delight 2) Safaa feminine first name

сәфаләт : *n* 1) poverty, destitution, penury, pauperism 2) distress, difficulties

сәфалы : *a* 1) pleasant, nice, giving pleasure 2) picturesque *n* 3) picturesque surroundings *a road, forest, etc.*

сәфарәт : *n* embassy, mission

сәфарәтхана : *n* 1) embassy 2) embassy-building

сәфеһ : *a* 1) stupid, foolish, reckless, rash *n* 2) fool, blockhead

сәфеһләмә : *vn fr.* **сәфеһләмәк**

сәфеһләмәк, сәфеһләшмәк : *v* 1) grow stupid/foolish, be in a stupor 2) become crazed

сәфеһлик : *n* stupidity, foolishness, rashness, abnormality

сәфеһ-сәфеһ : *adv* stupidly, foolishly, like a fool, muddle-headedly

сәфәр : *n* 1) journey, voyage, trip, march 2) sea-voyage 3) time

сәфәрбәр : *a* mobilized

сәфәрбәрлик : *n* 1) mobilization *a* 2) mobilization

сәфил : *a* 1) pitiful, pitiable, unfortunate 2) base, contemptible 3) poverty-stricken 3) outcast, cast out *n* 4) social outcast, vagrant, tramp, hobo

сәфилләшмәк : *v* become pitiful/pitiable, become poverty-stricken, become a vagrant/tramp/ hobo

сәфиллик : see **сәфаләт**

сәфир : *n* ambassador

сәфра : *n* bile, gall

сәфһә : *n* phase 1) a transitional factor in the developmental process of a phenomenon *astron* 2) one of the appearances or forms presented periodically by the moon and planets

сәхавәт : *n* generosity, lavishness, magnanimity

сәхавәт көстәрмәк : *v* spend lavishly, generously

сәхавәтлә : *adv* generously, lavishly, magnanimously

сәхавәтләнмәк : *v* become generous, magnanimous

сәхавәтли : *a* generous

сәһв : *n* 1) mistake, error 2) blunder, omission, slip of the tongue, misprint

сәһвән : *adv* mistakenly, erroneously, by mistake

сәһвсиз : *a* 1) faultless, unerring, infallible, impeccable adv 2) faultlessly, unerringly

сәһвсизлик : *n* infallibility, impeccability

сәһәнк : *n* large earthenware jug/pitcher for water

сәһәр : *n* 1) morning *adv* 3) in the morning *a* 2) morning

сәһәр-сәһәр : *adv* early in the morning, in the morning

сәһијјә : *n* sanitation, hygiene, health care

сәһифә : *n* page

сәһифәбағлајан : *n typ* senior compositor/typesetter

сәһифәбәсәһифә : *adv* page by page

сәһифәләмә : *n typ* composing stick

сәһифәләмәк : *v-tr typ* 1) compose, make up 2) turn pages, leaf, leaf through

сәһифәләнмәк : *v-intr typ* 1) be composed,be made up 2) be turned *of pages* , be leafed through

сәһиһ : *a* correct, right, authentic, reliable, accurate

сәһиһлик : *n* correctness, rightness, authenticity, reliability, accuracy

сәһләнкар : *a* 1) neglectful, negligent careless, inexact, unconcerned *adv* 2) negligently, neglectfully, carelessly

сәһләб : *n bot med* salep *dried tubers of species of the Orchis genus*

сәһләнкарлыг : *n* negligence, carelessness, inexactness, unconcern

сәһм : *n* share, stock

сәһмдар : *n* shareholder, stockholder

сәһн : *n* 1) portico, porch of a church, parvis 2) court[yard]

сәһнә : *n* stage; act *of a play* ; episode

сәһнәләшдирмә : *n* staging, dramatization, adaptation *for stage/screen*

сәһнәләшдирмәк : *v* stage, dramatize, adapt *for stage or screen*

сәһра : *n* desert

сәһһәт : *n* health

сәһһәти вүчуд : *exp* A healthy existence! *traditional greeting to a person who has just taken a bath or a shower. Persian, derived from Arabic*

сәчдә : *n* a deep bow, a bow down to the ground, prostration, 2) petition

сәчдәкаһ : *n* altar

сәчијјә : *n* character, nature

сәчијјәви : *a* characteristic, typical, peculiar *to*

сиан : *n chem* 1) cyanogen *a* 2) cyanogen, cyano- *lower or -ous* , cyanide of

сианат : *a chem* cyanol, aniline

сибир : *n* 1) Siberia *a* 2) Siberian

сибирли : *n* a Siberian *m/f*

сибирпорсуғу : *n zool* wolverine *fur-bearing animal, a variety of marten*

сибирсамуру : *n zool* 1) sable a 2) sable

сивил : *a* civilian

сивилчә : see **сазаг**

сивишгулу : **сивишгулуја дәм вермәк** take to one's heels, run for it

сивишкән : *a* slippery, evasive, shifty, sliding

сивишкәнлик : *n tech aero* 1) fairing *fig* 2) evasiveness, shiftiness

сивишмәк : *v* 1) slip off/away, slip, dart 2) dodge, evade

сиврә : see **күлгабы**

сиври : *a* sharp, acute, pointed

сигар : *n* 1) cigar *a* 2) cigar

сигарабәнзәр : *a* cigar-shaped

сигнал : *n* 1) signal *a* 2) signal

сигналчы : *n* signalman

сиғә : *n relig* Muslim marriage contract. *Sometimes refers to a temporary marriage;* see **кәбин**

сидик : *n* urine

сидиклик : *n* bladder*urinary*

сидр : *n bot* 1) cedar *tree a* 2) cedar

сиз : *pro* you *polite/plural*

сизинки : *a* your; yours, belonging to you

сизчә : *adv* in your opinion

сијасәт : *n* politics, policy

сијасәтчи : *n* 1) politician, political figure, diplomat 3) intriguer

сијасәтчә : *adv* politically

сијаси : *a* political

сијаһы : *n* list, inventory, register

сијаһыја салмаг : *v* introduce into a list, file

сијаһыјаалма : *n* census

сијәнәк : *n* 1) herring *a* 2) herring

сијимәк : *v* urinate

сијирилмәк : *v* 1) be stripped/flayed *of animal carcass* 2) be scraped *of dishes/pots/pans*

сијирмә : *n* 1) bolt, slide-bolt latch *a* 2) sliding *i.e. drawers*

сијирмәгылынч : *adv* with drawn swords

сијирмәк : *v* 1) strip, flay, scratch, peel shell, 2) clean the food from a plate using finger or a piece of bread 3) unsheathe, draw *e.g. a sword from a scabbard*

сијиртмә : see **сијирмә** 1)

сијитмәк : *v* cause to urinate

сиккә : *n* stamped/embossed/chased coin

сиккәвурма, сиккәкәсмә : *n* minting, coining, coinage; engraving, embossing

сиккәхана : *n* mint

сиклоид : *n geom* cycloid *curve described by a point on the circumference of a circle rolling along a straight line in a single plane*

сиклоидал : *a geom* cycloidal *resembling a circle/somewhat circular*

сиклоп : *n* Cyclops *legendary one-eyed giant*

сикдирмәк : *v vulg* kick *s.o.* out, get rid of *s.o.*

сикмәк : *v vulg* fuck

силаh : *n* 1) weapon, arms, armament *a* 2) arms

силаhгајыран : *n* gunsmith, armorer

силаhдаш : *n* companion-in-arms, comrade-in-arms

силаhландырылмаг : *v* be armed, be supplied with arms

силаhландырмаг : *v-tr* arm

силаhландыртмаг : *caus* of **силаhландырмаг**

силаhланма : *vn* fr. **силаhланмаг**

силаhланмаг : *v-intr* arm oneself, be armed

силаhлы : *a* armed

силаhлылыг : *n* level of arms/armament

силаhсыз : *a* unarmed

силаhсызландырма : *n* disarmament

силаhсызландырмаг, силаhсызлашдырмаг : *v-tr* disarm

силаhхана : *n* arsenal

силдирмәк, силдиртмәк : *caus* of **силмәк**

силәчәк : *n* cleaning-rag, rag for wiping

силикат : *n chem* 1) silicate *a* 2) silicate

силиндр : *n geom* cylinder

силиндрик : *a geom* cylindrical

силиндршәкилли : *a geom* cylindrical

силинмәз : *a* indelible, ineffaceable, ineradicable *stain*

силинмәк : *v-intr* 1) be wiped/washed 2) be struck out, be deleted/expunged, be effaced/rubbed out/obliterated

силисиум : *n chem* silica, silicon dioxide

силк : 1) stratum, section of the population, estate *inherited status in a traditional society*

силкдирмәк, силкдиртмәк : *caus* of **силкәмәк**

силкәләмә : *n* shaking

силкәләмәк : *v-tr* shake, rock, swing

силкәләнмәк : *v-intr* shake, rock, sway, swing

силкәмәк : *v-tr* 1) shake, shake off 2) beat (dust) out (of), shake (rugs)

силкинмәк : *v* shake oneself

силки : *n* rag *for wiping*

силл : *n med* see **вәрәм**

силлабик : *a* syllabic *poetic meter*

силлә : *n* slap in the face

силмәк : *v-tr* 1) wipe, dry, clean 2) strike out, delete, expunge

силсилә : *n* 1) chain, garland 2) row 2) ridge, range

силсиләви : *a* continuous

сил-сүпүр : *n* tidying up, cleaning up

сим : *n* 1) wire 2) string *med* 3) blood poisoning *from inflammation of a wound or injury*

сима : *n* 1) face, look, image, [outward]appearance 2) personality; person, individual

симасыз : *a* faceless, without personality/ individuality

симасызлашдырмаг : *v* depersonalize, make impersonal, remove/ eliminate personal responsibility

симасызлыг : *n* 1) absence of personal responsibility 2) facelessness, depersonalized/impersonal in nature

симитән : *a* see **ситал**

симич : *a* 1) stingy, miserly *n* 2) miser, skinflint, stingy person

симичлик : *n* stinginess, miserliness

симләмәк : *v* 1) string *e.g. an instrument* 2) set in/start *of blood poisoning*

симли : *a mus* string *i.e. instrument/quartet/section*

симметрија : *n* symmetry

симметријасыз : *a* asymmetrical

симметрик : *a* symmetric[al]

симметриклик : *n* symmetry, proportionality

симсиз : *a* 1) stringless, unstringed 2) wireless

симург : *n myth* 1) Phoenix, the Firebird 2) Simurg *male first name*

симфонија : *n* symphony

симфоник : *a* symphonic

синдесмолокија : *n* syndesmology *the study of the anatomy and physiology of the ligaments*

синә : *n* breast, chest

синәзән : *n* 1) Sinazan, songs of mourning *traditionally accompanied by breast beating* 2) Sinazan-singer

синәк : *n* fly ; see **милчәк**

синәкир : *n* an asthmatic; one who suffers from asthma

сини : *n* large brass or copper tray

синирмәк : *v* digest *food*

синиф : *n* 1) class 2) grade *at school* 3) social stratum *in Marxist ideology* *a* 4) class

синифләшдирмә : *n* classification

синифләшдирмәк : *v* classify

синифли : *a* class *re social stratum*

синифсиз : *a* classless

синк : *n* *chem* 1) zinc *a* 2) zinc

синкографија : *n* 1) zincography, etching on zinc *a* 2) zincographic

синли : *a* elderly, getting on *in years*

синмәк : *v-intr* take shelter, hide, conceal oneself, snuggle/cuddle *up to*

синн : *n* age

синоним : *n* synonym

синонимик : *a* synonymous

синор : *n* boundary, border, frontier, limit

синтаксис : *n* syntax

синтактик : *a* syntactic[al]

синтез : *n* synthesis

синтетик : *a* synthetic

синчаб : *n* *zool* gray squirrel

синччалан : *n* cymbalist

синч : *n* cymbals

сипәр : *n* shield; see **галхан**

сирајәт : *n* 1) spreading, dissemination 2) infection 3) contagion

сирајәтедичи : *a* infectious, contagious

сирдаш : *n* close/true/bosom friend

сирдашлыг : *n* close/bosom friendship, intimacy

сирән : *n* siran, young people's gathering *for recreation on winter evenings*

сиринсимәк : *v* grow/become damp, to lose crispness because of dampness

сирк : *n* 1) circus *a* 2) circus

сиркә : *n* 1) vinegar 2) nit *louse-egg* 3) *a* vinegar[y]

синкониум : *n* *chem* zirconium

сиркулјар : *n* circular, *official* instruction

сирли : *a* secret, mysterious, enigmatic, mystic, esoteric

сирлилик : *n* mysteriousness, mystery

сирр : *n* secret, mystery

сир-сифәт : *n* physiognomy, face

сис : *n* smog, haze

сисер : *n* *typ* pica *typeface*

сисәј : *n* *zool* cricket

систем : *n* system

систематик : *a* systematic, methodical

системләшдирмәк : *v* systematize

системли : *a* systematic

системлилик : *n* systematic character, system

системсиз : *a* 1) unsystematic, unmethodical *adv* 2) unsystematically, unmethodically

системсизлик : *n* unsystematic/unmethodical character

систерн : *n* cistern, tank

ситајиш : *n* 1) worship, adoration 2) deification

ситал : *a* obtrusive, nagging, impudent, barefaced

ситаллыг : *n* nagging, impudence, effrontery

ситәм : *n* constraint, torture, torment, hardship, oppression

ситәмкар : *n* 1) oppressor, despot, tyrant 2) torturer, executioner,

ситилдәмәк : *v* whine, pine *for* , languish, complain about o.'s fate

сифали : *n* see **бој-бухунлу**

сифал : *n* see **кирәмит**

сифариш : *n* order, commission, mission, errand, assignment,

сифаришчи : *n* customer, client

сиферблат : *n* dial, face *of a watch/clock/measuring instrument*

сифәт : *n* 1) face *gram* 2) adjective

сифраг : *n* vomiting, retching

сифтә : *n* 1) initial proceeds/earnings 2) beginning, start 3) first sale of the day

сичан : n 1) mouse a 2) mouse/mice['s]

сичанјолу : *n* 1) lead *the distance or interval by which s.o. or s.t. leads or precedes* 2) way out, loophole *opportunity or means by which one can slip out of a tight situation*

сичовул : *n* 1) rat *a* 2) rat['s]

сичилләмә : *adv* verbosely, wordily, at length, endlessly *of a narration or conversation*

сичим : *n* woolen cord

сығал : *n* 1) stroking or smoothing the hair 2) small trinket

сығалламаг : *v* stroke, smooth, caress, massage, rub

сығалланмаг : *v* be smoothed, be massaged/rubbed, caressed

сығаллатдырмаг, сығаллатмаг : *caus* of **сығалламаг**

сығаллы : *a* smooth, sleek, smoothed, ironed

сығдырмаг : *v-tr* put, place, find room (for), squeeze/cram (in/into)

сығым : *n* capacity

сығын : *n* *zool* 1) elk *a* 2) elk['s]

сығынаг, сығыначаг : *n* shelter, cover, refuge, asylum, haven

сығындырмаг : *v-tr* shelter, give refuge, harbor, give charitable support to

сығынмаг : *v-intr* take shelter, take cover

сығыр : *n* cattle

сығырчы : *n* cattle herdsman

сығырчын : *n* *zool* starling *genus Sternus*

сығыщдырмаг : *v* 1) suffer, bear, endure, stand *pain/wrong* 2) see **сығдырмаг**

сығышмаг : *v* see **сығмаг**

сығмаг : *v-intr* 1) find/have room *to fit in somewhere* 1) go in, be housed/accommodated

сығмаз : *a* incompatible

сығмамазлыг : *n* incompatibility

сығорта : *n* 1) insurance *a* 2) insurance

сызаг : *n* see **сызанаг**

сызаған : *a* permeable to liquids

сызанаг : *n* pimple, blackhead

сызанаглы : *a* pimply, suffering from acne

сызга, сызгах : *adv* in a weak stream

сызылдамаг : *v-intr* 1) ache 2) whimper, whine; weep softly and mournfully 3) complain about one's fate

сызылдашмаг : *v-intr* softly and mournfully weep together *of many people*

сызылты : *n* 1) pain, ache 2) whimpering, soft and mounful weeping 3) squeal[ing], screech[ing]

сызламаг : *v* see **сызылдамаг**

сызма : *n* percolation, seepage, leakage, oozing

сызмаг : *v-intr* 1) seep, trickle, percolate, pass liquids through s.t. 2) emit a small stream, leak, allow a liquid to pass through

сыјыг : *a* 1) liquid *n* 2) sludge, slurry, liquid mud; thin gruel

сыјыгланмаг : *v* see **сыјыглашмаг**

сыјыглатмаг : *v* see **сыјыглашдырмаг**

сыјыглашдырмаг : *v-tr* dilute, thin

сыјыглашма : *n* dilution, thinning *out*

сыјыглашмаг : *v-intr* be diluted/thinned, become diluted

сыјыглыг : *n* liquid, fluid

сыјылмаг : *v* 1) dilute, thin *fig* 2) give in *to,* be carried away *by* , have an inclination *for*

сылдырым : *a* 1) steep, precipitous, sheer *n* 2) precipice, steepness

сымсырыг : *n* dissatisfied facial expression, sullenness, gloominess

сымсырығыны салламаг : *v* frown; sulk

сынаг : *n* test; experience *derived from o.'s own practice*

сынагчы : *n* tester, experimenter

сынама : *n* test, trial

сынамаг : *v-tr* test, try, sound, probe,

сынанмаг : *v-intr* be tested/tried, be put to the test

сынатмаг : *v* *caus* of **сынамаг**

сынга : *n* *med* scurvy

сынгалы : *a* scorbutic

сындырма : *vn* fr. **сындырмаг**

сындырмаг : *v* 1) break 2) defeat, conquer, smash, shatter, rout *fig* 3) put on the spot, throw for a loss, put in an awkward position; wound/hurt *s.o.'s* feelings *fig* 4) dance with pleasure

сыныг : *n* 1) break/fracture of a bone 2) potsherds, shards, piece of broken crockery 3) bankrupt, insolvent *person* *a* 4) broken, fractured 5) defeated, routed, conquered, vanquished, smashed, shattered

сыныг-сыныг : *a* broken into pieces/fragments

сыныгчы : *n* bonesetter

сыныгчыхма : *n* bankruptcy, insolvency

сынырмаг : *v* digest food

сыныхмаг : *v* get/grow thin/emaciated, lose flesh

сынма : *n* 1) breaking, breakage *phys* 2) refraction

сынмаг : *v-intr* 1) break, smash 2) be routed, suffer defeat 3) go bankrupt 4) decrease, diminish, begin to decline, be on the wane *of cold or heat* 5) drop/decline in price 6) be offended/hurt

сынмајан : *a* infrangible, unbreakable

сыпа : *intj* 1) see **хотуг** *a* *fig* 2) fat, greasy, obese

сыпыхмаг : *v* see **сивишмәк**

сыра : *n* 1) row[s], line[s], formation, rank, file; 2) *mountain* range, chain, ridge 3) turn, place *in a line/queue*

сырави : *a* 1) ordinary, common mil 2) enlisted *non-officer*

сыраламаг : *v-tr* line up, place in line

сыраланмаг : *v-intr* get lined up, fall in

сыратаҕ : *n* arcade, row of arches, gallery of arches

сырача : *n med* scrofula

сырҕа : *n* earring

сырҕалыг : *n* earlobe

сырыг : *n* quilting, basting, stitching a seam

сырыглы : *a* 1) quilted *n* 2) quilted jacket

сырымаг : *v* 1) quilt, stitch, baste 2) impose, burden against the wills.*o*., force to accept *by ruses.intrigues/devices*

сырынмаг : *v-intr* be stitched, be quilted

сырытдырмаг, **сырытмаг** : *caus* of **сырымаг**

сырма : *n* stripe, chevron

сырмаламаг : *v* sew on stripes/chevrons

сырок : *n Ru* sweet cottage cheese

сырсыра : *n* icicle

сыртыг : *a* 1) shameless, unblushing, brazen *a* 2) impudent/insolent/cheeky fellow

сыртыглашмаг : *v* see **сыртылмаг**

сыртыглыг : *n* shamelessness, impudence, brazenness, insolence, effrontery, cheek

сыртылмаг : *v* become shameless, become importunate, brazen, become impudent/insolent/cheeky

сырф : *adv* exceptionally, exclusively, purely, absolutely, completely, entirely, wholly

сысга : *a* 1) sickly, puny, feeble, stunted, emaciated *n* 2) puny creature, starveling

сысгаланмаг, **сысгалашмаг**, **сысгалмаг** : *v* get/grow/become sickly/puny, feeble, be stunted, waste away, get/grow/become thin/emaciated

сысгалыг : *n* thinness, leanness, sickliness, puniness, emaciation

сысламаг : *v-tr* hush, silence

сыфыр : *n* 1) zero, nought *a* 2) zero

сых : *a* close, thick, compact, dense

сыхач : *n* clamp

сыхылабилән : *a* [being] squeezed

сыхылмаг : *v* 1) be squeezed/compressed, be squeezed/wrung out 2) be sad/melancholy, pine *for*, languish 3) feel shy/ashamed, be embarrassed/disconcerted/put out

сыхылмаз : *a* shameless, brazen, heartless

сыхынты : *n* 1) strain, hardship, straightened circumstances, need 2) sadness, melancholy, distress, low spirits

сыхынтылы : *a* burdensome, stressful, dreary, embarrassing, difficult

сыхычы : *a* 1) oppresssive 2) depressing, dreary

сыхышдырылмаг : *v* be oppressed, be driven out, be subjected to pressure, be burdened

сыхышдырма : *n* oppression, pressure

сыхышдырмаг : *v* oppress, keep down, drive/force out, press

сыхышмаг : *v-intr* be squeezed/ crowded/herded

сыхјарпаг : *a* with abundant/dense foliage or leaves

сыхлашдырылмаг : *v* be condensed/compacted

сыхлашдырма : *vn* fr. **сыхлашдырмаг**

сыхлашдырмаг : *v-tr* thicken, press, crowd, condense, compact

сыхлашма : *n* thickening, compressing, compression, condensing, condensation

сыхлашмаг : *v-intr* 1) thicken, be thickened, clot 2) crowd, be herded, be squeezed; be condensed/compacted 3) close up, be made close to one another, *as in the military expression "to close ranks"*

сыхлыг : *n* 1) thickness, density, frequency 2) compactness, cohesion 3) thicket

сыхма : *n* 1) pressing, squeezing, wringing 2) handful, hollow of the hand, cupped hand 3) sıxma *a dish made exclusively of green vegetables*

сыхма-боғма : *cmp* **сыхма-боғма вермәк**, **сыхма-боғма алмаг (салмаг)** drive into a corner, bring to bay

сыхмаг : *v-tr* 1) squeeze, press, wring, squeeze/press/ wring out 2) push, put pressure on, put restraint *on*, keep down, oppress

сых-сых : *adv* very densely, very closely, very close to one another

сыхчаламаг : *v-tr* 1) rumple, crumple, press *on* 2) pull *s.o.* about, bother/pester

сыхчаланмаг : *v-intr* 1) be rumpled/crumpled, be pressed down 2) be shabby/seedy *person*

сычрајыш : *n* jump, bound, leap, spring

сычрама : *vn* fr. **сычрамаг**

сычрамаг : *v-intr* 1) jump, leap jump/leap up/out, bob up and down 2) splash, spatter, sprinkle *e.g. water*

сычранты : *n* spray, jet of water

сычратмаг : *caus* splash, spatter, sprinkle

скамеjка : *n* bench

скандиум : *n chem* scandium *rare metal*

скарлатин : *n med* scarlet fever, scarlatina

славjан : *n* 1) Slav *a* 2) Slavic

славjанпәрәст : *n* Slavophile

славjанпәрәстлик : *n* Slavophilism

славjанчылыг : *n* Pan-Slavism

славjаншүнас : *n* Slavist, Slavonic scholar

славjаншүнаслыг : *n* Slavonic studies, Slavonic philology

следователь : *n Ru* investigator

сметана : *n Ru* sour cream

соба : *n* stove, oven, furnace, kiln

собачы : *n* stove maker

собственно говорjа : *exp Ru* basically, strictly speaking

совгат : *n* 1) gift, present *in return for hospitality or as a veiled form of bribe* 2) gift sent by a traveller en route

совет : *n hist* 1) soviet, council *a* 2) Soviet

советләшмә : *n hist* Sovietization

советләшмәк : *v-tr hist* Sovietize

совещание : *n Ru* conference, meeting

совмаг : *v* see **совушмаг** 2), 3)

совмәә : *n* cell; hermitage *monk's*

совмәәнишин : *n* see **дашакирән**

совру(г) : *n* bedsheet

совулмаг : *v-intr* be depleted, thin out, come to an end, be drawing to a close *i. e. the season for fruits and vegetables*, expire, run out

совуран : *n-cmp* **совуран машын** : winnower, winnowing machine

совурмаг : *v* 1) winnow 2) scatter, strew, disperse *fig* 3) spend, waste, squander

совуруг : *n* 1) snowstorm, blizzard 2) winnowing

совушмаг : *v-intr* 1) slip out, slip away, run away, make off, escape 2) pass, go by *of a season* 3) go by/past, fly by/past

совха : *a leg* 1) escheated *reverting to the state in absence of legal heirs* *n* 2) escheat *property reverting to the state in the absence of legal heirs*

соған : *n coll* 1) onions 2) onion *the plant a* 2) onion

соғанаг : *n bot* bulb, onion

соғанкүлү : *n bot* dahlia

соғанлы : *a* seasoned/flavored with onion

соғанлыг : *n* plot sown with onions

соғанча : *n* onions fried in butter

созалмаг : *v-intr* 1) turn/grow pale 2) fade,wither, wilt 3) weaken, grow weak[er]; become weak/sickly,

соj : *n* 1) family, kin, clan, race 2) breed, species, kind 3) origin, descent, parentage, extraction, lineage 4) name surname, family name

соjгырымы : *n* extermination, massacre, genocide

соjғун : *n* robbery, pillage, plundering, brigandage, burglary

соjғунчу : *n* 1) robber, brigand, bandit 2) extortioner, blackmailer

соjғунчулуг : *n* 1) robbery, brigandage, banditry 2) extortion, blackmail

соjма : *n* 1) skinning, flaying; peeling, shelling, removing a rind 2) robbery, extortion, blackmail

соjмаг : *v-tr* 1) peel, shell, remove a rind 2) rob, clean out completely, strip of possessions/valuables

соjуг : *n* 1) cold *a* 2) cold

соjугганлы : *a* cool, composed

соjугганлылыг : *n* sang-froid, coolness, composure, presence of mind

соjугдәjмә : *n* cold, influenza, flu

соjуглама : *vn* see **соjугдәjмә**

соjугламаг : *v-intr* catch [a] cold

соjуглашдырмаг : *v-tr* cool/chill gradually, cool/chill slightly

соjуглашмаг : *v-intr* grow cold, gradually become cool, cool down gradually, become somewhat colder

соjуглуг : *n* 1) coldness, coolness *in relationships* 2) carelessness, negligence 3) cold

соjуг-соjуг : *adv* in a cold state/condition

соjугтәһәр : *a* 1) chilly, rather cold *adv* 2) in a chilly manner

соjугча : *a* 1) slightly cold, on the chilly sdie *adv* 2) in a cold/ unwarmed/unheated state

соjуғадавамлы : *a* 1) cold-resistant *bot* 2) hardy

сојуғадавамлылыг : *n* 1) cold-resistance *bot* 2) hardiness

сојудулмаг : *v-intr* grow cold, be cooled/chilled, be cooled off

сојудучу : *a* 1) cooling, chilling, refrigerating, refrigeratory *n* 2) refrigerator

сојулмаг : *v-intr* 1) be skinned, peeled *of apples, potatoes* 2) come off, be peeled *of a skin/pelt* 3) be robbed, cleaned out *of valuables* , be fleeced

сојумаг : *v-intr* 1) cool, get cool, cool down, become cold, congeal *fig* 2) become indifferent, lose interest *in,* grow cool/ cold *towards* ,

сојундурмаг *:* *v-tr* undress *s.o. else*

сојундуртмаг : *caus* of **сојунмаг**

сојундурулмаг : *v-intr* be undressed

сојунмаг : *v-intr* undress *o.s.*

сојутма : *n* 1) cooling 2) cold roast meat

сојутмаг : *v-tr* cool. chill. let cool down

сок : *n* *Ru* juice

сол : *a* 1) left, left-hand, *naut* port *polit* 2) left-wing, left

сола : *adv* to the left

сола(ға)н : *a* not fast, liable to fade

солахај : *n* left-hander, left-handed person, southpaw

солғун : *a* pale, faded, withered

солғунлашмаг : *n* see **солмаг**

солғунлуг : *n* paleness, pallidity, pallor

солдат : *n* 1) soldier *a* 2) soldier's 3) jack, knave *playing cards*

солдатлыг : *a* 1) soldier's *n* 2) soldiering, soldiery *derog* 3) military service

солдыш : *n* best man *at a wedding*

солдурмаг : *v-tr* decolorize, bleach

соллуг : *n* 1) leftishness *adv* 2) more to the left

солма : *vn* fr. **солмаг**

солмаг : *v* 1) fade, lose color 2) pale, turn/grow pale 3) wither

солмаз : *a* 1) unfading, everlasting 2) Solmaz *feminine first name*

солмамазлыг : *n* everlastingness

солтан, султан : *n* monarch, sovereign

солуг : *a* withered, faded, discolored

солухмаг : *v-intr* fade, wither

сом : *a* massive

сомун : *n* *tech* nut

сон : *n* 1) end, ending, termination, finish, outcome, dĕnoument, finale *a* 2) last, final, extreme

сона : *n* *zool* 1) drake 2) a beauty *beautiful woman* 3) Sona *feminine first name in Azerbaijan and Armenia*

соналамаг : *v* try to find flaws/shortcomings in s.o./s.t.

сонбешик : *n* last-born child *lit. :"last cradle"*

сонлуг : *n* *gram* ending, termination

сонра : *adv* after, later, afterwards, then, later on

сонраја гојмаг : *v* delay, postpone

сонрадан : *adv* subsequently, afterwards, then, later on,

сонракы : *a* subsequent, succeeding, ensuing

сонралар : *adv* subsequently, afterwards, later on, at a later time

сонрасы : *n* continuation

сонсуз : *a* 1) endless, infinite, boundless 2) childlesss

сонсузлуг : *n* 1) endlessness, infinity, eternity 2) childlessness

сонунчу : *a* last, final

сончуг : *n* kicking

сончуглајан : *a* 1) given to kicking, kick-prone *n* 2) kicker

сончугламаг : *v* kick

сончуглатмаг : *v* cause to kick

сопа : *n* see **зопа**

сорағ : *n* 1) interrogation, questioning, cross-examination 2) news, piece of news, information

сораглашмаг : *v* make inquiries, gather information

сорғу : *n* question, questioning, interrogation, inquiry

сорғу-суал : *n* 1) questioning, cross-examination 2) inquiry, inquest

сорғучу : *n* interrogator, questioner

сордурмаг, сордуртмаг : *caus* of **сормаг**

сорма : *vn* fr. **сормаг**

сормаг : *v* 1) suck, suck out, suck dry 2) see **сорушмаг**

сорочка : *n* *Ru* shirt

сортухламаг : *v* suck intensely/strongly *of a baby*

сорулмаг : *v* be sucked, be sucked out, be sucked dry

соручу : *a* 1) sucking, sucking out, for extracting, for drawing out 2) interrogating

соруша-соруша : *adv* asking, inquiring

сорушма : *n* inquiry, interrogation, questioning

сорушмаг : *v-tr* ask, inquire, interrogate, question, make inquiries

сорушуласы : *a* 1) subject to interrogation *person* *n* 2) subject of inquiry *area of investigation*

сорушулмаг : *v* be questioned, be interrogated

сосиализасија : *n* socialization

сосиализм : *n* socialism

сосиалист : *n* 1) socialist *a* 2) socialist[ic]

сосиска : *n* *Ru* sausage, hot dog, frankfurter

софи : *n* 1) Sufi *follower of a system of Muslim religious mysticism* 2) very pious Muslim *derog* 3) sanctimonious person; canting religious hypocrite

соха-соха : *v* sticking/shoving/pushing in

сохмаг : *v* poke/stick/shove/thrust/push in, stab

сохулма : *n* climbing *in*, invasion, encroachment, incursion, intrusion

сохулмаг : *v-intr* 1) butt in, poke one's nose in, be poked/shoved/thrust in, shove/force one's way through, be pushed/shoved/forced/squeezed through 2) squeeze oneself *in/into* , be squeezed *in/into* 3) get in, climb in, flit/dart in 4) burst *into*, invade, intrude *into*, encroach *upon* *fig* 5) interfere, meddle *in*

сохулчан : *n* *zool* earthworm

сохушдурмаг : *v* 1) see **сохмаг** 2) insert/put in imperceptibly

сөвг : *v-cmp* **сөвг әтмәк** : direct, send, draw *in/into* , involve *in*

сөвги-тәбии : *n* instinct

сөвда : *n* *med* eczema

сөвдалы : *a* *med* eczematous

сөвдә : *n* deal, bargain, transaction

сөвдәкәр : *n* merchant, businessman

сөвдәләшмәк : *v* conclude a transaction/deal, strike a bargain

сөз : *n* 1) word 2) promise 3) rumor, hearsay, common talk, piece of information 4) gossip

сөз атмаг : *v* 1) hint 2) wound *s.o.'s feelings*

сөз гајтармаг : *v* contradict, cross *in a conversation*

сөз гачыртмаг : *v* blurt out

сөз гојмаг : *v* agree *to do s.t.*

сөз гошмаг : *v* 1) make up, compose *fig* 2) concoct *especially about rumors*

сөз еләмәк : *v* find fault *with*

сөз кәздирмәк : *v* gossip

сөз көтүрмәк : *v* endure *insult, offence etc*

сөзүнү кәсмәк : *v* interrupt *oneself or another person*

сөзарасы : *adv* by the way, à propos, incidentally

сөзарды : *n* epilogue, concluding remarks

сөзбаз : *n* gossip, rumor-monger

сөзбазлыг : *n* gossiping, rumor-mongering

сөзбирлик : *n* unanimity

сөзгајтарма : *n* contradiction

сөздәјишдиричи : *a* *gram* inflecting

сөздәјишдирмә : *n* *gram* inflection, accidence

сөздүзәлдичи : *a* *gram* word-forming

сөздүзәлтмә : *n* *gram* word formation

сөзәбахан : *a* obedient, dutiful, compliant, tractable, pliable, pliant, complaisant

сөзәбаханлыг : *n* obedience, compliancy, tractability, pliability, pliancy, complaisance

сөзәбахмаз, сөзәбахмајан : *a* 1) disobedient, naughty 2) disobedient person, naughty child

сөзкәздирән : *n* informer, tattletale, gossip, scaandalmonger

сөзкәздирәнлик : *n* informing, gossiping, scandalmongering

сөзкәлиши : *adv* by the way, for example, incidentally

сөзкүләшдирмә : *n* contradiction

сөзләшмә : *n* 1) agreement, compact, deal, understanding 2) argument, controversy, dispute,squabble, altercation

сөзләшмәк : *v* 1) arrange, agree, come to an agreement, come to an arraangement/understanding 2) argue, have an argument, squabble, fall out *with*

сөзлү : *a* oral, in words

сөзлүк : *n* dictionary, lexicon glossary

сөзсүз : *a* 1) unconditional, unreserved, unqualified, absolute, indisputable *adv* 2) unconditionally, unreservedly, absolutely

сөзтөрәдичи : *a* *ling* productive

сөзүдүз : *a* truthful, upright, true-to-one's-word, keeping-one's-word

сөзүкечән : *a* influential, authoritative

сөзүндәндөнән : *a* unfaithful-to-o.'s-word

сөзчүјәз, сөзчүк : *n dim* word

сөјдүрмәк, сөјдүртмәк : *caus* of **сөјмәк**

сөјдүрүлмәк : *v* be scolded, be railed at , be criticized severely

сөјкәк : *n* support, prop, brace, strut

сөјкәмәк : *v-tr* prop, lean *against* , rest *against*

сөјкәнәчәк : *n* 1) support, place of support 2) back *of piece of furniture*

сөјкәнмәк : *v-intr* rest *upon/against* , lean *against*

сөјләјә-сөјләјә : *adv* talking, telling, relating

сөјләмәк : *v* say, speak, talk, reiterate, tell, relate, narrate, state, express, pronounce, utter

сөјләнмәк : *v* 1) talk to oneself, mutter 2) grumble, growl, snarl 3) be told, be rumored

сөјләтдирмәк, сөјләтмәк : *caus* of **сөјләмәк**

сөјмәк : *v* scold, rail *against*, swear *at* , rebuke, curse, defame/revile *one another*

сөјүд : *n bot* willow *Salix*

сөјүдлүк : *n bot* willow grove, osier-bed

сөјүлмәк : *v* be cursed/scolded, be called names, be sworn at, be defamed/reviled

сөјүш : *n* bad language, swearing, invective, making obscene references to *s.o.'s* mother

сөјүшдүрмәк : *v* cause to swear at one another, cause to revile/defame *one another*

сөјүшкән : *a* see **сөјүшчү**

сөјүшмә : *n* squabble

сөјүшмәк : *v* swear at *one another*, exchange angry words, have words *with*

сөјүшчү : *a* cantankerous, quarrelsome *n* 2) quarrelsome persson

сөјүшчүл : *a* see **сөјүшчү**

сөкдүрмәк, сөкдүртмәк : *caus* of **сөкмәк**

сөкмәк : *v* 1) undo, break down, unpick, unstitch, rip, rip open 2) take apart, disassemble, dismantle, strip *piece of equipment/machine/engine* 3) take down, pull down, tear down, demolish *building/structure*

сөкүк : *a* 1) undone, unstitched, ripped open 2) partially dismantled/disassembled 3) dilapidated, partially demolished *structure*

сөкүлмә : *n* 1) undoing, unstitching 2) disassembly, dismantling, taking apart 3) pulling down, demolishing, demolition

сөкүлмәк : *v* 1) be broken, undone, be unstitched, be ripped open, be ripped 2) be disassembled, be dismantled, be taken apart 3) be demolished, be torn down

сөкүнтү : *n* 1) unstitched parts of clothing 2) pieces/parts *of a machine/ engine/building/structure*

сөндүрмә : *n* extinguishing, putting out, turning off

сөндүрмәк : *v* extinguish, put out, turn off

сөндүртмәк : *caus* of **сөндүрмәк**

сөндүрүлмәз : *a* inextinguishable, unquenchable

сөндүрүлмәк : *v* be extinguished, be put out/quenched, be turned off

сөндүрүчү : *n* extinguisher

сөнмә : *n* extinguishing, quenching, putting out, turning off

сөнмәк : *v* extinguish, quench, put out, turn off

сөнүк : *a* dull, dim, quenched, gone out *of fire*; colorless, insipid, drab

сөнүкләшмәк : *v* turn/grow pale, grow dim/dull

сөр-сөкүнтү : *n* see **сөкүнтү**

сөһбәт : *n* talk, conversation

сөһбәтчил : *a* loving to talk, knowing how to talk entertainingly

спасателны : *a Ru* rescue

спесификасија : *n* specification *document*

спирт : *n* 1) alcohol, spirit[s] *a* 2) alcohol[ic]

спиртли : *a* alcoholic, containing alcohol/spirits

спичка : *n Ru* match

спортчу : *n* sportsman

сраґакүн : *adv* the day before yesterday

сраґакүнкү : *a* day-before-yesterday's

стандарт : *n* 1) standard *a* 2) standard

стандартлашдырылмаг : *v* be standardized

стандартлашдырма : *n* standardization

стандартлашдырмаг : *v-tr* standardize

стансија : *n* 1) station *a* 2) station

статик : *a* static

статистик : *a* statistical

статистика : *n* statistics

статјая : *n Ru* article

стенка : *n Ru* large furniture unit

стереотип : *n* 1) stereotype *a* 2) stereotyped, stereotype

стереотипчи : *n* stereotyper

стәкан : *n* glass, tumbler, beaker

стэканалты : *n* glass holder *for use in drinking Russian tea*

стибиум : *n* *chem* antimony, Sb

стил : *n* style

стилләшдирмә : *n* stylization

стол : *n* table, desk

столүстү : *a* table, desk *intended for use on a table or desk*

стратежи : *n* 1) strategy *a* 2) strategic

стратосфер : *n* stratosphere

страхование : *n* *Ru* insurance

стул : *n* *Ru* chair

су : *n* 1) water 2) juice, sap 3) sauce, dressing, gravy

су анбары : *n* reservoir *of water*

су бәнди : *n* dam

су кәмәри : *n* waterpipe

суајырычы : *n* *geog* watershed

суал : *n* question

суаледичи : *a* 1) interrogative, questioning, inquiring, question *adv* 2) interrogatively, questioningly, quizzically

суалты : *a* underwater, submarine

субај : *a* 1) unmarried, single *n* 2) bachelor

субајла(н)маг : *v* be single, be a bachelor

субајлыг : *n* bachelorhood

субалдырғаны : *n* *bot* water hemlock *Cicuta virosa, poisoneous European herb*

субасан : *n* water tower

субасар : *n* 1) flood plain, bottom land, river valley *which is inundated during floods* *a* 2) flood plain, bottom land

субасгылы : *a* *geol* water-pressure

субибәри : *n* water pepper, smartweed *Polygonum hydropiper*

субити : *n* water bug *hemipterous insect of the family Belostomatidae*

субјект : *n* *phil* subject

субјектив : *a* subjective

субјективлик : *n* subjectivity

субтропик : *n* 1) the subtropics *a* 2) subtropical

суваг : *n* plaster, plastering

сувагламаг : *v* plaster

суваглanмаг : *pass* be plastered

сувaглатдырмаг, сувaглатмаг : *vn* *fr.* **сувагламаг**

сувагсыз : *a* unplastered

сувагчы : *n* plasterer

сувагчылыг : *n* occupation/job of plasterer

сувамаг : *v* 1) apply, smear *with*, spread *on* 2) see **сувагламаг**

суванмаг : *pass* be smeared *with*

сuварылмаг : *v* 1) be irrigated, be watered *of land, crops* 2) be watered *of livestock*

суварма : *n* 1) irrigation, watering *n* 2) watering *livestock* *a* 3) irrigation, irrigating

сувармаг : *v* 1) water *field, garden, etc.*, irrigate 2) water *livestock*

суват : *n* 1) watering place 2) swill, mash

суватдырмаг, суватмаг : *caus* of **сувамаг**

сувачаг : *n* sluice, lock

сувашган : *a* sticky, sticking, adhesive, viscous, glutinous

сувашганлыг : *n* stickiness, adhesiveness, viscosity

сувашдырмаг : *v* coat/smear *with* , apply

сувашмаг : *v* be smeared/coated *with*

сугабағы : *n* *bot* bottle-gourd, calabash *Lagenaria vulgaris*

сугамышы : *n* *bot* cattail, reed mace *Typha*

сугарангушу : *n* *zool* tern *bird related to the gull, subfamily Sterninae*

сугозу : *n* *bot* water-chestnut, water caltrop *Trapa natans*

сугузғуну : *n* *zool* kingfisher *genus Halcyon*

судур : *n* *med* see **сулуг**

сузанбағы : *n* *bot* water lily *genus Nymphaaea*

суи-гәсд : *n* plot, conspiracy

суи-гәсдчи : *n* plotter, conspirator

суи-истифадә : *n* abuse, misuse

суиланы : *n* *zool* grass snake

суи-нијјәт : *n* malicious intent

суити : *n* *zool* 1) seal *a* 2) seal

суjaдавамлы : *a* waterproof

суjaјатан : *n* 1) person seated in water *fig* 2) person amenable to persuasion

суjаран : *n* cutwater, nose *of a ship*

сукирписи : *n* *zool* sea urchin *class Echinoideae*

сулаг : *n* 1) boggy/swampy/marshy place 2) bog, swamp, marsh

суламаг : *v* pour, spray *on people* 2) see **сувармаг**

суланмаг : *v* 1) to pour/sprinkle on oneself 2) be irrigated 3) become moist/wet/damp 4) become filled with liquid/juice/sap/tears/saliva 5) be sprinkled/sprayed with water

сулатдырмаг, **сулатмаг** : *caus* of **суламағ**

сулгунчуг : *n* puddles formed after a rain

султан : *n* sultan, monarch, sovereign, lord, ruler

сулу : *a* 1) watery, liquid, wet, moist, damp, humid 2) juicy, sappy, succulent 3) aqueous, abounding in water

сулуг : *n* blister

сулугланмаг : *v-intr* blister, form blisters

сулуглашмаг : *v-intr* turn into blisters

сулулуг : *n* juiciness, sappiness, succulence

сулуф : *n* millet *Panicum miliaceum* . Used for chicken-feed

сулуча : *a* rather juicy, sappy, succulent

сулфат : *n chem* sulfuric acid

сумах : *n bot* sumac *Rhus*

сумағы : *n* purple *color*

сумбата : *n* 1) emery *impure corundum* 2) emery paper

сумбаталамаг : *v* polish with emery paper

сумбатлы : *a* decent, respectable, proper, honest, deserving, worthy

сунәркизи : *n bot* verbena, vervain *an herb*

суөлчән : *n* water meter, water gauge

супәриси : *n myth* mermaid, water nymph

супишиҹи : *n zool* stingray *family Dasyatidae*

сур : *n relig* the trumpet of the Day of Judgement. Occurs in the bound form : **сур дүдүјү** : the trumpet which will be blown by the archangel Israfel at the Last Judgement

сурәт : *n* 1) image, face, facial expression, physiognomy, appearance 2) look, appearance, aspect, shape, form 3) way, method, procedure 4) portrait, representation, image 5) copy 6) numerator

сурәтчыхаран : *n* copier, copyist

сурәтчыхарма : *n* copying

сурсат : *n* 1) provisions, food 2) supplies *military*

сус : *intj* Shut up!, Be silent!

сусамаг : *v* thirst, experience thirst; crave

сусамуру : *n zool* otter *genus Lutra*

сусдурмаг, **сусдуртмаг** : *v* cause to be silent

сусдурулмаг : *v* be compelled/forced to be silent

сусәпән : *n* watering can

сусәрчәси : *n zool* water ouzel, also called dipper *Cinclus*

сусичаны : *n zool* desman, muskrat *Desmana moschata*

сусичовулу : *n zool* water rat, European vole *genus Arvicola*

сусма : *n* silence, passing over in silence

сусмаг : *v-intr* 1) keep silence, be/keep silent, become/fall silent 2) fade, die away *of a noise/sound*

сусмаз : *a* unceasing, incessant

сусуз : *a* 1) waterless, without water 2) unwatered/deprived of water *i.e. domestic animal*, thirsty

сусузламаг : *v* see **сусамаг**

сусузлашдырма : *n chem* calcination, roasting, dehydration

сусузлуг : *n* 1) dryness, aridity, drought 2) thirst

сусүнбүлү : *n bot* pond weed, an aquatic plant *Potemogeton*

сутка : *n Ru* 24 hour time-period

сүүстү : *a* surface, above-water

суф : *n zool* pike perch *a pike-like percoid fish*

суфәрәси : *n zool* great snipe, double snipe, a bird *Capella media*

суфи : *n* Sufi, Islamic mystic

суфилик : *n* Islamic mysticism

суфлјор : *n* 1) prompter *a* 2) prompter[s], prompter-related

суфлјорлуг : *n* 1) occupation/job of prompter 2) prompting

сухары : *n Russ* rusk *a dried bread*

сухәрчәнки : *n med* noma, a gangrenous inflammation of the mouth, a form of stomatitis found especially in young children

суч : *n* fault, guilt

сучичәји : *n med* chicken pox *Varicella*

сучлу : *a* guilty

сучлулуг : *n* guilt, culpability

сучу : *n* water carrier

сучулуг : *n* occupation/ job of water carrier

сучә : *n zool* see **корамал**

сучинчилими : *n bot* chickweed, starwort *Stellaria*

сучуг : *n* fruit sausage with nut filling 2) boggy/swampy/marshy terrain, bog, swamp, marsh 3) see **сулуг**

сучуглуг : *n* marsh, swamp, quagmire

сучуллуту : *n zool* jacksnipe *Limnocryptes minimus , a marsh-dwelling sandpiper*

сушејтаны : *n zool* suşeytanı fresh-water mollusk *living in stagnant ponds*

сүбут : *n* proof, evidence, argument, reason

сүбутсуз : *a* 1) unsubstantiated, unproven, groundless *adv* 2) pro contra, groundlessly, unsupportedly

сүбутсузлуг : *n* disproof, counterevidence, confutation, groundlessness, baselessness

сүбһ : *n* 1) morning 2) dawn, daybreak

сувари : *n* horseman, rider, cavalryman, equestrian

сүд : *n* 1) milk *a* 2) milk

сүдашы : *n* see **сүдлүсыјыг**

сүдгабы, сүддан : *n* milk jug, milk can

сүдәмәр : *a* 1) nursing, suckling *of an infant* *n* 2) suckling-babe, nursling *fig* 3) greenhorn, raw youth, neophyte

сүдәчәр : *a* 1) born nearly every year *n* 2) children born one aafter another over a short period of time

сүдләјән : *n bot* milkwort, spurge *Euphorbia*

сүдлү : *a* 1) milk, lactic, lacteal, lactescent *adv* 2) with milk, with an admixture of milk 3) *n* high-milk-producer *cow*

сүдлүлүк : *n* milk-producing capacity *of a cow*

сүдлүплов : *n* milk-pilaf

сүдлүсыјыг : *n* milk-gruel, milk-porridge

сүдсатан : *n* see **сүдчү**

сүдсүз : *a* milkless, non-lactic, non-milk-producing/non-lactating/dry *of a cow*

сүдсүзлүк : *n* non-lactating state in a milch cow

сүдхана : *n* 1) dairy, creamery 2) dairy establishment

сүдчү : *n* milkman, dairyman, dairy maid

сүдчүлүк : *n* the dairy business, occupation/job of dairyman

сүжет : n 1) subject, topic, plot a 2) subject/topic/plot-related

сүздүрмәк, сүздүртмәк : *caus* of **сүзмәк**

сүзәнәк : *n med* gonorrhea, the clap

сүзәр : *n* tree-creeper *Certhis familiaris* a small oscine bird

сүзкәч : *n* 1) filter; distiller 2) strainer, colander

сүзкүн : *a* smooth

сүзмә : 1) *vn fr.* **сүзмә** 2) süzma sweetened, strained and thickened sour milk

сүзмәк : *v* 1) strain, filter, pass through a colander/strainer/sieve/filter 2) dance smoothly 3) soar, hover, float/sail through the air; fly glidingly 4) look s.o. up and down, measure with a glance

сүзүлмәк : *n* 1) be strained, be filtered 2) ooze, exude, trickle, flow/stream down 3) wear out, wear thin from age 4) be looked at up and down, be measured with a glance

сүзүнтү : *n* residue left after straining

сүјсүн : *n* withers *of a horse*

сүкан : *n* steering-wheel, rudder, helm

сүканчы : *n* driver, helmsman, steersman, coxswain, pilot

сүкунәт : *n* 1) peace, rest, quiet, tranquillity 2) silence, calm, lull

сүкут : *n* 1) silence, hush 2) pause

сүлалә : *n* dynasty

сүлејман : *n* Solomon *Hebrew king 1036-980 B.C.E.*

сүлејман балығы : *n zool* salmon

сүлејман дашы : *n min* garnet

сүлејмани : *n* corrosive sublimate, mercuric chloride

сүләнмәк : *v* hang around, loaf, loiter, mooch around

сүлүкән : *n* red lead, red lead oxide, minium *pigment*

сүлһ : *n* peace, accord

сүлһпәрвәр : *a* 1) conciliatory, peace-loving *n* 2) peace-lover, peacemaker

сүлһпәрвәрлик : *n* peaceableness, concord, amity

сүлһсевәр : *a* see **сүлһпәрвәр**

сүмсү : *n* hunter's whistle, bird-call *special whistle or instrument ussed for luring birds*

сүмсүк : *n* beggar, cadger

сүмсүнмәк : *v* beg, cadge

сүмүк : *n* 1) bone *a* 2) bone, bony, osseous

сүмүкалты : *a* sub-osseous

сүмүкарасы : *a* inter-osseous

сүмүкләшмә : *n* ossification, hardness

сүмүклү : *a* 1) bony, having many bones *meat, fish* 2) bony, big-boned

сүмүксүз : *a* boneless

сүмүрмәк : *v* suck, suck in, absorb, draw

сүмүрүлмәк : *v* be sucked in

сүнбә : *n* ramrod, cleaning rod

сунбәләмәк : *v* ram/pack in with a ramrod

сунбәли : *a* 1) ramrod-/cleaning rod-related 2) equipped/furnished with a ramrod/cleaning rod

сунбүл : *n* ear, spike *of grain, grass*

сунбүлгыран : *n zool* gopher *family Geomydaae*

сунбүлләнмәк : *v agric* form ears/spikes

сунбүллү : *a agric* full of ears, heavy-eared *corn etc*

сунбүлчичәји : *n bot* hyacinth *fragrant flower*

сун'и : *a* 1) artificial, man-made, synthetic *adv* 2) artificially, synthetically

сун'иләшдирмәк : *v* impart an artificial character *to an action*

сун'илик : *n* artificiality

сункәр : *n zool* sponge *Porifera*

сункәрдашы : *n* pumice, pumice stone

сункү : *n* 1) bayonet *a* 2) bayonet

сункүләмәк : *v* bayonet, stab with a bayonet

сункүлү : *a* equipped with/furnished with bayonet

сункүсүз : *a* bayonetless

сүннәт : *n* circumcision *the ritual practice in Islam, Judaism, et al.*

сүннәт дәриси : *n* foreskin

сүнни : *n* 1) Sunni *a major sect of Islam a* 2) Sunnite, Sunni

сүпүркә : *n* broom, besom, whisk-broom

сүпүркәләмәк : *v* see **сүпүрмәк**

сүпүркәсаггал : *n* house spirit *folklore*

сүпүркәчи : *n* 1) sweeper,street-sweeper *person* 2) charwoman, cleaning woman 3) broommaker, brushmaker

сүпүркәчилик : *n* 1) job of sweeper, street-sweeper 2) job of charwoman, cleaning woman 3) occupation of broommaker, brushmaker

сүпүрмәк : *v* sweep

сүпүртдүрмәк, сүпүртмәк : *caus* of **сүпүрмәк**

сүпүрүлмәк : *v* be swept, be swept out

сүпүрүнтү : *n* litter, sweepings, rubbish, trash, refuse

сүпүрүшмәк : *v* grapple with, come to grips with, struggle with, come to blows with, fight with

сураһи : *n* 1) handrail, railing, banister, balustrade 2) carafe

сүрбә : *n* flock, pack

сүрәк : *n* duration

сүрәкли : *a* long, prolonged, protracted

сүрәклилик : *n* duration, length

сүрәксиз : *a* brief, of short duration , short-lived, short-term, transitory

сүр'әт : *n* speed, velocity, quickness, rapidity, rate, pace, tempo

сүр'әтлә : *adv* quickly, rapidly, at an accelerated rate/pace/tempo

сүр'әтләндирилмәк : *v-intr* quicken, accelerate, speed up

сүр'әтләндирмә : *n* acceleration, increase/augmentation of rate/pace/tempo

сүр'әтләндирмәк : *v-tr* hasten, quicken, accelerate, increase the speed (of); increase the rate/pace/tempo, speed up

сүр'әтләнмә : *n* acceleration, accelerating, augmentation of rate/pace/tempo, speedup

сүр'әтләнмәк : *v-intr* quicken, accelerate, speed oneself up

сүр'әтли : *a* fast, quick, rapid, lightning, quick-as-lightning

сүр'әтлилик : *n* rapidity, quickness, celerity, rapidity of pace/tempo

сүркәч : *n* runner *of a sled*

сүркү : *n* 1) slide-bolt, bar, latch 2) bolt *of a gun*

сүркүн : *n* 1) exile, banishment, expulsion, ostracism *a* 2) exiled, banished, expelled 3) *n* exile *person*

сүркүнлүк : *n* see **сүркүн** 1)

сүрмә : *v n* 1) fr. **сүрмәк** 2) smut *fungus disease of grain in which the affected parts are transformed into a dusty black powder* 3) antimony *employed as a black coloring for eyelashes*

сүрмәји : *a* dark-blue, lilac, violet

сүрмәк : 1) drive, herd *i.e. cattle* 2) ride/guide *i.e. a horse* 3) drive *a vehicle* 4) plow, till 5) drive out/away, banish, expel, exile, evict *intr* 6) continue, last, drag on *of time tr* 7) spend *time*

сүрмәләмәк : *v* dye, darken *hair/eyes/eyelashes*

сүрмәли : *n* eyes or eyelashes *darkened with antimony or mascara*

сүр-сүмүк : *n* meat of poor or indifferent quality *made up largely of bones*

сүртдүрмәк : *caus* of **сүртмәк**

сүртәләмәк : *v-tr* rub in a circle, wipe dry, rub in

сүрткәч : *n* grater, grinder

сүртку : *n* 1) lubricant, grease, oil 2) salve, ointment, liniment *a* 2) lubricating

сүртмә : *vn* fr. **сүртмәк**

сүртмәк : *v* 1) rub, grind 2) oil, grease, lubricate 3) smear, spread,

сүртүк : *a* 1) ground, grated 2) effaced, obliterated, frayed, threadbare 3) impudent, insolent *n* 4) frock-coat *fr. Russ. "syurtuk"*

сүртүклүк : *n* 1) dilapitation, frayed/worn state ; faded, threadbare appearance 2) impudence, insolence *a* 3) pertaining to a frock-coat *fr. Russ. "syurtuk"*

сүртүлмәк : *v-intr* 1) rub, be rubbed 2) be effaced, be obliterated, be frayed 3)) be smeared, be spread 4) be lubricated/oiled/greased

сүртүнмә : *n* rubbing, friction

сүртүнмәк : *v-intr* rub against

сүртүшкән : *a* captious, faultfinding, bothersome, importunate

сүртүшкәнлик : *n* captiousness, faultfinding, pestering

сүртүшмәк : *v-intr* 1) rub against one another *fig* 2) bother, pester, find fault *with*, carp, nag *v-tr* 3) offend, hurt; tease

сүрү : *n* flock, herd

сүрүдүлмәк : *v* be dragged off, be carried away

сүрүк : *intj* Get out [of here]!, Beat it!, Scram!

сүрүкләмә : *n* 1) pulling/dragging *through/along* 2) pulling/drawing in, involving

сүрүкләмәк : *v* 1) pull, drag, pull/drag *through/along* 2) pull/ draw in, involve

сүрүкләндирмәк : *v* see **сүрүкләмәк** 2)

сүрүкләнмәк : *v* be drawn in, be dragged in, become involved

сүрүлмәк : *v* 1) be driven on, be urged on 2) be steered, be driven *of a vehicle* 2) be plowed/tilled 3) be exiled, be expelled, be banished, be sent away

сүрүмәк : *v* pull, drag

сүрүндүрмә : *n* procrastination

сүрүндүрмәк : *v* 1) dally, loiter 2) drag *ext* 3) drag out, delay *a matter*

сүрүндүрмәчи, сүрүндүрүчү : *n* red tape merchant, red tape monger, bureaucrat, one who drags matters out for no reason

сүрүндүрмәчилик : *n* red tape, deliberate bureaaucratic procrastination

сүрүнән : *a* 1) crawling, creeping *n* 2) crawler, creeper

сүрүнәнләр : *n* *zool* reptiles

сүрүнәрәк, сүрүнә-сүрүнә : *adv* on hands and knees, crawling on all fours, by crawling/creeping

сүрүнкәл : *n* narrow slippery places in mountains

сүрүнмәк : *v* 1) crawl, creep, drag oneself, drag oneself along 2) lead a miserable existence 3) grovel

сүрүнчәк : *a* slippery

сүрүтләмә : *v n* 1) fr. **сүрүтләмәк** 2) slippers; bedroom slippers

сүрүтләмәк : *v* drag, tow

сүрүтмәк : *caus* of **сүрүмәк**

сүрүчү : *n* 1) driver *of animal-drawn vehicle,* cabby, drayman, carter, waggoner, coachman 2) driver *of motor vehicle* , racer

сүрүшдүрмәк : *caus* of **сүрүшмәк**

сүрүшкән : *a* slippery

сүрүшмә : *n* 1) sliding *geol* 2) displacement, dislocation, landslide

сүрүшмәк : *v-intr* slide, slip, roll

сүрфә : *n* *zool* larva, grub, maggot

сүс : *n* see **зинәт**

сүсән : *n* *bot* iris *Iris pseudacorus*

сүсәри : *n* cricket

сүсләмәк : *v* beautify, adorn, decorate, array, dress up

сүст : *a* flabby, listless, limp, apathetic, inert, dull, phlegmatic; boring, uninteresting

сүстләшмәк : *v* become flabby, become listless, become apathetic, become dull/sluggish/inactive; become boring, uninteresting

сүстлүк : *n* flabbiness, sluggishness, apathy, inertness; boringness

сүтүн : *n* 1) column, post, pole, pillar 2) newspaper column *book-keeping* 3) column *of a table or page*

сүтүнлү : *a* columnar, columned

сүтүл : *a* 1) unripe *of grains, fruits, etc.* 2) undercooked, underdone *of food*

сүтүлләшмәк : *v* become almost ripe, approach ripeness

сүфтә : *n* initiative

сүфрә : *n* 1) tablecloth 2) covered/set table, meal fig 3) hospitality

сүфрәлик : *n* material suitable or intended for a tablecloth

сүхүр : *n* *geol* rock, rock layer, bed, stratum

сухурдоғуран : *a min* rock-forming, mineralizing, petrifying

схем : *n* diagram, scheme

схематик : *a* schematic

сепление : *n Ru* 1) gearshift 2) coupling *between railroad cars*

Т

т : twenty-fourth letter of Azerbaijani alphabet

та : *prep* 1) by *some time* , up to, before 2) any more, any longer, hence, and so, already 3) in order to, so that

таам : *n* food; eating

таариф : *v-cmp* **таариф еләмәк (етмәк)** regale *with* , treat *to* , entertain

таб : *n* 1) power, might, strength, force 2) endurance

таб еләмәк : *v* stand, endure

табдан салмаг : *v-tr* exhaust *s.o.*

табаг : *n* 1) hawker's/vendor's wooden tray/stand 2)) wash-tub, trough; tub, vat

табагчы : *n* hawker, vendor *selling wares from a tray, or stand*

табе : *a* subordinate, submissive, obedient, dependent, subject

табеетдиричи : *a* subduing, restraining, confining, strait- *as in strait-jacket*

табел : *n* table *e.g. data displayed in rows or columns*, time sheet

табелчи : *n* timekeeper

табели : *gram* **табели мүрәккәб чүмлә** complex sentence

табелик : *n* 1) subordination *a* 2) subordinating

табесиз : *gram* **табесиз мүрәккәб чүмлә** compound sentence

таблашмаг : *v* bear, stand, endure, suffer, withstand

таблы : *a* firm, steadfast, steady, staunch, hardy

табсыз : *a* weak, feeble, enfeebled, frail, exhausted

табсызлыг : *n* weakness, feebleness, frailty, debility, lack of staying power

табут : *n* coffin

табутгајыран, табутчу : *n* coffin maker, undertaker

тава : *n* frying pan

тавакабабы : *n* cutlet prepared with eggs

таван : *n* ceiling

тавана : *n* 1) power, might, strength, force 2) property, fortune, affluence

таванлы : *a* 1) strong, powerful, mighty 2) affluent, rich, wealthy, well-to-do, well-off

таванасыз : *a* 1) low-powered 2) indigent, poor, of modest means

тавар : *a* 1) large, great, prominent, major 2) big, strong, mature, grown-up 3) hardened, inveterate

тагт : *intj* bang! crash!

тагтылдамаг : *v-intr* knock, bang

тагтылдатмаг : *v-intr* knock, bang, rap

тагтылты : *n* knock, tap, knocking

тагәт : *n* strength, force, power, might

тагәтсиз : *a* weak, feeble, exhausted, powerless, frail

тагәтсизлик : *n* weakness, feebleness, debility, sickness, illness

тағ : *n* 1) arch, vault; straight-arch, crosspiece 2) arc 3) fringe *of hair* 3) plant, bush, vine *of melon, cucumber, etc.*

тағалаг : *n* see **гаргара**

тағбәнд : *a* arched, vaulted

тағлы : *a* arched, vaulted

тазијана : *n* 1) whip, lash *fig* 2) epigram

тазы : *n* hound

таинки : *prep* until

тај : *n* 1) bale, pack, pile, stack 2) each one of a pair 3) bank, shore, coast 4) side 5) leaf, fold *each of a pair of objects that open and close, e.g. a shutter or door* 6) fringe 7) point of division of a whole object into two parts *a* 8) like, equal *to,* match for

таја : *n* stack, rick

тајајаг : *n* see **ағачајаг**

таја-таја : *adv* in a stack/rick, in stacks/ricks

тајбағлајан : *n* packer, baler

тајбатај : *adv* wide open

тајбујнуз : *a* one-horned

тајганад : *a* one-winged

тајгылча : *a* one-legged

тајгулаг : *a* one-eared

тајгулп : *n* 1) mug, tankard 2) scoop, dipper, ladle

тајдәјишик, тајкеш, тајкешик : *a* unpaired, odd, not a pair

тајы-бәрабәри : *a* equal to oneself, on a par *with* , on a level *with*

тајкөз : *a* 1) one-eyed, blind in one eye *n zool* 2) crawfish

тајлашдырмаг : *v* group by similarity

тајтаг : *n* lame person *m/f*

тајтаглыг : *n* lameness, limping

тај-тај : *adv* in piles/heaps *when taking or giving something*

тајтыма : *n* lameness, limping

тајтымаг : *v* hobble, limp; be lame

тај-туш : *n* contemporary, person of the same age, buddy/chum/pal

тај-туш олмаг : *v* hang around together *especially of teenagers*

тајфа : *n* tribe, clan, kin, family, offspring, race, breed

тајфасыз : *a* without kin

такт : *n mus* time, measure

тактик : *a* tactical

тала : *n* glade, clearing

талаг : *n relig* divorce *Arabic talaq "severance of a bond"* refers to the action of the husband rejecting the wife

таламаг : *v* rob, ransack, plunder, loot, pillage

талан : *n* 1) pogrom, massacre, 2) robbery, burglary 3) devastation

таланмаг : *v* be robbed, be ransacked, be looted, be pillaged/plundered

таланчы : *n* robber, burglar, thug

таланчылыг : *n* robbery, burglary

талаша : *n* chip

талвар : *n* 1) awning, sunshade, parasol, umbrella 2) sunshade formed of grapevines growing over a lattice-work support

тале : *n* 1) fate, destiny, lot 2) happiness, good fortune, good luck 3) Tale masculine/feminine first name

талесиз : *a* 1) unfortunate, unlucky, ill-starred, ill-fated *n* 2) unlucky person, a failure

талесизлик : *n* 1) misfortune 2) a cruel, unlucky fate/destiny

талибә : *n* student, undergraduate *woman*

талиум : *n chem* thallium, Ti

талиум-сулфид : *n chem* thallium sulfide

талыш : *n* Talış an Iranian people living in south-eastern Azerbaijan, Leninakor Province.

талон : *n Ru* coupon, ration card

талк : *n* talc

там : *a* 1) whole, entire *a* 2) full, complete *adv* 3) just, exactly, sharp 4) fully, completely *n math* 5) integer 6) taste, smack, touch

тамада : *n* toast-master *Georgian loan-word*

тамам : *a* 1) whole, entire, full, complete, all *adv* 2) very, greatly, highly, quite, rather, absolutely, utterly, perfectly 3) wholly, completely, fully, in full

тамамән : *adv* in full

тамамилә : *adv* 1) as a whole, wholly, fully, completely, quite, in full measure 2) exactly, sharp, precisely

тамам-камал : *adv* in full; completely, entirely

тамамлајычы : *a* 1) final, closing, concluding, conclusive 2) additional, supplementary

тамамламаг : *v* supplement, complete, conclude, finish

тамамланмаг : *pass* be supplemented, be completed

тамамлатдырмаг, тамамлатмаг : *caus* of **тамамламаг**

тамамлыг : *n* 1) fullness, completeness *gram* 2) object

тамарзы : *n* one who feels a strong desire to have/acquire/partake/taste s.t.

тамас : *n* lath

тамаһ : *n* 1) mercenariness, avidity, greed 2) temptation

тамаһкар : *a* avid, greedy, money-grabbing, mercenary, covetous

тамаһкарлыг : *n* avidity, greed, selfishness, covetousness

тамаһла : *adv* avidly, greedily, covetously, selfishly

тамаһландырмаг : *v* tempt, allure, entice, arouse a desire/appetite *for*

тамаһланмаг : *v* be tempted, be enticed, covet, crave

тамаһсыз : *a* 1) disinterested, unselfish 2) generous, unselfish, selfless *adv* 3) unselfishly, in a disinterested manner

тамаһсызлыг : *n* disinterestedness, unselfishness, generosity

тамаһсыландырмаг, тамаһсылатмаг : *v* see **тамаһландырмаг**

тамаһсыланмаг : *v* see **тамаһланмаг**

тамаһсымаг : *v* see **тамаһланмаг**

тамаша : *n* 1) spectacle, sight, show, play, performance 2) contemplation

тамашачы : *n* spectator, onlooker

тамландырмаг : *v* flavor, spice , make delicious/tasty

тамлы : *a* 1) delicious, tasty, pleasant to the taste 2) smacking *of*

тамсыз : *a* tasteless, insipid, unpalatable

тамсынмаг : *v* smack one's lips while trying to determine what *s.t.* tastes like

тамһүгуглу : *a* enfranchised, enjoying full rights

тана : *n* see **сырға**

таныг : *n* see **шаһид**

танымаг : *v* 1) learn, find out, identify, recognize, discern 2) admit, acknowledge 3) know, be acquainted *with*

танынмаг : *v* 1) be well-known, become famous *for*, be reputed *to be*, pass for 2) admit, acknowledge, be acknowledged 3) be recognized

танынмаз : *a* unrecognizable

танынмыш : *a* well-known, famous, celebrated, renowned

танытдырмаг, танытмаг : *v* 1) acquaint *with*, introduce *to* 2) let know, manifest, display, show

таныш : *a* 1) acquainted, familiar *with* *n* 2) acquaintance

таныш еләмәк : *v* get acquainted, get familiar

танышлыг : *n* acquaintanceship, acquaintance

танк : *n* 1) tank *a* 2) tank

танкчы : *n* tank crew member

танры : *n* *relig* God

тапа : *n* see **тыхач**

тапан : *n* 1) finder *person* 2) guesser, diviner 3) tamping-machine

тапанча : *n* 1) pistol, revolver *a* 2) pistol, revolver

тапгыр : *n* saddle girth, belly-band

тапдаг : *a* well-trodden, beaten *of a path, road, etc.*

тапдаламаг : *v* trample down

тапдаланмаг : *v* 1) be trampled down, be trodden under foot *fig* 2) be oppressed/depressed

тапдалатдырмаг, тапдалатмаг : *caus* of **тапдаламаг**

тапдыг : *n* 1) foundling 2) find, godsend, windfall, catch

тапдырмаг, тапдыртмаг : *caus* of **тапмаг**

тапылма : *n* finding, discovering, discovery, detecting, detection

тапылмаг : *v* 1) be found 2) be discovered, be invented 3) be guessed, be divined 4) prove t*o be*, turn out *to be* , appear *to be* , be available

тапынма : *v* *n* see **тә'зим**

тапынмаг : *v* worship, adore

тапынты : *n* find, godsend, windfall

тапышмаг : *v* find one another, come together, become friends

тапма : *vn* 1) fr. **тапмаг** *n* 2) find, godsend, windfall, that which was found

тапмаг : *v* 1) find 2) guess, divine 3) discover, invent

тапмача : *n* riddle, rebus, puzzle, charade

тапочки : *n* *Ru* slippers; sports/gym shoes, sneakers

таппатап : *n* continuous knocking/tapping, unremitting tramping/stamping *of feet, hooves, etc.*

таппылдамаг : *v* 1) produce/emit *the sound of* 2) tramping/stamping, tap produce/emit knocking/rapping

таппылдатмаг : *v* clap, bang, slap, spank, smack

таппылты : *n* knock, tap, footstep, tramp/tramping/stamping

тапш : *n* *slang* bribe in the form of a present; providing employment/ promotion to one's relatives, friends etc.

тапшырыг : *n* 1) task, commission, mission, errand, assignment, order 2) mandate

тапшырыгверән : *n* 1) customer, client 2) person or official who appoints subordinates to perform tasks and assigns the tasks to be performed

тапшырылмаг : *v* 1) be assigned/ commissioned, be trusted/entrusted *with* 2) be ordered, be charged with responsibilities

тапшырма : *n* commission, mission, assignment, errand

тапшырмаг : *v* 1) commission, assign, [en]trust *with*, charge *with*, make responsibile *for* 2) order

тар : *n* *mus* 1) tar Iranian stringed instrument 2) perch for birds *a elev* 3) black, dim, dark, dull, gloomy *Persian* 4) pile of old unmelted snow *esp. in spring*

тарагта : *n* 1) fly swatter *mil hist* 2) petard

тараз : *a* 1) equal, equivalent *adv* 2) equally *tech* 3) balance wheel, counterbalance 4) level *the instrument*

таразламаг, таразлашдырмаг : *v* make even, balance

таразлашмаг : *v* become balanced, become equal, be at the same level

таразлыг : *n* equilibrium, balance, equipoise

тарач : *n* robbery, plunder, plundering, misappropriation; squandering

тараш : *a* cut, facetted

тарашчы : *n* lapidary, diamond cutter

тарзэн : *n* see **тарчалан**

тарих : *n* 1) history 2) date 3) era 4) chronology 5) chronicle

тарихи : *a* historical

тарихјазан : *n* chronicler

тарихли : *a* dated

тарихсиз : *a* undated

тарихчә : *n dim* 1) tale/story 2) story-teller

тарихчи, тарихшүнас : *n* historian

тарым : *a* 1) tight, taut *adv* 2) tight, tightly, tautly

тарла : *n* 1) field, ploughed field, grain-field 2) plantation 3) paddy

тарлагоруіан : *a* forest-protection

тарланмаг : *v* perch, roost *of chickens* 2) grow dim *fig* 3) take pleasure/delight *in*, enjoy

тарлачы : *n* field crop grower

тарлачылыг : *n* 1) field crop cultivation *a* 2) field crop cultivation-related

тар-мар : *a* 1) confused, messy, disordered 2) completely broken, destroyed

тартан-партан : *n* balderdash, nonsense, rubbish

тарчалан : *n* tar player *musician skilled at playing the tar q.v.*

тарчы : see **тарчалан**

тарчыг : *n* pasture, pasturage, grass

тас : *n* 1) basin, bowl 2) traditional fortune-telling using a bowl 3) tas *winning three games of nard, a backgammon-like game*

таса, таса-паса : *n* anger, wrath, malice, spite

тасар : *n* plan, scheme, project

тасарламаг : *v* plan, design, project

таскабаб : *n* taskabab *stewed meat cut into small pieces*

таскүлаһ : *n obs* helmet

таслаг : *n* sketch, draft, outline, scheme, layout

тат : *n* Tat *a minority people of Iranian speech in Azerbaijan and the Northern Caucasus*

татар : *n* 1) Tatar *a* 2) Tatar, Tatarian, Tataric

татары : *n* lash, whip

татарыламаг : *v* lash, whip, strike with a whip or lash

Татарыстан : *n* an autonomous republic in the middle Volga region

татарча : *adv* in Tatar, in the Tatar language

таун : *n med* 1) plague *a* 2) plague-related

тафлан : *n bot* cherry laurel *Prunus laurocerasus an evergreen tree*

тахыл : *n* grain, cereal-grain

тахылбити : *n zool* weevil *Curculionidae, agricultural pest*

тахылбичән : *n* reaper, harvester, reaping/harvesting machine

тахылгыран : *n zool* pine-sawyer *a longicorn beetle found in dead timber*

тахылгурду : *n zool* borer *a worm*

тахылгурудан : *n* grain dryer

тахылдөјән : *n* thresher

тахылмаг : *v* 1) be dressed in, have on 2) be hung/suspended *from* 3) be fastened/hooked *onto* 4) get stuck *on/in* 5) tie up

тахылсыз : *a* without grain, barren

тахылсовуран : *n* winnower, winnowing machine

тахмаг : *v* put on *clothes* , 2) pass through, insert, put in 3) fasten, hook on, stick *on/in*

тахт : *n* 1) throne 2) ottoman, cot, couch, plank bed

тахта : *n* 1) board, plank 2) strip, band, belt *a* 3) [made] of planks/boards

тахтабити : *n* 1) bedbug *Cimex lectularius a* 2) bedbug-related

тахталамаг : *v* cover with boards/planks, board up

тахталанмаг : *v* be covered/sheathed with boards/planks, be boarded up

тахталатдырмаг, тахталатмаг : *caus* of **тахталамаг**

тахта-пара : *n dim* small board/plank

тахтапуш : *n* 1) roof 2) roofing, roof-covering

тахтапушчу : *n* roofer

тахтачы : *n* lumberman

тахт-тач : *n* throne, royal throne

тахча : *n* 1) niche, recess 2) alcove

тач : *n* 1) crown, coronet *fig* 2) empire, monarchy

тачгојма : *n* coronation, crowning

тачдар : *n* monarch, sovereign, crowned head

тачик : *n* 1) Tajik *a* 2) Tajik

тачикистан : *n* Tajikistan

тачикчә : *adv* in Tajik, in the Tajik language

тачир : *n* merchant, businessman

творог : *n* *Ru* cottage cheese

театр : *n* 1) theater *a* 2) theatrical

тез : *adv* 1) fast, quickly, promptly, smartly 2) early

тезальшан, тезаловланан : *a* inflammable, highly inflammable

тезатан : *a* rapid-fire, quick-firing

тезбазар : *a* 1) transient, fleeting *n* 2) quick dĕnouement to an event

тезбөјүјән : *a* fast-growing

тездәјән : *a* see **фараш**

тездән : *adv* early, very early

тезәријән : *a* *tech* fusible

тезјетишән : *a* see **фараш**

тезкечән : *a* transitory, transient, fleeting

тезкедән : *a* 1) swift-footed, quickly-moving, nimble *n* 2) fast runner

тезкөрән : *a* sharp-eyed

тезләщдирмәк : *v-tr* 1) hasten, quicken, accelerate, speed up 2) make more frequent, increase the frequency *of*

тезлик : *n* 1) quickness, speed, velocity, swiftness *phys* 2) frequency

тезликдә : see **тезликлә** 1)

тезликлә : *adv* 1) before long, soon, in the near future 2) see **тез** 1)

тезликөлчән : *n* frequency gauge

тезликчә : *adv* a bit early, soon

тезсатылан : *a* saleable, marketable, quick-selling, best-selling *of goods or wares*

тезсезән : *a* sharp, keen-witted, quick on the uptake

тезсынан : *a* fragile, brittle

тез-тез : *adv* often, frequently, now and then, quite frequently, fairly often

тезчә : *adv* a bit faster, a bit more quickly

тејләсән : *n* dervishes' head-dress

тејха : *a* see **чылха**

тел : *n* 1) thread 2) bang[s] *of hair* 3) string *musical instrument* 4) wire 5) telegram 6) a hair 7) connections 8) ties

телбасан : *n* pinning

телевизија : *n* *Ru* television

телевизор : *n* *Ru* TV-set

телеграм : *n* telegram, wire

телеграф : *n* 1) telegraph *a* 2) telegraph[ic]

телеграфчы : *n* telegrapher, telegraph operator

телеграфчылыг : *n* the specialty of telegraph operator

телефон : *n* 1) telephone *a* 2) telephone, telephonic

телефонлащдырылмаг : *v* have telephones installed, have a telephone system set up

телефонлащдырмаг : *v* install telephones, set up a telephone system

телефонлашмаг : *v* get in touch over the telephone, speak on the telephone *to* , arrange*s.t.* on the telephone

телефонограм : *n* telephoned telegram *telegram read over the telephone*

телефончу : *n* telephone operator

телефончулуг : *n* specialty of telephone operator

телли : *a* wearing bangs

телсиз : *a* wireless

температур : *n* 1) temperature, fever *a* 2) temperature, temperature-related

теннис : *n* 1) tennis *a* 2) tennis

теннисчи : *n* tennis player

теорем : *n* theorem

термин : *n* *Ru* term

терминоложи : *a* terminological

терминолокија : *n* terminology

террор : *a* 1) terror *a* 2) terrorist[ic]

террорчу : *n* terrorist

террорчулуг : *n* terrorism

техника : *n* engineering, technics; technique; technology

техники : *a* technical, engineering; technological

техноложи : *a* technological

технолокија : *n* technology

теһран : *n* 1) Teheran *capital of Iran* *a* 2) Teheran['s]

теши : *n* spindle

тешт : *n* large copper basin

тәаруф : *n* ceremony

тәб : *n* 1) nature, character, disposition, inclination 2) inspiration; state of mind

тәбабәт : *n* medicine

тәбашир : *n* chalk, whiting

тәбаширләмәк : *v-tr* chalk, polish with whiting

тәбәгә : *n* *geol* 1) layer, stratum; stage 2) sheet, leaf *of a book*

тәбәгәләшмә : *n* stratification; exfoliation; lamination

тәбәгәләшмәк : *v-intr* exfoliate, divide into layers, become stratified

тәбәддүлат : *n* *rare* see **дәјишиклик**

тәбәә : *n* subject, citizen

тәбәәлик : *n* citizenship, nationality

тәбәнә : *n* see **гыјыг** 1)

тәбәр : *n* battle-ax, pole-ax

тәбәрзин : *n* *hist* halberd

тәбәррүк : *a* *relig* 1) blessed, blest, hallowed 2) rare, uncommon

тәбәссүм : *n* smile

тәбәххүр : *n* 1) see **бухарланма** 2) disappearance

тәбиб : *n* physician, doctor *more commonly* "**һәким**"

тәбиәт : *n* 1) nature, countryside 2) character, nature, disposition, temper

тәбиәтпәрәст : *n* 1) naturalist; nature-writer 2) nature-lover

тәбиәтпәрәстлик : *n* 1) naturalism *in literature and arts)* 2) love of wild nature

тәбиәтчи, тәбиәтшүнас : *n* natural scientist, naturalist

тәбиәтшүнаслыг : *n* natural science, natural history

тәбии : *a* 1) natural 2) elemental, native 3) spontaneous *adv* 4) naturally, of course

тәбиїјат : *n* natural history, natural science[s]

тәбиїјатчы : *n* natural scientist, naturalist

тәбииләшдирмә : *n* naturalization

тәбииләшдирмәк : *v-tr* naturalize

тәбиилик : *n* natural state

тәбил : *n* 1) drum *more commonly* "**нағара**" *a* 2) drum, drum-related

тәбилчалан : *n* drummer

тә'бир : *n* 1) expression 2) see **јозма**

тәблиғ : *v-cmp* : **тәблиғ еләмәк (етмәк)** disseminate propaganda, propagandize, popularize, tadvocate

тәблиғат : *n* propaganda

тәблиғатчы : *n* propagandist

тәбриз : *n* 1) Tabriz *city* *a* 2) appertaining to Tabriz

тәбрик : *n* 1) greeting, salutation, congratulation[s] *a* 2) welcoming, salutatory, congratulatory

тәбрик еләмәк : *v* congratulate

тәбрикнамә : *n* congratulatory letter, letter of congtratulation

тәвазө : *n* modesty

тәвазөкар : *a* modest, unassuming, unpretentious

тәвазөкарлыг : *n* modesty

тәвазөлү : *a* see **тәвазөкар**

тәвәггә : *n* request, petition 2) application, sollicitation; intercession, personal influence

тәвәггәчи : *n* intercessor, solicitor, petitioner

тәвәккүл : *n* 1) hope *esp. hoping and trusting in God alone* 2) risk

тәвәккүлү : *adv* 1) riskily, venturesomely, on the off chance 2) by putting oneself in God's hands

тәвәллүд : *n* birth

тәвәччөһ : *n* good will, liking *for*, sympathy *for*

тәгауд : *n* 1) pension 2) scholarship, grant

тәгаүдчү : *n* 1) pensioner; retiree 2) scholarship recipient/holder; grantee

тәгвим : *n* 1) calendar *a* 2) calendar

тәгдим : *n* 1) recommendation, representation 2) presentation

тәгдир : *n* appraisal, assessment, evaluation, approval

тәгдис : *n* sanctification, sanctifying, consecration, consecrating, hallowing 2) honoring, respect, esteem; reverence, worship

тә'гиб : *n* 1) following s.o. or s.t. 2) pursuit, persecution

тәглид : *n* imitation, aping *more commonly* **јамсылама**

тәглидини чыхармаг : *v* imitate, mimic ape

тәглидчи : *n* imitator, mimic; parodist

тәглидчилик : *n* imitation; mimicry, aping

тәгрибән : *adv* approximately, roughly, about

тәгриби : *a* approximate

тәгсим : *n* see **бөлмә**

тәгсир : *n* fault, guilt, blame

тәгсиркар : *a* see **тәгсирли**

тәгсирләндирән : *n* accuser, prosecutor

тәгсирләндирилән : *n* the accused, defendant

тәгсирләндирилмәк : *v* be accused *of*, be charged *with*

тәгсирләндирмәк : *v-tr* blame, accuse, charge *with* , incriminate, prosecute, indict

тәгсирли : *a* guilty, at fault

тәгсирлилик : *n* guilt, culpability

тәгсирнамә : *n* indictment

тәгсирсиз : *a* innocent, not guilty, guiltless

тәгсирсизлик : *n* innocence, guiltlessness

тәгти : *n* foot *prosody*

тәғјир : *n* change *more frequently* **дәјишмә**

тәғлит : *n* see **тәһриф**

тәдарүк : *n* 1) preparation, readiness, stocking up 2) procuring, procurement 3) supply, stock, reserve

тәдарүкчү : *n* procurement officer

тәдарүкчүл : *a* thrifty, provident

тәдбир : *n* 1) measure, step, arrangement 2) precaution, wariness, circumspection, discretion

тәдбир көрмәк : *v* take measures

тәдбир төкмәк : *v* think over, make a plan

тәдбирли : *a* wise, foresighted, cautious, prudent, sensible, judicious

тәдбирлилик : *n* sense, wisdom, foresight[edness], prudence, discretion

тәдбирсиз : *a* improvident, imprudent, incautious, careless

тәдбирсизлик : *n* improvidence, imprudence, carelessness

тәдбирсизчә, тәдбирсизчәсинә : *adv* improvidently, imprudently, carelessly

тәдгиг : *n* research, analysis, study, investigation

тәдгигат : *n* 1) investigation, research, analysis *a* 2) research

тәдгигатчы : *n* researcher, investigator

тә'дијә : *n* payment, paying off, repayment, remittance

тә'дијәчи : *n* payer

тәдрис : *n* 1) teaching, instruction 2) training, study, studies *a* 2) educational, study/school/training-related

тәдрич : *n* 1) gradualness, gradation *adv* 2) consecutively, in succession, in strict accordance/ conformity *with*

тәдричән : *adv* gradually, systematically, little by little

тәдричи : *a* gradual

тәдричлә : *adv* see **тәдричән**

тәдһиш : *n* terror

тәәссүб : *n* 1) fanaticism, bigotry 2) partiality toward one's kinfolk/neighbors

тәәссүбкеш, тәәссүбчәкән : *n* 1) fanatic, bigot *a* 2) partial toward one's kinfolk/neighbors

тәәссүр : *n* emotion

тәәссүрат : *n* experience, feeling, perception of external reality

тәәссүф : *n* regret, chagrin

тәәччүб : *n* surprise, amazement, astonishment, wonder

тәәччүб галмаг : *v* be surprised, amazed

тәәччүбләндирмәк : *v* astonish, surprise, amaze, dumbfound, take aback

тәәччүбләнмәк : *v* be astonished/ surprised/ amazed, be dumbfounded

тәәччүблү : *a* astonishing, surprising, amazing, odd, strange

тәәһһүд : *n* obligation, commitment

тәзад : *n* 1) contradiction 2) contrast 3) antagonism

тәзаһүр : *n* phenomenon, manifestation

тәзә : *a* 1) new, fresh, young *adv* 2) recently

тәзәбәј : *n* groom; newly-wed man

тәзәдәм : *n* fresh brew of tea

тәзәдән : *adv* anew, again, from the beginning/start

тәзәк : tazak *pressed cattle dung used as fuel*

тәзәләмә : *n* renewal, renovation, revival, freshening

тәзәләмәк : *v-tr* renew, renovate, revive, freshen

тәзәләндирән : *n* renewer, restorer, rehabilitator *person*

тәзәләндирмә : *n* see **тәзәләмә**

тәзәләндирмәк, тәзәләтмәк : *v* see **тәзәләмәк**

тәзәләндиртмәк : *caus* of **тәзәләмәк**

тәзәләнмәк : *v* 1) be renewed, be renovated, be revived, become fresh, freshen *up*

тәзәләтдирмәк, тәзәләшдиртмәк : *caus* of **тәзәләмәк**

тәзәлик : *n* freshness, novelty, newness, innovation

тәзәчә : *a* 1) brand new, very fresh *adv* 2) just now, just

тә'зијә : *n* mourning, requiem

тә'зим : *n* bow

тәзјиг : *n* 1) pressure 2) onslaught, onset

тәзкирә : *n obs* 1) narrative, history memoirs, biography 2) ticket, passport

тәзмәк : *v* run as fast as one can, run as fast as one's legs can carry one

тәзминат : *n* indemnity

тәјјарә : *n* airplane

тәјјарәчи : *n* pilot, aviator

тә'јин : *n* 1) appointment, assignment, determination, fixing, asscertainment *gram* 2) attribute

тә'јинат : *n* 1) appointment, assignment

тә'јинедичи : *a* 1) determining, determinative *gram* 2) attributive

тә'јини-мүгәддәрат : *n* self-determination, state of sovereignty

тәјјарә : *n* airplane, aircraft. *Russian самолет is also used colloquially*

тәјјарәвуран : *n* antiaircraft gun

тәјјарәсүрән, тәјјарәчи : *n* pilot, aviator

тәјјарәчилик : *n* aviation, aeronautics, aerostatics

тәк : *a* 1) odd; unpaired *a* 2) alone, by oneself, single, only, sole, without a companion 3) Tuesday

тәкаварлы : *a* single-oared

тәкаллаһлылыг : *n* monotheism, theism

тәкалты : *n* saddlecloth

тәкамүл : *n* 1) evolution *a* 2) evolutionary

тәкан : *n* 1) force, head, pressure-head *of liquid/steam* 2) push, shove jolt

тәкатлы : *a* one-horse

тәкбармаг : *n* mitten

тәкбашына : *adv* individually, independently, without outside help

тәкбәтәк : *adv* in private, privately, face to face, one-on-one

тәкбир, тәкдәбир : *adv* 1) sometimes, at times, from time to time, every now and then, occasionally *a* 2) single, solitary, individual

тәкдир : *n* blame, censure, reproach, disapproval

тәкә : *n* male goat *older than 2 years*

тәкәббүр : *n* pride, haughtiness, arrogance, conceit, superciliousness, putting on airs, swagger

тәкәббүрләнмәк : *v* swagger, be arrogant/ haughty

тәкәббүрлү : *a* 1) proud, haughty, arrogant, supercilious, conceited *adv* 2) proudly, haughtily, arrogantly, superciliously, swaggeringly, conceitedly

тәкәббүрлүлүк : *n* see **тәкәббүр**

тәкәр : *n* wheel

тәкәрли : *a* wheeled

тәкәрсиз : *a* wheelless

тәкәтәк : *adv* see **тәкбәтәк**

тәкзиб : *n* refutation, disproof, exposure as a liar, catching *s.o.* in a lie

тәкзибедилмәз : *a* irrefutable, incontrovertible, undeniable

тәки : *adv* 1) like, like this, this way 2) if only

тә'кид : *n* insistence, persistence

тә'кид етмәк : *v* insist

тә'кидлә : *adv* insistently, persistently

тә'кидли : *a* insistent, persistent

тә'кидлилик : *n* insistence, persistence

тәкир : *a* red-feathered *of birds* , red-finned *of fish*

тәкјеји-кәлам : *n* foreword, preface

тәкјә : *n* 1) support, place of propping; handrail, banister 2) site for sectarian worship

тәкјә етмәк : *v* 1) rely on 2) lean against, rest upon

тәккөзлү : *a* one-eyed, blind in one eye

тәкләмәк : *v* 1) see *s.o.* privately/in private 2) assault/attack *s.o.* taking advantage of the fact that he is alone

тәклик : *n* 1) loneliness, solitariness 2) solitude, seclusion 3) unit, unity, singleness, single occurence 4) state of being odd/unpaired

тәкликдә : *adv* privately, in private

тәклиф : *n* 1) offer, suggestion, proposal 2) direction 2) post, position

тәклифсиз : *a* unceremonious, offhanded, unduly familiar

тәклифсизлик : *n* unceremoniousness, undue familiarity

тәклифсизчә, тәклифсизчәсинә : *adv* unceremoniously, with undue familiarity,

тәклүлә : *n* single-barreled gun

тәкмә'налы : *a ling* monosemantic *having a single meaning*

тәкмә'налыг : *n ling* monosemy *condition of having only one semantic meaning*

тәкмил : *n* 1) completion, finishing, termination *n* 2) perfection *a* 3) all, whole, full *adv* 4) as a whole

тәкмилләшдирилмәк : *v* be perfected, perfect *o.s.*

тәкмилләшдирмә : *n* 1) advanced training, improvement, perfection 2) extention courses

тәкмилләшдирмәк : *v* improve, perfect

тәкмилләшмәк : *v* be improved/perfected, perfect *o.s.*

тәкнә : *n* tub, vat; bucket *of an excavating machine*

тәкнәгаjыран, тәкнәчи : *n* cooper

тәкнәчилик : *n* cooper's trade, occupation of cooper

тәкрар : *n* 1) repetition *adv* 2) again

тәкрарән : *adv* for the second time, once again, once more

тәкрари : *a* repeated, recurring

тәкрарлама : *n* repetition, reiteration

тәкрарламаг : *v* repeat, reiterate

тәкрарланмаг : *v-intr* be repeated, repeat

тәкрарлатмаг : *caus* of **тәкрарламаг**

тәкраролунмаз : *a* unique, inimitable

тәкрар-тәкрар : *adv* repeatedly, many times, over and over again

тәксәсли : *a* one-voice, solo

тәк-тәк : *adv* 1) singly, one by one, one at a time *adv* 2) by the piece, singly, by the unit 3) rarely, seldom; now and then, from time to time, occasionally *a* 4) rare, single, isolated, sporadic

тәк-тәнһа : *adv* 1) lonely, in a solitary state 2) quite alone, by o.s., deserted by everybody

тәктәсәррүфатчы : *n* individual peasant *one who refused to join a collective farm*

тәк-түк : *adv* see **тәк-тәк** 3)

тәкфир : *n relig* anathema, excommunication, accusation of heresy, damnation

тәкһечалы : *a gram* monosyllabic

тәкчә : *a* 1) sole, only *adv* 2) only, solely

тәлатүм : *n* 1) choppiness *of water* , atmospheric disturbance, storm *fig* 2) commotion, confusion, disarray, mess

тәлаш : *n* agitation, commotion, disarray, flurry; anxiety, alarm, haste

тәлашлы : *a* agitated

тәлашсыз : *a* imperturbable, unruffled, carefree, untroubled, unconcerned

тәлгин : *n* suggestion, instilling through suggestion, inspiring

тәлгинедичи : *a* imposing, impressive, inspiring

тәлә : *n* mousetrap, trap, snare, noose

тәлә јеми : *n* bait

тәләб : *n* 1) demand, request, requirement 2) insistance *econ* 3) demand *as in supply and demand leg* 4) action, suit, claim

тәләбат : *n* requirement, need, want, necessity

тәләбә : *n* 1) student, undergraduate *a* 2) student['s], student-related

тәләбәлик : *n coll* 1) the students, student body; student days *a* 2) student, pertaining to student[s]

тәләбкар : *a* 1) demanding, exacting, strict *n* 2) plaintiff, petitioner, claimant 3) creditor

тәләбкарлыг : *n* 1) exactingness, strictness 2) position of plaintiff/petitioner/claimant/ creditor

тәләбнамә : *n* demand, request *written*

тәләгуран : *n* pettifogger *one who engages in chicanery*

тәләм-тәләсик, тәләм-тәһтили : *adv* hastily, in a hurry, in a slapdash manner

тәләсдирән : *a* driving/speeding/urging on

тәләсдирмә : *n* driving/speeding/urging on

тәләсдирмәк : *v-tr* hurry, drive on, urge on

тәләсдиртмәк : *caus* of **тәләсмәк**

тәләсә-тәләсә : *adv* hurriedly, hastily, in haste

тәләсик : *a* 1) urgent, pressing, express, emergency *adv* 2) hurriedly, hastily, in a hurry, urgently, headlong

тәләсиклик : *n* hurry, haste

тәләситмәк : *v* see **тәләсдирмәк**

тәләскән : *a* hasty, hurried, quick, prompt; efficient

тәләскәнлик : *n* haste, hurry, quickness, promptness; efficiency

тәләсмә : *v n* fr. **тәләсмәк**

тәләсмәдән : *adv* unhurriedly, without haste/hurry, slowly, calmly

тәләсмәк : *v-intr* hasten, hurry, make haste, be in a hurry

тәләф : *v-cmp* **тәләф еләмәк (етмәк)** : destroy, do away (with), ruin, waste, squander

тәләфат : *n* loss, casualties, losses *in war*

тәләффүз : *n* pronunciation, accent, enunciation, articulation, diction

тә'лигә : *n* memorandum, letter, official paper, document *business document or paper sent by one organization or official to another*

тә'лим : *n* 1) teaching, instruction 2) training *animals*, schooling

тә'лимат : *n* 1) instructions, directions *a* 2) instructional

тә'лиматчы : *n* instructor

тәлис : *n* tarpaulin, canvas

тә'лиф : *n* work *of literature*

тәлл : *n* barrow, tumulus, embankment

тәлтиф : *n* rewarding, decorating

тәлх : *a* bitter

тәлхәк : *n* fool, jester, clown

тәмајүл : *n* 1) tendency, inclination 2) deviation *in political views* 3) branch of specialization

тәмајүлчү : *n hist* deviationist *Communist Party member in disagreement with the party line in the early 30's in the Soviet Union*

тәмас : *n* 1) touch 2) contacts, relations, intercourse

тәмәл : *n* foundation, base, basis

тәмәлчилик : *n polit* fundamentalism

тәмәнә : *n* see **гајыг**

тәмәнна : *n* 1) desire, wish, request 2) self-interested assistance

тәмәннасыз : *a* 1) unselfish *adv* 2) unselfishly, gratis, free of charge

тәмәссүк : *n* promissory note

тәмиз : *a* 1) clean, pure, neat, tidy 2) unsullied, unblemished, stainless; irreproachable, faultless; platonic *adv* 3) cleanly, purely, neatly

тәмизкар : *a* clean, neat, tidy

тәмизкарлыг : *n* cleanliness, neatness, tidiness

тәмизкарчасына : *adv* cleanly, tidily, neatly

тәмизләјичи : *n* 1) cleaner, cleanser, purifier *a* 2) cleansing, purifying

тәмизләмә : *n* cleaning, cleansing, purifying, refining, refinement, purification,

тәмизләмәк : *v* clean, cleanse, purify, refine, clean out, clean up

тәмизләнмәк : *v* be cleaned, be cleansed, be purified, be refined

тәмизлик : *n* cleanness, cleanliness, neatness, tidiness

тәмизүрәкли : *a* candid, sincere, frank, open-hearted, simple-hearted, artless

тәмизчә : *adv* very cleanly, spotlessly clean

тә'мим : *n* see **тә'мимнамә**

тә'мими : *a* circular

тә'мимнамә : *n* circular, instruction *official*

тә'мин : *n* 1) ensuring, securing, guaranteeing 2) security, guarantee

тә'минат : *n* 1) guarantee 2) security, social security

тә'мир : *n* 1) repair; repairing, mending, fixing *a* 2) repair

тәмјиз : *n leg* 1) cassation; appeal *a* 2) cassation-/appeal-related

тәмкин : *n* reserve, reticence, gravity, seriousness

тәмкинлә : *adv* restrainedly, reservedly, seriously, decorously gravely

тәмкинли : *a* restrained, reserved, pompous, staid, serious, grave

тәмр : **тәмр веркиси** : stamp duty

тәмрин : *n* exercise; rehearsal

тәмсил : *n* 1) assimilation, assimilating, likening 2) representation, representing 3) fable

тәмтәраг : *n* luxury, splendor, magnificence, pomp

тәмтәраглы : *a* luxurious, sumptuous, luxuriant, splendid, magnificent, pompous 2) flowery, high-flown, bombastic, florid *of speech*

тәмтәраглылыг : *n* 1) splendor, magnificence, pomposity 2) floridness, grandiloquence, magniloquence *of speech*

тән : *a* 1) equal, identical, the same *as adv* 2) equally

тәнасүб : *n* 1) proportionality, symmetry 2) proportion

тәнасүблү : *a* 1) proportionate, proportional 2) well-proportioned

тәнасүбсүз : *a* disproportionate, out of proportion

тәнасүбсүзлүк : *n* misproportion, lack of symmetry

тәнасүл : **тәнасүл аләти** : *n* penis

тәнбәки : *n* 1) pipe tobacco, makhorka *an inferior kind of tobacco a* 2) tobacco, makhorka-like

тәнбәл : *n* lazy person, loafer, idler, slacker

тәнбәлләнмәк : *v* loaf, idle, be lazy, be indolent

тәнбәлләшмәк : *v* 1) become/grow lazy 2) stagnate

тәнбәллик : *n* laziness, idleness

тәнбиһ : *n* punishment, penalty

тәнбиhсиз : *a* 1) unpunished *adv* 2) with impunity

тәнбиhсизлик : *n* impunity

тәнбөлән : *n* *geom* bisector

тәнгид : *n* criticism; critique

тәнгиди : *a* 1) critical *adv* 2) critically

тәнгидчи : *n* critic

тәнгидчилик : *n* profession/occupation of critic

тәнгит : *n* punctuation

тәндир : *n* deep oven for baking bread lavaş and chörak *Caucasian breads*

тәндүрүст : *a* healthy, strong, well-proportioned

тә'нә : *n* reproach, rebuke, reproof

тәнәззөh : *n* excursion, tour, trip, outing

тәнәззөhчү : *n* tourist, sightseer, excursionist

тәнәззүл : *n* decline, decay, collapse, regression, retrogression, fall, drop, degradation

тәнәк : *n* 1) grapevine 2) grape leaf

тәнәкгурду : *n* *zool* kind of worm *destructive to grapevines*

тәнәкгушу : *n* zool yellowhammer *Emberiza citrinella*, also called yellow-bunting *bird*

тәнәкә : *n* 1) tin *a* 2) tin

тәнәкәчи : *n* tinsmith

тәнәкәчилик : *n* occupation/profession of tinsmith

тәнәклик : *n* willow bush; place overgrown with vines

тәнәффүс : *n* 1) respiration, breathing, breath *n* 2) *recess in school* , intermission *at the theater* 3) rest, relaxation, break, respite 4) *a* respiratory

тәнзим : *n* regulation, adjustment, adjusting

тәнзиф : *n* gauze, cheesecloth

тәнк : *v-cmp* **тәнкә кәлмәк** : 1) eat one's heart out, consume/exhaust oneself *with* 2) **тәнкә кәтирмәк** exhaust, torment, vex, exasperate, bother, pester, bore

тәнкишдирмә : *n* irritation

тәнкишдирмәк : *v* 1) be too tight *of clothing* 2) anger, make angry, irritate, exasperate

тәнклик : *n* 1) tightness 2) burden, difficulty, hardships *in life*

тәнкнәфәс : *n* 1) gasping, breathing with difficulty 2) an asthmatic

тәнкнәфәслик : *n* 1) breathlessness, shortness of breath, asphyxia, suffocation *med* 2) asthma

тәнләшдирмәк : *v-tr* 1) compare equally 2) even, level, make level, smooth

тәнләшмәк : *v-intr* 1) be equal *to* 2) be made even, be leveled, be made level,

тәнлик : *n* *math* equation

тәнтәнә : *n* 1) festivity, celebration, solemnity 2) splendor, magnificence, pomp

тәнтәнәли : *a* 1) festive, holiday 2) solemn, splendid, magnificent

тәнтимәк : *v-intr* hasten

тәнумәнд : *a* stately, portly, imposing, dignified, impressive

тәнумәндлик : *n* 1) stateliness, portliness 2) imposing/dignified/impressive appearance/presence

тәнхаh : *n* wealth, riches, fortune

тәнhа : *a* solitary, lonely

тәнhалыг : *n* solitude, seclusion, loneliness

тәпә : *n* 1) crown, top of the head 2) hill, hillock, knoll, mound 3) height, top, summit, apex, crest, peak

тәпәјән : *a* 1) inclined to kick *n* 2) kicker

тәпәјәохшар : *a* shaped like/in the form of a hill or knoll

тәпәл : *a* with a star/blaze on the face *of livestock*

тәпәләшдирмәк : *v* gobble up, guzzle, wolf down, eat voraciously

тәпәли : *a* hilly

тәпәлик : *n* hilly terrain, hilly country, hilly locale

тәпәр : *n* energy

тәпәрли : *a* energetic

тәпәрлилик : *n* honest/courageous/energetic nature

тәпәрсиз : *a* inert, inactive, sluggish; lacking honesty, courage and energy

тәпәчик : *n* hillock

тәпик : *n* kick

тәпикатан : *a* 1) inclined to kick *n* 2) kicker

тәпикләмә : *n* kick

тәпикләмәк : *v* kick

тәпикләшмәк : *v-intr* kick, kick one another

тәпикчил : *a* see **тәпикатан**

тәпилмәк : *v-intr* be thrust/shoved *in*, be squeezed *in*, be crammed *in*, squeeze oneself *in/into*

тәпимәк : *v-intr* get dry, dry up

тәпинмәк : *v* threaten, berate *s.o.*

тәпитмә : *n* poultice of hot flour-paste

тәпишдирмәк : *v* guzzle, gobble, eat voraciously, devour, eat with gusto

тәпмә : *n* 1) fulling *of felt* 2) recoil *of a firearm*

тәпмәк : *v-tr* 1) stick, thrust, stick *in* , shove *in/into*, push *in/into* 2) full *felt* 3) kick, recoil *of a fire arm* 4) dig the ground with a spade

тәптәзә : *a* perfectly new, brand new, very fresh

тәр : *n* 1) sweat *a* 2) fresh, young

тәравәт : *n* freshness

тәравәтләндирмәк : *v-tr* refresh, freshen

тәравәтли : *a* fresh

тәранә : *n* melody, tune

тәрбијә : *n* education, training, discipline, upbringing; civility

тәрбијәләндирилмәк : *v* be educated, trained, brought up, disciplined

тәрбијәләндирмәк : *v* educate, bring up, rear, discipline

тәрбијәләнмәк : *v* become educated, be brought up, become disciplined

тәрбијәли : *a* well brought up, well-bred, refined, courteous, polite, decent, respectable, self-restrained, proper, correct

тәрбијәлилик : *n* breeding, good breeding, refinement, good manners

тәрбијәсиз : *a* 1) ill-bred, ill-mannered, discourteous, impolite *n* 2) hooligan, boor

тәрбијәсизлик : *n* ill breeding, bad manners, impoliteness, discourtesy, rudeness

тәрбијәчи : *n* educator

тәрбијәчилик : *n* work or profession of educator

тәрә : *n* 1) edible wild grasses 2) tara *bladed tool used by leather-workers in processing the inner side of hides*

тәрәвәз : *n* vegetable[s], greens

тәрәвәзсатан, тәрәвәзчи : *n* produce-merchant, greengrocer, vegetable vendor

тәрәгги : *n* progress, prosperity

тәрәггипәрвәр : *n* 1) a progressive, advocate of progress *a* 2) progressive, progress-minded, forward-looking

тәрәддүд : *n* 1) hesitation, vacillation, indecision 2) links, connections

тәрәддүдсүз : *a* 1) unhesitating, unshakable, steadfast *adv* 2) unhesitatingly, unshakably, steadfastly

тәрәддүдсүзлүк : *n* resoluteness, steadfastness, unshakability

тәрәзи : *n* scales, balance

тәрәзипулу : *n* weighage *duty or toll for weighing merchandise*

тәрәзичи : *n* weigher, weighman

тәрәк : *n* tarak, a confection similar to halvah made of flour and sugar cooked in butter

тәрәкәмә : *n* Tarakama 1) nomadic Azerbaijani ethnic group of cattle-herders formerly living in the steppes of western Azerbaijan and the adjacent areas of Armenia and Georgia 2) name of an Azerbaijani dance

тәрәлли : *n* taralli *variety of peach*

тәрәннүм : quiet and beautiful singing; dolcissimo singing

тәрәссүд : **тәрәссүд борусу** : 1) telescope 2) periscope

тәрәф : *n* side, direction

тәрәфдар : *n* patron, supporter, adherent, advocate, follower

тәрәфдарлыг : *n* weakness *for*, predilection *for* , partiality or bias *toward* adherence, attachment; intercession

тәрәфдарчасына : *adv* with partiality, with prejudice

тәрәфи-мүгабил : *n* the opposition, the opposite/opposing party

тәрәфкеш, тәрәфкир, тәрәфсахлајан : *n* see **тәрәфдар**

тәрәчә : *n* drying shelf *for drying cotton-bolls, etc.*

тәрз : *n* way, method, mode, manner, form, type, style

тәрзи-ифадә : *n* manner of expression, manner of expressing o.s.

тәрзи-һәрәкәт : *n* manner, mode of action

тәригәт : *n* *relig* sect

тәригәтчи : *n* *relig* member/adherent of a sect

тәригәтчилик : *n* *relig* sectarianism

тә'риф : *n* 1) definition, description, explanation 2) praise, approval

тә'рифә : *n* tariff

тә'рифәкәлмәз : *a* indescribable

тә'рифәлајиг : *a* praiseworthy

тә'рифләмә : *a* praise, praising, eulogy, glorifying, glorification

тә'рифләмәк : *v* praise, eulogize, glorify

тә'рифли : *a* much-vaunted, celebrated

тә'рифнамә : *n* certificate of merit, testimonial of good conduct and progress *in school*

тәрк : *n* 1) leaving, abandoning, abandonment, forsaking, deserting 2) horse's croup/crupper 3) bottom, depth

тәрки-адәт : *n* breaking/getting out of a habit; breaking/abandoning a tradition

тәркиб : *n* 1) composition, content; components, ingredients; 2) staff *of an organization etc* 3) collocation 4) parts of mugam musical works

тәркиб етмәк : *v* form, compose

тәрки-вәтән : *n* expatriate

тәрки-дүнја : n 1) ascetic, anchorite, hermit, recluse a 2) anchoritic, hermitical, solitary, secluded

тәрки-дүнјалыг : *n* asceticism, hermit's life, recluse's life, wandering life

тәркләшмәк : *v* ride double on one horse

тәрксилаһ : *n* disarmament, disarming

тәркитдирмәк : *v-tr* break *s.o.* of the habit of

тәркитмә : *n* breaking a habit

тәркитмәк : *v-intr* get out of the habit *of* , break *o.s. of* the habit *of*

тәрлан : *n* 1) hobby *Falco subbuteo* a small Old World falcon 2) Tarlan *masculine first name*

тәрләдичи : *a med* 1) sudorific, diaphoretic, inducing perspiration *ext* 2) involving/relating to sweatshop conditions

тәрләмә : *n* sweating, perspiration

тәрләмәк : v 1) sweat, perspire *ext* 2) loosen o.'s purse-strings, fork out, shell out, cough up money, pay up *unwillingly or by force*

тәрләтмәк : *caus* of **тәрләмәк**

тәрли, тәрли-тәрли : *a* sweaty, damp with perspiration, bathed in sweat

тәрпәниш : *n* movement, motion, animation

тәрпәнмәз : *a* 1) motionless, immovable, stationary *adv* 2) motionless[ly]

тәрпәнмәзлик : *n* immobility

тәрпәнмәк : *v-intr* 1) move, oscillate, vascillate; wave to and fro 2) stir, move, toss and turn, sway, wave, flutter, flicker

тәрпәтмә : *vn* fr. **тәрпәтмәк**

тәрпәтмәк : *v-tr* move, stir, turn, shift, shake, rock, swing

тәрпәшдирмәк : *v-tr* put in motion, shake

тәрпәшмәк : *v* see **тәрпәнмәк**

тәрс : *a* obstinate, stubborn, persistent, willful, intractable, unyielding, unmanageable

тәрс дамары тутмаг : *v* 1) jib, be restive *of horses* 2) be obstinate/ pig-headed

тәрсанә : *n* shipyard, dockyard

тәрсим : *n* drawing, outlining, tracing

тәрсими : *a* graphic, descriptive

тәрсинә : *adv* 1) on the contrary, opposite, counter to; inside out, wrong side out, the opposite way, 2) topsy-turvy, upside-down

тәрсләшдирмәк : *caus* of **тәрсләшмәк**

тәрсләшмәк : *v* be obstinate, be pigheaded

тәрслик : *n* obstinacy, stubbornness, persistence, pertinacity

тәрс-тәрс : *adv* 1) with hostility *only in compounds* 2) *v-cmp* **тәрс-тәрс бахмаг** look at with hostility/animosity/enmity, look at in an unfriendly manner

тәртәг : *n chem* lead oxide

тәртәмиз : *adv* perfectly clean, spotlessly clean

тәртиб : *n* 1) arrangement, order, manner; organization 2) compiling, drawing up, putting into final/official form 3) staff; group 3) composition, composing, type-setting

тәртибат : *n* drawing up, putting in final/official form

тәртибли : *a* 1) well organized, in good order 2) comfortable, well equipped, with good amenities 3) neat

тәртибсиз : *a* disorderly, unsystematic, unmethodical, disorganized, unorganized, untidy

тәртибсизлик : *n* disorderliness, lack of organization, lack of system/method

тәрхис : *n* demobilization

тәрхун : *n bot* tarragon Artemesia dracunculus

тәрчүман : *n obs* 1) interpreter, translator *in former times in Consulates in the Middle East fig* 2) echo, reflection, conductor

тәрчүмеји-һал : *n* biography

тәрчүмә : *n* translation *into another language*

тәрчүмәчи : *n* interpreter, translator

тәрчүмәчилик : *n* occupation or profession of interpreter/translator

тәс : *n* manure, dung *of domestic cattle*

тәсадүф : *n* occasion, chance, coincidence, meeting

тәсадүфән : *adv* accidentally, by accident, by chance

тәсадүфи : *a* 1) accidental, chance; casual 2) episodic[al], incidental

тәсбит : *n* reaffirmation; securing

тәсбиһ : *n relig* Muslim rosary

тәсвиб : *n* approval

тәсвибедичи : *a* approving, favorable

тәсвијә : *n* liquidation, abolition, elimination

тәсвијәчи : *n polit hist* liquidator

тәсвијәчилик : *n polit hist* liquidationism

тәсвир : *n* 1) description 2) representation, image, picture

тәсвири : *a* descriptive, graphic

тәсдиг : *n* affirmation, confirmation, corroboration, assertion, attestation, certification, sanction, approbation

тәсдигедичи : *a* affirmative

тәсдигләмәк : *v* 1) affirm, confirm, corroborate, certify, witness, attest; testify, assent 2) ratify 3) sanction

тәсдигнамә : *n* certification, attestation

тәсәввүр : *n* idea, imagination

тәсәввүф : *n* mysticism, theosophy

тәсәддүг : *n* alms, donation

тәсәк : *n* see **арагчын**

тәсәлли : *n* comfort, consolation

тәсәлливеричи : *n* 1) comforter, consoler *a* 2) comforting, consoling, consolatory

тәсәллисиз : *a* 1) inconsolable *adv* 2) inconsolably

тәсәллисизлик : *n* inconsolability

тәсәррүфат : *n* 1) economy, farm, household, homestead *a* 2) economic[al]; household

тәсәррүфатсызлыг : *n* thriftlessness, mismanagement; squandering

тәсәррүфатчы : *n* manager

тә'сир : *n* influence, effect, impression

тә'сирли : *a* effective, influential, impressive, touching, affective

тә'сирлик : *a gram* **тә'сирлик һал** : accusative case

тә'сирлилик : *n* 1) influence, state/quality/nature of being influential 2) impressionability

тә'сирсиз : *a* ineffective, ineffectual, having no influence

тә'сирсизлик : *n* inertia, inertness, lack of influence

тә'сис : *n* establishment, creation

тә'сиседән : *n* founder

тәскәрә : *n* see **табут**

тәскин : calming, quieting, soothing, comforting, consoling

тәскинлик : *n* calm, quiet, comfort, consolation

тәскинликверичи : *a* calming, quieting, soothing, comfort-ing, consoling, consolatory

тәслим : *n* 1) delivery, handing in, transfer handing over 2) surrender, capitulation

тәсниф : *n* 1) classification 2) compiling, compilation, writing *a book* 3) tasnif rhythmic folk melody

тәснифат : see **тәсниф** 1), 2)

тәснифатчы : *n* classifier

тәсриф : *n gram* conjugation

тәсһиһ : *n* correcting, correction, proofreading

тәтбиг : *n* use, application

тәтбиги : *a* applied

тәтик : *n* trigger *of a weapon*

тә'тил : *n* 1) strike 2) holidays, vacation

тә'тилпозан : *n* strikebreaker, scab

тә'тилчи : *n* striker

тәфавүт : *n* distinction, difference

тәфавүт гојмаг : *v* differentiate *between*

тәфәккүр : *n* thinking, thought

тәфәррүат : *n* details, trifles

тәфәррүатлы : *a* detailed

тәфригә : *n* dissidence, split

тәфригәчи : *n* dissenter, dissident

тәфсилат : *n* details

тәфсилатла : *adv* in detail, thoroughly

тәфсилатлы : *a* detailed, thorough

тәфсир : *n* explanation, explaining, interpretation, interpreting, commentary

тәфсирчи : *n* commentator *person who interprets, explains*

тәфтиш : *n* revision, inventory, inspection, control, examination

тәфтишчилик : *n* revisionism

тәхәллүс : *n* pseudonym

тә'хир : *n* postponement, deferment, adjournment, delay

тәхирә дүшмәк : *v* be delayed, postponed

тә'хирәсалынмаз : *a* pressing, urgent

тә'хирсиз : *adv* immediately, urgently, without delay

тәхмин : *n* 1) supposition, assumption, surmise, conjecture 2) state of affairs, juncture

тәхминән : *adv* approximately, roughly, about, almost

тәхмини : *a* approximate

тәхрибат : *n* 1) destruction, demolition; subversion, sabotage *a* 2) destructive, subversive

тәхрибатчы : *n* 1) saboteur, subversive *person* 2) diversionary, subversive, sabotage-related

тәхсисат : *n* loan, grant, credit; allowance, allotment; designated fund

тәхт : *n* see **тахт**

тәхти-рәван : *n* see **кәчавә**

тәһ : *n* see **диб** 1)

тәһвил : *n* delivery, handing over; capitulation

тәһвилверән, тәһвилчи : *n* delivery-person

тәһгиг : *n* 1) check, check-up, verification, adjustment *leg* 2) investigation, inquiry, inquest

тәһгигат : *n* 1) investigation, examination 2) interrogation, questioning

тәһгигатчы : *n* investigator, interrogator

тәһгир : *n* insult, offense, injury, wrong, abasement, humiliation

тәһгирамиз : *a* insulting, contemptuous, scornful, disdainful

тәһгиредичи, тәһгирли : *a* insulting, humiliating, degrading

тәһдид : *n* threat

тәһәр : *n* 1) way, method, procedure 2) opportunity, possibility, chance

тәһәрсиз : *a* 1) disproportionate, deformed 2) impossible

тәһким : *n* fastening, attachment; also *fig*

тәһкимли : *a* serf['s]; serf-owner['s]

тәһкимчи : *n hist* 1) serf, bond-servant 2) serf-owner, land-owner, landlord

тәһкимчилик : *n hist* serfdom, serf-ownership

тәһлил : *n* analysis

тәһлили : *a math* analytical

тәһлүкә : *n* danger, peril, threat, risk

тәһлүкәли : *a* dangerous, threatening, menacing, disastrous, unsafe, risky

тәһлүкәлилик : *n* danger, risk

тәһлүкәсиз : *a* safe, secure, protected

тәһлүкәсизлик : *n* safety, security

тәһрик : *n* encouragement, instigation, incitation, inspiration

тәһрикедичи : *a* encouraging, inciting, instigating, egging-on

тәһрикедичилик : *n* instigation, incitement

тәһрикчи : *n* instigator, inciter

тәһрири : *a* 1) written, writing *adv* 2) in writing, in written form

тәһриф : *n* distortion, perversion

тәһсил : *n* 1) education, studies; teaching, instruction, training *a* 2) educational, training, school, academic

тәһсилли : *a* educated

тәһсилсиз : *a* uneducated, unschooled

тәһсилсизлик : *n* lack of education

тәһтәлһесаб : *n* 1) accountable sum, sum paid out on account *a* 2) accountable, on account

тәчавүз : *n* aggression, violence, coercion, encroachment *upon* , infringement *upon*

тәчавүз еләмәк : *v* encroach

тәчавүзкар : *n* aggressor, violator

тәчавүзкарлыг : *n* 1) aggression, violence, coercion 2) violation

тәчәлли : *n* emanation, outflow

тәчәссүм : *n* embodiment, incarnation, personification

тә'чил : *n* acceleration, speeding up

тә'чили : *a* 1) fast, urgent, emergency, pressing *adv* 2) urgently, in a hurry

тәчрид : *n* 1) isolating, isolation 2) abstraction

тәчрүбә : *n* 1) experience, experiment, test, trial 2) practice, practical work

тәчрүбәләнмәк : *v* acquire experience, become experienced

тәчрүбәли : *a* experienced, sophisticated

тәчрүбәлилик : *n* experience, sophistication

тәчрүбәсиз : *a* inexperienced, unsophisticated

тәчрүбәсизлик : *n* inexperience, lack of sophistication

тәчрүбәчи : *n* probationer, student-intern *student engaged in practical work*

тәчрүби : *a* 1) practical, experimental 2) empirical, based on experience

тәчһиз : *n* supply, supplying, equipping, equipment, outfit, outfitting

тәчһизат : *n* equipment, equipping, supply, supplying

тәшвиг : *n* encouragement, instigation, incitement

тәшвигат : *n* 1) agitation *e.g. creation of public interest,* propaganda *a* 2) agitation/propaganda-related

тәшвигатчы : *n* propagandist, agitator *e.g. one engaged in stirring up of public interest*

тәшвиш : *n* trouble, uneasiness, alarm, anxiety; agitation, commotion

тәшвишлә : *adv* in an anxiously, uneasily, apprehensively

тәшәббүс : *n* initiative, undertaking, endeavor, beginning

тәшәббүскар : *a* 1) enterprising *n* 2) businessman, enterpreneur

тәшәббүскарлыг : *n* enterprise, enterpreneurial spirit

тәшәббүсчү : *n* initiator, organizer, trailblazer, pioneer, leader

тәшәккүл : *n* formation; organization

тәшәккүр : *n* 1) gratitude, thanks, thankfulness *a* 2) thanksgiving, expressing thanks

тәшәккүрлә : *adv* thankfully, gratefully

тәшәр : *n* see **давакар**

тәшәххүс : *n* pride, haughtiness, arrogance, swagger, conceit

тәшәххүслә : *adv* proudly, haughtily, arrogantly, pompously, grandly

тәшәххүсләнмәк : *v* be proud, take pride in, pride oneself on, put on airs, act haughtily/arrogantly, swagger, act conceited, turn up o.'s nose

тәшәххүслү : *a* proud, haughty, arrogant, pompous, grand, conceited

тәшкил : *n* formation, forming, organizing

тәшкил олунмаг : *v* become organized, formed

тәшкилат : *n* 1) organization *a* 2) organizational, organizing

тәшкилатчы : *n* organizer

тәшкилатчылыг : *n* organizing abilities

тәшнә : *a* thirsting/craving *for*

тәшриф : *n* advent, coming, arrival *of eminent personages*

тәшриф бујурмаг : *v* arrive *of the arrival of an important personage/ "big-wig"*

тәшрифат : *n* ceremony, etiquette

тәшрифатсыз : *adv* unceremoniously, with undue familiarity

тәшрифатсызлыг : *n* undue familiarity

тәшт : *n* copper basin

тәшхис : *n* diagnosis

тибб : *n* 1) medicine *a* 2) medical

тибби : *a* medical

тијан : *n* cast-iron caldron, large cast-iron pot

тијанча : *n dim* small cast-iron pot

тијә : *n* blade

тикан : *n* thorn, prickle, spike, burr; needle *of plants*

тиканлы : *a* thorny, prickly, needle-shaped, acicular

тиканлыг : *n* place overgrown with thorns/prickles

тикдирмәк, тикдиртмәк : *caus* of **тикмәк**

тикә : *n* bit, small piece, slice, lump, scrap

тикә-тикә : *adv* in bits, in small pieces

тикили : *n* 1) building, structure *a* 2) sewn, embroidered

тикилиш : *n* 1) cut, style, fashion, form, shape 2) sewing, embroidery

тикилмәк : *v* 1) be built, be erected, be constructed 2) be sewn, be embroidered

тикинти : *n* construction, building, structure, erection

тикичи : *n* 1) builder 2) one who sews/embroiders

тикичи говлуг : *n* folder

тикиш : *n* 1) sewing 2) seam *a* 3) sewing

тикишсиз : *a* seamless

тикмә : *n* 1) building, constructing, construction, erection 2) sewing, embroidery

тикмәк : *v* 1) build, construct, erect 2) sew, embroider

тил : *n math* edge *line of intersection of two planes*

тилиф : *n* oil cake, cotton cake, squeezings

тилишкә : *n* splinter

тилов : *n* fishing rod

тилсим : *n* talisman, amulet, charm

тилсимләнмиш, тилсимли : *a* bewitched, charmed

тимик : *n* acute angle; sharp corner, sharp protuberance

тимикли : *a* angular, pointed

тимиклилик : *n* angularity

тимов : *n* head cold

тимсал : *n* example

тимсаһ : *n* 1) crocodile *a* 2) crocodile

тин : *n* corner *of a street/house*

тинга : *n zool* tench *Tinca tinca, a freshwater cyprinoid fish*

тинк, тинки : *n* seedling, sapling

тип : *n Ru* type, sort

тираж : *n Ru* circulation *of a newspaper or periodical*

типи : *n* see **човғун**

типик : *a* typical, characteristic

тир : *n* 1) log, beam 2) shooting range 3) arrow

тир-тап узанмаг : *v* lie with one's arms and legs outstretched

тир-тир әсмәк : *v* tremble convulsively

тирә : *n* 1) faction, camp, bloc 2) tribe, race *geog* 3) mountain ridge 3) earthen embankment in front of the moat of a fortress

тирә-тирә : *v-cmp* **тирә-тирә олмаг** : split up into separate groups or blocs

тирјәк : *n* opium

тирјәки : *n* opium-smoker

тирјәкхана : *n* opium den

тирләнмәк : *v* lie stretched out at one's full length

тирли : *a* made of logs

тирмә : *n* tirma fine hand-loomed woolen cloth

тир-тап : *v-cmp* **тир-тап узанмаг** : lie at full length, to lie stretched out

тир-тир : *v-cmp* **тир-тир әсмәк** : shake/quiver greatly

титан : *n chem* titanium

титә : *n med* cataract, leucoma

титрәгуш : *a* 1) sensitive to cold *n* freezie-cat *person sensitive to cold*

титрәјиш : *n* trembling, shiver, quiver

титрәк : *a* trembling, quivering, shivering

титрәмә : *n* trembling, shivering, shaking, shudder, tremble, shiver, quiver, vibration

титрәмәк : *v* tremble, quiver, shiver, shake , vibrate

титрәтмә, титрәтмә-гыздырма : *n* fever, malaria

титрәтмәк : *v-intr* be feverish, have a fever, shake

титрәшмәк : *v* tremble, quiver, shiver, shake *many people together*

тифил : *n* child *rare fr. Persian*

тифтик : *n* nap *of cloth*

тифтикли : *adv* fluffy

тичарәт : *n* 1) trade, commerce *a* 2) commercial, trade, trading

тичарәтчи : *n* merchant, businessman

тыггылдатма : *n* knock, knocking, tap, tapping, tick, ticking

тыггылдатмаг : *v* knock, tap

тыггылты : *n* knock, tap

тығ : *n* huge pile

тығланмаг : *v* be gathered/collected in a huge pile

тын-тын : *a* nasal

тын-тынлыг : *n* nasality, nasal intonation, twang

тынчыхмаг : *v* be stifled/suffocated *by the heat*

тыппылдамаг : *v* flutter, palpitate, beat *of heart/pulse*, knock gently, tap

тыппылдатмаг : *caus* of **тыппылдамаг**

тыппылты : *n* fluttering, palpitation, beating of *heart/pulse*, gentle knock, tap

тырыг : *n* diarrhea

тырылдамаг : *v* crack

тырылдатмаг : *v* 1) tap with o.'s shoe in walking 2) snort

тырылты : *n* crackle, crackling, rattle, rattling

тырынты : *n* see **диринкә**

тыртыл : *n zool* 1) caterpillar *tech* 2) caterpillar track

тыртыллы : *a zool* 1) caterpillar 2) caterpillar/crawler band/tracked, full-tracked

тысбаға : *n* 1) turtle, tortoise *a* 2) turtle, tortoise

тысылдамаг : *v* breathe heavily and noisily through the nose

тых : *n* fish bones

тыхамаг : *v* push *in/into* , cram/stuff *in/into,* shove/thrust *in*, stop/cork up

тыханмаг : *v* be squeezed, be herded, crowd, be pushed/shoved *in* , be crammed/ stuffed *in/into* , be stopped up, be corked

тыхач : *n* cork, stopper, plug

тыхачламаг : *v* stop/cork up

тыхашдырмаг : *v* push/shove *in*, shove *under*, cram *in/into*, stuff *with*, pack full *with*

тыхылы-тәпили : *a* packed, chock-full

тыхылмаг : *v* squeeze oneself *in/into*, squeeze *in/into*, be shoved i*n/into*

тыхышдырмаг : *v* 1) shove/push *in* 2) devour, eat with gusto, eat one's fill

тыхлы : *a* bony *of fish*

тыхмаг : *v* guzzle, gobble, gobble *up* , gorge oneself *with*

тыхнашдырмаг : *v* push/cram/stuff *in/into*

тов : *n* twist, twisting, winding *thread/yarn*

товлама : *v n* 1) fr. **товламаг** *n* 2) twisting/spinning *yarn*

товламаг : *v* 1) deceive, cheat, trick, swindle, entice *with*, lure 2) wave, swing, shake

товланмаг : *v* be deceived, be enticed, be lured, be attracted/tempted *by*

товуз : *n zool* peacock

тогга : *n* 1) belt 2) buckle, clasp

тоггуш : *n* cry/shout used to stop a donkey

тоггушдурмаг : *caus* of **тоггушмаг**

тоггушма : *n* 1) clash, conflict, encounter, skirmish 2) collision, crash

тоггушмаг : *v* 1) run/dash *against/into s.o.* 2) collide *with s.o.*, bump *into s.o.*

тоғал : *n* cinder[s],ashes smell of burning

тоғлу : *n* young ram, lamb *just weaned; 10 months-old*

тоз : *n* dust; powder

тозанаг : *n* wind-borne dust ; great amount of dust

тозвары : *a* powdery, powder-like, pulvurulent

тозкөтүрән : *a* holding/containing much dust

тозламаг, тозландырмаг : *v* raise dust, fill the air with dust, cover with dust

тозланма : *n bot* pollination

тозланмаг : *v* 1) become dusty, be covered with dust *bot* 2) be pollinated

тозлу : *a* dusty

тозлуг : *n bot* anther

тозсоран : *n* vacuum cleaner *lit. dust-sucker*

тоз-торпаг : *n* thick/dense dust

тозчуг : *n bot* pollen

toj : *n* 1) wedding *a* 2) wedding, nuptial

тојгушу : *n zool* bustard *Otis tarda*

тојуг : *n* 1) hen, chicken *a* 2) poultry, hen's, chicken

тојугчичәји : *n med* see **сучичәји**

тојугчу : *n* poultry breeder

тојугчулуг : *n* poultry-breeding

толазламаг : *v* fling, hurl, toss, throw out, throw with all o.'s might

томағал : *n* see **кәкил**

томбаз : *n* pontoon

томбул : *a* see **тотуг**

томпал : *n* cocoon waste

тон : *n* 1) ton 2) tone

тонгал : *n* bonfire

топ : *n* 1) ball 2) gun, cannon 3) whole piece *of material/cloth* 4) ream *of paper* 5) rook, castle *chess*

топа : *n* heap, pile, lump, clod

топабасма : *n* cannonade

топал : *a* 1) lame *n* 1) lame man; cripple

топаламаг : *v* pile up, stock up

топалдыгач : *n* lapta *Russian ball game*

топаллыг : *n* lameness, limping

топа-топа : *adv* in small groups *people*

топатутма : *n* see **топабасма**

топдан : *adv* wholesale

топдансатыш : *n* wholesale trade

топданчы : *n* wholesaler

топлајан : *n* collector

топлајычы : *n* 1) collector *a* 2) collective

топлама : *v n* 1) fr. **топламаг** *n* math 2) addition *a* 3) assembled

топламаг : *v-tr* 1) assemble, collect, gather, accumulate, lay up, store up, in one place concentrate, pile or heap; recruit *math* 2) add

топланан : *n math* addend, item

топланыш : *n* 1) collection, assemblage, gathering, meeting, assembly, rally 2) harvesting

топланма : *n* assemblage, gathering

топланмаг : *v-intr* gather, collect, accumulate, be piled/heaped/stacked, unite, rally, concentrate, be concentrated, come together

топлашма : *v n* 1) fr. **топлашмаг** 2) conglomeration

топлашмаг : *v-intr* gather/collect/assemble in one place, accumulate, pile up

топливо : *n Ru* fuel

топлу : *a* compact, closely grouped, dense, congested, assembled, collected

топлулуг : *n* compactness, density, congestion

топографија : *n* topography *an applied form of geodesy*

топографик : *a* topographic

топпуз : *n* mace, club. cudgel

топпуш : *n* chubby lad; tot

топсаггал : *a* bearded

топтоп : *n* top-top *children's ball game*

топ-топ : *adv* 1) in reams *of paper* 2) in whole pieces *of material. cloth, fabric*

топ-топхана : *n* artillery

топуг : *n* ankle

топугвуран : *n* horse inclined to/apt to kick

топурча, топуш : *n* see **топпуш**

топ-чомаг : *n* bowling *game*

топчу : *n* 1) artilleryman 2) bombardier

топчулуг : *n* 1) the art or specialty of artillery 2) service of an artilleryman

тор : *n* 1) net, netting, snare *a* 2) dull, lusterless, mat

торағај : *n zool* lark

торалма : *n* darkening

торалмаг : *v* grow cloudy/foggy; fall *of dusk or twilight*

торалтмаг : *v-tr* cloud, dim fog, darken, black out

торан : *n* twilight, dusk, semidarkness

торанлашмаг : *v* get dark, fall *of twilight*

торба : *n* bag, pouch

ториум : *n chem* thorium *radioactive metal*

торлу : *a* netted, reticulated

тормоз : *n* 1) brake *a* 2) brake

тормозлама : *n* braking

тормозламаг : *v* brake, apply the brake

тормозланмаг : *pass* 1) be braked, be slowed down *v-intr* 2) brake, slow down

торначы : *n* turner, lathe operator

торначылыг : *n* 1) turning *the art or practice of turning wood or metal on a lathe* 2) lathe-operation *the occupation of a lathe operator*

торпаг : *n* 1) soil, ground, land, dirt *a* 2) soil, ground, land, dirt

торпагалты : *a* subsoil, underground, subterranean

торпагарысы : *n zool* bumblebee *fam. Bombidae*

торпагдашыјан : *n* dirt-hauler

торпагламаг : *v* cover with earth/dirt

торпаглы : *a* earthy

торпагсыз : *a* landless

торпагсызлыг : *n* lack of*arable* land

торпагсоран : *cmp* : **торпагсоран машын** hydraulic-dredge, suction-dredge

торпагшүнас : *n* soil scientist

торпагшүнаслыг : *n* soil science

торта : *n* sediment

тор-топ : *v-cmp* : **тор-топ олмаг** see **бүзүшмәк**

торф : *n* 1) peat *a* 2) peat

торфлуг : *n* peatbog

тосгун : *a* fat, obese, stout, corpulent, portly

тосгунлашмаг : *v* grow stout, put on weight/flesh, grow fat, become obese

тосгунлуг : *n* fatness, obesity, stoutness, corpulence

тотуг : *a* 1) chubby, plump *n* 2) chubby lad

тотуглуг : *n* plumpness, chubbiness, pudginess

тотуш : *a* see **тотуг**

тох : *a* 1) full, replete, sated, satiated, satisfied 2) saturated *ext* 3) wealthy 4) dark *color*

тоха : *n* hoe, mattock

тохалама : *vn* fr. **тохаламаг**

тохаламаг : *v* hoe, weed, loosen soil with a hoe

тохаланмаг : *v* be loosened by a hoe, be hoed 2) saturated *of soil*

тохан : *n* standing position of a talus with the broader side down *talus or knucklebone is a kind of die used in games of chance*

тохач : *n* rammer, tamp *the tool*

тохачлама : *n* ramming, tamping

тохачламаг : *v* ram, tamp

тохлуг : *n* 1) satiety, satiation, saturation *ext* 2) wealthiness

тохмаг : *n* 1) watchman's stick, or baton 2) heavy wooden mallet

тохмагламаг : *v* 1) strike with a watchman's stick 2) hit with a wooden mallet

тохмачар : *n* seedling

тохтаг : *a* 1) quiet, calm, tranquil *adv* 2) quietly, calmly

тохтахлыг : *n* calming, quieting, soothing

тохтамаг : 1) calm/quiet down, become calm/quiet 2) bear, endure, restrain oneself, wait a bit 3) reach *a place* 4) ease, abate *of pain*

тохтамаз : *a* unceasing, ceaseless, nonstop

тохтатмаг : *v* calm, quiet, soothe

тохум : *n* 1) seed, seeds 2) eggs *of insects*

тохума : *n* 1) weaving 2) knitting, braiding, plaiting *a* 3) braided, plaited, knitted

тохумаг : *v* weave, knit, plait, braid

тохумламаг : *v* go to seed

тохумлуг : *n* 1) seed, seeds *for sowing* *bot* 2) ovary

тохумсəпəн : *n* sower

тохумсуз : *a* seedless

тохумсузлуг : *n* lack of seeds

тохумчу : *n* seed grower

тохумчулуг : *n* seed growing

тохунан : *n* *math* tangent

тохундурмаг : *v-tr* knock together

тохунма : *n* 1) woven fabrics 2) weaving, knitting, plaiting, braiding 3) touch, touching *a* 4) knitted, braided, plaited, woven

тохунмаг : *v* 1) be knitted, be woven, be braided/plaited 2) touch, touch lightly, come in contact *with*, be contiguous 3) run against, stumble *on/across*, hit/strike *against*, collide with *s.o.*, run into *s.o.* 4) offend, hurt, wound, insult 5) have *s.t.* to do with

тохунулмаз : *a* inviolable

тохунулмазлыг : *n* inviolability

тохучу : *n* 1) weaver, textile worker *a* 2) weaving, textile

тохучулуг : *n* weaving, the art and practice of weaving

точно : *adv* *Ru* exactly, precisely

төвбə : *n* *relig* 1) confession, penitence, repentance, remorse 2) vow, pledge,

төвлə : *n* stable, stall

төврат : *n* *relig* the Torah, the Law; the Bible *esp. the Old Testament*

төвсиjə : *n* recommendation, advice, counsel

төвһид : *n* monotheism

төвшүjə-төвшүjə : *adv* panting, gasping, in a hurry, hurry-scurry

төвшүк, төвшүмə : *n* shortness of breath, panting, puffing

төвшүмəк : *v* pant, puff, gasp, be short of breath/ out of breath

төjчү : *n* *hist* quitrent, *pooling of resources to pay a tax or pay off common indebtedness)*

төкдүрмəк : *caus* of **төкмəк**

төкдүртмəк : *caus* of **төкмəк**

төкмə : *vn* 1) fr. **төкмəк** *a* 2) cast, founded, molded 3) poured *into*, filled *with*

төкмəк : *v* 1) pour, pour in, pour out, pour off *of liquids* 2) cast, found, mold *of metals* 3) pour, pour out, spill *of dry materials, e.g. sand, gravel* 4) fall, fall down, downpour

төкмəхана : *n* foundry

төкмəчи : *n* foundry worker

төкүб-төкүшдүрмəк : *v* throw about, scatter, strew

төкүлмə : n 1) shedding, falling out *of hair* *vn* 2) fr. **төкүлмəк**

төкүлмəк : *v-intr* 1) pour, pour out, spill *of liquid* 2) be cast/founded/molded 3) pour, pour out, spill, scatter *of dry material, e.g. sand, gravel* 4) fall, fall out, crumble 5) shed, fall out *of hair* 6) flow/fall into *of a river*

төкүлүшмəк : *v* attack, assault, rush *many people together*

төкүнтү : *n* waste, waste products, garbage, refuse, leavings *usually in liquid form*

төкүчү : *n* see **төкмəчи**

төкүшдүрмəк : *v* throw about, scatter, strew

төрəди : *n* upstart, parvenu

төрəдичи : *n* 1) sire, stud-animal 2) pathogenic organism

төрəмə : *n* 1) origin, beginnings, reproduction, propagation, formation, emergence, coming into the world 2) genesis 3) generation, breed, race

төрəмəк : *v* 1) multiply, propagate, breed, come into being 2) be formed, arise, originate, come from

төрəниш : *n* descent, origin

төрəнмəк : *v-intr* arise, multiply, propagate, come into the world, be created

төрəтмəк : *v-tr* procreate, produce, give birth *to* , bring into the world, beget, create

төрпү : *n* rasp *the tool*

төрпүкөрмəмиш : *a* unpolished, rough

төрпүлəмəк : *v* clear away/strip off with a rasp

төр-төкүнтү : *n* 1) rabble, riff-raff *a* 2) disorderly, untidy, slipshod *n* 3) vestiges, remnants

төр-төкүнтүлүк : *n* disorder, untidiness

төһмəт : *n* reprimand, rebuke, reproof, reproach

төһмəтлəндирмəк : *v* rebuke, reproach, reprove, reprimand

төһмəтлəнмəк : *v* receive a rebuke/reproach/reproof, receive a reprimand

төһмəтли : *a* reproachful; containing a rebuke or reproof or reprimand

төһфә : *n* gift, present

тракторчу : *n* tractor driver, tractor operator

тракедија : *n* tragedy

тракик : *n* tragedian, tragic actor

трамвај : *n* 1) streetcar *a* 2) streetcar

трамвајсүрән : *n* streetcar driver/conductor, tram operator

трамвајчы : *n* streetcar/tram worker

трансатлантик : *a* trans-Atlantic

транслјасија : *n* 1) transmission, relay *a* 2) transmission, relay

трап : *n Ru* gangway

трапесија : *n math* trapezium

тред-јунионизм : *n* trade-unionism

тригонометрија : *n math* trigonometry

тригонометрик : *a math* trigonometric[al]

трилјон : *n* trillion

трŏпик : *n* the tropics

тропйк : *a* tropical

тубургу : *n* birch-rod *for whipping/flogging*

тувалы : *n* a Tuvinian, or Tuva *member of the Tuvinian ethnic group*

тувача : *adv* in Tuvinian, in the Tuvinian language

туғ : *n relig* banner, standard

тула : *n* pointer *hunting dog*

туламбар : *n* stokehole, stokehold

туламбарчы : *n* stoker, fireman

тулани : *a* protracted, prolonged, lingering, long

туллајан : *n* 1) thrower *a* 2) to be thrown or launched

туллама : *vn* fr. **тулламаг**

тулламаг : *v* throw, throw out, throw off, cast, fling

тулланан : *n* jumper

тулланыш : *n* jump, spring, leap

тулланма : *n* see **тулланыш**

тулланмаг : *v* 1) jump, spring, leap, throw/fling oneself, rush *to* 2) be thrown *out/off* 3) jump up

тулланты : *n* garbage, refuse

туллатдырмаг, **туллатмаг** : *caus* of **тулламаг**

тулуг : *n* wineskin, water skin

тулугзурнасы : *n* bagpipe *musical wind instrument common to the Azerbaijanis and Armenians*

тулугзурначысы : *n* bagpiper, piper

тулуглуг : *n* skin, hide *intended for use as a wineskin or water skin*

тулумба : *n obs* oil-pump

тум : *n* 1) seed[s] 2) seed ; *fig* posterity

туман : *n* 1) pants, trousers, drawers 2) skirt *a* 3) skirt

туман-көјнәк : *n* underwear, underclothes, underclothing

туманчаг : *n* ragged person, ragamuffin

тумар : *n* 1) grooming/rubbing down*a horse* 2) smoothing *hair* 3) roll, scroll, parcel, bundle

тумарламаг : *v* groom/rub down *a horse* 2) tend, care for, pet, caress, smoothe

тумарланмаг : *v* 1) be groomed or rubbed down *of a horse* 2) be cared for, petted, caressed, smoothed

тумарлатдырмаг, **тумарлатмаг** : *caus* of **тумарламаг**

тумач : *n* 1) morocco leather, morocco *a* 2) morocco

тумурчуг : *n bot* bud, gemma; eye *of potato*

тунел : *n* tunnel

тунч : *n* 1) bronze *a* 2) bronze

тупурча : *n* tot, chubby lad

турач : *n zool* turaç, francolin *genus Francolinus, an Old World partridge*

турбин : *n* 1) turbine *a* 2) turbine

турбингајыран : *n* turbine builder

турна : *n* plait, braid; tourniquet

турп : *n* radish

турпәнк : *n bot* rape *Brassica napus* ,source of rapeseed oil

турш : *a* sour, acid

туршәнк : *n bot* sorrel, dock *Rumex*

туршлашдырмаг : *v chem* oxidize

туршмәзә : *a* sourish, acidulous

туршмәзәлик : *n* sourness, acidulousness, mild acidity

туршу : *n* 1) acid 2) see **шораба**

туршума : *n* oxidation; souring, going/turning sour

туршумаг : *v-intr* sour, turn/go sour

туршутмаг : *v-tr* make sour *chem* 2) oxidize

тутағач : *n* potholder

тутағачы : *n bot* mulberry tree *Morus*

туталға : *n* cause, ground[s], foundation, basis

туталғасыз : *a* groundless, unfounded

тутарлы : *a* 1) appropriate, pertinent, apt, accurate, undeniable; powerful *adv* 2) appropriately, pertinently, to the point, aptly

тутарсыз : *a* inappropriate, irrelevant, out of place, incoherent, disjointed, deniable, unreliable; weak, sluggish

туташма : *n* scuffle, melee, skirmish

туташмаг : *v* 1) grapple *with one another,* come to blows *with one another;* fight 2) find fault *with s.o.*

тутгач : *n typ* tenaculum *support for strengthening a manuscript set in type*

тутгун : *a* 1) dark, dull, mat, lusterless *of color* 2) cloudy, overcast, foul, inclement 3) gloomy, depressed, dispirited, sullen, morose 4) quiet, strangled *voice* 5) tense, strained 6) dark-brown *color*

тутгунлашмаг : *v-intr* 1) grow/get/become dark, darken; grow dim/turbid, grow dull, lose luster, pale 2) become darkened/clouded 3) be-come gloomy, depressed, dispirited, sullen 4) become strangled*voice* 5) become tense, strained

тутгунлуг : *n* depression, blues, gloom, gloominess

тутма : 1) *vn* fr. **тутмаг** *n* 2) fit, attack 3) *a* infectious, contagious *disease*

тутмаг : *v* 1) hold, keep, hold/keep to, catch hold *of*, grasp, grab, seize 2) catch, detain, arrest 3) rent, hire, lease 4) occupy *a place*, take up, fill 5) occupy, capture *intr* 6) catch, be infected *with* 7) fit, suit, become 8) combine 9) influence strongly

тутмалы : *a* possessed, obsessed

тутмуш : *adv part* beginning with/from

тутугушу : *n* parrot

тутуздурмаг : *v* slap, hit *s.o.*

тутулабилән : *a* perceptible

тутулмаг : *v* 1) be caught, be seized, be grabbed/grasped 2) be detained, be arrested 3) be eclipsed *of the sun or moon* 4) become confused, falter, stop short in confusion *about a person* 5) become hoarse *of o.'s voice intr* 6) catch, be infected *with*

тутулмаз : *a* imperceptible, subtle; incapable of confusion; ashamed, taken aback

тутум : *n* capacity

тутумлу : *a* capacious, spacious, roomy

тутумсуз : *a* not spacious/roomy, too small

тутушдурма : *n* comparison, collation

тутушдурмаг : *v* 1) compare, collate 2) cause to quarrel *with* , sow enmity or discord or dissension

тутушдурулмаг : *v* be compared, be collated

тутушма : *vn* 1) see **туташма** 2) ignition, inflammation 3) skirmish, melee

тутушмаг : *v* 1) see **туташмаг** 2) catch fire, ignite flame/flare up *of firewood* 3) dry up

тутһатут : *n* mass arrests

туфан : *n* 1) storm, thunderstorm, snowstorm, gale, hurricane, tornado 2) deluge, flood

туфанлы : *a* 1) accompanied by a snowstorm, storm, blizzard, hurricane, tornado, or thunderstorm 2) stormy, menacing, threatening

туфли : *n Ru* shoes

туш : *n* 1) front part of something 2) flourish 3) Indian ink 4) eye-liner 5) contact with a ball *in billiards , counted as a stroke a* 6) accurate *adv* 7) accurately 8) straight in the direction of something, directly

туш кәлмәк : *v* meet; coincide

тушатан, тушвуран : *n* marksman, sharpshooter

тушлајычы : *n* gunlayer, one who points out a target

тушлама : *vn* fr. **тушламаг**

тушламаг : *v* 1) aim, take aim, sight, point at a target *of a gun* 2) shade

тушланмаг : *v* be aimed, be directed at a target

туғјан : *n* mutiny, revolt, rebellion, insurrection, commotion, disarray

түк : *n* hair, down, fluff, feathers

түкәндирмәк : *v* exhaust, drain, wear out

түкәнмәз : *a* inexhaustible, interminable, never-ending, endless

түкәнмәк : *v-intr* end, come to an end, be exhausted, run low/short/dry

түкәнмәмәзлик : *n* inexhaustibility

түкәтмәк : *v* see **түкәндирмәк**

түкләнмә : *vn* fr. **түкләнмәк**

түкләнмәк : *v* become fully fledged, become hairy or shaggy, be covered with down or hair

түклү : *a* hairy, shaggy, long-haired, fleecy, covered with feathers, downy, fluffy

түклүлүк : *n* hairiness, shagginess, downiness, fluffiness

түксүз : *a* hairless, featherless

түкүкөдәк : *a* short-haired

түл : *n* see **чуна**

түләк : *n* shedding or molting of feathers

түләмәк : *v* shed, molt *of birds*

түлкү : *n* 1) fox *fig* 2) sham, dissembler, hypocrite, sly person *a* 3) sly, cunning

түлкүгујруғу : *n bot* foxtail grass *Alopecurus, a grass with spike-shaped inflorescence*

түлкүлүк : *n fig* slyness, cunning, pretense, dissembling, sham

түлу : *n* sunrise, daybreak, dawn

түлү : *n* see **түлүнкү**

түлүбашы : *n* inveterate cheat, sly person

түлүнкү : *n* cheat, scoundrel, rascal, sly person, old hand

түмән : *n* tuman *Iranian coin*

түнбазар : *n* covered bazaar

түнд : *a* 1) strong *of tea* , pungent, strong *of vinegar* 2) dark brown *color* 3) fast *of a horse* 4) stern, difficult *of disposition* 5) angry, furious, quick-tempered, hot-tempered, irascible 6) powerful, tough

түндлүк : *n* strength, pungency, sternness, fury, rage, quick/hot/tough temper

түндмәзач : see **түндхасијјәт**

түндрәнкли : *a* dark in color

түндхасијјәт, түндхасијјәтли : *a* hot-tempered, quick-tempered, irascible, furious; tough

түндхасијјәтлилик : *n* hot/quick temper, fury, rage, toughness

түнк : *n* catchment *a structure or drainage system that catches and collects water*

түнлүк : *n* the thick *of* , crush, jam, congestion, overcrowding, crowd

түнүк : *a* thin, weak, small, slight, lean

түнүкә : *n* coward

түнчү : *n* bull-calf *older than two years*

түпүрмәк : *v* spit, expectorate

түпүрчәк : *n* spit, spittle, sputum

түпүрчәкгабы : *n* spittoon

түпүрчәкләмәк : *v* beslobber, wet with saliva

түрбә : *n* tomb, mausoleum

түрк : *n* 1) Turk *a* 2) Turkish, Turkic

түркәсаја : *n* 1) simple-minded person, artless person, simpleton *a* 2) open-hearted, simple-minded

түркәчарә : *n* folk medical treatment or cure

түркәчарачы : *n* folk doctor, traditional healer; quack *male or female*

түркијә : *n* Turkey

түркмән : *n* 1) Turkoman/Turkman *a* 2) Turkmen

түркмәнчә : *adv* in Turkmen, in the Turkmen language

түркoложи : *a* Turcological

түркчә : *adv* in Turkish, in the Turkish language

түррә : *n* lock, curl, ringlet

түрүнч : *n* see **нарынч**

түстү : *n* 1) smoke, steam *a* 2) smoke, steam

түстүләмәк : *v* 1) smoke, fill with smoke, emit smoke, steam, fumigate *fig* 2) be timid, be frightened

түстүләнмәк : *v-intr* smoke, give off/emit smoke, be fumigated

түстүләтмәк : *v* emit smoke, smoke, fill with smoke

түстүлү : *a* smoky

түстүсүз : *a* smokeless

түтәк : *n mus* fife, pipe, reed pipe

түтәкчалан, түтәкчи : *n mus* fifer, piper

түтүн : *n* 1) tobacco *a* 2) tobacco

түтүнчү : *n* tobacco grower/planter

түтүнчүлүк : *n* 1) tobacco growing/cultivation *a* 2) tobacco growing/cultivation-related

түфејли : *n* 1) parasite, sponger *a* 2) parasitic

түфејлилик : *n* parasitism, sponging

түфәнк : *n* 1) rifle, gun *a* 2) rifle, gun

түфәнкгајыран : *n* gunsmith, armorer

түфәнкләнмәк : *v* arm oneself with a rifle

түфәнкли : *a* armed with a gun or rifle

түфәнксаз, түфәнкчи : *n* master-gunsmith

У

у : twenty-fifth letter of the Azerbaijanian alphabet

увертүра : *n mus* overture

уғрамаг : *v* 1) meet each other 2) undergo, suffer

уғратмаг : *v caus* of **уғрамаг**

уғрунда : *postp* for, for the sake of

уғулдама : *vn* buzzing, droning, honking

уғулдамаг : *v* buzz, drone, honk

уғулту : *n* buzz, drone, honk

уғултулу : *a* hollow; resounding, resonant, booming, rumbling

уғундурмаг : *v* *caus* of **уғунмаг**

уғунмаг : *v* burst into laughter

уғур : *n* 1) luck, success *adv* 2) unluckily, unsuccessfully

уғурлу : *a* 1) lucky, fortunate, successful *adv* 2) luckily. fortunately, successfully

уғурсуз : *a* unfortunate, unlucky, unsuccessful

уғурсузлуг : *n* lack of success, lack of fortune

удгунма : *vn* fr. **удгунмаг**

удгунмаг : *v* 1) swallow o.'s spittle 2) stammer

уддурмаг : *caus* of **удмаг**

удлаг : *n* gullet; throat

удлагүстү : *a* *anat* supraglottal *located above the gullet*

удма : *n* 1) winning 2) swallowing

удмаг : *v* 1) win 2) swallow

удостоверение : *n* *Ru* identification document

удузма : *vn* fr. **удузмаг**

удузмаг : *v* lose *a game*

удузмаз, удузмаjан : *a* 1) safe, sure, without risk of loss *n* 2) all-prize lottery *lottery in which no competitor loses*

удулмаг : *v* 1) be swallowed 2) be won

удум : *n* sip

удумлуг : *n* 1) sip *a* 2) sip

удучу : *n* 1) swallower *a* 2) swallowing *movement*

удуш : *n* victory, winning

удушлу : *a* winning; advantageous

удушсуз : *a* no-win, losing; disadvantageous

уже : *adv* *Ru* already

узаг : *a* 1) far, far away, remote *adv* 2) far off, far away, afar, afar off

узагвуран : *a* long-range *weapon*

узагда : *adv* far off

узагдакы : *a* 1) far, remote *n* 1) that which is far off

узагдан : *adv* from afar, at a distance

узагкөрән : *a* 1) sagacious, perspicacious *med* 3) far-sighted, presbyopic *n* 2) far-sighted/presbyopic person

узагкөрәнлик : *n* 1) sagacity, perspicacity *med* 2) far-sightedness, presbyopia

узагкөрүчү : *a* see **узагкөрән**

узагкөрүчүлүк : *n* see **узагкөрәнлик**

узаглашдырма : *n* estrangement, moving afar from; removal, dismissal

узаглашдырмаг : *v* 1) put, place afar, estrange 2) remove/put/place apart; eliminate 3) delay, postpone

узаглашмаг : 1) go afar from, distance o.s' from; become estranged, alienated

узаглыг : *n* distance, distant prospect, farness, remoteness

узаглыгөлчән : *n* range-finder

узаға : *adv* afar, at a distance, into the distance

узагы : *a* 1) farthest, remotest, utmost *adv* 2) not later than

узадылы : *a* extended, outstretched

узадылма : *n* stretching out, extending, lengthening

узадылмаг : *v* last; be prolonged/ outstretched/extended

узанабилән : *a* viscous, syrupy; malleable, ductile

узандырмаг : *v* *caus* of **узанмаг**

узаныглы : *a* lying down, recumbent

узанышмаг : *n* lie down *many together*

узанма : *vn* fr. **узанмаг**

узанмаг : *v* 1) lie down 2) stretch, stretch out 3) extend, pull out 4) grow, develop; cause to grow/to become longer 5) stretch o.s out 6) lengthen, become longer

узатма : *vn* see **узатмаг**

узатмаг : *v-tr* 1) prolong, protract, make longer, stretch, stretch out 2) postpone, put off, delay *fig* 3) talk in a long boring manner, ramble on 4) grow *nails, beard, moustache etc*

узлашдырылмаг : *v* be coordinated, correspond to each other; be in concord

узлашдырмаг : *v* 1) coordinate, bring into harmony with each other; to settle with *gram* 2) be in *grammatical* agreement, govern

узлашма : *n* coordination; compromise; settling

узлашмаг : *v* coordinate; compromise; settle

узун : *a* 1) long, lengthy, extensive 2) tall, lank[y] *person* *adv* 3) long, lengthily

узун кетмәк : *v* talk a lot

узун сүрмәк : *v* long, last

узунајаг : *a* 1) long-legged *ext* 2) restless, on the go

узунасына : *a* 1) longitudinal, lengthwise *adv* 2) longitudinally, lengthwise

узунбалдыр : *a* long-legged

узунбоғаз : *a* high *of boots*

узунбојлу : *a* 1) tall *n* 2) lanky person

узунбојун : *a* long-necked

узунбурун : *a* long-nosed

узунгол, узунголлу : *a* long-armed

узунгујруг : *a* long-tailed

узунгулаг : *a* 1) long-eared *n* 2) ass, donkey

узунданышан : *a* 1) garrulous, talkative *n* 2) talkative person; chatter-box

узундимдик : *a* long-beaked

узундраз : *a* 1) lanky, long-limbed, rangy *n* 2) lanky fellow, long drink of water

узунәтәк, узунәтәкли : *a* long-flapped, long-skirted *of a garment*

узунјал, узунјаллы : *a* long-maned

узунјунлу : *a* long-haired *of an animal*

узункөвдә, узункөвдәли : *a* long-boled, long-trunked *of a tree/plant*

узунлатмаг : *v* lengthen, prolong

узунлашмаг : *v* become longer, extend

узунлуг : *n* length

узунлүлә : *a* long-barreled

узунмүддәтли : *a* of may years, of many years standing, lasting, perennial,long-term

узунөмүрлү : *a* long-term

узунөмүрлүлүк : *n* longevity

узунпача : *a* long-legged

узунсаггал : *a* long-bearded

узунсач, узунсачлы : *a* long-haired

узунсов : *a* oblong

узунсүнкүл : *a* oval; oblong

узунсүрән : *a* continuous; protracted; chronic

узунтәһәр : *a* 1) somewhat long, longish *adv* 2) for a longish time, to a longish extent

узунту : *n* long-drawn-out proceedings; procrastination

узунтулу : *a* long-drawn-out, continuous,dilatory, procrastinating

узунтучу : *n* time-waster, one who generates long, tedious, boring procedures

узунтүклү : *a* long-haired *of animals*

узуну : *a* 1) longest *adv* 2) along, in the course of, during, within the period

узун-узады : *a* 1) long, time-consuming *adv* 2) long, a long time, protractedly

узунуна : *adv* along , longitudinally, longwise, lengthwise, at full length

узунчәкән : *a* long, lengthy, time-consuming

узунчу : *a* 1) garrulous, talkative, verbose *n* 2) talkative person; chatter-box

узунчулуг : *n* talkativeness, garrulousness, verbosity

ујар, ујарлы : *a* resembling, like, similar; fitting

ујғун : *a* corresponding, fitting, compatible, commensurate

ујғун кәлмәк : *v* fit, be suitable, be in harmony

ујғунлашдырылмаг : *v* be correlated, be adopted, be fitted

ујғунлашдырма : *n* linking, coordination, adaptation

ујғунлашдырмаг : *v* link, coordinate, adapt, fit, adjust

ујғунлашма : *n* adaptation, adjustment, coordination

ујғунлашмаг : *v* adapt, combine, become co-ordinated, get linked with

ујғунлуг : *n* harmony; compatibility; linkage; fitting

ујғунсуз : *a* unfitting, inharmonious, incompatible

ујғунсузлуг : *n* unfittingness, incompatibility, dissidence, dissention, lack of harmony

ујдур : *n tech* waste products *from silk production*

ујдурма : *vn* 1) fr. **ујдурмаг** *n* 2) fabrication, fable, fantasy, fiction, cock-and-bull story *a* 3) made-up, fabricated, fictitious, imaginary

ујдурмаг : *v* make up, fabricate, think up, compose

ујдурмачы : *n* inventor, fabricator, story-teller, faker; liar

ујдурулмаг : *v* 1) be made up/fabricated/invented 2) be adapted, be coordinated/adjusted/fitted, be accomodated to

ујма : *vn* fr. **ујмаг**

ујмаг : *v* 1) become keen on, get carried away with, yield to, give way to become prone to 2) be suitable, be corresponding to/similar to

ујсал : *a n* easy to get along with, congenial

ујсаллыг : *n* congeniality

ујуз : *a* mangy, scabby

ујумалашдырычы : *a* hallucinogen

ујушган : *a* sticky; viscous

ујушганлыг : *n* stickiness; viscosity

ујушдурмаг : *v-tr* combine

ујушма : *vn* fr. **ујушмаг**

ујушмаг : *v* be combined, be coordinated

ујушмаз : *a* irreconcileable, incompatible

ујушмазлыг : *n* incompatibility, irreconciliability

ујушуг : *a* benumbed, stiff with cold

украјналы : *n* Ukrainian

украјнача : *adv* in Ukrainian

улаг : *n* 1) pack-animal 2) ass, donkey *fig* 3) blockhead, dolt, fool,idiot

улајыш : *n* howl, wail

улама : *vn* fr. **уламаг**

уламаг : *v* howl, wail

улас : *n* *bot* hornbeam *Carpinus*

улашма : *n* fr. **улашмаг**

улашмаг : *v* howl, wail *in unison, many together*

улдуз : *n* 1) star *a* 2) star, stellar

улдузаохшар, улдузвары : *a* star-shaped, star-like

улдузлу : *a* stellar, star

улдузсуз : *a* starless

улдузшәкилли : *a* see **улдузаохшар**

ултиматум : *n* ultimatum

улу : *a* great, ancient; proto-

улу дил : *n* *ling* proto-world language

улу баба : *n* great grandfather

улу нәнә : *n* great grandmother

умач : *n* noodles

умачаг : *n* hope, expectation

умачашы : *n* kind of noodle soup

умма : *vn* fr. **уммаг**

уммаг : *v* hope, expect

умсуг : *a* 1) deceived, cheated *in expectations, in hopes* *n* 2) trap; temptation

умсундурмаг : *v* deceive, disappoint *in expectations, hopes*, discourage, disillusion

умсунма : *vn* fr. **умсунмаг**

умсунмаг : *v* be deceived, disappointed *in expectations, hopes*, be discouraged/ disillusioned

уму-күсү : *n* offense, injury; complaint about an offence or injury

ун : *n* 1) flour *a* 2) flour, floury, mealy, farinaceous

универсал : *a* universal, generic

универсаллыг : *n* universalism

университет : *n* *Ru* University

унитаз : *n* toilet

унификасија : *n* unification

унлама : *vn* fr. **унламаг**

унламаг : *v* sprinkle with/strew with flour, sprinkle/strew flour on

унлу : *a* sprinkled with flour

унсија : *n* ounce

унудулмаг : *v* be forgotten

унудулмаз : *a* unforgettable

унутган : *a* forgetful

унутганлыг : *n* forgetfulness

унутма : *n* forgetting, oblivion

унутмаг : *v* 1) forget 2) forget how *to*, lose the art *of*

упузун : *a* very long

ур : *n* swelling, tumor; outgrowth, excrescence; bump, lump

уран : *n* *chem* uranium

урин : *n* *chem* urea

урлама : *vn* fr. **урламаг**

урламаг : *v* call cattle to a watering place

уруп : *n* nut, female-screw

усал : *a* see **јолајахын**

усандырычы : *a* annoying, boring, monotonous

усандырычылыг : *n* annoyance, boredom, monotony, tedium

усандырмаг : *v* bore, get on the nerves *of*, bother; become a nuisance

усанма : *vn* fr. **усанмаг**

усанмаг : *v* be fed up with s.o.; be annoyed with *s.t.*

усанмаз : *a* indefatigable

усан(ма)мазлыг : *n* indefatigability

услу : *a* see **јаваш**

уста : *n* 1) master craftsman, foreman 2) expert in o.'s area of competence *a* 3) skilful, experienced, expert, adroit

устабашы : *n* chief master craftsman; top foreman

устад : *n* 1) teacher; maestro 2) virtuoso *a* 3) venerable

устадлыг : *n* virtuosity, skill, craftsmansship

усталашмаг : *v* become a master craftsman, become proficient/good at *s.t.* become a specialist

усталыг : *n* skilfulness, being a master; being a foreman

усталыгла : *adv* skilfully, adroitly, dexterously

устачасына : *adv* see **усталыгла**

устуб, **устублу** : *adv* quietly, carefully

утандырмаг : *v* put to shame, shame, place in an embarrassing position, embarrass

утанма : *n* shyness, constraint. confusion, embarrassment

утанмаг : *v* be shy, shamed,put to shame, be thrown into confusion/embarrassed

утанмагсызын, **утанмадан** : *adv* over-freely, over-familiarly, impudently, cheekily, brazenly

утанмаз : *a* 1) shameless, impudent, brazen, cynical *n* 2) shameless person, impudent/brazen fellow, smart aleck, smart-ass

утанма(ма)злыг : *n* cynicism, impudence, brazenness cynicism

утанмазчасына : *adv* shamelessly, impudently, cynically

утанчаг : *a* 1) bashful, shy, diffident *n* 2) shy, timid person

утанчаглыг : *n* shyness, timidity, bashfulness

уф : *intj* Oh!

уфулдамаг : *v* moan, groan

уфулту : *n* moans and groans

учаған : *n* *zool* lady-bug *fam. Coccinellidae*

уча-уча : adv ptc on-the-wing, flying around

учгун : *n* 1) falling, crumbling 2) landslide, slide, avalanche

учма : *vn* fr. **учмаг**

учмаг : *v* 1) fly, soar, swoop 2) fly away, vanish, disappear 3) collapse, fall in/apart/to pieces, cave in

учуг : *n* 1) ruins, wreck 2) fever-blisters, or rash on the lip *from a cold*

учуглама : *vn* fr. **учугламаг**

учугламаг : *v* become covered with fever-rash

учунма : *n* trembling, shaking

учунмаг : *v* 2) tremble, shake 1) swing *on child's swing*

учунчаг : *n* swing *child's*

учурдулмаг : *v* be ruined, wrecked, swept away

учурмаг : *v* ruin, wreck, sweep away

учуртмаг : *v* 1) ruin, sweep away 2) let fly away

учурум : *n* precipice, abyss; ravine; rapids

учуручу : *a* destructive, devastating, shattering, crippling *blow*

учучу : *a* flying

учучулуг : *n* *chem* volatility

учуш : *n* 1) flight; take-off *of an aircraft* *a* 2) take-off

учушмаг : *v* fly together, congregate *of birds*

уч : *n* end, tip

уча : *a* 1) high 2) loud *adv* 2) highly 3) loudly

учабој(лу) : *a* 1) lanky, tall *person*

учадан : *adv* loudly, aloud

учалан : *a* ascending, rising

учалыг : *n* 1) height, altitude, highness, 2) authority

учалма : *n* rise, increase, ascending

учалмаг : *v* rise, increase, ascend

учалтмаг : *v* make higher, raise, elevate

учбат : *adv* because of; due to; through *s.o.'s* fault

учгар : *n* 1) periphery; outskirts *a* 2) bordering, outlying

учгур : *n* *bot* see **сузанбағы**

учдантутма : *adv* every single one, without exception, altogether, in a row

учлуг : *n* head *of an arrow* ; tip, point

учсуз-бучагсыз : *a* endless, limitless, infinite

учсуз-бучагсызлыг : *n* endlessness, limitlessness, infinity

учубиз : *a* sharp, sharp-pointed, acute, acicular

учу-бучағы : *n* ends, corners and limits

учу-бучағы олмамаг : *v* be endless, infinite

учуз : *a* 1) cheap *adv* 2) cheaply

учузланмаг : *v* become cheaper, fall in price

учузлашдырма : *n* making cheaper, lowering/reduction of prices

учузлашдырмаг : *v* make cheaper, lower/reduce the price *of*

учузлашма : *vn* fr. **учузлашмаг**

учузлашмаг : *v* become cheaper, fall in price

учузлуг : *n* cheapness, low price, bargain price, inexpensiveness

учузча : *adv* at a very low price, very cheaply

учундан : *adv* through *s.o.'s* fault; because of; due to

учундан-гулағындан : *adv only in compound* : **учундан-гулағындан демәк (данышмаг)** say s.t. *unpleasant* about s.o.

ушаг : *n* 1) child, baby 2) fellow, guy *a* 3) infantile, childish

ушаға галмаг : *v* get pregnant

ушаг салмаг : *v* have a miscarriage

ушагланмаг : *v* behave like a child

ушаглы : *a* having a child *usually of a woman*

ушаглыг : *n* 1) childhood, babyhood 2) uterus

ушаглыгдан : *adv* since o.'s childhood

ушаг-мушаг : children, little kids

ушагпәрәст : *a* see **ушагсевән**

ушагпәрәстлик : *n* see **ушагсевәнлик**

ушагсалдырма, ушагсалма : *n* 1) abortion *a* 2) abortion[al]

ушагсевән : *a* child-loving

ушагсевәнлик : *n* love of children

ушагсыз : *a* childless

ушагсызлыг : *n* childlessness

ушагчанлы : *a* see **ушагсевән**

ушагчасына : *adv* childishly, in a childish manner

ушагчыг, ушагчығаз : *n dim* baby, child, kid, kiddie

Y

Y : twenty-sixth letter of the Azerbaijani alphabet

Yвәз : *n* bot rowan-tree *Sorbus aucuparia*

Yвәзлик : *n* grove of rowan-trees

Yдүләмәк, Yдүләјиб-төкмәк : *v* blurt out at one breath

Yз : *n* 1) face 2) front, right-side *of material* 3) surface 4) upholstery,covering *of furniture* 5) facet, facetting, edge *math* 6) period

Yз бағламаг : *v* form cream *on surface of milk*

Yз вурмаг : *v* pester *s.o.*

Yз дөндәрмәк : *v* betray, be unfaithful

Yз көрмәк : *v* show one's benevolence

Yз тутмаг : *v* address

Yз чевирмәк : *v* apply *to s.o.*, ask *s.o.* for a favor

Yз чәкмәк : *v* upholster; tile; panel

Yздән ираг : *expr* God forbid!

Yзә дурмаг : *v* rise *against,* protest *against*

Yзүнә бахмамаг : *v* disregard, neglect *s.o.*

Yзүнә салмаг : *v* be impudent, brazen

Yзүнү јазмаг : *v* copy, rewrite

Yзбары : *adv* see **Yз-Yзә**

Yзбәүз : *adv* face to face, facing each other; opposite, on opposite sides

Yзв : *n* 1) member; limb *anat* 2) organ

Yзви : *a* 1) organic; *adv* 2) organically

Yзвлүк : *n* 1) membership *a* 2) membership, membership-related

Yзвлүк һаггы : *n* membership fee

Yз-көз олмаг : *v* become alienated *from each other*

Yздә : *adv* in the face *of,* in the presence of *s.o.*

Yздән : *adv* superficially, in passing

Yзәкүлән : *a* flattering *words etc*

Yзән : *a* floating

Yзәнки : *n* stirrup[s]

Yзәнкивермәјән : *a* stirrup-shy, skittish *horse*

Yзәри : *prep/adv* along, on *the surface of*

Yзәриндә : *prep* on; over

Yзәрлик : *n bot* rue *Ruta graveolens*

Yзә-Yзә : *adv* swimming

Yзәчыхма : *n geol* 1) outcrop; erosion 2) bride's formal arrival at the home of her parents-in-law after the wedding-party 3) appearance of a fugitive *criminal or asylum-seeker* after a grant of immunity is promised

Yзкәч : *n* 1) fin 2) float

Yз-көз : *n* 1) face, physiognomy 2) facial expression

Yзкөрә : *a* 1) biased, partial, prejudiced *adv* 2) in a biased manner

Yзкөрә(н)лик : *n* bias, partiality

Yзкүн : *a* weak, exhausted; fragile

Yзкүнлүк : *n* physical weakness, fatigue, debility, fragility; exhaustion

үзкүчү : *n* swimmer

үзкүчүлүк : *n* swimming

үзләмә : *vn* 1) fr. **үзләмәк** 2) shallow-plowing

үзләмәк : *v* 1) sort out the best *agric* 2) shallow-plow, take off *turf/stubble* loosen *the soil*

үзләнмәк : *v* become loosened/unbound; grow impudent

үзләшдирмә : *n leg* confrontation

үзләшдирмәк : *v leg* confront

үзләшмә : *vn leg* see **үзләшдирмә**

үзләшмәк : *v* 1) run across, encounter 2) quarrel, squabble

үзлү : *a* 1) whole, unskimmed *milk* 2) unduly familiar, free-and-easy, shameless, impudent

үзлүк : *n* 1) mask 2) visor *of a helmet*

үзмә : *vn* fr. **үзмәк**

үзмәк : *v* 1) swim, float 2) pick off *flowers/fruit* 3) exhaust, wear out with work, torment 4) wear out *clothing*

үзр : *n* excuse; request for pardon

үзрә : *prep* 1) according to *adv* 2) in no time

үзрлү : *a* pardonable, justifiable, excusable

үзрсүз : *a* unexcusable, unjustifiable

үзрхаһлыг : *n* excuse

үзсүз : *a* skimmed *of milk*

үзүағ : *a* sinless, innocent, clear of conscience, having the right to look people in the eye

үзүашағы : *adv* downwards, in a downwards direction

үзүгара : *adv* ashamed, guilty

үзүгаралыг : *n* shame, disgrace

үзүгырмызы : *a* red-faced

үзүгојлу : *adv* prone, prostrate; face downwards

үзүдөнүк : *a* 1) changeable, inconstant, fickle; unfaithful *n* 2) traitor

үзүдөнүклүк : *n* treason; unfaithfulness

үз-үзә : *adv* face to face

үзүјола : *a* obedient, complaisant, tractable

үзүјолалыг : *n* obedience, compliancy, tractability

үзүјумшаг : *a* obedient, tractable, easy-going

үзүјумшаглыг : *n* obedience, tractability

үзүк : *n* 1) ring *a* 2) annular, ring-shaped

үзүкмәк : *v* show up; encounter, meet *with*

үзүкүләр : *a* jovial, friendly, hospitable

үзүкүләрлик : *n* joviality, friendliness, hospitality

үзүлмә : *vn* fr. **үзүлмәк**

үзүлмәк : *v* 1) wear out, become shabby 2) be racked with pain, suffer greatly, wear o.s. out 3) become exhausted/weakened; toil, languish

үзүлүшмәк : *v* settle accounts, get even with someone

үзүм : *n* 1) grape *a* 2) grape, vine

үзүмлүк : *n* vineyard

үзүмчү : *n* viticulturist

үзүмчүлүк : *n* viticulture

үзүндән : *adv* due to, because of, as a consequence of

үзүнтү : *n* distress, anxiety, sorrow

үзүрлү : *a* excusable, pardonable, justifiable

үзүрсүз : *a* unexcusable, unpardonable, unjustifiable, unforgivable

үзүчү : *n* 1) swimmer *a* 2) floating 3) exhausting, fatiguing, wearisome, tiring

үзүшмәк : *v* swim together

үзчијәз : *n dim* face *affectionately of a child, a loved one*

үјүдүлмәк : *v* be ground, milled

үјүтдүрмәк : *v caus* of **үјүтмәк**

үјүтмә : *vn* fr. **үјүтмәк**

үјүтмәк : *v* grind, mill *in a mill*

үлкәр : *n astron* Pleiades *constellation*

үлкү : *n* cloth-cutting

үлкүч : *n* razor

үлүш : *n* halvah-sandwich *given to beggars after funeral-service*

үмдә : *a* main, important, substantial, basic, essensial

үмид : *n* hope, aspiration

үмид бағламаг : *v* hope, rely *on s.o.*

үмиди кәсилмәк : *v* lose hope

үмидвар : *a* hoping

үмидверичи : *a* hope-sustaining, giving hope

үмидләндирмәк : *v* reassure, encourage

үмидләнмәк : *v* hope for, rely on, expect

үмидли : *a* 1) hopeful 2) hope-sustaining, giving hope

үмид-нәвид : *n* hope-and-encouragement

үмид-нәвид вермәк : *v* calm down, inspire with hope

үмидсиз : *a* hopeless

үмидсизлик : *n* hopelessness, despair

үмизсизчә, үмидсизчәсинә : *adv* hopelessly, despairingly

үмман : *n* ocean

үмум : *adv* all, entire

үмумдүнја : *a* universal, all-world

үмумгошун : *a* combined-arms

үмумдөвләт : *a* state , state-related

үмумән : *adv* see **үмумиjјәтлә**

үмумзавод : *a* plant, factory

үмуми : *a* 1) general, public; universal *econ* 2) gross, wholesale generic

үмумиjјәтлә : *adv* in general

үмумиләшдирилмәк : *v* 1) be generalized; be socialized/collectivized *of property*

үмумиләшдирмә : *n* 1) generalization 2) socialization, nationalization, collectivization

үмумиләшдирмәк : *v* 1) generalize 2) nationalize, socialize

үмумиләшмә : *n* generalization

үмумиләшмәк : *v* 1) become generalized 2) become socialized

үмумилик : *n* general/universal/generalized nature; community

үмумиттифаг : *a* all-union

үмумилли : *a* nationwide

үмуморду : *a* all-army

үмумрајон : *a* all-district

үмумтәһсил : *a* of general education, general-education-related

үмумфабрик : *a* all-factory

үмумхалг : *a* nationwide

үмумшәһәр : *a* all-city, city-wide

үн : *n* see **сәс**

үнван : *n* 1) address 2) title *various senses*

үнга : *n* see **симурғ**

үнсиjјәт : *n* 1) intercourse, comunication 2) relationship, attachment 2) sociability; social relations, friendship

үнсиjјәтли : *a* sociable, outgoing

үнсүр : *n* extraneous element

үрәјәјатан : *a* prepossessing,pleasant *of a person*

үрәјиачыг : *a* frank, sincere, simple-hearted

үрәјиачыглыг : *n* frankness, sincerity, simple-heartedness

үрәјигурдлу : *a* envious, jealous

үрәјидағлы : *a* heavy-hearted

үрәјиjумшаг, үрәјиjуха : *a* see **үрәјиназик**

үрәјиназик : *a* sentimental, impressionable

үрәјиназиклик : *n* sentimentality, impressionability, soft-heartedness ; compassion

үрәјитәмиз : *a* open-hearted

үрәк : *n* 1) heart 2) soul *fig* 3) courage, valor, bravery

үрәк вермәк : *v* inspire with hope, hearten

үрәк еләмәк : *v* dare; have the courage to do *s.t.*

үрәк кисәси : *n* *med* pericardium

үрәјә дәјмәк : *v* offend, insult

үрәјә јатмаг : *v* like, be to *s.o.'s* taste

үрәји кәлмәк : *v* dare *to do s.t.*

үрәји ағзына кәлмәк : *v* be repelled, revolted

үрәји долмаг : *v* be on the verge of tears

үрәји кетмәк : *v* faint

үрәјиндән кечмәк : *v* have the merest inkling of a thought

үрәкачан : *a* plausible, pleasant

үрәкбуландырычы : *a* 1) nauseating 2) outrageous, scandalous

үрәкбуланмасы : *n* sickness, nausea

үрәкдән : *adv* whole-heartedly, cordially

үрәк-дирәк : *n* hope-and-encouragement *lit : "heart and support"*

үрәк-дирәк вермәк : *v* give hope

үрәккечмә, үрәккечмәси : *n* 1) faint, fainting spell; heart attack *med* 2) cerebral thrombosis, stroke

үрәккетмә, үрәккетмәси : *n* see **үрәккечмә**

үрәкләндиричи : *a* encouraging

үрәкләндирмәк : *v* encourage

үрәкләнмәк : *v* become encouraged

үрәкли : *a* brave, courageous, valorous

үрәклилик : *n* bravery, courage

үрәкпартламасы : *n* heart failure

үрәксиз : *a* 1) timid; cowardly 2) indifferent *colloq* 3) heartless *This meaning is doubtless a calc under the influence of Russian "бессердечный" : heartless, cruel* *adv* 4) unwillingly, involuntarily

урәксизлик : *n* 1) timidity, cowardice 2) indifference *colloq* 4) heartlessness

урәксизчәсинә : *adv* 1) timidly, in a cowardly manner 2) indifferently *colloq* 3) heartlessly

урәксындыран : *n* 1) offender *a* 2) touchy, susceptible *to offence* , sensitive

урәксыхан : *a* 1) boring, tiresome 2) worrisome, troublesome, annoying

урәксыхынтысы : *n* 1) annoyance, nuisance, trouble 2) troublesome request

урәкчырпынтысы, урәкчырпынмасы : *n* strong heart-beat

урјан : *a* see **чылпаг**

уркә : *n* two-year old mare

уркәјән, уркәк : *a* timid, timorous, preternaturally shy

уркәклик : *n* timidity, timorousness, preternatural shyness

уркмәк : *v* be afraid of, frightened, timid

уркудулмәк : *v* be frightened, scared

уркутмәк : *v* frighten; scare away

уркушдурмәк : *v* scare, frighten

уркушмәк : *v* be frightened, be scared

урпәрмәк : *v* get goose pimples; stand on end *of hair*

урпәшмәк : *v* shudder, give a start *several together*

урф-адәт : *n* 1) ethics 2) moral traditions 3) manners, customs, ways

усјан : *n* rebellion, uprising, revolt, insurgency, mutiny

усјанчы : *n* rebel, insurgent

ускук : *n* thimble

ускул : *n* see **зәјәрәк**

услуб : *n* 1) literary style, literary manner 2) style, fashion

услубијјат : *n* stylistics

уст : *n* 1) top, upper part *math* 2) exponent, power *a* 3) top, upper

уст-баш : *n* clothes

устгурум : *n* superstructure

устдә : *adv* on top; upstairs

устдәнтулланма, устдәнhоппанма *n* leap-frog

устдән : *adv* from the top

устәләмәк : *v* surpass, be superior to *s.o.*, overshadow, overrun *s.o.*

устәлик : *adv* extra, additionally, as a supplement

устуачыг : *a* open, uncovered

устун : *a* surpassing, overrunning, overwhelming

устундә : *postp* 1) because of 2) on, on top of *s.t.* *location*

устундән : *postp* over, above *s.t.*

устунә : *postp* on *direction/motion*

устунлук : *n* supremacy; preponderance, primacy, preeminence

устуну ачмаг : *v* expose *s.o.'s meanness*

устун кәлмәк : *v* overcome

устуөртулу : *a* covered *on top*

уст-устә : *adv* 1) one on top of the other 2) in a body, en masse; in succession, running; making no selection or distinction

усул : *n* method, manner

усули-идарә : *n* *hist* regime *political*, form of government

усуллу, усуллуча : *adv* quietly, carefully

усулсуз : *a* unsystematic

утарид : *n* *astron* Mercury *planet*

утәлки : *n* *zool* shrike *fam. Laniidae*

утмә : *vn* fr. **утмәк**

утмәк : *v* scorch

уту : *n* *flat* iron

утук : *a* 1) scorched 2) brisk, nimble

утуклук : *n* nimbleness, briskness

утуләмә : *vn* fr. **утуләмәк**

утуләмәк : *v* iron, press

утуләнмәк : *v* be ironed, be pressed

утуләтдирмәк, утуләтмәк : *v* *caus* of **утуләмәк**

утулмә : *vn* fr. **утулмәк**

утулмәк : *v* be scorched

утулу : *a* ironed, pressed

утусуз : *a* 1) without an iron 2) unironed, unpressed

уфги : *a* horizontal

уфләмәк : *v* see **уфурмәк**

уфунәт : *n* stink, stench

уфунәтли : *a* stinking

уфуг : *n* horizon

уфурмә : *vn* 1) fr. **уфурмәк** *a* 2) blown out *fire*

уфурмәк : *v* 1) blow 2) blow out, extinguish *fire*

уфурулмәк : *v* 1) be blown up 2) be blown out/put down/extinguished

үч : *num* three

үчаjаг : *n* see **сачаjаг**

үчаjаглы : *a* three-legged

үчаjлыг : *a* three-month

үчаршынлыг : *a* three-arshin *an arshin is an old Russian measurement = 28 in. or 71 cm*

үчбармаг : *a* *zool* tridactylous, three-fingered

үчбашлы : *a* three-headed

үчбир : *adv* by threes

үчбучаг : *n* triangle

үчбучаглы : *a* triangular

үчвәзнли : *a* three-dimensional

үчгат : *a* 1) triple; three-layered 2) three-level; three-storeyed

үчдәбир : *num* one-third

үчдилли : *a* trilingual

үчдорлу : *a* three-masted

үчәси : *n* *of children* triplet

үчиллик : *a* three-year

үчjаш, үчjашар, үчjашлы : *a* three-year

үчкүнлүк : *a* 1) three day- *n* 2) three-day period, three days)

үчләмәк : *v* 1) make three *of*; triple 2) fold into three 3) divide into three parts

үчлү : *a* see **үчлүкдә**

үчлүк : *a* 1) tripartite, consisting of three parts *n* 2) three-man group/commission etc, triumvirate *mus* 3) trio; 4) three-ruble/manat/dollar etc bill

үчлүкдә : *adv* three together

үчманатлыг : *n* three-ruble bill

үчмәртәбә : *a* three-storeyed

үчрәгәмли : *a* *math* three-digit, three-figure

үчрәнкли : *a* three-colored, tri-colored

үчсәсли : *a* *mus* three-part

үчтарлалы : *a* *agric* three-field

үчүзлү : *a* *geom* trihedral, triangular

үчүн : *prep* for, for the sake of

үчүнчү : *a* *num* third

үч-үч : *adv* by three

үчһечалы : *a* three-syllable[d]

үчһәдли : *n* *math* 1) trinomial *a* 2) trinomial

үччә : *adv* only three, just three

үшкүрәк : *n* see **фышгырыг, фышдырыг**

үшүмә : *vn* fr. **үшүмәк**

үшүмәк : *v* be cold, freeze

үшүтмә : *n* shivering

үшүтмәк : *v* be feverish, shiver

ф

ф : twenty-seventh letter of the Azerbaijani alphabet

фабрик : *n* 1) factory *a* 2) factory

фабрикант, **фабрикчи** : *n* factory-owner

фагты : *n* pretender, sham, faker

фагтылыг : *n* pretense, sham, simulation,

фагтылыгла : *adv* hypocritically, deceptively

фағыр : *a* 1) poor, impoverished 2) timid

фағырлашма : *vn* fr. **фағырлашмаг**

фағырлашмаг : *v* 1) become poor 2) grow timid

фағырлыг : *n* 1) poverty 2) timidity

фағыр-фағыр : *adv* 1) plaintively, mournfully 2) timidly, meekly, obediently

фағыр-фүгәра : *n* the poor, impoverished people

фаиз : *n* percent, percentage; interest

фаизли : *a* percent, percentage; interest

фаизсиз : *a* interest-free

фаj : *n* *geol* fault, break

фаjда : *n* use, benefit, profit, the good, the sense, the point the advantage, *in doing something*

фаjдаландырмаг : *v* *caus* of **фаjдаланмаг**

фаjдаланмаг : *v* make use of, utilize, derive profit, take advantage of

фаjдалы : *a* useful, advantageous, helpful; profitable

фаjдалылыг : *n* usefulness, helpfulness, advantage; profitability;

фаjдасыз : *a* useless, disadvantageous, unprofitable

фаjдасызлыг : *n* uselessness, unprofitability, disadvantageousness

фаjтон : *n* phaeton *type of carriage*

фаjтончу : *n* phaeton coach-man

факт : *n* *Ru* fact

фактик : *a* factual, actual, real

факүлтә : *n* 1) department of a higher educational institution, faculty *a* 2) departmental

фал : *n* 1) fortune-telling; fate 2) egg deliberately placed under a hen

фалабахан : *n* see **фалчы**

фалагга : *n* *hist* falagga, a wooden instrument to which the feet of a convicted criminal were bound while the bastinado, or beating on the soles of the feet with a staff, was being administered

фалчы : *n* fortune-teller; sorcerer

фалчылыг : *n* sorcery, fortune-telling

фамилија : *n* last name

фамилијалы : *a* by the last name of . . .

фамилијасыз : *a* having no last name

фанер : *n* 1) veneer; plywood *a* 2) veneer; plywood

фани : *a* ephemeral; perishable; transitory

фанилик : *n* ephemerality ; perishability; transitoriness, mortality

фантазија : *n* fantasy

фантастик : *a* fantastic

фантастиклик : *n* fantastic nature, unreality

фанус : *n* lantern; flash-light

фарағат : *n* 1) leisure, rest *a* 2) quiet, calm, tranquil *adv* 3) quietly calmly, tranquilly *mil* 4) Attention! *command*

фарад : *n* *phys* farad

фараш : *a* *agric* 1) early *sowing* 2) early-ripening

фармаколог : *n* pharmacologist

фармаколожи : *a* pharmacological

фармаколокија : *n* pharmacology

фарс : *n* a Persian, an Iranian

фарсча : *adv* in Persian

фасилә : *n* 1) interval, space, distance 2) pause; break; intermission

фасиләли : *adv* off-and-on

фасиләсиз : *a* 1) incessant *adv* 2) incessantly

фасиләсизлик : *n* continuity

фасыг : *n* chronic complainer; chronic gossip

фасон : *n* 1) fashion,style, cut 2) arrogance

фасонлу : *a* 1) fashionable, luxurious 2) self-satisfied, smug, arrogant

фасонсуз : *a* cut simply, without style; humble, modest

фатеһ : *n* conqueror

фатманәнә ханасы : *n* rainbow *lit. "grandma Fatma's house"*

фаһишә : *n* prostitute, harlot, whore

фаһишәхана : *n* brothel, house of prostitution

фачиә : *n* 1) tragedy, drama 2) calamity, disaster, catastrophy

фачиәли : *a* 1) tragic, sad, doleful 2) disastrous, fatal

фашизм : *n* fascism

фашист : *n* 1) Fascist *a* 2) Fascism

феврал : *n* 1) February *a* 2) February

федерасија : *n* federation

федератив : *a* federative, federal

фејз : *n* welfare, prosperity

фејзјаб : *a* 1) prospering *being in s.o.'s good favor, enjoying advantages/grants etc* *n* 2) a prosperous individual *enjoying every advantage*

фејзјаб олмаг : *v* 1) be prosperous; be fortunate in all aspects 2) derive benefit/ enjoyment/ esthetic pleasure *from*

фе'л : *n* *gram* 1) verb *n* 2) action, act, deed *a* 3) verbal

фе'ли бағлама : *n* *gram* adverbial participle

фе'ли сифәт : *n* *gram* participle

фелдшер : *n* 1) physician's assistant, paramedic *fr. German via Russian* *a* 2) paramedical

фелдшерлик : *n* profession of physician's assistant/paramedic

фелдшпат : *n* *geol* feldspar, orthoclase

фе'лән : *adv* actually, basically, virtually

фе'ли : *a* verbal

фелјетон : *n* 1) feuilleton, satirical newspaper article *a* 2) feuilleton-related

фелјетончу : *n* feuilletonist, composer of satirical newspaper and magazine articles

феноложи : *a* *biol* phenological

фенолокија : *n* *biol* phenology

феодал : *n* 1) feudal lord *a* 2) feudal

феодализм : *n* feudalism

ферма : *n* farm

фестивал : *n* 1) festival *a* 2) festival, festive

фәал : *n* *hist* 1) activist element *the most active members of the Communist party* *a* 2) active *adv* 3) actively

фәалијјәт : *n* activity

фәалијјәтли : *a* active, energetic

фəалиjjəтсиз : *a* inactive, passive, inert, sluggish

фəалиjjəтсизлик : *n* inactivity, passivity, inertia, sluggishness

фəаллыг : *n* activity

фəввара : *n* fountain

фəгəрə : *n* 1) vertebra 2) happening, occasion, occurence 3) batch of goods *a* 4) vertebral

фəгəрəсиз : *a zool* 1) invertebrate *n* 2) invertebrate

фəгəт : *conj* but, however

фəгир : *a* see **фатыр** 1)

фəған : *n* outcry

фəда : *n* sacrifice, offering

фəдаи, фəдакар : *a* selfless, self-sacrificing

фəдакаранə : *adv* see **фəдакарчасына**

фəдакарлыг : *n* selflessness

фəдакарчасына : *adv* selflessly, self-sacrificingly

фəза : *n* space, spaciousness, expanse

фəзилəт : *n* 1) merit, moral superiority, moral perfection 2) virtue

фəлакəт : *n* calamity,catastrophe, disaster; crash, crack-up

фəлакəтли : *a* disastrous, catastrophic

фəлəк : *n* 1) heaven, the celestial sphere, the firmament, the vault of heaven 2) fate, destiny, fortune

фəлəкзəдə : *a* poor, unfortunate, unhappy, suffering, hapless, ill-starred,

фəлəстин : *n* Palestine

фəллаһ : *n* fellah *Egyptian peasant*

фəлсəфə : *n* philosophy

фəлсəфеjи-əглиjjə : *n phil* rationalism

фəлсəфи : *a* philosophic, philosophical

фəна : *a* 1) bad, poor, nasty, foul *adv* 2) badly, poorly, nastily

фəнд : *n* trick, dodge, evasion, subterfuge

фəндкир : *a* 1) evasive, shifty; resourceful 2) dodger, tricky fellow

фəндкирлик : *n* dodginess, shrewdness, craftiness resourcefulness

фəндчил : *a* see **фəндкир**

фəнəр : *n* flash-light; lantern, lamp, light

фəнн : *n* 1) subject, discipline 2) art, science, branch of knowledge, technique

фəнни : *a* 1) scientific *adv* 2) scientifically

фəраг : *n* separation *of a couple*

фəрари : *n* deserter; fugitive, runaway

фəрасəт : *n* 1) reason, intellect, sense 2) native wit, instinct, insight keenness, quick-wittedness

фəрасəтли : *a* keen, quick-witted, perspicacious, insightful

фəрасəтсиз : *a* slow-witted, unclever, slow on the uptake

фəрасəтсизлик : *n* incapacity, inability, slow-wittedness, stupidity, lack of insight

фəрг : *n* 1) difference *math* 2) difference

фəргләндирилмəк : *v* be differentiated, be distinguished

фəргләндирмə : *n* differentiation, distinguishing

фəргләндирмəк : *v-tr* differentiate, distinguish

фəргләнмə : *n* difference, distinction

фəргләнмəк : *v* be differentiated, be distinguished

фəргли : *a* different, distinguished *from*

фəргсизлик : *n* indifference

фəрд : *n* individual, personality

фəрдəн : *adv* individually, personally

фəрди : *a* 1) individual, personal *adv* 2) individually, personally

фəрдиjjəт : *n* individuality

фəрдиjjəтчи : *n* individualist

фəрдиjjəтчилик : *n* individualism

фəрдиләшдир(ил)мə : *n* individualization

фəрдиләшдир(ил)мəк : *v* individualize

фəрдиләшмəк : *v* become individualized

фəрə : *n* pullet, young hen

фəрəһ : *n* joy

фəрəһлə : *adv* joyfully

фəрəһләндиричи : *a* gladdening s.o.

фəрəһләндирмəк : *v tr* gladden, make glad/happy

фəрəһләнмəк : *v* be glad *at* be happy *at*, rejoice *in*

фəрəһли : *a* happy, merry, joyful

фəрəһсиз : *a* 1) unhappy *adv* 2) unhappily

фəрз, фəрзиjjə : *n* surmise, hypothesis

фəрjад : *n* outcry

фəрjад јетмəк : *v* come to the assistance of; get *s.o.* out of trouble

фəрли : *a* 1) good, useful, solid, decent 2) gifted, talented

фәрмајиш : *n* authority; command, injunction

фәрман : *n* decree, order, rescript

фәрсиз : *a* 1) unfitting, unsuitable, unusable, useless, invalid, 2) talentless, undistinguished *n* 3) passive/inert/sluggish person

фәрсизлик : *n* 1) unsuitability, unusability, invalidity 2) lack of talent, irresponsibility, capriciousness, passivity, inertness, sluggishness

фәрш : *n* small carpet, throw-rug, mat,

фәс : *n* fez

фәсад : *n* intrigues, plots, conspiracies

фәсадчы : *n* 1) intriguer, trouble-maker *a* 2) intriguing, trouble-making

фәсадчылыг : *n* intriguing, trouble-making

фәсаһәт : *n* 1) eloquence *n* 2) silver-tongued orator

фәсаһәтли : *a* 1) eloquent

фәсил : *n* 1) season 2) chapter, section

фәсилә : *n* *bot/zool* family

фәтир : *n* flat cake; cookie

фәтһ : *n* conquest

фәхр : *n* pride, object of pride

фәхри : *a* honorable

фәһлә : *n* worker

фәһләбашы : *n* foreman

фәһм : *n* 1) understanding, comprehension 2) reason, intellect, mind

фәһмли : *a* keen, quick-witted, insightful, clever, wise

фәһмсиз : *a* stupid, dull, slow-witted

фиғһ : *n* theology *Islamic*

физик : *n* *Ru* physicist

физика : *n* physics

физики : *a* physics, physical

физикшүнас : *n* physicist

физиоложи : *a* physiological

физиолоқија : *n* physiology

фикир : *n* 1) thought, reflection 2) idea 3) opinion 4) intention, purpose

фикир апармаг : *v* become thoughtful

фикир вермәк : *v* pay attention *to s.t.*

фикрә кәтирмәк : *v* imagine, fancy *s.t.*

фикриндән дашынмаг : *v* change one's mind

фикриндә олмаг : *v* intend

фикриндән чыхмаг : *v* forget

фикринә салмаг : *v* remind

фикирләшмә : *vn* fr. **фикирләшмәк**

фикирләшмәдән : *adv* rashly, thoughtlessly, precipatately

фикирләшмәк : *v* think, meditate, reflect, ponder

фикирли : *a* 1) thoughtful, preoccupied *adv* 2) thoughtfully, anxiously, worriedly

фикирсиз : *a* 1) thoughtless, reckless, careless 2) not carefully thought-out, not well-considered 3) thoughtlessly, rashly, carelessly

фикир-хәјал : *n* thoughts, reflections and ideas

фикрән : *adv* mentally, in thought

фикриачыг : *a* sober-minded, sensible, judicious

фил : *n* 1) elephant *a* 2) elephant['s], elephantine

филан : *pro* a certain, so-and-so, such-and-such

филан-бәһман : *deic* this and that frequently expresses irritation/impatience

филанкәс : *deic* this *person*, such-and-such

филан-филан : *deic* such-and-such *plural*, so-and-so

филармонија : *n* philarmonic society

филбан : *n* mahout, elephant-handler

филбаһар : *n* *bot* clematis

филдиши : *n* ivory

филиал : *n* branch *of an organization*

филиз : *n* ore

филм : *n* film, movie

филоложи : *a* philological

филолоқија : *n* philology

философија : *n* philosophy

философлуг : *n* philosophizing

фин : *n* 1) Finn *a* 2) Finnish

финландија : *n* Finland

финландијалы : *n* Finn

финчан : *n* cup

финчанабәнзәр, финчанаохшар : *a* cup-shaped

финчә : *adv* in Finnish

фираван : *a* 1) sufficient, abundant, wealthy, well-to-do *adv* 2) abundantly, sufficiently, wealthily

фираванлыг : *n* abundance , sufficiency, wealth

фиргəндə : *n bot* 1) layer, cutting 2) seedling, sprout

фирəнктојуғу : *n zool* guinea-fowl *Numida mileagris*

фирма : *n Ru* firm, company

фирни : *n* firni *sweet milk porridge*

фирон : *n* 1) Pharaoh *ext* 2) violent, tempestuous *ext* 3) wilful person; tyrant

фирузеји : *a* turquoise *color*

фирузə : *n min* turquoise *precious stone*

фисги-фүчур : *n* lechery, fornication

фит : *n* whistle, signal

фитə : *n* apron *worn in bath-houses in the Middle East*

фитлəмə : *vn* fr. **фитлəмəк**

фитлəмəк : *v* 1) whistle 2) instigate, incite, stir up against set *a dog* on

фитнə : *n* 1) intrigue, slander, machinations, plotting 2) provocation, dirty trick, instigation 3) confusion, disarray

фитнəкар : *n* intriguer, plotter, provocateur, instigator, blackmailer, trouble-maker

фитнəкарлыг : *n* intrigue, plotting, provocation, conspiring, blackmailing, stirring up trouble

фитнəчи : *n* see **фитнəкар**

фитрə-зəкат : *n* alms

фитри : *a* innate, inborn

фишəнк : *n* rocket, petard

фишəнкгајыран : *n* pyrotechnician

фылыг : *a* peeled; hulled

фындыг : *n* fındık *a variety of hazelnut*

фындыгбурун : *a n* snub-nosed

фындыглыг : *n* nut-tree forest, area

фынхырыг, фынхырты : *n* snorting, sniffing

фынхырмаг : *v* 1) snort, sniff 2) blow o.'s nose

фыр : *n* 1) abscess, boil 2) growth, tumor, lump; knob

фырыг : *a* bad, poor

фырылдаг : *n* humbug, fraud, tricks, machinations

фырылдагчы : *n* swindler, confidence man, swindler

фырылдагчылыг : *n* swindling, fraud, cheating

фырылдамаг : *v* 1) rotate; circle, whirl, turn/go around 2) fly down from, rush along, roll noisily

фырылдатмаг : *v-tr* 1) rotate; circle; turn around, whirl, cause to go around 2) roll along,wheel, trundle noisily 2) throw with force, fling, hurl, hurl out

фырылты : *n onom* whirling sound

фырын : *n* bakery oven

фырламаг : *v tr* see **фырландырмаг**

фырлана-фырлана : *adv* rotating, turning around, whirling, spinning like a top

фырланғыч : *n* see **фырфыра**

фырландырылмаг : *v-pass* be rotated, be turned around, be whirled around

фырландырмаг : *v* rotate, turn around, whirl around

фырланма : *vn* 1) fr. **фырланмаг** *a* 2) rotatory

фырланмаг : *v-intr* rotate, circle, turn around, go around, whirl around

фырлатмаг : *v-tr* 1) rotate, circle, turn around, whirl around 2) throw, fling, hurl

фыртыг : *n* mucus; snot

фыртыглы : *a* 1) snotty *n* 2) whimperer, sniveller; milksop

фыртына : *n* storm

фыртыналы : *a* stormy *of the sea*

фыртынасыз : *a* calm *of the sea*

фырфыра : *n* top *toy*

фырча : *n* brush

фырчылдатмаг : *v* sniffle

фысгыртмаг : *v* smoke *cigarette/pipe*

фысылдамаг : *v* 1) breath heavily and noisily through the nose 2) puff, put-put *of an automotive vehicle*

фысылты : *n* sniffling; puffing, put-putting

фысылтылы : *n* hissing, lisping

фыстыг : *n bot* 1) beech *Fagus a* 2) beech

фыстыглыг : *n* beech-grove

фышгырыг, фышдырыг : *n* whistle, whistling

фышгырмаг : *v* spurt; erupt, throw/cast out *sth.*

фышгырты : *n* spurting; eruption, ejection

фышгыртмаг : *v* cause to spurt/gush/spray out; sprinkle *with*

фышылдамаг : *v* hiss, fizz

фышылдајан : *a* hissing, fizzing, spitting

фышылты : *n* hissing, sparkling, fizzing; babbling

фышылтылы : *a* 1) hissing *ling* 2) sibilant/hushing *of a consonant*

фыш-фыш : *intj onom* 1) purling, babbling *of water*; rustling 2) murmuring, any sort of slight noise; whistling

флејта : *n* flute

флејтачалан, флејтачы : *n* flautist

фоје : *n Ru* foyer, lobby, lounge

фонд : *n Ru* fund

фолклор : *n* 1) folklore *a* 2) folkloristic

фолклорчу : *n* folklorist

фонетик : *a* phonetic

фонетика : *n* phonetics

форзас : *n* fly-leaf

форма : *n* 1) form; shape 2) uniform

формал : *a* formal, official

формалист : *n* pedant; one given to scrupulous observance of prescribed forms

формалистик : *a* formalistic

формалы : *a* having a given form

формасија : *n* formation *social, in Marxism*

формасыз : *a* shapeless

формасызлыг : *n* shapelessness

форс : *n* swagger

форсланмаг : *v* put on airs, get a swelled head, overestimate o.s.

форслу : *a* arrogant, haughty, overbearing

фото : *n* photo, snapshot

фотоапарат : *n* camera

фотографхана : *n* photo-shop

фотошәкил : *n* photo, snapshot

фөвгәл'адә : *a* unusual, extraordinary; emergency

фөвгәл'адәлик : *n* unusualness, remarkableness, singularity

фөвгәлбәшәр : *a* superhuman, beyond human capabilities

фөвгәлтәбии : *a* supernatural

фөвгәлтәбиилик : *n* unearthliness, supernatural character

фөврән : *adv* momentarily, instantaneously

фөври : *a* momentarily, instantaneous

фөвт : *n* destruction, ruin, degeneration, elimination

фразеоложи : *a* phraseological

фразеолокија : *n* phraseology

фраксија : *n* 1) faction *a* 2) factional

франса : *n* France

франсыз : *n* 1) a Frenchman *a* 2) French

франсызлашдырмаг : *v-tr* Frenchify, Gallicize

франсызлашмаг : *v-intr* Frenchify, be Frenchified

франсызча : *adv* in French

фрез : *n tech* cutter,milling cutter, mill

фронтал : *a anat* frontal, forehead

фуникулјор : *n* funicular railway

фургон : *n* van, station wagon

футбол : *n* 1) European football, soccer *a* 2) soccer, soccer-related

футболчу : *n* European football player, soccer player

фүзүл : *n* loudmouth, crude and annoying big-mouth interrupting conversations with long monologues

фүзүллүг : *n* garrulousness, disruption of conversions with boring monologues

фүләмәк : *v* see **үфүрмәк**

фүрсәт : *n* appropriate opportunity, the right moment

фүсүнкар : *a* charming, captivating, delightful

фүсүнкарлыг : *n* charm, attractiveness

фүтуһат : *n* conquest

фүфә : *n* yum-yum , num-num *food in baby talk*

X

x : twenty-eighth letter of the Azerbaijani alphabet

хавјар : *n* caviar

хавра : *n* synagogue *rare*

хадим : *n* public figure , statesman

хаин : *n* traitor

хаинанә : *adv* see **хаинчәсинә**

хаинлик : *n* treachery, betrayal, perfidy

хаинчәсинә : *adv* treacherously, perfidiously

хај : *n* calm *at sea*

хаја : *n anat* 1) groin 2) scrotum

хаки : *a* khaki

хал : *n* 1) mole 2) speck, spot 3) score; point

хала : *n* aunt *mother's sister*

халагызы : *n* cousin *maternal aunt's daughter*

халанәвәси : *n* second cousin, *maternal aunt's grandchild*;; also used loosely in reference to cousins other than first cousins

халаоғлу : *n* male second cousin *on the mother's side*

халвар : *n* khalvar *old weight measurement; 900-1000 pounds*

халг : *n* 1) people *a* 2) people's, popular

халгчы : *n* populist *calc of Russian "народник", representative of the Russian revolutionaries of the period 1860-90 +*

халгчылыг : *n* Populism calc of *Russian "народничество", revolutionary movement in 19th century Russia*

халгшүнас : *n* ethnographer

халгшүнаслыг : *n* ethnography

халдар : *a* see **халлы**

хали : *a* empty, desolate, uninhabited

хали јер : *n* virgin soil/ land

халис : *a* pure, genuine, true

халы : *n* large carpet

халлы : *a* 1) dappled, spotted 2) having a birthmark

халседон : *n min* chalcedony a semi-precious stone

халсыз : *a* without a mole/birthmark

халта : *n* leash

халталамаг : *v* leash, put on a leash *a dog*

халтура : *n* 1) pot-boiler, hack work 2) money made on the side, additional income *a* 3) relating to 1), 2)

халтурачы : *n* 1) person turning out pot-boilers, hack 2) moonlighter *person making money on the side by extra work* 3) truant, hookey-player

хал-хал : *a* dappled, spotted, speckled

халча : *n* carpet, rug

халчатохуҹан : *n* carpet-weaver, rug-maker

халчачы : *n* 1) carpet-weaver, rug-maker 2) carpet/rug-merchant

халчачылыг : *n* carpet-weaving, rug-making

хам : *a* 1) raw 2) undercooked 3) inexperienced, unversed 4) virgin land-related

хам јер : *n* virgin land

хама : *n* 1) sour-cream *geol* 2) bed, deposit 3) see **чаја**

хамыт : *n* horse-collar

хамытламаг : *v* put on a horse-collar

хамлама : *vn* fr. **хамламаг**

хамламаг : *v* lose a work skill

хамлыг : *n* 1) inexperience 2) lack of familiarity with terrain/with local conditions 3) uncooked/incompletely cooked state 4) raw, unprocessed state 5) unawareness

хаммал : *n* raw material

хамна : *n* raw silk

хамуш : *a* 1) silent, calm, taciturn *adv* 2) silently, taciturnly, calmly, soundlessly

хамушлуг : *n* silence, calm, soundlessness

хана : *n* 1) check *on material* 2) square

ханалы, хана-хана : *a* checked

ханәдан : *n* dynasty

ханәндә : *n* singer

ханәндәлик : *n* profession of singer

ханәнишин : *n* stay-at-home *one preferring to stay at home*

ханзад : *n* windfallen trees and branches

ханзадә : *n* 1) person of royal/noble descent *a* 2) of royal/noble descent

ханиман : *n* family, household

ханы, ханы балығы : *n zool* ruff *fish* 2) perch *fish*

ханым : *n* 1) madam, ma'am 2) noble lady *added, in polite speech, after a woman's first name*

ханым гыз : *n* Miss *polite address*

ханымбөчәји : *n zool* see **учачан**

ханымлыг : *n* status of noble lady

ханымсалланды : *n bot* see **нәстәрән**

ханахап : *adv* unexpectedly, unaware[s], taken aback

ханлыг : *n* khanate

хар : *n* 1) thorn 2) shame *a* 3) spongy 4) insect-pest

хара : *n hist* khara *a type of damask silk fabric*

хараб : *a* 1) bad, spoiled, rotten, broken, out of order 2) badly, poorly

хараба : *n* 1) ruins *a* 2) broken, devastated

харабазар, харабазарлыг : *n* ruins

харабедичи : *a* spoiling, going bad *i.e. foodstuffs*

харабламаг : *v* 1) spoil, mar, ruin, damage 2) foul, defile, soil, mess up

хараблащдырмаг : *v-tr* spoil, worsen, make rotten

хараблашмаг : *v* spoil, worsen, become rotten

харабчылыг : *n* disgraceful/outrageous/ shocking things

характеризә еләмәк : *v* characterize

характерик : *a* peculiar *to*, characteristic *of*

характерсиз : *a* lacking in character, weak willed

характерсизлик : *n* weak will, lack of character

харал : *n* large sack

харахапан : *a* 1) closed, locked 2) uninhabited, unpopulated

хардал : *n* 1) mustard *a* 2) mustard, mustardy

хардал јахысы : *n* mustard plaster

харигә : *n* miracle, wonder supernatural event or phenomenon

харигүл'адә : *a* unusual, extraordinary, supernatural

харигүл'адәлик : *n* extraordinary happening, supernatural phenomenon

харич : *a* 1) external, exterior 2) foreign *n* 3) appearance, exterior *of s.t.* 4) external, outside party/element

харичдә : *adv* 1) beyond 2) abroad

харичдән : *adv* 1) from outside 2) from abroad

харичә : *adv* outside, abroad *indicates movvement or position*

харичи : *a* 1) outward, external 2) foreign *n* 3) foreigner 4) member of another religious faith

харичиндә : *adv* outside, beyond the limits

харичдән : *adv* 1) outwardly, exteriorly 2) from the outside, from abroad

харылдамаг : *v* crunch, crackle; rustle

харылты : *n* crunching, crackling; rustling

харландырмаг : *v* candy, cause to beocme sugared

харланмаг : *v* be candied, become sugared

харланмыш : *a* candied; sweetened *jelly or jam*

харрат : *n* 1) joiner/cabinet-maker *a* 2) joiner's, cabinet-maker's

харратлыг : *n* occupation of joiner/cabinet-maker

харратхана : *n* joiner's/cabinet-maker's workshop

хартылдатмаг : *v* cause to crunch, to crackle

хартылты : *n* crunching, crackling

харбүлбүл : *n* *bot* orchis

хартут : *n* *bot* black mulberry *Morus nigra*

хас : *a* 1) peculiar, specific; 2) unfading *paint* 3) high quality 4) crisp, crispy; browned, toasted *bread* *n* 5) Tuesday

хас гырмызы : *n* *min* cinnabar

хасиј̇јәт : *n* character, quality, property

хасиј̇јәтнамә : *n* written appraisal of performance and personal characteristics

хассә : *n* peculiarity, quality, nature of s.t.

хата : *n* 1) mistake; error 2) trouble, danger

хата-бала : *n* trouble, grief, misfortune, danger

хатакар : *a* 1) dangerous, mean *person* 2) mischief-maker

хатакарлыг : *n* unpleasant, mean, dangerous behaviour

хаталы : *a* dangerous, risky

хатасыз : *a* 1) faultless, correct *adv* 2) faultlessly, infallibly

хатасызлыг : *n* infallibility; faultlessness

хатир : *n* 1) memory 2) respect; courtesy

хатират : *n* remembrances, recollections, memoirs

хатирә : *n* remembrance; memoirs; memory

хатирәкөрән : *a* obliging, accomodating, gracious

хатирәкөрәнлик : *n* favor, service *done for s.o.*

хатирчәм : *a* self-confident, calm, self-assured

хатирчәмлик : *n* self-confidence,self-assurance calmness

хатын : *n* see **ханым**

хатынбармағы : khatınbarmağı , a variety of grape *lit. ladies' fingers*

хатырламаг : *v* remember, recollect

хатырланмаг : *v* be remembered, be recollected

хатырлатдырмаг : *v* *caus* of **хатырламаг**

хатырлатмаг : *v* remind

хатырлы : *a* respected, honorable, trusted *person*

хатрына : *prep* for the sake of

хахам : *n* interpreter of religious law *in Judaism*

хаһиш : *n* solicitation, request

хач : *n* 1) cross fr. *Armenian* 2) cross

хач чәкмәк : *v* make a sign of the cross

хачвары : *a* cruciform, cross-shaped

хачпәрәст : *n* Christian

хачпәрәстлик : *n* Christianity

хачпәрәстчәсинә : *adv* in a Christian manner, as a Christian

хачә : *n* see **хәдим**

хаша : *n* *bot* esparsette, sainfoin *Onobrychis*

хашал : *a* big-bellied, pot-bellied

хаш-хаш : *n* *bot* poppy *Papaver*

хејир : *n* 1) benefit, advantage s.t. good; bargain, deal 2) good, the good, profit

хејир-дуа : *n* blessing; sage advice

хејирләшмәк : *v* make a bargain, strike a deal

хејирли : *a* 1) beneficial, useful 2) salutary

хејирсиз : *a* useless, disavantageous, unfavorable, non-beneficial

хејирсизлик : *n* uselessness, disadvantageousness lack of benefit

хејирхаһ : *n* 1) well-wisher, philanthropist, humanitarian *a* 2) benevolent, kindly

хејирхаһлыг : *n* benevolence, goodwill, kindness, benignity

хејирхаһчасына : *adv* benevolently, kind-heartedly

хејирхәбәр, хејирхәбәрчи : *n* bearer of good news

хејли : *adv* 1) considerably, much, by far 2) quite, a great deal of

хејмә : *n* tent; tabernacle; pavillion

хејмәкаһ : *n* temporary encampment, bivouac

хејр : *ptc* no

хејрат : *n* funeral repast

хејрә : *n* copper basin

хејри, хејрикүлү : *n* *bot* wallflower, gillyflower *genus Cheiranthus*

хејријјә : *n* 1) charity *a* 2) charitable

хејријјәчи : *n* philanthropist; benefactor

хејријјәчилик : *n* philanthropy; charity

хәбәр : *n* 1) news, information 2) notice notification, dispatch *gram* 2) predicate

хәбәр вермәк : *v* let know, inform

хәбәри олмаг : *v* be aware

хәбәрдар еләмәк : *v* warn

хәбәрдар : *a* 1) *n* knowing, knowledgeable, aware of *intj* 2) Watch it ! Coming through! Look out!

хәбәрдарлыг : *n* 1) warning, caution 2) information, notification;

хәбәр-әтәр : *n* some/any news, some/any information

хәбәр-әтәрсиз : *a* 1) unreported *adv* 2) without news, no news/information

хәбәр-әтәрсизлик : *n* unawareness, obscurity, lack of information

хәбәрләшмәк : *v* come to know, find out, inquire

хәбәрсиз : *a* 1) unaware, uninformed *adv* 2) without/no news, no one knows, God knows

хәбәрсизлик : *n* unawareness, lack of information

хәбәрчи : *n* 1) messenger, herald 2) gossip; informer, tale-bearer

хәбәрчилик : *n* gossiping; tale-bearing, informing *on* , reporting *to the authorities*

хәбис : *n* 1) thug; villain, scoundrel *a* 2) vile, foul, perfidious

хәбислик : *n* 1) vileness, loathsomeness, crime, evil deed 2) treachery

хәвличан : *n* *bot* see **гулунчан**

хәдәмә : *n* mosque-servant

хәдим : *n* eunuch

хәз : *n* fur

хәзан : *n* 1) autumn, fall 2) fall of the leaves *in autumn*

хәзәл : *n* dry fallen leaves *in autumn*

хәзәр : *n* 1) Caspian sea; *a* 2) Caspian

хәзәрләр : *n* *hist* Khazars *an ancient Turkic people, originally from the Transcaucasus who settled on the lower Volga in early medieval times*

хәзинә : *n* 1) Exchequer,Treasury, public purse 2) treasure, treasure-house

хәзинәдар : *n* treasurer

хәзнә : *n* 1) cartridge-chamber 2) warm-water pool *in middle-eastern bathhouses*

хәзри : *n* north wind *particularly in the Baku area*

хәјал : *n* 1) reverie 2) apparition, ghost, phantom, hallucination, vision 3) utopia

хәјалындан чыхмаг : *v* be completely forgotten, be completely gone from o.'s memory

хәјалат : *n* 1) chimera, utopia 2) melancholy

хәјалән : *adv* thoughtfully

хәјали : *a* 1) imaginary, spectral, fantasmal 2) romantic, utopian 3) alleged; phony

хәјалпәрәст : *n* 1) dreamer, romantic, idealist, visionary, utopian

хәјалпәрәстлик : *n* romanticism; idealism, utopianism

хәјалплов : *n* fantasy, flight of the imagination, fanciful invention, utopia

хәјалчы : *n* see **хәјалпәрәст**

хәјанәт : *n* treason, perfidy, betrayal 2) abuse *of*

хәјанәткар, хәјанәтчи : *n* traitor

хәкә : *n* coal dust

хәкәндаз : *n* iron scoop/shovel *for rubbish/garbage/debris*

хәлбир : *n* sieve

хәлбиралты, хәлбиркөзү : *n* residue

хәлбирләмә : *vn* fr. **хәлбирләмәк**

хәлбирләмәк : *v* sieve

хәлбирләнмәк : *v* be sieved

хәлбирләтдирмәк : *v* *caus* of **хәлбирләмәк**

хәлбирләтмәк : *v* *caus* of **хәлбирләмәк**

хәлвәт : *n* 1) solitude, seclusion, hidden/secluded place *a* 2) secret, secluded, sheltered *adv* 3) see **хәлвәтчә**

хәлвәти : *adv* see **хәлвәтчә**

хәлвәтләмәк : *v* find a secluded/hidden place; create conditions for secret talks

хәлвәтлик : *n* 1) solitude, seclusion 2) secrecy; confidentiality

хәлвәтчә : *adv* surreptitiously, on the quiet, on the sly, secretly, stealthily

хәләл : *n* 1) violation 2) harm, damage

хәләт : *n* 1) *traditional* robe 2) gift of a *traditional* robe, or of material to make it

хәләтлик : *a* suitable for sewing a robe *fabric*

хәләф : *n* 1) successor 2) posterity, descendant[s]

хәлитә : *n* 1) ingot, bar, bullion 2) alloy *tech* 2) charge, burden *of a smelter*

хәлифә : *n* *relig* *hist* Caliph *the spiritual and civil head of a Muslim state*

хәлифәлик : *n* Caliphate *the office, domain, or reign of a Caliph*

хәлфә : *n* *relig* 1) prefect, or senior student *of the student body of a religious school* 2) master of ceremonies *presiding at wedding parties and funerals* 3) sacristan, sexton

хәмир : *n* dough

хәмирашы : *n* see **әриштә**

хәмирјоғуран, хәмиркир : *n* 1) dough-kneader *a* 2) dough-kneading

хәмирләмәк : *v* cover/putty a crack with dough

хәмировуз : *n* dough reserved for future leavening

хәмирчәк : *n* cartilage, gristle

хәмрә : *n* leaven, ferment; leavened dough

хәмрә вурмаг : *v* leaven, ferment

хәмрәсиз : *a* unleavened *dough*

хәмси : *n* zool khamsa *small fish of the anchovy family*

хәмсин : *n* see **сәмум**

хәназир : *n* *med* mumps

хәндан : *a* 1) jolly, smiling 2) flourishing

хәндәк : *n* 1) gutter 2) deep ditch, trench

хәннас : *n* Satan

хәнчәр : *n* dagger

хәнчәргајыран, хәнчәрсаз : *n* cutler, swordsmith

хәрач : *n* 1) tribute 2) donation; contribution

хәрәзи : *a* haberdasher

хәрәк : *n* 1) stretcher 2) bridge *of a stringed instrument*

хәрәнкә : *n* 1) crafty/sly person; cheat, swindler *a* 2) crafty, cunning sly 3) arch

хәритә : *n* *geog* map

хәритәчәкән : *n* cartographer

хәриф : *a* 1) irresponsible, stupid, weak-minded *n* 2) idiot

хәрифләмәк, хәрифләшмәк : *v* become stupid, crazy, lose possession of o.'s faculties

хәрифлик : *n* irresponsibility

хәрчәнк : *n* *zool* 1) crayfish; lobster 2) *n* *med* cancer

хәрч : *n* expenses, expenditures

хәрч еләмәк : *v* spend, expend

хәрчини чәкмәк : *v* support *s.o.* materially; pay *s.o.'s* bills

хәрчләмәк : *v* spend, expend *money*

хәрчләнмәк : *v* be spent *of money*

хәрчлик : *n* money for current expenses, pocket money, petty cash, walking-around-money

хәсарәт : *n* damage; injury

хәсарәт јетирмәк : *v* damage

хәсис : *n* 1) miser, penny-pincher, niggard *a* 2) avaricious; stingy, tight

хәсисләшмәк : *v* become avaricious;/greedy; become stingy, niggardly

хәсислик : *n* greed, avarice; stinginess, niggardliness

хәсисчәсинә : *adv* avariciously, greedily, stingily

хәспуш : *n* see **чибкир**

хәстә : *n* 1) ill, unwell, sick 2) crazy

хәстәләндирмәк : *v* cause illness, sickness, dicease; infect

хәстәләнмәк : *v* fall sick, become ill

хәстәлик : *n* sickness, illness, ailment, disease, malady

хәстәликли : *a* see **чаназар**

хәстәхана : *n* 1) hospital *a* 2) hospital

хәтәр : *n* 1) threat, danger 2) harm

хәтәрли : *a* 1) threatening, dangerous, risky 2) harmful

хәтәрсиз : *a* 1) safe; painless 2) harmless

хәткеш : *n* ruler

хәтли : *a* linear; lined

хәтми : *n bot* marsh-mallow, hollyhock *Althaea*

хәтт : *n* 1) line, stroke 2) handwriting

хәттат : *n* calligrapher

хәттатлыг : *n* calligraphy

хәтти-һәрәкәт : *n* tactics

хәфә : *a* 1) stuffy; bleak, comfortless *n* 2) cramped, uncomfortable room 3) extinguisher *of a samovar*

хәфәләмәк : *v* cover/ block the air-inlet

хәфәнәк : *n vet* 1) heaves, broken wind, pulmonary emphysema *in horses and other animals med* 2) cardiac and bronchial asthma; shortness of breath;

хәфәнк : *n* upper part of a window or door; casement

хәфијјә : *n* 1) *criminal* investigation *a* 2) *criminal* investigatory

хәфијјәчи : *n* investigator; detective

хәфиф : *a* quiet, soft

хәчаләт : *n* shame, embarrasment, uneasiness

хәчаләтли : *a* shameful, embarrassed, uneasy

хәчил : *a* see **хәчаләтли** 1)

хәшә : *n* see **харал**

хәшәм : *n zool* chub *a carp-like fish*

хәшил : *n* khaşil *a liquid porridge made with flour and meat*

хидмәт : *n* 1) service 2) taking care of, caring for s.o.

хидмәт көстәрмәк : *v* do/ render a service, do a good turn

хидмәтиндә олмаг : *v* be at *s.o.'s* disposal

хидмәти : *a* service, service-related, official

хидмәткар : *a* obliging

хидмәткарлыг : *n* obligingness, disposition to do favors/services

хидмәтчи : *n* service-industry worker, office-employee/worker

хизәк : *n* sledge, sleigh

хијабан : *n* broad avenue

хијар : *n* 1) cucumber *a* 2) cucumber

хилас : *n* salvation, rescue, liberation,deliverance

хиласедичи : *n* emancipatory, rescue[ing], saving, deliverance, relief

хиласкар : *n* saviour, liberator, emancipator

хилаф : *n* 1) lie , untruth *adv* 2) against

хилафәт : *n* caliphate

хилафи-адәт : *adv* contrary to the usual way of things

хилафи-ганун : *a* 1) illegal *adv* 2) illegally

хилафи-сијасәт : *a* impolitic, politically incorrect

хиллә : *n* tusks

химирчәк : *n anat* cartilage, gristle

хинк : *a* confused, embarrassed

хинкал : *n* khingal *large Georgian-style dumpling*

хирид : *n* sale; marketing; merchandise

хиртдәк : *n* larynx, Adam's apple

хиртдәкләмәк : *v* grab s.o. by the throat; put a knife to s.o.'s throat

хиртдәнәк : *n* see **химирчәк**

хитаб : *n* address, appeal, proclamation

хитабнамә : *n* appeal, proclamation *written*

хиштәк : *n* wedge

хыж : *n* see **чингыл**

хыл : *n* band, crowd, gang

хылт : *n* 1) dregs, lees, sediment, deposition 2) inward resentment;

хылхын : *a* very old, worn-out, unfit for wear or use *furniture/clothing etc*

хымы : *n bot* cow parsnip *Heracleum*

хымыр-хымыр : *adv* on the sly, secretly, on the quiet, calmly, without attracting attention; without looking preoccupied

хымхырт : *n* small items, trifles, trivcialities

хына : *n* henna *powder used for hair coloring, and other cosmetic purposes*

хыналы : *a* painted with henna

хыначичәји : *n bot* balsam *genus Impatiens, a flower*

хынчахынч : *a* overfilled, overcrowded

хынчылоуз : *n bot* snowdrop *Galanthus, a flower*

хынчым-хынчым : *a* broken into small pieces/fragments

хыр : *n* see **бостан**

хырда : *a* 1) little, scanty 2) petty, trifling; fragmented 3) close, small *of handwriting adv* 4) fine, finely, into small particles *n* 2) small change, chicken-feed *money*

хырда чүллүт : *n zool* snipe *Genus Capella*

хырдабојлу : *n* 1) dumpy, tubby person *a* 2) short *in stature*

хырдават : *n* sundries, haberdashery items

хырдаватчы : *n* haberdasher; peddler

хырдадиш, хырдадишли : *a* small-toothed

хырдаіарпаг(лы) : *a* small-leafed

хырдакы : *n* chopped rice-straw

хырдалама : *vn* 1) fr. **хырдаламаг** 2) changing *money* , making change

хырдаламаг : *v* fragment, make small; change *money*

хырдалатдырмаг : *v* caus of **хырдаламаг**

хырдалатмаг : *v* fragment, make small, break up/divide up into smaller units

хырдалашдырылмаг : *v* be broken up/divided up into smaller units

хырдалашдырмаг : *v* see **хырдалатмаг**

хырдалашмаг : *v* become smaller

хырдалыг : *n* 1) smallness, littleness, small quantity 2) minority, immaturity, juvenile age

хырдамејвәли : *a* small-fruited, bearing small fruits *of a tree*

хырдамешәлик : *n* scrubby, forested with small or young trees

хырда-мырда, хырда-пара : *n* all sorts of/every kind of trifle/little things

хырдасүнбүллү : *a bot* small-eared/spiked *of corn/wheat etc*

хырда-хырда : *n* 1) small pieces, small fragments *adv* 2) little by little, gradually

хырда-хуруш : *n* see **хырда-мырда**

хырдачы : *n* hairsplitter, petty/greedy/trivial person, small-minded person, narrow pedant

хырдачылыг : *n* pettiness; triviality, narrow pedantry

хырдача : *a* 1) little, small, petty, tiny 2) insignificant, inconsiderable, unimportant

хырылдамаг : *v* speak hoarsely, wheeze

хырылты : *n* hoarse voice, hoarseness, huskiness, wheeze, wheezing sound

хырылтылы : *a* hoarse, husky, wheezing

хырым-хырда : *n* trifles, little things, petty stuff

хысин-хысин : *adv* on the quiet, on the sly, noiselessly, quietly and sweetly

хырман : *n* threshing-floor

хырманалты : *n* waste-products from the threshing-floor

хырмандөјән, хырманчы : *n* thresher

хырник : *n bot* 1) date *fruit of the date-palm a* 2) date

хырпаламаг : *v* grab someone by the throat

хырпылдамаг : *v* crunch; rustle

хыртылты : *n* crunching; rustling

хырхы : *n* see **мышар**

хырхыр : *a* 1) hoarse *n* 2) man with a hoarse voice

хырчы : *n* see **бостанчы**

хырчылдамаг : *v* grit/gnash the teeth

хырчылдатмаг : *v* 1) *caus* of **хырчылдамаг** 2) cause chattering of the teeth

хырчылты : *n* gnashing/gritting

хырчын : *a* hot-tempered, irascible; stubborn; cantankerous, capricious, hard-to-get-along-with

хысма : *n* closed handful *of s.t.*

хых : *v-cmp* **хых еләмәк** kill *in infantile speech*

хыш : *n* wooden plough

хышылдамаг : *v* 1) produce a rustling, rustle 2) produce a hoarse sound *in the thorax*

хышылдатмаг : *v-tr* rustle loudly

хышылты, хышырты : *n* 1) rustling, crunching 2) hoarse sounds *from the thorax*

хышламаг : *v* plough *with a wooden plow*

хышмаламаг : *v* crumple *s.t.* up

хлорид : *a* 1) chlorine, chlorous *n* 1) chloride of *the lower or "-ous"*

хлорламаг : *v* chlorinate

хлорланмаг, хлорлашдырылмаг : *v* become chlorinated

хов : *n* nap, pile

ховлу : *a* fleecy

хозал : *n* residue, siftings

хозан : *n* see **хөвшән**

холерин : *n* cholerine *a mild form of cholera*

холодилник : *n* *Ru* refrigerator

хонса : *n* 1) bisexual; hermaphrodite *a* 2) bisexual; hermaphroditic

хонча : *n* traditional ornamented tray

хор : *a* 1) mean, low, base, contemptible *n* *mus* 2) chorus, choir

хора : *n* 1) aftergrass, aftermath *the second grass crop of the season* 2) underripe leftover fruit crop 3) ulcer

хорна : *n* snoring

хорна чәкмәк : *v* snore

хортдан : *n* vampire, bloodsucker, monster

хортламаг : *v* *myth* rise from the dead, come back from the grave as a vampire, become transformed into a vampire,

хортулдамаг : *v* grunt

хортулту : *n* grunting

хортум : *n* trunk *of an elephant*

хоруз : *n* 1) rooster *also used as a general epithet* *a* 2) rooster['s]

хорузбечә : *n* little rooster *said of a little bully*

хорузланмаг : *v* be on o.'s high horse; swagger

хорузчасына : *adv* swaggeringly, in a swaggering manner

хорулдама : *vn* fr. **хорулдамаг**

хорулдамаг : *v* 1) snore 2) purr *of a cat*

хорулту : *n* 1) snoring, snore 2) purring *of a cat*

хорум : *n* ration of cattle-fodder *for one feeding*

хосдәвәнк : *n* background noise of whispering, general whispering

хосәк : *n* small cabin/hovel/shack

хосунлашмаг : *v* talk in a whisper

хоткә : *n* *zool* teal *Anas crecca a short-necked river duck*

хотуг : *n* donkey-foal

хоф : *n* fear, terror, horror

хофландырмаг : *v* intimidate, terrorize, horrify

хофланмаг : *v* be afraid, scared, intimidated, terrified, horrified

хофлу : *a* 1) dreadful, terrifying, horrifying 2) timid, timorous, fearful

хофсуз : *a* brave, courageous, fearless

хохан, хоху : *n* bogeyman; fairy-tale witch

хош : *a* 1) pleasant, good, kind, lovely 2) affable, cordial, affectionate *adv* 3) pleasantly, well, nicely, affably, cordially

хош көрдүк : *expr* Hello; Nice to see you; Welcome

хоша кәлмәк : *v* like, enjoy

хошаваз : *a* 1) pleasant-voiced *n* 2) pleasant-voiced person

хошавазлыг : *n* euphony

хошакедән, хошакәлән, хошакәлимли : *a* attractive, nice-looking, pleasant, likeable

хошакәлимлилик : *n* attractiveness, likeableness, pleasant appearance

хошакәлимсиз, хошакәлмәз : *a* unpleasant, inattractive, rebarbative

хошакәлмәзлик : *n* unpleasantness, unsightliness

хошакәлмәјән : *a* see **хошакәлимсиз**

хошаһәнк : *a* euphonious

хошаһәнклик : *n* euphony

хош-беш : *n* greetings, exchanging greetings

хошбәхт : *a* 1) happy, prosperous, blessed, blissful *n* 2) happy person, lucky man *adv* 3) luckily, happily

хошбәхтлик : *n* happiness, bliss, felicity, prosperity

хошгәдәм : *n* harbinger of happiness *person bringing good fortune*

хошәмәл : *n* righteous man/person, upright person, moral person

хошәтир : *a* fragrant, aromatic

хошәхлаг : *a* of highly moral, well-behaved

хошәхлаглыг : *n* high morality, rectitude, moral excellence, probity

хошәһвал : *a* 1) obliging, well-behaved, good-spirited, easy to get along with n 2) easy-dispositioned person

хошзаһир, хошкөркәм : *a* 1) attractive, good-looking, nice-looking *n* 2) good-looking/nice-looking person

хошлама : *vn* fr. **хошламаг**

хошламаг : *v* like, prefer

хошландырмаг : *v* amuse, bring pleasure

хошланмаг : *v* enjoy, have pleasure

хошлуг : *n* 1) pleasantness 2) good treatment

хошлугла : *adv* in a good way, in an amicable way, without compulsion

хошниііјәт : *a* well-intentioned, right-thinking, benevolent

хошнәвис : *n* see **хаттат**

хошрəфтар : *a* polite, well-mannered, sociable

хошрəфтарлыг : *n* good manners, politeness, sociability

хошсəсли : *a* pleasant-voiced, euphonious-voiced

хошсəслилик : *n* pleasant voice; euphony

хошсима : *a* comely; good-featured

хошсималыг : *n* comeliness good looks

хошсифəт : *a* affable, cordial, good-hearted; nice-looking

хошсифəтлик : *a* affability, cordiality, good-heartedness, friendliness

хошсөһбəт : *n* good/pleasant conversationalist

хошсурəт : *n* see **хошзаһир**

хоштəбиəт, хоштинəт : *a* 1) good-hearted; well-behaved *n* 2) good-hearted person

хошу : *n* coquette, flirt

хошфикир : *n* see **хошниjjəт**

хошхасиjjəт : *a* good-hearted, good-natured, well-mannered

хошхасиjjəтлилик : *n* good-heartedness, good nature, affability

хошһал : *a* equible, placid; good-humored

хошһаллыг : *n* good humor; equability, placidity

хөрəк : *n* 1) food *to be served and eaten* 2) meal; dish

хөрəкпаjлаjан : *n* waiter, waitress *rare*

хөтəк : *n* bull calf *between 6 months and 1 year old*

хризантем : *n bot* chrysanthemum

христиан : *n* 1) a christian *a* 2) christian

христианлыг : *n* christianity

хроматик : *a* chromatic

хромламаг : *v* plate with chrome, chrome plate

хромланмаг : *v* be plated with chrome

хромлу : *a* chrome-plated

хроноложи : *a* chronological

хронолокиjа : *n* chronology

хронометрик : *a* chronometric

худа : *n* God *Persian*

худаjа : *intj* God!

худанакəрдə : *hortative* God forbid! *Persian*

худаһафиз : God save you! God protect you! *polite leave-taking*

худаһафизлəшмəк : *v* say good-bye/farewell, take o.'s leave

худбин : *n* 1) egotist; self-centered person *a* 2) egotistic, self-centered

худбинлик : *n* egotism, selfishness

худбинчəсинə : *adv* selfishly, egotistically

худмани : *a* intimate

худпəсəнд : *n* see **худбин**

худсəр : a see **өзбашына**

хуз : *n* hump *deformity of the back*

хузлу : *a* 1) hump-backed, scoliotic *n* 2) hump-backed person, person with scoliosis

хузлулуг : *n med* scoliosis

хул : *n zool* bullhead, goby *fish*

хулин : *n* hoodlum

хулиганлыг : *n* hooliganism

хумар : *a* 1) languid, languorous, wistful *colloq* 2) tipsy, tight; hung-over

хумарландырмаг : *v* 1) become languid, languorous; become wistful 2) become tipsy, get tight

хумарланма : *n* 1) drunkenness, tipsiness 2) getting languid/languorous; becoming wistful

хумарланмаг : *v* become wistful, become languid/languorous, feel voluptuous

хумарлыг : *n* tipsiness; hangover

хумар-хумар : *adv* langorously, wistfully

хурафат : *n* 1) superstitions, prejudices 2) legends, fables, myths

хурд-хəшил : *a* crushed, broken to bits; crumpled

хурд-хəшил елəмəк : *v* break to bits/smithereens, crush, crumple

хурма : *n bot* 1) persimmon *Genus Diospyros a* 2) persimmon

хурмаjы : *a* chestnut *color*

хурмалыг : *n* grove of persimmon-trees

хуруш : *n* 1) dressing, sauce for pilaff 2) delirium, ecstasy

хурчун : *n* saddle-bag

хутуз : *n* see **чутгу**

худдам : *n* mosque attendant

хүдуру : *adv* in vain

хүласə : n 1) summary, generalization, résumé 2) conclusion; deduction, inference *expr* 3) in a word, to sum things up, to make a long story short

хүлjа : *n* fantasy, daydream, impossible/unattainable dream, chimera

хүлјачы : *n* fantasist, dreamer, day-dreamer, one living in a dream-world

хүлјачылыг : *n* inclination to dreams and fantasies

хүнк : *n* see **куниур**

хүсус : *n* matter, subject, topic

хүсусда : *prep* about, regarding, concerning

хүсусән : *adv* especially, particularly

хүсуси : *a* 1) special, particular, specific, peculiar 2) private, personal, own

хүсусијјәт : *n* peculiarity, property, specificity

хүсусијјәтчи : *n* property owner, landowner

хүсусијјәтчилик : *n* property-owning, state of being "landed"

хүсусилә : *adv* particularly, specifically

хүсусиләшмә : *n* *ling* isolation

хүсусиләшмәк : *v* *ling* become isolated

хүсусиләшмиш : *adv* *ling* in isolation

хүсусунда : *prep* concerning, regarding

хүтбә : *n* sermon; preaching

h

h : twenty-ninth letter of the Azerbaijani alphabet

hа : *intj* Ha! 1) indicates warning 2) indicates insistence 3) expresses irony 4) emphasizes the preceding statement

hабелә : *adv* also, as well as

hава : *n* 1) air 2) weather 3) climate 3) spirit, character *mus* 3) melody, tune; motif

hавадан : *adv* 1) from the air, from the sky 2) free of charge, gratis 3) effortlessly 4) unexpectedly

hавадар : *n* 1) defender; protector 2) supporter

hавадарлыг : *n* 1) defence; protection; support

hавадәјишән : *n* fan, ventilator

hаваjы : *a* 1) vain, useless 2) very cheap, free, gratuitous *adv* 3) in vain, to no purpose 4) for nothing, gratis, dirt cheap

hаваландырма : *n* 1) arousal, excitement, agitation 2) aeration, airing out, letting air in

hаваландырмаг : *v* agitate, excite, arouse, heat up

hаваланма : *vn* fr. **hаваланмаг**

hаваланмаг : *v* 1) raise in the air 2) become mad/infuriated 3) put on airs, have o.'s nose in the air

hавалы : *a* 1) haughty, arrogant 2) aroused, agitated, hot-tempered

hаваөлчән : *n* barometer

hавар : *n* 1) alarm bell, tocsin 2) cry for help

hавасат : *n* weather

hавасыз : *a* 1) airless 2) vacuum 3) stuffy

hавасызлыг : *n* airlessness; vacuum; stuffiness

hавахт : *pro* when

hавахтачан : *pro* for how long

hавачат : *n* songs, melodies

hавламаг : *v* bark *dog*

hавуч : *n* see **јеркөкү**

hагг : *n* *leg* 1) right 2) truth, verity 3) charge, recompense 4) payment, fee

hаггы : *exp* I swear. . . .

hаггында : *prep* about, concerning, regarding

hагг-hесаб : *n* 1) financial settlement 2) *official* report 3) payroll

hагг-hесаб чәкмәк : *v* settle a score *with s.o.*

hагда : *prep* see **hаггында**

hагламаг : *v* 1) witness, affirm *the accuracy of a statement* 2) catch up with

hаглашма : *n* settlement *financial or of a dispute*

hаглашмаг : *v* settle, settle accounts with

hаглы : *a* 1) fair, just, true 2) enjoying/having the right

hаглы чыхмаг : *v* turn out to be right/ correct

hаглылыг : *n* rightness

hагсыз : *a* 1) unfair, unjust 2) deprived of right[s], disfranchised, disenfranchised

hагсызлыг : *n* 1) unfairness, injustice 2) state of possessing no rights , complete disfranchisement/disfranchisement

hадисә : *n* 1) event 2) phenomenon 3) incident

hазыр : *a* 1) ready *adv* 2) in readiness

hазыр еләмәк : *v* prepare

hазыр-амадә : *adv* in readiness, ready, prepared

hазырда : *adv* 1) at present, at the present time 2) present, ready, prepared

hазыркы : *a* present, this, the given, of today, updated

hазырлама : *vn* fr. **hазырламаг**

hазырламаг : *v* 1) prepare, ready, get *s.t.* ready 2) develop

hазырланмаг : *v* get prepared, get *s.t.* ready

hазырлатдырмаг, hазырлатмаг : *v caus* of **hазырламаг**

hазырлашдырмаг : *v* get *s.o.* ready/prepared *for s.t.*

hазырлашма : *vn* fr. **hазырлашмаг**

hазырлашмаг : *v* get ready, get prepared

hазырлыг : *n* 1) preparedness, readiness 2) preparation

hазырлыглы : *a* ready, prepared, having preparation/training *for*

hазырлыгсыз : *adv* without preliminary preparation, impromptu

hазырчаваб : *a* 1) resourceful,witty, sharp-witted *n* 2) a wit,

hазырчаваблыг : *n* wit, wittiness, sharp tongue

haj : *n* 1) response *to an outcry* , help, assistance 2) alarm, alarm-bell, tocsin 3) fuss; outcry

hajды : *intj* Let's go !

haj-күj : *n* fuss, noise, racket, scandal

haj-күjсүз : *a* noiseless

haj-күjчү : *n* alarmist, panic-monger

hajлама : *vn* fr. **hajламаг**

hajлаз : *n* loafer; truant, absentee *from school*

hajламаг : *v* 1) call from a distance 2) drive a herd *of cattle etc*

hajланмаг : *v* 1) be called from a distance; be driven *cattle etc*

hajлатдырмаг, hajлатмаг : *v caus* of **hajламаг**

hajлашмаг : *v* call, shout *to one another*

hajхырыг : *n* phlegm, spittle, expectoration

hajхырыглы : *a* phlegm-like

hajхырмаг : *v* expectorate, spit out

haj-haj : *intj* Oh!, Wow!

haj-hapaj, haj-hyj : rumpus noise, hurly-burly, commotion outcry

haj-hyj гопармаг : *v* make a noise, set up a clamor, cause turmoil, raise an alarm

hаким : *n* 1) governor, ruler 2) judge *a* 3) governing, ruling, dominant

hакимиjjәт : *n* 1) power, authority 2) sovereignty 3) domination

hакими-мүтләг : *n* monarch, autocrat, authoritarian ruler

hакимлик : *n* power, domination, authority

hал : *n* 1) state, condition, situation, circumstances, mood 2) moment, time *gram* 3) case

hал апармаг : *v* faint, lose consciousness

hала кәлмәк : *v* regain consciousness

hалына галмаг : *v* take care *of s.o.*

hалына jанмаг : *v* feel pity, sympathetic, feel condolence *with s.o.*

hалаj : *n* circle

hалаjламаг : *v* surround, encircle

hалал : *a* 1) permitted *by shari'a, or Islamic law* 2) acquired , acquired by honest means

hалалсүдәммиш : *a* 1) respectable *n* 2) decent respectable person *one who was nourished with "halal" milk*

hалбуки : *conj* however, although; but at the same time; then

hалва : *n* halvah

hалвачы : *n* halvah-maker

hалга : *n* 1) ring; link *of a chain* 2) circle, rim, hoop round 3) loop

hалгавары : *a* annular, ring-shaped, round

hалгалама : *vn* fr. **hалгаламаг**

hалгаламаг : *v* surround, encircle, encompass; cordon off

hалгаланмаг : *v* be surrounded, encircled, cordoned off

hалгалы : *a* annular, annulate, consisting of rings, links

hалга-hалга : *adv* in rings/links

hаләт : *n* state, condition, mood, frame of mind

hалландырычы : *n* agent, stimulus;, inducer; exciter,actuator

hалландырма : *n gram* declension

hалландырмаг : *v gram* 1) decline 2) stimulate, induce, actuate

hалланма : *n gram* declension

hалланмаг : *v gram* be declined

hалланмаjан : *a gram* indeclinable

hаллашмаг : *v* 1) greet one another 2) inquire about one another's health

hалсыз : *a* weak, powerless *of a sick person*; helpless

һалсыз-әһвалсыз : *a* 1) impolite, unsociable, crude 2) cantankerous, peevish 3) fat and flabby

һал-һазыр : *n gram* present tense

һал-һазырда : *adv* at present, at this moment, at this point

һамам : *n* public bath-house, baths

һамамхана : *n* bathroom

һамамчы : *n* bath-house attendant

һаман : *deic* 1) that one, that very *adv* 2) immediately, right away

һаман-һаман : *adv* immediately, without any delays, right now, right away

һамар : *a* smooth, even

һамарлама : *vn* fr. **һамарламаг**

һамарламаг : *v* make *s.t.* even, smooth

һамарланмаг : *v* become even, smooth

һамарлатдырмаг, һамарлатмаг : *caus* of **һамарламаг**

һамарлыг : *n* evenness, smoothness

һамаш : *n* classmate

һамашыг : *n bot* raceme, inflorescence

һамашлы : *adv* together, clubbing together, going in together

һамашлыг : *n* clubbing/going in together/pooling resources *to buy something expensive*

һамбал : *n* porter; loader, stevedore

һамбаллыг : *n* occupation of porter/loader/stevedore

һами : *n* chief, protector, boss, patron

һамилә : *a* pregnant

һамиләлик : *n* pregnancy

һамилик : *n* protection, patronage

һамы : *pro* all, everybody, everything

һамыја : *adv* to all, to everybody, to everything

һамылыг : *a* 1) communal, general *n* 1) commune

һамылыгча : *adv* altogether, in one effort; in a body, en masse

һамысы : *pro* all, everything, everybody

һамлач : *n tech* blow torch

һампа : *a* 1) rich,wealthy, well-off *n* 2) wealthy man, rich man

һампалыг : *n* riches, wealth, affluence

һам-һам : *intj onom* bow-wow

һана : *n* warper,warp machine *textiles*

һанагуран : *n* warper *textile worker*

һаны : *pro* where, where is. . . ?

һанкы, һансы : *pro* which one

һапытты : *a* incautious, precipitate, hasty in conversation/talk

һара : *pro* see **һараја**. **һара**. . . **һара** in various combinations is used to express incomparability/incompatibility of quality/condition/state

һарада : *pro* where

һарадан : *pro* from where/whence

һараданса : *pro* from somewhere

һарај : *n* 1) shout, cry for help 2) alarm, tocsin

һараја : *pro* where to?

һарајадәк, һарајачан : *pro* to what place?

һарајлама : *vn* fr. **һарајламаг**

һарајламаг : *v* shout, cry out

һарајлашмаг : *v* exchange shouts, outcries, halloos

һарајчы : *n* one who parts two persons fighting; one who runs to give assistance

һаралы : *pro* from what place *of residence or birth*

һарам : *a* 1) prohibited by shari'a *Islamic law* 2) obtained by dishonest means

һарамзада : *a* 1) illegitimate, born out of wedlock *n* 2) bastard; swindler *colloq* 3) guy , man

һарамзадалыг : *n* swindling

һарамы : *n* outlaw, robber

һарамылыг : *n* brigandage, robbery, Mafiosi lifestyle, living outside the law

һарамхор : *n* parasite

һарын : *a* 1) satiated, fat and selfish 2) nouveau-riche 3) complaceent, self-saatisfied

һарынланма, һарынлашма : *vn* fr. **һарынланмаг**

һарынланмаг, һарынлашмаг : *v* 1) become fat and selfish 2) become self-satisfied/smug/complacent 3) become nouveau-riche

һарт : *n typ* type-metal

һасар : *n* fence, hedge

һасарлама : *vn* fr. **һасарламаг**

һасарламаг : *v* fence in, enclose with a fence or a hedge

һасарланмаг : *v* be fenced in, enclosed by a fence or a hedge

һасарлатдырмаг, һасарлатмаг : *caus* of **һасарламаг**

hасарлы : *a* fenced in, surrounded by a fence or a hedge

hасил : *n* 1) result; consequence 2) prey 3) bag *hunting* , catch *fishing* *math* 4) product

hасилат : *n* 1) product, production, output 2) gain, proceeds, profit 3) debit

hатәм : *a* lavish; magnanimous, generous

hафизә : *n* memory

hафизәли : *a* retentive, having a good memory

hафизәсиз : *a* forgetful

hафизәсизлик : *n* forgetfulness

hафизәсизләшмәк : *v* lose o.'s memory, become forgetful

hафылдама : *n* barking

hафылдамаг : *v* bark

hафниум : *n* *chem* hafnium

hаф-hаф : *intj* *onom* bow-wow

hача : *n* 1) forking, bifurcation, divarication, branching *a* 2) branching, forked, forking, furcate 3) a support with a bifurcated end

hачагујруг : *n* *zool* haçaguyrug *7cm long insect with bifurcated tail found in semi-arid areas of the Apsheron Peninsula*

hачадил : *a* having a bifurcated tongue

hачадырнаг : *n* cloven-hooved

hачалама : *n* bifurcation

hачаламаг : *v* become bifurcated

hачаланмаг : *v* 1) become forked, bifurcated 2) acquire an ambiguous meaning, become ambiguous

hачан : *pro* when

hачандан-hачана : *adv* after a long period of time, at last, in the end, after all

hачасаггал : *n* man with a bifurcated beard

hачәт : *n* tool, instrument, device, appliance

hачы : *n* Haji *honorific title of a Moslem who has made a pilgrimage to Mecca*

hачылејләк : *n* stork

hаша : *intj* God forbid !

hашалама : *vn* fr. **hашаламаг**

hашаламаг : *v* deny, negate

hашијә : *n* 1) *embroidered* edge, edging, border *of fabric* 1) margins of a book/notebook 3) marginal notes, footnotes 4) plinth, plinth course 5) frame

hашијәләмә : *vn* fr. **hашијәләмәк**

hашијәләмәк : *v* embroider, edge, frame

hашијәләнмәк : *v* be embroidered/edged, be framed

hашијәли : *a* having an embroidered border/edge

hашијәлик : *a* material for embroidered borders/edges

hашијәсиз : *a* without an embroidered border/edge

hej : *intj* 1) Hey!, Listen! *adv* 2) all the time, constantly *n* 3) energy, strength, capacity

hejбә : *n* saddle-bag

hejбәт : *n* 1) fear, terror, horror 2) severity, strictness

hejбәтли : *a* 1) terrible, horrible, dreadful 2) imposing *one's own views*

hejва : *n* *bot* 1) quince *Cydonia vulgaris* *a* 2) quince

hejван : *n* 1) animal, beast *a ext* 2) poor, pathetic, pitiable, unfortunate, eevoking compassion

hejванат : *n* 1) animal nature; animal life, nimal kingdom *a* 2) animal

hejвандар : *n* cattle-breeder, cattleman

hejвандарлыг : *n* 1) cattle-breeding/raising *a* 2) cattle-breeding/rąising

hejванлашмаг : *v* become an animal, become crude, beastly, unbearable, stupid

hejванлыг : *n* coarseness, grossness, uncivilized behavior

hejвансифәт : *a* stupid, beastly, cruel

hejванхана : *n* menagerie

hejванчасына : *adv* animalistically, in a beastly way, atrociously

hejвәрә : *a* 1) huge; ugly; clumsy 2) crude, coarse *n* 3) ugly monster, clumsy monster 4) boor 5) boob

hejвәрәлик : *n* 1) crudeness, crudity, coarseness, rudeness 2) hugeness, ugliness

hej'әт : *n* 1) staff, personnel 2) astrology

hejз : *n* menses, menstruation

hejкәл : *n* 1) statue, graven image *fig* 2) stick, block *person devoid of feeling or understanding* , blockhead

hejкәлтәраш : *n* sculptor

hejкәлтәрашлыг : *n* sculpture

hejран : *a* charmed, rapt, admiring

hejранедичи : *a* charming, captivating

hejраты : *n* *mus* heyratı a traditional Azerbaijani muğam

hejрәт : *n* surprise, astonishment, stupefaction

hejрәтамиз, **hejрәтәнкиз**, **hejрәтләндиричи** : *a* wonderful, miraculous, amazing, staggering, incredible

hejрәтләндирмәк : *v* surprise, astonish, shock

hejрәтләнмәк : *n* be surprised, astonished, shocked

hejрәтли : *a* surprising, astonishing, shocking

hejсиjjәт : *n* honor, merit, ambition

hejф : *adv* *intj* 1) A pity!, What a pity! *n* 2) revenge

hejфсиләнмәк : *v* feel pity; feel sorry

hejhат : *intj* Alas! What a pity!

hекаjә : *n* 1) story, short story, tale, narrative 2) fable, fairy-tale

hекаjә формасы : *n* *gram* indicative mood

hекаjәjазан : *n* fiction-writer

hекаjәнәвис : *n* see **hекаjәjазан**

hекаjәчи : *n* story-writer, short-story writer

hектар : *n* hectare

hектограф : *n* hectograph *duplicating machine*

hектографиjа : *n* hectography

hектографик : *a* hectographic

hекемон : *n* leader

hекемониjа, **hекемонлуг** : *n* hegemony

hесаб : *n* 1) counting, accounting; calculation 2) arithmetic

hесаб вермәк : *v* report, give an account *of s.t.*

hесаб еләмәк : *v* count, compute, calculate; consider

hесаб олунмаг : *v* be counted as, be taken into account, be considered

hесаб чәкмәк : *v* make calculation, computation; sum up

hесаба алмаг : *v* take into account, consideration

hесаба кечирмәк : *v* deposit, include, transfer *to an account*

hесабыны апармаг : *v* understand, make clear *to oneself;* make a conclusion; grasp

hесабаалма : *n* calculation, stock-taking, taking into consideration; registration

hесабакәлмәз : *a* countless, incalculable

hесабат : *n* 1) account; accountability *financial* a 2) financially accountable; account-related

hесабдар : *n* accountant

hесабдарлыг : *n* accounting

hесабы : *a* 1) correct, accurate 2) fair

hесаб-китаб : *n* bookkeeping, accounting

hесаблаjычы : *n* 1) meter, measuring device 2) computer *person*

hесаблама : *n* computation, calculation

hесабламаг : *v* compute, count, calculate, consider, figure out

hесабланмаг : *v* 1) be computed, counted, calculated; amount to 2) be figured out, be considered

hесаблатмаг : *caus* of **hесабламаг**

hесаблашма : *vn* fr. **hесаблашмаг**

hесаблашмаг : *v* 1) settle, pay out a debt 2) figure out, consider 3) take revenge on , revenge o.s. on; deal with

hесабсыз : *a* 1) unaccountable 2) innumerable, numberless, countless

hеч : *pro* 1) nothing 2) absolutely no; . . at all, absolutely 3) no. . . whatsoever *intj colloq* 4) Meaningless! Unimportant!

hеч кәс : *pro* nobody

hеч бир : *pro* no one; nothing

hеч вахт : *pro* never, under no circumstances

hеч дә : *pro* not at all, in no way

hеч еләмәк : *v* destroy, annihilate

hеч јердә : *pro* nowhere

hеч зад : *pro* nothing

hеч кәс : *pro* nobody

hеч нә : *pro* nothing

hеч олмазса : *pro* at least

hечдән : *adv* out of nothing

hечлик : *n* nothingness

hеч-пуч : *n* nothing, trifles

hеч-hечә : *adv* in a draw, in a tie

hеча : *n* syllable

hечаламаг : *v* read syllable-by-syllable

hечалы : *a* syllabic

hеча-hеча : *adv* by syllables, syllablically

hә : *n* 1) yes *intj colloq* 2) Go on!, Keep it up*! used to connote encouragement/incentive*

hәб : *n* pill

hәбәш : *n* 1) Ethiopian, Abyssinian 2) negro, black person

hәбс : *n* imprisonment, arrest, detention

hәбсхана : *n* prison, jail

hәбсханачы : *n* jailer, guard, warden, prison official

hәвалә : *n* 1) commission, assignment 2) payment transfer *to another party*

hәвали : *n* suburbs, outskirts

hәвва : *n relig* Eve *first woman*

hәввари : *n relig* apostle

hәвә : *n* carpet-weaver

hәвәнк : *n* mortar

hәвәнкдәстә : *n* mortar and pestle

hәвәс : *n* will, desire, wish, striving *for*, aspiration *to*, inclination *to do something*

hәвәсә кәтирмәк : *v* cause willingness *to do s.t.*

hәвәскар : *n* 1) enthusiast, amateur, devotee 2) dabbler, dilettant

hәвәскарлыг : *n* willingness; non-professionalism, amateurism

hәвәслә : *adv* willingly, with pleasure

hәвәсләндирилмәк : *v* be encouraged *to do s.t.*

hәвәсләндиричи : *a* encouraging

hәвәсләндирмә : *n* encouragement

hәвәсләндирмәк : *v* encourage

hәвәсләнмәк : *v* be enthusiastic *about* , be carried away *with*

hәвәсли : *n* 1) hobbyist, non-professional enthusiast *a* 2) hobby, amateur

hәвәссиз : *adv* unwillingly, without interest

hәгарәт : *n* insult, humiliation, disparagement

hәгарәтлә : *adv* insultingly, disparagingly, humiliatingly

hәгганиjјәт : *n* justice

hәгганиjјәтлә : *adv* justly, fairly

hәгганиjјәтли : *a* just, fair

hәгигәт : *n* 1) truth, verity 2) reality

hәгигәтән : *adv* truly, really, indeed

hәгиги : *a* true, veritable, actual, real, genuine

hәгигилик : *n* truthfulness, verity, actuality, genuineness

hәгир : *n* pitiable; humble; timid

hәгиранә : *adv* most humbly

hәгирлик : *n* humility; timidity

hәдд : *n* 1) frontier, border, limit 2) measure, degree *math* 3) member, term *of an equation*

hәдди-булуғ : *n* puberty, sexual maturity; coming of age

hәдә : *n* threat, threatening; intimidation, frightening, scaring

hәдәгә : *n anat* orbit, eye-socket

hәдәләмәк : *v* threaten, scare, intimidate, inspire fear *in*

hәдәр : *a* 1) useless, vain, ineffective *adv* 2) uselessly, vainly, ineffectiveely

hәдәрән-пәдәрән : *n* nonsense, lies, idle talk, verbiage

hәдәф : *n* aim, target

hәдәфә : *n mil* sight-aperture, peep-hole, rear hole *optical attachment for increasing the accuracy of a weapon*

hәдиjјә : *n* present, gift

hәдиjјәлик : *a* donated, presented as a gift

hәдик : *n* 1) barley; rye 2) wheaten kasha

hәдис : *n* hadith *religious traditions of the Prophet Mohammed*

hәдjан : *n* 1) swearing, cursing 2) using perjorative, four-letter words 3) nonsensical talk

hәдjанламаг : *n* 1) curse, use perjorative words 2) talk nonsense, talk rubbish

hәдjанчы : *n* foul-mouthed person

hәдсиз : *a* 1) limitless, unbounded, excessive, inordinate *adv* 2) limitlessly, unboundedly, excessively, inordinately *n* 3) a great number, a nultitude

hәдсиз-hесабсыз : *a* numberless, multitudinous, unlimited, countless, manifold

hәдсиз-hүдудсуз : *adv* unboundedly, limitlessly, countlessly

hәзарбута : *n bot* sweet-william *Dianthus barbatus*

hәзары : *n bot* hazarı variety of white grape

hәзарпешә : *n* 1) coffer, small chest 2) person without a specific profession

hәзз : *n* pleasure, amusement, enjoyment

hәзин : *a* 1) sorrowful, pitiful, mourning *adv* 2) sorrowfully, pitifully, mournfully

hәзин-hәзин : *adv* pitifully, mournfully

hәзм : *n* 1) digestion *a* 2) digestive

hәзми-рабе : *n* gobbling up, swallowing

hәзрәт : *n* 1) highness, majesty *a* 2) most honorable, most venerable

hәjа : *n* shame, shyness, timidity

hәjаланмаг : *v* become/grow ashamed, shy, timid

hәjалы : *a* ashamed, modest, timid

həjан : *n* 1) defence; protection 2) patronage, favor, support

həjасыз : *a* 1) shameless, impudent, brazen 2) cynical *n* 3) impudent fellow, smart aleck, smart ass 4) cynic

həjасызлыг : *n* 1) shamelessness, impudence 2) cynicism

həjасызлыгла, həjасызчасына : *adv* impudently, shamelessly, cynically

həjат : *n* life, existence

həjата кечирмәк : *v* accomplish

həjатбәхш : *a* see **həjатверичи**

həjатверичи : *a* enlivening

həjати : *a* life, vital

həjатилик : *n* life; vitality; viability

həjатсыз : *a* lifeless, inanimate; spiritless

həjәт : *n* yard; courtyard

həjәчан : *n* worry, alarm, nervousness

həjәчанландырмаг : *v-tr* worry, alarm, bother

həjәчанланмаг : *v* become/grow nervous, worried

həjәчанлы : *a* 1) nervous, worried, alarmed *adv* 2) nervously, worriedly

həjjә : *n astron* Ophiochus, Serpent-holder *constellation*

həкәм : *n coll* judges

həким : *n* 1) doctor, physician 2) philosopher, sage

həкиманә : *adv* 1) wisely, sagaciously *a* 2) wise, sagacious

həкимбашы : *n* chief physician *of a hospital*

həкимлик : *n* 1) profession of physician/doctor 2) doctoring, medical treatment

həкк : *n* 1) engraving 2) inlaid work, inlay

həкк еләмәк : *v* carve, engrave

həккак : *n* engraver

həккаклыг : *n* engraver's profession

həлак : *n* death, destruction, ruin, mortal danger, peril

həлак олмаг : *v* die *as a result of an accident, disaster, war etc.;* perish

həлакәт : *n* see **həлак**

həлакәтли : *a* death-dealing, mortal, fatal

həлвиjjат : *n* sweets, sweetmeats

həлгәви : *a* ring-shaped, annular

həлә : *pro* 1) not yet, not for a while yet; in the meantime, still 2) and what is more

həләзун : *n* 1) spiral 2) snail

həләзуни : *a* spiral, helical

həләлик : *adv* 1) yet, still, as it is now, for the time being *exp* 2) So long! Bye-bye!

həлә-həлбәт : *adv* certainly, without fail

həлим : *a* 1) timid, humble; soft in nature, calm *n* 2) broth, medical decoction

həлиманә : *adv* meekly, humbly, timidly

həлимашы : *n* wheat and meat porridge; jellied boiled wheat and meat *a breakfast dish*

həлимләнмәк, həлимләшмәк : *v* become meek, humble, timid

həлимлик : *n* meekness, humbleness, timidity

həлл : *n* 1) decision 2) resolution *of a problem chem* 3) solution 4) salvation, deliverance

həлл еләмәк : *v* solve; come to a decision

həллач : *n* wool-carder

həлледичи : *n* 1) solvent *a* 2) decisive, resolute

həлләм-гәлләм : *n* swindler, cheater, fraud

həлләнмәк : *v* have pleasure, fun, enjoy *s.t.*

həлләhуш : *n* swindler

həлләhушлуг : *n* swindling, fraud

həлмәшик : *n* 1) galantine, aspic, jellied meat or fish *a* 2) jelly-like

həм : *adv* also, as well as, too

həмаваз : *n mus* accord, consonance

həмавазлыг : *n* consonance

həмаjил : *n* 1) sword-belt, baldric, shoulder-belt 2) amulet

həмаhәнк : *a* 1) sounding, resounding in unison 2) harmonizing

həмбәтн : *a* uterine, born of the same mother

həмвәтән : *n* compatriate, fellow-countryman

həмвилаjәт : *n* see **həмjәрли**

həмгәбилә : *n* 1) fellow-tribesman *a* 2) related, of the same tribe

həмдәм : *n* 2) friend 2) collocutor, interlocuter *person with whom one is speaking*

həмдәрд : *n* companion in misery/grief/sorrow

həмәгидә : *n* see **həммәслик**

həмәл : *n astron* Ares, the Ram *constellation*

həмән : *pro* the same

һәмәрсин : *n* *bot* dog rose, sweetbrier, eglantine *Rosa canina*

һәмәср : *n* contemporary

һәмиjjәт : *n* zeal

һәмиjjәтлә : *adv* zealously

һәмиjjәтли : *a* zealous

һәмин : *deic* that very

һәмишә : *adv* always, constantly, forever

һәмишәбаһар : *n* 1) evergreen; always neat *bot* 2) peony *Paeonia*

һәмишәjашыл : *a* evergreen

һәмишәки : *n* 1) habitué, frequenter *a* 2) revisiting, haunting

һәмишәлик : *a* 1) eternal, life, endless, everlasting *adv* 2) forever, eternally, everlastingly, for life

һәмишәчаван : *a* 1) ever-blossoming 2) eternally young, never-aging *ironic*

һәмjаш : *n* 1) person of the same age

һәмjерли : *n* fellow-countryman, person from the same district

һәмкар : *n* colleague, fellow-worker

һәмкәндли : *n* felloow-villager, person from the same village

һәмлә : *n* attack, offensive

һәмли : *a* see **һамилә**

һәммәзһәб : *n* co-religionist

һәммә'на : *n* 1) synonym *a* 2) synonymous

һәммәнзил : *n* apartment-mate *in a communal apartment in the former Soviet Union)*

һәммәсләк : *n* like-minded person

һәммәһәллә : *n* neighbor, person living in the same neighborhood

һәмпиjалә : *n* 1) drinking-buddy, boon companion *fig* 2) bosom-friend

һәмрә'j : *a* 1) at one *with*, in sympathy *with* showing solidarity *adv* 2) collectively, jointly

һәмрә'jлик : *n* solidarity

һәмрәнк : *a* one-color, monochrome; of the same color

һәмсәрһәд : *a* adjacent, contiguous, bordering *on*

һәмсөһбәт : *n* interlocutor, collocutor

һәмфикир : *n* 1) like-minded person *a* 2) like-minded

һәмхана : *n* 1) lodger, tenant *of a rented apartment* 2) neighbor, apartment-mate *in a communal apartment*

һәмһүгуг : *n* equal, enjoying/possessing equal rights

һәмһүгуглуг : *n* equality of rights, possession of equal rights

һәмһүдуд : *a* see **һәмсәрһәд**

һәмчинин : *pro* also; as well as

һәмчинс : *a* 1) homogenous, uniform 2) related 3) of the same sex

һәмчинслик : *n* 1) homogeneity; relatedness 2) person[s] of the same sex

һәмшәһәрли : *n* person from the same city

һәндәвәр : *prep* 1) around, round, about *n* 2) outskirts, environs, vicinity

һәндәвәриндә : *adv* very close to, in the immediate vicinity

һәндәсә : *n* geometry

һәндәси : *a* geometric

һәнәк : *n* joke, joking, fooling around, buffoonery

һәнәкләшмәк : *v* keep joking, fool around, make fun of, play practical jokes

һәнәкчи : *n* joker, wag

һәнирти : *n* rustle, rustling, whisper, whispering, quiet, obscure sounds

һәнк : *n* rhythm, meter, measure, bar, beat, tempo, time

һәнкамә : *n* 1) fuss 2) show, spectacle, noisy performance

һәнчама : *n* hinge, joint-pin

һәпәнд : *n* mean, low, cheap, banal

һәпир-чупур : *n* rubbish, trash, junk, garbage

һәр : *pro* every, each

һәр бир : *pro* everybody, everyone

һәр jердә : *pro* everywhere

һәр кәс : *pro* everybody, everyone

һәраjлыг : *a* 1) monthly *n* 2) monthly basis

һәрами : *n* see **һәрамы**

һәрамилик : *n* see **һәрамылыг**

һәрарәт : *n* 1) heat, temperature *fig* 2) ardour

һәрарәтли : *a* hot, flaming, ardent

һәрб : *n* war

һәрбә-зорба : *n* threat, menace

һәрби : *a* military

һәрбиjjәли : *n* military serviceman

һәрбиләшдирилмәк : *v* be militarized

һәрбиләшдирмә : *n* militarization

һәрбиләшдирмәк : *v-tr* militarize

һәрбиләшмәк : *v* become militarized

һәрдәмхәјал : *a* impermanent, light-minded, unreliable

һәрдәмхәјаллыг : *n* impermanence, unreliability; instability, light-mindedness

һәрдән, һәрдәнбир : *adv* sometimes, occasionally, from time to time

һәрә : *n* each *person*

һәракат : *n* movement; traffic

һәрәкәт : *n* 1) movement, motion 2) action 3) deed, exploit, gesture, behavior 4) animation

һәрәкәтверичи : *a* moving, driving, imparting motion

һәрәкәтли : *a* 1) mobile 2) affected, coquettish, mannered

һәрәкәтсиз : *a* 1) motionless, inactive *adv* 2) motionlessly, inactively

һәрәкәтсизлик : *n* motionlessness, inactivity, apathy, immobility

һәрәм : *n* wife, spouse

һәрәмағасы : *n* eunuch

һәрәмхана : *n* 1) harem, seraglio *a* 2) harem

һәрзә : *n* 1) nonsense, rubbish, absurdity 2) obscene, bawdy 3) foul-mouthed person

һәрзәкар, һәрзәку : *n* 1) chatter-box, blowhard 2) foul-mouthed blatherskite

һәрзәлик : *n* foul-mouthed loquacity

һәри : *n* see **бәли**

һәрис : *a* 1) greedy, grasping, insatiable, passionate 2) inveterate, out-and-out *n* 3) fan, enthusiast

һәрислик : *n* greed, graspingness, avarice, insatiability

һәриф : *n* 1) rival,opponent 2) partner *fig* 3) strange/fishy/suspoicious character, phony

һәрки-һәркилик : anarchy, confusion, muddle

һәркүнкү : *a* daily, usual, ordinary, customary

һәркүнлүк : *a* 1) daily, quotidian *adv* 2) on a daily basis

һәрләмә : *vn* fr. **һәрләмәк**

һәрләмәк : *v* 1) roll, turn around, rotate 2) pursue, chase

һәрләндиричи : *a* rotatory

һәрләндирмәк : *v* 1) rotate, turn around 2) start to twirl 3) undertake a little work

һәрләнмә : *n* 1) rotation, turning around *a* 2) rotary

һәрләнмәк : *v* 1) rotate, turn around, go round 2) take a walk 3) hang around together

һәрләтмәк : *v* see **һәрләмәк**

һәррач : *n* auction, public sale

һәртәрәфли : *a* all-round, thorough, detailed

һәрф : *n* letter *alphabetical*

һәрфбәһәрф : *adv* letter by letter; literally

һәрфи : *a* literal

һәрфиjjән : *adv* literally, verbatim, word-for-word

һәрфи-һәрфинә : *adv* literally, verbatim, word-for-word

һәрф-һәдјан : *n* nonsense, rubbish

һәрф-һәрф : *adv* letter by letter

һәрчәнд : *conj* although, despite, in spite of

һәрчаји : *a* 1) unduly familiar, free-and-easy 2) inappropriate, out of place, inopportunely said, mal à propos

һәрч-мәрч : *adv* 1) completely, utterly 2) muddle, confusion, turmoil, upheaval *n* 3) chaos

һәрч-мәрчлик : *n* anarchy, turmoil, chaos, upheaval

һәсәд : *n* envy, jealousy

һәсир : *n* matting; mat

һәсирчи : *n* matting-maker

һәсирчилик : *n* occupation of matting-maker

һәсләмәк : *v* stop short and shy back, shy, balk *of animals*

һәср : *n* dedication, consecration

һәсрәт : *n* 1) grief, sorrow; 2) aspiration, desire

һәсрәт чәкмәк : *v* grieve

һәссас : *a* sensitive, impressionable

һәссаслыг : *n* 1) sensitivity, sensitiveness 2) impressionability

һәтта : *adv* even

һәфтә : *n* week

һәфтәарасы : *n* 1) week-long interval, interval between o.'s rest days/days-off *adv* 2) in the course of a week

һәфтәашыры : *adv* once in two weeks

һәфтәбечәр : *n* pickled vegetables

һәфтәлик : *a* 1) weekly, hebdomadal 2) weekly, sufficient for a week *adv* 3) every week, weekly

һә-һә : *intj* Oh, yes, sure!

həчв : *n* 1) treatise, booklet, pamphlet 2) satire, lampoon

həчвиjjат : *n* 1) collection of satirical articles 2) booklet of lampoons

həчвиjjə : *n* epigrammatic verse

həчвjазан : *n* see **həчвчи, həчвку**

həчвли : *a* satirical

həчвчи, həчвку : *n* satirist ; pamphleteer,writer of lampoons

həчəмəт : *n* 1) blood-letting *med* 2) cupping-glass

həчм : *n* 1) capacity 2) tonnage; volume, bulk

həчмли : *a* capacious, bulky, volumous

həчч : *n* hajj *the pilgrimage to Mecca required of every Muslim once in his life*

həшəм : *n* thatch, straw

həшəмəт : *n* magnificence, pomp, state, luxury

həшəмəтлə : *adv* magnificently; with pomp and state

həшəрат : *n* insect

həшəратjejəн : *a* 1) insectivorous *n* 2) insectivore

həшəри : *n* nymphomaniac

həшəрилик : *n* nymphomania

həшиш : *n* hashish

həштад : *num* eighty

həштадиллик : *n* eightieth anniversary

həштадынчы : *ord* eightieth

həштадjашлы : *a n* eighty-years old *a person*

həштəрхан : *n* Astrakhan *Russian city on the Volga*

hибрид : *n biol* 1) hybrid *a* 2) hybrid

hибридлəшдирилмə : *n biol* hybridization

hиддəт : *n* rage, fury, wrath; madness

hиддəтлə : *adv* madly, angrily, with rage, infuriatedly, wrathfully

hиддəтлəндирмəк : *v-intr* infuriate, madden, lash into fury

hиддəтлəнмəк : *v* become outraged, infuriated, lashed into fury

hиддəтли : *a* outraged, maddened infuriated

hидравлик : *a* 1) hydraulic *n* 2) hydrolics, hydromechanics

hидравлика : *n* hydraulics, hydromechanics

hидрокен : *n chem* hydrogen

hидроплан : *n* hydroplane

hиjлə : *n* trick, dodge, ruse, stratagem

hиjлəбаз, hиjлəкəр : *a* 1) tricky, crafty, wily *n* 2) sly person, sharper, cheat

hиjлəбазлыг, hиjлəкəрлик : *n* cunning, guile, craftiness, slyness

hиjлəкəрчəсинə : *adv* triclily, guilefully, craftily, slyly

hиjлəсиз : *a* simple-hearted, ingenuous, unsophisticated

hиккə : *n* wickedness, spite, meanness

hикмəт : *n* wisdom

hикмəтли : *a* wise

hил : *n bot* cardamom *Ellataria cardamomum*

hилал : *n* lunar crescent, crescent moon, half-moon

hилали : *a* lunar-crescent

hилали-əhмəр : *n* Red Crescent *Turkish organization similar to the Red Cross*

hим : *n* eye-signs, eye-gestures; hints

hимаjə : *n* 1) patronage 2) disdain, scorn 3) influence

hимаjəчи : *n* protector, patron

hимлəшмəк : *v* exchange winks and signs

hиммəт : *n* 1) persistent efforts, zeal 2) mercy, benevolence, magnanimity

hиммəт көстəрмəк : *v* 1) apply efforts 2) show generosity, magnanimity

hиммəтлə : *adv* 1) persistently, ardently, energetically 2) benevolently, magnanimously

hиммəтли : *a* 1) energetic, active, zealous 2) benevolent, magananimous

hимн : *n* hymn; anthem

hин : *n* 1) hen-house; hut, shack, hovel, cabin

hинд : *a* Indian

hиндгозу ағачы *n bot* coconut

hинддарысы : *n bot* sorghum

hиндистан : *n* India

hиндли : *n* American Indian, Native American

hинду : *n* Hindu

hиндушка : *n* turkey

hипноз : *n* hypnosis

hипнозчу : *n* hypnotist

hипотенуз : *n math* hypotenuse

hирс : *n* irritation, nervousness

hирслəндирмəк : *v* irritate, get on *s.o.'s* nerves

һирсләнмә : *vn* fr. **һирсләнмәк**

һирсләнмәк : *v* be irritated/angered

һирсли : *a* 1) irate, irritated *adv* 2) irritatedly, irately

һирслилик : *n* irascibleness, irritation

һирсли-һирсли : *adv* angrily, irately, irritatedly

һис : *n* soot

һисбасмыш : *a* sooty, covered with soot

һисләндирмәк : *v* get *s.t.* sooted over; smoke *s.t.* up

һисләнмәк : *v* get covered with soot

һисләтдирмәк : *caus* of **һисләтмәк**

һисләтмәк : *v* see **һисләндирмәк**

һисли : *a* smoked up, sooted, sooty

һисли-паслы : *a* grubby, filthy, dirty

һис-пас : *n* dirtiness, filth, pollution *lit. soot and rust*

һисс : *n* feeling, sentiment

һиссә : *n* 1) portion, share 2) component 3) military unit

һиссә-һиссә : *adv* in parts, in shares

һиссәчик : *n* particle

һисси : *a* sensitive; sensual; sentimental

һиссиз : *a* insensitive, devoid of feeling; unsensual

һиссизләшдирмә : *n* anesthesia, anesthetization

һиссизләшдирмәк : *v* anesthetize

һиссизлик : *n* 1) loss of consciousness 2) insensitivity, unfeelingness 3) absence of sensuality

һиссијјат : *n* 1) feelings, sensitivity 2) sentiment,sentimentality 3) sensuality

һисхана : *n* smoking shed

һифз : *n* protection, guard, patronage

һичаз : *n* 1) Hejaz *area of Western Saudi Arabia having its own constitution* 2) Hijaz *a mugam, or traditional Azerbaijani melody*

һичран : *n* separation, living apart

һичрәт : *n* resettlement, emigration

һичри : *n* Hegira flight of Mohammed from Mecca to Medina in 622 A. D., now taken as the beginning of the Muslim era.

һыгылдамаг : *v* groan

һыгтына-һыгтына : *adv* groaning while straining and faltering

һыгтынма : *n* groaning with effort

һыгтынмаг : *v* groan, strain with effort

һырылдамаг, һыртылдамаг : *v* laugh loudly, giggle on the slightest provocation

һырылты : *n* loud laughing; giggling

һыр-һыр : *n* one given to laughing for very little reason

һычгырыг : *n* see **һычгырты**

һычгырмаг : *v* hiccup

һычгырты : *n* hiccuping

һм : *intj* hm-m hm-m

һов : *n* 1) urgent help, assistance, aid 2) swelling, inflammation *of a wound*

һовланмаг : *v* swell, become inflamed *of a wound*

һовуз : *n* reservoir, cistern

һовур : *n* interval of time

һовур-һовур : *adv* relieving one another

һовхурма : *n* exhaling, breathing out

һовхурмаг : *v* exhale, breath out

һогга : *n* 1) joke, practical joke, conjuring trick, 2) clay pipe with a cup for smoking opium

һоггабаз : *n* 1) stage-magician, sleight-of-hand artist, clown, practical joker, buffoon *fig* 1) swindler, rogue, trickster

һоггабазлыг : *n* 1) sleight-of-hand,playing practical jokes, clowning 2) swindling, fraud

һодаг : *n* herder, herdsman, cowman

һозаки, һозу : *a* 1) clumsy, awkward *n* 2) clumsy/awkward person, lubber, fumbler

һојдуламаг : *v* hiss *off the stage* , catcall, boo

һојду-һојду : *n* hissing, catcalling, boo-ing

һол : *n* see **фырфыра**

һолландијалы : *n* Dutchman, Hollander, Netherlander

һопдурма : *n* *phys* absorption, soaking in

һопдурмаг : *v* absorb, drink in, suck in

һопдурмајан : *a* water-proof, impermeable, impervious *to moisture*

һопма : *n* *phys* absorption

һопмаг : *pass* be absorbed

һоппана-һоппана : *adv* jumping, hopping

һоппандырмаг, һоппандыртмаг : *caus* of **һоппанмаг**

һоппаныш : *n* jump

һоппанма : *n* jumping

һоппанмаг : *v* jump, hop

һоппулдатмаг : *v* swallow/wolf down in big pieces; devour

hoп-hoп : *n zool* hoopoe, a bird *fam. Upupidae*

hoppa : *n* 1) jelly, jelly-like porridge; any semi-liquid jelly-like substance *fig* 2) thick, deep mud

hoртлатмаг : *v-intr* choke

hoруг : *a* 1) quick, prompt, efficient *n* 2) quick, prompt, efficient person

ho-ha : *intj* shout or command used to halt harnessed bulls, or water-buffalos

hөвзә : *n* basin *region drained by a river*

hөвкә : *n* soldering iron

hөвкәләмә : *vn* fr. **hөвкәләмәк**

hөвкәләмәк : *v* 1) crumple, clump 2) concentrate, mass

hөвләки, hөвлнак : *adv* 1) in a panic, panicking 2) in a rush, hastily

hөвсәлә : *n* patience; endurance

hөвсәләли : *a* 1) patient 2) assiduous, persevering

hөвсәләсиз : *a* 1) impatient 2) unpersevering

hөвсәләсизлик : *n* 1) impatience 2) lack of assiduity/perseverence

hөвсәмә : *v* winnowing

hөвсәмәк : *v* winnow

hөвсәр : *n* winnowing-machine, winnower, fanner

hөкм : *n* 1) order *leg* 2) sentence

hөкмдар : *n* monarch, ruler, dictator

hөкмдарлыг : *n* dominion, sway, dictatorship

hөкмдарчасына : *adv* sovereignly *as a ruler/monarch/dictator*

hөкмән : *adv* without fail, unavoidably, necessarily

hөкмран : *n* 1) ruler, dictator *a* 2) ruling, governing, reigning

hөкмранлыг : *n* regime, dominion, sway, dictatorship

hөкмфәрма : *n* see **hөкмран**

hөкумәт : *n* government, power, authority

hөкумәтсизлик : *n* anarchy

hөнкүрмә : *vn* fr. **hөнкүрмәк**

hөнкүрмәк : *v* weep, sob

hөнкүртү : *n* weeping, sobbing

hөнкүр-hөнкүр : *adv* sobbingly,wailingly, lachrymosely

hөрәләнмәк : *v* swagger, boast

hөркү : *n* 1) laying/construction *of a masonry wall* 2) plaiting, basketwork, wickerwork

hөрмә : *vn* fr. **hөрмәк**

hөрмәк : *v* 1) weave, spin, plait, wattle 2) lay *a masonry wall* 3) brick up, wall up

hөрмәләмәк : *v* weave, spin; interlace; knit

hөрмәт : *n* honor, respect, prestige

hөрмәт бәсләмәк : *v* respect/ feel respect for *s.o.*

hөрмәткар : *a* see **hөрмәтчил**

hөрмәткаранә, hөрмәтлә : *adv* respectfully, politely

hөрмәтли : *a* respected, honored; respectable

hөрмәтсиз : *a* 1) not respected, held in contempt, disregarded *of a person* 2) crude, impolite

hөрмәтсизлик : *n* crudeness, crudity ; rudeness; impoliteness, discourtesy, bad manners

hөрмәтчил : *a n* polite, affable, cordial, considerate

hөрмәтчиллик : *n* thoughtfulness, affability friendliness

hөрүк : *n* braid *of hair*

hөрүкләмә : *n* braiding *of hair*

hөрүкләмәк : *v* plait *hair*

hөрүмчәк : *n* 1) spider *a* 2) spider['s], arachnoid

hөрүчү : *n* knitter

hөрүш : *n* wet, raw

hөчәт : *a* 1) stubborn, obstinate *n* 2) stubborn, obstinate, pig-headed person

hөчәтләшмәк : *v* argue, discuss hotly *one with another*

hөчәтлик : *n* stubbornness, obstinacy, pig-headedness

hубара : *n zool* bustard, a game bird *fam. Otididae*

hујухмаг : *v* be stunned, taken aback, struck dumb

hул : *a* 1) vertical *adv* 2) upwards

hулу : *n* peach

hумајун : *n mus* 1) humayun *a traditional Azerbaijani muğam a* 2) august, regal

hуманизм : *n* humanism

hуманист : *n* humanist

hуманитар : *a* humanitarian

hумус : *n* humus, black soil, chernozyom

hури : *n* houri. *In Muslim belief, one of the beautiful maidens alloted to those who attain Paradise*

hуш : *n* 1) consciousness memory 2) attention 3) somnolence, half-sleep, oblivion

hушјар : *a* alert, attentive, cautious

hушјарлыг : *n* alertness, attentiveness, cautiousness

hушјарчасына : *adv* alertly, attentively, cautiously

hуш-куш : *n* tension, attention

hуш-кушла : *adv* attentively, tensely, with concentration

hушлу : *a* quick-minded, bright, smart

hушлу-башлы : *a* see **hафизәли**

hушсуз : *a* 1) absent-minded; forgetful 2) unconscious *adv* 3) unconsciously

hушсузлашмаг : *v* become absent-minded, forgetful

hушсузлуг : *n* absent-mindedness, forgetfulness; amnesia

hүгуг : *n* 1) law; justice, legality *a* 2) legal, juridical

hүгуглу : *a* legal, lawful; just, fair

hүгугсуз : *a* 1) enjoying no rights, deprived of rights, disfranchised *n* 2) pariah, outcast

hүгугсузлуг : *n* lack of rights

hүгугшүнас : *n* lawyer, specialist in civil law, legal expert

hүгугшүнаслыг : *n* jurisprudence

hүдуд : *n* limit, border, boundary

hүдудлама : *n* delimitation, demarcation, placing limits/boundaries *upon*

hүдудламаг : *v* delimit, demarcate, establish/put boundaries *upon*

hүдудлу : *a* delimited, demarcated, having boundaries/demarcations

hүдудсуз : *a* limitless, unbounded

hүд-hүд : *n zool* see **hоп-hоп**

hүзн : *n* sadness, grief, sorrow

hүзнлә : *adv* sadly, mournfully, sorrowfully

hүзнлү : *a* sad, grief-stricken, sorrowful

hүзур : *n* presence *of another person*

hүлгум : *n anat* throat, gullet; pharynx

hүллүкчү : *n* cheat, fraud, swindler

hүндүр : *a* 1) high 2) loud *adv* 3) highly, loudly

hүндүрдән : *adv* 1) from the heights, from on high 2) loudly

hүндүрлүк : *n* 1) height, altitude, elevation *geog* 2) eminence 3) loudness

hүнәр : *n* 1) skill, capacity, gift, talent 2) exploit, deed 3) bravery, courage, heroism

hүнәрли : *a* 1) skilful, gifted, capable 2) heroic, brave, courageous

hүнәрсиз : *a* unskilful, ungifted, untalented

hүнү : *n* mosquito

hүрәјән : *a* 1) incessantly barking *n* 2) incessantly barking dog *fig* 3) quarrelsome person

hүркмәк : *v* be afraid, scared, frightened

hүркүтмәк : *v* scare, frighten, intimidate

hүркүтмүш : *v* scared to death; startled

hүркүч : *n* hump *of a camel*

hүрмә : *n* barking *of a dog*

hүрмәк : *v* bark *of a dog*

hүрриjјәт : *n* freedom, liberty

hүрийјәтпәрвәр, hүрийјәтсевәр : *a* 1) freedom-loving *n* 2) freedom-loving person/people

hүруфат : *n* 1) letters, alphabet 2) script

hүруфатөлчән : *n* typemeter, printer's rule *ruler for determining the size in points of a typeface*

hүрүш : *n* bark, barking

hүрүшмәк : *v* bark *many dogs together*

hүсн : *n* beauty, comeliness

hүсни-рәғбәт, hүсни-тәвәччөh : *n* favorable disposition/attitude, favor, good graces

hүсни-тәвәччөh көстәрмәк : *v* sympathize *with s.o.*

hүснхәт : *n* penmanship, skill in writing, calligraphy

hүчејрә : *n biol* cell

hүчејрәарасы : *a biol* intercellular

hүчејрәли : *a biol* cellular

hүчрә : *n* cell *monastic*

hүчрәнишин : *n relig* lay brother

hүчум : *n* attack, offensive, invasion

Ч

ч : thirtieth letter of the Azerbaijani alphabet

чаггал : *n zool* 1) jackal *fig* 2) coward

чаггылдамаг : *v* crack, crackle

чаггылдатмаг : *caus* of **чаггылдамаг**

чаггылты : *n* cracking, crackling

чаг : *n* 1) time, period of time 2) good mood *a* 3) full, well-fed, fat, plump

чаға : *n* baby, nursling

чағала : *n bot* ovary of a fruiting plant

чағаланмаг : *v* behave childishly

чағдаш : *a* contemporary

чағырылмаг : *v* be called/summoned/invited

чағырым : *n* shouting distance

чағырыш : *n* 1) call, summons; appeal 2) draft notice, conscription 3) convocationn 4) invitation; 5) subpoena *a* 6) call-up, draft; invitational; *gram* vocative

чағырышма : *n* roll-call

чағырышмаг : *v* call the roll

чағырышчы : *n* draftee, conscript

чағырма : *n* calling, summoning

чағырмаг : *v* 1) call; appeal 2) draft, conscript 3) invite; summon; subpoena

чағыртдырмаг, чағыртмаг : *caus* of **чағырмаг**

чағырты : *n* call, appeal, shout

чадыр : *n* tent; marquee

чадырлыг : *n* tent-cloth/fabric

чадра : *n* veil, chador *large veil worn by a Moslem woman to cover her body, dress, and most of the face*

чадралы : *a* wearing a chador, veiled

чадрасыз : *a n* without a veil/chaddor, unveiled

чај кандары : *n* rapids

чај : *n* 1) river 2) tea

чај јатағы : *n* riverbed

чајан : *n zool* scorpion

чајбасары : *n* river flood plain, high water

чајгарталы : *n* osprey, fish-hawk *Falco haliëtus*

чајдан : *n* teakettle; teapot

чајдашы : *n* cobblestone

чајыр : *n* bot couch-grass, quack grass *Agropyron repens*

чајырлыг : *n* thicket of couch-grass

чајыр-чәмән : *n* meadow

чајлаг : *n* wadi, dry riverbed

чајламаг : *v* serve tea to a large group

чајпулу : *n* tip, gratuity

чајсүнкәри : *n bot* a fresh water sponge *Spongia fluviatilis*

чајхана : *n* tea-house

чајхор : *n* tea-drinker, tea-fancier

чајчы : *n* 1) tea-house employee 2) tea-grower

чајчылыг : *n* 1) occupation of tea-house owner 2) tea-growing

чајчыхана : *n* see **чајхана**

чал : *a* 1) roan 2) gray 3) gray-haired, having hair streaked/touched with gray

чала : *n* pit; ravine; hollow, depression, hole

чалаған : *n zool* kite, *fam. Falconidae*

чалар, чаларлыг : *n* hue, shade *of color*

чала-чухур : *n* pot-holes, ruts *on a road*

чала-чухурлуг : *a* rutted, pot-holed *of a road*

чалбаш : *a* grey-haired, having hair streaked with gray

чалғы : *n* 1) music *n* 2) besom *small broom made of twigs a* 3) musical

чалғыламаг : *v* sweep with a besom

чалғычы : *n* musician

чалғычылыг : *n* profession of musician

чалдырмаг, чалдыртмаг : *v* see **чалмаг**

чалы : *n* bushes; bushy area

чалыгушу : *n zool* goldcrest, golden-crested kinglet *Regulus cristatus, a very small European bird*

чалынч : *n* mowing

чалынчан : *n* mower

чалышган : *a* 1) industrious, diligent, conscientious 2) hard worker, workaholic, enthusiastic worker

чалышганлыг : *n* industriousness, conscientiousness, diligence, zeal

чалышганлыгла : *adv* industriously, conscientiously, diligently, zealously

чалышдырмаг, чалышдыртмаг : *caus* of **чалышмаг**

чалышма : *vn* 1) fr. **чалышмаг** 2) exercise

чалышмаг : *v* 1) work, toil strive, try 2) exercise

чалламаг : *v* become gray/gray-haired

чалланмаг, чаллашмаг : *v* become gray-haired

чаллыг : *n* streaks of gray *in the hair*

чалма : *vn* 1) of **чалмаг** 2) turban

чалмаг : 1) play *a musical instrument* 2) beat in 3) knock 4) wave the wings 5) sting 6) be shot with *a color* 7) honk, whistle 8) mow 9) hit 10) steal 11) mix up *with s.t.* 12) sweep with a besom

чалмалы : *a n* turbaned, wearing a turban

чалмалыг : *n* turban fabric, fabric to be used for a turban

чалов : *n* scoop

чалсаггал : *a n* gray-bearded

чалсач : *n* gray-haired

чалха(ла)ма : *vn* fr. **чалха(ла)маг**

чалха(ла)маг : *v* 1) stir 2) splash 3) rock, roll 4) rinse, gargle

чалхаланмаг : *v* 1) be stirred be splashed 3) be rocked 4) be rinsed

чал-чарпаз : *adv* 1) criss-cross *a* 2) cross

чамадан : *n* suitcase, valise, bag

чампа : *n* rice *of low grade/quality*

чанаг : *n* 1) chanag, *old measurement of weight for dry substances, about 5 kilos* 2) vessel holding about 5 g dry weight *anat* 3) pelvis 4 wooden basin/bowl 5) sink, wash-basin 5) scoop, bucket

чанта : *n* handbag, bag, pouch

чап : *n* print; printing

чапа : *n* see **лөвбәр**

чапаг : *n zool* bream *a freshwater cyprinoid fish*

чапаған : *n* runner

чапалама : *n* floundering; convulsions

чапаламаг : *v* 1) flounder; convulse 2) fuss

чапар : *n* courier; messenger; envoy

чапараг : *adv* racing, running headlong

чапархана : *n* traditional inn; rest-stop

чапачаг : *n* large butcher knife, meat-cleaver

чапгын : *n* raid, foray, invasion, offensive

чапгынчы : *n* robber, brigand

чапгынчылыг : *n* robbery, brigandage

чапдырмаг, чапдыртмаг : *caus* of **чапмаг**

чапыг : *n* scar, scarification circatrice

чапылыб-таланмаг : *v* be ruined, go broke; go bankrupt

чапылмаг : *v* 1) be chopped, smashed 2) be attacked, be robbed

чапышма : *n* races, horse-races,

чапышмаг : *v* race, compete in races

чапма : *vn* fr. **чапмаг**

чапмаг : *v* 1) chop, cut apart 2) rush, gallop 3) rob

чаповул : *n* robbery, gangsterism, brigandage

чаповулчу : *n* robber, gangster, brigand

чаповулчулуг : *n* gangsterism, robbery

чапхана : *n* 1) printing-house, printshop *a* 2) typogrqphic

чапчы : *n* 1) printer 2) swindler, crook, confidence-man

чапчылыг : *n* poligraphy, graphic arts, printing trades

чар : *n* 1) Czar *a* 2) Czarist

чарвадар : *n* carrier, carter, cabman

чарвадарлыг : *n* occupation of carrier/carter/cabman

чаргат : *n* head-kerchief, head-scarf

чардаг : *n* attic, loft, garret

чарә : *n* means, method; way out

чарәсиз : *a* 1) incurable, beyond recovery, hopeless; 2) irreparable, irremediable 3) helpless 4) forced, compulsory, unavoidable *adv* 5) incurably, irrecoverably, hopelessly, unavoidably

чарәсизлик : *n* 1) incurability, hopelessness; helplessness 2) irreparability, irremediability 3) desperate situation, no-exit-situation

чаризм : *n* Czarism

чаричә : *n* Czarina, empress

чарыг : *n* bast sandals, *traditional peasants' footwear*

чарыглыг : *a n* suitable for/used to make bast sandals

чаркаһ : *n* charkah a traditional Azerbaijani muǧam

чаркүл : *a* square

чарлыг : *n* Czarism *as a political system* 2) reign *of a Czar*

чармых : *n* 1) cross 2) crucifixion

чар-начар : *adv* willy-nilly, like it or not

чарпаз : *a* 1) lying crosswise, crossing, intersecting *n* 2) fastening, fastener; clasp, buckle

чарпазлама : *n* 1) crossing, intersection *biol* 2) interbreeding

чарпазламаг : *v* intercross; interbreed

чарпазланма : *n* see **чарпазлашдырмаг**

чарпазланмаг : *v* be crossed, be crossbred

чарпазлашдырмаг : *v-tr* 1) interbreed 2) intersect

чарпазлашма : *n* interbreeding, intercrossing

чарпазлашмаг : *v* 1) interbreed 2) cross

чарпаjы : *n* bed

чарпанаг : *n* fragment, splinter *i.e. glass or metal*

чарпара : *n* castanets

чарпышма : *n* battle, fighting

чарпышмаг : *v* battle, fight, struggle

чарпмаг : *v* beat, smash *itself/oneself forcefully against something*

чарсу : *n* indoor market-place *in the Near East and the Transcaucasus*

чартылдамаг : *v* crack, crackle

чартылты : *n* crackle, crackling

чарх : *n* *tech* 1) wheel 2) grinding wheel, sharpener, lathe

чархламаг : *v* sharpen *on a grinding wheel*

чархланмаг : *v* be sharpened, pointed

чархлатдырмаг, **чархлатмаг** : *caus* of **чархламаг**

чархлы : *a* wheeled, equipped with wheels

чархсыз : *a* not wheeled, unequipped with wheels

чархчы : *n* knife-grinder/sharpener *person*

чархчылыг : *n* occupation of knife-grinder/sharpener

чарһовуз : *n* swimming-pool

чаршаб : *n* veil, chador

чаршәнбә : *n* Wednesday

чат : *n* 1) crack, gap 2) see **чатаг**

чатаг, **чатаглы** : *a* hobbled

чатагламаг : *v* hobble

чатагланмаг : *v* be hobbled, restrained

чатал : *n* double-boled trees

чатар-чатмаз : *adv* by the skin of o.'s teeth, by a gnat's whisker *referring to an action accomplished but barely so*

чатасы : *a* due to, owing to *money/payment to s.o.*

чаташыг : *a* grown together

чатдырма : *n* delivery, shipping and handling

чатдырмаг : *v* 1) deliver; ship and handle 2) have time to, manage to

чаты : *n* 1) woollen rope 2) bed-plate 3) roof-beam

чаты кәрәштәси : *n* rafters

чатыг : *n* joint, butt-junction

чатыламаг : *v* whip, flog

чатылы : *a* 1) loaded up; burdened 2) hobbled, tied up, shackled 3) stacked *rifles*

чатылмаг : *v* 1) be loaded; be burdened 2) be hobbled/tied up/shackled 3) be stacked *rifles*

чатырты : *n* cracking, crackling

чатыщдырмаг : *v* be barely on time

чатышмаг : *v* be enough, be sufficient

чатлаг : *n* 1) crack, crackle *a* 2) cracked, crackled

чатлаг-чатлаг : *a* cracked, chipped

чатламаг : *v* crack, burst out

чатлатмаг : *caus* of **чатламаг**

чатма : *vn* fr. **чатмаг**

чатмаг : *v* 1) reach, achieve 2) arrive 3) catch up 4) approach 5) be enough, suffice 6) be due to 7) load, burden 8) survive 9) hobble

чатмагаш : *a* having eyebrows grown together, with eyebrows meeting at the bridge of the nose

чат-чат : *a* see **чатлаг-чатлаг**

чахылы : *a* stuck into, plunged into

чахылмаг : *v* be stuck into, plunged into

чахыр : *n* 1) wine *a* 2) vinous

чахырсатан : *n* wine merchant; wine-salesman

чахырчы : *n* distiller

чахырчылыг : *n* distillation

чахычы : *n* stamper, calker

чахмаг : *n* 1) trigger *v* 2) release *a trigger* 3) strike *fire from a flint* 4) flash, strike *lightning* 5) plunge into, drive into 5) stamp

чахмагдашы : *n* flint *formerly used for striking fire with a piece of steel*

чахнащдырмаг : *v* 1) worry, bother, alarm, rouse *s.o.* 2) anger s.o., make s.o. indignant

чахнашма : *n* panic, commotion, rumpus

чахнашмаг : *v* worry, be anxious/uneasy, be alarmed

чах-чах : *n* rattle *watchman's, or child's* , clapper

чахчур : *n* wide trousers *formerly worn by Near Eastern women*

чаш : *a* 1) squint-eyed *adv* 2) obliquely

чаш галмаг : *v* be embarrassed/ misled confused

чашбаш : *adv* state of confusion, being mixed up

чашбашлыг : *n* confusion, perplexity, bewilderment

чашгын : *a* stunned, shocked, confused

чашгынлыг : *n* confusion, bewilderment, embarrassment

чашдырылмаг : *v* be misled, be confused, be discouraged, be embarrassed

чашдырмаг : *v* mislead, muddle, confuse, discourage

чашырмаг : *v* see **чашдырмаг**

чашмаг : *v* become misled, confused, muddled, discouraged, embarrassed

чевик : *a* 1) flexible, nimble, adroit, dexterous *adv* 2) flexibly, adroitly, nimbly, dextterously

чевиклик : *n* flexibility, adroitness, dexterity

чевирмә : *vn* fr. **чевирмәк**

чевирмәк : *v* 1) turn, overturn 2) turn upside down 3) transform 4) translate 5) turn clothes *in sewing, by reversing the fabric*

чевиртдирмәк, чевиртмәк : *caus* of **чевирмәк**

чеврә : *n* 1) circumference; outline; contour *math* 2) periphery

чеврәләмәк : *v* encircle, enclose in a circle

чеврәләнмәк : *v* be encircled, be enclosed in a circle

чеврәсиндә : *postp* around

чеврилиш : *n* revolution, coup d'état

чеврилмә : *vn* fr. **чеврилмәк**

чеврилмәк : *v* 1) be turned, be overturned 2) be turned upside down 3) be transformed 4) be translated

чејнәмә : *n* 1) chewing, mastication, rumination *a* 2) chewing, masticatory, manducatory

чејнәмәк : *v* 1) chew *fig* 2) repeat frequently

чејнәнмәк : *v* be chewed/masticated

чемодан : *n* suitcase

чемпион : *n* champion

чемпионлуг : *n* championship

червон : *n hist* 1) chervonets gold coin of 3, 5, or 10 rubles denomination; 10 ruble note in circulation 1922-47 *colloq* 2) ruble *corresponds to U.S. "buck"*

чери : *n* squint-eyed, cross-eyed

чертјож : *n* 1) drawing, sketch a 2) drawing

чертјожчу : *n* draftsman

чесунча : *n* tussore, also called tussah/tusseh silk, *a coarse silk usually undyed and left in its natural fawn color*

чет : *n* quarter *in various senses*

чех : *n* 1) a Czech *a* 2) Czech

чехчә : *adv* in Czech *language*

чечен : *n* a Chechen

чечәлә : *n* little finger, pinkie

чечәмәк : *v* choke *over*

чешид : *n* kind, sort, variety of something

чешидләјичи : *n* 1) see **чешидчи** *a* 2) sorting

чешидләмәк : *v* sort, sort out

чешидләтдирмәк, чешидләтмәк : *caus* of **чешидләмәк**

чешидчи : *n* sorter

чешмә : *n* spring, fountain

чешмәк : *n* eye-glasses, spectacles

чешмәкли : *a* wearing eye-glasses

чешмәкчи : *n* optician

чешни : *n* pattern *for sewing, embroidery etc*

чәјирдәк : *n* see **чәрдәк**

чәјирдәкли : *a* see **чәрдәкли**

чәјиртҝә : *n* locust, grasshopper

чәкдирмәк, чәкдиртмәк : *caus* of **чәкмәк**

чәкә : *a* tight, tense

чәки : *n* weight

чәкибалыгы : *n* see **сазан**

чәкил : *n bot* mulberry tree *Morus*

чәкили : *a* 1) weighed 2) drawn, sketched 3) embroidered; open-work[ed]

чәкилиш : *n* retreat

чәкиллик : *n* mulberry-grove

чәкилмә : *vn* 1) fr. **чәкилмәк** *geog* 2) ebb, ebb-tide

чәкилмәк : *v* 1) pull *os.* along, be pulled 2) retreat, get back, fall back 3) get away 4) be weighed 5) subside, sink

чәким : *n* pinch *of s.t.*

чәкиндирмәк : *v* talk *s.o.* out of doing *s.t.* ; disssuade *s.o.* from *s.t.*

чәкинә-чәкинә : *adv* timidly, faint-heartedly, meekly

чәкинкән : *a n* meek, timid, cowardly

чәкинмә : *n* abstinence; abstention

чәкинмәдән : *adv* importunately, stubbornly; unrestrainedly

чәкинмәз : *a* persistent, importunate, uncontrolled, unrestrained

чәкинмәк : *v* 1) avoid, abstain *from* , stand aside 2) be timid, not have the courage *to do s.t,* not dare *to do s.t.* 3) disdain, have an aversion *to do s.t.*

чәкинти : *n* cigarette butt

чәкисиз : *a* weightless

чәкисизлик : *n* weightlessness

чәкич : *n* hammer

чәкичвуран : *n tech* hammerer

чәкичләмәк : *v* 1) hammer *s.t.* 2) forge

чәкишдирмәк : *v* pull in opposite directions

чәкишмә : *n* 1) misunderstanding ; quarrel; litigation 2) bet, wager; dispute

чәкишмәк : *v* 1) quarrel, argue *with*, squabble, dispute 2) bet, wager

чәкмә : *vn* 1) fr. **чәкмәк** 2) shoe, boot *chem* 3) distillation, sublimation

чәкмәк : *v* 1) pull, push 2) attract, involve, go on, continue 3) pump out 4) smoke a pipe 5) distill 6) weigh 7) draw 8) resemble *s.o.* spiritually, be a kindred spirit to *s.o.* 9) take after *s.o.*

чәкмәсилән : *n* bootblack *person*

чәкмәчи : *n* bootmaker, shoemaker

чәкмәчилик : *n* occupation of bootmaker, shoemaker

чәкмәчә : *n* 1) drawer 2) cabinet

чәк-чевир : *n* measuring, trying; considering, thinking *s.t.* over

чәкчәки : *n zool* landrail, European short-billed rail, corncrake *Crex crex*, a bird, commonly frequenting grainfields

чәләнк : *n* wreath

чәләнкгојма : *n* wreathing, garlanding, crowning *with*

чәлик : *n* cane

чәлимсиз : *a* see **сысга**

чәлләк : *n* 1) two-handled tub 2) keg, small barrel

чәлләкгајыран, чәлләкчи : *n* cooper, barrel-maker

чәлпәшдирмәк : *v* confuse, mix up, muddle up

чәлпәшик : *n* confused, mixed up, muddled, complex

чәлпәшиклик : *n* muddle, confusion, mess, intricacy

чәлтик : *n* unshelled rice

чәлтиклик : *n* rice-field, rice-paddy

чәм : *n* 1) way, method, order 2) move, gambit

чәм-хәм еләмәк : *v* blow air; be unnecessary ceremonious; make too much fuss *about s.t.*

чәмән : *n* meadow

чәмәнкаһ : *n* large meadow

чәмәнкүлү : *n* see **тәзәк**

чәмәнлик : *n* meadow, pasture

чәмәнчилик : *n* grass farming, meadow cultivation

чәмкирмәк : *v* shout at *s.o* rudely and insolently.; be extremely rude with *s.o.*

чәм-хәм : *n* 1) affectedness, putting on airs 2) refusing, making excuses

чән : *n* 1) haze, mist, obscurity 2) tank, reservoir

чәнбәр : *n* 1) hoop, rim 2) bandage

чәнбәрләмәк : *v* put on a hoop *on a barrel*

чәнә : *n* chin

чәнәбазар : *n* bargaining *in a market*

чәнәбоғаз : *n* arguing, disputation, altercation

чәнәләшмә : *n* squabbling, altercation

чәнәләшмәк : *v* squabble, have an altercation

чәнк : *n* 1) numbness 2) cramp, convulsion 4) paw 3) see **дырмыг**

чәнкә : *n* handful tuft, whisp *of grass, hair etc*

чәнкәл : *n* 1) fork 2) hook, boat-hook

чәнкәләмәк : *v* 1) grab, take something with one's palm/with the whole hand 2) give a wash *to*

чәнки : *n* 1) stinker, a shit, a low disgusting person 2) whore, bawd, hussy

чәнли : *a* hazy, smoky, overcast, cloudy

чәп : *a* 1) oblique 2) cross-eyed 3) stubborn, obstinate *adv* 4) obliquely, indirectly

чәпбучаглы : *a* oblique-angled

чәпәки : *adv* obliquely, slantwise

чәпәр : *n* fence, hedge

чәпәрләмәк : *v* surround with a hedge or fence

чәпәрләнмәк : *v* be surrounded with a hedge or fence

чәпәрли : *a* surrounded with a hedge or fence

чәпәрлик : *a* suitable for use as fence or hedge material

чәпик : *a* 1) quick, adroit, dexterous 2) applause, clapping

чәпиклик : *n* quickness, adroitness, dexterity

чәпин : *n* trowel

чәпинә : *adv* obliquely, slantwise

чәпиш : *n* a one-year old male kid *goat*

чәпкән : *n* *chapkan* a light outer jacket of distinctive cut traditionally worn by men in the Caucasus

чәпкөз : *a* *n* cross-eyed, squint-eyed, strabismic

чәпләшдирмәк : *v* squint

чәплик : *n* *med* 1) strabismus *crossed eyes* 2) obstinacy, stubbornness 3) warp, bending, curve, skew

чәп-чәп : *adv* obliquely, aslant

чәр : *n* *vet* equine heart attack

чәрдәк : *n* stone/pit/seed *of a fruit*

чәрдәкли : *a* containing a stone/pit/kernel *of a fruit*

чәрдәксиз : *a* without a stone/pit/kernel *of a fruit*

чәрәз : *n* 1) dried fruit 2) dessert, dainty, delicacy

чәрәзхор : *n* person with a sweet tooth, one who likes sweets

чәрәк : *n* 1) quarter, one fourth part 2) see **гарыш**

чәрәнләмәк : *v* chatter, talk idly, schmooze

чәрән-пәрән : *n* nonsense, gibberish, absolute rubbish

чәрәнчи : *n* 1) chatterer, talker, windbag, phrase-monger, idle talker *a* 2) garrulous, talkative, windy

чәрәнчилик : *n* garrulity, loquaciousness, talkativeness

чәркәз : *n* Circassian

чәркәзи : *n* Circassian coat *a long, narrow, collarless coat worn by Caucasian highlanders*

чәрләмәк : *v* become exhausted, reach the end of o.'s rope

чәрләтмәк : *v* exhaust; drive to desperation

чәрмәки : *n* special hammer used to smooth and flatten the seams of leather,

чәрпәләнк : *n* kite *toy*

чәртик : *n* 1) cicatrice, scarification 2) incision

чәртикләмәк : *v* 1) make an incision 2) cicatrize

чәртили : *a* 1) excised, cut out 2) peeled; cleaned

чәртилмәк : *v* be pointed, sharpened

чәртмә : *n* 1) noose, snare, trap 2) misfire

чәртмәк : *v* 1) sharpen, point 2) incise 3) release the trigger 4) shut, close *a trap*

чәрхи-фәләк : *n* fate, fortune, lot

чәрчи : *n* 1) peddler, itinerant merchant *fig* 2) narrow pedant 3) greedy/avaricious person

чәрчивә : *n* frame

чәрчивәләмәк : *v* frame, install frames 2) embroider

чәрчивәләнмәк : *v* 1) be framed 2) be embroidered

чәрчилик : *n* 1) occupation of a peddler/itinerant merchant *fig* 2) greed, avarice 3) narrow pedantry

чәршәнбә : *n* see **чаршәнбә**

чәтәлә : *n* token, tag

чәтән : *n* wattle fencing

чәтәнә : *n* *bot* 1) hemp *Cannabis sativa* *a* 2) hemp[en]

чәтин : *a* 1) difficult, hard, troublesome, formidable; 2) burdensome, onerous 3) thorny, prickly 4) ticklish, delicate

чәтинбәјәнән : *n* 1) squeamish/fastidious person *a* 2) fastidious, squeamish

чәтиндејилән : *a* unpronounceable

чәтинәријән : *a* high melting; infusible *of metals*

чәтинләшдирмәк : *v* make difficult, complicate

чәтинләшмәк : *v* become more difficult, become more complicated

чәтинлик : *n* difficulty, hardship, snag, obstacle, complication

чәтинликлә : *adv* with difficulty, hardly, only just, barely

чәтинохунан : *a* not easily readable, difficult to read, obscure

чәтинсатылан : *a* not easily marketable, difficult to sell

чәтинтәһәр : *a* somewhat/a bit difficult

чәтир : *n* 1) umbrella 2) crest/top of a tree

чәһрајы : *n* rosy, pink

чәһ-чәһ : *n* modulation, trill, shake *of voice;*; warble

чәһ-чәһ вурмаг : *v* trill; warble

чибан : *n* *med* furuncle, carbuncle, boil, abscess

чибин : *n* fly

чив : *n* wedge

чивзә : *n* pimple

чивзәли : *a* pimply, pimpled

чиви : *a* see **чив**

чивләмәк : *v* wedge

чидар : *n* 1) hobbles, fetters *fig* 2) hindrance, obstacle

чидарламаг : *v* tie up, hobble,

чидарланмаг : *v* be hobbled, be tied up

чизки : *n* line, stroke

чизкиләмә : *vn* fr. **чизкиләмәк**

чизкиләмәк : *v* rule *draw lines on*

чизкиләнмәк : *v* be ruled with lines

чиј : *a* raw

чијә : *n* sour-cream

чијәләк : *n* 1) wild strawberries *a* 2) wild-strawberry

чијид : *n* cotton seed

чијин : *n* 1) shoulder *a* 2) humeral

чијнини атмаг : *v* shrug *one's shoulders*

чијинли : *a* broad shouldered

чијинлик : *n* shoulder-strap

чијин-чијинә : *adv* shoulder to shoulder

чијнидүшүк : *n* 1) person with sloped shoulders; 2) milksop

чијриндирмәк : *v* sicken, disgust, repel

чијринмәк : *v* be filled with disgust, be repelled

чил : *n* 1) covered with gray and white spots, dappled, spotted 2) freckled *a* 2) hazel-grouse *Tetrastes bonazia*

чил төкмәк : *v* become covered with freckles

чиләјән : *n* sprayer, atomizer

чиләкән : *n* lathe, batten *used under plastering*

чиләмә : *vn* fr. **чиләмәк**

чиләмәк : *v* 1) sprinkle, splash 2) drizzle, spatter *of rain*

чиләнмәк : *v* be sprinkled

чилик : *n* 1) handle, stock, grip *of a tool med* 2) splint, cast 3) tibia, shin-bone

чиликләмәк : *v* cut *a quantity of* small, short lengths of wood

чилинк : *n* peg

чилинкағачы : *n* children's game played with pegs

чилинкәр : *n* 1) machinist, metal worker; plumber *a* 2) machinist['s], metal worker['s]; plumber['s]

чилинкәрлик : *n* occupation of machinist/metal worker; plumber's trade

чилинкәрхана : *n* machine-shop, metal-working shop; plumber's shop

чилләә : *n* 1) pole, beam 2) forty-day period following a birth/wedding/funeral etc.

чилләә(н)мәк : *v* become covered with freckles

чилли : *a* freckled; dappled, piebald *of a horse*

чилчыраг : *n* chandelier

чим : *n* 1) layer of soil stripped of grass/turf 2) layer of dirty water *a* 2) all, whole, complete, total

чимдик : *n* 1) pinch, nip, tweak 2) pinch *of salt, snuff etc*

чимдикләмәк : *v* pinch, nip, tweak

чимдикләшмәк : *v* be pinched, pinch one another

чимдик-чимдик : *n* *s.t.* pinched off, plucked, picked

чимдирмәк, чимиздирмәк : *v* bathe *s.o.*

чимир : *n* nap, doze

чимишмә : *n* bathing

чимишмәк : *v* bathe *together*

чимләмәк : *v* cover a swamp/pond with top-soil and turf/sod

чимләнмәк : *v* cover with top-soil and turf, sod over

чимләтмәк : *v* *caus* of **чимләмәк**

чимлик : *n* area covered with top-soil and turf

чиммә : *n* see **чимишмә**

чиммәк : *v* bathe

чимчишмә : *n* 1) fastidiousness; squeamishness, disgust 2) shudder

чимчишмәк : *v* 1) be squeamish/fastidious *about* 2) shudder

чин : *n* 1) China 2) saw-toothed scythe 3) shoulder-boards, epaulets 4) layer of objects placed one on another 5) end of a journey/trip 6) woven row of a carpet

чинар : *n* *bot* plane-tree *Platanus orientalis*

чинарлыг : *n* plane-tree grove

чинәдан : *n* crop, craw *of a bird*

чинәчи : *n* cotton-picker

чини : *n* porcelain, china

чинләмәк : *v* layer, stratify, make in layers; pile up in neat layers

чинли : *n* Chinese *person*

чинразјанасы : *n* *bot* star anise *Illicium anisatum*

чин-чин : *a* 1) layered, laminated *adv* 2) in lamellar fashion

чинчә : *adv* in Chinese

чиншүнас : *n* sinologist

чиншүнаслыг : *n* sinology

чириш : *n* paste

чиришләмәк : *v* apply paste

чиришләнмәк : *v* be coated with paste, have paste applied *to*

чиришоту : *n bot* asphodel

чирк : *n* 1) dirt 2) pus *a* 2) dirty; purulent

чиркаб : *n* sewage

чиркин : *a* 1) unsightly, ugly, uncomely, disgusting 2) reprehensible, indecent *adv* 2) hideously, indecently

чиркинләтмәк, чиркинләшдирмәк : make ugly/dirty/disgusting/unsightly, uglify

чиркинләшмә : *vn* fr. **чиркинләшмәк**

чиркинләшмәк : *v* become ugly/unsightly/uncomely/disgusting

чиркинлик : *n* ugliness, unsightliness, uncomeliness

чирккөтүрән : *a* easily soiled

чирккөтүрмәјән : *a* soil/stain-resistant

чиркләндирмәк : *v* soil/dirty/stain *s.t.*

чиркләнмәк : *v* get/become dirty/stained soiled

чиркләтмәк : *v* see **чиркләндирмәк**

чиркли : *a* 1) dirty, besmirched, unhygienic 2) suppurating, purulent

чиркли-паслы : *a* slovenly,untidy, grubby, dirty, smudged

чирмәләмәк, чирмәмәк : *v* roll up *o.'s sleeves*

чирмәләнмәк, чирмәнмәк : *v* be rolled *up of sleeves*

чисәмәк : *v* drizzle

чисәнки : *n* drizzle

чискин : *a* 1) see **чисәнки** 2) drizzling and foggy

чит : *n* 1) chintz *a* 2) chintz

читәк : *n* small patch *on garments*

читә(лә)мәк : *v* 1) sew onto, stitch to 2) fasten

чифајда : *adv* unfortunately. . . but; no matter that. . . still;

чичә : *a* nice, new *in children's speech*

чичәк : *n* 1) flower; blossom 2) smallpox

чичәк дөјмәк : *v* vaccinate *especially of small pox*

чичәкверән : *a bot* flower-bearing, floriferous

чичәкдөјән : *n* vaccinator *health professional administering vaccine against smallpox*

чичәкдөјмә : *n* vaccination *against smallpox*

чичәклә(н)мә : *n* blossoming

чичәклә(н)мәк : *v* blossom

чичәкли : *a* flowery

чичәклик : *n* flower-bed, flower garden

чичәкчи : *n* flower-gardener, flower-grower

чичәкчилик : *n* flower-growing, floriculture

чытгат : *a* loose, not firmly seated

чытгылдамаг : *v* tick *of a time-piece*

чытгылты : *n* ticking *of a timepiece*

чыг : *n* avalanche

чығыр-бағыр : *n* noise, uproar

чығыр-бағырчы, чығыран : *n* shouter, bawler

чығырғанлыг : *n* clamorousness

чығырышма : *n* noise, racket, uproar *produced by a crowd*

чығырышмаг : *v* cry, shout *all together*

чығырмаг : *v* shout, bawl, yell

чығырты : *n* shouting, bawling, yelling

чығыртма : *n* çığırtma roasted lamb or poultry with eggs

чығыртмаг : *caus* of **чығырмаг**

чызгырмаг : *v* gush up/spurt up in a thin stream

чызгыртмаг : *v* cause to gush/spurt up in a thin stream

чылғын : *a* angry, irate, infuriated, wrathful

чылпаг : *a* 1) naked, stripped naked, bare, nude, *adv* 2) stark naked

чылпагландырмаг : *v* strip naked, undress

чылпагланмаг : *v* be stripped naked, get undressed, disrobe

чылпаглатмаг : *v* see **чылпагландырмаг**

чылпаглашмаг : *v* see **чылпагланмаг**

чылпаглыг : *n* nakedness, stark-nakedness, nudity

чымхырмаг : *v* yell at, answer with a snarl, be rude to

чынгыл : *n* cobblestones, paving material, pebbles, gravel,

чынгыллы : *a* paved with cobblestones

чынгыллыг : *n* place abounding in cobblestones/paving material

чыраг : *n* lamp, torch, lantern, floodlight

чырагалты : *n* see **чырагдан**

чырагбанлыг : *n* illumination

чырагдан : *n* lamp-support

чырма(ла)маг : *v* see **чирмәләмәк**

чырпы : *n* brushwood

чырпыг : *n* boon *the woody portion of flax left after retting and scutching*

чырпылмаг : *v* 1) be shaken out, be caused to fall by shaking 2) be hit against, be knocked against *s.t.*

чырпынмаг : *v* 1) toss and turn 2) shiver, shake; shake off, throw off *dust etc.* 3) pulsate 4) roll over

чырпынты : *n* beating, pulsating shaking, shivering, tossing and turning, rolling over

чырпышдырмаг : *v* pilfer, steal

чырпышма : *n* battle, fighting

чырпышмаг : *v* battle, fight

чырпмаг : *v* 1) shake off 2) hit, kick 3) pilfer, stealr

чырт : *n* spittle

чырт атмаг : *v* spittle

чыртдаг : *n* speck, speckle, spot

чыртдаглы : *a* specked, speckled, spotted

чыртдамаг : *v* get cracked; crack *nuts, oil-seeds etc.*

чыртыг : *n* snapping the fingers

чыртылдамаг : *v* see **чыртламаг**

чыртылты : *n* crash, crack, crackle

чыртламаг : *v* 1) eat, nibble, crack *sunflower seeds, nuts etc* 2) sparkle

чыртма : *n* crack; snap; flick, fillip *of the fingers*

чыртмаг : *v* cut into little pieces

чыртмаламаг : *v* hit *s.t.* with the fingers

чыр-чырпы : *n* 1) brushwood 2) kindling wood

чытызмаг : *v* 1) hint; remind; prompt; let know 2) understand, guess

чыхар : *n* 1) expenditure, expense 2) waste product[s], fumes

чыхарылмаг : *v* be taken out, be extracted

чыхарыш : *n* citation, exerpt

чыхартдырмаг : *caus* of **чыхармаг**

чыхар(т)маг : *v* 1) take out, carry out 2) extract 3) put out, dismiss, fire, exclude 4) dig up, pull out, pluck 5) put/set ashore, set aside 6) undress

чыхдаш : *n* spoilage, waste

чыхдашајыран, чыхдашчы : *n* quality inspector, sorter-out of deefective articles

чыхыг : *n* *med* dislocation

чыхылан : *n* *math* subtrahend

чыхылмаз : *a* hopeless, desperate

чыхынты : *n* 1) protruberance, projection *anat* 2) appendix

чыхыш : *n* 1) getting out, going out, walking out; starting 2) exit; exodus

чыхышлыг : *a* *gram* 1) ablative *n* 2) ablative case

чыхма : *n* 1) going/getting out 2) departure , exit *math* 3) subtraction

чыхмаг : *v* 1) get out, go out, walk out 2) appear, appear from nowhere, spring up 3) grow, begin to grow, push up *grass/plants/hair* *math* 4) subtract 4) protrude *med* 5) dislocate

чобан : *n* shepherd

чобаналдадан : *n* *zool* goat-sucker, whippoorwill, nighthawk *fam. Caprimulgidae a nocturnal, insectivorous bird*

чобанашы : *n* çobanaşı *thick milk porridge*

чобанбајатысы : *n* a traditional Azerbaijani miğam

чобанити : *n* çobaniti *a sheep dog*

чобаны : *n* see **чобанбајатысы**

чобанјастығы : *n* *bot* camomile *Matricaria*

чобанлыг : *n* occupation of shepherd

чов : *n* news

човғун : *n* snowstorm, blizzard

човдар : *n* *bot* 1) rye *Secale cereale* *a* 2) rye

човкә : *n* panic-monger, alarmist

човустан : *n* hut

човуш : *n* leader of a caravan of pilgrims

човушгушу : *n* *zool* hoopoe *fam. Upupidae,* a bird

чоған : *n* soap-root *Saponaria officinalis*

чодар : *n* 1) herdsman, drover 2) cattle-dealer

чолаг : *a* 1) crippled, lame, handicapped *n* 2) crippled, lame, handicapped person

чолма-чочуг : *n* kids, kiddies

чолпа : *n* cockerel, young rooster

чолуг-чочуг : *n* see **чолма-чочуг**

чомаг : *n* shepherd's club; shepherd's crook

чопур : *a* 1) pock-marked *n* 2) pock-mark

чор : *n* 1) disease of cotton and grape leaves; often used as an expletive

чорт : *n* nap, short period of sleep

чоткə : *n* abacus, counting frame

чох : *adv* 1) much, many 2) very 3) too, too much

чохаjаглы : *n* *zool* myriapod

чохаллаhлы : *n* polytheist

чохаллаhлылыг : *n* polytheism

чохалма : *n* 1) increase; growth 2) mutiplication

чохалмаг : *v* 1) increase; grow 2) multiply

чохалтмаг : *v-tr* 1) increase; grow 2) multiply

чохарвадлы : *n* polygamist

чохарвадлылыг : *n* polygamy

чохатомлу : *a* polyatomic

чохбашлы : *a* many-headed, polycephalic

чохбилмиш : *a* 1) quick-witted, keen-witted, quick-on-the-uptake *n* 2) pushy, intrusive person

чохбудаглы : *a* branchy

чохбучаглы : *n* *geom* 1) polygon a 2) polygonal

чохгатлы : *a* multi-layered

чохдан : *adv* for a long time; a long time ago

чохдан бəри : *adv* since time long past

чохданын : *a* see **чохданкы**

чохданышан : *a* talkative, garrulous, loquacious

чохданкы : *a* bygone, ancient, long-standing

чохдилли : *a* multilingual, polyglot

чохəрлилик : *n* polyandry

чохиллик : *a* of many years, of several years standing, long-term

чохjарпаг, **чохjарпаглы** : *a* many-leaved, *bot* polyphyllous

чохjашар, **чохjашлы** : *a* of many years, of several years standing, long-term

чохjеjəн : *n* glutton, heavy eater

чохjерли : *a* multiseater, multiplace *i.e. aircraft*

чохкүлəн : *n* 1) mocker, scoffer 2) giggler *zool* 3) mocking bird *fam. Mimidae*

чохлаjлы : *a* multi-layered

чохлары : *n* *coll* many people

чохлашмаг : *v* see **чохалмаг**

чохлу : *a* 1) numerous , a lot of *n* 2) multitude *adv* 3) many-many times

чохлуг : *n* 1) majority; multitude 2) abundance, plenty

чохлуча : *adv* rather much

чохмə'налы : *a* *ling* 1) polysemantic 2) very meaningful

чохмə'налылыг : *n* *ling* polysemanticism

чохмəртəбə, чохмəртəбəли : *a* many-storeyed, multistory

чохмилjонлу : *a* multimillion

чохмиллəтли : *a* multinational

чохрəгəмли : *a* *math* multiple digit *number* ,

чохрəнкли : *a* multicolored, polychrome

чохрəнклилик : *n* polychromy

чохсаhəли : *a* multi-branch *industry*

чохсəсли : *a* polyphonic

чохсимли : *a* *mus* many-stringed

чохтарлалы : *a* crop rotation *system using more than three fields*

чохтəрəфли : *a* multilateral

чохтиражлы : *a* published in large editions

чохторпаглы : *a* large land-owning, possessed of much land

чоху : *n* 1) the greater part, the majority, the maximum *adv* 2) in most cases, maximally

чохусу : *n* see **чоху**

чохушаглы : *a* having many children, large-family

чохүзлү : *a* many sided, multilateral, versatile

чохhечалы : *a* *gram* polysyllabic

чохhəдли : *n* *math* multinomial, polynomial

чохчичəкли : *a* *bot* multiflorous

чох-чох : *adv* by much, in plenty, in large numbers/quantities

чохчилдли : *a* multi-volume

чохшəкилли : *a* *biol* polymorphic

чохшəкиллилик : *n* *biol* polymorphism

чошга : *n* piglet

чошгаламаг : *v* farrow *of a pig*

чөздəлəмəк : *v* unwind

чөзə(лə)мəк, чөзмəк : *v* see **чөздəлəмəк**

чөкдүрмəк : *v* 1) besiege, lay seige to 2) make/compel to sit down

чөкə : *n* *bot* lime-tree, linden, basswood *Tilia*

чөкәбалығы : *n zool* small sturgeon, sterlet

чөкәк : *n* 1) pit, ravine 2) depression

чөкәклик : *n* 1) pit, ravine 2) depression, cavity

чөкәлик : *n* grove of lime-trees

чөкәлмәк : *v* lower, go down

чөкәлтмәк : *v* make a cavity/a depression, push in

чөкә-чөкә : *adv* in a squatting position, squatting

чөкмә : *n* landslide

чөкмәк : *v* 1) sink, settle, lower, go down 2) squat down

чөкүк : *a* hollow, concave

чөкүклүк : *n* hollowness, cavity, concavity

чөкүнтү : *n* 1) sediment *geol* 2) deposit 3) residuum

чөл : *n* 1) steppe, arid plain; desert 2) yard; court

чөлгазы : *n zool* barnacle goose *Branta leucopsis*

чөлгарангушу : *n* zool desert swallow *Glareola*

чөлдә : *adv* outside

чөлдонузу : *n zool* wild boar *Sus scrofa*

чөлешшәји : *n zool* onager *Equus onager, the wild ass of Asia*

чөлкәсәјәни : *n zool* steppe marmot

чүлкөјәрчини : *n zool* wild dove

чөллү : *n* peasant; country bumpkin

чөллүк : *n* open area; steppes, desert

чөлнохуду : *n bot* see **күлүл**

чөлөрдәји : *n zool* mallard *Anas platyrhynchos* a wild duck

чөлпишији : *n zool* serval, *Felis capensis,* a wild cat

чөлсичаны : *n zool* field mouse

чөлтојуғу : *n zool* hazel-hen, hazel grouse *Tetrastes bonasia,* a ruffed grouse

чөлүндә : *adv* outside

чөмәлмәк : *v* squat

чөмәлтмә : *n* 1) squatting *adv* 2) squatting, in a squat

чөмчә : *n* ladle

чөмчәбалығы : *n zool* sea-roach *fish*

чөмчәгујруг : *n zool* tadpole

чөнбәлмәк : *v* see **чөмәлмәк**

чөндәрмәк : *v* see **дөндәрмәк**

чөп : *n* small stick, straw

чөпатма : *n* drawing/casting lots

чөпәкүлән : *n* mocker, scoffer; one engaging in meaningless laughter

чөпрә : *n* zool loach, a fish *fam. Cobitidae*

чөпүк : *n* 1) loose clump 2) linen waste products *material left after scutching*

чөрәк : *n* bread

чөрәкағачы : *n* bread-winner, principal means of support

чөрәкбиширән : *n* baker

чөрәкгабы : *n* bread-basket

чөрәкдашыјан : *n* bakery-truck

чөрәкләмәк : *n* feed, keep, maintain, support materially

чөрәкли : *a* hospitable

чөрәкпулу : *n* money for bread; money to make both ends meet

чөрәксатан : *n* bakery product merchant

чөрәксиз : *a* 1) breadless 2) inhospitable

чөрәкчи : *n* baker

чөрәкчилик : *n* baker's trade

чөрәкчихана : *n* bakery

чөр-чөп : *n* small brushwood

чубуг : *n* 1) switch, birch, rod *used as a whip* 2) tobacco-pipe

чубугламаг : *v* whip with a birch/switch/rod

чубуглатмаг : *v caus* of **чубугламаг**

чубуглуг : *n* thin, short twig suitable for use as the stem of a tobacco pipe

чувал : *n* large sack

чуваш : *n* 1) Chuvash *a Tatar people of Turkic language living chiefly in the Chuvash Republic in the middle Volga region a* 2) Chuvash

чувашча : *adv* in the Chuvash language

чугун : *n* 1) cast iron a 2) cast iron

чугунәридән : *a* cast iron-smelting

чуғул : *n* informer, snitch, nark, stool-pigeon, stoolie

чуғулламаг : *v* inform, report on, snitch

чуғуллатмаг : *caus* of **чуғулламаг**

чуғуллуг : *n* snitching, informing, reporting

чуғулчу : *n* see **чуғул**

чуғундур : *n* beet, sugar-beet

чуғундурбөчәји : *n zool* leaf beetle *Cassida*

чуғундурчу : *n* beet farmer/grower

чуғундурчулуг : *n* sugar-beet-farming/growing

чул : *n* saddle-cloth, saddle-blanket

чулгах : *n* wrapper, envelope, cover, package

чулғаламаг : *v* 1) wrap up, wrap, cover, package 2) cover everything comprehensively, synthesize

чулғаланмаг : *v* 1) be wrapped up/wrapped/packaged/packed 2) be covered thoroughly/comprehensively, be synthesized

чулғамаг : *v* see **чулғаламаг**

чулламаг : *v* 1) cover with a saddle-cloth 2) put too much clothes on

чулланмаг : *v* 1) be covered with a saddle-cloth 2) put too much clothes on o.s.

чуллатмаг : *caus* of **чулламаг**

чуллу : *a* covered with a saddle-cloth

чулсуз : *a* without a saddle-cloth

чуст : *n* traditional Azerbaijani sandal

чустгикəн, чустчу : *n* sandal-maker *of the traditional Azerbaijani sandal*

чутгу : *n* bonnet *child's*

чуха : *n* chukha *a long overcoat worn by men in the Caucasus*

чухалыг : *n* fabric for a traditional Caucasian overcoat or chukha

чухур : *n* small pit, hollow, depression, cavity

чухурланмаг : *v* settle *of soil*

чүнки : *conj* because

чүрүк : *a* rotten, moldy

чүрүклүк : *n* rottenness, putridity

чүрүкчү : *n* bore, pedant, small-minded person

чүрүкчүлүк : *n* boringness, wearisomeness, pedanticism

чүрүмə : *vn* fr. **чүрүмəк**

чүрүмəк : *n* 1) rot, decay, go bad 2) curdle, clot *of milk*

чүрүнтү : *n* mold, rotten stuff; humus

чүрүтмəк : *v* 1) let rot, let decay 2) let curdle *fig* 3) be boring, bore with

Ч

ч : thirty-first letter of the Azerbaijani alphabet

чабəча : *adv* in its own place, in proper order

чаваб : *n* answer, response

чаваб гајтармаг : *v* object; give a brazen answer

чавабверəн, чавабдеһ : *n* 1) responsible person *leg* 2) defendant; respondent *a* 3) responsible

чавабдеһлик : *n* responsibility

чаваблы : *a* as a response, in answer

чавабсыз : *a* unanswered

чаван : *a* 1) young *n* 2) young man

чаваназəн : *n* young married woman *often with an implication that she might welcome advances)*

чаванјана : *a* suitable for the young

чаванламаг : *v* see **чаванлашмаг**

чаванлашдырмаг : *v* rejuvenate

чаванлашма : *n* rejuvenation

чаванлашмаг : *v* become younger, grow young again; become younger in appearance

чаванлыг : *n* youth, youthfulness

чаванпəрчими : *n* *bot* see **бојмадəрəн**

чаванча : *a* *dim* young

чаванчасына : *adv* youthfully

чаваһир : *n* 1) precious stone, gemstone *a fig* 2) pure, charming; precious

чаваһират : *n* precious stones; jewelry

чаваһирсатан, чаваһирфүрүш : *n* gem merchant, jeweller

чағ : *n* stockade

чағаны : *n* cağanı twigs, twiglets *a crisp, delicate pastry*

чағылдамаг : *v* 1) flow, fall noisily *of water* 2) scatter noisily/with a clatter *of nuts, pebbles etc*

чағылты : *n* noise produced by falling objects *i.e. water, nuts and pebbles*

чағламаг : *v* surround with a stockade

чағланмаг : *v* be surrounded with a stockade

чад : *n* millet

чадар : *n* crack *in the ground/soil/skin etc*

чадарланмаг : *v* become cracked

чадар-чадар : *adv* covered with cracks

чаду : *n* magic, sorcery

чадукәр : *n* magician, sorcerer

чадукәрлик : *n* magic, sorcery, witchcraft

чадуламаг : *v* practice witchcraft/sorcery

чаду-питик : *n* 1) written prayer 2) amulet 3) spell, incantation

чаз : *n* 1) jazz *a* 2) jazz, jazzy

чазибә : *n* 1) gravity, gravitation; attraction 2) attractive force 3) attraactiveness, charm

чазибәдар, чазибәли : *a* 1) attractive, charming, tempting 2) magnetic

чазибәлилик : *n* attractiveness, charm, temptation

чаиз : *a* persmissible, acceptable

чаjдаг : *n* lean, lanky, long-legged

чаjлаг : *n* *zool* see **арыjеjән**

чаjнаг : *n* claw

чаjнагламаг : *v* seize with claws

чаjнаглы : *a* 1) equipped with claws, clawed *fig* 2) grabby; tenacious

чакеш : *n* pimp

чакешлик : *n* pimping, occupation of pimp

чалаг : *n* 1) inoculation, grafting 2) trailer 3) stitching

чалагламаг : *v* see **чаламаг** 1), 2)

чалагланмаг : *v* 1) be inoculated; be grafted *of plants* 2) be stitched *of fabric/clothing*

чалаглы : *a* 1) inoculated *bot* 2) grafted, engrafted 3) stitched

чалаглылыг : *n* 1) scion, graft, cutting, slip *for grafting* 2) piece of cloth to be stitched

чалагсыз : a 1) ungrafted 2) unstitched

чалагчы : *n* grafter, grafting specialist

чалал : *n* 1) luxury, magnificence 2) grandeur, might

чалаллы : *a* luxurious, magnificent

чаламаг : *v* 1) engraft, inoculate 2) stitch 3) spill

чаланмаг : *v* 1) be engrafted, be inoculated 2) be stitched 3) be spilled

чалатдырмаг, чалатмаг : *caus* of **чаламаг**

чам : *n* iron basin

чамаат : *n* the public, people, crowd, the multitude

чамадар : *n* bath-house attendant *esp. one serving in the cloakroom*

чамадарлыг : *n* occupation of bathing-house attendant

чамал : *n* beautiful face, prettiness, beauty, fairness

чамәкан : *n* shop-window

чамыш : *n* *zool* buffalo cow

чан : *n* 1) soul, spirit 2) life

чан атмаг : *v* be eager *to do s.t.,* be very enthusiastic; be devoted *to s.t.*

чан вермәк : *v* be about to die

чан гоjмаг : *v* waste, spend all *o.'s* energy

чан jандырмаг : *v* be very conscientious *about one's work*

чан чәкмәк : *v* be lazy

чандан дүшмәк : *v* get tired, exhausted

чаны сыхылмаг : *v* be bored; long *to do s.t.*

чаны чыхмаг : *v* die

чанавар : *n* 1) wolf *fig* 2) beast, monster *of a rapacious and cruel man*

чанаварлыг : *n* atrocity, cruelty, brutality

чаназар : *a* 1) fragile, frail *n* 2) fragile, frail person

чаналан : *n* 1) tormenter, torturer *a fig* 2) charming

чанан : *n* 1) mistress 2) sweetheart, heart's desire

чанбаз : *n* rope dancer, tightrope walker

чанбазлыг : *n* rope dancer['s], tightrope walker['s] occupation

чан-башла : *adv* willingly, with pleasure, ardently, zealously

чанбир : *adv* harmoniously, in concord, at one *of two people*

чанвермә : *n* 1) agony, death-struggle *ext* 2) great enthusiasm *for s.t.*

чангуртаран : *a* life-saver, rescuer

чандәрди : *adv* heart-brokenly, unwillingly, against o.'s will

чан-дилдән : *adv* conscientiously, with enthusiasm

чани : *n* criminal; villaain, scoundrel

чанилик : *n* crime; evil deed

чанишин : *n* governor-general, viceroy

чаныбәрк : *a* tenacity of life

чаныjананлыг : *n* sympathy, compassion

чанынданкечән : *a* self-sacrificing, selfless

чанjандыранлыг : *n* conscientiousness, enthusiasm, zeal

чанландыран : *a* reviving, resurrecting *s.o.*

чанландырычы : *n* inspiring; life-giving

чанландырма : *n* enlivening; inspiring; resurrecting

чанландырмаг : *v* enliven; inspire; resurrect

чанланма : *n* enlivenment; inspiration; enthusiasm *for*, zeal *for*

чанланмаг : *v* 1) enliven; become inspired 2) become more corpulent, grow healthier

чанлы : *a* 1) vivid 2) inspired 3) healthy 4) *colloq gram* 5) animate

чанлылыг : *n* vivacity; good health

чансағлығы : *n* good health

чансыз : *a* 1) lifeless 2) weak, fragile *gram* 2) inanimate

чансызла(ш)маг : *v* become weaker, weaken, waste away

чансызлыг : *n* lifelessness, weakness, frailty, sickliness

чансыхан, чансыхычы : *a* boring. tiresome

чансыхычылыг : *n* weakness, lifelessness, frailty

чансүртəн : *n* bath-house masseur

чанфəшанлыг : *n* conscientiousness; zeal

чанчəкишмə(си) : *n* agony, death pangs

чан-чијəр : *a* 1) dear *n* 2) the most beloved, precious person *lit."soul and liver"*

чар : *n* exclamation, cry

чари : *a* current, ongoing

чарчы : *n* herald, announcer

часус : *n* spy; scout

часуслуг : *n*, espionage

чаһан : *n* world, universe

чаһанкир : *n* conqueror

чаһаншүмул : *a* worldwide

чаһил : *a* 1) ignorant, uneducated *n* 2) ignoramus

чаһиллик : *n* ignorance, lack of education

чаһыл : *a* young

чаһыллашдырмаг : *v* make look younger

чаһыллашмаг : *v* begin to look younger

чаһыллыг : *n* youth, youthfulness

чаһылча : *a dim* young

чаһ-чалал : *n* luxury, pomp, ostentation

чаһ-чалаллы : *a* luxurious, ostentatious

чејран : *n zool* gazelle

чејраны : *n* jeiranı *Azerbaijani folkdance*

чејраноту : *n bot* feather-grass *Stipa*

чентлмен : *n* gentleman

чеһиз : *n* dowry

чеһизли : *a* 1) dowried *of a bride n* 2) a dowried bride

чеһизлик : *a* 1) to be used as a dowry *n* 2) assets to be used as a dowry

чеһизсиз : *a* 1) undowried *of a bride n* 2) undowried bride

чечə : *n* oilcake

чечим : *n* jejim *home-spun carpet cloth*

чəббəхана : *n* 1) arsenal 2) armory; store-room

чəбə : *n* narrow mountain pass

чəбр : *n* 1) algebra 2) force, compulsion

чəбрајил : *n relig* Gabriel *archangel*

чəбрəн : *adv* by compulsion, by force

чəбри : *a* 1) compulsory 2) algebraic

чəбһə : *n mil* 1) front *a* 2) front, frontal, front-line

чəбһəчи : *n mil* 1) front-line soldier *ext polit* 2) member of the People's Front of Azerbaijan

чəвəрəн : *n* wicker basket

чəвчə : *n* see **чəһəнк**

чəдвəл : *n* 1) schedule; time-table; chart 2) payroll

чəдвəлчи : *n* timekeeper; scheduler; time-table-specialist; payroll clerk

чəдд : *n* ancestor

чəза : *n* 1) punishment, retaliation *a* 2) punitive, retaliatory

чəза вермəк : *v* punish

чəзаирбəнөвшəси : *n bot* periwinkle, creeping myrtle *Vinca minor*

чəзаландыран : *n mil* member of a punitive expedition

чəзаландырылмаг : *v* be punished/penalized

чəзаландырмаг : *v-tr* punish, penalize

чəзаланмаг : *v* be punished, penalized

чəзан : *n* extremity

чəзасыз : *a* 1) unpunished *adv* 2) with impunity

чəзб : *n* 1) attraction; gravitiation 2) sucking in, inhaling 3) charm, fascination, seduction, attractiveness

чəзбедичи : *a* charming, alluring, attractive

чəзвид : *n* Jesuit

чəзирə : *n* see **Ада**

чəјəн : *n* bast fibers

чəлаји-вəтəн : *n* vagabond

чəлб : *n* involvement; attraction

чəлбедичи : *a* attractive

чəлд : *a* quick, adroit, dexterous, mobile

чəлдлəшмəк : *v* become quick, adroit, dexterous

чəлдлик : *n* quickness, adroitness, dexterity, mobility

чəлə : *n* trap *hunter's*

чəллад : *n* executioner

чəлладлыг : *n* cruelty, brutality

чəм : *n* 1) aggregate, sum total; sum, total amount 2) assembly *gram* 3) plural, plural number

чəмадиjəл-ахыр : *n* Jomada-2 *sixth month of the Moslem calendar*

чəмадиjəл-əввəл : *n* Jomada-1 *fifth month of the Moslem calendar*

чəмалмал : *n* heirs who, unable to agree on sharing the patrimony, live together

чəмдəк : *n* carrion

чəмдəкjejəн : *n* vulture *carrion-eater*

чəми : *adv* in all, altogether

чəмиjjəт : *n* society, order; league; corporation

чəмиjjəтдəнгачан : *n* unsociable

чəмиjjəтəзид : *n* anti-social

чəмиjjəтпəрəст : *n* sociable person

чəмиси : *adv* in all, altogether

чəми-чүмлəтаны : *adv* altogether not to exceed. . . .

чəмлəмəк : *v* gather, assemble; sum up

чəмлəтмəк : *caus* of **чəмлəмəк**

чəмлəшдирмəк : *v* gather together; sum up, summarize; concentrate, focus

чəмлəшмəк : *v* be gathered together

чəнаб : *n* Mr., Sir

чəназə : *n* corpse, dead body

чəнк : *n* 1) war, battle 2) mold 3) rust, corrosion

чəнкавəр : *a* belligerent

чəнкавəрлик : *n* belligerence

чəнкəл, чəнкəллик : *n* jungles; thickets; underbrush

чəнкəри : *a* lilac *color*

чəннəт : *n* 1) paradise *a* 2) paradisical

чəнуб : *n* 1) south *a* 2) southern

чəнуб-гəрб : *n* south-west

чəнуб-гəрби : *a* south-western

чəнуби : *a* southern

чəнуб-шəрг : *n* south-east

чəнуб-шəрги : *a* south-eastern

чəнчəл : *n* mess, confusion

чəнчəлли : *a* complicated, confused in the extreme

чəнчəлчи : *n* litigator; nit-picker

чəрəjан : *n* 1) current *phys* 2) electric current 3) direction; flow

чəримə : *n* fine, penalty

чəримəлəмəк : *v* impose a fine/penalty, fine, penalize

чəримəлəнмəк : *v* be fined, penalized

чəркə : *n* row; ridge, chain

чəркəарасы : *n* space between rows

чəркəви : *a* in rows

чəркəлəмəк : *v* arrange in a row

чəркəли : *a* in rows

чəррah : *n* surgeon

чəррahлыг : *n* 1) surgery *a* 2) surgical

чəсарəт : *n* courage, bravery, valor, resoluteness, daring

чəсарəтлə : *adv* courageously, valorously, bravely, resolutely

чəсарəтлəндирмəк : *v* encourage, hearten, brace, rally

чəсарəтлəнмəк : *v* get encouraged/braced/rallied/imbued with valor/heartened

чəсарəтли : *a* brave, valorous, courageous, resolute

чəсарəтлилик : *n* bravery, courageousness, resoluteness

чəсарəтсиз : *a* timid, meek, cowardly, irresolute

чəсарəтсизлик : *n* lack of courage, faint-heartedness, irresoluteness

чəсəд : *n* corpse, dead body

чəсур : *a* see **чəсарəтли**

чəсурлуг : *n* courage, valor, bravery, resoluteness

чəфа : *n* sufferings, torments

чəфакеш : *n* sufferer, tortured/tormented person, martyr

чəфəнк : *a* absurd, crazy, senseless

чəфəнкиjат : *n* absurdity, nonsense, senselessness

чəфəнклəмəк : *v* talk rubbish, talk nonsense

чәфәнклик : *n* 1) talking rubbish, talking nonsense 2) idle talk, nonsense, absurdity

чәфәри : *n bot* parsley

чәфтә : *n* doorlatch

чәфтәләмәк : *v* latch, lock with a latch

чәфтәләнмәк : *v* be latched, be locked with a latch

чәфтәли : *a* 1) latched, locked by a latch 2) equipped/furnished with a latch

чәфтәсиз : *a* unlatched; not locked by a latch; without a latch

чәһаләт : *n* ignorance; obscurantism

чәһаләтпәрәст : *n* obscurantist

чәһаләтпәрәстлик : *n* obscurantism

чәһд : *n* 1) efforts; zeal 2) importunity

чәһдлә : *adv* industriously, conscientiously

чәһдли : *a* industrious, conscientious

чәһәнк : *n* corner of the mouth

чәһәннәм : *n* hell, inferno

чәһәннәм дашы : *n geol* silver nitrate, AgNO2, lunar caustic

чәһәннәм ол : *expr* get out! get lost!

чәһәннәмә : *expr* I don't care; who cares; I wouldn't give a damn for it

чәһәт : *n* 1) side, aspect 2) cause, reason

чәһрә : *n* spinning-wheel

чәһ-чәһ : *n* trill; warble *of a bird*

чиб : *n* pocket

чиб дәфтәри : *n* pocket notebook

чибкир : *n* pickpocket

чибәкирән : *n* see **чибкир**

чибкирлик : *n* occupation of pickpocket

чибләмәк : *v* pocket s.t. *take for o.'s own use*

чиблик : *n* material to be used for a pocket

чивар : *n* environs, neighborhood, vicinity

чивә : *n* mercury

чивәли : *a* mercuric

чивзә : *n med* acne

чивилдәмәк : *v* squeak, peep

чивилти : *n* squeaking, peeping

чивилтили : *a* squeaking, squeaky, peeping *voice*

чида : *n* pike, spear

чидди : *a* 1) serious, earnest, intensive *adv* 2) seriously, earnestly, intensively

чиддијјәт : *n* seriousness, earnestness; intensivity *of efforts*

чиддијјәтлә : *adv* earnestly, seriously; diligently, industriously, intensively

чиддиләшдирмәк : *v* impart a serious character to a matter

чиддиләшмәк : *v* become earnest, become serious

чиддилик : *n* earnestness, seriousness

чидд-чәһд : *n* seriousness, zeal, fervor

чизјә : *n hist* poll tax paid by non-Moslems in lieu of conversion to Islam

чијә : *n* thin rope, twine

чијәр (аҝ) : *n* lung

чијәр (гара) : *n* liver

чијәрли : *n* brave, manly, courageous

чијил : *n* see **кол-кос**

чијиллик : *n* see **кол-кослуг**

чијилти : *n* shriek, screech

чиккилдәмәк : *v* twitter, chirp

чикләшмә : *n* cockfight

чик-чик : *intj onom* Chirp! Chirp! *imitative of bird-song*

чил : *n* see **чығ**

чила : *n* 1) gloss, luster, shine 2) polish, French polish, varnish, shellac *a solution of shellac or resins in ethyl alcohol*

чилалама : *n* polishing

чилаламаг : *v* polish

чилаланмаг : *v* be polished

чилалы : *a* polished

чилачы : *n* polisher

чилвә : *n* coquetry

чилвәкар : *a* coquettish, playful

чилвәләнмәк : *v* be coquettish/affected/flirty

чилд : *n* 1) cover of a book 2) volume, copy *of a book* 3) leather, cover material

чилд астары : *n* fly-leaf

чилд үзлүјү : *v* supercover

чилдләмәк : *v* bind *books*

чилдләнмәк : *v* be bound *books*

чилдләтдирмәк, чилдләтмәк : *caus* of **чилдләмәк**

чилдли : *a* provided ed with a cover, bound

чилдсиз : *a* unbound, without a cover *book*

чилдхана : *n* bindery

чилдчи : *n* bookbinder

чилд-чилд : *adv* volume by volume

чиликләмәк : *v* pinch out/off

чилик-чилик : *a* broken into small fragments

чилов : *n* bridle; reins

чиловламаг : *v* 1) bridle *ext* 2) bridle, curb, control

чиловланмаг : *v* 1) be bridled *ext* 2) be bridled/curbed/controlled

чиловлатдырмаг, чиловлатмаг : *caus* of **чиловламаг**

чиловлу : *a* bridled

чиловсуз : *a* unbridled; loose, uncurbed

чин : *n* 1) evil spirit, demon 2) gin *machine for removing seeds from cotton*

чинајәт : *n* 1) crime *a* 2) criminal

чинајәткар : *n* criminal

чинајәткаранә : *adv* criminally

чинајәткарлыг : *n* criminality, delinquency

чинас : *n* pun, play on wordss

чинаһ : *n* wing, flank

чиндар : *n* shaman, sorcerer, practitioner of black magic

чинк : *n* *zool* 1) siskin *Spinus spinus* a variety of finch *onom* 2) ding-dong

чинкәнә : *n* baby, infant

чинкилдә(т)мәк : *v* ring, jingle

чинкилти : *n* ringing, jingling

чинкилтили : *a* *ling* voiced

чинкир : *n* see **чүрә**

чинләндирмәк : *v* tease, bedevil, enrage, infuriate

чинләнмә : *vn* fr. **чинләнмәк**

чинләнмәк : *v* get mad, infuriated

чинк-чинк : *intj* *onom* ding-dong *sound of a bell*

чинләтмәк : *v* see **чинләндирмәк**

чинли : *a* possessed, raging, raving

чинс : *n* 1) sex; gender 2) breed 3) ssort, kind, variety *a* 4) pure-blooded, pure-bred, thoroughbred, pedigreed

чинси : *a* sexual; gender-related

чинсијјәт : *n* sex; gender

чинсләшдирмәк : *v* 1) improve the quality 2) improve the breed of animals/plants

чинслик : *n* 1) pure-breeding, good quality 2) sexual appeal

чинчилим : *n* *bot* chickweed *Stellaria media*

чирә : *n* 1) food ration, diet 2) *bot* caraway *Carum carvi*

чисим : *n* 1) body 2) essence, being 3) object

чисимчик : *n* corpuscle

чисмани : *a* corporal

чиһад : *n* *relig* jihad, Islamic holy war

чиһаз : *n* appliance; device; equipment

чичи : *n* mother *affectionate*

чичи-бачы : *n* female friend *affectionate*

чичи-бачылыг : *n* close friendship *between women*

чыбырыг : *n* nut *peeled of the outer green integument*

чывата : *n* bolt; screw bolt

чыгта : *n* 1) forelock 2) plume *on a headdress etc*

чыгтылы : *a* tiny, very small

чыгтыр : *n* barely audible sound

чығ : *n* 1) weed 2) seaweed

чығал : *n* sportsman/player in a game who breaks a rule

чығалламаг : *v* deliberately break the rules in a game/a sport

чығаллыг : *n* deliberate infraction of game-rules

чығылдамаг : *v* squeak; peep

чығылдатмаг : caus of **чығылдамаг**

чығылдашмаг : *v* squeak, peep *many together*

чығылты : *n* squeaking, peeping

чығылтылы : *a* squeaking, peeping

чығыр : *n* 1) path 2) furrow *fig* 3) direction

чығырачан : *n* ploughshare

чығырдаш : *n* travel-companion

чығ-чығ : *a* squeaker

чыдыр : *n* horse-races

чыдырчы : *n* jockey

чыдыр мејданы : *v* hippodrome, *arena for horse shows*

чыз : *n* hot *children's speech*

чызбыз : *n* jızbız an entrée made with stewed offal

чызбызчы : *n* jızbız merchant

чызғы : *n* metal bar

чыздаг : *n* cracklings

чызыг : *n* line

чызыгламаг : *v* line

чызыглы : *a* lined *of paper, notebook etc*

чызыг-чызыг : *a* 1) crossed out, marked out 2) effaced wiith scratches

чызылдамаг : *v* make a whistling noise *of a samovar*

чызылмаг : *v* 1) be marked out, be crossed out 2) be scratched out

чызылты : *n* hissing

чызынты : *n* scratch

чызмаг : *v* 1) draw, outline; sketch 2) scratch

чызмагара : *n* scrawl, scribble *illegible wriing*

чызмагарачы : *n* scribbler, hack, literary drudge

чыjыг : *a* see **сыjыг**

чылғы : *n* goatskin cleaned of hair

чылыз : *a* gaunt, emaciated, weakly, frail, puny, fragile, exhausted

чылызланмаг, чылызлашмаг : *v* become emaciated, gaunt, frail, fragile, weak, exhausted

чылызлыг : *n* weakness, fragility, exhaustion

чылфыр : *a* 1) rash, hasty, thoughtless, frivolous, lacking in gravity 2) upstart, parvenu

чылха : *a* pure, unadulterated

чынгылдамаг : *v* ring, jingle; bang, clatter

чынгылдатмаг : *v* cause to ring/jingle; cause to bang/clatter

чынгылы : *a* see **чумбулу**

чынгылты : *n* quiet banging, ringing

чынгыр : *n* hardly audible noise *only in combinations*

чынгыров : *n* little bell

чында : *n* 1) whore, streetwalker 2) see **чындыр**

чындыр : *n* 1) rag *a* 2) ragged

чындырлы : *a* in rags, ragged

чындыр-мындыр : *n* rags

чындырчы : *n* junkman, ragman

чыр : *a* 1) wilding*wild fruit-bearing plant* ungrafted/uncultivated fruit-tree 2) shrill *voice*

чырыг : *a* 1) torn, shabby, ragged *n* 2) scar

чырыг-чырыг : *a* torn, shabby, ragged, tattered

чырылдамаг : *v* 1) squeak, creak 2) chirp *about a cricket* 3) chirr *of a grasshopper* 4) rattle, chatter *of a machine-gun etc*

чырылдатмаг : *caus* of **чырылдамаг** :

чырылдашмаг : *v* squeak; chirp; chirr, rattle, clatter *many together*

чырылмаг : *v* be/get torn apart

чырылты : *n* squeaking; chirping

чырылтылы : *a* squeaking; chirping

чырламаг, чырланмаг : *v* 1) degenerate *bot* 2) run wild, become wild

чырмаг : *v* 1) tear, tear apart, rend asunder *n* 2) see **чаjнаг**

чырмагламаг : *v* scratch with claws

чырмагланмаг : *v* be scratched, clawed

чырмаглашмаг : *v* scratch/claw one another

чырнаг : *n* see **чаjнаг**

чырнамаг : *v* 1) be angry 2) give up, give in, prove incapable

чырнатмаг : *v* 1) anger, vex s.o. 2) cause s.o. to give up/give in; cause s.o. to admit incapability

чыртгоз : *a* touchy, susceptible to offense, sensitive

чыртдан : *n* dwarf

чыр-чындыр : *n* see **чындыр-мындыр**

чырчырама : *n* *zool* dragon-fly *Odonata*

чоғрафи : *a* geographical

чоғрафиjа : *n* geography

чографиjачы : *n* geographer

чоғрафиjашүнас : *n* geographer

чод : *a* rough

чодjунлу : *a* rough-wool[ed]

чодлашмаг : *v* become rude, rough

чодлуг : *n* roughness

чомәрд : *a* generous, lavish, magnanimous

чомәрдләнмәк, чомәрдләшмәк : *v* be generous, magnanimous

чомәрдлик : *n* generosity, open-handed, magnanimity

чомәрдликлә, чомәрдчәсинә : *adv* generously, magnanimously

чораб : *n* sock; stocking; hosiery

чораббағы : *n* garter

чораблы : *a* wearing socks or stockings

чораблыг : *n* threads, yarn to be used to knit socks or stockings

чорабтохуjан : *n* stocking-maker/knitter

чошгун : *a* 1) agitated, aroused *adv* 2) ardently, emotionally

чошгунлуг : *n* state of agitation, arousal, impetuousness

чошдурмаг : *v* become angry; become agitated

чошма : *n* extreme agitation; sudden strong anger

чошмаг : *v* be in a state of rage or extreme agitation

чөвза : *n* *astron* Gemini *constellation*

чөвлан : *n* 1) walk, promenade 2) rotation

чөвланкаh : *n* area for walks, promenades

чөвүз : *n* see **гоз**

чөвүзгыран : *n* nut-cracker

чөвhәр : *n* *chem* 1) essence, extract, infusion *phil* 2) crux, essence, being 3) precious stone

чөвhәрнанә : *n* mint drops

чөhрә : *n* face *of a person*

чу : *n* 1) boundary, boundary strip 2) irrigation-channel

чувар : *n* person in charge of distribution of the irrigation water

чуггулдамаг : *v* twitter, chirp *of birds*

чуггулту : *n* twittering, chirping

чулфа : *n* 1) see **тохучу** 2) Julf *small city on the Araks river in the Nachichevan Autonomous Region near the Iranian border*

чумбулу : *a* very small, tiny

чумдурмаг : *v-tr* dip; plunge

чумма : *vn* fr. **чуммаг**

чуммаг : *v* 1) dip, plunge, dive 2) fall upon, go for; rush, dash

чумурт : *n* *bot* buckthorn *fam. Rhamnaceae*

чуна : *n* gauze, cheesecloth, tulle, *any thin, transparent fabric*

чунгуш : *n* baby

чур : *n* person of the same age or social rank, member of a demographic generational cohort

чуhуд : *n* 1) Jew *a* 2) Jewish

чуш : *n* emotion, agitation, arousal

чүббә : *n* a long ecclesiastical garment worn under the chasuble *similar to the western alb*

чүвәллағы : *n* swindler, cheater, fraud, confidence man

чүвәллағылыг : *n* swindling, cheating, fraud

чүз : *n* fragment, extract

чүзам : *n* *med* leper

чүзамлы : *a* *med* leprous

чүзи : *a* tiny, very small, insignificant

чүзиjjәт : *n* small, tiny thing, trifle

чүзилик : *n* insignificance, scantiness, unimportance, trifle, bagatelle

чүjүлдәмәк : *v* squeak, peep

чүjүлтү : *n* squeaking, peeping

чүjүр : *n* *zool* roe deer *genus Capreolus*

чүjүроту : *n* *bot* woad *Isatis tinctoria* . Plant from which blue coloring agent is extracted

чүллүт : *n* *zool* snipe *Capella gallinago, a game bird*

чүмә : *n* Friday

чүмлә : *n* *gram* 1) sentence 2) all 3) number, structure, category

чүмләпәрдазлыг : *n* phrase-mongering

чүмләси : *adv* altogether; total

чүмhуриjjәт : *n* 1) republic *a* 2) republican

чүмhуриjjәтчи : *n* Republican

чүр : *n* 1) kind, sort 2) way, method

чүрбәчүр : *a* various, assorted, variegated

чүрбәчүрлүк : *n* variety

чүрдәк : *n* clay jug with a narrow throat

чүрә : *a* 1) undersized, underdeveloped, dwarfish, small *n zool* 2) teal *Anas crecca*

чүр'әт : *n* courage, resoluteness; daring

чүр'әтлә : *adv* courageously, resolutely

чүр'әтләндирмәк : *v* enhearten, put spirit into, encourage

чүр'әтләнмәк : *v* become enheartened, encouraged

чүр'әтли : *a* 1) courageous, brave, daring *n* 2) brave person, person of courage

чүр'әтлилик : *n* courage, resoluteness

чүр'әтсиз : *a* timid, meek, irresolute

чүр'әтсизлик : *n* timidity, irresoluteness meekness

чүрләмәк : *v* sort, sort out

чүрүлдәмәк : *v* chirp *of a cricket*

чүссә : *n* body, figure, build, frame

чүссәли : *a* heavy-set *man*

чүт : *n* 1) pair; even number *n* 2) wooden plough *a* 3) even

чүтләмәк : *v* select pairs

чүтләшдирмә : *n* 1) coupling, pairing, mating 2) matching; crossing, interbreeding

чүтләшдирмәк : *v agr* 1) couple, pair 2) match; interbreed, serve, cover *animals*

чүтләшмә : *n* coupling, pairing, mating *of bull/stallion etc*

чүтләшмәк : *v* get bred; get mated

чүтчү : *n* ploughman

чүт-чүт : *adv* in pairs

чүчә : *n* chicken

чүчәрмәк : *n* spring, sprout, put out shoots *of seeds*

чүчәртмәк : *v-tr* grow *plants*

чүчү : *n* 1) insect, bug, midge 2) small

чүчүјејән : *a* insectivorous

Ш

ш : thirty-second letter of the Azerbaijani alphabet

шаб : *n* see **зај**

шабалыд : *n bot* chestnut-tree *Castanea sativa*

шабалыды : *a* chest-nut *color*

шабалыдлыг : *n* grove of chest-nut trees

шаблон : *n* 1) pattern; mold 2) cliché *a* 3) commonplace, unoriginal, stereotyped, routine

шагга : *n* half of a smoked, dried, or salted bird or other game

шаггаламаг : *v* chop into two halves lengthwise *of meat*

шаггаланмаг : *v* be cut into two parts lengthwise *of a butchered carcass*

шаггалатдырмаг, шаггалатмаг : *caus* of **шаггаламаг**

шаггалы : *a* broad-shouldered

шаггылдаг : *n* toy-pistol; rattle

шаггылдамаг : *v* 1) click, snap 2) sing trillingly *of a nightingale fig* 3) burst into laughter

шаггылдатмаг : *caus* of **шаггылдамаг**

шаггылты : *n* clicking; trilling; bursting into laughter

шаграг : *n* 1) bullfinch *genus Pyrrhula a* 2) jovial, merry *of laughter*

шагул : *n* vertical slope

шагули : *a* 1) vertical *adv* 2) vertically

шад : *a* 1) glad, happy, merry *adv* 2) gladly, happily, merrily

шад еләмәк : *v* make *s.o.* glad, happy

шадара : *n* fine sieve

шадјаналыг : *n* joy, gladness, rejoicing, festivities

шадландырычы : *a* gratifying, pleasing, comforting

шадландырмаг : *v* make happy

шадланмаг : *v* be glad, happy, merry

шадлашмаг : *v* become glad, happy, merry

шадлыг : *n* joy, gaiety, merriment, delight, pleasure

шадлыгла : *adv* happily, gladly

шад-хүррәм : *n* see **шад**

шаир : *n* poet

шаиранә : *adv* 1) poetically *a* 2) poetic

шаирә : *n* poetess

шаирлик : *n* talent, gift, calling/vocation of a poet

шајани-диггәт : *a* see **диггәтәлајиг**

шајәд : *adv* if, in the event that, just in case, to be on the safe side

шајиә : *n* 1) rumor, gossip, talk *adv* 2) by hearsay

шакәр : *n* habit, manner, way of doing

шакирд : *n* 1) student *elementary, middle school, high school* 2) apprentice

шакирдлик : *n* 1) student days, period spent as a student 2) period spent as an apprentice, apprenticeship period

шал : *n* 1) shawl *woolen* 2) cashmere

шалаг : *a* clumsy, awkward, unskilful

шалбан : *n* log, timber, beam

шалбанлыг : *n* tree suitable for use as timber/beam

шалвар : *n* pants

шалварлыг : *n* pants/trouser material

шалғам : *n* turnip

шаллаг : *n* whip

шаллагламаг : *v* whip

шам : *n* 1) candle 2) pine 3) supper 4) Damascus *city in Syria*

шам ағачы : *n bot* pine-tree

шамајы : *n zool* şamaja *Aspius cloides* , *a fish*

шамама : *n* small, fragrant but inedible, melon

шаман : *n* shaman

шаманлыг : *n* shamanism

шамдан : *n* candle-stick

шамлыг : *n* pine grove

шан : *n* 1) glory, brilliance 2) valor, honor 2) beehives

шана : *n* 1) pitchfork 2) trident

шанакүллә : *n* lotus

шанапипик : *n* *zool* hoopoe

шанлы : *a* glorious; honorable; valiant

шапалаг : *n* slap in the face

шапалагламаг : *v* slap *s.o.* in the face

шапалагланмаг : *v* get slapped in the face

шаппадан : *adv* suddenly, unexpectedly

шаппаламаг : *v* slap, thrash, flog, whip

шаппылдамаг : *v* splash; hit noisily against

шаппылты : *n* splashing with a plopping noise

шарылдамаг : *v* fall down noisily *of water*

шарылты : *n* splashing, falling down *of water*

шарф : *n* scarf

шатыр : *n* baker, bread-baker

шатырлыг : *n* baker's occupation , bread-baking

шатуј : *n* *zool* şatuy *Pelicus cultratis , fish*

шафталы : *n* 1) peach *a* 2) peach

шах : *n* 1) branch *a* 2) even, smooth

шах-будаг : *n* branching

шах-будаглы : *a* branchy

шахә : *n* see **шах** 1)

шахәләнмәк : *v* branch

шахыс : *n* levelling/level rod *used in surveying*

шахлама : *n* scraper *kind of a harrow used for working ploughed fields*

шахлы : *a* branchy

шахта : *n* 1) frost, severe cold 2) coal mine

Шахта Баба : *n* Santa Claus; *a literal translation of the Russian '**Дед Мороз**' Grandfather Frost*

шахталы : *a* frosty

шахтачы : *n* 1) coal-miner *a* 2) coal-miner['s]

шах-шах : *n* rattle

шаһ : *n* 1) shah, monarch 2) king *chess piece*

шаһад : *n* toll imposed at a mill for grinding grain

шаһанә : *a* 1) kingly, regal, magnificent, brilliant, beautiful *adv* 2) magnificently, beautifully, brilliantly

шаһбаз : *n* *zool* white falcon

шаһдамар : *n* *anat* aorta

шаһәншаһ : *n* king of kings *official title of Iranian shahs*

шаһзадә : n prince

шаһид : *n* witness

шаһидлик : *n* testimony

шаһин : *n* 1) falcon 2) Şahin *a common male first name*

шаһы : *n* five-kopek coin

шаһмар : *n* 1) şahı a large poisonous snake *fig* 2) the hair of a beautiful woman *in poetic language*

шаһмат : *n* chess

шаһматчы : *n* chess-player

шаһнамә : *n* Book of Kings *Biblical literature*

шеј : *n* 1) thing, article, item 2) object 3) piece

шејда : *a* 1) mad, crazy, senseless *of love* 2) madly infatuated

шеј-меј : *n* see **шеј-шуј**

шејпур : *n* horn, trumpet

шејпурчалан, шејпурчу : *n* trumpeter, trumpet-player

шејтан : *n* 1) Satan, devil, demon, unclean spirit *fig* 2) scoundrel, swindler, sly, cunning person

шејтанағачы : *n* *bot* honey-locust *Gleditschia triacanthus*

шејтанбазар : *n* flea-market

шејтандырнағы : *n* hangnail

шејтанламаг : *v* denounce, inform on, spy on

шејтанлатмаг : *v* *caus* of **шејтанламаг**

шејтанчы : *n* denouncer, informer, stool-pigeon

шејтанчылыг : *n* denunciation; libel, false accusation, tale-bearing, character assassination

шејтанчасына : *adv* devilishly, damnably

шејх : *n* 1) sheikh, tribal elder *in Arab societies* 2) head of a Dervish Order 3) venerable old man, estimable person

шејхүлислам : *n* Sheikh-ul-Islam. *Arabic; lit. the Chief of Islam. The chief judge of the Muslims of any of the larger towns and cities of the Muslim world, especially the Grand*

Mufti of Constantinople who was formerly the spiritual leader of the Muslim religion in the Turkish Empire.

шеј-шүј : *n* belongings, one's things, goods and chattels; junk

шенлик : *n* well-equipped area, area having modern conveniencces, inhabited area

шенликләндирмәк : *v* equip with services and utilities; settle, populate

ше'р : *n* 1) poem, verse 2) poetry

ше'ри : *a* poetic

ше'ријјәт : *n* 1) poetics 2) poetry;

ше'рләшмә : *n* poetic competition

ше'рләшмәк : *v* compete in writing or reciting poetry

шеф : *n* chief

шефлик : *n* patronage, sponsorship

шеh : *n* dew

шеhли : *a* 1) dewy, dew-covered 2) fresh *of fruit*

шеш : *n* 1) threading, thread *of screw etc* *num* 2) six *in the Persian backgammon game, called "nard"*

шешдрәнки : *n* şeşdranki *a sweet dressing used for pilaf*

шеш-беш : *n* a backgammon, or nard game *lit " five-six"*

шешә : *a* 1) haughty, arrogant 2) protruding, protuberant, sticking out

шешәбығ : *n* man with a thick, protruding, luxurious moustache

шешәләнмәк : *v* brag, boast

шешәлик : *n* arrogance, haughtiness

шә'бан : *n* Shaaban *eighth month of the Moslem calendar*

шәббу : *n* bot gillyflower, stock *Matthiola*

шәбәдә : *n* mockery, scoffing

шәбәкә : *n* 1) net; net 2) open-work, ornamentation 3) grating, grill, bars

шәбәкәли : *a* 1) reticulated, reticular, latticed, screen, net-like 2) open-work

шәбиh : *n* 1) resemblance *relig* 2) Shiite mystery play *reenactment of a calamity in Kerbede*

шәбкорлуг : *n* night-blindness, nectalopia

шәбнәм : *n* dew

шәбпәрә : *n zool* see **јараса**

шәввал : *n* Shawwal *tenth month of the Moslem calendar*

шәвә : *n* 1) agate *black precious stone a fig* 2) black*of eyes or hair*

шәддә : *n* thread *for stringing beads/pearls*

шәкәр : *n* 1) sugar *a* 2) sugar, sugary

шәкәргамышы : *n* sugarcane

шәкәрләнмәк : *v* sugar

шәкәрли : *a* sugary, saccharine

шәкәрчөрәји : *n* a shortbread *made of flour, sugar and eggs*

шәкил : *n* 1) picture, image, drawing, portrait; photo 2) shape, form, appearance 3) chart, lighted indicator-board 4) scene *in a theater*

шәкилли : *a* with pictures; illustrated

шәкилсиз : *a* 1) devoid of drawings or pictures 2) unillustrated 3) shapeless

шәкилчәкән : *n* photographer

шәкилчәкмә : *n* drawing

шәкилчи : *n gram* affix

шәкилчиләшмә : *n gram* affixation

шәкк : *n* doubt, skepticism

шәккак : *n* skeptic

шәккаклыг : *n* skepticism

шәкләмәк : *v* sharpen; prick up *one's ears*

шәклән : *adv* formally; superficially

шәкләнмәк : *v* be doubtful, suspicious

шәкли : *a* 1) suspecting, doubting 2) suspicious, doubtful, scepticial *n* 3) sceptic

шәксиз : *a* 1) undoubted, indubitable, certain *adv* 2) undoubtedly, doubtless certainly, beyond all question

шәлалә : *n* 1) waterfall 2) cascade

шәлә : *n* burden; bundle

шәләгујруг : *n* Şalaguyrug *nickname of a fox in folk tales lit. " bushy-tail"*

шәләкәт : *n* calm weather *at sea*

шәлә-күлә : *n* see **шеј-шүј**

шәләләмәк : *v* put/load onto o.'s back

шәләләнмәк : *v* be burdened/laden

шәләләтдирмәк, шәләләтмәк : *caus* of **шәләләмәк**

шәләли : *a* laden, burdened

шәлпә-шүлпә : *n* see **шеј-шүј**

шәлтә : *n* 1) panties, underpants *woman's* 2) slip, petticoat

шәлтәлик : material for slip/panties

шән : *a* 1) jolly, happy, merry 2) lively

шәнбә : *n* 1) Saturday *a* 2) Saturday['s]

шәнләндирмәк : *v* 1) cheer, gladden, make glad 2) enliven

шәнләнмәк, шәнләшмәк : *v* 1) become jolly/happy/glad 2) become enlovened

шәнлик : *n* 1) gaiety, merriment, jollity, happiness 2) festivity, celebration

шәр : *n* 1) wicked act/deed/action 2) calumny, slander

шәраб : *n* 1) wine *a* 2) wine, vinous

шәрабчы : *n* 1) wine-maker,vintner 2) wine-merchant

шәрабчылыг : *n* 1) wine-making *a* 2) wine-making

шәраит : *n* 1) conditions, situation 2) circumstances 3) atmosphere

шәракәт : *n* see **шәриклик**

шәрбаф : *n* braid-maker *i.e. gold/silver braid/galoon*

шәрбәт : *n* sherbet *a cooling drink*

шәрбәтчиоту : *n* hops

шәрг : *n* 1) east; the Orient *a* 2) eastern

шәрги : *a* 1) oriental, eastern *n* 2) song

шәргли : *a* 1) oriental *n* 2) person living in the East

шәргшүнас : *n* orientalist

шәргшүнаслыг : *n* oriental studies

шәрәлли : *n* variety of peach

шәр'ән : *adv* according to Shariat *the code of Moslem religious law*

шәрәф : *n* 1) honor, glory, ambition 2) object of pride, pride

шәрәфли : *a* honorable, glorious

шәрәфсиз : *a* 1) inglorious *adv* 2) ingloriously

шәрәфсизлик : *n* infamy, dishonor

шәриәт : *n* Shariat *Islamic code of religious law*

шәрик : *n* 1) companion, associate, joint-owner 2) participant, accomplice, confederate; partner

шәрикләшмәк : *v* 1) become companions, associates 2) agree with so.'s opinions

шәрикли : *adv* 1) together with, in company with *a* 2) inseparable

шәриклик : *n* corporation, company, association

шәрир : *a* 1) wicked, unkind *n* 2) wicked person, scoundrel

шәрит : *n* clothes-line

шәрт : *n* 1) condition 2) reservation, proviso

шәрти : *a* conditioned *by* , stipulated *for* , agreed upon

шәртләшмәк : *v* agree, make agreement, settle conditions

шәртнамә : *n* contract, agreement

шәртсиз : *a* 1) unconditional *adv* 2) unconditionally

шәрф : *n* scarf

шәрһ : *n* commentary, interpretation, explanation, clarification

шәрһчи : *n* commentator

шәст : *n* proud bearing, brave carriage

шәстлә : *adv* grandly, majestically

шәтәл : *n* dirty trick, cheating

шәтрәнҹ : *n* chess

шәфа : *n* recovery, recuperation, healing

шәфаверичи : *n* 1) healer *a* 2) healing, life-giving

шәфалы : *a* healing, curative

шәфгәт : *n* mercy, compassion, grace

шәфгәтли : *a* merciful, charitable, compassionate

шәфгәтсиз : *a* unmerciful, pitiless, without compassion

шәфгәтсизлик : *n* mercilessness, pitilessness, ruthless, unfeeling

шәфгәтсизҹәсинә : *adv* unmercifully, ruthlessly, unfeelingly

шәфәг : *n* 1) dawn, daybreak 2) sunrise 3) brightness, brilliance,radiance, luster,shining

шәфәгләнмәк : *v* shine, be lighted/illuminated

шәфәгли, шәфәгсачан : *a* shining, bright, radiant, lustrous

шәффаф : *a* 1) transparent *adv* 2) transparently

шәффафлыг : *n* transparence, transparency

шәхс : *n* 1) person, personage; fellow 2) individual

шәхсән : *adv* personally, individually

шәхси : *a* personal, individual, subjective

шәхси-гәрәз : *n* personal interest

шәхси-гәрәзлик : *n* personal hostility, malice, malicious intent

шәхсиј̌ј̌әт : *n* personality, individuality

шәхсли : *a* personal, individual

шәхссиз : *a* *gram* impersonal

шәһадәт : *n* testimony, evidence

шәһадәтнамә : *n* certificate, certification, attestation

шәһвани : *a* voluptuous, erotic

шәһвәт : *n* 1) lust, desire, voluptuousness flesh

шәһвәтпәрәст : *a* 1) lustful, voluptious, erotic *n* 2) voluptuary

шәһвәтпәрәстлик : *n* 1) voluptuousness, eroticism

шәһәр : *n* 1) city, town *a* 2) city, urban

шәһәрарасы : *a* interurban

шәһәрәтрафы : *n* 1) suburb *a* 2) suburban

шәһәрләрарасы : *a* see **шәһәрарасы**

шәһәрли : *n* city-dweller, urbanite

шәһәрсалма : *n* town-planning

шәһид : *n* 1) martyr *a* 2) martyred

шәһла : *a* 1) dark-blue *of eyes* 2) Şahla *feminine first name*

шәһрә : *n* open wound

шәчәрә : *n* genealogy

шив : *n* twig, sucker *on a tree*

шивә : *n* 1) accent, articulation, pronunciation 2) manner, habit 3) see **ишвә**

шивәбаз : *a* see **ишвәбаз**

шивәбазлыг : *n* see **ишвәбазлыг**

шивәкар, шивәли : *a* see **ишвәбаз**

шивән : *n* crying, weeping, sobbing

шивәрәк : *n* tall, slender

шиддәт : *n* 1) intensivity, vehemence 2) strength, power 3) abruptness, severity 4) extremity

шиддәтлә : *adv* 1) intensively, vehemently 2) strongly, powerfully 3) abruptly, severely 4) extremely

шиддәтләндирмәк : *v* intensify, arouse, stir up, aggravate

шиддәтләнмәк : *v* become stronger/tougher/more severe

шиддәтли : *a* 1) strong 2) severe 3) harsh

шиә : *n* Shiite

шикајәт : *n* complaint, appeal

шикајәтләнмәк : *n* complain

шикајәтчи : *n* complainer, nagger

шикар : *n* 1) hunt, hunting, catching 2) bag, catch

шикәст : *a* 1) broken; cracked 2) crippled, handicapped; maimed, mutilated *n* 3) invalid, crippled

шикәстә : *n mus* şikasta a traditional muğam *Middle Eastern melody*

шикәстәнәфс : *a* modest, unpretentious

шикәстәнәфслик : *n* modesty, unpretentiousness

шикәстлик : *n* 1) trauma; maiming, impairment, permanent disability 2) breakage, defect *med* 3) affection; lesion

шил : *n* 1) cripple, handicapped person *a* 2) crippled, handicapped

шилә : *n* 1) şila thick rice porridge 2) coarse red calico

шилим-шәһрә : *a* cut, slashed and crumpled all over

шил-күт : *a* crippled, maimed, handicapped

шиллә : *n* slap in the face

шилләләмәк : *v* slap *s.o.* in the face

шиллик : *n* disablement, incapacitation, infirmity

шимал : *n* 1) north *a* 2) northern

шимал-гәрб : *n* 1) north-west *a* 2) north-western

шимали : *a* northern

шималлы : *n* northerner

шималморуғу : *n* raspberry *Rubus saxatilis*

шималтүлкүсү : *n zool* Arctic fox, white fox *Alopex lagopus*

шимал-шәрг : *n* 1) north-east *a* 2) north-eastern

шимшәк : *n* lightning

шин : *n* tire *automotive*

шинәбуб : *n zool* see **шанапипик**

шинкилә : *n bot* Chondrilla *rubber-yielding plant*

шир : *n* 1) lion 2) enamel

ширдан : *n zool* abomasum *second stomach of a ruminant*

ширә : *n* juice, extract, infusion

ширәли : *a* juicy

ширәхак : *n* şirakhak a special clay used in boiling fruit juice to prevent fermentation

ширин : *a* 1) sweetish 2) fresh *adv* 3) sweetly

ширинданышан, ширindil(ли) : *a* 1) smooth-spoken, smooth-tongued; courteous 2) hypocritical

шириндил(ли)лик : *n* 1) courtesy 2) sweetness of speech 3) hypocrisy

ширинләндирмәк : *v* see **ширинләшдирмәк**

ширинләнмәк : *v* see **ширинләшмәк**

ширинләтмәк : *v* see **ширинләшдирмәк**

ширинләшдирмәк : *v* 1) make sweet, sugar *fig* enliven a conversation/a meeting

ширинләшмәк : *v* 1) become sweet/sweeter *fig* 2) become livelier/nicer looking/pleasanter

ширинлик : *n* sweetness

ширинтәһәр, ширинһал : *a* 1) sweetish, slightly sweet 2) sickly-sweet

ширинчә : *a dimin* 1) sweet *adv* 2) sweetly

ширин-ширин : *adv* very sweetly

ширкәт : *n* company, firm, corporation, partnership

ширләмәк : *v* glaze pottery/crockery

ширли : *a* glazed, enameled

ширни : *n* fruit drops, sweets, candy

ширниjjат : *n* sweets, candy

ширниjатсевән : *n* gourmand, person who likes sweets/delicacies

ширникдиричи : *a* encouraging; tempting; luring

ширникдирмә : *n* encouragement; temptation

ширникдирмәк : *v* encourage, tempt, lure

ширникмә : *n* excitement, passion

ширникмәк : *v* be enthusiastic about, be crazy about, be nuts about *s.t.*

ширпәнчә : *n med* see **гараjара**

ширпәнчәси : *n bot* lady's mantle *Alchemilla vulgaris*

шист : *n min* slate

шит : *a* 1) unsalted, plain 2) insufficiently/inadequately salted, *fig* 3) banal; frivolous, non-serious *of a person's character*

шитләндирмәк : *v* spoil *a child*

шитәнки : *n* spoiled child; pet, favorite

шитәнмәк : *v* play around; fool around, be mischievous

шитил : *n* seedlings

шитилләмәк : *v* put out seedlings, transplant seedlings

шитиллик : *n* seed-plot, greenhouse, hothouse, plant-nursery

шитлик : *n* 1) frivolity, light-mindedness; naughtiness 2) too little salt

шифаһи : *a* 1) oral *adv* 2) orally

шифер : n 1) roofing slate a 2) slate

шиш : *n med* 1) swelling, edema 2) tumor, lump, abscess 3) spit *for roasting* *a* 4) sharp

шишбаш : *a* dolichocephalic *having a long skull*

шишгулаг : *a* sharp-eared

шишәк : *n* a ram older than 4 years old

шиширдилмәк, шиширтмәк : *v* be blown up/inflated/swollen; bulge

шиширтмә : *n* exaggeration, inflation, blowing up

шиширтмәк : *v* 1) exaggerate, overplay 2) blow up, inflate

шишкин : *a* swollen, puffy

шишкинлик : *n* swelling, puffiness

шишман : *a* fat, pot-bellied, paunchy

шишманла(ш)маг : *v* become fat/pot-bellied

шишманлыг : *n* fatness, obesity, corpulence

шишмәк : *v* 1) swell, bulge 2) become fat/obese

шиштәпә : *n* peak *mountain*

шыг : *n* 1) chic, elegance *a* 2) chic, smart

шыггылдамаг : *v* crack the knuckles; snap the fingers

шыггылдатмаг : *v* click, crack *i.e. the knuckles;* snap *i.e. the fingers*

шыггылты : *n* snapping, cracking

шыглыг : *n* dandyism, foppishness; elegance

шыгчасына : *adv* foppishly, in a dandified manner

шығамаг, шығымаг : *v* 1) throw oneself on/attack *s.o.* 2) dive, swoop

шығыjычы : *n* diving, swooping

шыдырғы : *adv* 1) fluently, quickly *a* 2) fluent, fast, quick

шыллаг : *n* kicking

шыллагатан, шыллаглаjан : *n* see **шыллагчы**

шыллагламаг : *v* kick

шыллагчы : *a* 1) kicking *n* 2) kicker

шылтаг : *n* 1) whim, whimsy, caprice *a* 2) whimsical, capricious, fastidious

шылтаглыг : *n* see **шылтаг** 1)

шылтагчы : *n* whimsical, capricious, fastidious

шыппылты : *n* splash *of water*

шырылдамаг : *v* banble, murmur, gurgle *of water etc*

шырылты : *n* babbling, murmuring, gurgling *of water etc*

шырылтылы : *a* babbling, murmuring, gurgling

шырым : *n* furrow

шырымашыры : *n* strip farming

шырымламаг : *v* cut into strips ; cut furrows

шырым-шырым : *a* striped

шырынга : *n* 1) syringe 2) extrusion

шырнаг : *n* jet *of water*

шырран : *n* waterfall

шырты : *n* plain, banal, vulgar

шыртылашдырылмаг : *v* be/become popularized, become common/banal/hackneyed/trite

шыртылашдырма : *n* popularizing, making popular/common/hackneyed/trite/banal

шыртылашдырмаг : *v* popularize, make popular/common/hackneyed/trite/banal; use to death, work *an expression* to death

шыртылыг : *n* vulgarization

шыр-шыр : *n* see **шырран**

шкаф : *n* *generic term for any big piece of furniture serving as a storage space e.g. tallboy, dresser, cupboard, wardrobe, bookcase etc.*

шлеј : *n* breech-band, breast-band *part of a harness*

шлүз : *n* lock, sluice, floodgate

шлүзләмәк : *v* convey through a lock *a ship*

шовинизм : *n* chauvinism

шовинист : *n* chauvinist *a* 2) chauvinistic

шоггу : *n* see **шушәки**

шогәриб : *a* ill-fated

шоколад : *n* 1) chocolate *a* 2) chocolate

шоколадлы : *a* chocolate

шор : *a* 1) salted *n* 2) şor *salted cottage cheese*

шораба : *n* 1) marinade 2) marinated/pickled vegetables

шоракәт, шоран : *n* 1) salt marsh, saline/alkaline soil, salt bottoms *a* 2) brackish, briny, saliniferous

шоранлашма : *n* salination

шорба : *n* soup, broth

шоргогалы : *n* şorogalı *flaky spiced roll with salted cottage cheese*

шоркөз : *n* skirt-chaser, womanizer, wolf

шоркөзлүк : *n* lasciviousness, lechery, lust *of men*

шортмаг : *v* run

шорту : *a* frivolous; immoral; shameless

шортулуг : *n* 1) superficiality, frivolousness 2) immorality, shamelessness

шосе : *n* 1) highway, surfaced road *a* 2) highway

шофер : *n* 1) driver, chauffeur *a* 2) driver['s], chauffeur['s]

шоферлик : *n* occupation of a driver/chauffeur

шө'бә : *n* department, section, branch

шөвг : *n* 1) zeal, vocation, desire, will, inclination, enthusiasm

шөвглә : *adv* willingly, zealously, enthusiastically

шөвгләндиричи : *a* encouraging, inspiring

шөвгләндирмәк : *v* encourage, inspire

шөвгләнмәк : *v* become encouraged/inspired

шөвглү : *a* 1) zealous, fervent, thirsting after, strongly desiring 2) happy, glad, joyous, merry

шөвгсүз : *a* 1) reluctance *adv* 2) reluctantly, unwillingly

шөвкәт : *n* magnificence, grandeur

шөвкәтли : *a* magnificent, brilliant

шөк : *adv* with a push, with a poke

шө'лә : *n* shining, radiance

шө'ләләнмәк : *v* shine, radiate

шө'ләли : *a* shining, bright, brilliant

шөтдәмәк : *v* stitch hastily

шөһрәт : *n* glory; popularity, fame, reknown

шөһрәтбаз : *a* see **шөһрәтпәрәст**

шөһрәтләндирмәк : *v* glorify, make famous

шөһрәтләнмәк : *v* become glorified/famous/reknown

шөһрәтли : *a* famous, well-known, popular

шөһрәтпәрәст : *n* 1) vainglorious, ambitious person *a* 2) vainglorious, ambitious

шөһрәтпәрәстлик : *n* extreme ambition, vaingloriousness

шөһрәтсиз : *a* unknown, unpopular

шөһрәтсизлик : *n* anonymity, obscurity; lack of popularity

шприс : *n* syringe

шулуг : *n* 1) naughtiness, mischievousness 2) *a* naughty, mischievous

шулуглуг : *n* 1) naughtiness 2) disorder, mess, excess 3) looting

шулугчу : *n* 1) naughty child, mischief-maker, bundle of mischief 2) looter

шулугчулуг : *n* 1) naughtiness, mischief 2) rowdyism, brawling 3) looting

шум : *n* ploughing; ploughed field

шумал : *a* tall, slender

шумламаг : *v* plough

шумланмаг : *v* be ploughed

шумлатдырмаг, шумлатмаг : *caus* of **шумламаг**

шунгар : *n* *zool* gerfalcon *Falco rusticolus*

шур : *n* 1) ecstasy 2) an Azerbaijani muǧam or folk melody *a* 3) ecstatic

шура : *n* council

шуриш : *n* disarray, turmoil, confusion

шух : *a* 1) jolly, merry, playful, full of joie de vivre 2) bright *color*

шухлуг : *n* 1) playfulness, friskiness, joy 2) joke

шүа : *n* ray, beam

шүаланма : *n* radiation

шүаланмаг : *v* radiate, irradiate

шүалы : *a* radiating, radiant

шүар : *n* slogan

шүбһә : *n* doubt, suspicion

шүбһәләндирмәк : *v* evoke doubt/suspicion, give occasion/grounds/cause for doubts and suspicions

шүбһәләнмәк : *v* 1) suspect *that s.o. or s.t. is the cause* 2) be doubtful, doubt

шүбһәли : *a* 1) suspicious, doubtful *adv* 2) suspiciously, doubtfully, sceptically

шүбһәлилик : *n* 1) doubtfulness, suspiciousness, skepticism

шүбһәсиз : *a* 1) undoubted, indubitable, unquestionable 2) *adv* undoubtedly doubtless, beyond all question

шүбһәсизлик : *n* unquestionability, trustworthyness

шүвәрә : *n* letting *s.o.* down, putting *s.o.* on the spot

шүвүл : *n* pole

шүј : *n* stem/shoot *on a tree*

шүјүд : *n* *bot* dill *Anethum graveolens*

шүјүм : *n* shabby, unprepossessing appearance

шүкуһ : *n* pompousness, ambitions

шүкүр : *n* gratitude/thanks *to God*

шүлә : *n* distance between two outstretched hands *a traditional measure of length*

шүләмә : *n* whipping, flogging

шүләмәк : *v* whip, lash, flog

шүмшад : *n* 1) *bot* box, box-tree *Buxus sempervirens a fig* 2) tall, slender

шүрә : *n* desire for, or habit of doing *s.t. Only in combinations*

шүрәм : *n* see **зол, золаг**

шүру : *n* in comb. **шүру еләмәк (етмәк)** see **башламаг**

шүтүмәк : *v* rush, run fast

шүур : *n* consciousness

шүуралты : *a* subconscious

шүурланмаг : *v* become conscious/reasonable/sensible

шүурлу : *adv* 1) conscious, aware *a* 2) consciously

шүурлулуг : *n* awareness; intelligence, acumen

шүурсуз : *a* 1) irresponsible, not conscious *of adv* 2) unconsciously, involuntarily

шүурсузлуг : *n* irresponsibility, lack of consciousness of social obligations

шүчаәт : *n* valor, courage

шүчаәтлә : *adv* valiantly, courageously

шүчаәтли : *a* valiant, courageous

шүш : *adv* upright, erect

шүшә : *n* 1) glass 2) bottle *a* 2) glass

шүшәбәнд : *n* glassed-in, windowed gallery

шүшәбәндли : *a* having a glassed-in, windowed gallery

шүшәки : *n* hissing an actor/a speaker *off the stage . lit. whistling him off*

шүшәләмәк : *v* glaze, install window glass

шүшәсалан : *n* glazier

шүшәүфүрән : *n* glass-blower

шүшәчи : *n* see **шүшәсалан**

шүшәчилик : *n* occupation of glazier